HANDBOOK OF CLINICAL ASSESSMEN
OF CHILDREN AND ADOLESCENTS

VOLUME I

HANDBOOK
OF CLINICAL ASSESSMENT
OF CHILDREN AND ADOLESCENTS

VOLUME I

CLARICE J. KESTENBAUM
and
DANIEL T. WILLIAMS
Editors

NEW YORK UNIVERSITY PRESS
New York and London

Library of Congress Cataloging-in-Publication Data

Handbook of clinical assessment of children and
   adolescents.

   Includes bibliographies and index.
   1. Child psychopathology—Classification.
2. Adolescent psychopathology—Classification.
3. Mental illness—Diagnosis.   I. Kestenbaum,
Clarice J., 1929–   II. Williams, Daniel T.,
1944–
RJ500.5.H37   1987   618.92'89   87-20250
ISBN 0-8147-4592-X (v. 1)
ISBN 0-8147-4593-8 (v. 2)
ISBN 0-8147-4590-3 (set)

Clothbound editions of New York University Press
books are Smyth-sewn and printed on permanent and
durable acid-free paper.

Contents

VOLUME II

Preface

The problematic conceptual polarization of mind versus brain, which has plagued psychiatry since its inception, has never been demonstrated more vividly than in the area of child and adolescent assessment. This dichotomy is represented most starkly on the contemporary scene by intense and sometimes bitter disputes of a clinical, ideological, and political nature that are occasionally encountered when child psychiatrists who were primarily psychodynamically trained lock horns with those of primarily psychobiological persuasion. Often the intensity of these disputes seems directly correlated to the narrowness of training of the respective partisans. In a broader sense, the number of disciplines whose findings impinge in a clinically relevant way on the assessment of children and adolescents has proliferated in recent years. Even the best trained child psychiatrist must frequently call upon subspecialists from related fields for assistance. Yet the degree of specialization in training generated by these disciplines similarly can contribute to a narrowness of perspective of the type noted above. A child coming to a series of such specialists for clinical assessment is at similar risk as the elephant examined by the three blind men: each specialist produces an assessment sharply limited by the confines of his specialty's purview, with the quality and clinical utility of the assessment being markedly impaired as a consequence.

The roots of a broad-based contemporary perspective in the clinical assessment of children and adolescents with problems of emotions, behavior, and/or cognition spring from multiple sources. Naming only a few illustrates the breadth of the spectrum: the mental hygiene movement and the juvenile court system, which led to the child mental health clinics and agencies; education and cognitive as well as developmental psychology; behavioral psychology, with its emphasis on the paradigms of classical and operant conditioning; pediatrics and pediatric neurology, with their emphasis on physical developmental norms and the crucial role of underlying neurophysiological processes; and finally psychoanalysis, with its emphasis on childhood neurosis and the examination of children as a way of studying psychopathology in *status nascendi*.

Until the last twenty years there were no formal standards for child psychiatric evaluation. Fellowship training in child psychiatry was relatively informal and focused primarily upon the particular discipline that was the domain of the professor. Two or three child fellows had dozens of sometimes fascinating cases to discuss with a half-dozen supervisors and teachers. The chart notes often read like novels—

full of speculation, fantasy, hyperbole, and sometimes, a thoughtful analytic discussion of all the factors that lead to Johnny's inability to control his cursing or to his inordinate fear of dogs. Child psychiatry trainees met in small groups to review and discuss "important" child psychiatric papers. If the selections on one's reading list were sufficiently diverse and if one had the good fortune to have expert and diversely trained supervisors, one could learn how one's case could be evaluated and treated in a variety of ways: behaviorally, psychoanalytically, pharmacologically, or otherwise. There was no unified source to guide the trainee in this endeavor; efforts to understand more fully the role of diverse factors contributing to one's patient's condition required a direct appeal to a psychologist, pediatrician, social worker, educator, speech pathologist, and/or pediatric neurologist, among others, in search of not only relevant information, but help in integrating it into a unified perspective.

The past decade has seen numerous efforts to integrate the diverse approaches to psychiatric assessment generally, as witnessed, for example by the publication of the Third Edition of the Diagnostic and Statistical Manual of Mental Disorders (DSM-III) by the American Psychiatric Association. This volume is notable for its emphasis on phenomenological description of psychopathological entities, independent of diverse and often conflicting etiological formulations. Yet phenomenology, albeit clearly described and uniformly communicated, while a cornerstone of assessment, is only a beginning. The clinician seeking to minister to the psychopathological problems of youngsters must conduct an informed search for as many relevant etiologic contributants as possible, be they biological, psychological, social, or other. Only then is the clinician in a position to formulate a treatment plan that has the best prospects for effectiveness. In an era when no single clinician can master all the diverse areas of expertise that would be relevant and desirable as aids in assessment, it seems desirable to have a reasonably representative sample of the predominant contemporary approaches brought together as a reference and training resource. It is hoped that this volume, imbued with an eclectic biopsychosocial perspective, will be helpful in fostering this integrated approach.

John Sours, M.D., our late esteemed colleague, both reflected and advocated this broad-based biopsychosocial approach to clinical assessment of children and adolescents. This was reflected in his clinical work with patients, in his teaching over many years at the Columbia-Presbyterian Medical Center, and in his writings. It was he who was the moving spirit behind the genesis of this book, which we have carried through in light of his untimely death. While we have made some changes from his original design, we believe we have retained and implemented his guiding spirit.

Contributors

JULES R. BEMPORAD, M.D., is Director of Training and Education in the Department of Psychiatry of the Harvard Medical School, Massachusetts Mental Health Center.

STEPHEN L. BENNETT, M.D., P.C., is Assistant Clinical Professor of Psychiatry at the Columbia University College of Physicians and Surgeons. He is Chief of the Division of Child and Adolescent Psychiatry at the Harlem Hospital Center.

KAREN BERGER, M.S.W., is Research Social Worker at Children's Hospital National Medical Center in Washington, D.C.

MARCIA BERGTRAUM, M.D., is Director of the Pediatric Neurophysiology Laboratory at Schneider Children's Hospital in New Hyde Park, New York.

ANNI BERGMAN, PH.D., is Clinical Associate Professor of Clinical Psychology at the City College and Graduate Center of the City University of New York and Senior Research Scientist at the Margaret S. Mahler Psychiatric Research Foundation.

HECTOR R. BIRD, M.D., is Clinical Professor of Psychiatry at the Columbia University College of Physicians and Surgeons and Deputy Director of the Division of Child Psychiatry at Columbia University–New York State Psychiatric Institute.

IAN A. CANINO, M.D., is Associate Clinical Professor in the Department of Child Psychiatry at the Columbia University College of Physicians and Surgeons.

DENNIS P. CANTWELL, M.D., is Joseph Campbell Professor of Child Psychiatry and Director of Residency Training in Child Psychiatry at the UCLA Neuropsychiatric Institute. He has conducted extensive research in the areas of affective disorders, attention deficit disorder with and without hyperactivity, communication disorders, and other childhood disorders.

WILLIAM J. CHAMBERS, M.D., is an Associate Clinical Professor of Psychiatry in the Division of Child and Adolescent Psychiatry at the Columbia University College of Physicians and Surgeons and Director of the Pediatric Psychiatry Service at Babies Hospital, Columbia–Presbyterian Medical Center in New York City.

IRENE CHATOOR, M.D., is Associate Professor of Psychiatry and of Child Health and Development at George Washington University Medical School and Psychiatric Director of the Psychosomatic Program at Children's Hospital National Medical Center in Washington, D.C.

SANFORD J. COHN, PH.D., is Associate Professor of Education, focusing on the nature and education of gifted children, at Arizona State University.

SUSAN COATES, PH.D., is Director of the Childhood Gender Identity Unit at St. Luke's-Roosevelt Hospital Center in New York City.

CHERYL BETH DIAMOND, M.D., is Clinical Assistant Professor of Psychiatry at Cornell University Medical Center–New York Hospital.

JAMES EGAN, M.D., is Chairman of the Department of Psychiatry at the Children's Hospital National Medical Center in Washington, D.C., and Professor of Psychiatry at the George Washington University School of Medicine.

AARON H. ESMAN, M.D., is Professor of Clinical Psychiatry at Cornell University Medical College and Lecturer at the New York Psychoanalytic Institute.

RICHARD C. EVANS, M.D., is a child, marital, and family therapist with a private practice in Tarrytown, New York. He is Clinical Director of the Echo Hills Counseling Center in Hastings, New York.

HANS J. EYSENCK, PH.D., is Professor Emeritus at the University of London, at the Institute of Psychiatry, and the Maudsley and Bethlem Royal Hospitals.

CARL FEINSTEIN, M.D., is Director of the Program in Developmental Disabilities at Emma Pendleton Bradley Hospital in East Providence, Rhode Island, and Associate Professor of Psychiatry in the Division of Child Psychiatry at the Brown University Program in Medicine in Providence, Rhode Island.

RICHARD S. FELDMAN, PH.D., is Associate Research Scientist in the Department of Child Psychiatry at the New York State Psychiatric Institute, and the Department of Psychiatry at Columbia University, and is engaged in research and teaching in the areas of children's behavior and behavior therapy.

DAVID A. FREEDMAN, M.D., is Professor of Psychiatry and Associate Professor of Neurology at the Baylor College of Medicine in Houston, Texas. He is also a Training and Supervisory Analyst at the Houston-Galveston Psychoanalytic Institute.

ARNOLD P. GOLD, M.D., is Professor of Clinical Neurology and Professor of Clinical Pediatrics at Columbia University.

SHOSHANA MAFDALI GOLDMAN, PH.D., is with the Department of Medical Psychiatry at St. Luke's-Roosevelt Hospital Center and the Department of Psychology at Columbia University. She is a founder and the Director of the Language and Learning Unit in the Department of Child Psychiatry at St. Luke's-Roosevelt Hospital Center, St. Luke's Site.

JEROME D. GOODMAN, M.D., has a private practice in Saddle River, New Jersey. He is Assistant Clinical Professor at the Columbia University College of Physicians and Surgeons and Attending Psychiatrist at Valley Hospital in Ridgewood, New Jersey.

ARTHUR H. GREEN, M.D., is Medical Director of the Family Center and Therapeutic Nursery at the Presbyterian Hospital. He is Associate Clinical Professor of Psychiatry (in Pediatrics) at the Columbia University College of Physicians and Surgeons and a faculty member of the Columbia University Center for Psychoanalytic Training and Research.

WAYNE H. GREEN, M.D., is Associate Professor of Clinical Psychiatry at the New York University School of Medicine and Unit Chief of the Child and Adolescent Outpatient Clinic at New York University–Bellevue Medical Center.

STANLEY I. GREENSPAN, M.D., is Clinical Professor of Psychiatry and Behavioral Science and Child Health and Development, George Washington University Medical School, Washington, D.C., and has a clinical practice of child psychiatry and adult and child psychoanalysis.

HELEN HANESIAN, ED.D., is Assistant Professor of Clinical Psychology (in Psychiatry) at the Columbia University College of Physicians and Surgeons and Psychologist at the Pediatric Neuropsychiatry Service of Columbia Presbyterian Medical Center.

NEIL HARTMAN, M.D., PH.D., is Assistant Professor in the Department of Psychiatry and Biobehavioral Science at the UCLA School of Medicine and Chief of the Treatment Refractory Unit at the Veterans Administration Medical Center in Los Angeles. He was also the Fellow in Substance Abuse at Cornell University Medical College from 1981 to 1983.

MARGARET E. HERTZIG, M.D., is Associate Professor of Psychiatry at the Cornell University Medical Center.

GLENN HIRSCH, M.D., is Unit Chief of the Adolescent Inpatient Unit at Hillside Hospital, Long Island Jewish Medical Center.

MICHELLE HIRSCH, MD.D., is Assistant Clinical Professor of Psychiatry at Columbia University College of Physicians and Surgeons and Assistant Attending in Psychiatry at Columbia–Presbyterian Medical Center, St. Luke's-Roosevelt Hospital Center. She is also Coordinator of the lecture series in Child Psychiatry for Psychiatric residents and Supervisor in Child Psychiatry and Private Practice with Adults and Children.

ROBERT HUNT, M.D., is Director of Training and Research, Director of the Neuropsychiatric Unit and Clinic for Learning and Behavioral Disorders, and Associate Professor of Psychiatry in the Division of Child and Adolescent Psychiatry at the Vanderbilt University School of Medicine.

JOHN E. HUXSAHL, M.D., is Senior Associate Consultant in Child and Adolescent Psychiatry at the Mayo Clinic; and Instructor in Psychiatry at the Mayo Medical School.

JEANNETTE JEFFERSON JANSKY, PH.D., is Assistant Clinical Professor of Pediatric Psychology (in Psychiatry) at Columbia University and Education Director of the de Hirsch-Robinson Reading Clinic at Columbia–Presbyterian Medical Center.

WILLIAM H. KAPLAN, M.D., is Instructor in Clinical Psychiatry at the Columbia University College of Physicians and Surgeons and the Division of Child Psychiatry at the New York State Psychiatric Institute. He is also a supervising psychiatrist of children and youth at South Beach Psychiatric Center in Staten Island, New York.

PAULINA F. KERNBERG, M.D., is Associate Professor of Psychiatry and Director of Child and Adolescent Psychiatry at The New York Hospital–Cornell Medical Center, Westchester Division in White Plains, New York.

CLARICE J. KESTENBAUM, M.D., is Director of Training of the Division of Child and Adolescent Psychiatry at the New York State Psychiatric Institute and Clinical

Professor of Psychiatry at the Columbia University College of Physicians and Surgeons. She is also a faculty member of the Columbia University Center for Psychoanalytic Training and Research.

ELIZABETH T. KHURI, M.D., is the Clinical Director of the Adolescent Development Program of New York Hospital and Associate Professor of Clinical Public Health and Pediatrics at Cornell University Medical College. She is also a Visiting Physician at the Rockefeller University Laboratory of the Biology of Addictive Disease. She has worked in the field of substance abuse for the past seventeen years.

RACHEL GITTELMAN KLEIN, PH.D., has conducted clinical research with children with anxiety disorders. She is Professor of Clinical Psychology at the Columbia University College of Physicians and Surgeons and Director of Psychology at the New York State Psychiatric Institute.

HAROLD S. KOPLEWICZ, M.D., is Chief of Child and Adolescent Psychiatry at Schneider Children's Hospital and Hillside Hospital of Long Island Jewish Medical Center and Assistant Clinical Professor in Psychiatry at Columbia University.

ELLIOT M. KRANZLER, M.D., is Assistant Clinical Professor of Psychiatry at the Columbia University College of Physicians and Surgeons and at the New York State Psychiatric Institute.

LEO KRON, M.D., is Director of the Division of Child and Adolescent Psychiatry, St. Luke's-Roosevelt Hospital Center, St. Luke's Site and Assistant Clinical Professor of Psychiatry at the Columbia University College of Physicians and Surgeons.

KYU WON LEE, M.D., is with the Department of Psychiatry of the Harvard Medical School, Massachusetts Mental Health Center.

ALAN M. LEVY, M.D., is Associate Clinical Professor of Psychiatry at the Columbia University College of Physicians and Surgeons and Chief of the Forensic Child Psychiatry Clinic at the Columbia–Presbyterian Medical Center, Babies Hospital, New York City.

JULIA M. LEWIS, PH.D., is with the California State University in San Francisco and the center for the Family in Transition in Corte Madera, California.

JEROME H. LIEBOWITZ, M.D., is Clinical Assistant Professor of Psychiatry at the Cornell University Medical College. He is the former director of the Child and Adolescent Outpatient Department of the Westchester Division of New York Hospital–Cornell Medical Center in White Plains, New York.

ALEXANDER R. LUCAS, M.D., is Consultant in Child and Adolescent Psychiatry at the Mayo Clinic and Professor in Psychiatry at the Mayo Medical School.

ROBERT B. MILLMAN, M.D., is the Saul P. Steinberg Distinguished Professor of Psychiatry and Public Health at the Cornell University Medical College and Director of Drug and Alcohol Treatment Programs at the Payne Whitney Clinic–New York Hospital. He also serves as the Medical Director of the Employee Assistance Program Consortium at New York Hospital and affiliated institutions and the Employee Development Center.

WALTER J. MOLOFSKY, M.D., is Assistant Professor of Neuroscience and Pediatrics at the University of Medicine and Dentistry in Newark, New Jersey.

EDWARD D. MYSAK, PH.D., is Professor of Speech Pathology and Chairman of the Department of Speech and Language Pathology and Audiology at Teachers College, Columbia University.

HELEN ORVASCHEL, PH.D., is Assistant Professor of Psychiatry and Epidemiology and Program Director of the Department of Child Psychiatric Epidemiology at the Western Psychiatric Institute and Clinic of the University of Pittsburgh.

PATRICIO PAEZ, M.D., is Assistant Clinical Professor of Psychiatry at the Columbia University College of Physicians and Surgeons and Psychiatrist at the Pediatric Neuropsychiatry Service of Columbia–Presbyterian Medical Center.

GARY A. PAWL, M.D., is Instructor of Psychiatry in the Department of Child Psychiatry at the Albert Einstein College of Medicine. He is presently Director of the Child and Adolescent Crisis Service at the Bronx Municipal Hospital Center.

CYNTHIA R. PFEFFER, M.D., is Associate Professor of Clinical Psychiatry at Cornell University Medical College and Chief of Child Psychiatry, Inpatient Unit of the New York Hospital, Westchester Division, in White Plains, New York. She is President of the American Association of Suicidology.

RICHARD PLEAK, M.D., is Research Fellow in Child Psychiatry and Instructor in Clinical Psychiatry at the Columbia University College of Physicians and Surgeons.

JOHN D. RAINER, M.D., is Professor of Clinical Psychiatry at the Columbia University College of Physicians and Surgeons and Chief of Psychiatric Research (Medical Genetics) at the New York State Psychiatric Institute.

BORIS RUBINSTEIN, M.D., is Director of Pediatric Psychiatry Consultation and Liaison Service at Columbia–Presbyterian Medical Center and Assistant Clinical Professor of Psychiatry and Pediatrics at Columbia University College of Physicians and Surgeons.

M. BRUCE SARLIN, M.D., is Assistant Professor of Clinical Psychiatry at the Columbia University College of Physicians and Surgeons and Chief OPD of the Mental Health Clinic for the Deaf at the New York State Psychiatric Institute.

ROBERT SBRIGLIO, M.D., is Clinical Director of Liberation Programs, Inc., in Stamford, Connecticut. He was the Fellow in Substance Abuse at Cornell University Medical College from 1984 to 1986.

ALISON PEDICORD SCHLEIFER is an educator and independent educational consultant who works with students and families seeking school or college level placement. She is a member of the Independent Educational Counselors Association.

SHARON S. SCHAEFER, L.C.S.W., was a member of the Psychiatry Staff at Children's Hospital National Medical Center in Washington, D.C., and is currently a member of the Eating Disorders Team at Children's Hospital and in private practice.

DAVID SHAFFER, M.D., is Irving Phillips Professor of Psychiatry and Professor of Pediatrics at the Columbia University College of Physicians and Surgeons and Chief of Child Psychiatry at the New York State Psychiatric Institute.

MIRIAM G. SIEGEL, PH.D., has a private practice in New York City.

JOSEPH A. SILVERMAN, M.D., is Clinical Professor of Pediatrics at the Columbia

University College of Physicians and Surgeons and Attending Pediatrician at Presbyterian Hospital in New York City.

ARIETTA SLADE, PH.D., is Assistant Professor of Clinical and Developmental Psychology at the City College and Graduate Center of the City University of New York.

PHYLLIS L. SLOATE, PH.D., is Faculty and Supervising Psychologist in the Department of Child Psychiatry at St. Luke's Hospital and has a private practice in Larchmont, New York.

MARGARET ELLIS SNOW, M.D., is Assistant Professor of Psychology in Psychiatry at Cornell University Medical Center.

JOHN A. SOURS, M.D., now deceased, was formerly Clinical Assistant Professor of Psychiatry at Columbia University and a training and supervising analyst at both Columbia University Center for Psychoanalytic Training and Research and the New York Psychoanalytic Institute.

CAROLYN SNYDER, M.A., is a candidate within the CUNY Clinical Psychology Doctoral Program and an intern at the Naval Hospital in Bethesda.

LUDWIK S. SZYMANSKI, M.D., is Director of Psychiatry at the Developmental Evaluation Clinic of The Children's Hospital in Boston and Assistant Professor of Psychiatry at Harvard Medical School.

DIANA TOWNSEND-BUTTERWORTH, is an educational consultant working with young children and their parents in New York City. She was previously head of the Junior School at St. Bernard's School in New York City.

GILBERT J. VOYAT, PH.D., now deceased, was Professor of Clinical Psychology in the CUNY Clinical Psychology Doctoral Program, where his intelligence, wit, and commitment to scientific inquiry greatly enriched the lives of all who knew him.

JUDITH S. WALLERSTEIN, PH.D., is with the Center for the Family in transition in Corte Madera, California, and the University of California in Berkeley.

DANIEL T. WILLIAMS, M.D., is Associate Clinical Professor of Psychiatry at the Columbia University College of Physicians and Surgeons and Clinical Director of the Pediatric Neuropsychiatry Service at Columbia-Presbyterian Medical Center.

KENNETH J. ZUCKER, PH.D., is head of the Child and Adolescent Gender Identity Clinic of the Child and Family Studies Centre at the Clark Institute of Psychiatry in Toronto.

HANDBOOK OF CLINICAL ASSESSMENT OF CHILDREN AND ADOLESCENTS

VOLUME I

I

The Evaluation Process: Interview and Diagnosis

1

CLASSIFICATION OF CHILDHOOD AND ADOLESCENT DISORDERS

Dennis P. Cantwell

INTRODUCTION

This chapter will discuss the classification of child and adolescent psychiatric disorders. It asks, Why do we need to classify? What are the underlying basic principles that tell us how to classify? It discusses the various methods of classification, including current systems. Brief mention will be made of the relationship between the diagnostic classification system and the diagnostic process, and the chapter will end with some ideas about future research.

WHY DO WE NEED TO CLASSIFY?

Any psychiatric classification is likely to have multiple uses. Two of the most important are to provide for an orderly way to systematize the collection of current clinical data and to predict future patterns. Some include: communication with other professionals, development of scientific theories, information retrieval, research design, treatment planning, legal usage, funding issues, and qualification for specialized services. For a system to be useful and to be *used*, it must demonstrate clinical utility. An overly complicated system that is too difficult to use in everyday clinical practice cannot be considered successful. All professionals need shorthand ways in which to communicate about their patients' problems. A comprehensive diagnostic classification system allows clinicians and researchers of different theoretical persuasion to communicate with each other about disorders. Moreover, from the standpoint of information retrieval, a diagnostic classification system allows data accumulation at local, state, and national levels about the prevalence and types of mental disorders in infancy, childhood, and adolescence. Such data collection is often a first necessary step in convincing funding agencies of the nature and severity of problems and in obtaining the type of funding necessary for specialized intervention. From the standpoint of research design, it is axiomatic that some system is necessary for any advance in understanding etiology, natural history, and response to treatment of various psychiatric disorders. For example, to facilitate biological studies of a particular childhood disorder we must be able to classify children's problems into various groups so that we can consider a child to be depressed or not depressed, autistic or not autistic. The use of varying terminology and varying criteria for inclusion of children in certain studies has impeded scientific advancement. This is probably no more evident in child psychiatry than in the field of childhood psychosis, childhood schizophrenia, infantile autism, and related disorders. Many authors have proposed idiosyncratic ways of diagnosing and classifying these conditions, which means that studies from different centers using these idiosyncratic terms and criteria cannot be compared directly.

The same can be said of the use of diagnostic classifications for treatment planning. We recognize that no diagnostic classification system is perfect. Treatment decisions must be made, however, and the clinician must be able to call upon a body of literature to decide whether a certain type of treatment, or a combination of treatment interventions, is likely to be effective with a particular condition. This can be done only if there exists a body of literature about certain types of treatment intervention with certain types of conditions. If children are included in treatment studies in the absence of any type of diagnostic statement, then generalization from study to study is impossible. Thus, the treatment of any individual child becomes a research project in and of itself. Clinicians cannot afford to wait for a totally empirically validated classification to be able to make decisions about treatment planning.

Determining whether or not a child has a particular diagnosis may make a child eligible for certain intervention programs such as educational therapy, occupational therapy, language services, and so forth. From a legal standpoint classification provides a framework not only for provision of services but also possibly for mitigation in criminal issues. The prime requirement for any system to be used for clinical purposes is that the system be of utility for those who are practitioners of child psychiatry and related mental health specialties. If clinicians do not find the system useful in clinical work as a means of organizing information and facilitating decisions about treatment or about predictions of untreated natural history, then the system will not find general use.

HOW TO CLASSIFY

There are certain basic principles in any classification system of child and adolescent psychiatric disorders that are generally agreed upon by people of different theoretical persuasion. These have been discussed fully in previous publications (Cantwell 1980, 1985) but will be briefly reviewed here. It is generally recognized that there is no single right way to classify psychiatric disorders of childhood and adolescence. Most of the official classification systems in the past have been cate-gorical systems, and DSM-III and ICD-9 carry on that tradition. However, dimen-sional systems do offer an alternative approach.

Classification by etiology is generally not a fruitful way to organize these disor-ders. Many present with the same phenomenolgic system but may develop on the basis of different etiologic factors in different children. If one could isolate a specific pathophysiologic agent that would then lead to treatment and/or prevention, then classification on the basis of these pathophysiologic features would be preferable. However, that is not the state of the art in child and adolescent psychopathology at the present time.

Given the current state of the art, if the system is going to be used as a frame-work for communication among clinicians and researchers with different theoretical persuasions, then the classification system should be based as much as possible on factual information rather than on any particular theoretical framework. Psychoan-alysts, behavior therapists, family therapists, and others may agree that a child or adolescent is presenting with a significant depression even though they disagree as to why the depression is present and what ought to be done about it.

In order to keep one of the fundamental usages of the classification system, that of communication, it is important to base the classification of child and adolescent psychiatric disorders on features that can be observed and agreed upon by clinicians of different theoretical orientations. There is a relative lack of hard, concrete facts in the child and adolescent area regarding natural history, family pattern of illness, and response to treatment of various psychiatric disorders, compared to the more traditionally well-defined syndromes such as schizophrenia and affective disorder in adults.

For a system to be useful in the classification of child and adolescent psycho-pathology, the disorders must have reliability. Sources of unreliability in psychiatric diagnosis include: information variance, observation and interpretation variance, and criterion variance. Information variance or observation and interpretation variance are not affected by any system, but criterion variance can be minimized by specify-ing diagnostic criteria for each disorder.

Having a reliable system is not sufficient for either research or clinical purposes, although it is a starting point. For the system to be broadly useful, the disorders must be valid syndromes. Validity can consist of face validity, descriptive validity, predictive validity, and construct validity.

In our current state of the art, many of the disorders described in children and adolescents have only face validity—that is, a number of clinicians agree that such disorders exist. Some have descriptive validity in that they are characterized by symptoms not commonly seen in persons with other types of mental disorders or in individuals with no mental disorders. Data are accumulating to suggest that some of the disorders in childhood and adolescence, such as conduct disorder and atten-tion deficit disorder, have a good degree of predictive validity.

Any system of classification should attempt to describe disorders, not to classify children. Within a group of children presenting with a particular psychiatric disorder, there will not be homogeneity in many areas. A child or adolescent may present with one disorder at one phase of life and with another disorder or with none later in life. Thus, it is the disorder that is being classified, not the child.

The best system will have adequate differentiation between disorders and coverage of patients who present with different types of disorders. Ideally, children and adolescents who are evaluated will present with only one disorder, with one that is described somewhere within the particular classification system. In reality, at least 25 percent of psychiatrically ill adults will receive a diagnosis of "undiagnosed mental disorder" if one uses strict diagnostic criteria.

Fewer studies have been done with adolescent, grade school, and preschool age children; but it is likely that as one goes down the age range, since the repertoire of behaviors decreases with age, more young children will present with syndromes that do not meet a particular diagnostic criteria even though they may be considered to have a definitive psychiatric disorder in the sense that they have a disorder of emotions, behavior, relationships, or cognition severe and sustained enough to cause significant functional impairment.

The ideal classification system would also provide adequate differentiation among the categories described in the system. Child psychiatrists often see children presenting with conditions that are normal at one point in life but pathological in another. (For example, bed wetting at age two and bed wetting at age fourteen.) Moreover, as children and adolescents are developing, the same symptoms presenting at different ages may have different implications in terms of etiology, natural history, and response to treatment. The preschooler's refusal to go to school may have meanings quite different from the adolescent's.

In addition to distinguishing disorders from one another, a good system will clearly distinguish normality from abnormality. This problem is faced by all systems. Child psychiatrists have the added problem of meeting a system that defines normality for different ages at different developmental levels. Psychiatric classification systems that attempt to categorize psychiatric disorders of infancy, early childhood, and adolescence thus must have a developmental framework.

IS CLASSIFICATION HARMFUL?

There is a school of thought that suggests that classifying psychiatric disorders is merely "labeling people" and leads to harmful effects. Weiner (1982) has reviewed these potential harmful effects: psychological dehumanization, interpersonal stigma, and social and political deprivation.

Some think that to understand and help any individual with a psychiatric disorder the clinician must respect the uniqueness of the individual. Weiner pointed out that classifying persons by disorders prohibits the clinician from treating each patient as a unique individual. To learn something about a person may require an individual diagnostic formulation. To learn about a psychiatric disorder requires an adequate classification system. These are not mutually exclusive. A diagnostic formulation can tell us what is individually unique about a person who may have one type of disorder as compared to someone with the same type of disorder. Their sharing the same type of disorders tells us some things that they have in common. Moreover, complete abandonment of classification and attention *only* to individual characteristics will make treating each patient a research project for a clinician each time he sees a new individual. For if there are no shared characteristics, then there can be no body of knowledge accumulated from the general clinical practice of others and the previous experiences of those who have investigated and treated certain kinds of problems.

Weiner identified three types of interpersonal stigma that have been thought to result from classification: prejudice and rejection, negative expectations, and destructiveness in interpretation of behavior. One tenet of those who subscribe to the labeling theory is that if people are called psychiatrically disturbed, then other individuals will automatically look with disfavor on them and exclude them from everyday activities. If this in fact did occur, it would be difficult to justify classification on a regular basis. However, there are several studies that suggest that even though this may be a common belief, it is now clear that prejudice and rejection are not automatic consequences of classification. Weiner pointed to recent work that suggests that at least in the United States, increasing knowledge about psychiatric disorders has engendered increasing tolerance, and current attitudes are more accepting than rejecting. Secondly, it is not at all clear that rejection of a disturbed individual results from the classification per se rather than the disturbed behavior that he or she emanates. Rutter has also pointed this out with children.

Some have suggested that for children very little if any stigma is attached to simply carrying a label (whether it be psychiatrically disordered, mentally retarded, or learning disabled) and to receiving some type of special intervention such as special classroom placement. Rather, peers tend to be relatively open to changing attitudes depending on how the handicapped individual behaves.

One study by Budoff and Siperstein (1978) found that sixth-grade children labeled mentally retarded who performed poorly were viewed more positively than children who performed equally poorly but who did not carry the label of mental retardation. One explanation is that the label of mental retardation carried an explanation of why the poor academic performance might occur and made children more tolerant of those who were mentally retarded.

In an important book on classification of childhood psychiatric disorders, Hobbs (1975) pointed out that children given a label may be treated differently by parents or teachers. Thus, if teachers feel that a child is supposed to be a slow learner, then they may treat him differently and in fact encourage behaviors that make him perform worse. Likewise children labeled as high achievers may be called upon more in class, which will foster high achiever behavior. However, these effects apparently diminish fairly rapidly as teachers become better acquainted with their students.

Moreover, as Weiner pointed out, the fact that this type of negative expectation *can* occur as the result of a label does not mean that classification should be avoided—rather that it should be done better. Accurate expectations are promoted by careful and detailed classification and thus should foster correct expectations rather than negative ones. Thus, Weiner felt that negative expectations are not a necessary consequence of classification per se, but rather that they are unfortunate results of inadequate classification and can be avoided.

With regard to destructive interpretation of behavior, the Rosenhan (1973) study stands as a possible example. Rosenhan had eight normal individuals apply to admission to twelve different mental hospitals with the complaint of auditory hallucinations. These individuals were admitted with the diagnosis of manic depressive psychosis or schizophrenia. According to Rosenhan, the nonpatients, once they entered into the hospital, behaved in a normal fashion. However, nursing notes indicated that staff interpreted this "normal behavior" in pathological terms. He argued that once a patient was labeled "psychiatrically disturbed," all other behaviors were interpreted as abnormal. Rosenhan's work has received a lot of notoriety and has been criticized by Spitzer, Weiner, and others on a number of grounds: (1) As Weiner pointed out, patients who voluntarily admit to having auditory hallucinations and present to a hospital are likely to be admitted, and this is appropriate. (2) Weiner questioned from Rosenhan's own data whether these pseudopatients' behavior in the hospital was actually normal. (3) Rosenhan did not provide convincing data to suggest that these individuals' behavior was misinterpreted in any way, and indeed nurses' notes suggest that there was "no abnormal behavior" recorded on many occasions, indicating that they were perceiving these individuals' behavior correctly.

Whether or not Rosenhan's study demonstrates what it is supposed to, it is possible that a diagnostic label can influence how an observer perceives a child's behavior. Once again, however, such misinterpretation is not necessarily an inevitable consequence of classification but may in fact be prevented by adequate classification. More information about accurate diagnosis that conveys essential clinical information about patients' problems is likely to lead to less misinterpretation rather than more.

Finally, we must consider the question of social and political deprivation as put forth by authors such as Szasz (1961) and others. In reviewing this literature, Weiner asked two critical questions: (1) Is political and social deprivation an inevitable consequence of classification per se? (2) If it does occur, is classification indeed responsible for it?

According to the labeling theory, individuals who are labeled as sick, ill, disturbed, or crazy are labeled not because of their behavior but rather because of their economic characteristics, which may be different from the surrounding community. Moreover, according to the theory, the act of classification itself causes psychological maladjustment and does not lead to beneficial intervention. Weiner found little research support for the labeling theory. Any deprivation that may occur is an abuse of classification, not a proper use of classification.

Thus, a quick review of the arguments against classification indicates that the major ones suggesting that classification may be harmful actually have very little empirical support. It seems clear that benefits derived from classification far outweigh possible disadvantages.

WAYS TO CLASSIFY

"Official" classification systems of psychiatric disorders generally have been categorical systems. Categorical systems usually begin when clinical criteria are established for a particular diagnosis. Then, based on the diagnostic evaluation, it is determined whether or not the patient's disorder meets the criteria for one or more of these diagnostic categories. This categorical approach owes much to the medical model. An increasingly popular approach in classification does not begin with clinical criteria, but rather with mathematical and statistical methods to define dimensions of behavior. These behavioral dimensions are then scored so that a child can be rated on several dimensions of behavior; the result is a profile rather than a statement that the child's disorder meets the criteria for one or more diagnostic categories. This approach is generally known as the "dimensional approach." The categorical approach in psychiatric diagnosis, at least with adult disorders, owes much to the work of the Washington University Group in St. Louis under the direction of Eli Robins.

In 1972, Feighner and his colleagues (Feighner et al. 1972) published the Washington University criteria for the diagnosis of certain adult psychiatric disorders for research purposes. These criteria were offered in terms of their validation in a five-stage scheme, as follows: (1) clinical description; (2) delimitation from other disorders; (3) laboratory studies; (4) family studies; and (5) follow-up studies.

Delineation of a precise clinical picture including essential symptoms and associated symptoms, age of onset, demographic factors, and so on, is the first stage of the Washington University scheme. This is the equivalent of face validity. According to this scheme, if one defines a precise clinical syndrome and then demonstrates a characteristic natural history, family pattern, laboratory findings, and so on, one validates the original clinical picture. However, evidence from the other areas could in fact lead to a revision of the original clinical picture into several different distinct subgroups. A characteristic natural history would suggest that the original group did form a homogeneous patient population, while marked differences in natural history, such as the difference between complete recovery versus the development of a chronic disorder, would suggest that the original group was indeed a heterogeneous group. Perhaps by retrospectively looking at the two groups in terms of their initial clinical picture, one might be able to associate differences in initial clinical picture with differences in natural history. Likewise, family studies of adults with major types of psychiatric disorder have suggested that these disorders do tend to run in families, whether for genetic or environmental reasons or a combination of both. Thus, a characteristic family pattern linked with a particular clinical picture adds validity to the notion that the original clinical picture forms a distinct clinical psychiatric syndrome. Differences in family pattern may suggest differences in the original patient population that might be meaningful in terms of laboratory studies or some other type of measure.

Klerman et al. (1983) recently reviewed the approach of the NIMH collaborative study of affective disorders in adults in the evaluation of diagnostic classes. Their approach owes much to the work of Robins and Guze. He divided the concept of validity into internal validity and external validity. Once one has established criteria for a particular syndrome and collected reliable clinical data, the next step is the demonstration of internal validity. This essentially means determining the consistency of the symptoms that comprise the essential diagnostic criteria for the syndrome, usually done by correlation of statistical methods. The second step then is the validation of clinical syndromes by correlation with external validating criteria, much as described in the Robins scheme. The external criteria, outlined by Klerman, for the validation of the depressive syndromes in adults in the NIMH collaborative study would include:

1. *Epidemiological* (such as incidence rates, prevalence rates, lifetime expectancy, and morbid risk);
2. *Family aggregation studies* that look for patterns of psychiatric illness in the close family members of adult probands with certain types of affective disorder. As with the Robins model, this could mean genetic factors, environmental factors, or some type of interactive approach between genetic and environmental factors;
3. *Biological laboratory studies*, including biochemical, neurophysiological, and others, comparable to the laboratory study phase of the Robins scheme;
4. *Correlation with psychosocial factors*, such as life events, early childhood experiences, specific personality patterns, not found in the Robins scheme but analogous to biological laboratory correlates;
5. *Natural history studies* that look at various patterns of outcome;
6. *Response to treatment studies*. The outcome studies are the same as the follow-up study in the Robins scheme; the response to treatment studies does not occur in the Robins scheme.

Klerman divided the external validating criteria into antecedent, concurrent, and predictive correlates. Antecedent validators would include the family psychopathology, patterns of premorbid personality, and certain sociodemographic variables. Concurrent validation criteria would be, for example, life events associated with the onset of illness. Predictive validating criteria, which involve finding correlation with subsequent events, would include the follow-up studies and response to treatment studies.

Cantwell (1975) modified the original Washington University five-phase scheme. He outlined a six-stage system for the validation: (1) clinical picture; (2) physical and neurologic factors; (3) laboratory studies; (4) family studies; (5) follow-up studies; and (6) treatment studies. In this scheme, the first stage of clinical description includes a description of the essential clinical symptoms that must be present for the disorder to be diagnosed and also of associated clinical symptoms that *may* be present and are more likely present in these children than in children with other types of psychiatric disorder and/or normal children but that are not necessary for the diagnosis to be made. Nonsymptom factors such as age of onset, chronicity, and so on can also be a part of this phase. Inclusion criteria list factors by which the children can be diagnosed as having this condition, while exclusion criteria eliminate children with other conditions. Thus, the first phase in the Cantwell six-phase scheme combines the first two Washington University phases, clinical description and delimitation from other disorders.

This scheme is based on the premise that all child psychiatric disorders, with rare exception, are of multifactorial etiology. Children who meet strict diagnostic criteria for any condition probably form a heterogeneous group etiologically. In this six-stage model, studies of a large number of children who meet a precise clinical description such as that for major depressive disorder in childhood are likely to reveal subgroups of the initial population.

With regard to follow-up studies, it is unreasonable to expect that children who meet criteria for a definable psychiatric disorder will necessarily have the same untreated natural history. There are too many variables in a child's life not to expect that outcomes are going to be different. However, very marked differences in outcome may suggest etiologically distinct subgroups among the initial patient population, all of whom met the essential criteria for the disorder.

Family studies have not been used as much in child psychiatry as they have in adult psychiatry. However, the finding that the same disorders occur more often in close family relatives of patients with the disorder than they do in normal individuals or in families of children with other types of psychiatric disorder adds validity to the idea that the original population formed a distinct clinical syndrome. The delineation of family history positive and negative subgroups of the depressive syndrome may be a fruitful way of subdividing the population. Cantwell (1975) also added family interaction studies in his six-phase scheme. This is somewhat analogous to the correlation with psychosocial factors in the Klerman scheme but is not as broad, since the Klerman scheme takes in such things as life events and other psychosocial factors.

Finally, response to treatment in the Klerman scheme and the Cantwell scheme, particularly psychopharmacologic treatment, has been suggested as a way of adding validity to psychiatric syndromes. Some time ago, Klein and his colleagues (Klein et al. 1980) suggested the use of response to psychotropic drugs as a way of subdividing various adult psychiatric disorders. Cantwell (1975) suggested that it may be meaningful to subdivide the hyperactive child syndrome into groups of patients who get a distinctly positive response to treatment and those who get a distinctly negative response. The same case could be made for the depressive syndrome—it may also be fruitful to subdivide the population into those who respond positively to tricyclic antidepressants versus those who get a negative or neutral response.

In summary, Feighner, Robins, and their colleagues have put forth a scheme that is a useful way of validating categorical psychiatric diagnoses in adults. The Klerman scheme, which describes the evaluation of diagnostic categories used in the NIMH collaborative study of depression in adults, has many similarities. Both of these systems are similar to the six-phase scheme described by Cantwell for the validation of child psychiatric categorical diagnoses.

In classification of child psychiatric disorders, Achenbach (1982) has been one of the leading proponents of the multivariate statistical approach. His steps for creating such a classification system are as follows. Correlations are used to measure the tendency of specific items of behavior to occur together. Once correlation among individual items of behavior is computed, multivariate statistical analyses of the correlations can detect groups of items that regularly occur together. The user can decide subjectively which mathematical criteria to use. Once that is done, however, the computer will derive groups of items in a reliable fashion. So whoever does the analysis, once scores for a particular sample of children are selected, a particular way of analysis will always produce the same results. This eliminates observation unreliability.

Techniques such as factor analysis produce dimensions of behavior or factors. An item can load on one or more factors, and the loading will range from -1.0 to $+1.0$. The loading of an item on a factor will show how strongly the item correlates with a dimension defined by a particular factor. Thus, an item like "fidgets and can't sit still" may load on a hyperactivity factor and may also load on a conduct disorder factor. The higher the correlation of the individual item with a particular factor, the greater the loading on that particular factor. Factor analysis, however, classifies types of behavior; it does not classify *individuals*. Thus, a further step is cluster analysis, which derives syndromes of behavior. Cluster analysis can form groups of individuals that are mutually exclusive in that each individual is a member of only one cluster. This is a potential problem: individuals with borderline types of disorders or overlapping syndromes may receive two separate diagnoses such as attention deficit disorder and conduct disorder; in a categorical system they will be classified as one or the other by cluster, since by definition each individual can belong to only one cluster.

Achenbach and Edelbrock (1978) reviewed twenty-seven multivariate studies involving classification of psychiatric disorders in children and adolescents. There were several recurrent syndromes that tended to cut across all studies. In their own study of 2,683 sixteen-year-old boys and girls seen in a variety of different health facilities, Achenbach and Edelbrock found seven clusters of disorder in boys and eight among the girls.

In general the syndromes that are evolved from multivariate studies can be divided into "broad band" and "narrow band" syndromes. Achenbach made an analogy between the broad band and the narrow band syndromes and the broad (i.e., anxiety disorders) and more specific (i.e., separation anxiety disorders) diagnostic categories of DSM-III and other categorical systems. In several publications Achenbach (1980) has made detailed comparisons of DSM-III categorical syndromes and empirically defined narrow band syndromes; he has found that there were DSM-III disorders that did not appear to have empirical counterparts, that there were empirically derived syndromes that did not appear to have categorical counterparts, and that a significant number of syndromes were found both in the multivariate studies and in the categorical system.

A few authors have attempted to show how the multivariate techniques can be used in combination with the more clinically based approach for defining categorical syndromes in order to achieve a classification system. Pfohl and Andreasen (1978) outlined such a process. Their approach will be reviewed here along with a critique of certain aspects of the use of multivariate statistical techniques. Pfohl and Andreasen began with a simple and logical process of classification that involves four basic steps, each utilizing particular statistical techniques. The four steps include: (1) the selection of patients and variables to be studied; (2) the division of these patients into groups; (3) the development of diagnostic criteria (the criteria would be the essential features of the groups that were created in step 2); and (4) the evaluation of the diagnostic system created by steps one through three. The evaluation would be in terms of reliability and validity, and validity would be checked with regard to etiology, response to treatment, natural history, and other features such as family history of psychiatric illness. In their view the key is to see where each of the particular statistical techniques would fit into their four-step process. They pointed out that each of the four steps can be accomplished by combining clinical judgment with a particular statistical method. In their view, clinical judgment will continue to play a major and indispensable role in this process of creating diagnostic systems.

Step one involves the selection of patients. They rightly pointed out that the type of patients usually selected for study will influence both the complexity of the classification problems and also the variables that can be studied. Their view is that one should probably take a sample that includes patients who represent a broad diagnostic group (such as affective disorder or conduct disorder) that needs further subdivision. It should also be clear that the selection of the patient sample, or indeed a nonpatient sample as is in some cases with epidemiologic studies, will determine whether or not a particular dimension of behavior and (with further analysis) a cluster or syndrome will occur. For example, infantile autism is a relatively rare condition occurring in about five per ten thousand of the population. Thus, unless the patient sample base is extremely large, it is not likely that many autistic children will be included in the sample. If there are no autistics included in the sample, then an "autistic" or a "psychotic" factor will not emerge, and by extension, a psychotic syndrome representing infantile autism as a categorical diagnosis will not come up when mathematical techniques of cluster analysis are applied.

After the selection of patients, the next step is the selection of variables or symptoms to be measured. In studies with child psychiatric patients this is generally done by specifying items of behavior that are thought to represent commonly occurring psychiatric symptoms in children. It is axiomatic that if a symptom is not on a particular scale, then syndromes in which that symptom plays a predominant role will not be created when mathematical analysis takes place. It is also often overlooked that if the *meaning* of a particular symptom is misconstrued by a parent or a teacher, then syndromes can be created that have no "real" counterpart. For example, a common symptom on behavior rating scales for children is worded something like: "obsessive ideas, can't get mind off certain thoughts." This item is supposed to represent an obsessional thought. However, I have universally found that parents check this symptom off, and when I inquire about it, they usually say something like: "Well, what I mean by that is when he goes to Toys-R-Us and he gets his mind on having a certain toy, he just won't give up until we buy it for him." This is probably not the meaning attributed to it by those who created the rating scale. But without the opportunity for discussion of the meaning and significance of the symptom as it occurs in a parent interview, the computer will simply tabulate that as a positive symptom that occurs. This can be overcome by having parents or teachers write out descriptions of symptoms they check as positive.

Symptoms can be measured in a variety of ways: a dichotomous score of present or absent, a rank order score, a quantitative scale, or a nominal qualitative scale. Whatever the choice of measure, there should be good interrater reliability. A variety of different statistical methods is useful here.

Reduction of variables is the last phase of step one. As the number of variables per patient increases, the chance for spurious results increases greatly. Thus, investigators can intuitively combine variables in various theoretical ways to produce dimensions such as psychoticism, neuroticism, depression, and so on. It is here that factor analysis and principle component analysis find their greatest use. However, it should be pointed out that factor analysis and principle component analysis will produce statistically meaningful correlations between items, but that the *statistically* significant dimension of behavior created may not be *clinically* or *theoretically* meaningful. It also should be recognized that at this point there are various methods of factor analysis, and depending on the type of factor analysis done and the criteria used in combining the various symptoms, the same data will produce different results. Thus, there is some subjectivity and some clinical judgment in deciding what criteria and what method of factor analysis to use.

The second major step in Pfohl and Andreasen's scheme for construction of a classification system is division of the patient population into groups. This can be done on an intuitive and clinical basis, as has been done with depressed patients. These patients can be subdivided by certain clinical features, such as endogenous versus nonendogenous versus psychotic, or by family history, such as depressive spectrum disease, pure depressive disease, and sporadic depressive disease. Cluster analysis can also be used to subdivide the patients. Its use is based on the assumption that the patient group is indeed heterogeneous in terms of psychopathology *and* that the variables measured are indeed relevant to the heterogeneous nature of the population. It is often not recognized that while intuitive methods of grouping patients have some defects, the use of cluster analysis is not entirely an empirical method. Different methods of cluster analysis differ in the groupings that they produce. For example, some techniques will allow the investigator to determine how similar patients must be to be grouped together. Others require that the investigator give exactly the number of categories of classification. Some will allow for unclassified patients; others do not. Studies of adult patients have shown that depending on the methods of cluster analysis used, the same patients will be classified in different groupings. The use of cluster and factor analysis to produce syndromes in child psychiatry has also been complicated by the fact that often only one data source is used—most commonly a parent or teacher rating scale. The Isle of Wight study (Rutter, Tizard, and Whitmore 1970) showed that the parent and teacher rating scales are equally effective in picking out children who are ultimately determined to have a psychiatric diagnosis, but that they tend to pick out *different* children; it is therefore axiomatic that the use of parent and teacher rating scales *alone* with the same children will tend to produce different clusters of children even using the same methods of cluster analysis. How to amalgamate data from the different sources (parents, teachers, children, etc.) into a statistical analysis is a subject for future research.

Step three involves the development of diagnostic criteria. This can be an entirely intuitive clinical approach. A good example of such an approach was Kanner's original description of infantile autism in 1943. The criteria he used to identify those patients have stood the test of time some forty years later. With adult psychiatric disorders a number of specific criteria have been developed for greater diagnostic reliability. These include the Feighner criteria developed by the Washington University Group and the Research Diagnostic Criteria (RDC) developed by Spitzer, Endicott, and Robins (1978). The use of such criteria for child psychiatric disorders is in its infancy. The DSM-III criteria are essentially the first set of operational diagnostic criteria analogous to the Feighner criteria and the RDC developed for children. Discriminant analysis and stepwise discriminant function analysis are useful statistical techniques at this stage. These techniques determine which symptoms are most useful in discriminating one diagnostic group from another. However, there are statistical limitations. If the number of patients is relatively small compared to the number of variables, fictitious results are generally guaranteed. The number of variables has to be somewhat below 25 to 30 percent of the total number of patients. The test of this of course occurs when the original sample can be classified with an accuracy of close to 100 percent, but when the same discriminant equations are used with a new set of patients, classification is no more reliable than flipping a coin. Logical decision tree approaches such as CATEGO and DIAGNO have been developed, but in contrast to the discriminant analysis methods, different investigators will develop different systems of diagnoses even if they are given the same diagnostic patients as prototypes. Diagnostic decision trees require considerable user intervention in order to decide how the system evolves. Again, the test of this type of system is to classify a new set of patients.

Stage four in the creation of a diagnostic system according to Pfohl and Andreasen is evaluation of the system. The system to be used will stand or fall on its reliability and validity. For a system of classification of childhood disorders to be useful, it must be reliable. The kappa coefficient of agreement controls for chance and is probably the best statistic to use to test interrater reliability of psychiatric diagnosis.

Content, construct, and predictive validity are important. Content validity essentially means: are there real patients who present with problems that fit the nosological categories that are described in the system? A related issue is whether the various categories provide complete coverage for the types of problems children present with; is there a significant number of children who present with problems whose clinical pictures are not described anywhere in the system?

Construct validity essentially means: is the system consistent with various theories? Since etiologic theories are essentially unvalidated themselves for a large number of child psychiatric categories, construct validity is difficult to test for any diagnostic system in child psychiatry.

From the clinical standpoint, predictive validity is probably the most important. A clinician needs to feel that a particular diagnosis will predict some factor, such as untreated natural history, likely response or nonresponse to different types of therapeutic intervention, family pattern of psychiatric illness, and so on. With some disorders, predictive validity has been assessed by particular laboratory measures. For child psychiatry, untreated natural history, response to treatment, family patterns of psychiatric illness, and psychosocial factors such as life stress, are probably the most likely criterion for external validity.

Robins (1976) has compared the likely long-term utility of the categorical and dimensional approaches. He pointed out that the categorical approach has a long history in many areas in medicine. In his view, psychiatry does not have the laboratory tests that have been used to validate the categorical systems used in other areas of medicine. Until recently, there has been a lack of standard psychiatric definitions, large enough data bases, and acceptance of computer-rated psychiatric diagnosis by those in the psychiatric community. Psychiatry should tackle these three obstacles rather than abandon the categorical approach per se. Patients who present with more than one psychiatric illness or who are psychiatrically ill but whose condition is better classified as "undiagnosed" create problems for both the dimensional and the categorical approaches, but the categorical approach seems to have fewer problems with these patients. The categorical approach may become obsolete if the accuracy of the methods of obtaining information is not monitored, if more information is not obtained, if the normal and abnormal ranges to be expected for a given psychiatric disorder are not monitored, and if we are not prepared to change criteria if research shows that they need modification.

All of these factors are needed to prevent obsolescence of the dimensional approach as well, but in Robins' view there are additional issues. Changes in models will be necessary to prevent obsolescence of the dimensional approach. He feels that the use of cutoffs based on clinical experience in the categorical approach has an advantage over arbitrary cutoffs based on models in the dimensional approach. Robins feels that the additional limitations of the dimensional approach include: lack of standard clinical definitions, lack of a large data base that is sufficiently reliable, and difficulties presented by undiagnosed patients. Robins also points out that each dimensional model has certain underlying assumptions behind it. He feels that an assumption-free approach should be used with numerical data that come directly from psychiatric and other test results. The categorical approach is relatively easy to use with an assumption-free basis, but it may not be possible to obtain in a dimensional approach.

REFERENCES

Achenbach, T. M. (1980). DSM-III in light of empirical research on the classification of child psychopathology. *Journal of the American Academy of Child Psychiatry* 19:395–412.

———. (1982). *Developmental Psychopathology*. 2d ed. New York: Wiley, pp. 547–76.

———, and Edelbrock, C. (1978). The classification of child psychopathology: A review and analysis of empirical efforts. *Psychological Bulletin* 85:1275–301.

Budoff, M., and Siperstein, G. N. (1978). Low-income children's attitudes toward mentally retarded children: Effects of labeling and academic behavior. *American Journal of Mental Deficiency* 82:474–79.

Cantwell, D. P. (1975). *The Hyperactive Child: Diagnosis, Management, and Current Research*. New York: Spectrum.

———. (1980). The diagnostic process and diagnostic classification in child psychiatry—DSM-III. *Journal of the American Academy of Child Psychiatry* 19:345–355.

———. (1985). Organization and use of DSM-III. In D. Shaffer, A. A. Ehrhardt, and L. L. Greenhill (Eds.). *The Clinical Guide to Child Psychiatry*. New York: Free Press, pp. 475–90.

———.(In press). Clinical child psychopathology—diagnostic assessment, diagnostic process, and diagnostic classification: DSM-III studies. In M. Rutter, H. Tuma, and I. Lann (Eds.). *Assessment, Diagnosis and Classification in Child and Adolescent Psychopathology*. New York: Guilford Press.

Feighner, J. P., Robins, E., Guze, S. B., et al. (1972). Diagnostic criteria for use in psychiatric research. *Archives of General Psychiatry* 26:57–63.

Hobbs, N. (1975). *The Futures of Children: Categories, Labels and Their Consequences*. San Francisco: Jossey-Bass.

Kanner, L. (1943). Autistic disturbances of affective contact. *Nervous Children* 2:217–50.

Klein, D. F., et al. (1980). *Diagnosis and Drug Treatment of Psychiatric Disorder in Adults and Children*. Baltimore: Williams and Wilkins.

Klerman, G. L., et al. (1983). Major depression and related affective disorders. Presented at the American Psychiatric Association Invitational Workshop, DSM-III: An Interim Appraisal. Washington, D.C., October 12–15, 1983.

Pfohl, B., and Andreasen, N. C. (1978). Development of classification systems in psychiatry. *Comprehensive Psychiatry* 19:197–207.

Robins, E. (1976). Categories versus dimensions in psychiatric classification. *Psychiatric Annals* 6:39–55.

Rosenhan, D. L. (1973). On being sane in insane places. *Science* 179:250–58.

Rutter, M., Tizard, J., and Whitmore, K. (1970). *Education, Health and Behavior.* London: Longman Group.

Spitzer, R. L. (1976). More on pseudoscience in science and the case for psychiatric diagnosis. *Archives of General Psychiatry* 33:459–70.

Spitzer, R. L., and Endicott, J. (1968). A computer program for psychiatric diagnosis utilizing the differential diagnostic procedure. *Archives of General Psychiatry* 18:746–56.

———, and Robins E. (1978) *Research Diagnostic Criteria,* 3d ed. New York: New York State Department of Mental Hygiene, New York State Psychiatric Institute, Biometrics Research.

Szasz, T. S. (1961). *The Myth of Mental Illness.* New York: Harper and Row.

Weiner, I. B. (1982). *Child and Adolescent Psychopathology.* New York: Wiley, pp. 72–79.

2

A SEMISTRUCTURED APPROACH TO CLINICAL ASSESSMENT

Hector R. Bird and
Clarice J. Kestenbaum

INTRODUCTION

Child assessment is more complex than its adult counterpart. The child seldom attributes "patienthood" to himself. His defenses, like the rest of his personality, are in the process of development. Under the stress of being brought to a psychiatrist's office, he resorts to more primitive ways of dealing with life. More often than not, the clinician is faced with the child's denial, projection, and displacement. Adults can take over the diagnostic process and the negotiation of therapeutic measures. The parents may similarly distort the clinical picture in response to their guilt, anxiety, or anger at the child for his misbehavior. In order to obtain a comprehensive picture of the "patient," the clinician needs to rely on information provided by parents, teachers, other relatives, pediatricians, camp counselors, further testing done by a psychometrician or a learning specialist, as well as on the information provided by the child himself. Armed with this wealth of frequently conflicting data, the clinician must use his cumulative knowledge of personality development and psychopathology as well as his intuitive abilities to arrive at a tentative but operational diagnostic decision. Undoubtedly the clinician's biases enter into his ultimate judgment as to whose information is most accurate.

Whereas the clinician's goal in the process is to obtain the in-depth knowledge about a child implicit in the concept of "diagnosis," intervention measures often cannot wait for an assessment at a time of crisis—the child is about to be expelled or suspended from school or the family is in crisis because of his behavior. Moreover, most families who seek help for their children lack the sophistication or the financial resources to extend the process before some specific evaluative judgments and recommendations are provided. Whereas we agree with Gardner (1985) and others that a thorough evaluation is essential to ensure optimum service for the patient, practical and economic considerations move most clinicians toward a more structured approach to clinical assessment.

This chapter will focus specifically on two areas of assessment: interviewing approaches with parents and children, and the child mental status examination.

INTERVIEWING APPROACHES

There may be seemingly divergent opinions among clinicians and researchers as to which interviewing approach is likely to provide the most accurate and comprehensive information. Most will agree, however, on the types of information that are clinically useful. The approaches to interviewing range from the highly structured to the open-ended. So far neither extreme seems to satisfy the two requirements of diagnostic depth and diagnostic accuracy.

The issue of diagnostic validity is of paramount importance. Although there is no "gold standard" against which to measure the validity of clinical diagnosis, much attention is being cast on improving diagnostic reliability in both adult and child psychiatry. In a sense, the greater the reliability obtained through different diagnostic methodologies, the closer to the truth one can assume to be.

Endicott and Spitzer (1978) have attributed the problem of diagnostic unreliability to two major sources of error: criterion variance and information variance. Criterion variance results when operational criteria to define specific syndromes are lacking. Clinicians with different theoretical and experiential backgrounds may ascribe a diagnosis to a patient based on idiosyncratic and often highly personal criteria. Although not as frequently in recent years, we would often hear competent clinicians state: "I can diagnose a schizophrenic simply by the way he makes me feel." Labeling patients on such vague grounds is hardly justifiable or useful. Information variance poses an even greater problem, because it cannot be controlled. It is affected by many variables that are difficult to address or control, the most significant of which is recall.

With operational criteria based on descriptive symptomatology, DSM-III (1980) has attempted to reduce criterion variance. In adult psychiatry more structured assessments such as the Schedule for Affective Disorders and Schizophrenia (SADS) (Endicott and Spitzer 1978), the Diagnostic Interview Schedule (DIS) (Robins et al. 1981), or the Structured Clinical Interview for DSM-III (SCID) (Spitzer and Williams 1985) constitute attempts to improve diagnostic reliability by keeping information variance at a minimum. Similar efforts are taking place in the field of child psychiatry. Instruments such as the Kiddie SADS (Puig-Antich and Chambers 1978) and the Kiddie SADS-E (Orvaschel et al. 1982; Puig-Antich et al. 1980), the Diagnostic Interview for Children and Adolescents (DICA) (Herjanic et al. 1977), or the NIMH Diagnostic Interview Schedule for Children (NIMH-DISC) (Costello 1983) attest to this endeavor. Such efforts in child psychiatric assessment are further complicated by the multiple sources of information on which the diagnosis of child psychopathology is based. The additional element of informant variance enters into the picture (Kashani et al. 1985). The question of which source of information carries greater weight when conflicting data are obtained remains unresolved. The algorithms devised for the computerized use of these diagnostic instruments do not properly address this issue, and the measures of diagnostic interrater reliability obtained when they are put to the test are far from optimal. These instruments may be useful for research purposes, but they cannot presently be used to generate clinical diagnoses of individual children.

During the assessment process a clinician obtains information about developmental and past history as well as about family history. DSM-III nosology is based on criteria of current or recent symptomatic expressions that, clustered together, constitute a syndrome. With few exceptions these clusters fail to take into account developmental considerations. As Achenbach (1980) has pointed out, "the absence of positive adaptive behavior and the failure to progress along one or more dimensions of development are often more salient in childhood abnormalities than are symptoms like those considered pathognomonic of adult disorders" (p. 397). The issue of whether most of the DSM-III adult categories that can presently be applied to children truly have counterparts in childhood psychopathology is highly controversial and lies beyond the scope of this chapter. As clinicians we must deal with the current state of the art. Rutter (1975) has pointed out that with very few exceptions childhood disorders do not necessarily constitute diseases that differ qualitatively from normality; rather, individual children tend to differ quantitatively from the norm in a number of often unrelated parameters. The severity of dysfunctionality and associated impairment frequently leads us to consider the child "disturbed" and to intervene on his behalf, even when he may not fully meet the criteria for a specific disorder.

The instruments developed, or being developed, for the evaluation of child psychopathology are based on DSM-III criteria, or prior to that on RDC criteria; they consequently deemphasize the developmental dimension of child assessment. In addition, these instruments are usually designed so that they can be used by lay interviewers for research purposes. Thus, mental status and clinical observations, important dimensions of psychiatric assessment, are usually not recorded in these instruments or taken into account in the diagnoses they generate. Attempts at systematically gathering psychosocial and developmental data have been made (Brown and Rutter 1966; Lukens et al. 1983; NIMH 1973; Rutter and Brown 1966). In all likelihood, these instruments have not become incorporated into structured diagnostic instruments because the nosological systems themselves do not take into account this information for diagnostic purposes.

Thus etiological components traditionally attributed to developmental and familial factors have been purposely excluded from consideration in the systematic description of DSM-III disorders; but they unquestionably enter into a clinician's diagnostic considerations. A psychotic adolescent with hallucinations, constricted affect, and withdrawal is more likely to be judged schizophreniform by a clinician if there is a strong family history of schizophrenia than if there is a family history of affective disorder, or vice versa. Other issues of premorbid functioning and level of adaptation achieved throughout the patient's development will also enter into the picture.

Although structured diagnostic questionnaires have so far not proved to be the panacea for diagnostic accuracy, the open-ended, unstructured approach leaves much to be desired as well. A clinician's theoretical orientation, his preconceived notions about a patient's pathology, or even his own interest or area of highest competence may lead him to emphasize some aspects of the data obtained while neglecting or totally ignoring others that may be of equal or even greater significance.

The optimal interview format should include structured instruments that systematically investigate criteria applicable to the various diagnostic categories as well as developmental and family history; the clinician should be able to deviate from the instruments' structure to probe further. This semistructured approach can ensure that the data collection will be comprehensive but not circumscribed by a particular way of inquiring or wording. Dr. Orvaschel's chapter addresses the particular merits or deficiencies of existing structured instruments for child psychiatric assessment. Our opinion is that so far none of the existing instruments designed to provide child psychiatric diagnoses seems to be comprehensive enough; nor do they provide the desirable breadth and scope to the diagnostic parameters that need to be considered.

THE PARENT INTERVIEW

Parents generally provide more accurate information about developmental and past history than does the child. Orvaschel et al. (1981) noted that parents reported factual or time-related material such as duration of illness or treatment history more accurately than the child, whereas the child's own report was essential in assessing his own feelings and internal states. Mothers are reportedly more reliable informants than fathers (Evans and Nelson 1977).

Different clinicians approach the order of the interviews in a different fashion. Most will agree that with an intact family, at some phase of the assessment, one needs to see the parents alone, the child alone, and the whole family, or at least the triad together. It is important to see the parents alone to obtain information that the parents may feel uncomfortable discussing in front of their child. This should be scheduled without leaving the child out in the waiting room behind a locked door, fully cognizant of the fact that he is the central topic of the conversation. For similar reasons, the child must also be interviewed individually. It is highly unlikely that children will be able to reveal candidly negative feelings about their parents or maladaptive behaviors in front of their family. The family interview is equally important. At that point one can attempt to clarify contradictory pieces of possibly relevant information and observe family interactions, alliances and coalitions or collusions.

The parent interview can be useful to obtain information on current symptom-atology, its duration and its severity. A thorough outline for developmental and past history as well as family history is provided by Canino (1985). A child's develop-mental history must include data from the time of conception to the time when the evaluation takes place. The circumstances surrounding pregnancy and delivery as well as the child's early environment need to be explored. The infant's own charac-teristics and how these fit into parental expectations can reveal patterns of accep-tance or rejection that become established early in life. Although many parents are frequently inaccurate about the time at which developmental milestones are reached (Robins 1963), most can provide a fairly accurate assessment of their child's slow-ness or precociousness when compared to their other children or to other children of similar age. This evaluation should probe not only into areas of neurophysiolog-ical maturation, such as motor and language development, sphincter control, and sleeping patterns, but also into areas of emotional significance, such as attachment, relatedness, stranger and separation reactions, and emerging patterns of social in-teractions. An evaluation of the child's assets and areas of ego strength is equally important. Very often in our clinical zeal to help troubled people and to look for the roots of psychopathology, we may emphasize deviance and neglect to inquire about the child's assets and adaptive behaviors and capacities.

The parents are also the most accurate informants about the child's past medical history: illnesses, hospitalizations, serious injuries or trauma, and the impact of these factors on the child's life and activities. Parents will be most knowledgeable of de-tails related to the composition of the immediate as well as the extended family, as well as the history of psychiatric and other illnesses in the family, important life events and stresses, and the definition of family roles.

THE CHILD INTERVIEW

The child's interview should emphasize his report of his own feelings and inter-nal states, areas in which the child is considered to be the most reliable informant (Orvaschel et al. 1981). Kestenbaum and Bird (1978) have reported on the reliability of items in the Mental Health Assessment Form, an instrument for clinical assess-ment independent from other data. The first part of the MHAF scores mental status items on the basis of information gathered and observations made during the inter-view; the mental status examination will be discussed further. Whereas this pre-DSM-III instrument lacks the necessary specificity to generate diagnostic syndromes, its second part obtains and scores information on a variety of topics. These are re-lated to the child's perceptions of and feelings about his family and his family rela-tionships, school situation, relationships to his peers, fantasy life, and personality organization, including self-concept, moods, perceptions, and coping mechanisms. Scoring the instrument is facilitated by a semistructured interview; outlined on Table 2.1, this can serve as a guide to the interviewer.

TABLE 2.1 Outline of Suggested Semistructured Child and Adolescent Interview

School

What grade are you in?

What is your best subject? Which is worst?

Are you better in subjects in which you have to figure things out or ones which require memory?

Have you ever been held back in school?

Work

What would you like to be when you grow up?

Why do you think you would enjoy that?

Do you know any (name occupation choice)?

How good are your chances of becoming (occupation)?

What would you do if you couldn't be a (occupation)?

Have you ever had a job?

What did/do you do with the money you make?

Interpersonal Relations (Family)

Who lives at home with you?

Do you have brothers and sisters?

How do you all get along?

Who else is in your family?

When you have a problem, whom do you tell about it?

Does he/she help you with your problem?

Who is the closest person to you in your family?

Who gives you the most problems? Tell me about that.

How do you get along with your mother/father?

Who is their favorite?

Dependence-Independence with Family Members

Do your parents always tell you what to do or can you make some of your decisions?

What are the rules at home about going out alone or getting home, bringing friends home, etc.?

Have you ever been away from home at sleep-away camp or at a friend's home? How did you feel about being away?

What happens at home when you do something wrong or break the rules?

Interpersonal Relationships—Other Adults

What kind of relationship do you have with other adults (grown-ups) outside the family? (teachers, coach, minister, counselor, etc.)

Is there someone you especially admire?

Which adults do you respect the least?

Interpersonal Relations—Peers

Do you have friends?

Are most of your friends about your age?

Do you have friends who are older? younger?

Do you have a best friend?

How long has he/she been your best friend?

What sort of things do you do together?

Why did you pick him/her as your best friend?

How do you feel when something good (bad) happens to one of your friends?

Do you do what most kids want to do, or do they do what you want?

What happens when you can't get your own way?

Sexual Concepts and Behavior

What are the advantages of being a boy (girl)?

What are the disadvantages?

Do you like being a boy/girl?

Suppose you could start all over again, would you rather be a boy/girl?

(for adolescents)

Many people speak nowadays of the sexual revolution. How has this affected you?

Are kids in your group (school) very active sexually?

What is your opinion about kids your age "going all the way"? Have you done it yourself?

What do you think about homosexuality? Is homosexuality something you worry about?

There are a lot of old wives' tales about masturbation. What have you heard? Do you believe them?

Is masturbation a problem for you?

(female) Have you had your first period? Were you prepared? How do you feel during your periods?

(male) What did you feel was happening the first time you had a wet dream? Who explained it to you?

Self-concept

If I asked your parents what they think about you, what would they say?

Suppose I asked your friends?

If you could change anything about yourself, what would you change?

How do you compare yourself with your friends (in sports, looks, intelligence, personality)?

Do you like the way you are? Do people like you?

Conscience

What was your best deed?

What is the worst thing you've ever done?

Did it get you into trouble?

How did you feel?

Did you ever take something that didn't belong to you? What? What happened? How did you feel?

How do you feel when you do something you know is wrong?

Do you ever do it again?

(for adolescents)

How are your values different from your parents'?

Tell me about the drug scene among your friends. How about at school?

Have you tried any drugs? (Obtain names, frequency, amount.) How do you feel when you're high? How is this different from the way you feel most of the time?

When you get into trouble how do you get out of it?

Feeling States—General

How do you feel most of the time? (happy/sad)

How do you feel now compared to the way you usually feel?

What sort of things make you happy? sad?

What things do you enjoy doing most of all?

What was the happiest time in your life?

Feeling states—Anxiety

What things make you nervous?

What is the scariest thing that's ever happened to you?

What happens when you get scared like that?

When you are scared, does it bother you in other ways, like you can't sleep or get headaches, etc.?

Do you ever feel scared like that for no reason at all? What does that feel like?

Feeling States—Depression

What is the saddest thing that ever happened to you?

Do you ever feel sad even if there's no good reason? Tell me about that.

Do you ever think of dying? Have you ever thought of killing yourself? Have you ever tried to kill yourself?

When you feel sad like that, does it ever last many days in a row? How many days?

When you feel sad like that, does it bother you in other ways, like you can't sleep, appetite, etc.? Does that last many days in a row? How many days?

TABLE 2.1 (*continued*)

Did you ever feel the opposite, like you're on top of the world, for no reason at all? Tell me about it (duration, severity, other descriptive symptoms).

Feeling States—Anger
What do you do when you really want something and you don't get your way?
Do you have a "short fuse" (lose your temper easily)?
What sort of things make you angry?
What do you do when you get very angry?
Do you ever get into fights? with whom?
(if yes) Do you fight alone or in a group?

Reality Testing
Do you think there are people who can predict the future?
Do you believe in E.S.P.? Have you had experiences like that?
Some people when they get very nervous have funny experiences. Did it ever happen to you that you heard voices inside/outside your head? Were you fully awake? What did they say? (frequency, severity) What do you think that was?
Some kids have told me that they think their minds are controlled by something or someone else. Others believe someone is looking at them or talking about them when it really isn't so. Did something like that ever happen to you?

Fantasy
Do you have an active imagination?
When you're bored in school and looking out the window, what do you think about?
Make believe we just heard a loud noise outside the window, can you make up a story about what happened?
Do you dream a lot?
How often do you dream?
Are most of your dreams good dreams or bad dreams?
Tell me about a dream that you remember.
Did you ever (do you) have a make-believe friend? Tell me about him/her.
Do you keep a diary of your secret thoughts?

Other
What do you think the future will be like?
How do you see yourself in five to ten years?
What do you think happens to people after they die?
Do you play sports? Are you good in sports?
Do you have any hobbies?
Do you have any special talents (drawing, music, etc.)?

(for adolescents)

What is your particular philosophy of life?
Do you like jokes? Can you tell me a joke that you have heard recently?

Most of the items on the MHAF are scored on a scale of 1 to 5 ranging from "no deviation" to "marked deviation" from the expectable. It requires that the rater be a trained clinician who uses his clinical experience and theoretical knowledge to determine whether a particular item is to be scored as within the expectable range or deviant. Other items are dichotomous and are scored on a yes/no basis. The interview questions address the child's experience of his feelings, as well as his attitudes towards school, interpersonal relations, adaptive abilities, and inner life. They are geared to elicit information that will enable the rater to score the items on the MHAF. Although the interviewer is expected to cover all the topics in the interview, he is nonetheless encouraged to adapt the wording to his personal style as well as to what he perceives is the most comprehensible language for his subject. Furthermore, the interviewer is also expected to deviate from the interview format and to add questions or probes he may consider necessary to elicit information from a particular child. With few exceptions the child's responses to the interview questions are not item specific; consequently, the scoring of each item is based on the rater's evaluation and measure of the particular child's normality or degree of deviance. Given this subjective and noncategorical approach to rating, it was surprising to find, on many important items, high Pearson correlates of interrater reliability among three child psychiatrists observing videotaped interviews of deviant and nondeviant children.

Although the instrument was not designed to rate children on the basis of diagnostic categories, items in it could certainly be incorporated into more structured instruments to provide measures on some of the dimensions that these instruments lack. The interview outlined in Table 2.1 provides a semistructured format that can be administered to most children between the ages of seven and sixteen years with only minor modifications consonant with their particular age and cognitive level. The entire interview can be completed in from thirty to forty-five minutes.

THE MENTAL STATUS EXAMINATION

The Mental Status Examination is another essential dimension of the diagnostic process in child psychiatry. Extensive discussions of the child mental status examination are provided by Goodman and Sours (1967) and Simmons (1981). The mental status report documents the clinician's observations of his patient's appearance, behavior, speech and use of language, social relatedness, affect, cognitive functioning, and thought processes. The clinician must record equally the patient's descriptions of feeling states or perceptual distortions. As clinicians, we are prone to infer feeling from behavior. It is of utmost importance that the mental status examination be as devoid of inference as possible and that we record what we see and hear, rather than what we think it means. The mental status should note perceived areas of ego strength (exceptional beauty, talents, interests, capacity to abstract, use of vocabulary, and so on), as well as deviations from the norm. There are five broad areas that need to be assessed; these are also included in the Mental Health Assessment Form and consist of physical appearance, motoric behavior and speech, relatedness during the interview, affect, and language and thinking.

Whereas one's esthetic appreciation of beauty or ugliness is ultimately a matter of personal taste, most people will agree about the extremes of exceptional beauty or exceptional ugliness. How one is perceived by others undoubtedly has an impact on self-concept. To be attractive to others is an ego asset; to be disliked because one is overweight or too short or too tall for one's age can be a liability and a stumbling block to successful adaptation. The clinician should judge how his patient compares in these parameters to other children of the same age and sex. He should note any deviations in physical characteristics—scars, burns, acne, hypertelorism. The patient's neatness or lack of it, his clothes, and any clues as to deviations in sexual identity formation can also help to delineate characterological psychopathology.

The clinician should note the child's level of motor activity. Can he sit still during the interview or is he aimlessly moving around the office? Is he clumsy and uncoordinated? Other observations should be made about unusual patterns of motor behavior such as tics, nail biting, thumb sucking, scratching, and so on. The child's speech patterns are also important. Does he stutter or lisp? Is the quality of his speech whining or monotonous or does he speak too loudly or too softly?

Most children are usually brought to a psychiatrist because someone considers their behavior to be deviant. In a child's mind, deviant behavior is equated with misbehavior, which is often the case. He therefore considers himself a bad child. The fact that he is meeting a strange adult in a strange setting is sufficient to provoke a high level of anxiety. If that is compounded by the fact that he is there to attend to his "meanness," then anxiety must be high indeed. When in spite of all these sources of anxiety the child is able to relate to the clinician, this tells us something about his ego defenses and his capacity to adapt. As clinicians we still need to assess the quality of his relatedness: in the face of this anxiety, does he withdraw or become inordinately mistrustful? Can he establish a rapport and make eye contact? How long does it take him to warm up? How responsive is he to reassurance? Does he become excessively compliant and overly positive?

In evaluating the child's affect it is neccessary to note not only the quality but the intensity of a particular affective expression. Is his affect sad or depressed or is it inappropriate? Does he exhibit a full range of affective expression or is it constricted? Does anxiety paralyze him to the point that the interview must be terminated?

Cognitive functioning is usually best evaluated through formal psychometric testing. However, as clinicians we must estimate a child's cognitive abilities so that we can make appropriate referrals for further tests and not subject the child or his family unnecessarily to the added expense, time, and effort involved. An experienced clinician has a normative mental set he can use to evaluate cognitive functions. The child's ability to remember and reason, the vocabulary he uses, and his capacity to understand and conceptualize provide clues to his cognitive level. An assessment of his reality testing is also of diagnostic importance. Through the content of the interview and through direct questioning, one can usually detect a persecutory trend that has not reached delusional proportions; occasionally, particularly in the adolescent age group, one finds frank delusions and hallucinatory experiences. The patient seldom volunteers information about such frightening phenomena; one needs to ask. The child's use of language can not only provide clues to his cognitive level, but also suggest problems with central language processing. His choice of words may be inappropriate, as may be his grammar or syntax. One must be specially attentive for neologisms or echolalic speech as well as for other aspects of an expressive language disturbance. Goodman and Sours (1967) questioned whether thought disorders exist in young children; they suggested that a judgment be made about the pervasiveness of primary process thinking in the child, quoting specific examples in the mental status report.

In essence, the mental status examination must be a cross-sectional profile of the child based strictly on observation and on the child's own report of his feeling states and perceptions. It should contain concrete examples and verbatim quotes of what the child says. Other professionals who examine the patient in the future will welcome this level of objectivity.

SUMMARY

The complexities of child psychiatric assessment can be simplified through the use of a semistructured approach to diagnostic interviewing. The two extremes of structured instruments or open-ended lack of structure can lead to lack of depth on the one hand or to unnecessary bias on the other. The application of adult syndromal clusters of DSM-III to the diagnosis of childhood psychopathology may lead to inaccuracies, because this nosology tends to deemphasize the developmental dimension of childhood disorders.

A semistructured approach to data gathering that avoids duplication in the data obtained seems a better alternative than either excessive structure or the lack of it. The parental inquiry should focus on the areas in which they have proven to be most accurate, such as issues of family and developmental history and their child's manifest behavior. The child interview should emphasize the patient's report of his own feelings, internal states, and perceptions of the world.

REFERENCES

Achenbach, T. M. (1980). DSM-III in light of empirical research on the classification of child psychopathology. *J. Am. Acad. Child Psychiat.* 19:395–412.

Brown, G. W., and Rutter, M. (1966). Measurement of family activities and relationships: A methodological study. *Human Relations* 19:241–63.

Canino, I. (1985). Taking a history. In D. Shaffer, A. A. Ehrhardt, and L. L. Greenhill (Eds.). *The Clinical Guide to Child Psychiatry.* New York: Free Press, pp. 393–408.

Costello, A. (1983). Preliminary Report on the Diagnostic Interview Schedule for Children (DISC) (unpublished manuscript).

Endicott, J., and Spitzer R. L. (1978). A diagnostic interview: The schedule for affective disorders and schizophrenia. *Arch. Gen. Psychiat.* 35:837–44.

Evans, I., and Nelson, R. (1977). Assessment of child behavior problems. In A. Ciminero, K. Calhoun, and H. Adams (Eds.). *Handbook of Behavioral Assessment.* New York: Wiley, pp. 603–81.

Gardner, R. (1985). The initial clinical evaluation of the child. In *The Clinical Guide to Child Psychiatry*. pp. 371–92.

Goodman, J. D., and Sours, J. A. (1967). *The Child Mental Status Examination*. New York: Basic Books.

Herjanic, B., and Campbell, W. (1977). Differentiating psychiatrically disturbed children on the basis of a structured interview. *J. of Abnormal Child Psychology*. 5:127–34.

Kashani, J. H., et al. (1985). Informant variance: The issue of parent-child disagreement. *J. Amer. Acad. Child Psychiat*. 24:437–41.

Kestenbaum, C. J., and Bird, H. R. (1978). A reliability study of the mental health assessment form for school-age children. *J. Amer. Acad. Child Psychiat*. 17:338–47.

Lukens, E., et al. (1983). Reliability of the psychosocial schedule for school-age children. *J. Amer. Acad. Child Psychiat*. 21:29–39.

NIMH (1973). *Children's Personal Data Inventory*. ECDEU: Assessment Battery for Psychopharmacology. Rockville, Md.: NIMH.

Orvaschel, H., et al. (1981). Assessing psychopathology in children of psychiatrically disturbed parents: A pilot study. *J. Amer. Acad. Child Psychiat*. 20:112–22.

Orvaschel, H., et al. (1982). Restrospective assessment of prepubertal major depression with the Kiddie SADS-E. *J. Amer. Acad. Child Psychiat*. 21:392–97.

Puig-Antich, J., and Chambers, W. (1978). *The Schedule for Affective Disorders and Schizophrenia for School-Age Children* (Kiddie SADS). New York: New York State Psychiatric Institute.

Puig-Antich, J., et al. (1980). *The Schedule for Affective Disorders and Schizophrenia for School-Age Children—Epidemiologic Version* (Kiddie SADS-E). New York: New York State Psychiatric Institute and Yale University School of Medicine.

Robins, L. N. (1963). The accuracy of parental recall of aspects of child development and child rearing practices. *J. Abnorm. Soc. Psychol*. 66:261–70.

Robins, L. N., et al. (1981). National Institute of Mental Health diagnostic interview schedule: Its history, characteristics, and validity. *Arch. Gen. Psychiat*. 38:381–89.

Rutter, M., and Brown, G. W. (1966). Reliability and validity of measures of family life and relationships in families containing a psychiatric patient. *Social Psychiatry* 1:3–53.

Rutter, M. (1975). *Helping Troubled Children*. New York: Plenum.

Simmons, J. E. (1981). *Psychiatric Examination of Children* (3d ed.). Philadelphia: Lea and Febiger.

Spitzer, R. L., and Williams, J. B. (1985). *Instruction Manual for the Structured Clinical Interview for DSM-III* (2/1/85 Revision). New York: New York State Psychiatric Institute, Biometrics Research Department.

3

STRUCTURED AND SEMISTRUCTURED PSYCHIATRIC INTERVIEWS FOR CHILDREN

Helen Orvaschel

This chapter will review several psychiatric interviews appropriate for use with pediatric populations. The interviews selected for review are well-designed and together represent considerable progress in the field of child and adolescent psychiatric assessment. Their structure and format are based on extensive empirical experience with primarily clinically referred populations. They all assess behaviors that provide diagnoses according to DSM-III criteria, and they all use parent (or primary caretaker) and child informants. Finally, they all have psychometric data available that show good test-retest and/or interrater reliability and all have face and content validity. Two of the interviews are structured and will be presented first, followed by reviews of the three semistructured interviews.

DIAGNOSTIC INTERVIEW FOR CHILDREN AND ADOLESCENTS

The Diagnostic Interview for Children and Adolescents (DICA) was developed at Washington University by Herjanic and Welner. The 1981 version of the DICA was modeled after the Diagnostic Interview Schedule (Robins et al. 1981) and is designed to assess child psychopathology according to the DSM-III criteria (Welner et al. 1985). Discussion of the DICA will refer to the 1981 revision unless otherwise specified.

The DICA is a highly structured psychiatric interview designed for use in clinical and epidemiologic research. It can be administered by clinicians or trained lay inter-

Supported, in part, by the William T. Grant Foundation Faculty Scholars Award #5-33584 and NIMH Grant #5-37171.

viewers and requires no clinical judgment on the part of the interviewer. The DICA is appropriate for use with children aged six to seventeen years, while its parallel, the DICA-P, is administered to the parent about the child. It takes approximately sixty to ninety minutes to administer to each informant.

The DICA and DICA-P are comprised of three parts. Part one, the same for both instruments, is a joint interview with the parent and child, introducing the interview and obtaining baseline and general demographic information. Following these initial nineteen questions, parent and child are separated and interviewed individually by different interviewers. Part two of the child interview is comprised of two hundred forty-seven questions, grouped according to category of disorder. The items ask about symptoms for the following disorders: attention deficit disorder (and hyperactivity), oppositional disorder, conduct disorder (all types), tobacco dependence, other substance abuse and dependence, major depression, adjustment disorder with depressed mood, mania, separation anxiety disorder, overanxious disorder, phobic disorder, obsessive compulsive disorder, anorexia nervosa, bulimia, somatization disorder, enuresis, encopresis, and psychotic symptoms. The interview also includes questions about menstruation (for girls), gender identity, sexual experience and abuse, and psychosocial stressors.

Part three of the DICA provides the interviewer an opportunity to rate eight categories of observational items. Part two of the DICA-P is the same for the parent as for the child but is written in the third person (that is, Does he . . .). Part three of the DICA-P asks the parent about pregnancy complications, the child's infancy and early development, stuttering, medical history, siblings, and additional diagnostic information about the child that is best obtained from the parent (for example, autism, elective mutism, pica, stereotyped movements, and avoidant disorder).

Symptoms on the DICA are generally rated as present or absent, and no severity scoring of positive symptoms is available. Questions on duration, onset, and offset of disorders are included. Questions are phrased in the present tense for all children. If a child is on medication for a behavioral or emotional problem, the interviewer may determine if a problem was present before the medication. Children aged twelve or over may be asked if a particular problem was true in the past, if it is not present now. Therefore, some information on past psychiatric symptoms is obtained. All items are precoded, and computer derived diagnoses are possible.

Data available on the DICA include parent-child agreement on items and diagnostic categories, test-retest reliability, and diagnostic comparisons between interviews and charts. Parent-child agreement on items, calculated with the kappa statistic, ranged from 0 to .87 (Herjanic and Reich 1982). According to the authors, items with high agreement between informants were objective, concrete, and serious, while low agreement items required judgment or were subject to misinterpretation. Diagnostic agreement between parents and children was also quite varied, but tended to show more disagreement than agreement on earlier versions of the interview (Reich et al. 1982). On the more recent version of the DICA, an increase in mother-child agreement was noted (Welner et al. 1985). Test-retest reliability has thus far been quite high, while comparisons of DICA diagnoses with chart diagnoses have been more moderate. These rather preliminary validity data must await more extensive testing, since chart comparisons are not generally the best standard against which to compare research interview assessments.

Overall, the DICA is a well-written diagnostic interview with considerable value in clinical and epidemiologic research. Much of the interview structure and phrasing has been the product of sound research and thoughtful development. An additional asset is that it can be administered by lay interviewers. However, the DICA's dichotomous scoring of items as positive or negative and its lack of symptom severity ratings result in a less sensitive measure of change in follow-up assessments requiring the evaluation of treatment. In addition, diagnoses are derived separately for parent and child interviews, and no method for aggregating information from both is provided. Therefore, clinicians must contend with discrepant diagnoses and difficult data analytic decisions. These disadvantages must be weighed against the advantages of other aspects of this diagnostic assessment instrument.

DIAGNOSTIC INTERVIEW SCHEDULE FOR CHILDREN

The NIMH Diagnostic Interview Schedule for Children (DISC) was developed by Anthony Costello, Craig Edelbrock, Mina Dulcan, Robert Kalas, and Sheree Klaric, under contract to the Division of Biometry and Epidemiology of the National Institute of Mental Health. The initial version of the DISC was written by Keith Conners, Barbara Herjanic, and Joaquim Puig-Antich and was structured similar to the DICA. Subsequent changes by Costello and his colleagues resulted in the version currently available (Costello et al. 1984). The DISC is a highly structured psychiatric interview designed primarily as a survey instrument for use in large-scale epidemiologic research. It can be administered by clinicians or trained lay interviewers and requires no clinical judgment. The DISC is appropriate for use with children aged six to seventeen years, while its parallel, the DISC-P, is administered to the parent about the child. It takes approximately fifty to seventy minutes to administer to each informant (Costello et al. 1984).

The wording and order of questions on the DISC are completely specified, and the interview structure is explicit. Items are to be asked as written and the line of inquiry has been predetermined. Therefore, a "yes" to a particular item may be followed by one series of questions and a "no" may be followed by another series of questions, but the choice of follow-up is indicated in the interview and the examiner need make no other choices. Items are precoded and questions are rated as "not true" (0), "somewhat" or "sometimes true" (1), and "very" or "often true" (2), or "no"(0)/"yes" (2). Questions on duration and onset are included for some behaviors and categories of disorder. Severity of problems is based on quantitative symptom scores or by summing the 0-1-2 reponse codes for each item. Symptoms are rated primarily for the past year. Parents and children are interviewed separately.

A training manual is available that provides a general interviewing guide and specific instructions on administering the DISC.

The DISC contains two hundred sixty-four items; the DISC-P contains three hundred two items. The structure is symptom-oriented with questions organized according to subjects (family, school, friends, and so forth). The interview begins with some general questions about the child's family and proceeds to cover the behaviors and symptoms needed to assess most Axis I DSM-III categories of disorder. Algorithms are available for obtaining computer-derived diagnoses based on DISC interview data. Questions provide information on the following DSM-III categories of disorder: attention deficit disorder (and hyperactivity), oppositional disorder, conduct disorder (all subtypes), alcohol abuse and dependence, other substance abuse and dependence, major depression, dysthymic disorder, cyclothymic disorder, mania, anorexia nervosa, bulimia, enuresis, encopresis, separation anxiety, avoidant disorder, overanxious disorder, phobic disorder, panic disorder, obsessive compulsive disorder, schizophrenic disorder, and psychosexual disorders. The DISC-P contains questions for the following additional disorders: elective mutism, stereotyped movement disorders, pervasive developmental disorders, and dissociative disorders.

Data available on the DISC include test-retest and interrater reliability, parent-child agreement and comparisons with clinicians' diagnoses. Test-retest reliability for parent reports on two hundred forty-two clinically referred children ranged from .44 to .86, with an average intraclass correlation of .76. The reliability for behavior/conduct problems was somewhat higher than for affective/neurotic problems (Edelbrock et al. in press). Reliability of parent interviews for DSM-III diagnoses ranged from .35 to .81, with an average kappa of .56 (Edelbrock et al. 1985). Test-retest reliability for child reports ranged from .28 to .78, with an average correlation of .62. Again, reliability was higher for behavior/conduct symptoms (.69) than for affective/neurotic symptoms (.57). Reliability was also found to increase with the child's age for most symptom areas (.43, .60 and .71 for children aged six to nine, ten to thirteen and fourteen to eighteen, respectively (Edelbrock et al. in press; Edelbrock et al. 1985).

Interrater reliability for symptom scores ranged from .94 to 1.00, with an average correlation of .98 (Costello et al. 1984). Parent-child agreement for 299 clinically referred children ranged from .04 to .68, with an average correlation of .27. Agreement was higher for questions concerned with overt behavior (r = .42) than for questions on affect (r = .19). Parent-child agreement was also associated with the age of the child (.10, .27 and .35 for six to nine, ten to thirteen and fourteen to eighteen year olds, respectively) (Edelbrock et al. 1985). Diagnoses based on the DISC and the DISC-P showed poor agreement with diagnoses based on clinicians' standard assessments. The reasons for these poor agreement rates are as yet unclear. Results of DISC interviews did correlate significantly with clinicians' ratings of adaptive functioning with parents, teachers, and child ratings of children's problem behaviors, social functioning, school performance, peer relations and self-concept (Costello et al. 1984).

In summary, the DISC is a highly structured psychiatric interview of potential use in large-scale epidemiologic research, requiring lay interviewer administration. The interview is symptom-oriented, but comprehensive computer algorithms and data dictionaries are available for generating diagnoses according to DSM-III criteria. Diagnoses are derived separately for parent and child interviews. Therefore, investigators must contend with discrepant diagnoses based on different informants. Resolution of these problems must be considered along with the advantages of using this assessment instrument.

CHILDREN'S ASSESSMENT SCHEDULE

The Children's Assessment Schedule (CAS) was developed by Kay Hodges at the University of Missouri in collaboration with Leon Cytryn and Donald McKnew of the National Institute of Mental Health. The interview was designed to facilitate rapport while systematically collecting comprehensive clinical information (Hodges et al. 1982a). In its current form, the CAS is a semistructured psychiatric interview designed for clinical or research assessments. When it is used by clinicians, information can be qualitatively analyzed to determine a diagnosis and treatment plan. For research purposes, investigators may derive a total score of problems or symptoms, separate scores for specific content areas, or scores for symptom complexes similar to many DSM-III diagnostic categories. The CAS is appropriate for use with children aged seven to sixteen years, with a parallel form for use with parents (P-CAS). Administration time is approximately forty-five to sixty minutes for each informant. Parents and children are interviewed separately, but no method of resolving discrepant information is specified by the author.

The CAS is comprised of three parts. Part one is the semistructured interview composed of approximately seventy-five questions about school, friends, activities and hobbies, family, fears, worries, self-image, mood, somatic concerns, expression of anger, and symptoms of thought disorder. Items are grouped according to what the author refers to as natural topics of conversation, so that the child experiences the interview as a discussion about various areas of his/her life. The time frame of the interview is current or recent past (last six months). Items are rated a positive, negative, ambiguous, not applicable, or no response. Part two of the CAS allows the interviewer to record information on the onset and duration of positive symptoms of Part one. In the third section of the interview, the interviewer rates fifty-three observational items.

A manual accompanying the CAS is available. The manual discusses each of the interview's content areas, provides suggested probes for items, identifies problematic issues in scoring, defines terms, suggests guidelines for establishing interrater reliability with the CAS, and offers a good overview of general interviewing techniques. The manual also provides information on various methods of scoring the interview, including the specification of items needed for obtaining a number of DSM-III diagnoses. The diagnostic categories covered by the CAS are: attention deficit disorder (and hyperactivity), conduct disorder (all subtypes), oppositional disorder, separation anxiety, avoidant disorder, overanxious disorder, phobic disorder, obsessive compulsive disorder, major depression, dysthymic disorder, manic episode, cyclothymic disorder, anorexia nervosa, bulimia, enuresis, encopresis, panic disorder, generalized anxiety disorder, schizoid disorder, psychotic disorder, substance abuse disorder, sleepwalking disorder, and sleep terror disorder.

Data available on the CAS include interrater reliability and discriminant and concurrent validity. Agreement between interviewers for items ranges from .44 to .82, with a total CAS correlation of .90. Kappa coefficients for items ranged from .47 to .61 (Hodges et al. 1982b). The CAS was reported to discriminate inpatients, outpatients, and controls on the basis of total scores and individual category scores. Correlations were reported to be significant between child interviews and CBCL scores obtained from mothers, while child scores on a depression and anxiety self-report were moderately correlated with CAS symptom complexes on affect. Concordance between results on the CAS and the K-SADS-E (Orvaschel et al. 1982) ranged from moderate to high agreement, with the exception of overanxious disorder. Kappa coefficients were better when information from parent and child was combined (.59 to .60) and better for parents alone than for child alone. Agreement for conduct disorder was reported to be good for both informants (Hodges et al. 1985).

In summary, the CAS provides a standardized method for obtaining information on a broad range of child behaviors relevant to many Axis I DSM-III categories of disorder. The interview format is fairly structured but written primarily for clinician administration. While organization of the interview is symptom-oriented, a scoring system for deriving diagnoses is provided. No gradations of severity are available on positively rated items, but treatment effects may be estimated on the basis of a reduction of total number of symptoms. In addition, the manual accompanying the CAS is well-written and provides many useful guidelines for the administration and interpretation of this interview and for interview techniques in general. The resolution of discrepant findings between parent and child interviews is not discussed and remains an area of practical clinical importance.

INTERVIEW SCHEDULE FOR CHILDREN

The Interview Schedule for Children (ISC) was developed by Marika Kovacs. The first version was constructed in 1974 for a research project on childhood depression. Since that time, it has undergone numerous revisions and additions, resulting from psychometric testing, extensive experience, and expanded research needs. The remaining discussion of the ISC refers to the version currently used and its accompanying addenda.

The ISC is a semistructured psychiatric interview designed primarily for research assessments of childhood depression. Administration of the interview requires an experienced clinician trained in its use and familiar with the DSM-III diagnostic criteria. The ISC is appropriate for use with children aged eight to seventeen years. Mothers are interviewed about their children and children are then interviewed directly by the same clinician. Interviews with children take approximately forty-five to sixty minutes and interviews with parents between ninety and one hundred and twenty minutes. A follow-up ISC is also available to assess change over time (Kovacs 1983).

The ISC is comprised of the core interview and the addenda. The addenda provide questions that assess additional symptoms necessary for determining DSM-III criteria and categories of disorder not included in the core interview. The ISC begins with an unstructured interview focusing on an overview of the child's problems, the history of the complaints, and their duration. Following this, the interviewer inquires about the presence and severity of forty-three symptoms of psychopathology and records a global rating of the child's functional impairment. Also included in this section are additional items asked if certain symptoms are recorded as positive. The remaining questions that constitute the approximately one hundred items in the core interview include ratings on psychotic symptoms and developmental milestones. The interviewer also rates twelve observational items (for example, pressure of speech), records his/her clinical impressions, any DSM-III diagnoses, their duration, duration of symptoms, and then dictates a summary. Addenda items include questions relevant to most other Axis I DSM-III categories of disorder and several Axis II diagnoses. In the core ISC interview, information on the following DSM-III disorders is obtained: Conduct disorder (all subtypes), dysthymia, major depression, mania (and hypomania), adjustment disorder with depressed mood, schizophrenia, schizo-affective disorder, obsessive compulsive disorder, separation anxiety disorder, phobic disorder, substance abuse (drugs and alcohol), and enuresis/encopresis. Additional Axis I disorders assessed in the addenda include attention deficit disorder (with hyperactivity), avoidant disorder, oppositional disorder, overanxious disorder, and panic disorder. Axis II categories covered in the addenda include borderline, compulsive, histrionic, schizoid, and schizotypal personality disorders.

Most items in the core ISC are rated on an eight-point scale, with specific anchor points indicated for scoring level of severity. Behaviors assessed in the addenda are rated only as present or absent. For most symptoms, ratings reflect behavior for the past two weeks. Acting-out behavior is assessed for the past six months, while mental status is rated for "current," and examiners' observations and impressions are rated on the basis of interview behavior. The Follow-up ISC allows the recording of symptom ratings between interviews and for the past two weeks. It also includes "interim ratings" that reflect any significant changes in the severity of acting-out behaviors.

The ISC is symptom-oriented and precoded. Specific questions are provided for each of the items to be rated. Interviewers have considerable discretion regarding the order of behaviors they assess and the extent of questioning needed to determine a particular rating. Items are rated on the basis of mothers' reports, children's reports, and clinicians' overall evaluation from both informants. Diagnoses are based on the clinician's summary ratings and are generally verified by consensus of the clinicians involved in the evaluation. The ISC interview is accompanied by instructions on its administration and by a description of the clinical rules developed to assure reasonable decision-making uniformity of diagnoses (Feinberg and Kovacs 1983).

Data available on the ISC include interrater reliability and parent-child agreement. Interrater reliability was ascertained for interviews of thirty-five clinically referred children. Intraclass correlations of corated symptoms ranged from .64 to 1.0. Agreement on observational items ranged from .53 to .96; the correlation for ratings of current disorder was .86. Parent-child agreement for seventy-five clinically referred children ranged from .02 to .95 for symptoms and .32 to .86 for syndromes, with an average correlation of .61. Variability in parent-child agreement was generally a function of the internality versus externality of the symptoms assessed (Kovacs 1983).

In summary, the ISC is a semistructured, symptom-oriented psychiatric interview that provides a systematic procedure for assessing most Axis I and several Axis II DSM-III categories of disorder. Severity ratings are provided for depressive symptomatology and for a number of additional areas of behavior. A follow-up version of the ISC is also available to record change over time. Diagnoses are based on an integration of information from parent and child informants and are a function of consensual clinical judgment. Experienced and well-trained clinicians are required for the administration of the ISC.

KIDDIE-SADS

The Kiddie-SADS (K-SADS) was developed by Joaquim Puig-Antich and William Chambers at the New York State Psychiatric Institute as a children's version of the Schedule for Affective Disorders and Schizophrenia developed for adults by Endicott and Spitzer (Endicott and Spitzer 1978). The interview was originally constructed as a diagnostic instrument for the assessment of ongoing episodes of psychiatric disorder in pediatric treatment studies of childhood depression. The original version of the K-SADS was constructed in 1977 and was revised in 1978. The current 1983 version is a revision developed on the basis of reliability data reported for the 1978 version; it incorporates six years of experience with the interview.

In its current form, the K-SADS is a semistructured psychiatric interview designed for clinical or research assessments. Administration of the interview requires a trained clinician experienced in child psychiatric assessments. The K-SADS is appropriate for use with children aged six to seventeen years. Mothers (or primary caretakers) are interviewed about their children and children are interviewed directly by the same interviewers. It takes approximately sixty minutes to administer to each informant.

The K-SADS is comprised of three parts. The first part of the interview is relatively unstructured. The informant is asked to identify all presenting problems and symptoms so that the interviewer can obtain and record a chronological picture of the ongoing episode, its mode of onset, and duration. The child's treatment history is then recorded; the informant is asked to identify the time during the current episode or during the previous year (whichever is shorter) when symptoms were the most severe. The second part of the K-SADS includes questions on approximately two hundred specific symptoms or behaviors relevant to most Axis I DSM-III diagnoses. Information on the following DSM-III disorders is obtained: major depression, manic disorder, other affective disorders (minor depression, dysthymia, hypomania, cyclothymia), anorexia nervosa, bulimia, panic, separation anxiety, phobias, obsessive compulsive disorder, generalized anxiety (overanxious) disorder, conduct disorder, schizophrenia, schizophreniform disorder, brief reactive psychosis, paranoid disorder, schizo-affective disorder, and schizotypal disorder. Additional behaviors that are rated include depersonalization, derealization, impulsivity, unstable interpersonal relationships, and identity disturbance. Part three of the K-SADS includes sixteen observational items rated by the interviewer and a rating on the children's version of the Global Assessment Scale. Information on age of onset and duration of disorder(s) is also recorded.

Most items on the K-SADS are rated on a six- or seven-point range of severity, with specific criteria indicated for scoring levels. Most symptoms are rated twice: the first rating is for symptom severity during the worst period of the present episode, the second rating records symptom severity during the previous week. The second rating is used for comparison when investigators wish to assess change (for example, following completion of a treatment trial or at specified intervals during a protocol).

Administration of the K-SADS requires an interview with the parent first, followed by an interview with the child. Responses are recorded separately for each informant on an accompanying scoring sheet. The same clinician interviews both informants and records summary ratings for all items on the basis of information from parent, child, and any additional sources of data available. Discrepancies between parent and child responses are resolved by the clinician during the course of the interview. Summary ratings reflect the interviewer's best clinical judgment of the presence and degree of symptomatology reported. The final diagnostic assessment of the child is based on the clinician's summary ratings, which also become the standard against which to measure change.

The K-SADS is organized primarily according to diagnostic category. Sample questions are provided for all the items to be rated. These sample questions have been found most helpful with previous child interviews and are provided as a guide to the clinician. The presence of these questions is not intended to limit the interviewer, who should feel free to ask whatever is necessary to arrive at an accurate rating of each specific item.

In order to obtain a past history of psychiatric disorder or to assess chronic or episodic disorders requiring past history, the interview can be supplemented by the administration of the K-SADS-E (epidemiologic version) (Orvaschel et al. 1982). The K-SADS-E includes the diagnostic categories of attention deficit disorder, alcohol abuse and dependence, other substance abuse and dependence, and a section on suicidal behavior. Most of the previously mentioned Axis I DSM-III disorders are also included in the epidemiologic version, which does a lifetime assessment of all major Axis I psychiatric disorders. The administration and structure of the K-SADS-E is much the same as the K-SADS-P (present episode) described above, except that items are rated as present or absent, no symptom severity ratings are provided, and no item ratings for past week are recorded.

Data available on the K-SADS include test-retest reliability, mother-child agreement, interrater reliability, and sensitivity of ratings due to pharmacologic treatment. Agreement between raters for individual symptoms and major diagnostic syndromes on the second version of the K-SADS-P ranged from .65 to .96. Comparisons following imipramine treatment of depressed children indicated K-SADS ratings to be sensitive to changes due to drug trials (Puig-Antich et al. 1978). Mother-child agreement has ranged from −.08 to 1.0, with most items and syndromes in the acceptable range (>.50) (Orvaschel et al. 1982; Chambers et al. 1985). Test-retest reliability of depressive symptoms ranged from .28 to .88 with the vast majority of ratings over .50. Items relevant to the diagnosis of depression scored between .63 and .81 on test-retest and had internal consistency ratings between .65 and .84. Test-retest for conduct disorder was .89; for psychotic symptoms it ranged from .10 to .53. Anxiety diagnoses also demonstrated low test-retest reliability.

Overall, the K-SADS is a semistructured psychiatric interview that provides a standardized method of obtaining and recording behaviors necessary for the assessment of most Axis I DSM-III categories of disorder. The organization of the interview is primarily by category of disorder; items are generally rated for gradations of severity during episode and during the past week. A clinician experienced in child and/or adolescent psychopathology is required for the administration of the K-SADS.

CONCLUSIONS

The psychiatric interviews reviewed here were designed for different purposes, and each has its merits and deficiencies. Nevertheless, the use of a structured or semistructured pyschiatric interview will provide a more reliable and often more comprehensive assessment of the signs and symptoms of psychiatric disorder. As has been noted, however, these instruments should be supplemented with additional evaluation material relevant to diagnostic formulation and treatment recommendations. As with any branch of medicine, the psychiatric practitioner must integrate information based on physical examination, past history, and intellectual functioning, in addition to the problems reported by patients or their parents. The use of instruments such as those reviewed above should add to the overall quality of the psychiatric assessment of the child, but it is not a substitute for other appropriate clinical assessments.

REFERENCES

Chambers, W. J., et al. (1985). The assessment of affective disorders in children and adolescents by semistructured interview: Test-retest reliability of the K-SADS-P. *Arch. Gen. Psychiat.* 42:696–701.

Costello, A. J., et al. (1984). Report on the NIMH Diagnostic Interview Schedule for Children (DISC).

Edelbrock, C., et al. (Submitted 1985). Parent-child agreement on child psychiatric symptoms assessed via structured interview.

Edelbrock, C., et al. (In press). Age differences in the reliability of the psychiatric interview of the child. *Child Development.*

Endicott, J., and Spitzer, R. L. (1978). A diagnostic interview: The SADS. *Arch. Gen. Psychiat.* 35:837–53.

Feinberg, T. L., and Kovacs, M. (1983). Research diagnosis in a study of the depressive disorders in childhood: The formulation of clinical decision making. (Unpublished manuscript).

Herjanic, B., and Reich, W. (1982). Development of a structured psychiatric interview for children: Agreement between child and parent on individual symptoms. *J. Abn. Child Psychol.* 10:307–24.

Herjanic, B., et al. (1975). Are children reliable reporters? *J. Abn. Child Psychol.* 3:41–48.

Hodges, K., et al. (1982a). The development of a child assessment interview for research and clinical use. *J. Abn. Child Psychol.* 10:173–89.

Hodges, K., et al. (1982b). The Child Assessment Schedule (CAS) Diagnostic Interview: A report on reliability and validity. *J. Amer. Acad. Child Psychiat.* 21:468–73.

Hodges, K., et al. (Submitted 1985). Diagnostic concordance between two structured interviews for children: The Child Assessment Schedule and the Kiddie-SADS.

Kovacs, M. (1983). The Interview Schedule for Children (ISC): Interrater and parent-child agreement. (Unpublished manuscript).

Orvaschel, H., et al. (1982). Retrospective assessment of child psychopathology with the Kiddie-SADS-E. *J. Amer. Acad. Child Psychiat.* 21:392–97.

Puig-Antich, J., et al. (1978). Prepubertal major depressive disorders: A pilot study. *J. Amer. Acad. Child Psychiat.* 17:695–707.

Reich, W., et al. (1982). Development of a structured psychiatric interview for children: Agreement on diagnosis comparing child and parent interviews. *J. Abn. Child Psychol.* 20:325–36.

Robins, L. N., et al. (1981). National Institute of Mental Health Diagnostic Interview Schedule. *Arch. Gen. Psychiat.* 38:381–89.

Welner, Z., et al. (Submitted 1985). Parent-child agreement, reliability and validity studies of the Diagnostic Interview for Children and Adolescents (DICA).

4

GENERAL ISSUES IN THE CLINICAL ASSESSMENT OF CHILDREN AND ADOLESCENTS

Cheryl Beth Diamond

The diagnostic assessment of children and adolescents is an extraordinarily complex and challenging task. Children are often in the midst of rapid and continuous developmental and environmental changes. The child is continuously exposed to the supports, tensions, and demands of his immediate and extended families, his school culture and peers, his neighborhood and other cultural factors, and to ever-changing physical, emotional, and characterological traits and capacities. By virtue of a youngster's limited autonomy and independence, it is difficult to evaluate him at a single point in time and to consider that representative of his general functioning.

One is often called upon to evaluate youngsters in situations that do not allow for a complete assessment, in which questions are geared to a very particular environment or set of circumstances. Whether the evaluation is performed in the classroom or school, the pediatric ward or clinic or emergency room, the child-care agency or court, significant modifications in the scope and technique of the evaluation must be made. Yet the age, capabilities and vulnerabilities of the particular youngster under study must always be kept in mind. In most instances, the clinician is responsible to an adult who has asked for the assessment. Yet we must be mindful of the helplessness of the children or adolescents being evaluated; we must be protective of their immediate emotional needs. There are instances in which very limited, or even no, evaluation is required. At times, pursuing certain lines of inquiry is beyond the current capabilities of a youngster and might be too emotionally traumatic. For example, this is often the case when a youngster is a witness to or the victim of crime or physical or sexual abuse. Insensitive assaults on the child—a barrage of questions and demands for details—by a series of "well-intentioned" professionals will overwhelm the youngster. A thorough inquiry may be necessary and indeed therapeutic, but careful selection of the interviewer and when, how, and where the interview will take place will go a long way to ease an already intensely frightening and painful situation.

The task of child assessment requires the following: a well-grounded knowledge of normal child development and psychopathology; competence and sensitivity in interviewing techniques with adults and children; and a mix of patience, versatility, creativity, humor, and wonder. It also requires the self-assurance to admit igno- rance, and one's own limitations, and those of the discipline. The evaluator may also have to put forth a diagnosis or suggest interventions that may be painful or threatening to the children and adults who will be affected by them. One also needs a broad understanding of the childhood environments: the nursery, middle school, high school, playground, religious and ethnic institutions, and geographic region. It is also extremely important to be familiar with the possible sources of fantasy in the world of youngsters: current literature and television programs and movies; enter- tainment and sports figures of particular popularity, and current events that have particular poignancy for children: notorious crimes, newsworthy international and local disasters. All or some of the patient's family members, friends, and significant others, such as teachers, pediatricians, orthodontists, music teachers, coaches, housekeepers, baby-sitters, dogs, cats, hamsters, and snakes, may also need to be considered in the evaluation.

What will follow is a discussion of some of the major areas involved in assessing children and adolescents, largely from the private practice perspective: I will explore the office, the referral, the interview with the parents, the interview with the child or adolescent, evaluations by and interviews with ancillary professionals, diagnostic formulation and treatment planning, and communication of recommendations to parents, child, and others.

THE OFFICE

The need for flexibility quickly becomes apparent in arranging the physical as- pects of one's office. An ideal office is large and bright, with a separate playroom or play area designed for working with small children, child groups, and families. Most people manage with a good deal less. An accessible toilet and a good-sized waiting room are desirable to accommodate whoever will be escorting younger children to their sessions. Childproofing and soundproofing are important considerations, as is a good working relationship with officemates, especially if they don't work with children. Sturdy, colorful, washable decor and furnishings are "in"—precious an- tiques, silks and art objects are "out." Things should be attractive but replaceable. It is helpful to have room enough for a child-sized table and chairs, but most furni- ture can be modified on a temporary basis with pillows and so on to accommodate youngsters comfortably. Folding furniture offers one solution to this problem and is also useful for family interviews. It is best not to care too deeply for anything in the office or waiting room. I have found that if one sets a tone by keeping things reasonably clean and tidy patients and families follow suit. Friendly doormen and neighbors are helpful to have, though usually such factors are beyond one's control. An ideal office location may be difficult to find, but it is optimal to locate in an area in which many children reside, near good public and private schools, with good access to public transportation and parking facilities. It is best if older children can get to the office comfortably and safely on their own; parents and sitters appreciate convenience. Nearby stores in which parents and siblings can shop or stroll while waiting are advantageous, as is proximity to a park or playground and a good coffee shop or a delicatessen, especially if one is inclined to work with children outdoors or to provide food treats on special occasions like birthdays or holidays. A visit to a nearby art gallery played a significant role in the treatment of one youngster with whom I worked, and an occasional restaurant visit was important in furthering the socialization of another. These factors are less important in the course of an evaluation, but on occasion can prove useful.

Inside the consulting room, a closet, shelves, or toy box can be set up to store necessary evaluation and treatment materials. It is ideal if one can provide individual storage space for each child, but at least one can make available a file folder or slim box to hold drawings and small toys. Even during an evaluation children appreciate being given some sense of temporary belonging. On the subject of toys: select them to be bright, sturdy, replaceable, and limited to just a few for each age group. Especially for evaluation purposes, more is *not* better and distracts from the purpose at hand. Toy supplies can be expanded to meet the particular evaluation or treatment needs of a specific youngster: Star Wars figures for a young astronaut, popsicle sticks for an older puppeteer. Handicapped youngsters may require special toys or modifications in the evaluation and treatment setting. One must know one's own limitations; over time they will become apparent. Be careful about introducing active toys. I quickly switched from a wiffle ball to a nerf ball; some people should avoid both. Felt-tip markers are safer than oil paints. One has to decide if snacks will be provided, but it is difficult to say no to youngsters who bring their own. They are usually famished after school and the custom with tutors, music teachers, and sports groups is to supply snacks or at least to permit them. If one is nervous about the carpet, a tray and a few napkins will usually alleviate the anxiety. Since during evaluations one's time is more limited than in an ongoing treatment, it may be necessary to avoid snacking. Most children can refrain for the evaluation period, and, by sensitively setting such a limit, one may make important observations about a youngster's response to immediate deprivation. I always have sheets of blank paper for children to draw self portraits, family portraits, and layouts of their apartments, to illustrate dreams and stories, to write me notes on unmentionable topics, and to make paper airplanes. I also have a few diagnostic tools available: a Peabody Picture Vocabulary Test, Bender cards, and a few objects to test for soft neurological signs.

THE REFERRAL

It is important to consider one's referral sources. One needs to ascertain their perspective on the problem, the questions they want answered, the recommendations or help they expect to receive, the time framework, and the nature of their continued involvement with the child and family after the evaluation. One needs to know if a formal report would be useful or required and to whom it would be addressed and available. Frequently, parents make the initial contact; professional referral sources are contacted during the course of the evaluation. In emergency or time-limited evaluation situations, where one needs to gather a great deal of information rapidly, immediate consultation with referral sources and ancillary contacts may be necessary. It is nonetheless still important to avoid severely restricting the inquiry or basing judgments on the informant's particular prejudices or point of view. One must also bear in mind that though referral may be made by any number of individuals, the right to share the information obtained in the evaluation is determined by the parents or legal guardian of the youngster, and they may refuse later communication with the referral source or other concerned professionals unless they have abrogated their rights of guardianship as determined by court authority.

THE INTERVIEW WITH THE PARENTS

Once a referral has been made, arrangements are made for the evaluation. In the initial phone call, it is helpful to get a brief statement of the main problem and the names, addresses, phone numbers, and ages of the principal parties—usually the identified patient, the parents, and the siblings. I record the identifying data on a card that will constitute the patient's record. This card will eventually contain the diagnosis, the names and phone numbers of involved professionals, the fee, the dates of visits, charges and payments, and the disposition, if referral is made to someone else for treatment. Be prepared to be asked about fees and prognosis at this time, and encourage parents to wait to discuss these issues in the consultation. It is usually preferable to see both parents in the course of the evaluation. There are many ways to approach this; some clinicians prefer to see the entire family at the outset and later to interview individuals, parent-child, or sibling pairs. Estranged parents are often seen separately; however it is valuable if you can see them together at some point to help them develop some degree of accord in viewing their child's problems and the recommendations for alleviating them. The child should not be left with the impression, which he often maintains as an unconscious or conscious fantasy, that his problems will reunite his parents; however, it is important to try to convey that they can be united at least with regard to his problems and needs. In such instances, it is important to establish who will be emotionally, legally, and financially responsible for the evaluation. Also, it is important to be clear about custody issues; otherwise, one may be in a very uncomfortable and untenable position at some later date.

Give parents, or adolescents, who may insist on being the first to be seen, clear directions for getting to the office building and for finding the office. Let them know if they must ring the doorbell, if the door is locked or open, and the location of coat racks and bathrooms. It makes people feel much more welcome and much less helpless and frightened if some of these concrete issues are spelled out.

I arrange a first meeting at a time when I can see parents for a double session. In this session, I establish a working alliance with the parents, gather a comprehensive history of the current difficulties, the child's development, and the family and wider environment. Though the evaluator must have informational goals in mind, the order in which goals are met is not the relevant issue. The task is equally to help the parents tell the story freely as they see it. This may require various tactics. Some parents feel at ease first presenting the story and can accept specific questioning only after they feel they have the clinician's sympathy. Others respond better to a structured history taking during which they become more able to expand on various points after encouragement from the clinician.

There are a number of excellent models that describe the factual material needed from the parents (Canino 1985; Cramer 1975; Goodman and Sours 1967; Simmons 1981). Again, the order does not necessarily reflect the order in which the material was obtained. In addition, in reality one rarely if ever accumulates such an abundance of detail, and one must take from these guidelines what seems most clinically relevant, bearing in mind that will necessarily differ from child to child as the history unfolds.

During the initial interview, it is important to observe and note both parental attitudes and feelings towards historical information and congruent and divergent views between them, and to weigh their potential strengths and weaknesses in coping with developmental and environmental stresses. These data shed light on the etiology of pathology and influence the course of intervention. Parents are often anxious in these sessions and may feel very guilty for their child's difficulties. They may be very eager to exact premature diagnoses, prognoses, and treatment strategies. The clinician must tactfully resist these pressures and convey empathy for the anxious parent but stress that only with more complete clinical knowledge can the best understanding and planning be accomplished.

Occasionally in the course of the evaluation a parent will realize some part of his own behavior is injurious to his child, and will ask for permission to change. In such circumstances, it is best to support the parent's observation gently and to encourage him to alter his behavior if he feels he can. Some parents do, and report back that changing their own behavior at home has eased their child's difficulties. This process not only may provide some immediate therapeutic relief, but diagnostically and prognostically carries favorable weight. If the parents are unsuccessful, one can only encourage them to wait for the planning conference to make further interventions and tell them they need to know more about themselves and their child before they can hope for success.

If parents balk at revealing certain aspects of the history, most often in areas that are personally embarrassing such as sexual beliefs or behaviors and marital circumstances, it is useful to explain how this information can help one to understand the child and therefore to design a solution to the presented problems. Delicate information that may be avoided in the beginning of an evaluation may be more freely discussed later, once the parents have confidence in the assessor's good intentions. Obviously, if certain areas are consistently avoided one can surmise they represent areas of significant conflict for the parent and, most likely, for the child.

I use a semistructured interview format. I often introduce a topic, such as discipline, and then invite the parents to tell me in their own words about that area of family life. If they seem unable to use this format, I may resort to a more straightforward question-and-answer style, but I continually invite them to expand more fully. Similarly, after parents tell their story, I will ask them to fill in areas that may have been overlooked or to expand on items that seem confused, contradictory, or that provoke disproportionate affect.

Usually one can gather sufficient historical information and form a preliminary diagnostic picture of the parents in the double session. Occasionally, with extremely anxious, circumstantial or controlling parents, or those seen at a time of enormous emotional upheaval (such as serious illness, death, or separation), one must see the parents again before seeing the child. I encourage parents to call or drop a note if important things occur to them that they neglected to tell because of the anxiety surrounding their visit. In the parental sessions, one needs to establish the parameters of the evaluation process: how many sessions will be involved, the fee, and payment and cancellation policies.

At this point, it is often appropriate to request reports from pediatricians, former therapists, or evaluators, schools, and so on, if they have not already been presented by the parents. One may also need to involve other professionals in the evaluation; it may be advisable to arrange for such consultations before the evaluation is completed. It is necessary to have access to a number of reliable specialists to perform adjunctive evaluations such as psychological testing or speech, hearing, ophthalmologic, and neurological examinations. It is wise to have preprinted release-of-information forms handy so that the parents can authorize such exchanges. Some parents may be very cautious about allowing one to consult with various ancillary professionals. Clearly they need to be educated about this process and to be reassured that you will not disclose anything they object to. Some parents cannot tolerate such contacts till later in the evaluation process, when they are more secure about the clinician's alliance with them and their youngster. There remain some parents, however, who continue to refuse such contacts; the reasons for their refusal may need to be explored in future parental guidance or treatment, particularly if the blocking of such communication will significantly interfere with optimal treatment planning.

At the end of the history-taking sessions, parents must be shown how to inform their child about the evaluation. A child who is confident that his parents are comfortable with the consultant and the evaluation is infinitely more accessible than one who is convinced that his parents are sending him to someone because they are angry with him or frightened about his condition or the possible need for treatment. Begin by asking the parents to relate how they propose to inform their youngster. This permits the clinician to observe how the parents feel about the evaluation and the interviewer. One can also see how the parents speak with their children: how appropriate their explanation is to the age and reported capacities of their child; how freely they share information with him; how much they reveal in their tone and choice of words their attitudes and prejudices, in this case, regarding the evaluator, the evaluation, and the child.

INTERVIEW WITH THE CHILD OR ADOLESCENT

One should insist that a parent accompany the child to the first visit and to others as needed. With teenagers, it is helpful if parents offer but do not demand to come along. Caution parents not to be disappointed if they are turned down, since this is the usual case. Their offer, however, is usually appreciated and sets a positive tone for the evaluation process.

The interview begins in the waiting room, where one can observe the youngster together with his parent or parents. How are they seated? Are they communicating? What is the affectual tone, and how does the child relate to being introduced to the clinician? How does he separate from the parents? Waiting room observations may serve as a starting place for discussion with the child, particularly if the scene reveals a positive interaction or some aspects of the problems reported earlier by the arents. It is a here-and-now behavioral document that allows for a higher degree of consensual validation than reported information, since the clinician, parents, and child have observed it.

Once in the consulting room, I show youngsters where toy and art supplies are stored and offer them a choice of seats. I observe how they explore the room: Are they inhibited, spontaneous, or impulsive? Do they seek permission or ignore prohibition? Are they anxious or eager? I note how they hold themselves, how they are dressed and groomed, how they get into the chair or sit on the couch or floor. I observe how much they insist on having a toy right away or if they can tolerate sitting and talking for a while. I review with youngsters, even very young ones, why they are coming and what the evaluation process is all about. I do not always do this at the beginning of the interview. One must assess what will make any particular youngster most comfortable, judging this by his age and capacities. I may choose to discuss waiting room or office events, ask him if he can tell me why he has come to see me, ask if he has anything he'd like to ask me or to tell me about himself. Children need to know what one's policy is about confidentiality and that one will be discussing one's findings and recommendations with their parents at the end of the evaluation.

There are pros and cons to doing an evaluation if one doesn't have treatment time available. Sometimes it is easier for parents to accept the recommendation of a consultant who will not be administering the treatment; they may feel that the recommendation is more objective and less self-interested. However, if one will not be the therapist one should make that clear to the parents and child in order to limit, at least consciously, the degree to which they become invested in the relationship.

Some youngsters are most comfortable beginning with a discussion of their problems or telling you about their family or peer and school life; others need some concrete activity to help them get more comfortable: drawing tasks or a neurological exam for "soft signs"; with the most anxious children, a board or card game may be the only type of interaction removed enough for them to be initially comfortable. This behavior must be evaluated in the context of the entire interview or series of interviews. Youngsters who are quick to relate verbally may be very secure and comfortable with themselves and adults, or they may be superficial and glib and actually reveal little. A certain degree of circumspection would be appropriate when one is being interviewed by a strange adult, and a somewhat shy or withdrawn youngster may prove to be extraordinarily revealing when permitted to time his interactions appropriately to his emotional capacities. I usually structure the interview format to move from the more superficial to the deeper, more conflicted, more unconsciously revealing types of tasks, but some very troubled, severely traumatized youngsters may need to open up immediately; in contrast, others need to develop more of a sense of trust in the clinician before doing so. Prelatency and latency youngsters love performing the easy physical tasks of the neurological exam. Being active early in the interview can help them tolerate being more sedentary later on. Hyperactive youngsters may find these tasks relieve them of a certain anxiety, since they can be active and yet structured by the examiner. However, a youngster who is known to have severe learning or coordination problems might be overly discouraged and humiliated if these tasks are required before he has developed a positive relationship with the clinician.

I find a flexible, semistructured interview approach to be most fruitful (see Bird and Kestenbaum, this volume). Almost any task or topic of conversation can open lines of inquiry that the examiner intends to cover. I have performed an entire interview with a resistant preadolescent youngster by discussing a movie he was pleased to tell me about. Once I had listened patiently and attentively to his report, he was willing to explore with me how he, his family, and his situation related to the movie. I could observe his cognitive functioning and style, his affectual range and appropriateness, his reality testing, and the degree of idiosyncratic quality in his thought processes. I could estimate his level of object relations, describe his appearance, mannerisms, speech quality, and relatedness to me. I got some sense of his superego development from the standpoint of both ego ideal and conscience. Basically all the areas of the mental status exam, with the exception of more particular neurological measures, were made accessible through this interview. After this discussion, he was quite willing to complete those aspects of the assessment and to draw first some figures from the movie, and then his family. Youngsters are often quite willing to approach an interview through drawing and will "talk" this way initally about their families, classrooms, pets, conflicts, dreams, and fantasies. There are many variants of these techniques: Winnicott's squiggle game, Gardner's mutual storytelling with the addition of drawing, and so on (Gardner 1971; Kestenbaum 1985; Winnicott 1971). Younger children who cannot draw figuratively may carry on the same storytelling with small dolls that offer sufficient variety in age, sex, and ethnicity to allow for a free-ranging imagination.

At the end of the interview I invite the child to ask me any questions he may have or to tell me or show me anything else about himself that will help me understand him and his family. I may then present a simple formulation if I have been able to arrive at one, but at the very least, I review with a youngster what he and his parents have revealed to me about themselves and their problems, and I will state simply what areas of strength and weakness need to be considered in addressing the problems. I inform the youngster that I will tell his parents about my findings and that they and I will plan what is to follow. I let him know that his parents will tell him what plans we have made and that he will be included as much as possible. There are situations in which the youngster can be present at the recommendation conference, where his active input in the planning is both welcomed and advisable. Some clinicians arrange this almost routinely (Gardner 1971; Simmons 1981). In some instances, this may be the last time you will see the youngster, so you must put some closure on the relationship and at least say a tentative goodbye.

EVALUATIONS BY AND INTERVIEWS WITH ANCILLARY PROFESSIONALS

During the course of the evaluation, it may seem advisable to gather additional information from other professional sources. One must convince the parents that this additional data is necessary and gain their permission to pursue these other informational avenues.

It is necessary to gain the cooperation and respect of other professionals; tell them you need their input to help understand the child in question. Empathize with their difficulties if they have been affected by the adverse behaviors of the youngster or family; let them know how evaluation may be important to them as well as to the child and family. One must ask clear, if tentative, questions to help focus the interviews, which of necessity often must be brief and by telephone. When one is requesting an evaluation, provide a concise list of questions in addition to the general evaluation that may routinely be provided. Sample questions to the ophthalmologist, neurologist, psychologist, and so on, might be: how does any pathology uncovered relate to this youngster's behavioral or emotional difficulties? How might it limit his ability to function in his family, peer groups, normal classroom setting? How might corrective measures be implemented in light of the youngster's and family's strengths and weaknesses? The more specifically one can frame one's questions, the more focused are likely to be the consultants' reports. One must be careful, however, not to limit the breadth of the consultation, or one may miss the best chance to uncover unsuspected pathology.

Provide consultants with appropriate helpful information from one's own evaluation, again keeping in mind that parental permission is required and that the greatest tact must be used, resist the temptation to disclose material that may be interesting but is not germane to the other consultant's task. In my experience, the members of some disciplines are not as mindful of the need for confidentiality as are mental health personnel. One must be similarly cautious in disclosing diagnostic labels, since one cannot control how they will affect the life of the child and his family. It is better to state briefly and simply the nature of the problem and one's observations about the probable etiology and strengths and weaknesses of those involved. Other professionals operate under similar constraints, and at times one must push them to disclose information beyond generalities. For example, parents, children, schools, and agencies are often privy to psychological test results, and psychologists may properly make their reports simple and observational at the expense of suppressing a wealth of data that may be useful to the evaluation. Speaking with the psychologist personally or indeed reviewing the actual test material with him can prove extremely useful, especially in cases with ambiguous diagnostic possibilities.

One must clarify who will review the ancillary evaluation results with the parents and child. I find it best for each professional to have an evaluation session with the family, but to inform me clearly what he told the family so that I may review the information with them.

One must judge if it is necessary to wait for all ancillary evaluations to be complete before formulating one's own diagnosis and treatment plan. Often, it becomes clear before all ancillary evaluations are completed that certain educational, psychotherapeutic, or environmental interventions are appropriate; however, these evaluations are likely to provide information that will refine the diagnosis and treatment planning. Be sure to acknowledge receipt of the evaluations and to consult with the evaluators if further questions remain. It is also best if one can offer to provide follow-up to the consultant—again, if the parents are willing. In this way one can establish a professional support system around child and family that is useful in furthering treatment goals and in facilitating future diagnostic input and studies.

DIAGNOSTIC FORMULATION AND TREATMENT PLANNING

Through one's own evaluation and ancillary evaluations, an enormous amount of information is collected, which must be organized and evaluated in order to arrive at diagnoses and recommendations. There are many formats for organizing the data from a merely factual point of view: identifying data, a statement of the current problem and its history, mental status examination, and general psychiatric and developmental history (Cramer 1975; Fish and Shapiro 1965; Freud 1965; Goodman and Sours 1967; Greenspan 1981; Simmons 1981). This type of organization may be sufficient for arriving at a DSM-III diagnosis, which is based on a collection of more or less discrete descriptive symptoms. But it is insufficient, no matter how lengthy and complete, for formulating a meaningful working diagnosis. This must be much more descriptive: outlining the nature of the individual and family problems; evaluating their severity and chronicity in comparison with developmentally appropriate norms; stating the individual's and the environment's assets and weaknesses and how they will affect treatment strategies. One must determine who will best be able to address each problem area. It is best to think in terms of ideal strategies and to modify them as the need arises. A very complex diagnostic picture requiring a complicated and vigorous set of interventions can be accepted only in a treatment plan that involves the parents and eventually educates them to the need for more far-reaching interventions. For example, many families cannot readily accept the need for hospitalization of a very fragile or manipulative borderline or prepsychotic youngster. Only after they observe the difficulties in treating their youngster on an outpatient basis, and after they have worked through some of their own guilt, frustration, anger, and conflicts over separation can they face such a recommendation.

COMMUNICATION OF RECOMMENDATIONS TO PARENTS

When I am ready to discuss my recommendations with parents, I usually set aside a double session. Occasionally, a follow-up session is needed so that parents can further integrate my observations and treatment recommendations. I review the presenting complaints and symptoms and the reports of other professionals. I relate my observations and explain their significance. I try to list the child's strengths as well as weaknesses and to indicate how the former can be used in promoting improvements in the latter. I indicate what further evaluation, follow-up, or treatment may be necessary.

If I am recommending treatment, I help parents formulate how to tell their child. The sensitivity of the parents' approach can have a profound effect on the child's ability and eagerness to participate in the treatment process. Parental reluctance is usually reflected in whining, silent, or uncooperative children. I explain to parents that they will be seen regularly to provide information about the child and the family, especially if they have a small child who is not an accurate reporter. Seeing parents is also crucial in maintaining the treatment alliance. The frequency of parental contact is determined by the needs of the family and the treatment.

Not infrequently, it becomes clear that one or both parents require treatment as well. Clearly, one must be tactful in making such a recommendation and be able to recommend competent colleagues who are sensitive to the issues of child treatment and parenthood.

If I intend to be the therapist, I discuss the parameters of the treatment situation: fee, payment, cancellation, vacation policies, appointment times, and amount and type of continuing parent contact. Some put their policies in writing and give a copy to parents at the end of the evaluation. It is best to deal with these difficult issues at the outset to avoid unpleasant complications later on. I inform parents that at the beginning and end of each school and treatment year, I will review with them and their youngster why he is in treatment, what gains have been made, and what conflicts and symptoms remain to be addressed.

Some therapists arrange to maintain periodic contact with parents or patients after termination. If this practice is introduced at the beginning of therapy, it need not place too great a burden on the closure of termination. Parents and youngsters may welcome such an arrangement as an indication of professional diligence and interest, an assurance that if problems arise after the termination, help will be available. If one has a particular research interest, one may wish to maintain this contact even with families and youngsters one evaluates but does not treat.

SUMMARY

In my discussion of assessment strategies, I have offered my experience and philosophy of evaluating children and adolescents in a private office setting. I have tried to stress the need to establish an inviting, confidence-inspiring, sympathetic physical and emotional setting for the interviews. I believe that the manner in which one sets the stage for the clinical assessment is crucial in motivating the parents and child to reveal the material necessary to making the best diagnoses and recommendations. It also sets the stage for the therapeutic process that may follow.

The process of assessment can be very rewarding for the clinician. In addition to the satisfaction in helping the child and parents, the clinician can expand his experience in exploring developmental variants, new family patterns and adaptations to stress, as well as different evaluation strategies—all of which will prove useful in his approach to future clinical assessments.

REFERENCES

Bird, H., and Kestenbaum, C. J. (1988). A Semistructured Approach to Clinical Assessment. This volume, Chapter Two.

Canino, I. (1985). Taking a History. In D. Shaffer, A. A. Erhardt, and L. L. Greenhill (Eds.). *The Clinical Guide to Child Psychiatry*, pp. 393–407. New York: Free Press.

Cramer, J. (1975). Psychiatric Examination of the Child. In A. Freedman, H. Kaplan, and B. Sadock (Eds.). *The Comprehensive Textbook of Psychiatry*, vol. 2, pp. 2055–60. Baltimore: Williams and Wilkins.

Fish, B., and Shapiro, T. (1965). A typology of children's psychiatric disorders—Application to a controlled evaluation of treatment. *Journal of the American Academy of Child Psychiatry* 4(1):32–52.

Freud, A. (1965). *Normality and Pathology in Childhood.* New York: International Universities Press.

Gardner, R. A. (1971). *Therapeutic Communication with Children: The Mutual Storytelling Technique.* New York: Jason Aronson.

Goodman, J. D., and Sours, J. A. (1967). *The Child Mental Status Examination.* New York: Basic Books.

Greenspan, S. I. (1981). *Psychopathology and Adaptation in Infancy and Early Childhood.* New York: International Universities Press.

Kestenbaum, C. J. (1985). The Creative Process in Child Psychiatry. *American Journal of Psychotherapy.* 39 (4): 479–89.

Simmons, J. E. (1981). Psychiatric Examination of Children. 3d ed. Philadelphia: Lea and Febiger.

Winnicott, D. W. (1971). *Therapeutic Consultations in Child Psychiatry.* New York: Basic Books.

II

Psychological Assessment of Cognition and Personality in Childhood and Adolescence

5

COGNITIVE AND PROJECTIVE TEST ASSESSMENT

Miriam G. Siegel

Testing children requires intimate knowledge of normal sequences of child development and of its clinical disturbances. In order to differentiate among normal, deviant, and intervening grey areas, the psychologist should be alert to signs of age appropriateness, acceleration, and retardation. These simultaneous progressive and regressive forces, whether temporary or lasting, coexist as conflicting influences that eventually mold individual personality from infancy through toddlerhood into school age, adolescence, and beyond. Within the narrow confines of time and space that constitute the psychological examination, examiner and child establish a contact that is transitory yet intimate. This subjective experience of the child has qualities belonging to the realms of both fantasy and reality. For the child, the boundaries between the real and the imaginary worlds are more ephemeral. In comparison to big, overpowering adults in his surroundings, his actual physical smallness may generate conscious or unconscious feelings of inferiority. His ego is in a rudimentary stage, his developmental tempo is unstable, and he is excessively vulnerable to life's vicissitudes and to those external influences that he eventually assimilates as internal experiences.

To see the world through the eyes of a child is an exceptional talent. Testing the child sharpens clinical sensitivities. The examiner must disengage himself, if only temporarily, from the world of his contemporaries and enter into the mind and feelings of a child. With sympathetic identification, a sense of humor, flexibility, and readiness to depart from rigid blueprints, he sets aside some of the accretions of his adult personality.

Examiner and child share common responsibilities in regard to different yet closely interrelated demands that are placed upon them. In some tasks, such as the formal intelligence test, the child is asked to engage in conventional logical thinking, free

This chapter is adapted from *Psychological Testing from Early Childhood Through Adolescence* by Miriam G. Siegel, New York: International Universities Press, 1987.

from distractions of inner fantasies and emotions. In other instances, particularly the projective techniques, he is encouraged to suspend his ideational approach and to share his imagination and feelings.

USES AND LIMITATIONS OF PSYCHOLOGICAL TESTS

Discussing the use of tests in a child guidance clinic, Anna Freud (1945) has noted that they are meant to be "a shortcut to reveal what the child hides, willingly or unwillingly, and what the psychiatrist is unable to see." And in her earlier writing she said, "[Tests] are nearly indispensable in cases where a differential diagnosis has to be made between mental deficiency and defective awareness of reality through denial" (1945, p. 49).

The verbally facile child without inner cognitive substance may masquerade as brighter then he actually is. Conversely, the child whose intellectual inhibitions are environmentally or emotionally induced presents a spurious impression of mental limitations. The tests provide specific information about discrepancies between intellectual potential and achievement. They distinguish between fixed and transitory impairments of functioning; as a signal contribution, they confirm or contradict an equivocal diagnosis. To the dynamic orientation of the psychotherapist, they add an understanding of specific areas of conflict, of affective organization, defenses, transference phenomena, motivation and potential for change. When tests are used as a parallel technique and not as a substitute for other clinical methods, they fulfill their special challenge—that is, the portrayal of the unique child.

Inherent in testing procedures are cautions and restraints that must be applied to all clinical techniques. For some professional workers, the scope and expectations of testing are overextended, and for others, too limited. Misuse of tests and too heavy dependence on their results have disadvantageous effects on the developing skills of inexperienced clinical workers. For some clinicians, the worth of tests is doubtful, and their results suspect. The child becomes the ultimate victim of such misconceptions that interfere with productive interdisciplinary teamwork. Routine testing of every child presented for clinical evaluation is neither economically practical nor psychologically fruitful. It is superfluous when clinical interviews and information from the parents and school are sufficient for understanding the child.

THE TEST BATTERY

Although there is no standard test battery, a comprehensive evaluation of the child requires a balanced group of intelligence and projective tests. The choice of tests is determined by the age of the child, relevance to his particular needs, opportunities for investigation of broad areas of functioning, and judgment and training of the psychologist. A wide range and diversity of tasks complement one another and allow for cross-checking of the child's performance in various areas.

The assortment of developmental and intelligence tests available to the psychologist covers a broad range. Among those commonly used for infants are: the Gesell and Amatruda Developmental Schedule; the Cattell Infant Intelligence Scale; the Bayley Scales of Infant Development; and the Merrill Palmer Scale of Intelligence. For children of preschool and school age, there are the Stanford-Binet Revised Form L-M; the Wechsler Preschool and Primary Scale of Intelligence (WPPSI) for ages 4 to 6; the Wechsler Intelligence Scale for Children, Revised (WISC-R) for ages 5 through 16; the Wechsler Adult Intelligence Scale, Revised (WAIS-R) for age 16 through adulthood. The widely used projective techniques are the Rorschach Inkblots, the Human Figure Drawings, the Children's Apperception Test (CAT) for ages 3 to 16, and the Thematic Apperception Test (TAT) for age 10 and through adolescence and adulthood. There are many other tests that the examiner may prefer or add to the battery.

Group tests, unlike individually administered tests, are designed for rapid mass screening of large numbers of children. They provide crude estimates of intelligence and are useful when more sophisticated methods are unavailable or impractical. They do not, however, offer an opportunity for qualitative assessment of a child's behavior, motivation, attention, emotional rapport, or other factors that influence his performance and capacities. They do retain a general predictive value in regard to school achievement and may help to identify those children who need further assessment, but they may lead to serious errors in the evaluation of an individual child's intellectual potential.

The fundamental conditions that determine the usefulness of a test are its objectivity, validity, and reliability. Standardization on large representative groups and uniform norms and procedures for administration, scoring, and interpretation are essential. A valid test measures that particular characteristic it is designed to measure. A reliable test yields consistent results when it is repeated over a period of time by a different examiner. The following discussion of tests is neither exhaustive nor comprehensive. It represents one clinician's extensive experience with many different children from different environmental backgrounds, with varying degrees of mental health and illness.

QUALITATIVE IMPRESSIONS

Children do not voluntarily appear for a psychological examination. The troubled child cannot help but inflict his disturbance on others; he creates sufficient disruption in his family equilibrium to motivate a professional consultation that often includes a psychological examination. His behavior during his examination presents the first sketchy contours of his unique personality picture. He may transform the examiner into a loving or threatening parental surrogate or duplicate his reactions at home, in his classroom, or in therapy sessions. However, the change in physical milieu and the introduction of stress associated with test demands may reveal changes of attitude. In the final psychological assessment of the child, qualitative impressions are incorporated into the structural framework of a total test performance. The examiner remains alert to the rich flow of information, verbal and nonverbal, that comes from the child, and in many instances, from his parents. A clinician over-identified with the child's predicament is liable to lack sympathetic regard for the parents' distress. With compassionate understanding he must remain sensitive to the parents' feelings of guilt and their level of defensiveness, which ultimately have destructive influences on the child. For many parents, the preliminary arrangements prior to actual testing are smooth and the separation from the child easy and natural. A troubled parent may transmit his own unreal expectations, forebodings, and ambivalence to the child, who perceives and is affected by these attitudes.

Separation anxiety can vary from mild uncertainty to open terror; if it is present beyond preschool age, it usually has a deviant significance. It has many disguises: fervent farewells, as though the child were embarking on a perilous journey; loving reunions; and body-merging contacts. The child may focus his separation anxiety on an inanimate object that is a symbol of an emotionally meaningful adult in his life. He brings with him a cherished toy or stuffed animal that he uses to assuage his feelings of inner sadness and loneliness. As a magic amulet it introduces a note of security into the unfamiliar testing situation. In order to avoid the test demands, he may attempt to use the familiar object as a diversionary tactic. As an interested third party, the toy can also facilitate the flow of communication from the child.

The separation anxiety that a child initially controls may erupt during his examination. He provides critical evidence of his chronic discomfort or sudden intrusions of anxiety. A specific test stimulus—particular Rorschach card, apperception test picture, or intelligence test item—may produce increased hyperactivity, a demand for food or the bathroom, flight to Mother, or any of the multiple ways through which a child signals his distress. His anxiety may range from mild uneasiness that responds to reassurance to overwhelming panic about abandonment that can be alleviated only by a visit to the parent in the waiting room. As another extreme, a young child's lack of appropriate separation anxiety and quick adhesive attachment to the unfamiliar examiner often appear in his tests as diffuse, indiscriminate object relations. In those unusual circumstances when the examination must be conducted with a parent in the office, there is increased opportunity to observe their overly intense interaction.

A child's physical size relative to his chronological age impinges on his self-image in his test productions. His personal hygiene and dress, while sometimes outside the realm of his responsibility, are often linked to conflicts about exhibitionism in his tests. An assessment of the child's speech and language usage is based on developmental expectations, educational status, and possible pathological deviations, such as dysnomia, aphasia, and related disorders of central nervous system

origin. The examiner listens for impediments, infantilisms, stuttering, errors in articulation and grammar, habitual tempo, and nuances in inflection, pitch, and volume.
Unfamiliar words and idiomatic expressions derived from a particular ethnic and
geographical background are differentiated from oddities of language and bizarre
verbalizations.

Significant differences in the child's expressive language on the structured intelligence test and projective techniques reflect variations in his approach to reality and
fantasy tasks. He may use language to facilitate or avoid communication. The dull
talkative child may use an excess of empty words to compensate for a meager vocabulary and paucity of ideas. The aim of excessive garrulousness during the examination is often obfuscation rather than clarification. The language of the obsessive child is doubt-ridden, pontifical, and pedantic; he uses words as weapons, and
the atmosphere of the tests is one of parry and thrust; he rejects simple solutions
and engages in elaborate discourses; he assumes a grave philosophical front, seeks
out all possible ramifications, chooses words with precision (though malapropisms
are not unusual), and may end up far from his reality goal. Verbal inhibitions, protracted delays, or a nontalking stance may originate in inadequate language skills,
avoidance of phobic-laden words and ideas, distrust, and attempts to control the
adult.

As the child grows older and his verbal repertoire is expanded, he relies less on
his body to make his wants known and to establish contact with the outside world.
His body language may be as subtle as a flicker of his eyelid or as explicit as certain
voluntary or involuntary kinesthetic responses: tics, facial grimaces, sniffing, hand-
wringing. The restless child rocks, gyrates in his seat, hoists himself up and plops
down with visible erotic excitement. When oral determinants are dominant he yawns,
extrudes his tongue, and sucks or bites his fingers, fingernails, or other objects. He
chews gum, sings, whimpers, giggles, blubbers his lips.

The examiner notes excessive tautness or looseness in muscular posture and
gait, special skills, or impairments in fine and gross motor coordination that are
frequent components of the "organic" syndrome. It is important to distinguish between neurological and psychogenic causes of the child's motor excitement. The
restlessness of the fidgety child who is without acceptable outlets for his body tensions may be misinterpreted as organic in origin. The child who is physically active
or deficient in linguistic ability often resorts to dramatic body language.

Most children are readily engaged in the tests and friendly exchange with the
examiner. The trained examiner distinguishes between genuine investment in the
tests and chameleonlike compliance. An overly agreeable exterior often masks the
silent oppositionalism and passive-aggressive ambivalence that may present more
formidable obstacles to testing than frank resistance. The child's eye contact may be
direct, forthright, furtive, or adhesive. He may be so deeply immersed in his fantasy
life and obsessive ruminations that his emotional responsiveness and intellectual
energies are reduced. If he is overly involved in scrutiny of his surroundings, he
cannot relax his guards; he must maintain constant vigilance against potential as-

sault from the outside world. Such sensory hyperalertness must be distinguished from the excessive vulnerability of a neurologically impaired child who is bombarded by multiple extraneous stimuli impinging upon his consciousness.

The child's approach reflects pleasure in the completed task or quick acceptance of defeat. One child relies on trial-and-error methods; another surveys the problem in its entirety, and solves it in his initial attempt. The intellectually challenged child with inner motivation is not directly dependent on praise or approval from adults. In spite of intermittent anxiety and frustration, he keeps sight of his long-term goal, the successful closure of the task. The less challenged or motivated child may dissolve into helpless dependency with consequent loss in self-esteem. His shifts between an active and passive approach are often determined by specific differences in the test demands. External reassurance usually cannot relieve the anxiety of the child whose boasting and unrealistic aggrandizement of his test performance feed his fantasies of magic omnipotence. The grandiose expectations that he maintains in such a tenuous way may lead to distortions in his reality judgment. He may cling to the denials that are typical of the very young child, challenge the worth of the tests, and project his shortcomings onto the outside world: "This is impossible," "A piece is missing," "Can you do it?" The child who has suffered from severe deprivation—socioeconomic, emotional, or both—sometimes makes insatiable, unreasonable demands for material tokens of acceptance and approval. If his craving reaches inappropriate proportions, the examiner must exert firm limitations.

Testing the "unstable" child presents a particular challenge. He usually is not responsive to formal testing procedures, nor can he communicate to others his feelings of inner futility and inadequacy. In such a case the examiner must be familiar with a wide variety of children's tests from which bits and pieces are chosen, usually in nonsequential order. As the child drifts in and out of reality, he becomes, during his object-focused periods, accessible to one or another item in the intelligence or projective tests.

During the several sessions that are necessary for testing the "untestable" child, an expansion of his external environment beyond the physical confines of the office can provide experiences that allow him to reveal himself in ways different from his response to formal test demands. Such flexibility of test procedures does not, however, mean that the expectations of test performance are discarded. Although the child's anxiety may by this means be diminished, the traditional framework of the examination must be maintained. If the examiner does not encourage performance at the level of his capabilities or deficiencies, the child's personal boundaries, which are at best precarious, are loosened, and he becomes overwhelmed by disorganizing panic. Although the test reactions of the severely disturbed child are minimal and fragmented, they are useful aids to the determination of his developmental status and potential for future growth.

INTELLIGENCE

In spite of wide variations and ambiguity of textbook definitions of intelligence, there is general consensus about its multidimensional nature and its relation to purposive and adaptive behavior. Psychologists have long since abandoned the earlier concept of a predetermined fixed intelligence in which the constancy of the IQ was based on a traditional assumption that the child's intellectual ability responded more or less automatically to successive steps of physical maturation. That rigid belief stemmed from a narrow concentration on genetic factors to the exclusion of nonintellectual influences. The current viewpoint takes into consideration effects of cultural background, environmental idiosyncrasies, early learning experiences, and, as a derivation from ego psychology, affective organization, motivation, and drives that facilitate or impede intellectual growth. Particularly in children, whose development is in a state of flux, the IQ is an unstable index that measures only the current level of intellectual efficiency.

The three Wechslers (WPPSI, WISC-R, and WAIS-R) measure essential functions that develop in a sequential order from early childhood through adolescence and adulthood. The tests are constructed in two parts consisting of a Verbal scale and a Performance scale; they yield three IQs: Verbal, Performance, and Full. The Performance tests can be administered without verbal instructions, an important consideration for the child from a non-English-speaking home or with a special handicap such as a hearing impairment. When the child has completed the Wechsler test, the examiner is presented with a vast amount of data that he must eventually incorporate in his final summation of the total test findings. Normal developmental expectations and interrelationships between strengths and weaknesses are basic factors in analysis of the Wechsler pattern. The test is much more than a psychometric device; it is a clinical instrument that provides crucial dynamic and diagnostic information.

Quantitative and Qualitative

The IQ is a composite, condensed mathematical measure derived from a statistical average of the child's successes and failures on a wide variety of intellectual tasks of graded difficulty. The greater the range of test samples and choice of intellectual processes, the more accurate the assessment of the child's intellectual functioning. Intelligence is distributed in a statistical bell-shaped normal curve with half of the population in the average range from IQ 90 to IQ 109. At either of the extremes, above or below the normal range, each comprising 2.2 percent of the population, children are classified as intellectually superior or mentally retarded. The IQ alone is insufficient basis, however, for such classification; other criteria—historical, clinical, social, and emotional—are of critical importance in the identification of the exceptional child. Without other personality assets, an IQ of 130 and above does not necessarily characterize a child as intellectually gifted. Neither does an IQ of 70, particularly in the borderline zone, establish inadequate functioning because of low intelligence.

Scatter is the configuration of weighted scores based on significant inconsistencies in the child's test performance. The selective impact on intellectual functioning of emotional disturbance and different rates of maturational growth is implicit in the concept. Scatter assumes three forms: 1) Scatter in IQs: A full scale IQ can be derived from vastly different scores on the verbal and performance scales. A verbal IQ much elevated over a performance IQ is characteristic of the obsessive ideational child. A performance IQ that exceeds a verbal IQ indicates sparse language skills and is typical of a child whose competence is in nonverbal areas. A fifteen or twenty point difference in IQ in either direction, verbal or performance, is usually an alerting signal of an uneven development. The moderate discrepancies of the normal child relate to individual growth patterns, genetic disposition, special interests and predilections, and range of experience. 2) Interest scatter is determined by the relationships among subtest scores. These distributions cluster or diverge from a central mean tendency. They also reflect normal differences in maturational rate, relative strengths and weaknesses, and areas of intellectual acceleration or impairment. 3) Intratest scatter refers to patterns of success and failure within a single subtest; e.g., the child fails easy items and passes difficult ones. Such lacunae indicate "holes" that may be rooted in emotional conflict or developmental anomalies. Various forms of scatter are useful aids to determine a child's intellectual potential beyond his actual functioning efficiency.

Since intelligence is not a distinct entity that can be separated from other personality functions, use of the intelligence test merely as a psychometric device neglects clinical insights that can be gained from the child's responses. Qualitative analysis of the Wechsler bridges the gap between the child's response to the structured intelligence test and unstructured projective techniques.

THE VERBAL TESTS

Information

If a child's intellectual maturation proceeds unimpeded and he maintains active curiosity, he accumulates a steadily increasing amount of information from the outside world. The Information component matches the Vocabulary subtest as a verbal function that is directly regulated by the intellectual wealth or poverty of the child's home environment. Eventually the school assumes a more decisive role in formal learning. As one aspect of global intelligence, the Information component is dependent on numerous interrelated factors: intrinsic intellectual endowment; impairments associated with brief or protracted periods of emotional disturbance; environmental and cultural orientation. A street-wise ghetto child with an inquiring mind may be knowledgeable about matters within his special range of experience, but his fund of formal information as measured by the intelligence test is limited. A disturbance in acquiring appropriate information may begin at an early age, and if it continues it has a destructive influence on the child's learning and future development. The overideational child indulges in a sterile garnering of facts; such pedantry contrasts with pseudostupidity that results in meager information. A conspicuously high score in Information without corresponding acceleration in cognitive ability in the Similarities and other tests suggests obsessive strains toward labeling and classification of objects rather than conceptual thinking. The examiner is alert to unpredictable lacunae, temporary forgetting, and bizarre content. A ten-year-old engaged in a learned discourse on "Hieroglyphics," but he could not name the two countries that border the United States. As an isolated phenomenon such an internal contradiction may not be significant, but it alerts the examiner to other test evidence of developmental deviation.

Similarities

The Similarities subtest measures the child's ability to recognize a connection between two disparate objects or ideas. As development proceeds, this ability facilitates a high level of abstract thinking. The sameness that a child establishes between a cat and a mouse illustrates developmental gradations between concrete and abstract thinking. His generalization may be irrelevant: "They are little"; "They chase each other." As one step upward on the developmental scale, he fastens onto isolated body features or functions: "They have fur . . . legs . . . tails." In these instances the part assumes the properties of the whole; the choice is too limited and not sufficiently exclusive. "Animals," the third and highest level of abstraction, indicates advanced progress toward organized thinking and concept formation.

It is important to differentiate between pathological ideation as a form of maladjustment and the offkey thinking of a bright child whose intellectual curiosity leads him toward original exploration of his inner world of ideas. A genuinely creative child who is escaping from the conventional mold may engage in divergent thinking, yet he maintains healthy respect for reality. Clinicians are familiar with the stress-related regression and ease with which a child slips back from age-appropriate thinking. If this slippage is habitual, the disturbance appears in symptoms (and in the tests) as defensive mechanisms, usually involving denial, repression, dissociation, and regression.

Arithmetic

Mathematics is a form of pure logic. Arithmetic, in contrast to the other subtests on the verbal scale that rely primarily on language skills, involves conscious effort to examine, choose, and organize established patterns, a task demanding most scrupulous attention. At its earliest level arithmetic is dependent on memory. Later on the child learns to solve problems by mental manipulations of numbers and numerical symbols and in this way Arithmetic is closely related to Similarities as a measure of capacity for abstract thinking. The child's performance on this subtest reflects one aspect of his secondary process development. To solve the arithmetic problems, he must exclude from his consciousness irrelevant content that disturbs his concentration. Disruptive anxiety, imaginative reveries, obsessive ruminations, or weakened impulse controls have a particularly adverse effect on Arithmetic. A child with an idiosyncratic distribution of developmental skills may maintain a capacity for such exclusionary concentration in Arithmetic, but not in the other subtests. As a single precocious aptitude, it reaches a pathological extreme in the idiot savant. In the truly gifted child without such developmental anomalies, mathematics is one of a cluster of skills that belong within the domain of science and music.

An intellectually disciplined 7-year-old boy who had mastered the intricate game of chess showed his capacity for complex organization and visual memory, his patience and ability in long-term planning in Arithmetic and many other tests. His special skill in mathematics was an early precursor of subsequent creative achievements during adolescence. Conversely, an adolescent girl with hysterical inclinations engaged in histrionic complaints about her utter incompetence in this area. She dissolved into convulsive laughter, and her threat of imminent collapse was only partially averted by the examiner's reassurance.

Vocabulary

As the child matures, continuing expansion of his intellectual and emotional experiences requires increased vocabulary and mastery of verbal skills. Through symbolic language and thought, the child can exert restraints on immediate action. The Wechsler Vocabulary is a relatively stable function, and once achieved, it is among those less susceptible to deterioration. Since the development of vocabulary relies so heavily on early environmental stimulation, losses at this stage result in fundamental defects that are not readily overcome by subsequent school and life experiences. The child from a culturally impoverished home may enter first grade with inadequate language skills. Because of a popular fallacy that equates verbal skills with intelligence, a full battery of tests is of crucial importance in the assessment of the inarticulate child, who can readily be mistaken as intellectually limited. As he lacks words for objects and ideas outside his limited range of experience, the number of words he can define cannot be used as an accurate gauge of his intellectual capacity. Other measures of a nonverbal variety provide a more valid impression of his intellectual potential and of those restraining forces that prevent optimal use of his abilities. In contrast, the verbal deficiency of the mentally retarded child is one aspect of pervasive developmental arrests that are deeply embedded in stereotyped thinking and paucity of ideas.

The child's vocabulary definitions range from a high level of precision and clarity of expression, to mild affective coloration within an appropriate context, to pathological deviation. When certain words are heavily endowed with fantasy and affect, their definitions mirror thought content laden with emotional conflict. A verbally precocious 7-year-old girl defined "fable" as "a make-believe story, like a myth, when animals talk"; and she proceeded with a dramatic rendering of *The Fox and the Grapes*. To an 11-year-old boy who lacked her verbal talents, "fable" means "You tell a lie." He expounded on the "bad" consequences of falsehood: "Your teacher finds out you didn't do your homework and you're in big trouble." Defensive manipulations in the Vocabulary subtest may parallel those that appear in Information. One child applies his "not knowing" indiscriminately to words and facts; another indulges his exhibitionistic aims through verbal and factual pyrotechnics on both subtests. The gibberish, neologisms, or mutism of an autistic child also reflect the private meaning he attaches to words.

Comprehension

The Comprehension subtest explores soundness of judgment based on knowledge of facts and interrelations among them, and the ability to draw inferences, control impulses, and engage in thoughtful deliberations before acting. The unstructured personality of the very young child, with his uncertainties about himself in relation to the objective world and his still immature superego, can lead to diffuse, volatile, or indiscriminate reactions. Later on, he seeks adult approval, yet his judgment is determined by learned rules and regulations rather than internalized standards. When he enters school and the community beyond his circumscribed family environment, he absorbs rules about group acceptances. To deal effectively with his rapidly expanding intellectual, emotional, and social universe, the latency child must learn modes of age-appropriate behavior.

On the Comprehension subtest, too facile verbalizations that lack emotional conviction are typical of the overly adaptive, pseudorelated child who uses social talents for manipulative purposes. In matters of conscience, some children are too rigid, others too lenient. Some cling to passive dependency, others struggle for self-reliance. In the WPPSI, "Why should you go to the toilet before going to bed?" provides clues to the child's readiness to assume responsibility for his body management. "Mommy makes me" signals his mechanical response to external demands; "So you won't make in bed" indicates age-appropriate control of body functions. The proper response may come from a bed-wetter; he indicates a knowledge that is age-appropriate, but not necessarily appropriate control.

On the WAIS-R, "What should you do if while in the movies you are the first person to see smoke and fire?" requires careful choices and organization of facts that will result in immediate relevant action. The mature decisive child who is aware of the total situation calls on the appropriate figure of authority. At the other extreme, an unhesitating "Yell fire" usually signals the defective judgment of the impulse-ridden child. On the other hand, a mature adolescent with an IQ of 140 and excellent performance throughout his tests also said, "Yell fire." He was not really impulse-ridden but vulnerable to sudden anxiety. If he is engaged in an obsessive struggle with his impulses and anxiety, he asks, "What should I do or what would I do? I know I shouldn't yell fire, but I might panic." A narcissistic adolescent with grandiose ideas about his competence described his take-charge procedures: "First I'd notify the person next to me. Then I'd stop the picture and I'd order the people to walk quietly to the nearest exit. Then I'd grab the fire extinguisher and I'd put it out myself."

Digit Span

The Digit Span subtest in the WISC-R and WAIS-R consists of two parts. The first requires repetition of numbers spoken by the examiner; the second requires repetition of numbers in reverse sequence. The total score is misleading if it masks a significant discrepancy between both parts of the test. Although the Digit Span is considered to be a test of memory in general, its actual function is confined to immediate short-term auditory, rather than remote, memory. The child must cope with three processes of repetition, retention, and recall. His failure to focus on the immediate task indicates a disturbance in concentration associated with varying degrees of anxiety that may be temporary or chronic. Poor performance on this subtest may also be attributed to fatigue, boredom, depression, psychotic or organic disorganization, or a combination of these factors.

A disturbance in memory, a recurrent factor in numerous diagnostic categories, has significant meaning for the child's approach to learning. An unusually high, isolated success in Digit Span, coupled with a low Similarities score, suggests a learning style based on rote memorization rather than on logical reasoning. The child's reliance on routine, often prolific associative activity rather than on abstract thinking may stem from a modest intellectual endowment or specific inhibitions that limit learning and intellectual development.

THE PERFORMANCE TESTS

Picture Completion

In the Picture Completion subtest, the child is presented with drawings of commonplace objects in which one essential part is missing. His task is to discover the gap in the pattern, the basic inconsistency. To reach such a sense of closure, a complex interrelationship of visual imagery, visual memory, concentration, anticipation, and awareness of figure-ground relations is required. If his interpretation of the picture is too literal, he introduces an object that is not intended to be there. His focus on the ideal, as he wishes it to be, results in a loss of appreciation of the drawn picture as the reality stimulus. The culturally deprived child is unfamiliar with many objects within the experience of an advantaged child. Children who suffer from neurophysiological dysfunction and related learning deficiencies, particu-

larly spelling and writing, often do poorly in the Picture Completion. A conspicuously elevated or depressed score on the Picture Completion is determined, on the
one hand, by unusual accuracy of visual perception and on the other, by suspicious
hyperalertness to the surroundings. A low score may be based on reality distortions,
depression, general withdrawal of interest from the environment, or a combination
of these factors. The obsessive doubter worries about irrelevancies in symmetry and
identification of the object itself. Complaints about strangeness of commonplace objects are often linked to disturbed self-object representations and tendencies toward
depersonalization. The child may enliven, with kinesthetic gestures, the dynamic
interplay between visual perception and body-image anxiety. A 6-year-old who immediately recognized that the doll's arm was missing grasped his own arm as though
to reassure himself about his body intactness. Worry about body mutilation was a
major theme throughout his projective tests.

Picture Arrangement

In the Picture Arrangement subtest, the child must organize a scrambled series
of pictures into a sensible story. Success in this area requires attention to visual
details, recognition of plot, planning and sequencing, intact reality testing, and understanding of future consequences based on initial events. As a corollary to the
Comprehension subtest on the verbal scale, the Picture Arrangement measures the
child's social judgment and the ease with which he translates it into actual behavior.
The moralistic sermons delivered by a delinquent adolescent on the Comprehension
are belied by his infantile impulsive reactions on the Picture Arrangement. The inarticulate child without such devious aims may reveal appropriate judgment that he
cannot express verbally. Some children spontaneously share their fantasy about their
story sequence. A fearful 8-year-old girl who had correctly arranged the Fire series
became anxious and excited; she pointed to a barely distinguishable dot in the window of the flaming house. "That's my Mommy. She's stuck in the fire." The child
read the appropriate meaning of the pictures but she was threatened by guilt and
anxiety.

Perceptual-Motor Tests

Several Wechsler subtests are designed to assess the child's perceptual motor-
functioning: on the WISC-R and WAIS-R, Block Design, Object Assembly, Coding
or Digit Symbol; on the WPPSI, Block Design, Geometric Designs, Animal House,
Mazes. The scores are based on time and accuracy.

On the Block Design, the child is asked first to reproduce with colored blocks
the examiner's demonstrations, and later, two-dimensional geometrical forms on a
card placed before him. This subtest measures motor coordination, pattern analysis,
and pattern construction. The Object Assembly is a productive, not reproductive
task that involves two processes—visual recognition and spontaneous progression

to motor action. It uses jigsaw combinations of familiar objects—a manikin, horse, human profile, and others. In the Coding and Digit Symbol, the child is shown a sample line of symbols and numbers on the top of the sheet. He is asked to write in the empty squares the symbol associated with that number in the sample. The WPPSI Animal House is designed for the young child who has not yet developed symbol-number associations. He is presented with a board with animal pictures and different colored cylindrical pegs. He has to find the right color house for each animal; he must follow directions and work under time pressure. The functions involved are similar to, but not as habitual as, principles of writing, spelling, and drawing.

The Mazes, an integral part of the WPPSI and a supplementary test in the WISC-R taps several interrelated functions: visual-motor coordination, spatial orientation, sense of direction and dimension, capacity for observation, planning, and learning from errors. In the Geometric Designs, the child is asked to copy designs that are presented to him one at a time. Since the fine muscular coordination of the young child is not yet developed, gross irregularities are more significant than minute deviations.

The perceptual-motor tests involve several successive procedures. First, the child must see the stimulus; second, he must perceive or understand the visual image; finally, he must convert his perception into coordinated motor action. This complicated integrative process, which is so dependent on physical and neurological maturation, requires a delicate balance between the receptive and expressive functions. In his approach to these tasks, the well-organized child surveys the situation, plans his strategy, and proceeds in an orderly, deliberate way. The hasty, impulsive child plunges ahead without sufficient forethought; he relies on trial-and-error methods, and his movements are aimless, unguided, and time-consuming. The particular functions measured by the tests, the pervasive or selective nature of the child's skills and impairments, and the intensity of his emotional stress may produce very diverse test reactions. A child who demonstrates superior integrative ability on the relatively impersonal Block Design may dissolve into disorganizing panic on the Object Assembly, since the latter often evokes feelings about his body's integrity or vulnerability.

An overideational child may easily grasp verbal abstractions, but may regress to a piecemeal concretistic approach on the perceptual-motor tests. In contrast, a child with deficient language skills (low verbal scores) may display a high level of competence in nonverbal organization. Obsessive drive may prolong a struggle with these tasks beyond the allotted time limit. Depressive lethargy and psychomotor retardation result in minimal performance. As a reaction to his primary deficit, the child may display helplessness or an overconfidence that approaches grandiosity. Regression, projection, and denial are common defenses of the child who does poorly on perceptual-motor tests. A 4-year-old's score on the Mazes was noticeably lower than her other subtest scores. She interrupted her slow, anxious progress toward the mother chick with a plaintive question, "Why can't the Mommy meet me halfway?"

THE PROJECTIVE TECHNIQUES

The child's responses to structured test demands represent one aspect of his psychological organization. In contrast, his reactions to ambiguous perceptual stimuli that are without the firm boundaries of the intelligence test are the principal concern of the projective test. When used with clinical skill and sensitivity, the projective techniques are the most effective instruments for penetrating deeper recesses of personality. A projective test is a method of studying personality and conflict through an unstructured medium. The child is asked to create something, to tell a story, to draw a picture, to find a visual image in amorphous inkblots. Since he is not hampered by conventional patterns, through his interpretation of ambiguous material he divulges unconscious mental processes and content. Because there are no right or wrong answers, he rarely can recognize the deeper psychological significance of how he handles the task. This indirect method reveals the specific human substance that eludes more mechanical procedures concerned with personality isolated traits.

The projective test is derived from the concept of projection as a defense mechanism whose aim, similar to other defenses, is to shield the individual from feelings of narcissistic pain, anxiety, and guilt. Freud broadened his original application of the term beyond the realm of psychopathology, to include inner perceptions of ideational and affective experiences that, like sensory perceptions, are used to shape the outside world.

The child's projective test responses reflect myriad variations of developmental normality and disturbance. When he temporarily relaxes his external guards, he may indulge in adventurous exploration of his imagination. Rare poetic sensitivity colors the flights of fancy of the truly gifted child. Differential diagnosis requires careful distinction between pathological fantasy and imaginative creativity supported by accurate reality testing. There has been a vast proliferation of projective tests, some useful, some trivial. Beyond central issues of their validity, reliability, and respect for sound personality theory, projective tests vary in their purpose, material, kinds of response elicited, and interpretive procedures. In accordance with the basic principles of the psychological examination, a single projective test produces only a one-sided picture of the child. To ensure diversity, samples from various types of projective tests are essential.

THE RORSCHACH TEST

The Rorschach is the most widely used projective test in the psychodiagnostic battery. The development of norms for different age groups have resulted in expanded use of the test in clinical practice with children. The ten Rorschach inkblots with their various nuances of shading and color are handed to the child one at a time, in a prescribed order. He is asked, "What could this be? What does this look like?" His initial exposure constitutes the Performance Proper. After the ten blots have been presented, he is asked to look at them again. The second procedure, the Inquiry, provides an opportunity to clarify ambiguous responses and to elicit latent, previously repressed content. The very young child does not find the Rorschach an appealing task; he does not differentiate it from the structured tasks of the intelligence test. Like the disorganized hyperactive school-age child, he cannot submit to formal methods of testing. He lacks the patience and memory to go through the procedure a second time, and he cannot point out with certainty the specific location or qualities of the blot that determined his association. Although the scoring of his responses may lack finesse, the experienced examiner can usually catch the drift of things. The administration of the Rorschach to the school-age child can usually be conducted along traditional procedures used with adolescents and adults.

The first step in the interpretation of a Rorschach protocol is the numerical tabulation of formal scoring categories and percentages. The categories include: 1) Location, Whole, large detail or small detail; 2) Determinants, in single or various combinations of Form, Color, Movement, Shading; 3) Content; 4) Popular or Original perceptions. The composite Rorschach picture is based on reciprocal relationships between the formal structure and dynamic content of the responses. Like other tests, the Rorschach indicates that a developmental liability may represent a strength in another area. When viewed from the perspective of a developmental continuum, with various shades of normality and disturbance, the task of the psychologist is to determine whether a Rorschach trend represents a consolidation or disruption of psychological growth.

APPERCEPTION TESTS

The *Thematic Apperception Test* (TAT) conceived by Murray (1938) and developed by Bellak (1949) is widely used for older children and adolescents. The *Children's Apperception Test* (CAT) devised by Bellak and Bellak (1949) is geared to an approximate age range of 3 to 10. A series of pictures are handed to the child, one at a time, and he is asked to tell a story about each. In order to determine whether further probing may be fruitful, the sensitive examiner reads clues in the child's attitude and content. Questions that deal with identification of the hero, particular environmental circumstances, eventual outcome, and other significant factors are abandoned in the case of an overly suspicious or anxious child. Though such questions are couched in gentle terms, he sees them as punitive or prying, or as evidence of the adult's dissatisfaction with his story. Some adolescents are particularly concerned about what they construe to be violation of privacy.

The child's story reflects an integration of his past experiences and current emotional state. The dynamic interpretation, derived from concepts of ego psychology, takes into account content and narrative style. The examiner is alert to choice of language, imagery, ambiguities, and smooth or disrupted sequential development of the theme. The child reveals his moods, fantasies, anxieties, conflicts and defenses, and his perception of his environment, of his parents, his siblings, and himself. The child with a rich, imaginative inner life may respond with a flood of fantasy. The productions of a constricted child may be impoverished and drab; his brief descriptive enumerations are often tedious, and his repetitive concerns with daily routines may stem from several simultaneous sources: lack of language and imaginative skills, antagonism to the task, conscious or unconscious withholding, or mental retardation.

In the first TAT picture, a boy sits contemplating a violin that rests on a table in front of him. The child's story reveals his motivation, his wish to learn, his perseverance, and his aspirations for the future—in the face of challenge and frustration, he retreats into passivity and inertia. If his reality perceptions are disturbed, he transforms the violin into a broken train, a kite, a gun. Special needs or a dominance of aggressive or sexual drives determine individual distortions in identifying the object. The child with grandiose expectations introduces a fantasy of magic omnipotence. Without active mobilization of personal effort and energies, he daydreams of becoming a world-famous musical prodigy. A child without such fantasy resources views the boy as depressed, discouraged, fatigued, or uninvolved with the task. The violin as a cherished though fragile family heirloom is often associated with oedipal, castration, or masturbatory themes. Alternatives of play and work and conflicts about competition appear in overt or disguised form. The child's oppositionalism may take the form of verbal refusal or aggressive attack: "smashing" the violin; he may respond with forced unenthusiastic compliance; by devious means and shrewd manipulations, he may outwit adult authority.

The *Children's Apperception Test* pictures portray animals in typical human situations in the familiar anthropomorphic style of storybooks. The young child feels a closer kinship with animals than with his bewildering, often intimidating world of human adults. Animals play a special role in his fantasies and phobias. The high percentage of animals and relative infrequency of human figures in the Rorschachs of young children reinforce their close connection to the animal figure whom they perceive as friend or foe. The CAT evokes an exciting world of childhood experiences—eating, sleeping, elimination, aggression, pregnancy, and birth of siblings.

For example, Picture V is of a darkened room with a large bed in the background; in the foreground is a crib in which there are two baby bears. This picture evokes numerous variations of primal scene experiences, one seems to have his eyes open. The child's story reflects curiosity, observations, confusions, and conjectures about the parents' sexual activities. Common themes are mutual exploration between the siblings, loneliness, separation anxiety, and fear of abandonment. The fantasy figures that the child conjures up may be extraneous to the reality stimulus of the picture. The independent child by energetic efforts overcomes worry about mysterious dangers that the dark scene suggests; the phobic child is overwhelmed by them: he tells about neglectful parents who do not hear their child's cry for help, or who assuage his fears and feelings of isolation in an appropriate way. The panic of another child is relieved only by a visit to the big bed, where he remains cuddled between his parents. The parents' encouragement or rejection of such intrusion is relevant to seductive and infantilizing attitudes that reinforce the child's fears and regressive goals.

HUMAN FIGURE DRAWINGS

During his examination the child is asked to draw a person; he is then asked to draw a person of the opposite sex. A house and a tree, a family group and spontaneous pictures of his own choice also lend themselves to projective interpretation. Originally, clinicians used drawings as an intelligence scale based on the number of body details included. It soon became apparent that drawings also reveal significant personality characteristics. The projective drawings are especially useful in the assessment of a negativistic or inarticulate child who is less accessible to verbal tests.

The child's human figure drawing may represent a self-portrait, an ideal self, a perception of an emotionally meaningful person in his life such as a parent or sibling, or a fusion of various figures. His concept of the figure stems from pleasurable or painful experiences with his own body. From a developmental perspective, a child's drawing gradually changes from a loose assemblage of fragments to a unified body concept. The very young child's concentration on the head and face is assumed to derive from his earliest infantile contacts with his mother as the source of his anticipations, gratifications, and frustrations. At the age of 3 or 4, when he becomes engaged in active exploration and mastery of his environment, the legs appear, often as extensions of the head. If this "tadpole" phase continues beyond the age of 6, it generally indicates a lag or deviation in development. At the next stage he incorporates a torso into his body concept; it appears as a circle smaller in size than the head, with a prominent navel. As he develops a sense of himself as a separate entity, single dimensions give way to double dimensions, proportions are more accurate, and details more precise and elaborate. For purposes of manipulation and environmental contact, he adds hands and fingers. In later stages of latency, prepuberty, and adolescence, when the body becomes a major psychological issue, symbols of strength and prestige appear as enhancement of the self. The frail adolescent who draws a powerful muscular figure presents his ideal masculine stereotype. The female adolescent is involved with exhibitionistic clothing, a glamorous gown, jewelry, and a fancy hairdo. A physical defect usually appears only if it has intruded into the child's psychological consciousness as a sign of inadequacy.

The size of the child's drawing reflects his perception of himself in his physical environment. If he consistently draws tiny helpless figures, he may feel overwhelmed by the powerful world of adults; conversely, exaggerated large size suggests defensive self-aggrandizement. Arm movement toward the environment may be wooden, timid, searching, or aggressive. An overdetermined smile exposes dangerous teeth; the intent is friendly but the manifest image is sadistic. The eyes are rich in interpretive possibilities. The gaze may be direct and candid; a vacant unseeing stare betrays emotional isolation, while a piercing glance expresses hostile intentions. The facial expression may be friendly and affectionate, or depressed, angry, and bewildered. The choice of the opposite gender as the initial drawing suggests ambivalence about sexual identification. The body representation may be active or passive, emotionally removed or engaged, complete or fragmented, endowed with lively excitement or weighted down by depressive lethargy. In conjunction with the dynamic interpretation of the child's figure drawing, one must also consider his increasing facility in psychomotor expression and any artistic skill or its absence.

BENDER-GESTALT DRAWINGS

The Bender-Gestalt Drawings were adapted from those used by Wertheimer (1923) in his studies of Gestalt concepts involved in visual perception. The child copies on a blank piece of paper nine figures of varying complexity that are presented to him one at a time. In a subsequent recall procedure, when he is asked to reproduce them from memory, kinesthetic memory reinforces his short-term visual memory. The Bender is a nonverbal test that has a wide range of applications to all age groups and to populations with different cultural and experiential backgrounds. Extensive experimentation and standardization (Koppitz 1963) have established objective scores and age norms that aid in assessment of special competence or weakness in the perceptual-motor sphere. When viewed from developmental and clinical perspectives, the Bender-Gestalt drawings yield important information about developmental lags, neurophysiological deficits, mental retardation, and emotional disorders.

A significant relationship exists between intelligence and accuracy of Bender reproductions. The child supplies clues to his approach to learning and to the ease with which he acquires psychomotor skills and organizes his written work on a page. In a young child, the test is generally a reliable predictor of future writing and spelling ability or disability; studies of first-grade children (DeHirsch, Jansky, and Langford 1966) indicate close correlation between their performance on this test and subsequent educational achievement. The child's Bender drawings are compared to his performance on related tasks—the intelligence test, figure drawings, and the like. The different yet interrelated demands that each makes upon him may produce consistencies or contradictions in his perceptual-motor functioning. The Bender-Gestalt test can also be used as a projective device. The absolute precision that one child demonstrates in his response to the relatively impersonal Benders may dissolve into chaotic body representations in his human figure drawings. A child who struggles for perfection spends an inordinate amount of time and energy in copying the designs; he builds armatures, reinforces lines, continually erases, and remains dissatisfied with his reproduction. A hasty slapdash execution is typical of the impulse-ridden child who lacks the capacity for sustained effort and concentration required for this task.

INTEGRATION OF TEST RESULTS

It is the responsibility of the psychologist to translate into clinically meaningful language an integrated summary of the child's total test reactions that will have practical usefulness in the diagnostic and therapeutic formulations. This process involves weaving together cross-sectional data and logical, systematic organization of test structure and content, with special attention to chains of inferences, bases of the inferences, and conclusions that can be drawn from them. The testing psychologist is concerned with the active interplay of test functions and the ways in which assets and liabilities reinforce, contradict, or impinge upon each other. In one child a personality trend serves an adaptive purpose; in another it has a maladaptive role. The focus on test interpretation has shifted from the instrument to the child and the examiner. The experienced tester avoids certain extremes of test assessment such as the test-bound report, reflecting a sterile, mechanical preoccupation with fragmentary personality traits rather than their convergence into a living picture of the child. Another approach with limited effectiveness relies on pyramiding conjectures and speculations that lack solid empirical foundation. No single test in the battery provides conclusive evidence of a child's developmental and clinical status; whatever disturbance appears may encroach on some functions while others are intact. The interpretation of test results requires flexible application and familiarity with special problems of each age group. The categories that follow are not to be considered as separate entities, although they do help the clinician toward logical consistency and clarity of thinking.

1) Intelligence: Level and range of functioning, reality testing, cognitive style, discrepancies between potential and functioning efficiency, influence of emotional stress, symbolic meaning attached to intelligence, and its relation to motives, drive derivatives, and conflicts.
2) Experience of self apart from the environment: At different levels of awareness, feelings of strength or weakness, competence or incompetence, acceptance or abandonment by adults and contemporaries; early identification with parental models as reflected in the tests culminates in the ultimate individual personality pattern.
3) Experience of external world: Object relations, transference reactions, perceptions of others as differentiated or vague, stable or inconsistent, loving or threatening.
4) Affects and their organization: Propensity for action over fantasy and thought; mood swings, liability of feelings expressed directly in impulsive behavior or body symptoms; conversely, obsessive overdependence on thought as a defense against feared action, as derived from Freudian theory of thinking and Rorschach's Experience Balance.
5) Anxiety: Presence is not in itself significant, as some degree of anxiety is a normal and universal phenomenon; intensity of the child's anxiety in relation to impulses and conflicts that have induced it, and the motivation and capacity to master it.

6) Defenses: Appropriate or inappropriate, effective or ineffective, malleable or rigid; the means, age-appropriate or not, by which effort is made to maintain psychic equilibrium; extent to which defenses may be constructive or crippling influences on development.

7) Overlapping themes usually incorporated in the previous discussion: Psychosexual fixations, age-appropriate or fixated at an early stage of development; central conflicts centered on aggression and sexuality; intensity of drive derivatives, prohibitions against them, and means of discharge; character traits, oppositionalism, stubbornness, excessive compliance; motivation for change.

8) Diagnosis: The basis for diagnostic classification of children's test responses is taken from current psychiatric nomenclature. Although the classifications are not absolute and continue to undergo modification, parallels do exist between specific test patterns and traditional clusters of symptoms. The real child rarely conforms to the diagnostic model, and no single trend occurs exclusively in any one diagnostic category. Only minute differences distinguish a borderline psychotic condition from a neurophysiological dysfunction. Organicity, like "schizophrenia," is a vague term that encompasses a wide assortment of disorders. The "organic" child does not present a standard test pattern because of differences in localization and diffuseness of cerebral damage, specific diseases of a static or degenerative nature, and varying degrees of reversibility and irreversibility. The diagnostic impressions of the tests take into account overlapping aspects of the child's deficits: generalized or specific, acute or chronic, native or acquired, structural or functional.

9) Ego strengths: Adult standards cannot be imposed on the child, whose ego strength, as defined by his tests, is intergral to a developmental progression that depends on the ability to maintain a balance between overall forward drives and individual regressive forces. The evaluation of a child's inner resources, which may not be apparent on the surface, refers to cognitive functioning, emotional disposition, interpersonal relationships, fantasy activity, intensity of psychic drives, pressures of the superego, amount of available energy, ability to integrate needs with demands of reality, personal experiences of distress, and inner motivation toward change. Absence of pathology is not in itself an indication of ego strength.

PREDICTION AND RETESTING

More so for the child than the adult, prediction of developmental outcome or response to therapy on the basis of tests is approached with caution. Particularly for children whose development is in a state of continuous flux, predictions must be tentative and limited in scope. The younger the child, the less differentiated his test picture, and the less precise the statements that can be made regarding diagnosis and prognosis. Studies of long-range prediction on the basis of infant scales (Bayley

1933) show a poor correlation between quantitative developmental quotients and later intelligence quotients. An understanding of the whole child and the world in which he lives determines the usefulness of predictive test impressions; the degree of support that can be received from the family and school is a practical consideration in setting up therapeutic goals. An unfavorable environment may precipitate dormant pathology; fortunate life experiences may help to restrain a latent illness.

In longitudinal studies, tests provide a baseline for the later determination of development and of response to therapy. The primary purposes of serial testing are to evaluate psychological growth during a specific time interval; that is, the quantity and quality of change, the areas in which it has occurred and its adaptive or maladaptive directions. Although quantitative measures may not hold up longitudinally, the quality of the child's functioning shows continuities from one age level to another. Small differences that cumulatively become larger may have an important impact on the child's life situation.

Evaluation of retest results is a complicated process that cannot be reduced to a simple formula. Changes in IQ have different meanings for different children. A loss in IQ in the early years, when major skills are developing, especially in language, is likely to appear in the culturally deprived child. A rise in IQ in an intellectually inhibited child, who in the past relied on defensive pseudostupidity, is a decisive sign of improved intellectual efficiency. An increased verbal IQ and persistent scatters in an overideational child may represent either negative reinforcement of obsessive-compulsive defenses, or a continuing defense against an underlying thought disorder.

In general, retests tend to confirm clinical impressions of the child's development. Tests, however, may show greater pathology than is evident on the surface, particularly in children with a narcissistic and borderline disturbance. It is important to distinguish between manifest changes expressed as relief from symptoms and fundamental modification in personality organization. The embryonic deviation that a young child reveals in his tests may or may not develop into a pathological disturbance during adolescence. The experienced psychodiagnostician recognizes the potential rather than the actual risk during periods of future crisis.

COMMUNICATION OF TEST RESULTS

The responsibility for interpreting test results to parents and child varies in different clinical settings. The older child or adolescent may participate in a joint family session or he may prefer an individual interview. The psychological examination is only one approach to the complex process of clinical assessment and formulation of treatment plans and test results may be equivocal. The psychologist may recommend further exploration—psychiatric, medical, neurological, or other examinations.

Parents have different illusions and expectations of the tests; they may feel hopeful or threatened by the outcome. The interpretation of test results requires discretion and sensitivity to their fears and apprehensions. A description of the child's developmental status, his success or failure in achieving age-appropriate expectations, and the stresses that interfere with his mastery of skills and deprive him of opportunities for personal gratification, are more meaningful to parents than diagnostic labels and numerical quotients. For them test results are emotionally charged and often evoke anxiety, guilt, and ambivalence, as well as unconscious needs and fantasies. It is important to identify with parental resistances and defenses, to adopt a supportive posture, and to establish a commonality of therapeutic goals.

A child who represents a narcissistic extension of his parents becomes the vehicle for fulfillment or frustration of their aspirations. Because of their irrational expectations they may deny painful aspects of the test results or they may project blame onto the school or another environmental agency. Occasionally, a parent, having an inner need to deny any self-reproach for his child's condition, anticipates confirmation of a preferable view that the child is in some way organically and irreversibly impaired; he greets evidence to the contrary with dismay and attacks the validity of tests and the examiner's qualifications. It is often found that in pathologically disorganized families, a disturbed or mentally limited child may preserve a tenuous equilibrium. In other cases, a parent with a bias about psychological tests expresses disappointment that the child's IQ has not risen sharply or that his behavior, considered unacceptable, cannot be radically altered. The parents' determination to seek a second opinion should be supported.

The child's problems that motivated professional consultation are generally a main focus of parental concern. A restricted emphasis on his deficits may unduly neglect his potential abilities and special competencies. The assets and liabilities within the child and his environment provide a logical basis for appropriate choice of treatment modality, psychoanalysis, psychotherapy, educational remediation, change in school placement, or a combination of these alternatives. In order not to overwhelm the parents, priorities must be established in regard to the child's most immediate needs, to their acceptance of one form of treatment rather than another, and to realities that may include financial considerations.

Communication between the psychologist and other mental health practitioners is a two-way process that provides mutual educational opportunities. The test report that fails to make the expected impact on the understanding of the child may result from lack of training, skill, or professional experience of the examiner, or from inadequate data from the referral source. Because of differences in their conceptual approach, educational and professional background, family physicians, social workers, school counselors, and teachers have expectations of the tests that differ from those of clinicians; tailoring a report for a particular audience is a challenging task. The report, written or oral, should avoid technical jargon, derogatory or accusatory comments about the parents, or any information that has not yet been shared with them. The psychologist should be familiar with his professional code of ethics and with statutes about confidentiality and rights of privacy, which vary from state to state.

REFERENCES

Ames, L. B., et al. (1974). *Child Rorschach Responses: Developmental Trends from Two to Ten Years.* Rev. ed. New York: Brunner/Mazel.

———, Metraux, R. W., and Walker, R. N. (1971). *Adolescent Rorschach Responses: Developmental Trends from Ten to Sixteen Years.* 2d ed. New York: Brunner/Mazel.

Anastasi, A. (1982). *Psychological Testing.* 5th ed. New York: Macmillan.

Bayley, N. (1933). *Mental Growth During the First Three Years: A Developmental Study of 61 Children by Repeated Tests.* Genetic Psychology Monographs, vol. 14, no. 1.

Beck, S., and Beck, A. (1978). *Rorschach's Test,* vol. 2, *Gradients in Mental Disorder.* 3d ed. New York: Grune and Stratton.

Bellak, L. (1949). *The T.A.T and CAT in Clinical Use.* 2d ed. New York: Grune and Stratton, 1971.

———, and Bellak, S. (1949). *Children's Apperception Test,* manual, 4th ed. Larmont, N.Y., CPS, 1974.

Bender, L. (1938). *A Visual Motor Gestalt Test and Its Clinical Use.* Research Monograph No. 3, American Orthopsychiatric Association.

Chukovsky, K. (1971). *From Two to Five.* Berkeley: University of California Press.

Cronbach, L. (1969). *Essentials of Psychological Testing.* 3d ed. New York: Harper and Row.

DeHirsch, K., Jansky, J., and Langford, W. (1966). *Predicting Reading Failure.* New York: Harper and Row.

DiLeo, J. (1970). *Young Children and Their Drawings.* New York: Brunner/Mazel.

———. (1973). *Children's Drawings as Diagnostic Aids.* New York: Brunner/Mazel.

Flavell, J. H. (1977). *Cognitive Development.* New York: Prentice-Hall.

Ford, M. (1946). *The Application of the Rorschach Test to Young Children.* Minneapolis: University of Minnesota Press.

Freud, A. (1945). A psychoanalytic view of developmental psychology. In *Psychoanalytic Psychology of Normal Development,* vol. 8. New York: International Universities Press, 1981.

———. (1965). *Normality and Pathology in Childhood: Assessments of Development,* vol. 6. New York: International Universities Press.

Freud, S. (1922). Some neutonic mechanisms in jealousy, paranoia and homosexuality. *Standard Edition,* 18(pp. 203–26). London: Hogarth Press, 1955.

Fromm, E. (1960). Projective aspects of intelligence tests. In A. Rabin and M. Haworth (Eds.). *Projective Techniques with Children.* New York: Grune and Stratton.

Gardner, H. (1979). *Artful Scribbles, the Significance of Children's Drawings.* New York: Basic Books.

Goodnow, J. (1977). *Children Drawing.* Cambridge: Harvard University Press.

Gould, S. (1981). *The Mismeasure of Man.* New York: Norton.

Halpern, F. (1953). *A Clinical Approach to Children's Rorschachs.* New York: Grune and Stratton.

Hammer, E. F. (1968). *The Clinical Application of Projective Drawings*. 6th ed. Springfield, Ill.: Charles C. Thomas.

Harris, D. B. (1963). *Children's Drawings as Measures of Intellectual Maturity*. New York: Harcourt Brace Jovanovich.

Hassibi, M., and Breuer, H. (1980). *Disordered Thinking and Communication in Children*. New York: Plenum Press.

Haworth, M. (1966). *The CAT: Facts About Fantasy*. New York: Grune and Stratton.

———. (1986). Children's Apperception Test. In A. I. Rabin (Ed.). *Projective Techniques for Adolescents and Children*. New York: Springer.

Hertz, M. (1960). The Rorschach in adolescence. In A. Rabin and M. Haworth (Eds.). *Projective Techniques with Children*. New York: Grune and Stratton.

Hunt, J. McV. (1969). *Intelligence and Experience*. New York: Ronald Press.

Hutt, M. L. (1971). *The Hutt Adaptation*. 3d ed. New York: Grune and Stratton.

Koppitz, E. M. (1963). *The Bender Gestalt Test for Young Children*. New York: Grune and Stratton.

———. (1968). *Psychological Evaluation of Children's Human Figure Drawings*. New York: Grune and Stratton.

Kwawer, J. S., et al. (Eds.). (1980). *Borderline Phenomena and the Rorschach Test*. New York: International Universities Press.

Machover, K. (1949). *Personality Projection in the Drawing of the Human Figure*. Springfield, Ill.: Charles C. Thomas.

———. (1960). Sex differences in the developmental pattern of children as seen in human figure drawings. In A. I. Rabin and M. Haworth (Eds). *Projective Techniques with Children*. New York: Grune and Stratton.

Magnussen, M. (1979). Psychometric and projective techniques. In J. D. Noshpitz (Ed.). *Basic Handbook of Psychiatry*. New York: Basic Books.

Moriarty, A. (1966). *Constancy and IQ Change*. Springfield, Ill.: Charles C. Thomas.

———. (1968). Normal preschoolers' reactions to the Children's Apperception Test: Some implications for later development. *Journal of Projective Techniques and Personality Assessment*, 32, no. 5: 413–19.

Mundy, J. (1971). The use of projective techniques with children. In B. B. Wolman (Ed.). *Manual of Child Psychopathology*, New York: McGraw-Hill.

Murray, H. (1938). *Explorations in Personality*. New York: Oxford University Press.

———. (1943). *Thematic Apperception Test Manual*. Cambridge: Harvard University Press.

Oakland, T., and Matuszek, P. Using tests in nondiscriminatory assessment. In T. Oakland (Ed.). *Psychological and Educational Assessment of Minority Children*. New York: Brunner/Mazel.

Piaget, J. (1952). *The Origins of Intelligence in Children*. New York: International Universities Press.

Pitcher, E., and Prelinger, E. (1963). *Children Tell Stories*. New York: International Universities Press.

Pruyser, P. (1979). *The Psychological Examination*. New York: International Universities Press.

Rabin, A. I. (1965). Diagnostic use of intelligence tests. In B. B. Wolman (Ed.). *Handbook of Clinical Psychology*. New York: McGraw-Hill.

————. (1986). *Projective Techniques for Adolescents and Children*. New York: Springer.
————, and McKinney, J. P. (1972). Intelligence tests and childhood psychopathology. In B. B. Wolman (Ed.). *Manual of Child Psychopathology*. New York: McGraw-Hill.
Rapaport, D., Gill, M., and Schafer, R. (1968). In R. Holt (Ed.). *Diagnostic Psychological Testing*. New York: International Universities Press.
Schachtel, E. (1966). *Experiential Foundations of Rorschach's Test*. New York: Basic Books.
Schafer, R. (1948). *The Clinical Application of Psychological Tests*. New York: International Universities Press.
————. (1954). *Psychoanalytic Interpretation in Rorschach Testing*. New York: Grune and Stratton.
————. (1967). *Projective Testing and Psychoanalysis*. New York: International Universities Press.
Siegel, M. G. (1975). Psychological testing. In G. Wiedeman (Ed.). *Personality Development and Deviation*. New York: International Universities Press.
————. (1987). *Psychological Testing from Early Childhood Through Adolescence: A Developmental and Psychodynamic Approach*. New York: International Universities Press.
Wechsler, D. (1958). *The Measurement and Appraisal of Adult Intelligence*. 4th ed. Baltimore: Wilkins and Wilkins.
————. (1966). *Wechsler Preschool and Primary Scale of Intelligence*. New York: Psychological Corporation.
————. (1974). *Wechsler Intelligence Scale for Children*. Rev. ed. New York: Psychological Corporation.
————. (1981). *Wechsler Adult Intelligence Scale*. Rev. ed. New York: Psychological Corporation.
Wertheimer, M. (1923). Studies in the Theory of Gestalt Psychology. *Psychologische Forschung*. 4:301–50.

6

PIAGETIAN ASSESSMENT: AN INTEGRATIVE APPROACH

Phyllis L. Sloate, Gilbert J. Voyat,
and Carolyn Snyder

In this chapter, we will discuss the Piagetian clinical method of observation and its application to the assessment of children and adolescents. Our purpose is twofold: to demonstrate the ways in which stages of cognitive development to some degree determine and limit the range of affective possibilities, and to further the links with psychoanalytic developmental theory. Following a brief overview of Piaget's epistemological perspective and some significant criticisms of his theory by psychoanalytic researchers, we will present various Piagetian tasks in detail. Our discussion will consider the relationship between the attainment of a qualitatively different cognitive organization and the implications for the level of affective functioning.

THE EPISTEMOLOGICAL VIEW

Piaget's contribution provides us with a formal theory of normal cognitive development: the construction of conflict-free, secondary process cognitions. His primary intent is an epistemological one: understanding the construction of knowledge. Within his theoretical framework, "knowing" is a construction derived from stage-sequential progressive reorganizations, in which internal structures are increasingly elaborated, differentiated, and coordinated with each other. The child constructs reality, which is both defined and limited by his knowledge of the logical necessities (invariant relationships between objects) and possibilities of a given stage (Piaget 1952).

Development procedes by way of the functional invariants of organization and adaptation, which strive towards establishing a state of inner balance, or equilibrium. The infant's reflexes gradually become well-organized action sequences, or schemata, an outgrowth of the invariant processes of assimiliation and accommodation that underly adaptation and explain internalization. Assimilation, an incorporative process, refers to the taking in of the novel, while accommodation is the reciprocal process of adjusting existing schemata to these experiences.

Affectivity is always functionally related to intelligence; "these two aspects cannot be reduced to a single aspect, they are nevertheless, inseparable and complementary" (Piaget 1969, p. 23). Within this conceptualization, however, the subject constructs reality, and the objects are of secondary significance to that process of construction. Although Piaget (1954) did assign a primary motivational role to the child's relationship with the mother insofar as she stands at the confluence of the infantile schemata, this relationship is treated as a neutral constant. According to Piaget, affectivity does not create or modify cognitive structure, cannot impinge on its invariant, sequential unfolding. Both Anthony (1956) and Wolff (1976) have criticized this view, as it neither accounts for the realm of individual differences nor considers affects as structure-building forces in the psychic economy that might modify the nature and content of cognitive structure. Greenspan (1979) has also criticized Piaget's unsatisfactory treatment of the issue of anxiety and the mechanism by which exclusion of specific content from consciousness occurs.

As development proceeds, thought is transformed across four qualitatively different stages of mental development; sensorimotor, preoperational, concrete operational, and formal operations. Functional continuities obtain throughout, as the child redoes what has gone before at each new level of mental representation. While each stage has its characteristic structural organization, all later transformations of thought are rooted in sensorimotor schemes and their partial conservations of invariant aspects of early experience.

The transition to each new stage is always accompanied by a heightened egocentrism on the emerging plane of representation. Thus, the preperational child is newly "centered" on his own intents and actions and on the immediate perceptual aspects of objects; he lacks both reflective awareness and an appreciation of the other's perspective in relation to the self. "Decentering" from this orientation is a lengthy task and will not be completed until the onset of concrete operations, between 5 and 7 years of age. A similar increase in stage-specific aspects of egocentrism accompanies the inception of concrete operations and, later on, the transition to formal thought.

Although functional continuities remain, the completion of each stage is conceptualized as a moment of structural discontinuity and the emergence of a new mode of cognitive organization. Henceforth, the child's view of reality itself is different, as are the internal means at his disposal to comprehend that reality. Each successive transformation of the relation to reality has crucial implications for affective development, insofar as it potentiates new modes of object relations and significantly alters the patterns of defense available for drive discharge.

For illustrative purposes, let us briefly consider the interweaving of several developmental threads as the sensorimotor stage draws to a close, propelling the child into the rapprochement subphase of the separation-individuation process (Mahler et al. 1975). The transformation from external actions to the realm of representational intelligence reflects a coordination of three new, interrelated capacities: permanence of person and object, construction of sensorimotor causality, and the ability to represent internally the group of displacements, whereby movements of the self and objects in space are organized and endowed with permanence. External reality is stabilized by these partial conservations and exists independent of the child's immediate perceptions and actions on it. In the process, however, it has become a different reality.

This shift in the toddler's fundamental relation to reality precipitates a highly significant affective experience: the inevitable awarness of one's separate existence and the perception that mother cannot satisfy all wants. Even so, these new cognitive constructions contain within themselves those functional capacities through which the rapprochement crisis may be resolved. The need to be close to mother is preserved internally through the mental representation of the relationship with her, while the delay and displacement of drive energies is increasingly facilitated and mediated by the symbolic function, including language.

Although functional continuities remain, structural discontinuity marks the moment of transformation from one stage to another, as earlier stages are reorganized and reintegrated within succeeding ones. This notion of structural discontinuity is in direct contrast with psychoanalytic propositions, which stress the continuity of development, the ego's relative autonomy, and the potential for regression under the impact of the drives.

Piaget's inability to accept psychoanalytic notions of drive-related, dynamically unconscious forces that influence behavior, repression, the role of anxiety, and affects or memories tied to unconscious representations, constitutes true areas of theoretical difference. A full discussion of areas of complementarity and incompatability between the two theories is beyond the limited scope of this chapter. For this the reader is referred to Anthony (1956), Wolff (1976), and the more recent work of Greenspan (1979). We now turn to our presentation of the Piagetian clinical tasks.

THE CLINICAL/NATURALISTIC METHOD OF OBSERVATION

This method is derived from Piaget's theory of how we come to construct and "know" the real. It is a means of understanding the child's comprehension of his world across the four stages of development he delineated. The operational concepts of Piagetian tasks differ from standardized testing procedures in various ways that are useful to distinguish and discuss. In this context, we shall maximize the differences to highlight these contrasts in conceptualization and method.

The operational tasks are embedded in a comprehensive theory of the acquisition of knowledge; standardized tests reveal the child's acquired knowledge in terms of pass/fail percentages distributed normally on the Gaussian curve. Standardized tests yield a quantified result and measure performance, the result of an equilibrium between mental organizations and functioning. Though both procedures assess what the child "knows," Piagetian tasks also indicate how that knowledge was derived from earlier notions. Piagetian tasks lead us to a qualitative analysis of a state of equilibrium of thought processes, adding a performance potential to the standard test battery. Is the child delayed or advanced in relationship not to his age, but to his expectable stage of cognitive development? As the tasks are used to infer underlying structure and provide a detailed analysis of component thought processes, they may be used to complement and augment standardized tests in order to arrive at cognitive maps (Voyat 1982).

An important advantage in the Piagetian tasks is their conceptual robustness. As their basis is logical, rather than statistical, they are less susceptible than standardized tests to the vagaries and distractions of the test situation. Like the semi-structured therapeutic interview, they offer the advantage of being both open-ended and conceptually structured and can be adapted to individuals who need to be encouraged to respond without vitiating the results.

When processes rather than products are studied, a child's learning and developmental capacities and potential for growth can often be ascertained. Piagetian tasks have proven particularly useful in assessing deficiencies and potentials within more deviant populations: the brain damaged, the mentally retarded, and the severely disturbed. The reader interested in relevant clinical research applications is referred to the Appendix. Frequently, by comparing the results of Piagetian tasks to those of the standardized tests, one can compare optimal learning conditions and cognitive potential with performance measures administered under somewhat less flexible testing conditions. This comparison can only broaden one's understanding of the child's current strengths and weaknesses while allowing for recommendations based upon a knowledge of underlying potential.

TASK ADMINISTRATION

In contrast to the administration of standardized testing, the clinical method offers a great deal of flexibility. There are no pass/fail answers or time limits, for the technique consists in adapting the interview continually to the responses of the child. The inquiry is not codified; there is only a structural framework from which the questions and the justifications are derived.

The task protocols contain both a precise recording of the conversation between examiner and child and an exact description of the child's movements, nonverbal communications, constructions, explanations, and emotional responses. With each task, the child is first presented with the material in a uniform manner; this is the moment of anticipation of the logic required to fulfill the task. There is no intervention by the examiner, as the focus is on the spontaneous thoughts of the child. Following the child's initial responses, the Piagetian clinical method is applied to establish the level of thought the child has reached or may reach. This method usually consists of various manipulations of the task materials by the child and the examiner. A final period of generalization to similar material follows, where the child is observed using what he has gained during the experience.

The justification is central, as it reveals the underlying processes involved and the stage of thinking that the child has attained. Each time the child gives an answer, either verbally or through behavior, he is asked for a justification: "Why?", "How do you know?", "What would you do to show that's correct?", and so on. The three possible arguments that constitute the justification are: 1) Identity: nothing was taken away, the appearance changes but not the thing itself. 2) Compensation: one dimension increases as another dimension decreases. 3) Reversibility: it can be restored to the original form.

Following the child's justification, the technique known as contraproof is employed. Here, a countersuggestion is given by the examiner, who might say, "But, you know, another child said just the opposite. Was he wrong? Are you wrong?" With this technique it becomes clear how strongly the child maintains the conviction of his beliefs as to the solution to the problem. The functions of the contraproof then, are to establish further the validity of the obtained results, to aid in the differentiation of borderline cases, and to distinguish the operatory (logically organized) and nonoperatory levels of functioning.

Certain points should be emphasized in the Piagetian clinical method:

1) The method of presentation of the task gives the examiner an opportunity to motivate the child favorably and to develop rapport by putting the child directly in contact with the material. For example, a story might introduce a task, or the child might be asked to make up a story. Such techniques can be used to learn the child's language, so that the examiner can follow suit.
2) Through varying the factors implied in the task (which is not possible in standardized tests), one can obtain reliable results. If it is uncertain whether a child has offered a conceptual or perceptual solution to a problem, the perceptual factors may be further varied and results noted.
3) Varying the way or the order in which questions are asked reveals the child's understanding of the task. If the child does not understand the task, it is not administered, for some initial understanding is a prerequisite of participation.
4) When there is no question about the validity of the answers obtained, portions of the task may be omitted.

We will now present selected tasks from the domains of Piagetian testing: aspects of conservation, elementary logic, and the construction of space. Both the normal cognitive unfolding during the stage of concrete operations and the method of task administration will be demonstrated through the various subtests, and the clinical implications of these cognitive acquisitions will be discussed. Following this, we will present a limited number of the tasks that may be assessed during adolescence and discuss their interrelationship with the normal psychodynamic shifts of this stage of development. The reader interested in a complete presentation of Piagetian tasks is referred to the work of Voyat (1982).

CONSERVATION

One-to-One Correspondence

The child is presented a set of objects (A) and is asked to arrange an equal number of different objects (B) so that there is one A for each B. This task involves the child's understanding of logical invariance after manipulating a set of objects. He is then required to affirm equality of quantity as a logical invariance after optical correspondence has been broken by a further manipulation (C) after spacing the set of referent objects apart.

The equivalence relationship in terms of A = B is understood around 5 years of age. This represents the budding of number concept as well as a logical proposition that is extended in the transformation of A into C, so that if A = B = C, then A = C. Not until the child is between 6 and 8 years will he be able to justify his belief in the proposition A = C by means of one of the following arguments: identity (nothing was taken away) or reversibility (it can be restored to the original).

Substage 1.   The 3- to 5-year-old displays little understanding of the concept of equivalence as a logical invariance. Cognitively, he might respect an ordinal reference but not a cardinal reference.

Substage 2.   At around 5 years, the child understands the placement of objects in one-to-one correspondence and knows their cardinal value without counting. When optical correspondence is broken the child no longer conserves. Usually, he asserts that the extended row contains more objects, although the compact row may be thought to contain more by virtue of its density.

Substage 3.   The concept of number is established between 6 to 8 years and persists even when optical correspondence is broken.

Clinical Implications of One-to-One Correspondence

Conservation, regardless of the context of its application, rests upon the child's ability to comprehend the notion of invariance despite perceptual changes. One-to-one correspondence, in particular, delineates the emerging ability to differentiate numbers from their perceptual features. The understanding of equivalence and invariance is the conceptual prerequisite to the understanding of number. Dynamically, this acquisition reinforces the child's increasing capacity to sustain the invariant aspects of emotional relationships; it contributes to feelings of self-sameness despite changes and transformations.

Matter

This task requires the child to acknowledge two equal quantities of matter (two equal balls of clay) before and after transformations (pie-shape, sausage-shape, and pieces). The concepts of equivalence and logical invariance are required. Six- to 8-year-olds are transitional, conserving on some transformations but not on others. By the age of 8, the child conserves and justifies his belief with one of the three possible arguments. Of the three justifications, identity is the most primitive and the most common.

Substage 1.   The child of 5 or 6 believes that the quantity of matter changes after transformation, misled by the perceptual properties of the stimulus. Typically, the child responds that the sausage-shape contains more than the ball.

Substage 2.   Between the ages of 6 and 8, the child displays a transitional understanding as he oscillates between negation and affirmation. The contra-suggestion is usually accepted.

Substage 3.   By the age of 8 the child understands the concept of equivalence of matter.

Weight

This task requires the child to determine whether an object weighs the same after its shape is transformed (a clay ball is rolled into a pie-shape, a sausage-shape and broken into pieces). Seven- or 8-year-olds exhibit transitional conservation, alternately affirming and denying equivalence. By age 9, children are able to conserve equivalence of weight after transformation of shape has occurred. Justification by reversability, compensation or identity will be offered.

Substage 1.   At 6 to 7 years, weight is not understood as a property dependent on mass and density, but more as a function of shape. The child will be misled by his perception of which appears to be more.

Substage 2.   Around 7 to 8 years, some understanding of the concept of weight conservation emerges, as the child displays the typical transitional "on-off" conservation. At the end of this substage the child realizes that shape does not influence the quantity of matter.

Substage 3.   By the age of 9 the child detaches from the concrete, perceptual qualities of the object and conserves weight by focusing upon abstract properties.

Volume

This task requires simultaneous coordination between weight and mass and their displacement in water. The child is asked to affirm equality in size between two objects (balls of clay), and the equality of the water levels in two equal containers. He is then asked to anticipate the water level as a result of immersing the object in the container of water. One ball of clay is then transformed (pie-shape, sausage-shape and pieces), and the child is asked if the water level will rise more, or less, or be the same. Next, the child is presented with a metal ball of equal size and allowed to feel the differences in weight. He is again asked to anticipate the results. Not until 10 or 11 are weight and matter conserved, although the concept of displacement by mass is not understood to be independent of weight. Around 11 or 12, children understand not only that matter is invariant in its displacement properties after transformation, but also that weight is not a relevant factor. Conservation is justified by arguments of identity, compensation or reversibility.

Substage 1.   The child of 6 to 7 years displays no understanding of the problem. Responses such as "This one has more water, because this ball has more, because this one is heavy and this one is light and if you put them in the water that one will go up more" are typical.

Substage 2.   Around 7 or 8, children display transitional conservation after optical transformation, but are unable to recognize the unimportance of weight in the displacement of water.

Substage 3a.   At about 10 or 11 weight is conserved after the shape of the object is transformed. The child displays transitional conservation when an object of equal size but different weight is introduced.

Substage 3b.   The 11- or 12-year-old coordinates all the parameters involved in conservation of volume and disregards weight as a variable.

Clinical Implications of Conservation of Matter, Weight, and Volume

The consolidation of these particular aspects of conservation speaks to the child's increasing ability to maintain invariance despite perceptual changes; that is, the comprehension of a logical order beyond the immediate spatial organization. This, in turn, lends further coherence and orderliness to the internal world, reinforcing ego boundaries and enhancing secondary process functioning. From the concrete transformations of matter, touching upon anal and phallic issues, to the abstraction of the conservation of volume, the child must comprehend the inherent properties of objects and the myriad relationships that obtain between them; he then must integrate this knowledge into a network that is at once combined, interrelated, and capable of being separated. These tasks are also primary component features of those cognitive specifications that make oedipal development and resolution possible. The fantasy of the oedipal baby ignores the realities of relative size, volume, and weight, while simultaneously bypassing the true order of relationships within the family.

Length: Displaced Sticks

The child is asked to choose two equal sticks from an array placed contiguously before him. Small toys (e.g., horses) are placed on each stick and the child is asked which toy has to walk farther along his path, or if they walk the same distance. One stick is then displaced an inch or two to the right and the question is repeated, following which the stick is alternately displaced the same amount to the left and the question is repeated. Finally, each stick is displaced simultaneously in opposite directions and the question is repeated. The 7- or 8-year-old is capable of conserving transitionally. The child of 9 years coordinates both visual parameters of displacement and conserves equality of length as a necessary logical invariant with justification through identity, reversibility or compensation.

> *Substage 1.* The child of 5 or 6 is unable to conserve length when optical transformations take place. Three characteristic errors are made at this substage: 1) he states that the displaced stick is longer because it overpasses the other one at a certain point; 2) he compares the two end points and reports that the lengths are unequal because they do not take up the same space; 3) the third type of error is a composite of the first two or of various responses not clearly the first or second type.
> *Substage 2.* The child of 7 or 8 is transitional, vacillating between affirmation and negation as logic and perception alternately dominate his judgment.
> *Substage 3.* Around the age of 8 or 9 the child conserves length as a logical invariant.

Length: Sectioned Sticks

The child is asked to affirm the equality of length between two sticks, one of which is divided into four segments (B) equal to the other stick (A). When B is transformed into C, the child is asked to affirm the equality of length as a necessary logical invariance after transformation of configuration, and so on for D and E. This task requires an understanding of the notion of parts in relation to the whole. Around 7 or 8, the child becomes transitional, though not until the age of 9 or so will he conserve length as a logical invariance and justify this belief with an argument of identity, reversibility or compensation.

> *Substage 1.* The 5- or 6-year-old makes global comparisons based on his perceptions. When optical correspondence is broken, equality is disavowed.
> *Substage 2.* The child of 7 or 8 is transitional in his ability to conserve length.
> *Substage 3.* The 9-year-old conserves length as a logical invariant.

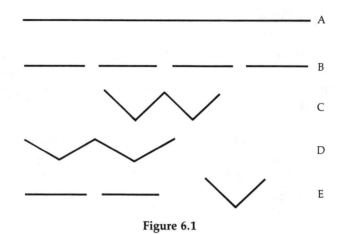

Figure 6.1

Clinical Implications of Conservation of Length and Sectioned Sticks

Conservation of length requires comprehension of the equality of two objects displaced in space. Sectioned sticks necessitate a similar affirmation of equality and an understanding of parts in relation to the whole. The recognition of equalities freed from the pull of immediate perceptions is reversible and implies a knowledge of inequality as well. The child's knowledge of parts and wholes and relations of equality and inequality furthers oedipal resolutions. This new understanding of the position and relation of an individual element within a system clarifies and stabilizes his perception of where he stands vis-à-vis other family members. This objectification of reality means that he is both less prone to personalized interpretations of relationships, and in a better position to infer similarities and differences from relationship to relationship. By implication, these new recognitions also facilitate the child's movement into the peer group and his adaptation to the school situation. Aspects of human relationships are also better conserved across their inevitable transformations. We speculate that the emerging ability to coordinate empty and filled spaces resonates affectively with the affirmation of one's personal identity and sustains libidinal constancy during moments of anger, disappointment, and loss.

SPACE

Conservation of Area: Euclidean Space

This task involves presenting the child two equal cardboard fields onto which thirty-two objects (e.g., houses) and two animals (e.g., horses) have been arrayed. The child is asked to affirm the equality of the fields and to divide the houses equally in two. The examiner places a house in the upper right corner, stating that a house is built, and so some of the grass must be taken away. The child is asked if the horses have the same amount of grass to eat. If inequality is affirmed, he is asked how it can be reestablished. If the child suggests removing the house, another solution is requested. The examiner continues placing houses simultaneously on fields A and B, arraying objects on A in a column and on B by dispersing the objects. On placing the third, fifth, seventh, tenth and fourteenth house, the child is asked to verify equivalence and to give justifications. The houses are then removed and replaced one by one with seven houses per field, field A having columns and field B dispersed houses. It is inquired whether there is the same, more, or less grass. If the child does not affirm equality, a contrasuggestion is offered.

The child of around 7 years conserves transitionally when offered the contrasuggestion. This transitional stage has three substages in which vacillation is gradually replaced by affirmation of the contrasuggestion; the child agrees that the appearance is unequal but the quantity is equal. By 8 years, surface area is conserved and the concept of subtraction of area is understood. As the global perceptual space is differentiated, the concept of numerical quantity is conceived as a result of a logical invariance of quantity. The child justifies his beliefs by arguments of identity, compensation, or reversibility.

Substage 1.   The child of 5 or 6 has little understanding, focusing on the perceptual configurations of the objects. When offered the contrasuggestion, he readily accepts it.

Substage 2a.   The 7-year-old alternately affirms and negates conservation when offered a contrasuggestion.

Substage 2b.   The child affirms conservation only when offered the contrasuggestion.

Substage 2c.   The child consistently affirms the contrasuggestion and agrees that the two surfaces only look different.

Substage 3.   By the age of 8 conservation of euclidean space is spontaneously affirmed.

Islands

The child is presented a blue field said to be water on which are located islands, represented by blocks A, B, C, and D (see Figure 6.2). He is then told that the people on island A want to move to B and that he must take cubes and make the same amount of room for people to live as they had on A. This task requires the use of addition and multiplication.

There is a progressive mastery of one, two and finally three dimensions of displacement. Conservation emerges between 10 and 12 years of age when children discover the geometric coordination between area and volume, such that when the products are the same, the multiplicative sum of the volume must also be equal as a logical invariant.

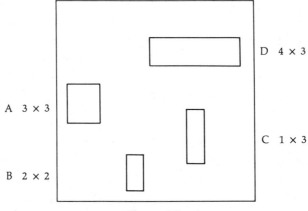

Figure 6.2

Substage 1a.   Between 5 and 7 the child reconstitutes volume in one dimension only. Although aware of a difference, he is unable to compensate the area of the base by increasing height. In the reconstruction, the child uses only ordinal references, that is, the perimeter as a standard for reconstituting the "island."

Substage 1b.   The child of 5 to 7 begins to apply multiplication or addition to the different dimensions of the problem. He applies trial-and-error methods, increasing the height of the construction but not sufficiently and only qualitatively.

Substage 2a.   Between 7 and 9, the child understands that the solution to the problem involves a relationship between three dimensions, but he still is unable to adjust the height correctly.

Substage 2b.   Around 9 years, the child's concept of measure is sufficiently differentiated to enable him to approach the problem in terms of metrical units. The concept of multiplication is not applied to the task, and he succeeds only when doubling one dimension is required.

Substage 3.   The mathematical relationship between area and volume is discovered by the child of 9½ to 12 years.

Rotation

The child is presented with two fields upon which objects are arrayed (house, horse, tree, lion); he is asked to construct the landscape as the experimenter or lion sees it. This task calls for the ability to entertain different viewpoints. The board is rotated 90° and the question is repeated, with two successive rotations. In a second series of rotations, the board remains stationary and the lion is moved in rotation from P1 to P4. Finally, the lion is placed in a corner diagonally in view. The child is asked to replicate the viewpoint of the lion, coordinating perspective and spatial relationships. The transitional child anticipates relative spatial relationships but cannot represent the different viewpoints accurately. By the age of 10, children are sufficiently decentered to understand simple perspective from a number of view-points in terms of the relative position of the observer.

Substage 1 .   The 4-year-old is characteristically unable to understand the problem posed by this task.

Substage 2a.   The child of 5 is egocentric and cannot account for a view other than his own. In performing the task, no spontaneous inversions of right, left, forwards or backwards are made.

Substage 2b.   Around 6 years one sees the beginnings of spontaneous re-groupment and hence awareness of alternate viewpoints, but with inaccuracy in placing the objects in proper relation to one another. The concept of per-spective is still rudimentary and dependent upon the position of the observer in some elements of the configuration.

Substage 3a.   Increasing differentiation and coordination of perspectives establishes partial relativity around the age of 6 to 7. The child attempts to cor-rect the relative viewpoint of the observer, but cannot make whole sponta-neous conversions. The notion of relativity is present but not fully coordinated.

Substage 3b.   By 8 years both perspective and relativity are understood. Objects are spontaneously regrouped, so that their spatial relationship is con-gruent with altered vantage points.

Horizontality

The child is shown bottles of various size filled with colored liquid, each taken from its own opaque bag one at a time. They are rotated at different angles and replaced in their respective bags, and the child is asked: 1) his spontaneous notion of the water level; 2) to copy the level from a model; 3) to point blindly at the correct model and to draw it; 4) to generalize these schemas to a different bottle shape. This task requires imagining the horizontality of the water level independent of the po-sition of the bottle. Children are misled by the position of the container until the age of nine, when the physical constancy of the water level is understood to be a logical invariance independent of the container.

Substage 1.   The child of 5 or 6 is usually able spontaneously to repro-duce the correct water level when the model is visually present in an upright, square container, using the base as a visual cue. Rounded bottles present diffi-culty at this substage, and the child is inconsistent in his responses.

Substage 2a.   The 7-year-old has begun to understand the water level as a planar surface, but cannot reproduce it without the aid of visual models. When visual models are present, the child will not reproduce horizontal water levels for tilted bottles. In tilted bottles, the water level is drawn near the neck of the bottle, displaying the notion of spilling.

Substage 2b.   The child of 8 applies trial and error persistently in his gropings. Although his drawings may depict the water level as parallel to the base, there is some indication that the concept of horizontality is understood, either through pointing or by making corrections.

Substage 3a.   Beginning around 8 years, the child acquires the capacity to extend his reference systems and to construct coordinate axes encompassing the entire spatial field. Construction of horizontals for all positions of the container is approached with the trial-and-error method.

Substage 3b.   The 9-year-old child demonstrates his successful coordination of all aspects of the problem.

Clinical Implications of Conservation of Area and Space

Euclidean space pertains to the child's ability to organize a surface into its various constitutive segments. Islands, like Horizontality, obliges the child to coordinate several dimensions spatially with each other, having first separated them into constituent terms. All three tasks require knowledge of the relationship between a content and a context.

These cognitive consolidations constitute important underpinnings of the complex internal reorganizations that occur during the transition from oedipal to latency phase development. The child becomes capable of viewing intrafamilial relationships from more realistic multiple perspectives, and he better understands his status within that constellation. Decreasing confusion between his own perspective and that of others further differentiates and stabilizes internal self and object representations and favors a decline in the use of projective mechanisms. Affectively, the objectification of perspective promotes mutuality and empathy, furthering the ability to form friendships and deepening the appreciation of social situations. Reality testing and secondary process are also enhanced as the child increasingly sustains an objective attitude toward the data of reality. This increased capacity to maintain objectivity supports the development of observing ego and the capacity for insight; knowledge of the relationship between a content and a context conserves the knowledge of social rules and behaviors in different situations. Sarnoff (1976) has referred to this new dependability as "behavioral constancy," a significant achievement of the latency stage.

ELEMENTARY LOGIC

Seriation

The child is presented ten seriated sticks and one intermediary stick. The difference between each stick is approximately 0.5 cm. He is first asked to construct a "staircase" and asked how he chose the sticks; he is then asked to build the same staircase behind a screen, with the experimenter taking the sticks one by one. Not until age seven is the child able to grasp the logic behind a systematic approach to seriation, which involves comparisons based on reciprocal relationships.

Substage 1a.   The 4- or 5-year-old child shows no understanding of the task.

Substage 1b.   The 5-year-old demonstrates rudimentary comprehension of the task by making seriations of two or three sticks without relationship to the larger group. While he is able to find the longest and smallest sticks spontaneously, intermediary elements are arranged between the two extremes without respect for their logical order.

Substage 2.   Around 6, he approaches seriation by trial and error, beginning with smaller groups and gradually extending the coordination of sticks until all are seriated. He is only gradually capable of comparing more than two or three objects at a time and may have difficulty placing the intermediary stick or do so only with trial and error.

Substage 3.   The 7-year-old applies systematic comparisons to the task. The smallest and longest sticks are found first and then the next longest and smallest until all, including the intermediary stick are correctly placed. He also succeeds in building the same staircase behind a screen.

Clinical Implications of Seriation

Seriation requires an affirmation of relationships of order and comparisons based on the construction of the reciprocal. Here the child uses the comparative to organize relative differences. Two unequal objects are seen in their logically necessary relationship to a third, introducing a new element into an overall context, and actualizing an abstract concept.

Following Greenspan (1979), we infer that a knowledge of seriation is a necessary component for the development and resolution of oedipal conflict. The preoedipal child is essentially involved in ordinal, dyadic relationships; the comparison of two in relation to a third constitutes the essential triangularity of the oedipal dilemma. The ability to compare oneself with parental figures (bigger/smaller, stronger/weaker, more/less) as they are simultaneously perceived in a reciprocal relation to each other and oneself promotes reality testing and ultimately confirms the impossibility of the child's desires.

With the attainment of seriation, wishes, affects, and feeling states are also more subtly differentiated and coordinated. Complex gradations of feelings enable the child to experience himself and others in relative, rather than absolute, terms. This decline in absolute qualities further stabilizes internal object relations through a reduction in tendencies toward splitting; it strengthens reality testing. Relativity also supports the defense of rationalization, insofar as one is more or less good or bad in relation to someone else (Greenspan 1979).

Dichotomy

The child is presented four large circles of equal size, two red and two blue, and four small squares of equal size, two red and two blue, and is asked to dichotomize the figures by group criteria: color, shape, and size. This task elicits the child's understanding of separating objects based on their similar and different characteristics; it requires flexible grouping criteria that allow an object to belong to more than one class simultaneously. Developmentally, the child groups according to criteria of color and shape before size. Children of 5 or 6 years group objects according to one criteria, but flexibility, which indicates coordinating past with future operations, is not yet evident. By age 7, the child correctly anticipates flexible criteria for grouping sets of objects, through trial-and-error method. Around the age of 8 a change of criteria does not present a problem as flexibility of criteria is established.

Substage 1.   The 5- or 6-year-old discriminates some criteria of classification, but cannot shift criteria.

Substage 2.   The child of 6 or 7 tends to use an ascending mode of classification. He begins with a number of subcollections corresponding to the lowest rank of an ordered classification and combines them step by step until one or more dichotomies are achieved. At times, he uses a descending mode of classification that begins with grouping into broad categories and lacks anticipation of all the possibilities. When asked to change criteria, the child resorts to trial-and-error groupings.

Substage 3.   The child of around 8 begins to dichotomize using a descending mode of classification and has no difficulty in changing criteria.

Clinical Implications of Dichotomy

Dichotomy requires the child to elaborate a construction and organize sets. The mental fluidity demanded by the changing criteria calls upon the child's resources for making appropriate, flexible responses in rapidly changing situations. This task necessitates both an appreciation of complexities of relationships and a coordination of the past experience and future anticipations of various perspectives of these relationships. It is not difficult to perceive the relationship between this cognitive operation and the child's capacity for more flexible, appropriate social responses to others. As one can have different criteria for membership in a particular set, one can also have separate criteria for behaviors and feelings towards family and friends.

Class Inclusion

In this task the child is presented with twelve horses and two lions and asked to state how many there are of each. He is then posed a series of questions related to the notion of class inclusion, such as: Are horses and lions animals? Are there more horses than lions? Are there more horses or more animals?

The concept of classification requires a complicated series of coordinated operations, as the elementary logic of intention and extension of a class is involved. Intention is the numerical sum of common qualities being designated by the class, whereas extension is the number of objects in the class. The capacity to construct the inverse and the subtraction of subclass from class are also involved; they are based upon the concept of some versus all.

Around the age of 6, the child groups objects on the basis of similar attributes. Subgroup classifications are not distinguished because the child fails to grasp the notion of intention of class as characteristics defining their membership in the group; the concept of extension of class is also lacking. The some-versus-all concept is understood around age 7, when the child distinguishes, inconsistently at first, between attributes of a class but not the subtraction of subclass from class. By age 8, children are able to coordinate intention and extension of class, as well as subtraction of subclasses from class.

Substage 1. The child of 6 or so groups objects according to their similarities and differences but cannot differentiate between subcategories and class; hence he is unable to coordinate the intentions of a class, nor can he conceive of class extension of the class. The notion of some and all is inadequately understood. He is perceptually bound by the objects and does not understand the notion of subtraction of a class.

Substage 2. The 7-year-old has difficulty with intention and extension of the class and groups inconsistently, according to similar attributes. The idea of class inclusion cannot be sustained. The child usually succeeds with one of the three questions, most often substraction of class.

Substage 3. The 8-year-old understands logical classification according to intention and extension of class. All questions are answered correctly.

Classification of Animals

The child is asked to sort pictures into three classes: A = five ducks; B = five birds, no ducks; C = five animals, no birds. He is asked to name the animals, to make piles, and to find a label for each pile. The labels DUCKS, BIRDS, and ANIMALS are placed in three separate transparent bags of increasing sizes and labeled DUCKS, BIRDS, and ANIMALS respectively. The child is then asked if the bag labeled DUCKS can be placed in the bag labeled BIRDS and if BIRDS can be placed inside the bag labeled ANIMALS. The child is asked if the bag labeled BIRDS can be placed inside the bag labeled DUCKS and still retain its label.

Substraction of class is tested by telling the child to imagine that all the ducks have been disposed of and by asking him if any birds remain. He is then asked to imagine the reciprocal. By asking if the extension of class requires logically more ducks, birds, or animals, we see how well the intention of class characteristics has been understood. Not until the eleventh year is there an appreciation of hierarchies based upon seriation and class inclusion that are coordinated into the classification of animals.

Substage 1. The child of 7 may understand the intention and extension of class, but he does not fully understand the concept of class. He is unable to answer all the questions.

Substage 2.   The 7- or 8-year-old has difficulty with the concept of hierarchies of classification, but answers several of the questions and gives an adequate explanation of class inclusion.

Substage 3.   By 10 or 11, intention and extension of class as well as hierarchies of classification are understood.

Clinical Implications of Class Inclusion and Classification of Animals

These operations require the child to demonstrate conceptual understanding of the relationship between subordinate and supraordinate class, then to coordinate this with a comprehension of hierarchy based upon a knowledge of seriation. Together they necessitate the application of the concept of reversibility by inversion and reciprocity, the cognitive constructions that also underly the three-way system of oedipal relationships. We suggest that the emerging concept of some versus all may play an important part in the process of oedipal resolution. The child must forego his grandiose fantasies and resign himself to the reality of participation in some, rather than all, parental activities; he must be content with only some of each parent's affection.

Processes of identification with the same sex parent and the further consolidation of gender identity are enhanced through an understanding of class and subclass relationships. Greenspan (1979) has discussed in detail the ways in which these class/subclass distinctions also enable the child to maintain one set of feelings towards his entire family, while experiencing quite different specific feelings towards individual family members and yet another complex set of distinct feelings towards the peer group and school situation.

In all, classification (with seriation) has a differentiating and organizing effect on wishes, affects, and feeling states. The child simultaneously becomes increasingly capable of appreciating the more subtle aspects of human relationships and has a more realistic understanding of their possibilities and limitations. Consolidation of these operations thus adds an important sense of stability and continuity to the child's perception of himself and his world.

Implications of Cognitive Level for the Latency Child's Affective Functioning

The structure of concrete operations introduces logical necessity into the life of the latency child, limiting the realm of infantile grandiosity and magical possibilities in favor of an increasingly reality-oriented "knowing" of the world. While the affective resolutions of oedipal phase development rest with individual emotional factors, the cognitive construction of conservation through inversion and reciprocity constitutes a necessary backdrop for the oedipal experience. Indeed, it would be difficult to account fully for the range and intensity of oedipal wishes, fantasies, and affects without consideration of their associated cognitive features. Could one fantasize an oedipal baby if conservation of weight, volume, and matter were already established operations? Would the castration fears of the oedipal period be as acute if conservation of length were consolidated? Without inversion and reciprocity how could the child know that to possess mother means the loss of father's love? Would it be possible to experience or resolve the oedipal triad without knowledge of seriation, class inclusion, and the concept of some versus all? Pine (1980, pp. 217–33) has discussed the consequences of new cognitive specifications for the differentiation and expansion of the affect array. Greenspan (1979) has commented upon the consolidation of affect dispositions and the reduction in tendencies towards splitting of the object world into all good or all bad components that is supported by the cognitive intercoordinations and regulations established at the onset of the concrete operational period of thought. He has also linked the attainments of the concrete operational stage with phase-specific defensive operations of the ego.

Conservation by inversion and reciprocity is the crucial knowledge of what remains invariant in a relationship across transformations; it is an essential feature of an organized system of thought. This cognitive achievement resonates powerfully with the child's emotional life, insofar as it contributes to oedipal phase development and the organization and modulation of affective experience. Feelings and relationships are no longer so absolute and irrevocable. The concept of some rather than all and the knowledge of relativity potentially temper more primitive affective states; subtle distinctions and blends of feelings are more readily available to the child.

As elements of this system are organized in relation to each other and to the total system, relationships within the family and in the larger world are stabilized and more likely to be sustained through moments of strain. This integration permits more flexible ego functioning, enhances reality testing, and modulates drive expression through the use of more refined channels for discharge. Identity and object relations are further stabilized by the multiple conservations of an organized system.

Despite all the advances we have described, the latency child is limited in his cognitive abilities. His perspective remains egocentric insofar as he fails to differentiate between subjective and objective relationships. "It is this lack of differentiation between assumption and fact that constitutes the egocentrism of the concrete operational period" (Elkind 1970, p. 55). The latency child builds assumptive realities based on limited amounts of information, then egocentrically adheres to his position even when confronted with new or contradictory data. He entertains hypotheses, but chooses facts selectively to be consistent with them.

As his reasoning does not go beyond the real and concrete, the past is linked with the present, but the future remains an enigma. Reality is not understood as only one indication of the possible; possibility remains subordinated to reality and cannot expand into a set of hypotheses. The latency child's powers of reflection are similarly restricted. Lacking the capacity for second-order thoughts with which critically to evaluate his own thinking, he also lacks the basis for true theory formation. He can use the inverse and the reciprocal, but not as a coordinated system capable of synthesizing multiple variables. In all, his new-found capacities remain unintegrated into the total system of logic that is the achievement of the level of formal thought.

The Transition to Formal Operations

From a psychodynamic perspective, adolescence is a time of restructuring, consolidation, and synthesis. In the process, far-reaching modifications and realignments of existing component substructures of the personality will occur. The expansion of ego functions, intensification of the drives, further maturation of the superego and ego ideal, and the resurgence of early developmental conflicts create a situation of inner disequilibrium, as the adolescent seeks to disengage from the internalized objects of his childhood. These intrapsychic transformations have their observable manifestations in the adolescent's frequently turbulent relationships with parents, peers, and the larger society.

By comparison, the cognitive transformations and ensuing structural disequilibrium of this period are no less dramatic. At the formal level of thought, as at previous levels, emerging cognitive structures comprise a backdrop for the conflicts of the phase, while the consolidation of this higher level of thought contains within itself those functional capacities necessary for the resolution of complex emotional issues.

Signs of the final restructuring of thought may be discerned in the child of 9 or 10 years, although the process of transformation will not be completed until mid to late adolescence. The years in between are a time of cognitive instability: new operations are in process of simultaneous construction; a coordinating metastructure is absent, so that the residua of concrete operations persists alongside the abstractions to be; egocentrism, typical of every new cognitive stage, is heightened; and the fundamental nature of the relationship to reality is being revised through the reversal of reality and possibility. As Flavell (1963) has pointed out, this reversal of reality and possibility underlies formal thought. The use of propositional thinking, the hypothetico-deductive method, and the combinative system follow from an understanding of the real as only one instance of the possible.

Six new operations that may be assessed (Inhelder and Piaget 1958) develop during adolescence. We will not elaborate on Piaget's explanatory model for the origins of formal thought. We will limit ourselves to a description of those new constructions of primary importance and a discussion of their implications for emotional development.

As the adolescent moves away from simple operations into whole systems and abstractions, his maturing intellect begins to construct complex networks of interconnected thoughts whose organization constitutes a logical network. A prime example of this new ability is the INRC model, which represents a combinative network and group of transformations, that is, two complimentary aspects of a new whole structure taking in every operatory mechanism found at this level. I = direct operations; N = the opposite of I; R = the operation and reciprocal of N; C = NR, the negative of the reciprocal; and I (identity) = NRC (Inhelder and Piaget 1958, p. 34). INRC represents inversion, reciprocity, negation of the reciprocal or the correlative, and the synthesis of all these separate elements into a single, flexible system of totality. Prior to this time, the two forms of reversibility—inversion/negation characterized by logic and mathematical reasoning, and reciprocity, which is reversibility applied to personal and social relationships—were parallel but not connected. Within this system of totality, different variables can be held constant and compared with all other variables, and all variables can be compared with all other variables. From a cognitive perspective, this extension and integration of inversion and reciprocity is used to construct hypotheses and deduce necessary consequences through logical reasoning. It also furthers the ongoing dissociation of form from content; increasingly, an abstract form of intelligence that utilizes hypothetico-deductive-inductive reasoning to generate hypotheses and theories is observed.

This new system of totality fosters logical operations of a second power; that is, operations acting upon operations, of which proportion is a prime example. Thought is increasingly an object of thought, as reversibility now includes an expanded capacity for mental detours and reflection, perhaps the most salient trait of the act of intelligence (Elkind et al. 1969). An emerging capacity to understand probabilities through proportions and the ability to form permutations further undo the egocentric certainty of middle childhood.

Propositional logic, the consideration of the value of propositions in terms of their truth and/or falsity, facilitates the reversal of the real and the possible, requiring a final synthesis with the logically necessary (Piaget and Voyat 1976). This final coordination occurs as "if . . . then," the essence of the hypothetico-deductive model, is consolidated. The definitive reorganization of the relation to reality frees the adolescent's thought from the immediacy of the here and now; concrete reality is increasingly known to be but one example of an infinite set of possible realities. With this reversal of reality and possibility, the adolescent is capable of projecting his thoughts across time and space, creating hypothetical time that will be, thus linking the past and the present with potential futures.

Implications of Cognitive Level for Adolescent Affective Functioning

Opportunities for emotional growth are vastly enlarged by the cognitive forces we have described. Even so, these new levels of abstraction and symbolic expression create additional psychological stress prior to their consolidation into a system of totality. As in previous cognitive stages, there is an initial rise in egocentrism, during which there is "a failure to distinguish between the ego's new and unpredicted capacities and the social or cosmic universe to which they are applied . . . the adolescent goes through a phase in which he attributes an unlimited power to his own thoughts" (Inhelder and Piaget 1958, p. 345f). Simultaneously, reality becomes "immersed in a sea of possibilities"; logical necessity as a regulatory element is a partial construction at this moment in adolescent development (Piaget and Voyat 1976). As all becomes possible, no idea is too extreme or outrageous, and grandiose flights of imagination that approach the fantastic are unleashed. Enamored of his new abstract abilities and convinced of the superiority of his thoughts, the adolescent imbues his ideas with the conviction of an immediate, attainable, concrete reality. This almost "magical" belief in the power of his own thoughts is reminiscent of the semiconceptual thought of the preoperational child.

Residua of concrete operational thinking also persist over time. For several years the adolescent oscillates between the earlier concrete form of thought and partially understood abstractions. He lacks a metastructure that would achieve the differentiation and coordination necessary to regulate and modulate the intensity of his thought processes per se. This confluence of cognitive factors is a partial explanation of the particularly fluid nature of adolescent thought and its fluctuating, alternately adult and childlike quality. By implication, heightened egocentrism, lingering aspects of concrete thought, and an incomplete discrimination of real from possible relationships also contribute to the adolescent's frequent confusions about his own internal life and his relationships with others. This is particularly noticeable during early adolescence when object removal is at its peak.

Cognitive advances and their consequent imbalances underlie the adolescent's egocentric orientation. Coordination of perspectives, a related issue, is also revived as a function of this unstable structure (Inhelder and Piaget 1958). The failure to coordinate the individual and societal perspective constitutes a true lack of differentiation on the plane of formal thought; it is simultaneously exacerbated by the adolescent's belief in the power of those thoughts and the subordination of reality to possibility. Thus, while he wishes to reform the world, it must be reformed his way, and at this very moment. The adolescent consistently overvalues his ideas and egocentrically fails to coordinate his more grandiose and extreme notions with the larger social context and the demands of reality. The narcissistic self-absorption that characterizes adolescence, therefore, is not only an outcome of ongoing dynamic shifts, but also derives from the conditions created by the half-formed structures of formal thought.

Via the implicative structure of propositional logic, the adolescent explores the nature of value systems and relationships and projects the possibilities of his own destiny into an unknown and seemingly limitless future. His readiness for impassioned discussions may be laden with dynamic meanings, but his love of discussion per se stems from a need to practice his new structures: the implicative "if . . . then" and the dysjunctive "either . . . or."

Thinking about thought further stimulates his interests in abstractions. In concert with propositional logic, it fuels the adolescent's interest in ideological issues and value systems. Potentially, his challenging and reevaluation of parental and societal rules and his testing absolute limits will also promote changes in the superego (Sarnoff 1976).

Propositional logic and the reversal of reality and possibility contribute to the restructuring of the ego ideal, insofar as they foster processes of deidealization and devaluation of internal parental images. As cognitive advances occur, the adolescent's perspective on the possibilities of human development is broadened; simultaneously, flaws and shortcomings in the parents and their value systems are more readily perceived. The exaggerated response to this more realistic appraisal, however, speaks to the adolescent's earlier creation of the internalized parents as larger-than-life figures out of infantile narcissistic needs (Blos 1974). Tendencies to idealize and condemn (Blos 1967) and the emotional propensity for seeking out alternative objects for idealization are not solely a consequence of the fragmentation of parental images. These trends also reflect the lack of coordination and immaturity of the cognitive structures themselves, during the moment of their transformation.

During early to midadolescence, the realm of the possible is not tempered by logical necessity, and the full discrimination of real from possible relationships is not readily available. At the same time, the conceptual distinction between some and all is being reworked on the plane of abstraction. These particular immaturities of thought promote the formation of more extreme idealizations around persons, ideologies, and life plans.

Residual egocentrism, the "sea of possibilities" (Piaget and Voyat 1976), a partial understanding of propositional logic, and the emerging combinative network also influence the process of adolescent identity formation. As the adolescent projects himself into a limitless future, an infinite variety of equally attainable life plans and social roles unfolds before him. By implication, this transitional world of unlimited choices and possibilities intensifies those identity issues that occur on an emotional basis.

The integration and consolidation of these structures leaves the adolescent with a greatly expanded and more realistic knowledge of human relationships, potential life plans, and appropriate social roles. We infer that as these cognitive elements are clarified and consolidated, they assist the adolescent in his struggles to accept both his and his parents' frailties and limitations.

Separation from the parents is a major task of adolescence. In his consideration of the topic, Greenspan (1979) proposes that the emerging capacity to discriminate between the real and the possible may facilitate this process, as separation is now seen as a realistic possibility. Hypothesizing alternate future relationships is an important concomitant ability, as the anticipation of alternate relationships introduces a note of hope into the adolescent's frequently stormy forays into the world of heterosexual relationships. With cognitive maturation, it becomes possible to consider a future independent of one's parents that also includes specific features of their life plans and goals, such as career, marriage and parenthood. We propose that processes of partial identification are facilitated by cognitive advances, insofar as they support the individual's separateness yet allow for the incorporation of subtle, symbolic aspects of the parents and their value systems.

As we have demonstrated, the emerging structural properties of formal operations create a series of imbalances that underlie and resonate with the emotional conflicts of adolescence. As a system of totality, formal operations contains within itself those functional capacities necessary, but not sufficient, for the resolution of those conflicts. Nevertheless, this systemic consolidation will constitute a powerful counterbalance to the emotional disequilibrium of adolescence, adding a particular unity and coherence to the emerging personality organization.

As at previous stages, the coordination of a new structure influences the level of affective functioning. The combinatorial network, hypothetical thought, and the knowledge of probabilities potentially modulates the experience of intense feeling states and their associated impulses, insofar as the current emotional state is known to be only one of many possible states. These advances also allow feeling states to acquire more refined shades of meaning, while the classes and subclasses of wishes and affects that can be directed towards any internalized relationship becomes vastly more complex (Greenspan 1979). As it is possible to reconcile multiple, discrepant feelings and attitudes related to internal representations of self and object, object relations are accordingly more stable and realistic, and the flexibility of the ego is increased. Identity formation is also advanced and stabilized by this new synthesis as past, present, and future are better understood in relation to each other and are experienced as a continuum.

Our discussion has focused on the normative unfolding of cognitive and affective features of adolescent development. The reader should bear in mind that more pathological outcomes are also possible. Ehrlich (1978) has linked the combination of burgeoning symbolic capacities, egocentrism, and lingering aspects of concrete thought to certain cases of adolescent suicide. It is also possible that the ability to build systems and the defensive use of intellectualization promote the consolidation of paranoid ideation into a cohesive, organized structure.

CONCLUSION

At every level of development, cognitive transformations influence ego maturation and the drive progression. These advances and their consolidations create new pathways for the discharge of impulses and the integration of affects, promote more complex defenses, and facilitate the development of more mature object relations. As an independent yet interrelated determinant, cognitive acquisitions inevitably have consequences for emotional development.

The precise nature of these consequences, however, awaits further explorations, as many questions remain unanswered. What is the relationship between an advance or delay in the acquisition of conservation at the concrete level of thought, and a pathological outcome of oedipal development? If a child has sustained himself with highly idealized parental images, how severe is his reaction likely to be when propositional logic stimulates their fragmentation? How does a delayed or premature recognition that it is realistically possible to establish a life separate from one's parents facilitate or impede the process of object removal?

At the present time, we can answer these questions only in a most general way.

Cognitive transformations produce their own tensions; whether they will be experienced as a ripple in the ongoing flow of development or as an overwhelming flood tide is contingent upon the emotional status of the child.

SUMMARY

In this chapter, we have presented an overview of the epistemological perspective and demonstrated the clinical method through a presentation of Piagetian tasks. Features of normal cognitive development during the concrete and formal operational periods have been described, and several areas of compatability with psychoanalytic developmental theory were discussed. The structure of concrete operations was interrelated with aspects of the transition from the oedipal phase into latency and preadolescence. During adolescence, heightened egocentrism, the reversal of the real and the possible, and the residua of concrete operational thought were shown to be central to the marked fluctuations in thought characteristic of this stage. The cognitive transformations of latency and adolescence were discussed in relation to psychoanalytic developmental theory, stressing the ways in which the level of cognitive development to some degree determines and limits the quality of affective functioning. It was also suggested that cognitive transformations generate their own independent pressures on development.

APPENDIX

Anthony, E. J. (1957). The regression of the object in the psychotic child. *Proceedings of the Second International Congress of Psychiatry.*

Dudek, S. Z. (1972). A longitudinal study of Piaget's developmental stages and the concept of regression II. *Journal of Personality Assessment* 36 (4):380–89.

Ertel, D., and Voyat, G. (1982). Sensorimotor analysis of early onset childhood psychosis. *Teachers College Record* 84 (2):423–51.

Halpern, E. (1966). Conceptual development in a schizophrenic boy. *Journal of Child Psychiatry* 5 (1):66–74.

Inhelder, B. (1966). Some pathologic phenomena analyzed in the perspective of developmental psychology. *Merrill Palmer Quarterly* 12 (4):311–19.

———. (1976). Operatory thought processes in psychotic children. In B. Inhelder and H. Chipman (Eds.). *Piaget and His School.* New York: Springer.

Lefevre, A. (1970). A propos d'un cas de "Dyscalculie" de la rééducation a la psychothérapie. *Perspectives Psychiatriques* 4 (30):39–56.

Modgill, S. (1969). *The relation of emotional adjustment to the conservation of number.* Unpublished master's thesis, University of Manchester.

Schmid-Kitsikis, E. (1973). Piagetian theory and its approach to psychopathology. *American Journal of Mental Deficiency* 77 (6):694–705.

———. (1976). The cognitive mechanisms underlying problem solving in psychotic and mentally retarded children. In B. Inhelder and H. Chipman (Eds.). *Piaget and His School.* New York: Springer.

Sloate, P. (1981). *A structural analysis of affect and cognition in a psychotic child.* Unpublished doctoral dissertation, City University of New York.

Sloate, P., and Voyat, G. (1983). Language and imitation in development. *Journal of Psycholinguistic Research* 12 (2): 199–219.

———. (1983). Cognitive and affective features in childhood psychosis. *American Journal of Psychotherapy* 37 (3):376–85.

Voyat, G., and Shakelford, M. (1982). A Piagetian analysis of thinking in severely disturbed children. In J. Steffen and P. Karoly (Eds.). *Autism and severe psychopathology: Advances in child behavior analysis and therapy,* vol 2. New York: Lexington Books, 257–85.

REFERENCES

Anthony, E. J. (1956). The significance of Jean Piaget for child psychiatry. *British Journal of Medical Psychiatry* 29:20–34.

Blos, P. (1967). The second individuation process of adolescence. *Psychoanalytic Study of the Child* 22:162–86.

———. (1974). The genealogy of the ego ideal. *Psychoanalytic Study of the Child* 29:43–88.

Ehrlich, H. (1978). Adolescent suicide: Maternal longing and cognitive development. *Psychoanalytic Study of the Child* 33:261–77.

Elkind, D. (1970). *Children and Adolescents.* New York: Oxford University Press.

Elkind, D., Barocas, R., and Johnsen, P. H. (1969). Concept production in children and adolescents. *Human Development* 12:10–21.

Flavell, J. H. (1963). *The Developmental Psychology of Jean Piaget.* Princeton: Van Nostrand.

Freud, S. (1914). On narcissism. In *Standard Edition,* vol. 14. London: Hogarth, 1957, pp. 69–102.

Greenspan, S. I. (1979). *Intelligence and Adaptation: An Integration of Psychoanalytic and Piagetian Developmental Psychology.* New York: International Universities Press.

Inhelder, B., and Piaget, J. (1958). *The Growth of Logical Thinking from Childhood to Adolescence.* New York: Basic Books.

Mahler, M., Pine, F., and Bergman, A. (1975). *The Psychological Birth of the Human Infant.* New York: Basic Books.

Piaget, J. (1952). *The Origins of Intelligence in Children* (2nd ed.). New York: International Universities Press.

———. (1954). Three lectures (the stages of the intellectual development of the child; the relation of affectivity to intelligence in the mental development of the child; will and action). *Bulletin of the Menninger Clinic* 26 (1962):120–45.

———. (1969). *The Psychology of the Child.* New York: Basic Books.

Piaget, J., and Voyat, G. (1976). The possible, the impossible and the necessary. *The Genetic Epistemologist* 6 (1):1–12.

Pine, F. (1980). On the expansion of the affect array: A developmental description.

In R. Lax, S. Bach, and J. A. Burland (Eds.). *Rapprochment: The Critical Subphase of Separation-Individuation*. New York: Jason Aronson.

Sarnoff, C. (1976). *Latency*. New York: Jason Aronson.

Voyat, G. (1982). *Piaget Systemized*. Hillsdale, N.J.: Lawrence Erlbaum.

Wolff, P. (1976). The developmental psychologies of Jean Piaget and psychoanalysis. *Psychological Issues* 2:1 (1960) Monograph 5. New York: International Universities Press.

7

MEASUREMENT OF PERSONALITY

Hans J. Eysenck

Measurement in science is crucially dependent on theory. Qualitative decisions concerning *what* to measure must precede any attempts to carry out such measurements; unless we know what to measure, how can we know how to measure it? Thus, measurement in personality presupposes some kind of theory, or at least some form of descriptive framework; without such a framework we are working in the dark. Many psychologists have used a psychiatric or psychoanalytic framework for their studies, but these are clearly insufficient. Psychiatric systems of diagnosis are based on categorical, qualitative distinctions between medical disorders (hysteria, schizophrenia, obsessive-compulsive neurosis, manic-depressive disorders, and so on). Yet, it is well known that such diagnoses even with the increased precision and specificity afforded by DSM-III are essentially the formulations of committee-based consensus, often without empirical validation (Spitzer and Fleiss 1974). Furthermore the hypothetical qualitative differences between diagnostic categories are not always empirically demonstrable. In reality, we most often seem to be dealing with *dimensions* of psychopathology, along which each individual can be placed in terms of his position on this dimension or framework (Eysenck 1970a, 1970b). Psychoanalytic hypotheses, while clearly much more in line with this dimensional theory, are too vague and inconsistent to be quantifiable, and consequently cannot serve as a basis for scientific measurement (Eysenck and Wilson 1973).

It might be thought that the introduction of DSM-III had brought a measure of order to this confused field. The description of various disorders in DSM-III has certainly been more precise, but this has in no way increased the *validity* of the diagnoses, which are still based on an entirely heuristic model. Eysenck, Wakefield, and Friedman (1983) have given a thorough review of DSM-III and have put the criticisms of this essentially categorical system in more detail than can be done here; they have also discussed the many reasons why a dimensional system is more in line with the facts, and is superior to any categorical system based on false analogies with the medical disease model (Eysenck 1970a).

There is a large body of evidence, summarized by Royce and Powell (1983) indicating that there are three major factors that can be used to describe human be-havior and even the behavior of animals (Eysenck and Eysenck 1985). These three factors, which have emerged from many hundreds of different correlational and factor analytic studies of widely different populations in many different countries, have been differently named and labeled by different investigators. For our present purpose we shall use the terms neuroticism-stability, extraversion-introversion, and psychoticism-superego functioning, abbreviated into N, E, and P. Very little work has been done with children on the P dimension, and hence we will concentrate on the E and N factors as these are measured on the Junior Eysenck Personality Inven-tory (Eysenck and Eysenck 1964) and the Junior Eysenck Personality Questionnaire. (Eysenck and Eysenck 1975). Many other tests give scores which are similar to those obtained from the Eysenck Personality Inventory or Questionnaire; thus Cattell's Anxiety and Axia-Invia factors are very similar to N and E. We will not detail here the many alternative approaches that correlate highly with this system; a full pre-sentation of these results is given by Morris (1979). Eysenck and Eysenck (1985) discuss relationships among P, E, and N on the one hand, and other measures of personality on the other, in detail.

EXTROVERSION-INTROVERSION

Figure 7.1 shows in diagrammatic form the various traits that make up the two dimensions involved. A person may have any position along such a dimension, from one extreme to the other; there is no intention to sort all children into extra-verts and introverts. The term "ambivert" has become useful in denoting children whose scores lie in the middle between the extreme extravert and the extreme intro-vert.

NEUROTICISM-STABILITY

The behaviors characteristic of extraverted and introverted high N scoring chil-dren was derived from a factor analysis of data on large numbers of child guidance clinic children furnished by Ackerson (1942). Two major factors were extracted from the matrix of intercorrelations and labeled neuroticism (the horizontal axis) and introversion-extraversion (the vertical axis). There are very marked differences be-tween the personality problems shown by the introverted children, who show be-haviors marked as sensitive, absent-minded, seclusive, daydreamy, depressed, inefficient, queer, changeable mood, feeling inferior, nervous, mental conflict, emo-tionally unstable, irritable, and so on; and the extraverted children who show conduct problems variously designated as truancy, stealing, lying, destructive, swearing, disobedient, fighting, disturbing influence, violent, rude, egocentric, fan-tastic lying, temper tantrums, and so forth. The general finding that children who

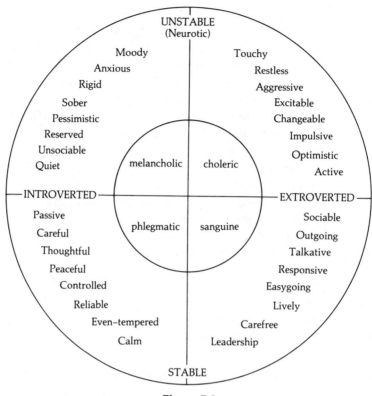

UNSTABLE
(Neurotic)

Moody   Touchy
Anxious   Restless
Rigid   Aggressive
Sober   Excitable
Pessimistic   Changeable
Reserved   Impulsive
Unsociable   Optimistic
Quiet   melancholic   choleric   Active

INTROVERTED — EXTROVERTED —

Passive   Sociable
Careful   phlegmatic   sanguine   Outgoing
Thoughtful   Talkative
Peaceful   Responsive
Controlled   Easygoing
Reliable   Lively
Even-tempered   Carefree
Calm   Leadership

STABLE

Figure 7.1

are emotionally unstable and introverted tend to be neurotic, while those who are unstable and extraverted tend to be antisocial and criminal, has also been found in many adult samples (Eysenck 1977). There are obvious similarities between these data and the Child Behavior Profile of Achenbach (1978; Achenbach and Edelbrock 1981; Edelbrock and Achenbach 1980), a rating scale widely used in the United States.

In essence, the question of measurement then becomes one of obtaining objective, valid, and reliable indices of a person's standing on the two personality dimensions of E and N. We do not suggest that these scales cover the whole of personality; clearly such a claim would be absurd. It is merely suggested that these two factors cover a considerable part of the total variance in the personality field, and that knowledge of a person's standing in this two-dimensional framework will give us more information than any other two measures could possibly. So far we have been concerned with a descriptive framework, and of course there have been many criticisms of trait theory in general (of which this is a particular example) and of attempts to describe personality along these lines, in particular. Mischel (1968) in particular has been highly critical of this approach, but his arguments are largely invalid (Eysenck and Eysenck 1980). This is not the place to discuss these criticisms, and we shall proceed on the assumption that the trait approach is valid and reasonable. (See Eysenck 1983a, 1983b; 1984; 1985a.)

DETERMINANTS OF PERSONALITY: NATURE VERSUS NURTURE

In order to arrive at suitable measures of personality, the descriptive approach has to be supplemented by a causal theory. Such a theory has been suggested by the author (Eysenck 1967). It is an hypothesis based on the demonstration that genetic factors play a large part in the position of a given child on the two dimensions of E and N (Fulker 1981). This evidence, deriving from studies of monozygotic twins reared apart from each other, differences in similarity between monozygotic twins, familial intercorrelations, studies of adopted children, and various other methods, shows that approximately two-thirds of the total "true" variance in these personality factors are contributed by genetic factors, and only one-third by environmental factors (Eaves and Eysenck 1986). In this, the results are similar to those obtained with intelligence testing (Eysenck 1979), where a large portion of the variance is also accounted for in terms of inheritance. There are, however, important differences between these two fields. In intelligence, nonadditive genetic factors, particularly dominance and assortative mating, play an important part. In the personality field there seems to be no question of dominance and very little evidence for assortative mating. On the environmental side, too, there are important differences. Geneticists consider two kinds of environmental variation, namely that due to between-family factors, and that due to within-family factors. In the case of intelligence, between-family environmental factors are roughly twice as important as within-family environmental factors, whereas in the case of personality, between-family environmental factors seem to be almost completely absent.

This is an important finding, also reported by Loehlin and Nichols (1976), the implications of which have not been widely realized. Many psychiatric theories posit as a factor in the origins of neurotic and psychotic disorders family factors such as the personality of the mother. The genetic analysis demonstrates quite clearly that such factors play little part in the genesis of personality differences, and hence they present an insuperable obstacle to the adoption of Freudian and other similar theories (Eysenck 1985b).

The fact that genetic factors are so important in the genesis of personality differences suggests immediately that in looking for a causal theory we should look at biological factors in the field of physiology, morphology, hormone secretion, and so on (Eaves and Eysenck 1986). It is clear that behavior as such cannot be inherited; all that can be inherited is morphology, anatomy, and physiology of the central and autonomic nervous systems; these, in interaction with environmental determinants, must predetermine the individual to react to various stimuli in a certain predictable manner. Such a theory has been advanced by the author (Eysenck 1967, 1981) and will now be discussed very briefly.

THE ROLE OF THE LIMBIC SYSTEM (VISCERAL BRAIN)

It is suggested that the visceral brain or limbic system is responsible for differences in the N dimension. In other words, people whose limbic system is unusually labile and responsive to emotion-producing stimuli will tend to have high N scores, be emotionally unstable, and develop neurotic disorders easily. The evidence for such a theory has been discussed in great detail by Stelmack (1981), and as the relationship between emotion and the limbic system is widely recognized it will hardly be necessary to argue in favor of this theory.

As regards extraversion-introversion, the writer has hypothesized that such differences are largely due to differences in cortical arousal, mediated by the ascending reticular activating system (Eysenck 1967). This system governs to a large extent the state of arousal of the cortex (although of course the cortex reciprocally innervates the reticular system); the hypothesis states that extraverts are characterized by a low state of cortical arousal, introverts by a high state. This statement, of course, refers to the resting state, when the individual is neither in receipt of strong afferent impulses nor in a state of sensory deprivation. The importance of this qualification will become clear later (see also Mangan 1982, and Strelau 1983).

The statement of the hypothesis just made may seem paradoxical, because a state of high arousal (introversion) is related to a type of behavior that would seem to be underaroused, rather than the opposite. The reason for this apparent paradox is that the function of the cortex is largely an inhibitory one; it inhibits the lower centers from independent activity, and hence strong cortical arousal leads to the suppression of outer activity. Alcohol is a depressant drug, and its depression of the activity of the cortex leads to a release of activity in the lower centers, resulting in more extraverted behavior.

The strong genetic determination of our model of personality suggests that it should not be confined to Western countries, but be universal. Cross-cultural studies using the EPQ have now been carried out in over two dozen cultures in Africa, South America, and Asia, as well as in North America and Europe, and the results have shown remarkable congruence, in that identical factors (defined as factors whose indices of factor comparison are in excess of .98) have been found in all the countries studied (Barrett and Eysenck 1984; Eysenck and Eysenck 1983). This cross-cultural identity of factors suggests that we may be dealing here with the beginnings of a paradigm of personality description (Eysenck 1983a), which must not be disregarded in our attempts to describe and explain the aberrant behavior of children and adults.

MEASUREMENT OF PERSONALITY DIMENSIONS

We have now outlined a general descriptive and causal theory of the major dimensions of personality; we must now turn to the question of measurement. The most widely used, most convenient, and probably the most accurate measure available is the questionnaire. For children able to read, the questionnaire has been found to be a useful and valuable method of ascertaining the child's position on the dimensions of personality in question. It is, of course, assumed in such measurement that the child is not motivated to tell lies, and the Eysenck questionnaires include lie scales that make it possible to determine the degree of dissimulation that has taken place. It has been found (Michaelis and Eysenck 1971) that it is possible to detect with considerable accuracy the degree to which a particular testing situation motivates the child or adult to dissimulate, and if need be scores can be corrected in terms of the degree of dissimulation involved. For most research purposes, it seems that children and adults are very ready to cooperate and to tell the truth as they see it; dissimulation has not normally been a problem, except when people are highly motivated to lie (as in applying for employment, or other similar situations). There is, therefore, a great deal to be said for using questionnaires in work with children, and such use has demonstrated its value in relation to many important practical problems. A list of one or two such uses will illustrate the relationship between questionnaire responses on personality inventories, on the one hand, and responses to life situations (in this case educational) on the other.

IMPLICATIONS OF PERSONALITY MEASUREMENT

New methods of instruction, when compared with older methods, are seldom found to be either superior or inferior; the null hypothesis is usually supported by the outcome of the experiment (Cronbach and Snow 1977). It is the writer's view (Eysenck 1978) that this is due in large measure to the fact that different children react differently to the different types of methods in question, and that therefore the main effects, calculated over all children, are relatively small and may be insignificant. What is significant is the interaction between main effects and personality, and many studies are cited in the paper referred to above (Eysenck 1978) to illustrate this point. Consider as an example the so-called "discovery" method, which was introduced some time ago in English schools and has been very popular. There has been no demonstration that it is superior to the traditional methods of direct instruction (reception learning), and Leith (1974) proceeded to examine the possibility that "there is a greater readiness of extraverts to become bored by routines but likely to respond to stimulus variation, and of introverts to be disturbed by changes of set but able to maintain attentiveness to a highly prompted task, could result in a methods x personality interaction" (p. 32). Teaching materials for a basic course in genetics were carefully prepared to offer equal amounts of learning and transfer in randomly chosen groups of students; "the materials were so chosen as to cover a range of personal discovery, tolerance for uncertainty and error-making as well as the differences which may be described as plunging into the deep end or stepping into the shallow end of the pool" (p. 134). Two hundred students took part in the experiment; they were tested one and five weeks after the end of the course with a series of largely transfer items. The major finding was a highly significant interaction between personality and method. On both testing occasions introverts and extraverts learned equally well *on the average;* thus there is no overall superiority of one method over the other. But extraverts learn much better than introverts with the discovery method, while introverts learn much better than extraverts with the direct teaching (reception) method. For the second test (delayed test) the difference in score between extraverts and introverts is thirty versus eighteen; in other words, extraverts do almost twice as well as introverts! This experiment illustrates very clearly the danger of comparing different methods of teaching without measuring personality at the same time and looking for different reactions of different personality types to the methods of teaching under examination.

As a second example, consider an experiment by McCord and Wakefield (1981). These two investigators were concerned with the effects of reward and punishment on the learning achievement of extraverted and introverted children. Gray (1972, 1973) had suggested a modification of Eysenck's (1967) theory such that extraverts achieve best under conditions of reward, while introverts achieve best under conditions of punishment. This proposal had been supported experimentally by results reported by Gupta (1976) and Gupta and Nagpal (1978). Wakefield (1979) has applied the interaction of extraversion and reward-punishment to the elementary classroom in order to influence academic achievement. He suggested that to improve achievement in the classroom, extraverts should be lavished with praise and continually reminded of the rewards available for adequate performance. Yet praise should do little to enhance the achievement of introverts. The careful use of threats of punishment and reminders of the consequences of inadequate performance should improve achievement for this group. Subjects were fifty-two girls and forty-nine boys in five fourth- and fifth-grade arithmetic classrooms in a California public school. Teachers in these five classrooms were observed over lengthy periods of time, and the proportion of praise and blame administered to the pupils recorded. In exploring the regressions of residual arithmetic achievement on introversion-extraversion for different ratios of reward to punishment, it was found that there was a close and highly significant relationship between treatment and extraversion, corresponding to a correlation of .59, in the expected direction. In addition, correlations between treatment and personality were also found for psychoticism ($-.58$) and neuroticism ($-.30$), both of them significant.

These two examples are given to illustrate two points. In the first place, they indicate that the personality inventories are both reliable and valid; if they were not both reliable and valid, then it would be impossible to obtain highly significant results from using them in checking predictions from the theory of extraversion and introversion. In the second place, the studies indicate the practical importance in education of having such questionnaire measures of personality qualities of this kind. From the point of view of scientific measurement, in laboratories and for purposes of research, we may often wish to go beyond questionnaires and to test more directly the underlying hypothetical structures believed to be causally related to personality factors; in that case we must have recourse to more experimental procedures that can be predicted on the basis of the theory briefly presented above to be related to extraversion and neuroticism, and that have in past research been shown to be very significantly correlated with other measures of E and N, such as questionnaires, ratings, symptomatology, and so on.

PSYCHOPHYSIOLOGICAL CORRELATES: THE EEG

The most obvious set of variables for this purpose is a selection of psychophysiological measures, particularly the EEG. It is the EEG that was originally primarily concerned in the definition of cortical arousal, although on an intraindividual rather than an interindividual basis. Under external conditions promoting high arousal, it was found that the tested subject's alpharhythm showed high frequency and low amplitude, while under conditions of low arousal alpha showed low frequency and high amplitude. The most obvious prediction, therefore, for interindividual comparisons would be the following: the more introverted a subject, the faster should be his alpharhythm, and the lower the amplitude of the waves recorded; whereas, the more extraverted the subject, the slower would be the alpharhythm, and the larger the amplitude of the waves recorded. Gale (1973) has reviewed the evidence on this point and has concluded that the situation is by no means as simple as this statement seems to imply. In particular, he drew attention to the fact that the stimulating situation, the situation under which the brain waves are recorded, can vary from being one of great boredom (stimulus deprivation) through moderate interest to strong arousal, and that these varying conditions must be taken into account in interpreting the results obtained. When this is done, it is found that, as predicted, introverts show the expected EEG rhythms under conditions of low and middling arousal. Contrary evidence seems to be forthcoming under conditions of very low and very high arousal; these seem to be explainable as favoring the theory in terms of a very important general law, enunciated by Pavlov as the law of transmarginal inhibition, but more widely known in American psychology as the Yerkes-Dodson Law, or the law of the inverted U relation between drive and performance.

What all these laws suggest essentially is that the relationship between drive, stimulation, and strength of unconditioned stimulus on the one hand, and response, conditioned reaction, or performance on the other, is not linear, but that there is an optimal point beyond which performance will decrease. According to personality theory, this optimal point should occur at a lower level of stimulation for introverts (because of their high cortical arousal) than for extraverts, and this difference in optimal point itself can be used to measure degrees of extraversion and introversion.

As an example, we may perhaps use an experiment reported by Zuckerman et al. (1974). They used two groups of subjects, one extraverted (high disinhibitors), the other introverted (low disinhibitors). Using the averaged evoked potential amplitude as their measure of reaction (in particular the P_1N_1 wave amplitude), they recorded these amplitudes as a function of stimulus intensity for the two groups. Results indicated that while there is a linear relationship between stimulus intensity and amplitude for the extraverted group, the introverted group shows clear evidence of transmarginal inhibition. This is only one of many examples of this curvilinear relationship between stimulus intensity and response amplitude. The laboratory measurement of personality is by no means as simple and straightforward as it might appear at first sight. Transmarginal inhibition is only one of many factors that have to be considered; several others will be mentioned later. When we bear in mind the transmarginal inhibition law, the data so far considered fall in line with the theory of extraversion-introversion outlined above.

PSYCHOPHYSIOLOGICAL CORRELATES

Salivary Reactions

Another example may be taken from a rather different type of psychophysiological measurement: salivary reaction to putting four drops of lemon juice on the tongue of the subject. This produces an increment in salivation, which, according to theory, should be greater for introverts than for extraverts. A study, conducted by Eysenck and Eysenck (1967) on a sample of fifty male and fifty female subjects, subdivided according to their introversion-extraversion scores into five groups, yielded interesting results. First, the actual resting rate of salivation was measured for each subject, then the four drops of lemon juice were put on his or her tongue, and the increment in salivation was then ascertained. The increment was certainly much larger for the extreme introvert group; it decreased linearly with an increase in introversion, until for the most extraverted group there was no increment at all. The correlation between the questionnaire score and the mean increment score on this very simple physiological test is in excess of .7, and this experiment itself is a replication of an earlier one carried out in a different laboratory, giving similar results. What appears to be a very simple and straightforward psychophysiological test can have quite high correlations with an apparently much more complex introspective report of a wide range of behavior, as incorporated in the Eysenck Personality Inventory. Such a demonstration argues for the validity of the questionnaire as well as for the essential correctness of the theory underlying the use of this test.

Transmarginal Inhibition

Can we introduce transmarginal inhibition into this experimental setup? Eysenck and Eysenck (1967) have reported a study in which they attempted to do this by increasing the effectiveness of the lemon juice by asking subjects to swallow it. Under these conditions the positive correlation between introversion and increase in salivation was turned into a significant negative one; in other words, under these conditions transmarginal inhibition could again be demonstrated. In all psychological experiments involving extraversion-introversion (and probably also involving neuroticism) it is vitally important to adjust the intensity of stimulation in accordance with theory and to test several different intensities for their effects on the individual's reactions. Only in this way can we be sure to cover both the ascending and descending limb of the inverted-U relationship. Using the wrong intensity of stimulation can transform a positive into a negative correlation, or vice versa.

Many other psychophysiological measures are available and have been used in attempting to measure E and N. The chapter by Stelmack (1981) gives a good survey of the available literature. Researchers interested in pursuing this line of work should also, however, be aware of the recent very extensive studies reported by Myrtek (1980) and Fahrenberg et al. (1979), which illustrate the considerable difficulties in this type of work, which make it difficult if not impossible for anyone but the most expert and experienced to pursue this line of research. The psychophysiological measurement of personality is beset by many experimental artifacts and other difficulties that should not be disregarded.

IMPACT OF PERSONALITY DIMENSION ON CONDITIONED RESPONSES

We will now turn to a consideration of experimental studies of personality along laboratory lines that use the concepts of arousal and automatic activation only indirectly, as a means of making predictions that can be tested in the laboratory. An obvious example, one that for many reasons is particularly important, is Pavlovian conditioning (Eysenck 1983c). In our own work we have mainly used eyeblink conditioning, in which a puff of air delivered to the eyeball is the unconditioned stimulus, a sound delivered over earphones the conditioned stimulus, and closure of the eyelid the unconditioned and conditioned response. The prediction was made that individual differences in rate of conditioning would be determined by the cortical arousal of the subject, in the sense that higher cortical arousal would lead to better conditioning. This leads to the prediction that under unfavorable conditions, such as low intensity of the unconditioned stimulus, introverts would condition much better than extraverts, whereas under favorable conditions, such as strong UCS, extraverts (because of transmarginal inhibition) would condition better than introverts. Eysenck and Levey (1972) have reported such a study. Under unfavorable conditions (weak UCS, short CS-UCS interval, partial reinforcement) introverts condition very much better than extraverts. Extraverts begin to show real evidence of conditioning only after thirty-six four-trial locks, by which time introverts have already reached a 45 percent frequency of conditioned responses. After forty-eight four-trial blocks, extraverts have not yet reached a 20 percent frequency of CRs, but already seem to have reached an asymptote, whereas introverts have reached a level approaching 60 percent and seem still to be increasing the frequency of CRs.

Under conditions of strong UCS, long CS-UCS intervals, and 100 percent reinforcement, extraverts condition significantly better than introverts, reaching a level of 90 percent frequency of CRs by the end of the experiment, while introverts only reached a level of slightly below 60 percent. Here again, we note verification of two essential hypotheses: 1) conditioning is a function of extraversion-introversion along the predicted lines, and 2) transmarginal inhibition is vitally concerned in the direction of the correlation between personality and conditioning. This fact must be taken into account in all attempts to measure personality by means of Pavlovian conditioning experiments.

IMPACT OF ANXIETY (NEUROTICISM) ON CONDITIONED LEARNING

Spence (1964) has postulated that anxiety (neuroticism) should show a positive relationship to Pavlovian conditioning; using eyeblink conditioning very much as we have done, he showed that the predicted correlation did in fact occur; he also failed to find any correlation between eyeblink conditioning and extraversion-introversion. As Eysenck (1981) has pointed out, this apparent contradiction can in fact be resolved by looking at the conditions under which the testing took place. Spence did not reassure his subjects that no electric shocks would be forthcoming (a perennial fear of subjects in psychological experiments!), he did not hide the apparatus from the sight of the subjects, and the whole experiment was carried out in such a way as to increase the anxiety of the subjects in their strange situation. In our own experiments, great care was taken to reassure the subjects, reduce their anxiety as far as possible, hide all the apparatus in a different room, assure the subject that no electric shocks would be forthcoming, and in all these ways attempt to reduce the influence of emotional reactions in the testing situation. Under the Spence conditions, the strong anxiety present in many subjects (particularly those high on N) would produce differential degrees of cortical arousal and hence produce a correlation with N. The strong influence of anxiety would rub out the rather smaller differences in cortical arousal produced by differences in extraversion-introversion; these would appear only under conditions of relative equanimity on the part of the subject. Thus in addition to transmarginal inhibition we have here another variable that must be considered carefully: the emotional state of the subject, as determined by instructions, testing conditions, and other similar factors. Unless these are controlled in line with the theory being tested, results may not be in line with prediction.

PERSONALITY DIMENSION AND RESPONSE TO AROUSAL

Figure 7.2 introduces another line of testing the hypothesis that arousal is responsible for differences between extraverts and introverts; it also introduces new ways of measuring this personality dimension. The abscissa indicates level of stimulation, from left (low stimulation or sensory deprivation) to right (high sensory stimulation, resulting in pain). We shall discuss level of stimulation in terms of intensity of stimulation, but other "collative" (Berlyne 1974) properties, such as complexity, can be substituted for simple intensity of sensory stimulation. On the ordinate is given the positive or negative hedonic tone resulting from stimulation of a given intensity; the central curve shows that, in general, middling levels of stimulating are preferred (give rise to positive hedonic tone, are pleasant), while too strong or too weak sensory stimulation is unpleasant (negative hedonic tone). The indifference level is also indicated in the diagram. Support for this general hypothesis, which dates back to Wundt, is found in Berlyne (1974).

The theory of personality advocated here predicts that the position of introverts and extraverts will be displaced towards the left and right, respectively, because of the high and low level of arousal of introverts and extraverts. In other words, introverts will experience as "strong," and extraverts will experience as "weak," inten-

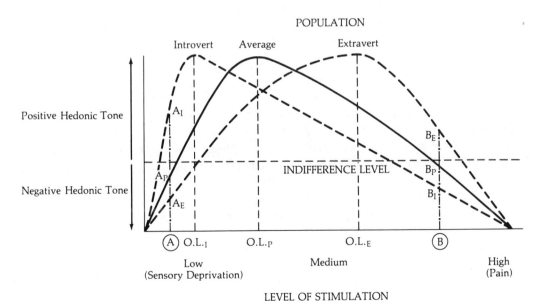

Figure 7.2

sities of sensory stimulation that to the average person will appear neither strong nor weak, but intermediate. Thus the optimal level of stimulation (O.L.) of the introverts will be displaced towards the left, and that of extraverts towards the right, of the average (O.L.$_P$). As indicated in the diagram, at point A, the average person will react to such low levels of stimulation with indifference, introverts with positive, and extraverts with negative hedonic tone. At point P, again the average, the ambivert person will react to such fairly strong stimulation with indifference, the extravert with positive and the introvert with negative hedonic tone. It follows from these arguments that introverts would be more tolerant of sensory deprivation, and extraverts of pain, and a large literature indicates that both these predictions are in fact borne out by the experimental evidence (Eysenck 1981). Thus tests of pain tolerance and sensory deprivation may be used as measures of personality.

Weisen (1965) has shown how this argument can be turned into a laboratory test of personality. Comparing groups of introverted and extraverted subjects, he measured behavior indicative of preference for presence or absence of strong sensory stimulation. Colored lights and loud music constituted the stimulation in question; silence and darkness constituted its absence. The subject pressed a key against a spring, the strength of his push constituting his selected behavior for reinforcement. Under "onset" conditions the room was dark and quiet, and a push of predetermined strength produced noise and light for a three-second period; unless the button was again pushed with predetermined strength, noise and light would then cease. Subjects would therefore ensure continuance of sensory stimulation by constantly pushing the button strongly, or they could ensure absence of stimulation by pushing the button weakly. Under "offset" conditions the opposite state of affairs prevailed; strong pushing was required to produce periods of silence; weak pushing ensured continuance of light and noise. For the first five minutes of the experiment (operant lever period) no reinforcement was given; this period established the natural strength of button pushing of members of the various groups. This was followed by a ten-minute conditioning period, and finally by a five-minute extinction period. Results indicate that both groups were similar in their behavior under operant conditions, but they behaved quite differently under experimental conditions. The extraverts increased their rate of correct responses when these were reinforced by stimulation and decreased their rate when absence of stimulation was a consequence. Introverts increased their rate of correct responses when these were reinforced by absence of stimulation and decreased their rate when stimulation was a consequence. These results are in good agreement with prediction and may be regarded as replications, as the subjects in the "onset" conditions were not the same as those in the "offset" conditions.

There are many other forms of experiments involving intensity modulation; reprints of some of these will be found in Eysenck (1971, 1976). The important work of Petrie (1967) has linked her own method of measuring intensity modulation with various social behaviors such as mental abnormality, criminality, and so on. Many different measures of personality can be derived from this extension of Eysenck's hypothesis.

Hundreds if not thousands of experiments have been done to test the theory linking E and N to physiological mechanisms in the cortex, the paleocortex, and the hindbrain; all of these can be used, under suitable conditions, for the measurement of personality. A detailed account is given elsewhere (Eysenck 1967, 1981); we have attempted here to give a rough indication of some of the types of tests used. All such experiments require careful attention to the control of relevant parameters; we have already indicated the importance of intensity modulation (Pavlov's transmarginal inhibition).

Time of day may have important effects; introverts show relatively greater arousal early in the day, while extraverts show comparatively greater arousal during the afternoon and evening. Thus time of testing may crucially affect the results of the test. Similarly, extraverts perform better in groups, introverts in isolation; this could be predicted from theory, but must be taken into account in evaluating the results of psychological experiments. In other words, the measurement of personality is not an easy task comparable to measuring a person's height with a tape measure; it requires considerable psychological sophistication, competence in the administration of the psychophysiological and laboratory tests, and acquaintance with personality theory in order to interpret the results.

PRECISION IN PERSONALITY TESTING

Measurement in science has always been a skilled, complex, and difficult task; the man-in-the-street is familiar only with such relatively obvious types of measurement as using a thermometer to gauge fever or a pair of scales to weigh ingredients for a cake. The great majority of scientific measurements are not like that at all, and while anyone can administer a questionnaire, proper scientific measurement, involving theories of personality, general psychological laws, and the skilled use of apparatus, is in a very different class. It is my firm belief that for most purposes the so-called experimental type of measurement is to be preferred to any other, although for many practical purposes questionnaires are much cheaper and easier to administer. Indeed, the often quite high correlation between questionnaires and experimental laboratory tests suggests that questionnaires may be used with advantage in many practical situations; but it should always be remembered that the interpretation of questionnaire results and their application to specific situations, whether in education, clinical work, industry, or elsewhere requires a thorough grasp of the theoretical principles on which they were constructed, and of the kinds of predictions that can be made as a consequence. The irresponsible way in which many people not properly trained in psychology are permitted to use questionnaires, IQ tests, and other types of psychological measures for purposes that may have serious consequences for children and adults is reprehensible and merits more careful monitoring by appropriate professional organizations.

In the course of this chapter we have purposely eschewed any discussion of projective tests such as the Rorschach or the TAT. The reasons for this omission are obvious. The evidence suggests strongly that none of these projective tests has sufficient reliability or validity to permit of any kind of practical use; even in experimental work they have not been found scientifically valuable (Zubin et al. 1965). The fact that in spite of these inadequacies projective techniques are still widely used, particularly in the clinical field, is another indictment of psychology as a science. There certainly is an esoteric art form that consists in the interpretation of such so-called projective devices, but it is a far cry from the existence of such an art form to its scientific validation, and no such validation has hitherto been reported. Until it is, we must read any results reported on the basis of such investigations with extreme caution, and the honorific of "measurement" cannot at the moment be bestowed upon such manifestations.

The general philosophy on which this whole discussion has been predicated will be alien to many personality psychologists, clinical workers, and applied psychologists; the demands for practical application of psychological devices having far outrun the scientific underpinning of these measuring instruments, it is small wonder that the public has become disenchanted with the results of the application of what purports to be a science to these various practical problems. Psychology may fail to gain the status of a science, to which it has always aspired, if it encourages too early and too cheap an application of methods of measurement of personality, intelligence, and other individual differences without the necessary backing of long-continued, disciplined, and patient research. The methods here suggested are more expensive and more time-consuming, and require more scientific expertise than do those currently practiced; but selection, clinical diagnoses, and other practical purposes for which personality tests are used have serious implications for the future health and happiness of many people, and it is unethical to fob them off with tests and measures that do not meet the minimum standard of scientific requirement. Science is always complex, difficult, and demanding; it is not unlikely that a science of human beings and their behavior will be even more complex, difficult, and demanding than has been the study of physics, chemistry, and astronomy. If that is so, then it is time we ceased to pretend that the problems of measurement of personality have already been solved; they have hardly begun to be touched.

REFERENCES

Achenbach, T. M. (1978). The Child Behavior Profile: 1. Boys aged 6–11. *Journal of Consulting and Clinical Psychology* 46:478–88.
———, and Edelbrock, C. S. (1981). Behavioral problems and competencies reported by parents of normal and disturbed children aged four through sixteen. *Monographs of the Society for Research in Child Development* 46:82.

Ackerson, L. (1942). *Children's Behavior Problems*. Chicago: University of Chicago Press.

Barrett, P., and Eysenck, S. B. G. (1984). The assessment of personality factors across twenty-five countries. *Personality and Individual Differences* 5:615–32.

Berlyne, D. E. (Ed.) (1974). *Studies in the New Experimental Aesthetics*. London: Wiley.

Cronbach, L. J., and Snow, R. E. (1977). *Aptitudes and Instructional Methods: A Handbook for Research on Interactions*. New York: Irvington.

Eaves, L., and Eysenck, H. J. (1986). *The Genetics of Personality*. New York: Academic Press.

Edelbrock, C. S., and Achenbach, T. M. (1980). A typology of child behavior profile patterns: Distribution and correlates for disturbed children aged 6–16. *Journal of Abnormal Child Psychology* 8:441–70.

Eysenck, H. J. (1967). *The Biological Basis of Personality*. Springfield, Ill.: C. C. Thomas.

———. (1970a). A dimensional system of psychodiagnostics. In A. R. Mahrer (Ed.). *New Approaches to Personality Classification*. New York: Columbia University Press.

———. (1970b). *The Structure of Human Personality*. 3d ed. London: Methuen.

———. (1971). *Readings in Extraversion-Introversion*. (3 vols.). London: Staples Press.

———. (Ed.) (1976). *The Measurement of Personality*. Lancaster: M.T.P.

———. (1977). *Crime and Personality*. London: Routledge and Kegan Paul.

———. (1978). Personality and learning. In S. Murray-Smith (Ed.). *Melbourne Studies in Education*. Melbourne: Melbourne University Press, pp. 134–87.

———. (1979). *The Structure and Measurement of Intelligence*. New York: Springer.

———. (1981). *A Model for Personality*. New York: Springer.

———. (1983a). Is there a paradigm in personality research? *Journal of Research in Personality* 13:369–97.

———. (1983b). Personality as a fundamental concept in scientific psychology. *Australian Journal of Psychology* 35:289–304.

———. (1983c). The social application of Pavlovian theories. *The Pavlovian Journal of Biological Science* 18:117–25.

———. (1984). The place of individual differences in a scientific psychology. *Annals of Theoretical Psychology* 1:232–85. New York: Plenum Press.

———. (1985a). The place of theory in a world of facts. *Annals of Theoretical Psychology* 3:17–72. New York: Plenum Press.

———. (1985b). *Decline and Fall of the Freudian Empire*. London: Viking Press.

———, and Eysenck, M. W. (1985). *Personality and Individual Differences: A Natural Science Approach*. New York: Plenum.

———, and Eysenck, S. B. G. (1964). *Manual of the Eysenck Personality Inventory*. San Diego: EDITS.

———. (1967). On the unitary nature of extraversion. *Acta Psychologica* 26:383–50.

———. (1975). *Manual of the E.P.Q.* London: Hodder and Stoughton.

———. (1983). Recent advances in the cross-cultural study of personality. In J. N. Butcher and C. D. Spielberger (Eds.). *Advances in Personality Assessment*. Hillsdale, N.J.: Lawrence Erlbaum, pp. 41–69.

———, and Levey, A. (1972). Conditioning, introversion-extraversion and the strength of the nervous system. In V. D. Nebylitsyn and J. A. Gray (Eds.). *Biological Bases of Individual Behavior*. London: Academic Press.

———, Wakefield, J. A., and Friedman, A. (1983). Diagnosis and clinical assessment: The DSM-III. *Annals Review of Psychology* 34:167–93.

————, and Wilson, G. D. (1973). *The Experimental Study of Freudian Theories*. London: Methuen.

Eysenck, M. W., and Eysenck, H. J. (1980). Mischel and the concept of personality. *British Journal of Psychology* 71:191–204.

Eysenck, S. B. G., and Eysenck, H. J. (1967). Psychological reactivity to sensory stimulation as a measure of personality. *Psychological Reports* 20:45–46.

Fahrenberg, J., et al. (1979). *Psychophysiologische Aktivierungsforschung*. München: Minerva.

Fulker, D. (1981). The genetic and environmental architecture of psychoticism, extraversion and neuroticism. In H. J. Eysenck (Ed.). *A Model for Personality*. New York: Springer.

Gale, A. (1973). The psychophysiology of individual differences: Studies of extraversion and the EEG. In P. Kline (Ed.). *New Approaches in Psychological Measurement*. London: Wiley, pp. 211–56.

Gray, J. A. (1972). The psychophysiological nature of introversion-extraversion: A modification of Eysenck's theory. In V. D. Nebylitsyn and J. A. Gray (Eds.). *The Biological Basis of Individual Behavior*. New York: Academic Press.

————. (1973). Causal theories of personality. In J. Royce (Ed.). *Multivariate Analysis and Psychological Theory*. New York: Academic Press.

Gupta, B. S. (1976). Extraversion and reinforcement in verbal operant conditioning. *British Journal of Psychology* 67:47–52.

————, and Nagpal, M. (1978). Impulsivity-sociability and reinforcement in verbal operant conditioning. *British Journal of Psychology* 69:203–6.

Leith, G. O. (1974). Individual differences in learning: Interactions of personality and teaching methods. In *Conference Proceedings, Personality and Academic Progress*. London: Association of Educational Psychologists.

Loehlin, J. C., and Nichols, R. C. (1976). *Heredity, Environment and Personality*. Austin: University of Texas Press.

McCord, R. R, and Wakefield, J. A. (1981). Arithmetic achievement as a function of introversion-extroversion and teacher-presented reward and punishment. *Vulnerability and Individual Differences* 26:145–52.

Mangan, G. (1982). *The Biology of Human Conduct: East-West Models of Temperament and Personality*. London: Pergamon Press.

Michaelis, W., and Eysenck, H. J. (1971). The determination of personality inventory factor patterns and intercorrelations by changes in real-life motivation. *Journal of General Psychology* 118:223–34.

Mischel, W. (1968). *Personality and Assessment*. London: Wiley.

Morris, L. W. (1979). *Extraversion and Introversion*. New York: Wiley.

Myrtek, M. (1980). *Psychophysiologische Konstitutionsforschung-Ein Beitrag zur Psychosomatik*. Gottingen: Hogrefe.

Petrie, A. (1967). *Individuality in Pain and Suffering*. Chicago: University of Chicago Press.

Royce, J. R., and Powell, S. (1983). *Theory of Personality and Individual Differences: Factors, Systems and Processes*. Englewood Cliffs, N.J.: Prentice-Hall.

Spence, K. W. (1964). Anxiety (drive) level and performance in eyelid conditioning. *Psychological Bulletin* 61:129–39.

Spitzer, P. L., and Fleiss, J. L. (1974). A reanalysis of the reliability of psychiatric diagnosis. *British Journal of Psychiatry* 125:341–47.

Stelmack, R. M. (1981). The psychophysiology of extraversion and neuroticism. In H. J. Eysenck (Ed.). *A Model for Personality.* London: Springer.

Strelau, J. (1983). *Temperament, Personality, Activity.* London: Academic Press.

Wakefield, J. A. (1979). *Using Personality to Individualize Instruction.* San Diego: EDITS.

Weisen, A. (1965). Differential reinforcing effects of onset and offset of stimulation on the operant behavior of normals, neurotics, and psychopaths. Unpublished Ph.D. thesis, University of Florida.

Zubin, J., et al. (1965). *An Experimental Approach to Projective Techniques.* New York: Wiley.

Zuckerman, M., et al. (1974). Sensation seeking and cortical augmenting-reducing. *Psychophysiology* 11:535–42.

III

Assessment of Normal Development and Its Variations

8

THE ASSESSMENT OF TEMPERAMENT

Margaret E. Hertzig and Margaret Ellis Snow

Current interest in the study of temperament can perhaps be said to date from the initiation of the New York Longitudinal Studies of Thomas, Chess, and their co-workers in the mid 1950s (Thomas and Chess 1977; Thomas, Chess, and Birch 1968; Thomas et al. 1963). During the past quarter-century, the temperamental attributes of large numbers of children living in a wide variety of social and cultural circumstances have been examined, and the accumulated evidence lends support for the view that individual differences in temperament play an important role in development and in the emergence of behavior disorders (Thomas and Chess 1977; Rutter 1982; Berger 1985). This chapter will examine the current status of research on the functional significance of temperament and will consider implications for clinical practice.

WHAT IS TEMPERAMENT?

Temperament may best be understood as a general term that refers to the *how* of behavior. As Thomas and Chess (1977, 1980) use the concept, the temperamental attributes of behavior are to be distinguished from content, which denotes *what* an individual does; from motivation, which seeks to account for *why* an individual does what he or she does; and from ability, which is concerned with measuring *how well* a particular behavioral act is executed. Temperament, by contrast, characterizes the *way* in which an individual behaves. For example, two children may throw a ball with comparable accuracy and have the same motives for so doing. Yet they may differ with respect to the vigor of the toss, the mood they express or their readiness to shift to a new activity.

In common parlance temperament and personality are frequently used interchangeably. Indeed, both terms reflect ways of characterizing differences among individuals. Although historically the construct of personality has evoked much debate (Thomas and Chess 1980), personality has come to be used clinically to refer to enduring aspects of how human beings perceive, relate to, and think about their environment and themselves. Personality, therefore, encompasses a multiplicity of characteristics that, when considered together, uniquely constitute the individual. By definition temperament refers only to the *way* that individual behaves.

In their New York Longitudinal Studies, Thomas et al. (Thomas et al. 1963; Thomas, Chess, and Birch 1968; Thomas and Chess 1977, 1980, 1984; Chess and Thomas 1984) have identified nine categories of temperament in the behavior of infants as young as two months of age. These nine categories, which have continued to be measurable through early adult life are: activity level, rhythmicity (regularity of biologic functions), approach or withdrawal to new situations, adaptability in new or altered situations, sensory threshold of responsiveness to stimuli, intensity of reaction, quality of mood, distractibility, and attention span/persistence.

In addition, the New York Longitudinal Study group has called attention to the following constellations of temperamental attributes: *The Easy Child* pattern is characterized by regularity, positive approach responses to new stimuli, high adaptability to change, and mood experiences that are only mild or moderate in intensity and predominantly positive. *The Difficult Child* pattern, at the opposite end of the temperamental spectrum, is characterized by irregularity in biologic functions, negative withdrawal responses to new situations, nonadaptability or slow adaptability to change, and intense mood experiences that are frequently negative. *The Slow-to-Warm-Up-Child* is characterized by a combination of negative responses of mild intensity to new situations with slow adaptability after repeated contact.

Several other temperamental schema have since been developed (see Hubert et al. 1982). Buss and Plomin (1975) have reported a classification of temperament utilizing four categories: activity, emotionality, sociability, and impulsivity; while Plomin and Rowe (1977) have directed attention to the following six temperamental traits: sociability, emotionality, activity, attention span/persistence, soothability, and reaction to food. Fastidiousness (Graham, Rutter, and George 1973) and vigilance (Kagan 1982) have been suggested as additional dimensions along which the *how* of behavior can be described and categorized.

Although the scientific study of temperament is relatively recent, the idea of grouping human beings into basic behavioral types is centuries old. Historically temperamental individuality has been considered to originate as a consequence of individual differences in biologic organization. Thus Hippocrates and later Galen described four basic temperaments—choleric, melancholic, sanguine, and phlegmatic—which were attributed to a preponderance of one or another of four cardinal humors. In more modern times Kretchmer (1936) as well as Sheldon (Sheldon and Stevens 1942) have proposed schemes of basic temperament and have examined their relations to various bodily types. In common parlance the meaning of the term temperament has come to encompass a characterization of fundamental elements of behavioral organization, constitutional in origin and persistent over extended periods of time.

It is important to recognize, however, that neither constitutionality nor immutability is an inherent part of the definition of temperament as the *how* of behavior. Temperament has become a categorical term without any implications as to etiology or immutability. Nevertheless, empirical findings from twin studies are reasonably consistent in showing that genetic factors play an appreciable but not exclusive role in individual variation of at least some temperamental attributes (Torgersen and Kringlen 1978; Matheny 1980; Goldsmith and Gottesman 1981). Several longitudinal studies have examined the question of temporal stability (Buss and Plomin 1975; Thomas and Chess 1977; Moss and Susman 1980). Consistency of temperamental style tends to vary inversely with the amount of elapsed time between repeated measures. Substantial consistency has been reported over periods of several months up to a year or two, but correlations extending over a period of several years are generally quite low. Moreover, group trends are of only modest value in defining temperamental variation in individual children over time. Qualitative analysis of the New York Longitudinal Study data has revealed that while some subjects remain temperamentally similar, others change significantly between early childhood and the early adult years (Chess and Thomas 1984). In this regard temperament is similar to such psychological phenomena as intellectual competence, value systems, patterns of adaptation, and coping or defense, which are affected by environmental circumstances. The developmental course of patterns of temperament as well as the nature and consequence of particular temperament–environment interactions are empirical issues to be addressed in the course of systematic research.

METHODOLOGICAL ISSUES IN THE STUDY OF TEMPERAMENT

Despite the clarity of the definition of temperament as the *how* of behavior, there is still much to be determined about the measurement of temperamental attributes. The relative merits and weaknesses of various approaches to assessment have generated ongoing conceptual and methodologic debate. Rutter (1982) and Berger (1985) have highlighted the following problems.

A first set of issues concerns the selection of the behaviors to be sampled. The number of different situations encountered by a young infant are limited so that choice is necessarily restricted. However, diversity increases with increasing age, and selection becomes more problematic. For example, is it appropriate to assess temperament in terms of children's behavior in their own typical predictable everyday situations, where the child's environment may be adjusted specifically to control any tendency towards extreme behavior? In the context of expectable, everyday routines, differences among children may tend to become muted. In contrast, assessing children in terms of how they respond to the demands of a new situation might offer an opportunity for individual differences to be manifest in an amplified form. Although one aspect of temperament, approach/withdrawal, is directly related to behavior in novel situations, other aspects of temperament (e.g., mood, activity, intensity) might be measured in new situations as well. However, it would be extremely difficult to standardize the degree of novelty in a "new" situation, given differences in the past experiences of individual children.

A second set of issues concerns the development of criteria for rating the selected behavioral sample. One problem arises out of the fact that the characteristics being measured, although tied to specific types of behavior, are relative. In examining the *how* of behavior, a comparison of the child in question with all other children, or with a norm or baseline for a specific subset of children, becomes implicit. When a child is described as "protesting mildly," "giving up easily," or "calming down quickly," the baseline for these relative judgments is not always clear. Rutter (1982) suggested that most people, in describing a child, apply a norm for comparison based on other known children of the same age. Perhaps individuals also adjust their norms according to expectations based on gender or socioeconomic factors. The usefulness of describing the *how* of behavior in relative terms is likely to increase in instances where these implicit norms are specified and used consistently.

Another problem in the establishment of criteria has to do with whether or not to consider social context in measuring specific aspects of temperament. For example, as Rutter (1982) noted, it is not obvious which type of behavior indicates a higher activity level: squirming and fidgeting while watching television or pacing about on the sideline of a sports match. One activity is clearly a greater expenditure of physical energy than the other; however, the difference could be due to situational demands rather than to actual individual differences in activity level.

A third set of issues arises in attempting to trace the course of temperament over time. This is because from year to year the same behavioral expression may change in terms of its underlying functional meaning. For example, as Rutter (1982) suggested, crying in a 6-month-old and a 16-year-old may have divergent and unrelated functional meanings, and the sense of correlating the two for evidence of temperamental continuity should be seriously questioned. There is also the possibility that different behavioral expressions at different ages may have the same underlying functional meaning. Thus, low correlations between behaviors at different ages may actually reflect temperamental continuity. The task of determining the functional equivalence of various behavioral aspects of temperament from one age to the next is clearly a complex one.

A final set of issues involves the more concrete problems involved in selecting appropriate tools for measuring temperament. For research purposes, issues of time, expense, subject commitment, and data manageability typically necessitate that investigators select one of the three commonly employed methods of measuring temperament: parent interview, parent questionnaire, and direct observation of the child. However, none of these three modes of measurement is without methodological weaknesses. Although interview data have the advantage of being based on long periods of close observation of the child in numerous situations, the potential for distortion of information as a result of parental bias must be considered. This problem is least likely to surface when interview questions call for specific, detailed descriptions of actual behavior in circumscribed situations, as opposed to global perceptions of temperamental characteristics. This type of detailed interview is very time consuming. Questionnaires are quicker and easier to administer; however the possibility that responses reflect distorted parental perceptions and not actual child characteristics may be even greater than is the case with more detailed, comprehensive interviews (Dunn and Kendrick 1980; Bates, Freeland, and Lounsbury 1979). Direct observations of the child offer the opportunity to obtain data that are free from the contamination of parent bias. However, watching the child in one or two specific observation sessions is unlikely to provide enough information for making valid judgments of how that child *generally* behaves, across different situations and at different times of the day.

Despite these problems, researchers have continued to develop instruments for measuring temperament; a review appearing in 1982 (Hubert et al. 1982) estimated twenty-six different temperament instruments in use at that time. Most of these employ the questionnaire approach, although interview and observational measures were also represented in the total count. Analysis of the psychometric properties of these instruments revealed high interrater reliability for most measures (correspondence between two independent scorings of the same record), moderate internal consistency, and moderate but inconsistent levels of test-retest reliability. Data on interparent reports suggest low to moderate levels of agreement between mothers and fathers. Data on stability over time suggest moderate stability for some, but not all aspects of temperament. Attempts to measure the validity of these instruments suggest low convergent validity (agreement between different instruments attempting to measure the same characteristics), inconsistent concurrent validity (correspondence between aspects of temperament and other aspects of development measured at the same point in time), and moderate predictive validity (correspondence between aspects of early temperament and other aspects of development at later points in time). Among the questionnaires that have been developed to rate temperament at various age periods are the Revision of the Infant Temperament Questionnaire for children between 4 and 8 months of age (Carey and McDevitt 1978), the Toddler Temperament Scale for children between 1 and 3 years of age (Fullard, McDevitt, and Carey 1984), the Behavioral Style Questionnaire for 3- to 7-year-old children (McDevitt and Carey 1978), and the Middle Childhood Temperament Questionnaire for children between 8 and 12 years (Hegvik, McDevitt, and Carey 1982). Instruments have also been developed for the assessment of temperament during adolescence (Lerner et al. 1982) and early adult life (Thomas et al. 1982).

The psychometric limitations of temperament instruments when used singularly lead Hubert et al. (1982) to encourage the use of the multitrait-multimethod approach to data collection originally described by Campbell and Fisk (1959). Although time-consuming, this way of combining information from numerous sources and through various techniques would be optimal in providing the most comprehensive data set upon which to base judgments about child temperament.

In summary, currently available research instruments developed for the study of temperament reflect a compromise between fidelity and convenience (Berger 1985). The measures in current use are an amalgam of intrinsic behaviors of the child, idiosyncratic perceptual biases of the primary observers, arbitrary classification decisions of the investigators, and situational effects.

MAJOR RESEARCH FINDINGS

There is a rapidly growing body of research on the relations between temperament and other aspects of behavioral functioning. Although temperament researchers have only partially resolved the formidable conceptual and methodologic problems facing them, the findings of these studies are of particular interest to clinicians in that they suggest significant associations between particular temperamental constellations and a diverse array of behavioral problems in children.

The prototype of temperament research is the New York Longitudinal Study (Thomas and Chess 1977; Thomas, Chess, and Birch 1968; Thomas et al. 1963). In this investigation of one hundred thirty-three children deriving from eighty-five families, an inductive content analysis of the information obtained during the course of parental interviews led to the establishment of nine individual temperamental dimensions as noted earlier. *The Difficult Child* pattern, characterized by irregularity in biologic functions, withdrawal in new situations, nonadaptability or slow adaptability to change and intense negative expressions of mood, has generated the greatest interest. Although difficult children comprised only 10 percent of the NYLS sample, 70 percent of those who were classified as difficult during the first three years of life developed clinically evident behavior problems during early and middle childhood. The risk of developing behavior problems is even greater among difficult children with physical handicaps or mental retardation (Thomas and Chess 1977).

Rutter (1977) has also reported that aspects of children's early temperament were predictive of disordered behavior both at home and at school. Childhood behavioral problems were likewise found by Wolkind and DeSalis (1982) to be related to difficult temperament in infancy. Negative mood and intensity as assessed by direct observation in nursery school as well as by teacher reports served to identify children who required psychiatric referral during a subsequent five-year period (Terestman 1980). Earls (1981) has reported that among preschool children low adaptability, low distractibility, and high intensity are closely linked to behavioral adjustment. Night awakening (Carey 1974), colic (Carey 1972), and accidental injury (Matheny, Brown, and Wilson 1971; Carey 1972) are also most likely to occur in infants and young children who are temperamentally difficult.

The predictive value of difficult temperament persists through the middle school years. Graham, Rutter, and George (1973), in studying children with one psychiatrically disordered parent, found those with difficult temperaments to be at greater risk for psychiatric disorder in middle childhood. In a general population study of French-Canadian children, those whose temperaments were determined to be difficult at age 7 were found to have more clinical disorders at age 12 that qualified for a DSM-III diagnosis than a matched group who were temperamentally easy (Maziade et al. 1985).

Temperament has also been found to affect educational experience. In a series of studies by Keogh and Pullis (Keogh and Pullis 1980; Pullis and Cadwell 1982; Keogh 1982), teachers' estimates of children's intellectual ability, perceptions of their classroom behavior, and decisions about classroom management were found to be biased by temperamental characteristics of the children. Research by Gordon and Thomas (1967) and Carey et al. (1977, 1979) also found teachers' perceptions of intelligence and adjustment to be biased by aspects of child temperament.

Efforts to identify possible mechanisms that may underlie the associations between difficult temperament and behavior disorder have led a number of investigators to examine associations between child temperament and family relationships. Dunn and Kendrick (1982), in a study of first-born children's reactions to the birth of a sibling, found adverse reactions to be related to certain aspects of difficult temperament. Temperamental differences were also found to be associated with the quality of mother-child interaction and the nature of children's behavior toward their mothers while mothers were interacting with the new sibling. Stevenson-Hinde and Simpson (1982) found difficult child characteristics to relate to negative types of interaction across the following dyadic combinations: mother-child, father-child, mother-father, and sibling-child. Mothers' efforts to teach their babies have also been influenced by temperament, especially in the case of boys. In a study by Maccoby, Snow, and Jacklin (1984), mothers of difficult sons were found to reduce their efforts at direct teaching over time, while mothers of more easy-going boys increased their teaching efforts. In families with a psychiatrically disordered parent, children with difficult temperamental characteristics were found to be targeted as objects of parental criticism (Rutter 1978). Maziade et al. (1985) have shown that the risk of behavior disorder among temperamentally difficult children increases if parents show little consensus and if family rules and demands lack clarity, firmness, and consistency.

CLINICAL RELEVANCE OF RESEARCH FINDINGS

Research findings over the past twenty years clearly indicate that temperament constitutes a variable of considerable predictive power (Rutter 1982). However, to identify temperament as a risk factor in the development of behavior disorder in children is, in and of itself, of little value to the clinician in the assessment and treatment of individual cases. What is needed is a clinical framework within which to interpret research findings. Rutter (1982, p. 287) has maintained that the lack of empirically based information on the implications of specific temperamental characteristics or clusters for individualized clinical management limits the clinician's ability to utilize research findings effectively. Observational skills may be sharpened in the course of obtaining information about temperament; discussions about the interactive nature of development may help relieve guilt in both parents and children, or reliable information about temperament may help define particular management strategies. Berger (1985) has suggested that whether and how the clinician uses currently available information about temperament is a matter of individual choice.

By way of contrast, Thomas and Chess (1977, 1984, 1986) have used an interactionist model of developmental process to provide a framework within which data on temperament can be incorporated into clinical practice. The model

> demands that behavioral attributes must always be considered in their reciprocal relationship with other characteristics of the organism and in their interaction with environmental opportunities, demands, and stresses. This process produces consequences which may modify or change in behavior. The new behavior will then affect the influence of recurrent and new features of environment. New environmental influences may develop independently or as a consequence of previous or on-going organism-environment interactive process. At the same time, characteristics of the organism, either talents or abilities, goals and motives, behavioral stylistic characteristics, or psychodynamic defenses may be modified or altered as the result of this continually evolving reciprocal organism-environment influence. Development thus becomes a fluid dynamic process which can modify and change preexisting psychological patterns. (Chess and Thomas 1984, p. 20).

The tracing of individual developmental sequences is guided by the concept of "goodness of fit" and the related ideas of consonance and dissonance. Thomas and Chess (1977, 1984; Chess and Thomas, 1984) considered goodness of fit to result when the child's capacities, motivations, and style of behaving are in accord with the demands and expectations of the environment. *Consonance* between child and environment potentiates optimal development. Conversely, poorness of fit reflects *dissonance* between individual and environment so that maladaptive functioning and distorted development may occur. Neither goodness of fit and consonance nor poorness of fit and dissonance are abstractions; but they acquire meaning only in terms of the values and demands of a given culture or socioeconomic group.

Thomas and Chess (1977, 1984; Chess and Thomas 1984) cautioned that goodness of fit does not preclude the presence of stress or conflict. These are inevitable concomitants of development, during which new expectations and demands for change and progressively more complex levels of functioning occur continuously.

> Demands, stresses, and conflicts when in keeping with a child's developmental potentials, temperamental characteristics, and capacities for mastery, are constructive in their consequences. It is rather excessive stress resulting from poorness of fit between environmental expectations and demands and the capacities of the child at a particular level of development that [may] lead to disturbed behavioral functioning. (Thomas and Chess 1984, p. 8).

It should be noted that this theoretical framework in no way implies that temperament is the sole determinant of behavior disorder in children. As conceptualized by Thomas and Chess, temperament is but one significant attribute of the individual and "must at all times be considered in its internal relations with abilities and motives and its external relations with environmental expectations and demands" (Thomas and Chess 1984, p. 4).

Qualitative analyses of the data of the New York Longitudinal Study have led Thomas and Chess (1986) to conclude that the delineation of temperament is an important facet of psychiatric assessment. In some instances the clinician may be required to distinguish between what may be extremes of normal temperament and symptoms of psychiatric disorder. In others, specification of particular temperamental attributes may alert the clinician to sources of dissonance between child and environment.

Extremes of temperamental traits or clusters that are within the normal range may appear as deviant or abnormal to parents, teachers, or others who interact with the child on a regular basis. Slow-to-warm-up children may be labeled timid and anxious because they stand at the periphery of any group. Highly active children may be considered hyperactive, while children whose activity levels are at the low end of the distribution may be viewed as developmentally retarded. Attention deficit disorder may be suspected in highly distractible children, especially if they are also highly active. The irregularity, intense negative responses to new situations or demands, and slow adaptability of the temperamentally difficult child may suggest the presence of a conduct disorder. Differential diagnosis is important because recognition of extremes of temperament may allay parental anxiety and provide a basis for the formulation of specific recommendations for optimal management and care (Thomas and Chess 1986; Turecki and Tonna 1985).

If the expectations and demands made upon a child are excessive because of one or another temperamental characteristic (poorness of fit), the possible consequences are many and varied. Thomas and Chess (1977, 1986) have described interactive sequences that involve the pathologic exaggeration of particular temperamental traits or constellations. For example, if a slow-to-warm-up child is repeatedly pressured to adapt quickly to new social situations, such unrealistic and stressful demands may lead to more widespread social inhibition. A highly active child expected to sit still for long periods without opportunities for motor discharge, as in school, may fidget when restrained and exhibit marked overactivity and impulsivity when released. An exaggeration of intense negative reactions or frequent temper tantrums may result if the temperamentally difficult child is expected to adapt immediately and cheerfully to new places and people. Such behaviors often evoke intensification of environmental demands. Over time these maladaptive responses may become generalized or other symptoms may appear as mechanisms of defense are elaborated.

The task of the clinician involves separating a deviant behavior pattern into its component parts—temperament, motivation, and ability—and examining the interplay among these three factors as well as their relation to important aspects of the familial and broader social environments (Thomas and Chess 1986).

THE ASSESSMENT OF TEMPERAMENT IN CLINICAL PRACTICE

The assessment of temperament in clinical practice does not require special techniques or interviews. Information about temperament can be obtained in the course of the clinician's usual diagnostic procedures. Instruments designed to assess temperament for research have limited value in clinical settings. When data on temperament is obtained during interviews with the child, the parents, and other significant adults in the child's life, the clinician has an opportunity to explore in detail those aspects that from the informant's initial responses appear most relevant to the problem at hand. Face-to-face contact permits the identification of attitudes, feelings, and ideas that add to the richness of the data base. Contradictions may be clarified and any confusions or misunderstandings the informant may have can be explored. These advantages far outweigh any additional time that might be required to adequately assess temperament in a clinical setting.

The following general principles help the clinician determine which temperamental qualities, if any, may be of importance in the etiology and evolution of the child's current pattern of behavior. First of all, significant temperamental traits are most likely to be at the extremes: high or low intensity rather than a moderate level, high or low persistence rather than an intermediate level, markedly distractible or nondistractible rather than a mid-range, high or low activity, rather than fairly active, or a definitely difficult or easy temperamental pattern rather than a borderline classification.

Secondly, it usually requires information about the child's behavior in a wide range of situations and circumstances to identify a particular behavioral pattern as temperamental. The hallmark of temperament is its nonmotivational character. A specific behavioral pattern in a specific environmental setting may be an expression of a particular temperamental trait. Similar behaviors, however, may be consciously or unconsciously motivated, or indeed may reflect the contribution of both temperamental and motivational factors. The child who stands at the edge of the group at a new nursery school may be temperamentally slow-to-warm-up or may have been made anxious by the requirement to separate from mother, or may be both slow-to-warm-up and anxious. If this child has behaved in similar ways in other new settings, but with increasing familiarity has gradually become an active participant, it is likely that the nursery school behavior is a manifestation of a slow-to-warm-up temperamental pattern. If, on the other hand, such a child continues to remain aloof when children or adults who are no longer strangers attempt to draw him into activities that require distance from mother, it is more probable that the pattern represents a defensive response to anxiety.

Finally, information about temperamental attributes is most likely to be accurate if the objective details of behavior in specific situations are obtained. Global statements often provide clues about parents' attitudes towards their child, but they do not yield the information necessary to identify temperamental characteristics. The parent should be asked to illustrate general statements by specific examples. Thus, if a child is described as "stubborn and self-willed" or as "having a tantrum every time he doesn't get his own way," the parent should be asked to describe several recent incidents in detail. The parent should be specifically requested to indicate how the sequence began, how he responded to the child's behavior, how the child reacted, and so on until the episode was brought to a close. The clinician who obtains several examples of such behavioral sequences is in a better position to estimate whether the child has a difficult temperamental pattern that the parents are perhaps handling less than optimally, or whether other factors may be operating as well.

THE PARENT INTERVIEW

The clinician will want to obtain an inventory of the child's current temperamental attributes as well as those that characterized his or her functioning during the infancy period. In some cases the chief complaint may suggest pertinent temperamental issues that can be explored as part of the investigation of presenting problem. For example, a chief complaint of continued crying and temper outbursts in school persisting for a month after entering kindergarten might suggest a temperamentally intense child with a predominantly negative mood who is slow-to-warm-up in new situations. A chief complaint of a school-aged child who is uncooperative, fails to finish assigned tasks despite constant reminders from an increasingly irate mother, who dawdles over dressing, and who is always "forgetting" even things she plans and looks forward to doing might be a description of the temperamental quality of high distractibility. A child described as "hyper," "always on the go," or "never still even in sleep" might be a youngster who is temperamentally highly active.

In other instances the role of temperament will be less clearly defined, and the clinician can begin an inventory of temperamental attributes by indicating that he wishes to understand more about what the child is like and how he or she behaves in daily life situations.

Activity level may be estimated by inquiring about the child's behavioral preferences. Would he rather play ball than sit quietly, drawing or reading? When required to sit still for long periods as in the classroom or on a long car trip is he restless?

Rhythmicity can be explored through questions about the regularity of the child's habits. Does he get sleepy at regular and predictable times? Does he snack regularly after school or in the evening? Are his bowel movements regular?

Approach/withdrawal, or the child's characteristic response style to new situations or people, can be explored through questions about the nature of reactions to new clothing, new children, a new school, a new teacher. Will the child try new foods or new activities easily or not?

Adaptability can be assessed by considering the way in which the child reacts to changes in the environment. Are changes in family routines taken in stride? Will the child accept substitutes? Can the child go along with other children's preferences or do things always have to be his way?

Threshold of responses to environmental stimuli is difficult to explore in an older child, but sometimes children are described as either unusually sensitive or unresponsive to noise, bright lights, or rough or itchy clothing.

Intensity of reaction can be determined by inquiring about how the child displays disappointment or pleasure. When unhappy does he fuss quietly or bellow with rage or distress? Are expressions of joy mildly enthusiastic or ecstatic?

Quality of mood can usually be estimated by asking parents if the child is predominantly happy and contented, or is he a frequent complainer, more often unhappy than not?

Distractibility, even when not part of the presenting complaint, will become apparent as parents describe routines of daily living. Does the child start off to do something and become easily sidetracked?

Persistence can be assessed by inquiring about how much effort the child expends to master games, puzzles, athletic activities, or school work if these prove to be initially difficult. Once the difficulty is overcome, the length of the child's *span of attention* for and concentration on these same kinds of activities can be inquired about. (Thomas and Chess 1977, 1986).

It is frequently important to obtain a picture of the child's temperament during infancy as well. Difficult children are more likely to develop behavioral problems than those who are temperamentally easy. Moreover, any temperamental attribute may be the source of "poorness of fit" between the child's characteristics and parents' attitudes, expectations, and child-care practices, and thus may serve as a nucleus for a cycle of negative parent-child interactions (Turecki and Tonna 1985).

Parents' recall of temperament during infancy may be distorted by particular biases influencing the recollection of the past. The problem of retrospective recall is not unique to temperament, but applies to other historical information as well. The accuracy of parental recall is likely to be increased if the questions focus on the infant's behavior and the parent's handling of it in specific age/stage related situations. General questions such as "Was he easy or hard to take care of as a baby?" are least likely to evoke accurate recall (Robbins 1963; Chess, Thomas, and Birch 1966).

The following outline provides the clinician with a guide for identifying temperament during the infancy period. The protocol may appear burdensome and excessively time-consuming. However, not all items need to be covered in depth. In each individual case the chief complaint, history of the present illness, and assessment of current temperament may well suggest which temperamental attributes require detailed exploration and which need only to be more quickly surveyed. In obtaining information about temperament during infancy it is useful to request parents to respond in terms of their child's behavior at 6 ± 2 months of age.

Activity Level. Did the baby lie quietly during diaper changes or did constant motion make the job difficult? During dressing and undressing was it a struggle to get kicking arms and legs where they belonged or was it quite easy because the baby held fairly still? Did the baby tend to remain in the same position during sleep or did he move all over the place?

Rhythmicity. Did he awaken at about the same time every morning? Was the timing and duration of naps consistent from day to day? Was the baby hungry at about the same time each day? Did you know when he would have a bowel movement?

Approach/Withdrawal. How did the baby react to new events such as new foods, new clothing, being cared for by a new person for the first time? Did he fuss, show no discernible reaction, or did he seem to enjoy the novelty?

Adaptability. If the baby didn't take to a new situation immediately could you count on his getting used to it quickly or did it take a long time? For example, if his first reaction to a new person was a negative one, how long (in days or weeks) did it take the child to become comfortable with the person? If he didn't like a new food the first time it was offered how long would it take for him to come to like it (if ever)?

Threshold Level. How would you estimate the child's sensitivity to sound, light, heat, cold, and textures of clothing? For example, did you have to tip-toe about when the baby was sleeping to avoid awakening him? Did bright lights or bright sunshine make him fuss or cry? Did he seem to be bothered by roughly textured clothing? Did you have to wash new clothes before they were worn?

Intensity of Reactions. When the baby was hungry did he fuss mildly, cry loudly, or was it somewhere in between? If he resisted going to bed or was offered a food he didn't like was his protest mild or vigorous? If he liked something, did he usually smile or coo, or laugh vigorously?

Quality of Mood. Was the baby generally pleasant or did he fuss a good deal? When he fussed or cried, did this happen mostly with definite discomfort like hunger, sleepiness, or a soiled diaper? Or were there many times when he seemed uncomfortable or upset and you couldn't tell what was the matter?

Distractibility. If he was hungry and fussy could you divert him easily so that he stopped crying while you got his food ready? Or would nothing seem to distract him? When he was feeding and someone walked by did he go on feeding or did he stop and turn his head to watch? If he was resisting being changed or dressed, could you get him to lie still by giving him a toy or did nothing stop his fussing?

Persistence and Attention Span. Can you estimate the longest time he remained engrossed in an activity such as playing with a cradle gym or watching a mobile all by himself? If he wanted something like a toy in the bathtub and couldn't get it easily, would he keep after it or give up very quickly?

The survey of the child's temperamental attributes in the current period and during infancy can be coupled with inquiries about what aspects of the child's temperament the parents found difficult or upsetting and why, as well as how they handled these issues. With these data the clinician will then be in a better position to identify those aspects of the child's temperament which might have significant factors in the development of the behavior problem. Further information can then be obtained about these characteristics at other ages between infancy and the present time. In addition the reactions of other family members, teachers and peers to the child's temperament can be ascertained. (Thomas and Chess 1977, 1986).

THE DIRECT EXAMINATION

The direct examination of the child provides the clinician with the opportunity to assess the temperamental attributes of a sample of behavior. With the exception of rhythmicity of biological functioning, which requires data over a more extended period of time, the clinician can assess whether the child engages quickly and easily or requires more time to warm up (*approach/withdrawal*); whether he sits quietly, fidgets, or engages in gross motor activities (*activity level*); whether or not he is aware of minor visual, auditory, or other stimuli (*threshold*); whether he shows mildness or *intensity* of expression; whether he is generally positive or negative in mood; whether or not he accepts suggestions and rules (*adaptability*); whether he appears to be predominantly *distractible* or nondistractible; whether his *attention span* is long or short; whether or not he is *persistent* when confronted with a demand he finds difficult or not.

Children's descriptions of their routines of living, likes and dislikes, adjustment at home, school, and in various social situations are a source of additional information about temperament. These accounts can be amplified by direct questions. For example, *activity level* can be explored by asking the child how he feels when there is no opportunity for physical activity, as during a long car ride. Does this make him restless and uncomfortable, or doesn't it bother him? One can also estimate whether active sports play an important part in his life or not. *Approach/withdrawal* can be explored by asking if he was bothered by a move to a new home, attending a new school, being assigned a new teacher, or meeting new children as in summer camp. If any of these new situations was upsetting, did he adjust quickly or slowly (*adaptability*) or did he do his best to avoid further contact. The clinician will utilize this information together with other data to distinguish between slow adaptability as a temperamental trait and defensive withdrawal. If there are several interviews the rate of *adaptability* can also be estimated by the tempo of the child's accommodation to the clinician, the office environment, and to the discussion of disturbing topics.

Quality of prevailing *mood* can be evaluated, once rapport has been established, by noting the manner in which peers, routines, adults, and tasks are discussed. The child with a predominantly positive mood will comment cheerfully on these activities and experiences. Such a child may also view any setback as due to temporary ill luck. By contrast, the youngster with predominantly negative mood is more likely to make comments such as "With my luck, I won't get chosen for the basketball team."

Intensity of expression can be rated in the play of facial expression, in the tone of voice, and in the content of ideas. Comments such as "I don't mind" and "I guess it's alright" are more characteristic of low intensity, while such phrases as "I always get so mad" or "I had a terrific time" would be more indicative of high intensity.

Threshold is not often an issue in older children. However, a child with a *low threshold* (high sensitivity to touch or taste) may avoid exposure to situations in which he may experience discomfort. If the history or prior discussion suggests this possibility, a direct question that reveals an appreciation for such sensitivities will often prompt acknowledgment and a description of the various devices used to cover over and avoid embarrassment.

The child's flow of ideas can provide some measure of *distractibility*. If a youngster repeatedly jumps to a new idea but readily picks up the original thread when the digression is called to his attention, it is likely that this is a stylistic component and not a measure of anxiety. *Low distractibility* will show itself by the firmness with which a topic is maintained despite the intrusion of other stimuli.

Rhythmicity is unlikely to be a significant aspect of problem behavior among older children. Only if there are strong idiosyncratic responses in which regularity of sleep or of appetite conflicts with rigid expectations may this be important. Should the history suggest such a possibility, the child may be asked directly about his needs for sleep and food. Such inquiry may well elicit a response that clarifies the issue, for example, "I get so sleepy that I have to go to bed by 10:00 even if I want to stay up later" or "My parents make a big fuss if I don't eat everything they put on my plate but my appetite isn't the same every day and then they accuse me of filling up with junk food."

In some instances it may be desirable to query teachers or other adults familiar with the child's behavior. For example, the parents may be so anxious or so much in conflict with each other that only limited reliable descriptive details of the child's behavior may be obtained from them. Information obtained during direct examination of the child may be sufficient to clarify the vagueness, ambiguities, or contradictions of the parents' histories. In other instances, however, the data obtained from the child may only partially illuminate an important issue such as the child's adaptability to new people or new demands over time. In these situations a teacher's description of the child's behavior in these specific areas may be useful. On some occasions another adult, such as a relative, babysitter, or close family friend, may have been in a position to observe the child closely and may therefore be able to give an objective description of specific aspects of the child's temperamental style. If the child has had psychological testing, the psychologist may also be able to provide useful information on the crucial dimensions of temperament as these attributes were exhibited during testing.

In evaluating information from different sources the clinician must bear in mind that an individual's temperament may not be expressed identically in different life situations or with different people. Thus a child may be intensely reactive temperamentally, but this characteristic will be more pronounced in a permissive home environment than in a formal structured schoolroom. A child's positive mood may be more evident in a play group or in school than in a stressful home setting. If the clinician obtains conflicting reports from different sources of information, he will have to assess the significance of the contradictory data. Contradictions may indicate that a particular setting is a significant source of stress.

CASE VIGNETTE

Mark K.'s mother consulted one of us in October of his kindergarten year. Her desire for an evaluation was prompted by a meeting with Mark's teacher, who said Mark was having problems adjusting to school. Of specific concern to the teacher were Mark's frequent temper outbursts, his inflexibility and need to do things his own way, and his tendency to resist social overtures made by other children. Mrs. K. referred to this meeting with Mark's teacher as "the last straw." Mark had always given her problems, she declared. She perceived her son as willful and defiant, but also as extremely sensitive. She described him as ignoring rules on purpose and deliberately antagonizing people, but also as being likely to burst into tears or fly into a rage at minor frustrations. He was unpredictable, she said, and always a potential embarrassment. Mrs. K. compared Mark to his brother David, two years older, who she felt rarely ever posed a problem. She stated she had always treated the boys equally, yet David was usually cheerful, friendly, and cooperative, while Mark was typically stubborn, irritable, and disobedient.

Mrs. K.'s initial global description raised the possibility that Mark's problems might be symptomatic of an oppositional disorder. However, questions about situation-specific behaviors revealed an ongoing pattern of difficult temperamental characteristics originating in infancy. Mark had been irregular as a baby, both in eating and sleeping patterns; he had been quick to fuss and difficult to soothe; he had displayed prolonged stranger anxiety; and he had been slow to adapt to changes in his established routines. When Mark began nursery school at age three, this pattern of temperamental characteristics made classroom adjustment slow and difficult. However, with time and the help of a flexible, patient nursery school teacher, Mark became more adaptable, gained better control of his emotions, and developed a few close friendships. Now, upon changing schools, a resurgence of Mark's difficult characteristics appeared to be occurring.

A brief developmental history of Mark's older brother, David, revealed a striking contrast. A relaxed, cheerful baby with regular biological routines, David had maintained the constellation of easy temperamental characteristics throughout the years. It appeared that Mrs. K. had developed a set of expectations and a mode of parental behavior consonant with the temperamental characteristics of her older son, David. What had created a "good fit" in this parent-child relationship appeared to be creating a "poor fit" in Mrs. K.'s relationship with her second son, Mark. It is likely that Mark's school adjustment difficulties were especially upsetting to Mrs. K. because her expectations were so dissonant with her child's capabilities. And it is possible that the dissonance of this relationship may have had an exacerbating affect on Mark's already difficult behavior.

A play session with Mark revealed behavior suggestive of the difficult temperamental pattern but not of an oppositional disorder. Although he was initially reluctant to enter the office, Mark's behavior was not provocative or defiant, but suggestive of wariness and mild anxiety. When reassured that his mother would remain in the waiting area, he hesitantly entered the office. With furrowed brow and a somber expression he tentatively examined the toys and games. When asked if he would like to play checkers, he first responsed, "I don't like that game." However, as he watched the checkerboard being set up improperly he could not resist offering a lesson in correct checker placement. He then commanded, "Let's play. I'll teach you." During the game Mark talked freely, and his lengthy explanations of the rules of checkers reflected language and reasoning skills beyond age-level expectations. He played seriously and clearly wanted to win. Each victorious move was accompanied by a fleeting smile, while losses were followed by exclamations of frustration, fist-banging, and at one point brief tearfulness. When it was suggested to him that we might bend the rules and play the game a slightly different way, he became agitated and upset, saying, "No, you can't, you can't, don't!" This was quickly followed by a look of embarrassment, and he added, "Well, you really can play however you want, but let's stay with regular rules just for today, OK?" The game of checkers was followed by a block-building activity, in which Mark became noticeably more relaxed and cheerful. When it was almost time for the session to end Mark's initial response was to whine and declare his unreadiness to leave. However, when told we could have five more minutes to play he brightened and said, "Oh thanks, let's play really fast so we'll be finished by then." Mark skipped out to his mother at the session's end, responding to her query, "How was it?", with, "Great! She had good toys and I taught her checkers."

A call to Mark's school teacher clarified her impressions of Mark. Her view was not that he was willfully negativistic, but that his adjustment problems were in fact a source of distress to him. She described him as a bright, well-meaning child who had an awareness of his difficulties and who appeared to be actively striving to control his maladaptive behavior.

The conclusion of the evaluation, which was communicated to Mr. and Mrs. K., was that Mark was not suffering from any behavior disorder that required treatment. Rather, it was likely that because of the novel demands of the new school placement, what was occurring was a temporary intensification of his difficult temperamental characteristics. It was hoped that with time, as had been the case in nursery school, Mark's classroom problems would significantly decrease. Parent counseling was initiated to guide Mr. and Mrs. K. in dealing appropriately with their son's difficult behavior and to help them develop a set of expectations more consonant with Mark's temperament. Although because of his difficult temperament Mark continues to be at risk for the development of more serious problems, he is now in second grade and progressing well both academically and socially.

SUMMARY

Temperament refers to the *how* of behavior, and as such is to be distinguished from content, motivation, and ability. Despite formidable conceptual and methodological problems, the findings of studies conducted over the past twenty years consistently confirm significant associations between particular temperamental constellations and a diverse array of behavioral problems in children. Thomas and Chess (1986) have used an interactionist mode of development to bridge the gap between research findings and clinical practice. In this model, the tracing of individual developmental sequences is guided by the concept of "goodness of fit" and the related ideas of consonance and dissonance. When the child's capacities, motivations, and temperament are consonant with demands of the environment, this "goodness of fit" potentiates optimal development. Poorness of fit reflects dissonance between individual and environment and increases the probability of maladaptive behavior.

The delineation of temperament is an important facet of psychiatric assessment of children. The clinician may be required to distinguish between what may be extremes of normal temperament and symptoms of psychiatric disorder; or particular temperamental attributes may suggest sources of dissonance between child and environment. Information about temperament can be obtained in the course of the clinician's usual diagnostic procedures. Alertness to the possible significance of temperamental issues directs the clinician's attention to the exploration of the role of specific temperamental attributes, both in the present and in the past. Inquiry is most likely to yield reliable information if the objective details of behavior in specific situations are obtained. While significant temperamental attributes are most likely to be at the extremes, information about the child's behavior in a wide range of circumstances is required to identify a particular behavioral pattern as temperamental. Information obtained from parents is augmented by observing the child and talking with him about *how* he behaves. Reports from teachers and descriptions of behavior during psychological testing are additional sources of data that can be exploited to increase the comprehensiveness and accuracy of the evaluation of temperament in clinical practice.

REFERENCES

Bates, J., Freeland, C., and Lounsbury, M. (1979). Measurement of infant difficultness. *Child Devel.* 50:794–803.

Berger, M. (1985). Temperament and individual differences. In M. Rutter and L. Hersov (Eds.). *Child and Adolescent Psychiatry: Modern Approaches.* London: Blackwell Scientific Pubs.

Buss, A. H., and Plomin, R. (1975). *A Temperament Theory of Personality Development.* New York: Wiley.

Campbell, D. T., and Fisk, D. W. (1959). Convergent and discriminant validation by the multitrait-multimethod matrix. *Psychol. Bull.* 56:81–105.

Carey, W. B. (1972). Clinical applications of infant temperament measurements. *J. Pediatrics* 81:823–28.

———. (1974). Night waking and temperament in infancy. *J. Pediatrics* 84:756–58.

———, and McDevitt, S. C. (1978). Revision of the infant temperament questionnaire. *Pediatrics* 61:735–39.

———, and Baker, D. (1979). Differentiating minimal brain dysfunction and temperament. *Devel. Med. Child Neurol.* 21:765–72.

———, Fox, M., and McDevitt, S. C. (1977). Temperament as a factor in early school adjustment. *Pediatrics* 60:621–24.

Chess, S., and Thomas, A. (1984). *Origins and Evolution of Behavior Disorders from Infancy to Early Adult Life.* New York: Brunner/Mazel.

———, and Birch, H. G. (1966). Distortions in developmental reporting made by parents of behaviorally disturbed children. *J. Am. Acad. Child Psychiatry* 5:226–34.

Dunn, J., and Kendrick, C. (1980). Studying temperament and parent-child interaction: Comparison of interview and direct observation. *Devel. Med. Child Neurol.* 22:484–96.

———, and Kendrick, C. (1982). Temperamental differences, family relationships, and young children's response to change within the family. *Ciba Foundation Symposium* 89:87–105.

Earls, F. (1981). Temperament characteristics and behavior problems in three-year-old children. *J. Nerv. Ment. Dis.* 169:367–73.

Fullard, W., McDevitt, S. C., and Carey, W. B. (1984). Assessing temperament in one- to three-year-old children. *J. Ped. Psychol.* 9:205–17.

Goldsmith, H. H., and Gottesman, I. I. (1981). Origins of variation in behavioral style: A longitudinal study of temperament in young twins. *Child Devel.* 52:91–103.

Gordon, E. M., and Thomas, A. (1967). Children's behavioral style and the teacher's appraisal of their intelligence. *J. School Psychol.* 5:292–300.

Graham, P., Rutter, M., and George, S. (1973). Temperamental characteristics as predictors of behavior disorders in children. *Am. J. Orthopsychiatry* 43:328–39.

Hegvik, R. L., McDevitt, S. C., and Carey, W. B. (1982). The middle childhood temperament questionnaire. *J. Devel. Behav. Pediatrics* 3:197–200.

Hubert, N., et al. (1982). The study of early temperament: Measurement and conceptual issues. *Child Devel.* 53:571–600.

Kagan, J. (1982). Heart rate and heart rate variability as signs of a temperamental dimension in infants. In C. Izard (Ed.). *Measurement of Emotion in Children.* Cambridge: Cambridge University Press.

Keogh, B. (1982). Children's temperament and teacher's decisions. *Ciba Foundation Symposium* 89:269–85.

————, and Pullis, M. E. (1980). Temperament influences on the development of exceptional children. *Advances in Spec. Ed.* 1:239–76.

Kretchmer, E. (1936). *Physique and Character: An Investigation of the Nature of Constitution and the Theory of Temperament.* London: Routledge.

Lerner, R. M., et al. (1982). Assessing the dimensions of temperamental individuality across the life span: The dimensions of temperament survey (DOTS). *Child Devel.* 53:149–59.

Maccoby, E., Snow, M., and Jacklin, C. (1984). Children's dispositions and mother-child interaction at 12 and 18 months. *Devel. Psychol.* 20:459–72.

McDevitt, S. C., and Carey, W. B. (1978). The measurement of temperament in 3–7-year-old children. *J. Child Psychol. Psychiatry* 19:245–53.

Maziade, M., et al. (1985). Value of difficult temperament among 7 year olds in the general population for predicting psychiatric diagnosis at age 12. *Am. J. Psychiatry* 142:943–45.

Matheny, A. P. (1980). Bayley's infant behavior record: Behavioral components and twin analysis. *Child Devel.* 51:1157–67.

————, Brown, A. M., and Wilson, R. S. (1971). Behavioral antecedents of accidental injuries in early childhood: A study of twins *J. Pediatrics* 79:122–24.

Moss, H. A., and Susman, E. J. (1980). Longitudinal study of personality development. In O. G. Brim and J. Kagan (Eds.). *Constancy and Change in Human Development.* Cambridge: Harvard University Press.

Plomin, R., and Rowe, D. C. (1977). A twin study of temperament in young children. *J. Psychol.* 97:107–13.

Pullis, M. E., and Cadwell, J. (1982). The influence of children's temperament characteristics on teachers' decision strategies. *Am. Ed. Res. J.* 19:165–81.

Robbins, L. (1963). The accuracy of parental recall of aspects of child development and of child rearing practices. *J. Abnorm. Soc. Psychol.* 66:261–68.

Rutter, M. (1977). Individual differences. In M. Rutter and L. Hersov (Eds.). *Child Psychiatry: Modern Approaches.* Oxford: Blackwell Scientific Pubs., pp. 3–21.

————. (1978). Family, area and school influences on the genesis of conduct disorder. In L. Hersov et al. (Eds.). *Aggression and Antisocial Behavior in Childhood and Asolescence.* Oxford: Pergamon Press, pp. 95–113.

————. (1982). Temperament: Concepts, issues and problems. *Ciba Foundation Symposium* 89:1–19.

Sheldon, W. H., and Stevens, S. S. (1942). *The Varieties of Temperament.* New York: Harper and Brothers.

Stevenson-Hinde, J., and Simpson, A. E. (1982). Temperament and relationships. *Ciba Foundation Symposium* 89:51–65.

Terestman, N. (1980). Mood quality and intensity in nursery school children as predictors of behavior disorder. *Am. J. Orthopsychiatry* 50:125–38.

Thomas, A., and Chess, S. (1977). *Temperament and Development.* New York: Brunner/Mazel.

————. (1980). *The Dynamics of Psychological Development.* New York: Brunner/Mazel.

————. (1984). Genesis and evolution of behavioral disorders from infancy to early adult life. *Am. J. Psychiatry* 141:1–9.

————. (1986). *Temperament in Clincial Practice.* New York: Guilford Press.

Thomas, A., Chess, S., and Birch, H. G. (1968). *Temperament and Behavior Disorders in Children.* New York: New York University Press.

Thomas, A., et al. (1963). *Behavioral Individuality in Early Childhood.* New York: New York University Press.

———, et al. (1982). A temperament questionnaire for early adult life. *Ed. Psychol. Measurement* 42:593–600.

Torgersen, A. M., and Kringlen, E. (1978). Genetic aspects of temperament differences in infants. *J. Am. Acad. Child Psychiatry* 17:433–44.

Turecki, S., and Tonna, L. (1985). *The Difficult Child.* New York: Bantam.

Wolkind, S., and DeSalis, W. (1982). Infant temperament, maternal mental state and child behavioral problems. *Ciba Foundation Symposium* 89:221–39.

9

EMOTIONAL AND DEVELOPMENTAL PATTERNS IN INFANCY

Stanley I. Greenspan

Recent understanding of both normal and disturbed emotional functioning in infants and young children makes it possible to explore new comprehensive approaches to understanding early development and implementing patterns of well-baby care. The newly delineated Emotional Milestones (Greenspan 1979, 1981; Greenspan and Greenspan 1985) can be added to the well-known sensory-motor and cognitive milestones. The operationalization and assessment of infant-caregiver and family patterns at each developmental phase permits the cross-sectional delineation of adaptive or maladaptive behavior. Furthermore, recent studies of cumulative risk suggest that family and interactive patterns during infancy correlate with later cognitive and behavioral performance at age 4. For example, children with four or more infancy risk factors have a twenty-five-fold increase in the probability of marginal IQ scores, in comparison to children with only a few risk factors (Sameroff et al. in press).

This chapter will outline an approach to emotional development, including a guide for screening. Basic concepts relevant to considering emotional factors as part of routine developmental care include: 1) the importance of considering multiple lines of development (as compared to only physical or cognitive); 2) the components of a comprehensive approach; and 3) the Developmental Structuralist approach to the Emotional Milestones.

MULTIPLE LINES OF DEVELOPMENT

It is perhaps self-evident that the infant develops along multiple lines—physical, cognitive, social-emotional, and familial, but this perspective is not always put into practice. An intervention strategy that takes into account the existence of multiple lines of development will best facilitate development in all areas of the infant's life. For example, babies who have been nutritionally compromised improve physically and gain weight more efficaciously when nutrition is provided together with adequate social interaction. A baby born with an auditory or tactile hypersensitivity will tend to withdraw when talked to or held. A clinical approach would combine gentle exposure to the potentially noxious stimuli in low doses, with soothing experiences, such as rocking and comforting sounds. At the same time, recognizing the youngster's tendency to withdraw, the clinical staff might formulate special patterns of care that would help the parents woo the baby into greater emotional relatedness.

In contrast, an approach that focused only on cognitive stimulation might attempt to enliven a withdrawn, seemingly slow baby through sensorimotor stimulation. Yet if a youngster actually has an undiagnosed sensory hypersensitivity, the child could become even more irritable and less available for human relationships as a consequence of this type of intervention.

Failure to consider multiple lines of development in infancy may lead to impairment at a later age. In general, a youngster who responds to human stimulation with irritability, rigidity, and gaze aversion may very well be alert and show interest in the inanimate world with inanimate stimulation. From the point of view of physical and neurological development, such a child might develop adequate cognition during the first 12 to 18 months. However, the impairment of human relationships and capacity to organize and differentiate animate experience (coping and adapting skills) might not become clearly noticeable until the latter part of the second or early in the third year. It is during this period, when relationships with peers become important, that complaints related to unsocialized behavior or patterns of withdrawal (refusal to play with others) are heard from parents.

COMPONENTS OF A COMPREHENSIVE CLINICAL APPROACH

A comprehensive clinical approach includes the parents, other family members, and relevant social structures. This approach would explore, for example, the parents' predominant attitudes and feelings, family relationships, and other crucial contextual factors, such as the system of health and mental health services and relevant community structures. More isolated intervention strategies, while working to stimulate an infant's cognitive capacities, may limit other involvement with parents to help only with issues such as food and housing.

A comprehensive clinical approach must begin with the assessment of a number of conceptually consistent categories that take into account multiple lines of development in a longitudinal manner. This approach attempts to deal with the full complexity of clinical phenomena and, therefore, has methodological limitations for research. For example, the ideal assessment protocol would define a limited number of key outcome criteria and would specify reliable and valid instruments to assess them. The variables assessed to plan interventions would differ from variables employed to assess outcome, in order to avoid the possibility of "teaching the test." However, a clinical orientation demands a detailed study of a minimum number of key clusters of personality variables for both clinical planning and assessment. Therefore, rather than prior selection of a few variables, the following six core areas of assessment must in one way or another be described.

1. *Prenatal and Perinatal Variables.* These variables all have some impact on the infant's constitutional status and development tendencies, although the extent of the impact is unknown. The prenatal variables include: familial genetic patterns; mother's status during pregnancy, including nutrition, physical health, and illness, personality functioning, mental health and degree of stress; characteristics of familial and social support systems; characteristics of the pregnancy; and the delivery process including complications, time in various stages, and the infant's status after birth. The perinatal variables include maternal perceptions of her infant, maternal reports of the emerging daily routine, and observations of the infant and maternal-infant interaction.

2. *Parent, Family, and Environmental Variables.* These include evaluations of parents, other family members, and individuals who relate closely to the family, as to their personality organization and developmental needs, child-rearing capacity, and family interaction patterns. Evaluations of the support system (extended family, friends, and community agencies) used or available to the family and of the total home environment (both animate and inanimate components) are also included.

3. *Primary Caregiver and Caregiver-Infant/Child Relationship Variables.* Evaluations in this area focus on the interaction between the infant and his or her important nurturing figures. Included are the quality of mutual rhythm, feedback, and capacity for joint pleasure, as well as their flexibility in tolerating tension and being able to return to a state of intimacy. Later in development, capacities to experience differentiation, form complex emotional and behavioral patterns, and construct representations are important.

4. *Infant Variables: Physical, Neurologic, and Physiologic.* These variables include the infant's genetic background and status immediately after birth, including his general physical integrity (size, weight, general health), neurologic integrity, physiologic tendencies, rhythmic patterns, and levels of alertness and activity. Special attention should be paid to the infant's physical integrity and how this factor could foster or hinder the child's capacities to experience internal and external stimulation, regulate internal and external experience to reach a state of homeostasis, develop human relationships, interact in cause-and-effect reciprocal patterns, form complex behavioral and emotional patterns, and construct representations to guide behavior and feelings.

5. *Infant Variables: Sensory, Motor, and Cognitive.* The variables in this category include the development, differentiation, and integration of the infant's motor and sensory systems, and the relationship of the infant's sensorimotor development to his cognitive development.

6. *Infant Variables: Formation and Internalization of Human Relationships.* The fol-

lowing variables involve the interrelationships and capacities for relationships among the infant, parents, and other family members. These early relationships help the infant develop the capacity for a range of emotions (dependency to assertiveness) in the context of a sequence of organizational stages. These stages include the capacity for purposeful interactions, complex, organized social and emotional patterns, constructing representations, and differentiating internal representations along self versus non-self time and space dimensions.

There also are variables that focus on the mother and involve her capacity to reach out and foster attachment; provide physical comfort and care; perceive basic states of pleasure and discomfort in her infant; respond with balanced empathy, that is, without either overidentification or isolation of feeling; perceive and respond flexibly and differently to the infant's cues; foster organized complex interactions; and support representational elaboration and differentiation.

DEVELOPMENT STRUCTURALIST APPROACH TO MILESTONES

Aspects of physical, sensorimotor and impersonal cognitive development are already included in many approaches to infants and their families. Comprehensive clinical approaches to diagnosis and preventive intervention require equal attention to emotional, social, and socially relevant cognitive development.

The focus on the infant and his or her family from multiple aspects of development has allowed new concepts of developmental stages that focus on the infant's social and emotional functioning. These milestones are based on an impressive number of studies of normal and disturbed infant development. A brief overview of an approach to developmental stages, with a table summarizing the stages of early development, will illustrate the specificity with which developmental progress can be followed.

Although there are no large-scale studies of infants' and young children's affective patterns at different ages, there is extensive literature on the emotional development of presumed normal infants. Interestingly, during the past fifteen years there has been considerably greater documentation of normal emotional development in infants than of any other age group.

It is now well documented that the infant is capable, either at birth or shortly thereafter, of organizing experience in an adaptive fashion. He or she can respond to pleasure and displeasure (Lipsitt 1966); change behavior as a function of its consequences (Gewirtz 1965, 1969); form intimate bonds and make visual discriminations (Klaus and Kennell 1976; Meltzoff and Moore 1977); organize cycles and rhythms such as sleep-wake and alertness states (Sander 1962); evince a variety of affects or affect proclivities (Tomkins 1963; Izard 1978; Ekman 1972); and demonstrate organized social responses in conjunction with increasing neurophysiologic organization (Emde, Gaensbauer, and Harmon 1976). From the early months, the infant demonstrates a unique capacity to enter into complex social and affective interactions (Stern 1974a,b, 1977; Brazelton et al. 1974). This empirically documented view of the infant is generally consistent with Freud's early hypotheses (1911) and Hartmann's postulation (1939) of an early, undifferentiated, organizational matrix. That the organization of experience broadens during the early months of life to reflect increases in the capacity to experience and tolerate a range of stimuli, including stable responses to social interaction and personal configurations, is also consistent with recent empirical data (Emde, Gaensbauer, and Harmon 1976; Escalona 1968; Stern 1974a,b; Sander 1962; Brazelton, Koslowski, and Main 1974; Murphy and Moriarty 1976).

Increasingly complex patterns continue to emerge as the infant further develops, as indicated by complex emotional responses such as surprise (Charlesworth 1969) and affiliation; wariness and fear (Ainsworth, Bell, and Stayton 1974; Sroufe and Waters 1977); exploration and refueling patterns (Mahler, Pine, and Bergman 1975); behavior suggesting functional understanding of objects (Werner and Kaplan 1963); and the eventual emergence of symbolic capacities (Piaget 1962; Gouin-Decarie 1965; Bell 1970).

In these studies there is a consensus (and there are no dissenting studies) that by 2 to 4 months of age at the latest, and often much earlier, healthy infants are capable of responding to their caregivers' faces, smiles, and voices with brightening or alerting and often with a smile and reciprocal vocalizations (suggesting positive affect) as well as other reciprocal responses. Furthermore, the infant-caregiver interaction patterns become progressively more complex as development proceeds.

In addition to the studies on normal infant emotional development, important observations on disturbed development fill out the emerging picture of new integrated milestones. Interestingly, the study of psychopathology in infancy is a new area, even though the historical foundation for identifying disturbances in the early years of life is very impressive. Constitutional and maturational patterns that influenced the formation of early relationship patterns were already noted in the early 1900s, with descriptions of "babies of nervous inheritance who exhaust their mothers" and infants with "excessive nerve activity and a functionally immature" nervous system (Cameron 1919).

Winnicott, who as a pediatrician in the 1930s began describing the environment's role in early relationship problems (1931), was followed in the 1940s by the well-known studies describing the severe developmental disturbances of infants brought up in institutions or in other situations of emotional deprivation (Lowrey 1940; Hunt 1941; Bakwin 1942; Spitz 1945; Bowlby 1951). Spitz's films resulted in laws in the United States prohibiting care of infants in institutions.

Both the role of individual differences in the infant based on constitutional maturational and early interactional patterns, and the "nervous" infants described by Rachford in 1905 and Cameron in 1919, again became a focus of inquiry, as evidenced by the observations of Burlingham and Freud (1942); Bergman and Escalona's descriptions of infants with "unusual sensitivities" (1949); Murphy and Moriarty's description of patterns of vulnerability (1976); Cravioto and DeLicardie's descriptions of the role of infant individual differences in malnutrition (1973); and the impressive emerging empirical literature on infants (Sander 1962; Brazelton, Koslowski, and Main 1974; Lipsitt 1966; Stern 1974a,b; Emde, Gaensbauer, and Harmon 1976; Gewirtz 1961; and Rheingold 1966, 1969).

We undertook an in-depth study of normal and disturbed developmental patterns in infancy in order to develop a systematic comprehensive classification of adaptive and maladaptive infant and family patterns. Table 9.1 summarizes the observations of the adaptive and maladaptive infant and family patterns (Greenspan 1979, 1981; Greenspan, Lourie, and Nover 1979; Greenspan and Lourie 1981).

The capacities described by the stages are all present in some rudimentary form in very early infancy. The sequence presented suggests not when these capacities begin, but when they become relatively prominent in organizing behavior and furthering development.

The first stage is the achievement of homeostasis, that is, self-regulation and emerging interest in the world through sight, sound, smell, touch, and taste. Once the infant has achieved some capacity for regulation in the context of engaging the world and central nervous system (CNS) maturation is increasing between 2 and 4 months of age, the infant becomes more attuned to social and interpersonal interaction. There is greater ability to respond to the external environment and to form a special relationship with significant primary caregivers.

A second, closely related stage is formation of a human attachment. If an affective and relatively pleasurable attachment (an investment in the human, animate world) is formed, then with growing maturational abilities, the infant develops complex patterns of communication in the context of this primary human relationship. Parallel with development of the infant's relationship to the inanimate world where basic schemes of causality (Piaget 1962) are being developed, the infant becomes capable of complicated human communications (Brazelton, Koslowski, and Main 1974; Stern 1974a; Tennes et al. 1972; Charlesworth 1969).

When there have been distortions in the attachment process, as occurs when a mother responds in a mechanical, remote manner or projects some of her own dependent feelings onto her infant, the infant may not learn to appreciate causal relationships between people at the level of compassionate and intimate feelings. This situation can occur even though causality seems to be developing in terms of the inanimate world and the impersonal human world.

Causal relationships are established between the infant and the primary caregiver, as evidenced in the infant's growing ability to discriminate primary caregivers from others. The infant also becomes able to differentiate his or her own actions from their consequences—affectively, somatically, behaviorally, and interpersonally. Usually by 8 months of age or earlier, the process of differentiation begins along a number of developmental lines including sensorimotor integration, affects, and relationships.

The third stage is somatopsychologic differentiation, indicating processes occurring at the somatic (sensorimotor) and emerging psychological levels. (In this con-

TABLE 9.1 Developmental Basis for Psychopathology and Adaptation in Infancy and Early Childhood

Stage-Specific Tasks and Capacities	Capacities		Environment (Caregiver)	
	Adaptive	*Maladaptive (Pathologic)*	*Adaptive*	*Maladaptive*
Homeostasis (0–3 mo) (self-regulation and interest in the world)	Internal regulation (harmony) and balanced interest in world	Unregulated (e.g., hyperexcitable). Withdrawn (apathetic)	Invested, dedicated, protective, comforting, predictable; engaging and interesting	Unavailable, chaotic, dangerous, abusive; hypostimulating or hyperstimulating; dull
Attachment (2–7 mo)	Rich, deep, multisensory emotional investment in animate world (especially with primary caregivers)	Total lack of, or nonaffective, shallow, impersonal, involvement (e.g., autistic patterns) in animate world	In love and woos infant to "fall in love"; affective multimodality pleasurable involvement	Emotionally distant, aloof, and/or impersonal (highly ambivalent)
Somatopsychologic differentiation (3–10 mo) (purposeful, cause and effect signaling or communication)	Flexible, wide-ranging affective multisystem contingent (reciprocal) interactions (especially with primary caregivers)	Behavior and affects random and or chaotic, or narrow, rigid, and stereotyped	Reads and responds contingently to infant's communications across multiple sensory and affective systems	Ignores infant's communications (e.g., overly intrusive, preoccupied, or depressed) or misreads infant's communication (e.g., projection)
Behavioral organization initiative, and internalization (9–24 mo)	Complex, organized, assertive, innovative, integrated behavioral and emotional patterns	Fragmented, stereotyped, and polarized behavior and emotions (e.g., withdrawn, compliant, hyperaggressive, or disorganized toddler)	Admiring of toddler's initiative and autonomy, yet available, tolerant and firm; follows toddler's lead and helps him organize diverse behavioral and affective elements	Overly intrusive, controlling; fragmented, fearful (especially of toddler's autonomy); abruptly and prematurely "separates"

Representational capacity, differentiation, and consolidation (1½–4 yr) (the use of ideas to guide language, pretend play, and behavior and eventually thinking and planning)	Formation and elaboration of internal representations (imagery) Organization and differentiation of imagery pertaining to self and nonself; emergence of cognitive insight Stabilization of mood and gradual emergence of basic personality functions	No representational (symbolic) elaboration; behavior and affect concrete, shallow, and polarized; sense of self and other fragmented and undifferentiated or narrow and rigid; reality testing, impulse regulation, mood stabilization compromised or vulnerable (e.g., borderline psychotic and severe character problems)	Emotionally available to phase-appropriate regressions and dependency needs; reads, responds to, and encourages symbolic elaboration across emotional behavioral domains (e.g., love, pleasure, assertion) while fostering gradual reality orientation and internalization of limits	Fearful of or denies phase-appropriate needs; engages child only in concrete (nonsymbolic) models generally or in certain realms (e.g., around pleasure) and or misreads or responds noncontingently or nonrealistically to emerging communications (e.g., undermines reality orientation; overly permissive or punitive
Capacity for limited extended representational systems and multiple extended representational systems (middle childhood through adolescence)	Enhanced and eventually optimal flexibility to conserve and transform complex and organized representations of experience in the context of expanded relationship patterns and phase-expected developmental tasks	Derivative representational capacities limited or defective, as are latency and adolescent relationships and coping capacities	Supports complex, phase- and age-appropriate experiential and interpersonal development (i.e., into triangular and post-triangular patterns)	Conflicted over child's age-appropriate propensities (e.g., competitiveness, pleasure orientation, growing competence, assertiveness, and self-sufficiency); becomes aloof or maintains symbiotic tie; withdraws from or overengages in competitive or pleasurable strivings

Source: S. I. Greenspan. Psychopathology and adaptation in infancy and early childhood: Principles of clinical diagnosis and preventive intervention. *Clinical Infant Reports*, No. 1. (New York: International Universities Press, 1981).

text, *psychological* refers to higher level mental processes characterized by the capacity to form internal representations or symbols as a way to organize experience.) While schemes of causality are being established in the infant's relationship to the interpersonal world, it is not at all clear whether these schemes exist at an organized representational or symbolic level. Rather, they appear to exist mainly at a somatic level (Greenspan 1979), even though the precursors of representational capacities are observed. Some are perhaps even prenatally determined (Lourie 1971).

With appropriate reading of cues and systematic differential responses, the infant's or toddler's behavioral repertoire becomes complicated and communications take on more organized, meaningful configurations. By 12 months of age, the infant is connecting behavioral units into larger organizations as he or she exhibits complex emotional responses such as affiliation, wariness and fear (Ainsworth, Bell, and Stayton 1974; Sroufe and Waters 1977). As the toddler approaches the second year of life, in the context of the practicing subphase of the development of individuation (Mahler, Pine, and Bergman 1975), there is an increased capacity for forming original behavioral schemes (Piaget 1962) and imitative activity and intentionality.

A type of learning through imitation evidenced in earlier development now seems to assume a more dominant role. As imitations take on a more integrated personal form, it appears the toddler is adopting or internalizing attributes of his or her caregivers.

To describe these new capacities it is useful to consider a fourth stage, that of behavioral organization, initiative, and internalization. As the toddler approaches the end of the second year, internal sensations and unstable images become organized in a mental representational form that can be evoked and is somewhat stable (Piaget 1962; Bell 1970; Gouin-Decarie 1965). While this capacity is fragile between 16 and 24 months, it soon becomes a dominant mode in organizing the child's behavior.

A fifth stage is the formation of mental representations or ideas. The capacity for "object permanence" is relative and goes through a series of stages (Gouin-Decarie 1965); it refers to the toddler's ability to search for hidden inanimate objects. Representational capacity refers to the ability to organize and evoke internal organized multisensory experiences of the animate object. The capacities to represent animate and inanimate experiences are related and depend both on central nervous system myelination and appropriate experiences. The process of "internalization" can be thought of as an intermediary process. Internalized experiences eventually become sufficiently organized to be considered representations.

At a representational level, the child again develops capacities for elaboration, integration, and differentiation. Just as causal schemes previously were developed at a somatic and behavioral level, now they are developed at a representational level. The child begins to elaborate and eventually differentiate those feelings, thoughts, and events that emanate from within and those that emanate from others. The child begins to differentiate the actions of others from his or her own. This process gradually forms the basis for the differentiation of self-representations from the external world, animate and inanimate, and also provides the basis for such crucial personality functions as knowing what is real from unreal, impulse and mood regulation, and the capacity to focus attention and to concentrate on learning and interaction.

The capacity for differentiating internal representations becomes consolidated as object constancy is established (Mahler, Pine, and Bergman 1975). In middle childhood, representational capacity becomes reinforced with the child's ability to develop derivative representational systems tied to the original representation and to transform them in accord with adaptive and defensive goals. This permits greater flexibility in dealing with perceptions, feelings, thoughts, and emerging ideals. Substages for these capacities include representational differentiation, the consolidation of representational capacity, and the capacity for forming limited derivative representational systems and multiple derivative representational systems (structural learning [Greenspan 1979]).

At each of these stages, pathological as well as adaptive formations are possible. These may be considered as relative compromises in the range, depth, stability, and personal uniqueness of the experiential organization consolidated at each stage. The infant can form adaptive patterns of regulation in the earliest stages of development. Internal states are harmoniously regulated and the infant is free to invest in the animate and inanimate world, thereby setting the basis for rich emotional attachments to primary caregivers. On the other hand, if regulatory processes are not functioning properly and the infant is either hyposensitive or hypersensitive to sensations, he or she may evidence homeostatic difficulties. From relatively minor compromises, such as a tendency to withdraw or become hyperexcitable under stress, to a major deviation such as overwhelming avoidance of the animate world, the degrees to which the infant, even in the first months of life, achieves a less than optimal adaptive structural organization can be observed.

Thus, the early attachments can be warm and engaging or shallow, insecure, and limited in their affective tone. There are differences between an infant who reads the signals of the caregivers and responds in a rich, meaningful way to multiple aspects of the communications (with multiple affects and behavioral communications) and one who can respond only within a narrow range of affect (for example, protest) or who cannot respond at all in a contingent or reciprocal manner (for example, the seemingly apathetic, withdrawn, and depressed child who responds only to internal cues). As the toddler becomes behaviorally more organized and complex patterns appear that reflect originality and initiative in the context of the separation and individuation subphase of development, we can observe those toddlers who manifest this full adaptive capacity. They may be compared with others who are stereotyped in their behavioral patterns (reflect no originality or intentionality), who remain fragmented (never connect pieces of behavior into more complicated patterns), or who evidence polarities of affect, showing no capacity to integrate emotions (the chronic negativistic aggressive toddler who cannot show interest, curiosity, or love).

The child who can organize, integrate, and differentiate a rich range of affective and ideational life can be distinguished from one who remains either without representational capacity or undifferentiated (that is, one who has deficits in reality testing, impulse control, and focused concentration), or who may form and differentiate self and object representations only at the expense of extreme compromises in the range of tolerated experience (for example, the schizoid child who withdraws from relationships). Similar adaptive or maladaptive structural organizations can be observed in later childhood (the triangular phase), latency, and adolescence.

A more detailed discussion of this framework, including principles of prevention and intervention, is available (Greenspan 1979, 1981). It should also be pointed out that, through videotaped analyses of infant-caregiver interactions (Greenspan and Lieberman 1980), these patterns evidence temporal stability and can be reliably rated and new raters trained and kept at high levels of reliability (Hofheimer et al. 1981, 1984; Poisson, Lieberman, and Greenspan 1981; Poisson et al. 1983).

The ability to monitor developmental progress with explicit guidelines facilitates the early identification of those infants, young children, and families who are progressing in an inappropriate or less than optimal manner. For example, it is now possible to evaluate infants who continue to have difficulty regulating their states and developing the capacity for focused interest in their immediate environments, or who fail to develop a positive emotional interest in their caregivers. It is also possible to assess an infant's difficulty in learning cause-and-effect interactions and complex emotional and social patterns, or inability, by age 2 to 3, to create symbols to guide emotions and behavior. In exploring the factors that may be contributing to less than optimal patterns of development, the focus on multiple aspects of development offers many advantages. Some infants, for example, show evidence of a motor delay because of familial patterns where explorativeness and the practice of the motor system is discouraged. In other infants there may be a maturational variation that, together with family patterns, is contributing to a motor lag. In still other cases, genetic maturational factors may completely explain the delay. Even with a symptom as common as a motor lag, unless all aspects of all contributing factors are explored, it is likely that important contributing factors will go unrecognized. The focus on multiple aspects of development, in the context of clearly delineated developmental and emotional landmarks, opens the door to a comprehensive assessment, diagnosis, and preventive intervention strategies.

The following section will present a guide to screening for the Emotional Milestones in the context of brief screening for sensorimotor, cognitive, and language development, as well.

EMOTIONAL HEALTH CHECKLIST: CHARTING EMOTIONAL MILESTONES FOR INFANTS AND CHILDREN

This section highlights some of the infant's unique abilities in each stage of development. It helps to identify the steps involved in an infant's learning to see the world as comforting, interesting, and loving, as well as his learning to create ideas to integrate dependency needs with assertiveness, curiosity, and greater autonomy. While watching for particular steps, it is important to remember that infants also enjoy many other things. Even though a parent will want to encourage a baby to smile or respond, the baby also needs time to relax, look around, or just suck on his fist if he wants to. When an infant enjoys his new abilities only some of the time, he is showing both his mastery of them and his selectivity. So, although over time one should expect an infant to be more vocal when one talks to her or initiates greater interaction, parents and professionals should not expect her to do so all the time.

As more of an infant's new abilities unfold, the earliest accomplishments continue to be refined. It is often useful to review the chart from the beginning even if the child is not a newborn. When expected progress is not occurring, however, it is especially important to review the earlier milestones for those areas of functioning in which there are lags. Noting which expected milestones are not occurring and the degree of the lag will help to identify areas deserving of constructive practice and understanding.

General Parenting Patterns
(By History and/or Direct Observation)

1. *Tend pleasurably to engage their infant* in a relationship (by looking, vocalizing, gentle touching, etc.), rather than to ignore their infant (by being depressed, aloof, preoccupied, withdrawn, indifferent, etc.).   Yes/No/Unsure

2. *Tend to comfort their infant*, especially when he or she is upset (by relaxed, gentle, firm holding, rhythmic vocal or visual contact, etc.), rather than to make their infant more tense (by being overly worried, tense or anxious, or mechanical or anxiously over- or under-stimulating).   Yes/No/Unsure

3. *Tend to find appropriate levels of stimulation to interest their infant* in the world (by being interesting, alert and responsive, including offering appropriate levels of sounds, sights, and touch—including the caregiver's face—and appropriate games and toys, etc.), rather than to be hyperstimulating and intrusive (e.g., picking at and poking or shaking infant excessively to gain his attention).   Yes/No/Unsure

General Parenting Patterns (*continued*)

4. *Tend to read and respond to their infant's emotional signals and needs in most emotional areas* (e.g., respond to desire for closeness as well as need to be assertive, explorative, and independent), rather than either to misread signals or to respond to only one emotional need (e.g., can hug when baby reaches out, but hover over baby and can't encourage assertive exploration or vice versa).   Yes/No/Unsure

5. *Tend to encourage their infant* to move forward in development, rather than to overprotect, "hold on," or infantilize; for example,   Yes/No/Unsure
   a) help baby crawl, vocalize, and gesture by actively responding to infant's initiative and encouragement (rather than overanticipating infant's needs and doing everything for infant);
   b) help toddler make shift from proximal, physical dependency (e.g., being held) to feeling secure while being independent (for example, keep in verbal and visual contact with toddler as he or she builds a tower across the room);
   c) help 2- to 3-year-old child shift from motor discharge and gestural ways of relating to the use of "ideas" through encouraging pretend play (imagination) and language around emotional themes (for example, get down on floor and play out dolls hugging each other, separating from each other, or soldiers fighting with each other);
   d) help 3- to 4-year-old take responsibility for behavior and deal with reality, rather than "giving in all the time."

General Infant Tendencies (All Ages)

1. Is able to be calm and/or calm down and not be excessively irritable, clinging, active, or panicked.   Yes/No/Unsure

2. Is able to take an interest in sights, sounds, and people and is not excessively withdrawn, apathetic, unresponsive.   Yes/No/Unsure

3. Is able to focus his or her attention and not to be excessively distractable.   Yes/No/Unsure

4. Enjoys a range of sounds including high and low pitch, loud and soft, and different rhythms and is not upset or confused by sounds.   Yes/No/Unsure

General Infant Tendencies (*continued*)

5. Enjoys various sights, including reasonably bright lights,   Yes/No/Unsure
   visual designs, facial gestures, moving objects and is not
   upset or confused by various sights.

6. Enjoys being touched (on face, arms, legs, stomach, trunk,   Yes/No/Unsure
   and back) and bathed and clothed and is not bothered by
   things touching his or her skin.

7. Enjoys movements in space (being held and moved up and   Yes/No/Unsure
   down, side to side, etc.), does not get upset with movement or does not crave excessive movement.

8. Enjoys a range of age appropriate foods and is not both-   Yes/No/Unsure
   ered (e.g., with abdominal pains, skin rashes or other
   symptoms) by any age-appropriate, healthy food as part of
   a balanced diet.

9. Is comfortable and asymptomatic around household odors   Yes/No/Unsure
   and materials and is not bothered by any routine levels of
   household odors such as cleaning materials, paint, oil or
   gas fumes, pesticides, plastics, composite woods (e.g., ply-
   wood), synthetic fabrics (e.g., polyester), etc.

SUMMARY

This chapter has presented the rationale for an in-depth emotional approach to infants to complement traditional developmental approaches. It suggested a brief screening outline to facilitate attention to emotional factors. The framework presented here, both theoretical and practical, may also prove useful for guiding the comprehensive clinical evaluations that are indicated when an infant's emotional progress lags or shifts into a disordered configuration. Careful history taking, clinical interviews, observations of infant-caregiver and family interaction, and formal testing of sensory/motor and cognitive abilities will help the clinician assess the following: 1) if the infant and family have reached a certain emotional milestone, like attachment, purposeful communication, or representational capacities; and 2) if there are constrictions in the emotional domains engaged at that level. Can the intentional 8-month-old, for example, initiate dependency (reaching out to be cuddled), assertive curiosity (exploring Daddy's mouth) as well as anger and protest (looking Mom in the eye and throwing the food on the floor), or are the intentional patterns limited only to dependency, with assertiveness and anger being dealt with at more primitive levels.

Determining overall developmental level and behavioral and emotional range at that level (see *The Clinical Interview of the Child*, Greenspan 1981) helps the clinician pinpoint the nature of the psychopathology. Symptoms such as sleep problems,

| | From History | | | | If during health visit there is opportunity to observe this function | |
	On Time and Present Now	Late But Present Now	Not Present Now- Present Earlier	Has Never Been Present	Present	Absent
I. BY 4 MONTHS: Calming down and taking an interest in the world, and falling in love (as illustrated by a special interest and joy in the caregiver).						
Primary-Emotional: Responds to environment by brightening to *sights* (by alerting, calming and focusing on objects rather than ignoring or becoming overexcited by bright lights or interesting objects)						
Responds to environment by brightening to *sounds* (same as above)						
Looks at person with great interest						
Responds to social overtures with some vocalization, smile, arms or leg movements						
Emotional: Looks at a person with a special joyful smile						
Joyfully smiles when spoken to						
Joyfully smiles in response to interesting facial expressions						
Vocalizes back when spoken to						
Can maintain focused interest on caregiver (e.g., looking, listening, and showing some pleasure) for 1 minute or more						
Able to calm down when comforted						
Can sleep for four hours or more at night						
Enjoys touch (e.g., stroking on arms, legs, stomach)						
Enjoys being cuddled and held firmly						
Cognitive, Sensory or Motor						
Shows selective attention (special interest) in some sights or sounds						
Coos with two or more different sounds						
Enjoys moderate movement in space (up and down, side to side)						

and neither gets upset with gentle movement nor craves excessive movement

Easily follows moving object or person

Turns head in the direction of a pleasant sound (rattle or voice)

Holds and waves a small rattle

When quiet and alert, hands are mostly open

Lifts head by leaning on elbows while on stomach

Holds head steady when sitting supported on your lap

II. BY 8 MONTHS: Communicates intentionally (cause and effect) and begins to learn how people and things work.

Primary-Emotional: Initiates simple interaction (e.g., expectantly looks for the caregiver to respond to his facial expressions) and responds to gestures with gestures in return (e.g., when you go to pick her up she responds by raising her arms and leaning forward)

Emotional: Initiates joy and pleasure (woos caregiver spontaneously)

Initiates comforting (reaches up to be held)

Responds to simple social games with pleasure, such as peek-a-boo or pat-a-cake, smiles or laughs when you do something silly like duck your head or pretend to sneeze

Shows assertiveness by reaching out for or going after an interesting toy that was taken away or put out of reach

Shows special interest in and cautiousness toward new people or unusual objects (e.g., usually examines from a distance before approaching)

Cognitive, Sensory, Motor or Language

Can focus on toy, object or person for 2 or more minutes

Explores a new toy (e.g., turns it to look at its different parts, mouthes, shakes, and bangs toy on a surface)

Likes to make things happen (bangs spoon on a pot, bangs two toys together, knocks down a stand-up toy)

Follows an object as it goes out of sight (e.g., mother's face, food

(continued)

	From History				If during health visit there is opportunity to observe this function	
	On Time and Present Now	Late But Present Now	Not Present Now–Present Earlier	Has Never Been Present	Present	Absent
or a toy that falls to the floor) and searches for it when out of sight (looking under a chair for a favorite ball)						
Reaches out and grasps an object or toy on a table while on your lap						
Can pick up small objects like a Cheerio or raisin						
Can drink from a cup or glass held by an adult						
Can imitate sounds (e.g., tongue click, fake cough, raspberry)						
Makes sounds from the front of mouth (da, ba, ma) and begins repeating them						
Rolls back to stomach						
Sits unsupported and plays from that position						
Can creep or crawl						
Can pull to stand in the crib or holding onto furniture						
III. BY 12 MONTHS: Beginning to develop a complex sense of self by organizing behavior and emotion.						
Primary-Emotional: Initiates complex interactions (e.g., hands parent toy to make it go, rolls a ball back and forth, uses gesture or vocalization to communicate the need for a desired object or food)						
Emotional: Uses complex behavior to establish closeness (e.g., pulls your leg *and* reaches up to be picked up)						
Asserts self through organized behavior such as pointing and vocalizing at desired toy or exploring for desired objects or people						
Responds to limits set by your voice or gesture						
Recovers from distress after ten to fifteen minutes						

Seems to know how to get you to react (which actions make you laugh, which actions make you mad)

Cognitive, Sensory, Motor or Language

Plays on own in a focused organized manner for ten minutes or more

Can copy simple gestures (waving bye-bye, shaking head, "no")

Uses hands and eyes more than mouth to examine a new object or toy

Looks at simple pictures in a book with your help

Can drop objects such as blocks or toys into a container

Can feed self small finger food

Can chew a Cheerio without choking

Throws a ball forward

Walks holding on to furniture

Understands simple words or commands like "shoe" or "give me a kiss"

Uses sounds for specific objects, like "ba-ba" for bath or "dup" for cup

Jabbers

IV. BY 18 MONTHS: Continues to develop a complex sense of self by intentional planning and exploration.

Primary-Emotional: Shows intentional planning and exploration in interactions and play. For example, chooses a toy, finds mommy and indicates with word or gesture she is the play partner

Communicates needs and feelings from across the room as well as close up, in gesture, or words, with touch or holding (e.g., can look at caregiver's admiring glance or hear reassuring word, smile happily and return to organized play, or indicate interest in having caregiver join in play)

Emotional: Uses gestures and vocalizations to get parent's interest and a sense of closeness from across the room

Can easily ask for help from adults with either play activities or to get food, etc.

(continued)

	On Time and Present Now	Late But Present Now	From History Not Present Now-Present Earlier	Has Never Been Present	If during health visit there is opportunity to observe this function Present	Absent

Balances a desire for independence and closeness (e.g., explores across the room and then comes back for a touch or cuddle)

Can show assertiveness by organizing complex behavior as meet own needs (e.g., going to refrigerator, opening door and pointing to food) or by refusing to comply with an adult or another child by saying "no" and doing something else

Can protest or be angry using voice and gestures, without having to cry, hit, or bite

Can recover from anger or upset within fifteen minutes

Can use role playing as part of complex play (e.g., cooking with pots or washing dishes in play sink, driving toy fire engine with fireman's hat on)

Cognitive, Sensory, Motor or Language

Searches for a desired object such as a toy in more than one place

Plays on own in a focused organized manner for fifteen minutes or more

Shows intentional planning and exploration by choosing a toy and then going to get it for play and exploration

Uses objects such as stuffed animals, toy telephone, etc., in play (e.g., putting animal to sleep, pretending to talk on the phone)

Can imitate something seen a few minutes earlier

Recognizes many simple pictures in a favorite book

Recognizes pictures of familiar objects (such as a dog, a baby, a ball, etc.)

V. BY 2–2½ YEARS: Creating new feelings and ideas.

Primary: Engages in pretend play (feeds doll and puts doll to sleep, has cars or trucks race)

Uses words and/or gestures to express what he wants

Emotional: Uses words or gestures to get you to participate in his play (e.g., "come here," "hold dolly")

Uses words to communicate desire for closeness ("hug," etc.)

Uses simple repetitive play sequences to indicate interest in closeness (e.g., dolls being cuddled)

Uses words for expressions of assertiveness ("me went!", "give me")

Uses simple repetitive play sequences to indicate interest in assertiveness (a truck race)

Communicates anger with gesture, word or word-like sounds with insistence that you comply

Recovers from anger or temper tantrum after ten minutes

Cognitive, Sensory, Motor or Language

Can play in a focused organized manner twenty minutes or more

Searches for favorite toy where it was the day before

Engages in pretend play alone

Can do simple shape puzzles with a few pieces

Plays with blocks with some order or design (builds a tower or lines up blocks in a train)

Can copy a circle

Catches a large ball from a couple of feet away using arms and hands

Balances momentarily on one foot

Jumps with both feet off the ground

Can walk up steps putting two feet on each step before going to the next

Can run

Uses simple two-word sentences ("go bye-bye," "more milk")

Understands simple questions ("Is mommy home?")

VI. BY 3–3½ YEARS: Emotional Thinking.

(continued)

	From History				If during health visit there is opportunity to observe this function	
	On Time and Present Now	Late But Present Now	Not Present Now-Present Earlier	Has Never Been Present	Present	Absent

Primary: Pretend play that conveys human dramas becomes more complex, so that one pretend sequence leads to another (e.g., instead of repetition where the doll goes to bed, gets up, goes to bed, etc., the doll goes to bed, gets up, and then gets dressed; or the cars race, crash, and then go to get fixed)

Knows what's real and what isn't (e.g., knows that cartoons are "pretend")

Emotional: Uses another person's help and some toys to play out complex pretend drama dealing with closeness, nurturing, or caretaking (taking care of a stuffed animal or doll that has fallen down and hurt itself)

Uses another person's help and some toys to play out pretend drama dealing with assertiveness, exploration, or aggression (e.g., a truck race, monsters and soldiers fighting, a trip to grandma's house)

Follows rules

Remains calm and focused for thirty minutes or more

Feels optimistic and confident

Realizes how behavior, thoughts and feelings can be related to consequences (if behaves nicely, makes you pleased; if naughty, gets punished; if tries hard, learns to do something)

Uses relationship between feelings, behavior and consequences to assert himself (e.g., bargains, "eat broccoli later!")

Interacts in socially appropriate way with adults

Interacts in socially appropriate way with peers

Cognitive, Sensory, Motor or Language

Can play in a focused organized manner without another person for twenty minutes or more

Pretend play elements are logically connected (e.g., "dolly is spanked because she messed up")

Puts pop beads together

Spatial designs become more complex and have interrelated parts so that a block house has rooms or maybe furniture, cars have different places to go such as the store and the house or garage

Can draw a man by putting indications of facial features or limbs on a circular shape

Can walk up stairs alternating feet

Can catch a large ball using both hands

Can kick a ball

Sentences become complex with logical connecting words between, phrases (e.g., "because" or "but" is used, "No like fish because icky")

Asks "why" although not necessarily interested in the answer, and may repeat

Guidelines for Catergorizing Patterns and for Recommending and Conducting Comprehensive Evaluations

I. If any *primary* capacity is not present at the time of screening, full evaluation is indicated.

II. If over half of emotional capacities are not present, a detailed evaluation is indicated.

III. If over half of cognitive, sensory, or motor capacities are not present, that area requires a detailed evaluation.

IV. If any *single* capacity is not present, whether in the emotional, cognitive, sensory, motor, or language area, it should be reviewed historically and followed closely. If that function does not show progress on follow-up visits, or if the precursors to that function were not present from history or prior observation, full evaluation is required. As a general rule, progress is indicated when on one- to two-month follow-up the relative lag has been reduced in relation to age expectations.

V. If relative progress is made, that area should nevertheless be encouraged and continually monitored.

VI. If no lags are present, overall development should be encouraged and monitored.

Note: Comprehensive evaluations for all areas of functioning are required even if there is a lag in only one general area of functioning (e.g., motor).

eating difficulties, or impulsive behavior may be part of an overall developmental lag or a more limited constriction in the range of emotional domains engaged in by the infant and family. The approach to treatment would differ considerably, depending on the nature of the psychopathology (Greenspan 1981). Whether to monitor normal emotional functioning or to screen for disordered emotional functioning, attending to the emotional milestones is important in a comprehensive framework to early development and preventive well-baby and child care.

REFERENCES

Ainsworth, M., Bell, S. M., and Stayton, D. (1974). Infant-mother attachment and social development: Socialization as a product of reciprocal responsiveness to signals. In M. Richards (Ed.). *The Integration of the Child Into a Social World.* Cambridge: Cambridge University Press, pp. 99–135.

Bakwin, H. (1942). Loneliness in infants. *Am. J. Dis. Childhood* 63:30.

Bell, S. (1970). The development of the concept of object as related to infant-mother attachment. *Child Devel.* 41:219.

Bergman, P., and Escalona, S. (1949). Unusual sensitivities in very young children. *Psychoanal. Study Child* 3–4:333.

Bowlby, J. (1951). *Attachment and Loss.* New York: Basic Books.

Brazelton, T. B., Koslowski, B., and Main, M. (1974). The origins of reciprocity: The early mother-infant interaction. In M. Lewis and L. Rosenblum (Eds.). *The Effect of the Infant on Its Care Giver*. New York: Wiley, pp. 49–76.

Burlingham, D., and Freud, A. (1942). *Young Children in Wartime*. London: Allen and Unwin.

Cameron, H. C. (1919). *The Nervous Child*. London: Oxford Medical Publications.

Charlesworth, W. R. (1969). The role of surprise in cognitive development. In E. Elkind and J. H. Flavell (Eds.). *Studies in Cognitive Development: Essays in Honor of Jean Piaget*. London: Oxford University Press, pp. 257–314.

Cravioto, J., and DeLicardie, E. (1973). Environmental correlates of severe clinical malnutrition and language development in survivors from kwashiorkor or marasmus. In *Nutrition, the Nervous System and Behavior* Pan American Health Organization Scientific Publication No. 251—Washington, D.C.

Ekman, P. (1972). Universals and cultural differences in facial expressions of emotion. *Nebraska Symposium on Motivation*. Lincoln: University of Nebraska Press.

Emde, R. N., Gaensbauer, T. J., and Harmon, R. J. (1976). Emotional expression in infancy: A biobehavioral study. *Psychological Issues*, Monograph No. 37, New York: International Universities Press.

Escalona, S. K. (1968). *The Roots of Individuality*. Chicago: Aldine.

Freud, S. (1911). Formulation on the two principles of mental functioning. *Standard Edition* 12:218–26. London: Hogarth Press, 1958.

Gewirtz, J. L. (1961). A learning analysis of the effects of normal stimulation, privation and deprivation on the acquisition of social motivation and attachment. In B. M. Foss (Ed.). *Determinants of Infant Behavior*, Vol. 1. London: Methuen.

———. (1965). The course of infant smiling in four child-rearing environments in Israel. In B. M. Foss (Ed.). *Determinants of the Infant Behavior*, Vol. 3. London: Methuen.

———. (1969). Levels of conceptual analysis in environment-infant interaction research. *Merrill-Palmer Quarterly* 15:9.

Gouin-Decarie, T. (1965). *Intelligence and Affectivity in Early Childhood: An Experimental Study of Jean Piaget's Object Concept and Object Relations*. New York: International Universities Press.

Greenspan, S. I. (1979). Intelligence and adaptation: An integration of psychoanalytic and Piagetian developmental psychology. *Psychological Issues*, Vol. 12, No. 3/4. Monograph, pp. 47–48. New York: International Universities Press.

———. (1981). Psychopathology and adaptation in infancy and early childhood: Principles of clinical diagnosis and preventive intervention. *Clinical Infant Reports*, No. 1. New York: International Universities Press.

———. (1984). A model for comprehensive preventive intervention services for infants, young children and their families. In S. I. Greenspan, et al. (Eds.). Infants in Multirisk Families; Case Studies of Preventive Intervention, *Clinical Infant Reports*, No. 3. New York: International Universities Press.

———, and Greenspan, N. T. (1985). *First Feelings: Milestones in the Emotional Development of Your Baby and Child from Birth to Age Four*. New York: Viking Press.

———, and Lieberman, A. F. (1980). Infants, mothers and their interactions: A quantitative clinical approach to developmental assessment. In S. I. Greenspan and G. H. Pollock (Eds.). *The Course of Life: Psychoanalytic Contributions Toward*

Understanding Personality Development, Vol. 1, Infancy and Early Childhood, DHHS Publication No. [ADM] 80–786. Washington, D.C.: Government Printing Office.

————, and Lourie, R. S. (1981). Developmental structuralist approach to the classification of adaptive and pathologic personality organization: Application to infancy and early childhood. *Am. J. Psychiatry* 138:6.

————, and Porges, S. W. (1984). Psychopathology in infancy and early childhood: Clinical perspectives on the organization of sensory and affective-thematic experience. *Child Devel.* 55: 49–70.

————, and Wieder, S. I. (1984). Dimensions and levels of the therapeutic process. *Psychotherapy* 21 (1):5–23.

————, Lourie, R. S., and Nover, R. A. (1979). A developmental approach to the approach to the classification of psychopathology in infancy and early childhood. In J. Noshpitz (Ed.). *The Basic Handbook of Child Psychiatry,* Vol. 2. New York: Basic Books, pp. 157–64.

Hartmann, H. (1939). *Ego Psychology and the Problem of Adaptation.* New York: International Universities Press.

Hofheimer, J. A., et al. (1981). The reliability, validity and generalizability of assessments of transactions between infants and their caregivers: A multicenter design. Working Paper, Clinical Infant Development Program, NIMH.

————, et al. (1984). Short-term temporal stability of mother-infant interactions in the first year of life. Unpublished paper.

Hunt, J. M. (1941). Infants in an orphanage. *J. Abnorm. Soc. Psychol.* 36:338.

Izard, C. (1978). On the development of emotions and emotion-cognition relationships in infancy. In M. Lewis and L. Rosenblum (Eds.). *The Development of Affect.* New York: Plenum.

Klaus, M., and Kennell, J. H. (1976). *Maternal-Infant Bonding: The Impact of Early Separation or Loss on Family Development.* St. Louis: Mosby.

Lipsitt, L. (1966). Learning processes of newborns. *Merrill-Palmer Quarterly* 12:45.

Lourie, R. S. (1971). The first three years of life: An overview of a new frontier for psychiatry. *Am. J. Psychiatry* 127:1457.

Lowrey, L. G. (1940). Personality distortion and early institutional care. *Am. J. Orthopsychiatry* 10:546.

Mahler, M. S., Pine, F., and Bergman, A. (1975). *The Psychological Birth of the Human Infant.* New York: Basic Books.

Meltzoff, A. N., and Moore, K. M. (1977). Imitation of facial and manual gestures by human neonates. *Science* 198:75.

Murphy, L. B., and Moriarty, A. E. (1976). *Vulnerability, Coping, and Growth.* New Haven: Yale University Press.

Piaget, J. (1962). The stages of the intellectual development of the child. In S. I. Harrison and J. F. McDermott (Eds.). *Childhood Psychopathology.* New York: International Universities Press, 1972.

Poisson, S. S., Lieberman, A. F., and Greenspan, S. I. (1981). Training manual for the Greenspan-Lieberman Observation System (GLOS), NIMH. Unpublished manuscript.

————, et al. (1983). Inter-observer agreement and reliability assessments of the GLOS Measures of caregiver infant interaction, NIMH. Unpublished manuscript.

Rachford, B. K. (1905). *Neurotic Disorders of Childhood.* New York: E. B. Treat.

Rheingold, H. (1966). The development of social behavior in the human infant. *Monographs Society Res. Child Dev.* 31, No. 1:1966.

––––––. (1969). Infancy. In D. Sills (Ed.). *International Encyclopedia of the Social Sciences.* New York: Macmillan.

Sameroff, A. J., et al. (In press). IQ scores of 4-year-old children: Social-environmental risk factors. *Pediatrics.*

Sander, L. (1962). Issues in early mother-child interaction. *J. Am. Acad. Child Psychiatry* 1:141.

Spitz, R. A. (1945). Hospitalism. *Psychoanal. Study Child* 1:53.

––––––. (1965). *The First Year of Life.* New York: International Universities Press.

Sroufe, L., and Waters, E. (1977). Attachment as an organizational construct. *Child Devel.* 48:1184.

Stern, D. (1974a). Mother and infant at play: The dyadic interaction involving facial, vocal, and gaze behaviors. In M. Lewis and L. Rosenblum (Eds.). *The Effect of the Infant on Its Caregiver.* New York: Wiley.

––––––. (1974b). The goal and structure of mother-infant play. *J. Am. Acad. Child Psychiatry* 13:402.

––––––. (1977). *The First Relationship: Infant and Mother.* Cambridge: Harvard University Press.

Tennes, K., et al. (1972). The stimulus barrier in early infancy: An exploration of some formulations of John Benjamin. In R. Holt and E. Peterfreund (Eds.). *Psychoanalysis and Contemporary Science*, Vol. 1. New York: Macmillan.

Tomkins, S. (1963). Affect, Imagery, Consciousness, Vols. 1 and 2, New York: Springer.

Werner, H., and Kaplan, B. (1963). *Symbol Formation.* New York: Wiley.

––––––. (1972). The stages of the intellectual development of the child. In S. Harrison and J. McDermott (Eds.). *Childhood Psychopathology.* New York: International Universities Press.

Winnicott, D. W. (1931). *Clinical Notes on Disorders of Childhood.* London: Heinemann.

10

THE CLINICAL ASSESSMENT OF TODDLERS

Arietta Slade and Anni Bergman

INTRODUCTION

Over the course of the past decade, the theory and practice of infant psychiatry has become a discipline in its own right. Thus, infants and toddlers who show signs of developmental difficulty are being referred with increasing regularity to psychiatrists, psychologists, social workers, and other child mental health specialists. In the past, it was rare for any other than the most developmentally delayed children to be referred for treatment, and in the event that less severe cases were referred for evaluation, few guidelines existed for assessment or treatment.

Parents have long recognized the significance and vulnerability of early childhood, and in many cases diagnose problems long before they receive proper professional attention. Pediatricians are usually the first to be appraised of parental concerns and anxieties by virtue of their regular professional contact with families. And yet, while they are in a unique position to evaluate and refer children, pediatricians vary greatly in their psychological sophistication and/or their willingness to hear out and evaluate parental inquiries. It is not uncommon for parents' concerns to be minimized, or for psychological symptoms to be treated as medical ones. Until recently, however, even the most conscientious and psychological pediatricians had few options available to them should psychological assessment be required.

In this chapter we will discuss the clinical assessment of toddlers—children between the ages of 12 and 36 months of age. We place special emphasis upon the toddler period as a "phase" in infancy for several reasons. For one, infants under a year of age rarely come to our attention. Of equal importance, however, is the fact that this period—marked by "developmental explosions" in physical, cognitive, object relations, and psychosexual development (Galenson 1980; Roiphe and Galenson 1981)—has been viewed as one of particular vulnerability (Pine 1982) and developmental upheaval (Mahler et al. 1975). In the sections that follow, we will focus on three areas relevant to diagnosis and treatment during this period: 1) processes of normal development; 2) the tasks of consultation and assessment; and 3) diagnostic considerations.

A VIEW OF THE TODDLER PERIOD: CHILD AND PARENT PERSPECTIVES

The toddler period spans nearly two years of the child's life and is a period of rapid emotional, cognitive, and physical development. While other notions of development during this period have been proposed (for a recent and provocative perspective, see Stern [1985]), our discussion will focus upon assessment of development from the perspective of separation-individuation theory. Separation-individuation is the term used by Margaret Mahler and her colleagues (Mahler et al. 1975) to describe the process by which the child develops a sense of himself as psychologically separate from his primary caregivers. Mahler and her colleagues systematically observed infants and their mothers from 5 through 30 months of age. These observations made it possible to describe in considerable detail emotional and object relations development during the preoedipal period and, in particular, to draw attention to the critical significance of the toddler period for later personality development. The process of separation-individuation is thought to begin when the child is around 5 months old. Prior to this point in development, the infant is thought to be in a relatively undifferentiated state and thus does not distinguish himself from others in a meaningful or significant way. At around 5 months, however, the baby begins to notice and be more actively curious about the world outside of the "mother-child orbit," and he enters the first phase of the separation-individuation process. This process was found to unfold in regular, predictable patterns and was thus divided into four overlapping subphases: differentiation (5 to 10 months), practicing (10 to 16 months), rapprochement (16 to 28 months), and "on the way to libidinal object constancy" (28 to 36 months). All but the first stage, then, take place during the toddler period.

The infant becomes a toddler as he takes his first upright steps, usually sometime around his first birthday. The shift from crawling and creeping to upright, freestanding locomotion dramatically alters the child's relationship to his world. It ushers in the "practicing subphase proper," which is characterized by the child's narcissistic investment in mastery, and a "love affair with the world." In the months that follow the child becomes increasingly steady and proficient at walking, running, and climbing; such large motor proficiency is matched by increasing manual dexterity and fine motor control. He can hold eating utensils, toys, crayons, begin to dress himself, and—often to his parents' dismay—he opens drawers, cabinets, medicine bottles, and so on. During the second year of life, capacities develop that make autonomy and independence increasingly possible. A mood of elation accompanies the development of these new competencies. The child feels "omnipotent" during this period and has the sense that he is without limitations. The child's capacity to invest in himself, his body, and his limitlessness is of critical developmental significance. While his sense of pleasure and self-worth will depend in part upon what he is actually capable of, it will also depend upon his parents' ability to mirror and affirm his joy in his new capabilities.

Until this time, according to Mahler, the child is for the most part unaware of his separateness from mother and father. It is as if they were with him at all times, whether or not he is able to see them—thus the careless abandon with which newly ambulatory toddlers will wander far away from their parents. However, the gradual development of object and person permanence (Piaget 1945; Pine 1974) during the latter half of the second year is accompanied by the child's recognition of his own separateness. This heralds the child's move into the "rapprochement" subphase, which parents aptly refer to as the "terrible twos." The awareness that he is separate from his parents and in particular from his mother brings with it a rapid deflation of mood as the toddler comes to realize the fact of his own vulnerability and smallness. It often provokes desperate attempts to restore the sense of unity and oneness with mother. Separation anxiety, clinging, shadowing, demandingness, and coercion express his wish to restore lost closeness and intimacy. At the same time, the child may express a strong need to "do" for himself, to insist doggedly upon his own autonomy, and to resent what he perceives as parental interference or intrusion. The tension between these two sets of feelings contributes to the rapid switch from happiness to rageful tantrums and to despair that are the norm for this period. This is also the period designated in traditional psychoanalytic theory as the anal phase, marked by the child's increasing interest in and attention to his bodily functions, and—in particular—to his efforts to control (or not control) these functions. Once again, fluctuations between regression and control or autonomy are typical.

Under optimal circumstances, this period of upheaval begins to diminish in the months following the child's second birthday. The sense of self as separate from mother and others becomes increasingly stable and coherent; the affect storms, moodiness, and aggression of rapprochement diminish; and the child begins to develop relationships outside the immediate family unit. The image of mother as available and nurturant is sufficiently internalized and integrated to permit the establishment of other relationships. These developments constitute the core achievements of the fourth and final subphase of the process, termed by Mahler "on the way to emotional object constancy."

Cognitive developments provide a critical backdrop for these changes. The development of language and conceptual skills allows the child to express his wishes and the widening range of his affective experience (Stern 1985), and permits him to understand better parental explanations and limits. For the toddler struggling with feelings of helplessness, loss and anger, such accomplishments are of major psychological significance. The child labels people and things and ascribes feelings and intentions to himself and others in increasingly complex and meaningful ways. The capacity to express himself in symbolic play allows the child the means to experience a range of conflicts in a safe way, to lend increasing structure and dimension to his sense of self and others, and to "play" out a variety of developing identifications (Slade 1986). The beginning development of a sense of time through the accretion of symbols affords him a means both to anticipate the future and to tolerate the frustration of delay. Through the accumulation of both cognitive and affective experiences, the child gradually gains a sense of his own agency and effectiveness. The tangible, pleasurable, and at times frightening knowledge of his own capacity to have an effect (Pine 1982) greatly enhances his self-esteem and diminishes his need for the desperate battles that had characterized earlier functioning. Accompanying this realization of agency, and thus others' agency, is the capacity for concern (Winnicott 1965, 1971), the hallmark of the beginnings of true object relationships.

Along with an increased sense of his own efficacy comes a sense of self-control and containment. Affects can be modulated with increasing effectiveness, as can drive states. The child can also exercise a modicum of control in his relationships and interactions in ways that add to his sense of mastery and independence. Reality—feelings, ideas, relationships—no longer seems as fluid and unstable as it previously had, and constancy is a dominant emotional experience. For the first time in development, the child may have a sense that he is truly "captain of his own ship" (Lichtenberg 1984).

Both Winnicott and Mahler have emphasized the importance of parents' providing a "facilitating" or "holding environment" as the child moves from absolute to relative dependence, particularly when the child is angry, rejecting, or in Winnicott's words, "ruthless." For parents to do so during this period poses a challenge surpassed only by that posed by the turbulence of adolescence. In large part, the difficulty rests in its contradictions: parents are faced with the challenge of being at once flexible and firm, imperturbable and greatly admiring, tolerant and playful, and so on. The toddler's drive for autonomy may be experienced by his parents as a loss, making it difficult indeed to enhance and encourage his independence (Mahler, et al. 1970). The emotional availability of the parents—which in point of fact refers to a number of parental attributes—seems to be especially crucial at this moment. They are asked to be both tolerant of the child's omnipotence and ambivalence (often expressed quite vehemently) and appreciative of the child's need to be made safe by firmness and limits. At times, the vehemence of a toddler's outbursts or the intensity of his rage will so hurt and anger parents that their response is retaliatory and impulsive, and may be guided by the implicit assumption that the child's provocation was deliberate. It is quite difficult to maintain an empathic stance vis-à-vis a toddler's feelings of vulnerability and anxiety in the face of one's own anger and feelings of rejection. And yet, imperturbability and stability are crucial to the child's gradual relinquishment of omnipotence.

Parents must also be able to be playful and understanding of their toddler's primary process communications. The toddler often takes great delight in pretend games and is particularly eager to share these games with his parents. Play of this kind requires parents to relinquish certain of their own rules—allowing themselves to make a mess, crawl on the floor or to be passively fed—in the service of the child's ego development and his enjoyment of playful intimacy. At the same time, the parent's observing ego maintains the boundaries of the play, contains the child's activity level, and provides a crucial bridge between reality and fantasy.

Another demand on parents is to allow their toddler a measure of self-determination. This may run the gamut from the child's demanding particular foods or rituals, to his insisting that he be allowed to dress himself or to touch, explore, and experiment. Parents' assertion of their authority at such junctures may only increase the child's feelings of smallness and vulnerability. A component of allowing a child such autonomy is parental willingness to admire and affirm their child in his accomplishments, to bolster their child's self-esteem. It is at this point in time that his sense of himself, his competence, his effectiveness, and his worth are being established. As Pine (1982) noted, the "self" is infinitely more vulnerable once it has been "born" and is thus recognizable as *me*.

As the "space" between mother and child widens (Winnicott 1971), with the child gaining a sense of his autonomy and independence, qualities such as tenderness and affection must often be expressed by the parents across space through distal modalities—facial expressions and words (Bergman 1980). Parents often find this shift difficult to manage and may relinquish physical displays of affection altogether; or in an attempt to "undo" such separateness, they may constantly touch, caress, and handle the child, even when parent and child are engaged in separate activities. Mothers who find this task less difficult often "check back" to their child visually, maintaining positive contact at a distance or offering affectionate touches or looks when the child returns to them.

It is our conviction that the successful navigation of the subphases of the separation-individuation process—which encompasses the resolution of psychosexual conflicts, the integration of infantile sexuality and the emergence of representational and symbolic capacities—constitutes a core developmental issue of the period and forms the basis for the unfolding of the oedipal phase. Thus, our emphasis will rest with evaluating progress toward and deviation from such resolutions.

It has been our intention in this section not to recapitulate separation-individuation theory in its entirety, but rather to highlight those areas that may prove most significant for purposes of assessing a toddler in his family and elaborating areas of child and parent functioning that have received less comprehensive study in the literature.

THE PROCESS OF ASSESSMENT AND CONSULTATION

The range of problems children and their parents present at the time of the initial consultation is considerable and runs the gamut from behavioral and interpersonal difficulties (excessive negativism, aggressive acting-out, sleep disturbance, and so on), to somatic complaints (eating disturbances, eliminatory disturbances, gastrointestinal upsets, allergic disorders), to motor and/or cognitive/attentional delays.

From the perspective of psychoanalysis, symptoms cannot be evaluated outside of the developmental context in which they occur (A. Freud 1965). Thus, while parents may focus their discussion upon a particular symptom (for instance, chronic constipation, late-night awakening), evaluation will necessarily rest on an exploration of a variety of other factors. The central issue with respect to assessment involves an evaluation of: (1) the child's physical and intellectual development; (2) the nature of separation-individuation, object relations, and psychosexual development; and (3) the parents' own capacity to remain emotionally available to the child while facilitating his autonomy and individuation.

While the range of interactions among these variables defies easy classification, we have found it useful to distinguish among: (1) subphase specific problems of development, in which subphase functioning has for the most part been uninterrupted; and (2) developmental deviations, in which some major aspect of development—affective, cognitive or both—is thought to be significantly off course. This may include situations in which parental disturbance or anxiety appears to be the major source of discordance in the dyad. Specific examples falling within each of these categories will be presented below. Before turning to these examples, however, we will first review the process by which such assessments are made.

Assignment to any one of these categories requires evaluation of the child on a number of dimensions simultaneously. In addition to assessing the age-adequacy of the child's physical and cognitive development, the clinician must evaluate the degree to which symptomatology does or does not interfere with normal subphase functioning. Each subphase is characterized by a particular set of behaviors, affects, and interaction patterns. While these patterns will vary, there are certain constellations that typify each subphase. In assessing toddlers we look for evidence that these constellations are indeed present; in the practicing subphase, for instance, we look for evidence of elation, pleasure, and investment in newly developing physical capacities, and relatively low levels of separation distress and concern for mother's whereabouts; in rapprochement, we expect greater degrees of anger and anxiety, greater separation distress and wish to be near mother, expressed via wooing, shadowing, and so forth. Subphase adequacy may be disrupted in one of two ways: by distortions or disturbances within the subphase itself or by the failure to resolve the tasks or issues of previous subphases, such that the present subphase cannot be fully experienced or ultimately resolved. Distortions or disturbances may be expressed via the absence or exacerbation of typical subphase patterns of affect and behavior. Thus, the child who shows little delight in his new ability to walk, or who greets such developments with trepidation or fear will be at risk for a variety of problems around mood and self-esteem regulation. By the same token, exacerbation of subphase specific conflicts may be equally disruptive. Thus, a child whose temper tantrums, separation anxiety, and coercive behaviors fail to diminish over the course of the rapprochement subphase, and who shows few signs of developing object constancy or the stabilization of mood, is at risk for a variety of disturbances resulting from faulty processes of internalization. Failures to resolve the tasks of previous subphases may similarly upset developmental progress. For instance, a child for whom chronic attentional disturbances impaired self-regulation throughout the first year of life would have few experiences of narcissistic delight and self-absorption that typically characterize practicing.

At the same time that subphase adequacy is assessed, parental capacities for empathy, differentiation and emotional availability must be evaluated; of equal importance is the degree to which such parental capacities mesh with the givens of a particular child's endowment and temperament. What may be "good enough" for a particular child may not be so for a baby with greater sensitivities.

The assessment of subphase adequacy and overall development in toddlers as well as of the nature of the "facilitating environment" requires both time and flexibility on the part of the clinician. While assessments of older children often progress according to a relatively standard formula for consultation and treatment, the same cannot be said for the evaluation of young children and their parents. In working with toddlers, treatment cannot always be distinguished from consultation. While more severe developmental deviations and parental pathology may require intensive intervention, in many cases within the range of subphase specific disturbance—even those where discrete symptomatology is present—the evaluation process itself may constitute the treatment. Winnicott described the aim of consultation as setting the developmental process in motion so that the child can once again make use of his family as a facilitating environment. Within the course of brief or extended evaluations, the developmental guidance, facilitation, and interpretation offered by the clinician may well provide the "push" needed to restore the course of development.

There is no time limit on the course of evaluations, nor are there clear definitions as to when consultation ends and treatment begins. There are times when a single meeting with parents (in rare cases, a phone consultation) will provide the clinician with enough information to make a diagnosis and to intervene in such a way that development can resume its progress. In other instances, the evaluation may require a more lengthy period of consultation with both parents, including observations of the child with parents and, if possible, alone.

The decisions regarding the length and depth of the consultation are often made as the consultation proceeds and as the clinician has an opportunity to observe the impact of the developmental guidance that naturally occurs during the course of such meetings. *Children react quickly to changes in parental attitudes and handling of conflicts.* Thus, the changes in management that often result from a consultation may lead to marked changes in the child and the quick disappearance of symptoms. Parents will often wish to discontinue the evaluation following such symptom remission; in many cases, this is indeed an appropriate course of action. Such rapid termination need not be viewed as resistance on the part of parents. It may simply be that they feel and are expressing the fact that their capacity to function as a family has been restored. By contrast, some parents will find it so uncomfortable to consider treatment for their toddler or to reveal their own parenting difficulties that their resistance will take the form of premature termination; only careful attention to the clinical material provided during the sessions will make such differential diagnosis possible. In some cases, a superficial willingness to engage in consultation and/or treatment belies serious resistance to following the developmental guidance offered by the clinician. It may not always be possible for the clinician to analyze these resistances; in some cases, changes in management may occur long after the consultation or treatment has ended.

There are many instances, of course, when it becomes clear that consultation coupled with developmental guidance will not be adequate. In cases where developmental delay is noted, such as in language acquisition, motor development, or visual motor coordination, an extended consultation with child and parents and with specialists in the areas of neurological and cognitive development will generally be required. Often, psychological testing will be necessary, as will—in the case of severe language delays—audiological and language evaluations. Neurological and developmental optometric examinations can be very useful in diagnosing perceptual, motor, and attentional deficits. It is often the case that children whose parents seek consultation are manifesting the kinds of developmental deviation and delay that requires multimodal assessment and treatment based on restoring biological as well as psychological inadequacies (Resch, Grand, and Meyerson 1981). Careful evaluation and testing can be crucial in making differential diagnoses and in establishing adequate and appropriate treatment plans.

EVALUATION AND DIAGNOSIS: CASE ILLUSTRATIONS

Expectable, Phase-Specific Disturbances. Within normal development, transient disturbances of all kinds are to be expected (A. Freud 1965). These will certainly include separation problems, lability of mood, sleep disturbances, eating disturbances, and the like. Late-night awakening and distress are not at all uncommon in two-year-olds who have for many months been maintaining regular, through-the-night schedules. Food fads, food refusals, compulsive rituals, stutters, and mannerisms are also common. So are mood swings, extremes of anger, sadness, glee, and frantic activity. Disturbances of this type may intensify beyond the expectable in response to unavoidable environmental stresses such as family vacations, moves, or sibling births. The nature of parental response to the child at these times will be crucial in determining whether the disturbance remains transient and within expectable limits or whether it constitutes a warning signal indicating more severe pathology.

Experienced parents come to expect such upheavals and rarely seek consultation for them. Primiparous parents, or those with some conflict or anxiety around their own capacities to parent, may often find these transient disturbances most unsettling. Particularly stressful are their own feelings of rage, helplessness, guilt, and uncertainty toward the child.

Case #1

The parents of 14-month-old Jessie were extremely concerned about sudden manifestations of separation anxiety in their otherwise well-adjusted and bright daughter. Devoted psychologically sophisticated parents, they worried a great deal about the fact that they had to leave their child with baby-sitters while working. They knew about the problems of attachment and wanted to be sure that their child recognized them as her primary care-takers. Thus, they decided to use several baby-sitters so that their child would not get attached to any one of them in particular. The recommendation was simple: to allow the child to become attached to one or two substitute care-takers, the mother was also given permission to follow along with her natural desire to stay at home with her daughter on those days when she seemed especially concerned about being left, and when she could afford to take time off from work. Follow-up indicated that the extremity of separation anxiety abated as soon as these changes were made.

Case #2

Jamie's mother asked for consultation following her 21-month-old daughter's particularly severe and prolonged (five-week) bout of constipation. Medical attempts at alleviating her great distress had been unsuccessful. In addition, she had begun to masturbate frequently and openly, as if to alleviate the discomfort of her constipation. The baby, while perhaps overly tied to her mother, seemed to be quite verbal, well-related, and friendly. Over the course of a long discussion with mother, it was learned that she was pregnant with a second child and that she had been quite depressed and withdrawn in recent weeks as she tried to decide whether to carry this unexpected pregnancy to term. When it was suggested to the mother that her depression had been experienced as an abandonment by her rapprochement toddler, she quite agreed. It was further suggested that mother try to reestablish the comfortable intimacy that had previously characterized their relationship. Later follow-up found complete remission of symptoms, and a much relieved mother and baby.

Case #3

A mother who had decided on the advice of her pediatrician to wean her 27-month-old daughter from the bottle reported that upon having the bottle taken away from her Michelle became extremely fretful and unhappy and stopped sleeping through the night. Separation anxiety increased markedly. Michelle had recently entered a new daycare program; the mother also reported that she and her husband were in the midst of a marital crisis, and the child had been privy to a good deal of fighting and upheaval. It was suggested to the mother that this might not be the best time abruptly to foster her daughter's independence, and that weaning might be reintroduced when Michelle seemed better able to manage it. The mother seemed both relieved and anxious at hearing this suggestion, but agreed to try it. Within a few days, what had appeared to be a reactivation of Michelle's rapprochement crisis diminished altogether. Several months later both weaning and toilet training were achieved without incident.

In these cases, the presenting symptoms were clearly age-adequate, and the contact was sufficient to convince us that there was no evidence of more serious difficulties requiring examination and possible treatment. In cases like this, it is frequently sufficient to relieve the anxiety of the parents and to effect a change in caretaking practices. It should be stressed, however, that it is the availability of this type of consultation that often prevents later, more serious difficulties.

There are some instances in which parents bring their children in for consultation and it quickly becomes clear that the child's development is proceeding quite normally and that the developmental guidance must address parental anxieties. In some instances, such interventions will not suffice, and individual treatment for the parent is recommended.

In the following example, the mother's anxieties had little to do with her baby's development.

Case #4

Mrs. P. sought consultation because she was concerned that her 10-month-old had never shown any signs of stranger anxiety. Examination of her and her baby quickly showed us that she had understood stranger anxiety in a very narrow way. It was true that the little boy was exceptionally friendly and did not cry when approached by a stranger. However, he demonstrated what Mahler has called stranger curiosity. The concept of stranger anxiety has expanded in the course of observational research to include a variety of reactions ranging from curiosity to wariness to distress. In this case, it was quite easy to see that the child had developed a specific attachment to the caretaker, and the mother could easily be reassured. What appeared as a danger signal to the concerned and observant mother in fact did not turn out to be a disturbance at all. It would have been a danger signal if the child indeed had not shown any reaction to the stranger, that is, if the child had not developed a specific attachment to the caretaker.

Parents will at times use their infants as a means of seeking help for themselves. Often it will be clear to the clinician that the parent is in fact the identified patient; at others, the parent's pathology will require that they be treated together in order to maintain a parent's sense of intactness or control (Bergman and Slade 1984).

Expectable, Phase-Specific Disturbances Which Have Reached Symptomatic Proportions. In such cases, symptom pictures per se do not differ from those in the first group. What does differentiate these children from those in the first group, however, are the intensity, severity, and duration of their symptoms. In severe cases, deviations may be such that there are gross divergences from the usual timing, intensity, or persistence of a particular subphase experience. For example, a child seen regularly from 12 to 30 months became progressively more clinging, angry, despondent, and demanding, following a prolonged separation from her mother at 14 months. Little of the elation or joy of practicing was observed, as the separation from her already quite ambivalent mother quickly deflated her sense of magical omnipotence and shattered the illusion of mother-child unity. By the time she was 18 months old, she was cranky, clinging, quite fearful of separation, provocative, and excessively wary of strangers. She appeared sad and woebegone. At 24 months, these patterns were unchanged. The phase-specific elation of practicing had given way to a flattening of affect and a premature awareness of separateness. Our observations led us to suspect that this resulted in a premature and especially intense rapprochement crisis. The sequelae of these distortions of subphase timing and intensity appeared to have lasting impact on the development of this child's character as well as her capacity for object relations.

In this case, like many in this category, parental response (or lack of response) to both phase-specific needs as well as transient disturbances may set such pathological cycles in motion, prolonging and intensifying a developmental problem to the point of more severe pathology. The mother who feels she has nothing to offer a child other than food may battle his normal food refusal, thus escalating a relatively innocuous manifestation of his need for control into an eating disorder. Similarly, the father who refuses to "give in" and cuddle with his panicky, tired toddler, wide awake and miserable at 4 A.M., may well find himself awake many more nights in succession as the child becomes more desperate in his quest for nurturance and physical affection.

Case #5

Lisa was seen in consultation at the age of 2½. She was highly verbal and bright. Mother reported that the child was extremely negativistic, possessive, and unable to share with other children. Mrs. L. felt she had to amuse Lisa constantly, respond to her demands, cart her hither and yon— or face the child's temper outbursts and provocations. Mrs. L. was unhappy and exasperated, though trying valiantly to hide this from Lisa. There were also family difficulties and impending divorce. During the course of the consultation, Lisa repeatedly admonished and scolded the dolls. This was quite surprising to Mrs. L., who thought Lisa aware only of her tolerant, helpful side. She remarked that she didn't realize Lisa had seen this side of her feelings, though it was evident she had. Lisa was expressing feelings of anger at her mother's ambivalence and withdrawal, as well as an identification with her. These interpretations were made to the mother and child over the course of the extended assessment. In view of the effectiveness of this work, it was decided to postpone the decision about further treatment. Contact with the mother was maintained with the idea that Lisa might well need treatment later on.

A second case illustrates some of the ways in which an extended assessment, though it appeared to have been thwarted by the parents, did in fact alleviate pressures on both parents and child and allowed developmental movement to continue.

Case #6

The evaluation was of a little boy, 3 years old, who had not achieved resolution of his rapprochement crisis. His parents were devoted and overly anxious to please him. The little boy was extremely demanding, immature, easily fatigued, and unable to play. Following an initial interview, a number of play sessions were conducted with the child in the presence of both parents. During these sessions the parents realized that their child was actually capable of tolerating more frustration than they had thought. The little boy responded well to these play sessions and quickly became quite attached to the therapist. Summer vacation intervened and the family did not resume contact in the fall. A letter to the therapist, written several months later, said:

> We would like you to know that we did benefit from our sessions with you and that we seem to be understanding our roles as parents more fully. Joey is doing well and is more fun for us now. I hope we are for him.

A third case illustrates an instance in which while symptom relief did occur, termination seemed somewhat premature.

Case #7

Bobby was seen in consultation when he was nearly 3 years old. He was an extremely bright, gregarious, and social child, whose parents reported that since 10 months of age he had refused to move his bowels unless diapered and lying on his stomach, usually in the middle of the living room. He delayed doing so until the last possible moment, and steadfastly refused to be toilet trained. The parents had sought (and received) extended gastrointestinal workups for the child, the result being that laxatives were prescribed and regularly administered. Thus, his stools were soft and difficult to withhold; his prone position also made comfortable elimination virtually impossible. The parents described a variety of family upsets (including two deaths) over the year preceding the consultation, and the mother reported that she was currently 5 months pregnant. Both parents were themselves somewhat phobic with respect to elimination and other bodily functions. They were quite resistant to seeing Bobby's inability to be trained (or to be *near* the toilet, for that matter) as a problem, although they reluctantly agreed to treatment once evaluation suggested that Bobby had a number of fantasies about his bowel movements, the toilet, his parents' feelings, and the like. Parent sessions were also scheduled; the first specific suggestion made was to move all eliminatory activity into the bathroom. Bobby could lie on the floor and move his bowels in the bathroom, but was to be discouraged from doing so in the living room. The parents were astonished to find that Bobby agreed to this. In his own sessions Bobby played out a variety of anal concerns and began specific play around elimination. Within three weeks of his beginning individual sessions Bobby was able to use the toilet in the usual fashion, and had begun to use the toilet at nursery school. At this point, the parents discontinued treatment and refused to bring Bobby in even for a final session. The therapist sent him a "goodbye" note, and treatment was terminated. While there were many issues that might well have been addressed with both parents and child in this case, it was clear that the parents were not open to such interventions. The symptom itself *did* remit, however; thus, a single and important goal of treatment was attained.

Disturbances in Response to Environmental Failures. In some instances, behavioral difficulties, somatic complaints, and even cognitive or motor delays may result from major environmental failure such as a lengthy separation from a parent, the death of a parent, maternal deprivation, severe parental psychopathology, or traumatic divorce. Such traumas may also lead to infantile mood disorders, especially depressed, flattened mood or frantic hyperactivity. Shallow, superficial object relationships or intense object-related affect—aggression or sadness—may also be noted. We should add here disturbances of the "false self" variety (Winnicott 1965), that is, overly great compliance and/or precocity.

Nellie, an only child, was 28 months old when her mother was killed in a car accident. Compounding this loss was her father's severe depression, which led to his withdrawal and unavailability. Nellie was placed in the care of her paternal grandparents, who up until then had been favored and frequent caretakers. Nellie's development had been quite normal prior to her mother's death; at this point, however, despite adequate nurturance from her also bereaved grandparents, she became demanding, provocative, and engaged in instances of soiling and messing. Her sleep patterns became quite erratic; this previously giving toddler suddenly seemed an unreachable stranger. Treatment was recommended by Nellie's nursery school teacher and was promptly begun. The work entailed not only treating the child, but also working with the father and his therapist to reestablish the bond between them; their capacity to reach one another would be vital to the family's psychological survival.

It would be rare for treatment of the child not to be recommended under such circumstances. The disruption to development that follows from the death of a parent, abandonment, or severe parental psychopathology can rarely be overcome without significant and sustained intervention. If the child is under two, this will most likely entail tripartite treatment with the child and caretaker. In older children, individual work may be possible in addition to tripartite or family treatment.

Developmental Deviations. This grouping represents the most serious deviations along the continuum described thus far and is considered appropriate for children whose development is decidedly out of sync with the usual milestones and affect/

behavior constellations. It is also the least homogeneous of the groupings presented here, for the possibilities for derailment in this period are myriad and defy easy classification. Delays in walking, talking, and in the general development of the symbolic function fall into this category. Also typical are the absence of developing object relationships and evidence of distortions in affective expression, as in the symbiotic and autistic syndromes (Mahler 1968; Resch et al. 1981). While there may be rare instances in which parental pathology can be considered the prime etiological agent, it is most often the case that biological and neurological causes are thought to interact with environmental influences.

Danny and his mother came for consultation just after his third birthday. Danny's parents had recently separated, following months of violent upheaval and the father's psychotic decompensation. The mother—an obese, extremely passive woman now living with her own mother—reported a chronic sleep disturbance, long-standing difficulties in concentration and attention, and a high level of distractibility. He had a history of severe ear infections and had suffered some hearing loss. The mother's report suggested that the child had not developed the capacity for self-regulation and homeostasis at any point. Currently, Mrs. D. found it impossible to control Danny's provocative and aggressive behavior: he repeatedly tore the house apart, flew into panicky tantrums, and in general thwarted her attempts at discipline.

Danny was an angelic looking child who sat close to his mother throughout our meetings. While superficially friendly, he seemed most concerned with maintaining control over his mother through a constant barrage of questions and demands. His articulation and motor control were immature. Play was fragmented, and generally of a practice variety. Symbolic sequences were quite brief. He appeared quite anxious and was enormously distractible.

Because of this child's obvious immaturity and the need to rule out organic causes for his somewhat disorganized and hyperactive behavior, psychological tests were administered. In addition, developmental optometric and audiological work-ups were conducted. All test results fell within normal limits. Mother-child psychotherapy and placement in a therapeutic nursery were recommended. It was also recommended that developmental guidance and individual psychotherapy be offered to the mother. These recommendations were made in view of both the mother's (and family's) limitations as well as the child's inability to maintain subphase adequacy in spite of average endowment. Follow-up suggested considerable improvement, though regressions were common for both mother and child.

As in cases of children where environmental failures have led to developmental delay, these cases require thorough consultations (often including a variety of kinds of testing and evaluation) and careful referral for treatment. Therapeutic nurseries are often the most appropriate form of treatment. These may include individual treatment for parents in addition to group and individual treatment for children.

SUMMARY

We have outlined a plan for toddler assessment that is based on thorough knowledge of normal development along the lines of psychosexual phases, ego development, and object relations. We have stressed the developmental process of separation-individuation because we feel that its completion is the crucial developmental achievement of the toddler period. Since the period from 1 to 2½ or 3 is one of enormous change in a relatively short time as well as of considerable turmoil, we have emphasized the difficulty in determining the difference between "normality and pathology" (A. Freud 1965). We have emphasized the crucial importance of the ongoing relationship of the toddler with both parents and have urged that both parents be involved in the assessment process whenever possible, as well as in treatment of toddlers if it is suggested. Since the toddler period is a time of such rapid developmental flux, as well as a time in which intrapsychic conflicts are not yet consolidated, a derailed developmental process can often be put back on track relatively quickly with the availability of a facilitating environment.

We have suggested a flexible approach to evaluation, but have at the same time attempted to offer some definite guidelines. We have also urged an approach of tolerance and understanding toward parents who often need support during this difficult period in development. In particular, it is helpful for parents to know that development does not progress in a straight line, and that what might seem like a regression (for example, the recurrence of extreme separation anxieties during the rapprochement period) is in fact an expectable phenomenon during a particular developmental period. Living with small children can be extremely lonely for mothers who often do not have their own families nearby. The availability of consultation can be of great help.

We have stressed the importance of knowledge of normal developmental phases and in particular of the separation-individuation process for the clinician evaluating toddlers. It is, of course, equally important to recognize and respect the wide variations that fall within the norm of adequate mothering styles as well as the wide variations in children as they develop from infants to toddlers and from toddlers to preschoolers.

REFERENCES

Ainsworth, M. D., et al. (1978). *Patterns of Attachment: A Psychological Study of the Strange Situation*. Hillsdale, N.J.: Lawrence Erlbaum.

Bergman, A. (1980). Ours, yours, mine. In R. Lax, S. Bach, and L. A. Burland. *Rapprochement: The Critical Subphase*. New York: Jason Aronson.

————.(1982). Considerations about the development of the girl during the separation-individuation process. In D. Mendell (Ed.). *Early Female Development: Current Psychoanalytic Views*. New York: Spectrum.

————, and Slade, A. (1984). *The Clinical Assessment of the Toddler*. Paper presented at the Margaret Mahler Symposium, Philadelphia, Pa.

Brazelton, T. B., Koslowski, B., and Main, M. (1974). The origins of reciprocity. In M. Lewis and L. Rosenblum (Eds.). *The Effect of the Infant on Its Caregiver*. New York: Wiley.

————, and Als, H. (1979). Four early stages in the development of mother-infant interaction. *Psychoan. Study Child* 34.

Fraiberg, S., et al. (1980). *Clinical Studies in Infant Mental Health*. New York: Basic Books.

Freud, A. (1965). *Normality and Pathology in Childhood*. New York: International Universities Press.

Galenson, E. (1980). Characteristics of psychological development during the second and third years of life. In S. I. Greenspan and G. Pollock (Eds.). *The Course of Life*, vol. 2. Washington: DHHS (ADM) Publ. #80–786.

Greenspan, S. I. (1982). *Psychopathology and Adaptation in Infancy and Early Childhood*. New York: International Universities Press.

————, and Lieberman, A. F. (1980). Infants, mothers and their interaction: A quantitative clinical approach to developmental assessment. In S. I. Greenspan and G. Pollock (Eds.). *The Course of Life*, vol. 1. Washington: DHHS (ADM) Publ. #80–786.

Lichtenberg, J. (1984). *Psychoanalysis and Intent Research*. New York: Analytic Press.

Mahler, M. S. (1968). *On Human Symbiosis and the Vicissitudes of Individuation*. New York: Basic Books.

————, Pine, F., and Bergman, A. (1970). The mother's reaction to her toddler's drive for individuation. In E. J. Anthony and T. Benedek (Eds.). *Parenthood: Its Psychology and Psychopathology*. Boston: Little Brown.

————. (1975). *The Psychological Birth of the Human Infant*. New York: Basic Books.

Piaget, J. (1945). *The Origins of Intelligence in Children*. New York: Norton.

Pine, F. (1974). Libidinal object constancy: A theoretical note. *Psychoanal. Contemp. Science* 3:307–13.

————. (1982). The experience of self: Aspects of its expansion, formation and vulnerability. *Psychoanal. Study Child* 37.

Resch, R., Grand, S., and Meyerson, K. (1981). From the object to the person: The treatment of a two-year-old girl with infantile autism. *Bull. Menninger Clinic* 45:281–306.

Roiphe, H., and Galenson, E. (1981). *Infantile Origins of Sexual Identity*. New York: International Universities Press.

Sander, L. (1977). The Regulation of Exchange in the Infant–Caretaker System and Some Aspects of the Context–Content Relationship. In M. Lewis and L. Rosenblum (Eds.). *Interaction, Conversation and the Development of Language*. New York: Wiley.

Slade, A. (1986). Separation-individuation and symbolic play: A naturalistic study. *Bull. Menninger Clinic*.

Stern, D. N. (1971). Microanalysis of the mother-infant interaction. In C. Rexford, L. Sander, and T. Shapiro (Eds.). *Infant Psychiatry*. New Haven: Yale University Press.

Stern, D. N. (1974). Mother and infant at play. In M. Lewis and L. Rosenblum (Eds.). *Interaction, Conversation and the Development of Language*. New York: Wiley.
————. (1985). *The Interpersonal World of the Infant*. New York: Basic Books.
Winnicott, D. W. (1965). *The Maturational Process and the Facilitating Environment*. New York: International Universities Press.
Winnicott, D. W. (1971). *Playing and Reality*. New York: Basic Books.

11

THE OEDIPAL AND LATENCY YEARS

John A. Sours

> *My mother died*
> *unrocked, unrocked*
> Ann Sexton, *The Death Baby*
>
> *Daddy, daddy, you bastard, I'm through.*
> Sylvia Plath, *Ariel*

The phallic-oedipal phase of maturation and development is known by a number of terms. Educators refer to it as the nursery school years or the preschool years, whereas in psychoanalytic terminology it is also known as the stage of initiative versus guilt. This phase of maturation and development usually occurs between the ages of 3 and 6 years, although the actual onset and offset of this phase are not clearly demarcated.

The lines of maturation and development through the phallic-oedipal years of childhood include changes in many instinctual life and ego functions: 1) the shift from dependency toward adult object relationships; 2) the transition from suckling to eating; 3) going from wetting and soiling to bladder and bowel control; 4) irresponsibility changing to responsibility in body management; 5) growth from egocentricity to companionship; 6) the transitions from body concentration to the toy world, and from play to work; and changes in the structure and function of 7) dreams, and 8) fantasies. Some of these lines are better understood than others, and, in the case of phallic-oedipal development, more completely understood in the male child.

Many developmental issues during this phase of development extend beyond the age span of 3 to 6 years. Central to all development is psychosexual progression and personality formation. The vicissitudes, influences, and transformations of the phallic-oedipal stage of psychosexuality affect every part of the developmental continuum and contribute enormously to the genesis of psychopathology.

Psychosexual development, in general, entails many more preadolescent changes than those seen in connection with physical development. This is especially true for

Originally published as "Lines of Maturation and Development through the Phallic-Oedipal Years of Childhood" in Jules R. Bemporad (Ed.). *Child Development in Normality and Psychopathology*. New York: Brunner/Mazel, 1980. Reprinted by permission.

the phallic-oedipal phase, in which children become aware of genital differences, are more inclined toward masturbatory activity and genital explorations, are preoccupied with making up theories of reproduction, and begin to manifest an attraction toward the opposite-sex parent. The phallic-oedipal period is, of course, the phase in which the Oedipus complex comes into full bloom, and at the same time it is the stage at which boys and girls experience intense castration anxiety. All the associated vicissitudes of this stage of psychosexual development occur independently of hormonal changes. During this stage of human development there are no significant primary or secondary changes in physical sexuality. The production of sexual hormones is limited to very small quantities of estrogen and androgen. Androgen production, however, increases in both sexes, more so in boys, after the phallic-oedipal stage when children enter late latency, after which there is a subsequently sharp rise in adolescence. Androgen production is somewhat different from that of estrogen excretion, which increases gradually in both sexes starting at about age 7.

There are a number of components to the phallic-oedipal phase of development. The undercurrent of this phase is infantile sexuality, which entails erotic-genital interest and exploration, sexual play, the discovery of sexual differences, the attraction to the opposite-sex parent with the eventual sense of loss of love, as well as the sense of injury and retaliation from the same-sex parent, along with the experience, for both sexes, of castration anxiety. In many respects, the pivotal force of this phase of development is castration anxiety, which is central to the creation and dissolution of the oedipal situation.

In order for the child to reach this stage of development, it is essential that he has completed many aspects of development in the anal-muscular phase, which precedes phallic-oedipal development. The former phase of development starts between 10 to 14 months, at which time creeping, crawling movements occur, and extends to the third year, when the child has attained libidinal object constancy. In order to proceed, it is essential that the child during the toddler years develop motor skills, language, ego defenses, and cognitive capacities preparatory for separation-individuation and autonomy. It is during this time that the child grows from cooperative babyhood to toddlerhood, a period that Erikson has labeled "autonomy versus shame and doubt." During this time, the erogenous zone shifts from the mouth to the anus-rectum, marking the beginning of anal eroticism and the associated conflictual, biological mode of fecal retention and elimination. Now the toddler shows self-assertion that is aimed at the furtherance of separation-individuation and autonomy. Through autonomy, the toddler can combat his sense of doubt and shame. Nevertheless, psychological, physical, and social dependency, frustrations, and disappointments foster serious doubts about his ability and freedom in asserting himself. At this time, the toddler experiences self and object images with blurring and confusion of the percepts. He wants to fall down and let go, not only with his hands, but also with his mouth, eyes, and sphincters. Now the mother begins to give increasingly more prohibitions to prevent him from hurting himself.

Oppositional behavior at this time is common and should not be confused with negativism. The latter appears when the toddler believes he must protect the anal-muscular developmental process by turning his oppositional behavior into mutism, bowel and bladder incontinence, and willfulness in food refusal and outright battles with mother. The toddler reaches separation-individuation through ego stages that are determined in part by the rate of neuromuscular and language maturation. In language development, maturation and learning go hand in hand, but the maturation of motor functions appears to be independent of learning. Language increases the child's sense of belonging to the family and allows him to use secondary process thinking and expressions.

The 2-year-old toddler shows little interest in reciprocal play and contacts with peers. He is interested in building materials for the purpose of construction and destruction. It is not until later, during the preschool years, that the child learns to play cooperatively. Before that, play is mainly exploratory and is aimed at learning a safe range of autonomy. As he enters the phallic stage, the child expresses masculine and feminine trends in solitary role playing, often with toys displaying oedipal objects and phallic exhibitionism. Later, the child stages the Oedipus complex in group play.

When the toddler enters the phallic-oedipal phase of development, he experiences once again a burst of energy, initiative, and curiosity. As Erikson has put it, the phallic child seems to be "on the make," likes "making," and displays great pleasure in the "conquest" of his mother. This intrusive quality is more apparent in boys, yet it has its parallel in girls insofar as they, as Erikson said, are out for "a catch," giving the appearance of "being on the make" and clearly wishing to be attractive and endearing to the opposite sex.

At this point in development, the child shows his capacity to imagine his place in the family and his relationship to people in his immediate environment. Mahler has demonstrated that at the end of the fourth subphase of separation-individuation, the child has reached the level of libidinal object constancy and is capable of establishing mental images of the parents and his own self. He sees himself as having a social role in his group, which helps him in defining his self-object representations. Ever since the age of 3, the phallic child has been reminded that he is no longer a baby. He hopes to meet this challenge but quickly finds that his energy and intrusiveness lead him to experience frustration and pain when he discovers that he is incapable of doing what adults do. As a result, narcissistic defeat and humiliation are commonplace in his life in the family, nursery school, and peer group.

During separation and individuation, the genital zone becomes increasingly important as a source of endogenous pleasure; it thereby enhances a sense of sexual identity and object relatedness and affects basic mood states as part of the early genital phase, which according to Galenson and Roiphe is a preoedipal antecedent to oedipal development.

Prior to the phallic-oedipal years, the male and female child have an undifferentiated primary identification with the mother. In the ensuing months, however, the child internalizes parts of both mother and father. Before she is 2 years old, a girl imitates her mother and starts flirting with her father. Then the little girl is mostly involved with her mother, and in a sense her investment with the mother is basically the negative Oedipus complex. At the time of separation-individuation, the little girl moves toward the positive Oedipus complex and then reaches out more affectionately and aggressively to the father. She devalues the mother. For the boy aged 2 to 3½, the psychosexual identification begins to shift from the mother to the father. Likewise, the boy experiences a negative Oedipal complex whereby aggressive feelings are attached to the mother, whom he regards as overprotective, nongiving, and potentially engulfing. Ideally, in a few months the boy is able to make a shift in his allegiance to his mother; he then transfers his aggression to his father, thereby permitting the mother to be overvalued and desired. Now the father is seen as a competitor for the mother.

The phenomena of infantile sexuality are clearly apparent during child treatment. The phenomena are also apparent in the direct observation of children, sexual perversions, sexual foreplay, florid psychosis, and states of regression. Adult psychoanalytic reconstructions of infantile sexuality are also helpful to our appreciation of the early years. But child analytic work provides the most convincing evidence for infantile sexuality. The child analyst has the unique opportunity of observing the child over a period of time. He is able to see the variations and transformations of instinctual drive and ego development as well as the importance of core gender-identity, learning experiences, cognitive styles and functions, and language.

Infantile sexuality is the keystone not only of clinical psychoanalytic theory but also of concepts of human development in general. When Freud first published his *Three Essays,* in which he reviewed the past contributions to the subject of infantile sexuality as well as his own clinical experience, his work was considered a sacrilegious attack against the innocence of children. His view was also questioned because of his belief that infantile sexuality had a great effect on an individual's subsequent personality development. What was particularly upsetting to people at the turn of the century was that infantile sexuality was said to leave an affective residue in childhood experience that continued to express itself outside of awareness throughout the individual's life. Freud also suggested that disturbances in the development of sexuality led to neurosis, "the negative of a perversion." In addition, Freud formulated developmental psychosexual stages (oral, anal, phallic-oedipal, latency, and genital) through which a child passes toward the completion of his development. Freud pointed out the universal oedipal constellation and the role of the incest taboo. His view of infantile sexuality suggested a mechanistic-biological concept that excluded environmental influences. With the development of ego psychology, however, the role of environment, as well as the development of the ego (perception, cognition, motility, defensive organization and adaptive-coping skills) took on more important roles. Infantile sexuality, therefore, acquired a more general meaning, including both internal and external influences and vicissitudes.

Freud was able to show that the sexual wishes of the adult's unconscious not only can lead to psychoneurosis but also can play a part in many of the normal everyday aspects of adult life such as play, superstition, dream, fantasy, wit, and religion. These wishes, either ungratified or gratified during childhood, continue in the unconscious of the adult and motivate him. Clinical observations of children confirm Freud's views of infantile sexuality. Infantile masturbation, erections, genital and oral play in infancy, and the toddler's curiosity about his excrement are all phenomena of infantile sexuality. In addition, normal nongenital lovemaking of adults satisfies many infantile sexual needs. The kiss demonstrates the importance of the mouth in lovemaking, as do many endearments such as "sweetie" and "honey." Playful spanking and biting as part of foreplay are other examples. Likewise, obscenity has a universal meaning to people because it is unambiguous in its connection to infantile modes of pleasure. Another proof of infantile sexuality is sexual perversions. Psychoanalytic studies of perverts demonstrate that they experience what is desired unconsciously by adults and openly by infants. On another level, sexual fantasies are the wishes of infantile sexuality, especially apparent when they are floridly evidenced in psychotic delusions and manifest content of dreams. Another type of evidence for infantile sexuality is the fact that amnesia for childhood events prior to 6 years is extremely common. Yet we know in watching young children that this is a time of intense emotional experience and excitement.

Historical study of the discovery of child sexuality has revealed that Freud's concepts in *Three Essays* were hardly his own observations. His theories of child sexuality were a composite of numerous observations of children. In 1867, the English psychiatrist Henry Maudsley pointed out examples of child sexuality. Later, before the turn of the century, others wrote extensively about infantile sexuality. It is apparent from the historical study of Stephen Kern that it remained for Freud to synthesize the earlier data, through his extensive clinical experience, into a consistent theory of infantile sexuality.

We see in boys various manifestations of infantile sexuality as they enter and pass through the phallic-oedipal years. They are increasingly aware of the triadic relationship of family life, and even without the birth of a sibling, wonder about pregnancy and delivery and how they came to be born. Even in the most sophisticated families, where sexuality is not a forbidden subject for discussion, the child must create his own theories of intercourse, pregnancy, and birth. He wonders whether his mother will have more children and even thinks about his own ability to make a baby. Often, he will openly tell his mother that he wants to marry her. Maybe they could have their own baby, he thinks, and go off someplace and live wherever his fantasies and wishes take him. He may suspect babies are made by oral impregnation and delivered anally; he may view coitus as sadistic, especially if he has witnessed his parents making love, and he is convinced of the universality of the penis—all views equally held by the oedipal girl.

He is soon confronted by the reality of his own being and the world in which he lives. There is no escape from his sense of inferiority and increasing anxiety and guilt about his wishes. He simply knows that he cannot do the many things that father does handily each day. Furthermore, in a healthy family the son realizes that the quality of the mother's affection for father is something that he will never share, much less her sexual love with the father. However strong the denial of his smallness is, it cannot save him at that time from the awareness that he is smaller than his father in every respect. Consequently, the phallic-oedipal child, much like the toddler in his toilet-training experience, meets with frustration and defeat.

The little girl in the phallic-oedipal period has no happier time of it. Failure and frustration are her everyday experiences. She can help her mother with chores, but never is she able to equal or excel the mother in this capacity. If she is lucky, she is told to take care of her little brother or sister, whom she resents and would like to hurt. By way of identification with the mother, she demonstrates her first interest in having a baby. At the same time, she fancies herself as a better mother, not to mention a better wife and lover than her mother. It is hard for the little girl to imagine why father stays with this woman who happened to have given birth to her a few years before. She dresses up for her father, scrambles to meet him at the door, and tries in every way to make him feel important. Instead, she quickly realizes that during the course of the evening the father's interest will be directed to the mother.

Direct observation of children, as well as our clinical experience, indicates that for the phallic child to reach this level of psychosexual development and to complete resolution of the Oedipus complex, a considerable degree of maturation and learning is necessary. This maturation and development cut right across all levels of ego development at a time when the development of the ego has reached a point where some degree of synthesis and consolidation is possible.

From about age 3 to 5 years, children grow rapidly. The average boy grows about five inches and gains ten pounds. The girl tends to be somewhat shorter and lighter. The organ that develops most rapidly is the central nervous system; by the time the child is 5 years old, over 90 percent of the nervous system tissue has attained an adult level of maturation, with myelin now deposited in the higher brain centers, particularly cortical and subcortical structures. Genitally, neurobiological organization is sufficiently developed to allow erotic excitation and orgasm, although, of course, ejaculation and menstruation cannot yet occur. It is not until puberty that genital functions are possible. Also during this time, psychomotor coordination and digital dexterity are greatly increased. Language development has progressed beyond basic phonemes to morphemes. The child is now increasingly able to understand logical rules and syntactical structures. The phallic child is able to use language as a means for classifying, describing and comparing the objects that he encounters every day in his world. Nuances of language are possible by age 5, and words can now be differentiated into meanings applicable to specific objects and events.

In object relations, the child continues to be egocentric up to the age of 5. It is hard for him to empathize with other individuals, but as he passes through the phallic-oedipal period, his relationships become more sociocentric. Imaginary companions are no longer needed, and there is less need for dramatization of different roles. Perceptual capacities of the phallic-oedipal child increase as he enters this phase of development. Now he is able to differentiate stimuli in his environment by using specific language labels for them, attending to both the whole and its parts. Spatial organization, however, is still not a particularly relevant dimension for the child. The phallic-oedipal child has now formed, to use Piaget's term, a representational world. Because of acquisition of language, increased memory capacity, especially evocative memory, his heightened ability to differentiate perceptual experiences, and his increasing knowledge of the rules of arithmetic and logic, he is capable of increased intellectual performance. By the time the child has left the toddler stage, he is no longer in what Piaget called the sensorimotor stage of intelligence and is at the level of true conceptual intelligence. He is now capable of symbolizations. Simple representations or intuitions begin to occur at ages 4 to 5, later followed by articulated representations or intuitions that occur between the ages of 5 and 7. At the age of 7, the child has entered the stage of concrete operations, at which time he is able to conceptualize coherence, groupings, and serializations. From ages 11 to 15 he enters a period of formal operations, when new structures, visuomorphic groups, and lattices of logical algebra are possible. What must be kept in mind, however, is that during the phallic-oedipal stage the child's understanding of concepts is partially colored by the perceptual aspect of the stimulus. For instance, at age 4 his concept of quality is dependent upon conceptual aspects of the stimulus. Piaget's famous experiment with beads in a tall cylinder jar illustrates this fact quite concretely. The phallic child is apt to consider beads in a tall cylinder as greater in quantity than beads in a short, squat jar that actually contains the same number of beads. From the ages of 5 to 7, however, as the child passes through the phallic-oedipal years into the middle childhood years, he begins to understand that the amount of beads is constant regardless of the change in the shape of the container in which they are held. Consequently, one can see that the phallic-oedipal child has added thought to his perception and is in general more thoughtful about the world in which he is living.

Dreams of children in the early phallic years demonstrate a tendency toward narration of events in very simple concrete terms. It is hard for a child of this age to tell the difference between a dream as a private experience and a dream as a shared experience. Furthermore, dreams are often depersonalized; dream images are iconic, usually involving monsters and threatening animals. Death is everywhere in these dreams, as the happy wish-fulfilling dreams of the earlier years are replaced by images of anxiety and guilt. Dreams of nakedness and embarrassment are their concern, as well as those of failing examinations, falling, flying, swimming, and having teeth pulled.

Play during these years also changes. Children now want to play out various roles such as doctor, cowboy, ship captain, nurse, and jet pilot. The play fantasy often aims at denying the anxiety associated with the child's smallness and relative overall inability to perform adult tasks. He wants to be big and to do what big people do. Oedipal play is dramatic, often grandiose, filled with feelings of invulnerability, invincibility, triumph, and eternal happiness.

Oedipal fantasies are universal and contain elements of the oedipal myth. The central figure of such fantasies is a hero, rescued from abandonment by someone from a lowly station in life, raised to adulthood when he follows a prophecy leading him to a rival whom he vanquishes and kills, only to realize his mistake and live forever with his guilt. These images can be transformed in fantasies of monsters, of attacking animals, of castration by a father, and of self-castration. The fantasies make up for an unpleasant oedipal reality, allow wish fulfillment, blind terror, and provide punishment for oedipal strivings.

The phallic-oedipal years of development are also important for psychosocial development. The phallic child's relationships with peers begin to change as he enters this stage. Up to the end of his toddler life, his peers were not particularly important to him. Reciprocal play seldom was enjoyed. As he enters nursery school, he becomes more aware of the external world, particularly of the fact that teachers and peers are not so readily accepting of his behavior, nor do they tend to view him as quite as special as his parents. He is encouraged to mix with the other children, to go from solitary to parallel play, and then to cooperative play. Finally, at the end of the phallic years, he is capable of reciprocal play in which there is greater opportunity for the discharge of instinctual drive and motor energy but also for the chance to try out new roles and skills.

The phenomena of the phallic-oedipal years demonstrate the change in erotic pleasures of the young child. Bowel-bladder pleasure and its transformations into personality development have already taken place. Anal erotism has been experienced during defecation and is connected with anal masturbation and anal retention. It is the stimulation of the mucous membrane lining the anus and the anal canal which leads to this kind of erotism. The pleasure is autoerotic although, of course, it may be enhanced by external sources. During bowel and bladder training, the child must negotiate with the mother, and it is by this kind of interaction that the erotism becomes related to the object. Ideally, at the end of the anal phase, the child repudiates anal wishes and sublimates this energy into activities such as playing with sand, painting, and staying clean. At this stage of development, if erotic development is interfered with, the child is apt to excessively use mechanisms of reaction formation and repression to ward off these impulses, thereby jeopardizing his entry into the phallic-oedipal phase of development. Erotic interest shifts at the time of change to the phallic phase from the anus to the penis and clitoris.

The phallic child is now in a second phase of infantile masturbation. In this second phase, the boy's specific aims are penetration and procreation. This erotism is different from genital erotism of adolescence and adulthood as the phallic impulses are to penetrate but not to discharge semen. The impulses to hit, to press in, to knock to pieces, to tear open and to make a bull's eye are part of the male child's fantasy. Even if a child is sexually knowledgeable from discussions with his parents, as well as information obtained from the "street," he is still puzzled in the attempt to understand phallic penetration in intercourse. As a result, he must fall back on other ideas of sexual contact and pregnancy, ideas which have occurred to him in his everyday childhood experiences and feelings. Phallic wishes lead him to want to penetrate through the mouth, the anus, the navel and in this manner create a baby. This is the act of phallic erotism; on the other hand, the passive aim is to be penetrated and to bear a baby, a feeling that little boys are apt to have in the early phase of phallic development as part of the negative Oedipus complex in which the wish to be castrated becomes a necessary condition for being penetrated and is usually fantasied as anal penetration.

Under the impetus of wishes, sexual knowledge comes to the young child through perceptions and fantasies. Initially, the child believes there is only one sexual organ, namely, the penis, but later the child must face the perception that the female has no penis. Since this perception is not acceptable, he must disavow it, something which he cannot later do because of a reality sense which prevents him from maintaining the belief that there is no perceptual difference between the sexes. In order to maintain this belief, he then has to elaborate a series of fantasies along the lines that the girl's penis will later grow back. Consequently, as a defense, the male child may develop fantasies and neurotic symptoms related to the female genitalia as a way of avoiding anxiety. These fantasies are usually repressed at the phallic-oedipal stage as the child enters latency. This is, however, not the case with perverts who find no solution to the Oedipus complex. They are stopped short between disavowal of the perception and the denial through fantasy. As Freud put it, the pervert is confronted with the fact that his mother has no penis and in order to fill this gap, he must create a fetish or face a phobia.

Early in the male phallic psychosexual development, he becomes cognizant of his anatomical gender differences. His awareness of the male genitalia enhances his identification with his father and encourages him in this competitive direction. Furthermore, he begins to have fantasies of parental lovemaking which can be reinforced by either hearing or seeing the parents making love, as well as by whatever fantasies that the boy may have of his parents. Parens suggests that a "primary heterosexuality" in boys, as well as girls, pushes the boy toward the mother and starts the Oedipus complex. At this point, the boy wants to show his mother his penis and at the same time to look at her breasts and genitals. His innate sense of the penis as a penetrating instrument and source of great pleasure are manifested in masturbation, exhibitionism, and sexual role playing. He may play games in which he is protective of his mother and in other respects imitates his father. He will make up stories and fantasies about larger rivals whom he easily vanquishes, as in "Jack and the Beanstalk." Soon his view of his father is so threatening that he lives in dread of injury by the hand of his father. This threat forms the basis of castration anxiety, which brings into his development a new theme, a theme that usually exists only in the child's fantasies but is reinforced by parental punishment and by the strength of his oedipal fantasies. The anxiety coming from the castration threat eventually leads to repudiation of the boy's oedipal wishes through suppression and repression, which shifts the ego defensive organization. Evidence for this developmental shift is found in the everyday play of children as well as in fairytales and fantasies. Children's graphic productions, anthropological studies of totemic animals, and the data from child analysis and psychoanalytic adult reconstructions are also supportive of these developmental trends.

Soon the mother indicates her unwillingness to respond to the boy's wishes, sending him perhaps into a jealous rage that may lead to a wish to kill her and to be loved by the father in her place. This is the negative type of Oedipus complex, which also leads to a dread of injury and castration because of the passive wishes involved. Fear of castration is a universal fear among young boys because of the erogenous quality of the phallus itself; pleasure and phallic tumescence enhance fears that erotic fantasies will be revealed. Earlier experiences in losing the breast in weaning and later losing feces in defecation are antecedents to the overall sense of castration anxiety and body fragmentation. Because of castration anxiety, the boy finally relinquishes the maternal object and replaces the mother in the ego by way of an identification with her. At the same time, there is an introjection of the father into the boy's representational world, and concomitantly an identification is made with this introjection, which strengthens masculinity in the boy's character. Thus the boy's libidinal wishes for the mother are in part desexualized and sublimated and partly inhibited and transformed into impulses of affection for her.

Female phallic psychosexual development is much more complicated than male development and less well understood. Freud initially assumed that sexual development in both boys and girls proceeded in a similar manner, a view he later modified after realizing that the little girl has to change not only her primary sexual object from the mother to the father, but also eventually her erogenous zone, from the clitoris to the vagina. In the beginning, however, the girl, much like the boy, starts off with the mother as the main libidinal object. Again like the boy, her earliest erotic fantasies are directed toward the mother. Between the ages of 2 and 3 years, however, she begins showing a preference for the father. Masturbation using the clitoris in lieu of the penis increases at this time as it does with masturbation for the boy. It is at this time, however, that gender differences in psychosexual development emerge. Her desire to play the man is not brought to an end by castration anxiety. It is, in fact, castration fear that propels the little girl toward the Oedipus complex. For now she blames her mother for the genital difference and looks to her father with the hope that he will repair her body damage and allow her to become a man like him. Even if she is aware of her vagina at this time, the clitoris remains the erogenous zone through phallic-oedipal development and usually the adolescent years when a switch from the clitoris to the vagina is made. It is during the time when the girl shifts her libidinal interest from the first object, the mother, to the father that she becomes aware of genital differences. At first, she wishes to repudiate her recognition of sexual difference. She tries to deny her fantasy of having been deprived of a penis. If successful, this denial increases her antagonism toward the mother and enhances her fear of more retaliation from the mother. Likewise, the wish for a penis increases interest in the father and any brothers. It is at this time that penis envy and its manifestations (inferiority, jealousy, shame, and rage) are evident. Castration anxiety is manifested by negative affects, like sadness, worry, anguish, and despondency, connected with comments and comparisons of the external genitalia, and by anxiety evidenced by phobias, sadism, rage, and anxious preoccupations. The girl's passive wish is then turned toward the father's penis as he becomes the principal object. The rivalry with the mother, however, may be interrupted by brief negative oedipal erotic feelings for her. Soon, however, she is rebuffed by the father and is forced to renounce her oedipal wishes. Thus, she is thrown back on her mother, with whom she must emotionally remain until adolescence when she starts to move toward heterosexual objects.

The child's awareness and observations of the parents' sexuality play an important part in psychosexual development. Awareness of parental intercourse (so-called primal scene experiences) are stimulating and often very exciting and frequently lead to fear, dread, and disgust. These experiences are ubiquitous but often not remembered in later life by the adult, and frequently not recalled at all by the parents even after their occurrences. The repression of primal scene experiences occurs for both the parents and the child. All children experience at least auditory primal scenes. They hear the parents' movement in bed, changes in breathing rate that suggest excitement or struggle, sounds of the mother's giggles, father's heavy breathing as well as various noises emitted at the time of orgasm. All these sounds are very stimulating to the child's fantasies and become even more graphic if the child has witnessed the parents having sex. In general, primal scenes are confusing for the child because he does not know who is doing what to whom. The younger child is particularly upset by the separation experience he feels as he witnesses the primal scene. Because his cognitive equipment is confused by what he perceives, parental intercourse is viewed as an act of aggression. Also connected with primal scene experiences is a child's fear that the mother will become pregnant. Pregnancy is another difficult fantasy during this stage of development because it stirs up old sibling rivalry feelings.

Freud considered the Oedipus complex the "cornerstone" of psychoanalysis, the central core of psychosexual theory of development and, in some respects, the phenomenological nucleus to his theories of infantile sexuality. It is a theory that is substantiated by a great deal of clinical and anthropological data. Rutter's critique of infantile sexuality, an objective overview of the literature, reviews empirical data supporting Freud's phallic-oedipal formulations. The Oedipus tragedy, from which Freud drew much of his view of the Oedipus complex, is found in the *Odyssey*, which leads us to suspect that the legend is older than the seventh century, when the Homeric epics were being written down. It is an ancient and universal myth.

The Oedipus complex is basically a triadic developmental family phenomenon in which a child's sexual strivings for the same-sex parent bring him face to face with his erotic feelings and phallic wishes toward the parent of the opposite sex. The Oedipus-complex further differentiates the object-relatedness of the child. The desire for affection and stimulation from the parent of the opposite sex pushes the child into a competitive relationship with the parent of the same sex. For the boy, this competition leads to fear of castration; for the girl, castration anxiety intensifies her hostility and ambivalent feelings toward her mother, magnifies her romantic inclinations toward her father, stimulates her wish to own or have her own baby, and heightens her desire to be like her father and be a member of the male world. Thus, the Oedipus complex is an apprenticeship for heterosexuality and an essential developmental step for male and female psychosexual identity. In girls, the wish to have a baby, often evident at the beginning of the third year, marks the awakening protogenital sexuality that gives rise to the Oedipus complex; this early sensuality suggests an innate primary feminine disposition that appears at the end of senior toddlerhood as an early form of genitality. Thus at this age the girl's psychic activity is dominated by a heterosexual genital drive preprogrammed to appear at this time. Parens, Pollock, Stern, and Kramer suggest that the heterosexual genital drive pressure may be a stronger factor than castration anxiety for the girl's entry into the Oedipus complex.

The incest taboo, a strong deterrent to acting out of the Oedipus complex, is universal. No society has ever allowed an individual to mate with members of his or her family for procreation. The reason why it is universal has been debated over the years. The resolution of the Oedipus complex, therefore, takes place with changes in both the aims and objects of the instinctual drives. Love-dependent and erotic aspects of objects are dissociated, and new object relations develop with people such as teachers and friends, who are free of the incestuous taboo. The child identifies with the authority of the father, who is introjected into the ego as the authority of the superego, thereby perpetuating the incest taboo and preventing the ego from returning to an earlier libidinal position with the parents. The libidinal components of the Oedipus complex are thus desexualized, sublimated, partially inhibited in their aims, and partially transmuted into impulses of affection. The overall outcome of this psychosexual phase and the resolution of the Oedipus complex is the structural formation of "precipitates" in the ego, which consist of true identifications in some way united with each other, a combination that gives rise to the ego ideal and the superego. Freud was quick to point out that because of the gender differences in the resolution of the Oedipus complex, the little girl's superego formation is quite different. The breakup of the girl's infantile genital organization comes from her increasing awareness during later development that her wish to have a child with the father can never be fulfilled. Consequently, Freud believed that the woman's superego is never impersonal or independent of its emotional origin, as in the resolution of the male Oedipus complex.

The triadic interaction of the Oedipus complex does not occur only in the phallic-oedipal period of development. In adolescence, there is a resurgence of many aspects of the Oedipus complex as the adolescent tries to rework previous developmental issues. Often in adulthood, prior to a son's marriage there is an upsurge of oedipal feelings on the part of the father toward his future daughter-in-law. The same response, of course, can occur in a mother's feelings for her newfound son-in-law. And in later life, grandparents may also have a return of their rivalrous feelings toward a son-in-law or daughter-in-law after the birth of a grandchild. Toward the end of the life, if aging has been complicated by brain deterioration resulting in loss of cognitive control and instinctual delay, a man may give vent to long repressed oedipal urges and make sexual advances toward young girls.

There are various reasons why the Oedipus complex may not be resolved and the child may be unable to develop in latency. The child may not be able to enter latency because he lacks the capacity to form symbols and use fantasies. Or the child may regress in his ego latency structure so that he acts out impulses rather than discharging them by way of fantasies. The child may also simply regress to prelatency behavior whereby pregenital fantasies dominate behavior, interfering with impulse control, learning, and peer relationships. If a child has had multiple deprivations in his childhood and a poor relationship with parents, these experiences may very well lead to tenuousness in his relationship with parental objects, leading to a limited control of aggressive and sexual impulses along with little capacity for sexual pleasure. Oedipal attachment may also be hindered if the child has been through extreme frustration or extreme overindulgence during this phase of psychosexual development. If a parent of the opposite sex has been out of the home at the time of the child's phallic development, the child's relationship with the parent of the same sex may be affected. The child may be overly involved with the parent of the same sex, a situation that will make it difficult for him to be sufficiently free of this parent to form a heterosexual object choice later in life. If the opposite-sex parent is seductive toward the child and overstimulates him with unresolved oedipal feelings, the child's oedipal situation may never be tempered. If the parent of the same sex dies or deserts the family during the oedipal period, this may be the soil for conflict, since the event coincides with the child's oedipal aggression toward this parent. It is best for the resolution of the Oedipus complex if the parent of the same sex is attractive, nonpunitive, and a satisfactory model for identification. At the same time, the opposite-sex parent should not be emotionally unpredictable, seductive, or unduly punitive, so that the child will be able to place confidence in objects of the opposite sex. It is also important that the parents do not indicate any rejection of the child's genetic sex. It is best for the resolution of the Oedipus complex that the child identify with a happy concept of marriage, seeing his parents' marriage in terms of pleasure, security, and comfort.

Between the ages of 3 and 5, the child struggles with his oedipal relationship and his competitive dependency vis-à-vis siblings and parents. During this time, he enjoys a happy illusion of being a miniature adult, but from age 5 to 7, he must come to terms with the illusion, often using fantasies that substitute for the primary objects in his family. Then he enters the stage of latency, or, in Erikson's terms, the stage of "industry versus inferiority." The physical onset of this stage is marked by the shedding of the first deciduous teeth, at which time the child ideally enters a period of repressive calm. At this point, if development has proceeded normally, the Oedipus complex has been resolved; narcissistic investment in the body and its various orifices and functions is diminished until the prepubertal growth spurt of adolescence, when instinctual drives are markedly heightened under the influence of increased androgenic production.

In the latency years, the child is not satisfied with merely "playing around" and doing "make-believe." This is a time when he turns to people outside the home with whom he hopes to identify. People who appeal to him for identificatory purposes are those who seem to have a great deal of competence and strength. The latency child's own feeling of competence and achievement is often illusory; he cannot yet trust himself to his wishes. He increasingly turns to industry with the idea that workmanship is now most important. Less time is spent with the family, and now there is more concentration on tools, objects, and work. Unlike his attitude during the phallic-oedipal years, he now emphasizes real goals, which he wants to take to completion. He also at this time begins to learn to read and write with a sense of competence.

Differentiation of male and female gender roles is furthered during the middle childhood years. Children are encouraged to develop skills and show interest in gender-appropriate achievement. Nevertheless, some children want to retreat to the earlier years because they are unable to enjoy the work situation and they feel inadequate. They long to return to the comfort of mother. The sense of failure and tendency toward regression are particularly marked if the child's mastery during the phallic-oedipal years was marginal. Furthermore, he misses out in developing his identity if work is something that he cannot be comfortable with. The latency child knows in his own way that part of what he will be in the future is determined by what he does now. It is at this level of development that work becomes a motivational force in the development of identity. Harry Stack Sullivan was well aware of this when he referred to the latency period as the juvenile era, a time when the child is concerned with competition and compromise and is bent on the achievement of social competence.

Peer group participation and school activities further the differentiation of sexual identification. Peers help the latency child learn his role in society, ease his way into associative-cooperative play, teach him to subordinate his individual needs and wishes to the group, give him a new idea of his value relative to other people, and help him learn his role in society. It is at this time that the latency child develops his academic skills, and it is also during these years that superego and ego ideals are strengthened. The superego authority is invested in the introjection of the parents and occurs at the oedipal resolution. Now during the latency years, its power is available to help the ego in controlling id impulses. The structures of the superego and ego ideal are further modified and amended as the child passes through middle childhood years into adolescence.

There has been much confusion about the instinctual life of the latency child. Freud in 1896 considered latency a time in which repression first appeared. Freud believed that latency lasted from age 8 to age 10. He felt that sexuality was quiescent in the latency years. Further, he thought that the resolution of the Oedipus complex led to repression as a typical latency defense. Reaction formation, sublimation, and the furtherance of superego development were important outcomes during that period. In addition, he believed that sexual energy was displaced in its gratification since its aims were inhibited. Later, in 1905, Freud indicated a change in his view. He thought that latency started at age 6, but he continued to adhere to the belief that sexual quiescence was present between the resolution of the Oedipus complex and the time of puberty. Sarnoff has pointed out in his review of latency that Freud continued to believe that phylogenesis resulted in the ego functions of latency. In other words, Freud continued to adhere to a biological view of latency throughout his career. Subsequent child developmentalists have questioned this view. They conclude that sexuality during the latency years is simply less observable, often repressed but more commonly suppressed because of the child's increasing social awareness. They also believe that masturbation in girls continues by way of indirect stimulation of the clitoris.

During latency, the child constantly has to fight against regression to a period in his life before the phallic-oedipal years. These pregenital impulses that haunt him are much more troublesome for boys. The child has to work out defenses against such drives, and these defenses are a large part of the psychological work of latency. It is a time when secondary process thinking is consolidated, and the reality principle is firmly established. Positive object relations and identifications are now established. Personality is in large part formed during latency; but contrary to Freud's view, personality development continues through life, as long as a person is not bound by rigid fixations and pathological defenses.

Latency is not characteristic of mammals. Man is the only mammalian that has a latency period. Apes and monkeys, for instance, show nothing like latency in their development. Consequently, latency is now viewed as a cultural phenomenon. Sexual quiescence does not exist; libidinal drive strengths are maintained but not increased until prepubertal hormonal changes occur. Nevertheless, clinical data, as well as Kinsey's research data, show that sexual experimentation and curiosity continue through the latency years. Masturbation and sexually colored play are quite common in these years. The sexuality of latency is also characterized by increased social awareness of sexuality and by increased circumspection about sexual behavior, especially in the presence of adults. The only latency children who openly masturbate and exhibit their sexuality in public are mentally defective children or psychotic children.

Fantasies change during the early latency years when children defensively show dissatisfaction with parents. Often adoption fantasies appear, especially if there were deprivations early in childhood, and they are precursors to the "family romance," as are fantasies of having a twin, imaginary companions, and animal fantasies, all containing objects that love the child more than the parents. These fantasies soon change in latency into "family romance" fantasies granting a new origin to the child, making him into a hero, whereby he gains strength and a refurbished identity.

There are two subphases during the latency years. In a sense, they are somewhat different. The first subphase occurs between the ages of 6 and 8 years, when the child is especially fearful. It is a time when repression, suppression, and aggression are most apparent. The child makes an attempt to control masturbation. He is vulnerable to regression to pregenitality, with the reaction formations of disgust, shame, and guilt. The superego is very strict, and often it feels like a foreign body haunting him. In relationships with others, the superego is ambivalent and crude, especially in relationships with the same-sex parent. Sexual impulses must be controlled by the superego. The child does not want to view his parents as sexual objects, although he is well aware of sexuality in general. He hopes to restrict the discharge of his sexual drive to fantasy and masturbation. And it is best that he continue masturbation; this provides him with an easy outlet for sexual feelings. At this time we see masturbatory equivalents, particularly in children who are fearful of masturbating. They appear as scratching, head banging, nail biting, and sadomasochistic behavior in varying degrees. Castration anxiety can continue, especially for girls, during this time. Penis envy frequently is prominent during this phase of latency. Secondary process thinking does not show any consistency. Often the child dips back into primary process thinking.

The second subphase of latency, ages 8 to 10, is a period of increasing cognitive control and reality testing. Sublimation now is fuller and more successful, and the child suffers less over masturbation. His external world is more gratifying and he tends to rely less on his fantasies. The superego is less severe and alien. In this phase, the child's sense of omnipotence is decreased, and his defenses and affects are more ego-syntonic and less involved in simple impulse control. Sexuality is more prominent and pressing, and from ages 8 to 11, the latency child is apt to flee from sexual and heterosexual curiosity and interests.

Six- to 9-year-old children spend a great deal of time learning how to get along with others and competing with peers. Rules in this regard are viewed as absolute and immutable, partly because of the severity of the superego and partly because of cognitive immaturity. By age 9, however, the child has some notion of reciprocity with other people. Now he can change the rules. These new rules apply to everybody. Between the ages of 11 and 12, children develop feelings of equity and fairness; they may even give concessions to handicapped players, realizing that other children's needs may be different from their own. Thus, they are able to transcend egocentrism, shift perspective, and be emphatic with peers. The child is now more involved with his peer relationships, dependent on them to impart and point out external reality to him, help him control inappropriate impulses, show him new ways of coping and developing skills, as well as means for repairing damage to self-esteem and mitigating the sting of narcissistic injuries. The group helps one another through maintaining its own controls. In a sense, the peer group provides an auxiliary ego to the late latency child.

At about age 8, the child develops a sense of time. Death is now seen as something permanent around which he will build, depending on family and culture, an ideology of afterlife. He tries to trust in the future and to be objective with himself. To some extent, he can detach from himself and other people so that he no longer narcissistically equates himself with others. Cause and effect are now less magical. Trust, autonomy, initiative, and industry are all part of his expanding cognitive awareness and strengthen his position vis-à-vis his identity and role in the culture.

In latency years, there is a deceleration in physical growth. Boys surpass girls at this time in that they are slightly taller and heavier, stronger, better coordinated, and have a faster reaction time. This gender differential in growth usually ceases at pubescence, when girls become slightly taller than boys and continue to be so until they are about 15 years old.

As boys and girls enter school in the latency years, there is a difference in their behavior, attitudes, and accomplishments. Girls are frequently fearful. Initially very tearful about being in school, they show more motor inhibition and less inclination to activity in school, and tend to stay closer to their mothers. In the toddler years, the female central nervous system develops faster than that of boys. Accelerated growth and deposition of myelin occur several years earlier in girls. Girls show a left hemispheric dominance manifested by better language arts skills, which, however, are only a temporary advantage until mid latency. Girls are more alert to new situations with schematic differences and discrepancies. This alertness is partly responsible for their cautiousness and greater need for conformity.

Boys, on the other hand, are more given to activity, which buffers their fearfulness. They are less skilled in the language arts and better able to see spatial relationships and do mechanical tasks. They evidence right hemispheric dominance in the early latency years. Male aggression is more prominent because it is displayed through physical activities and less so through words. In the early school years, boys often shun the school situation because they associate many of the activities such as drawing, cutting out, pasting, and so on with femininity. These activities are encouraged by teachers who are usually women. Unfortunately, in our culture few men teach in the lower grades. This is one reason why gender stereotyping is so readily maintained. Coeducation helps to remove gender stereotyping. It is my opinion that coeducation helps to neutralize the biological gender differences of the classroom, dampens the aggressive potential of boys, encourages girls to compete in sports, and fosters gender equality.

The socialization in school confronts a child with the fact that he is just another child in the school and neighborhood. He is forced by circumstances into an associative-cooperative mode of play where new patterns of aggressive behavior as well as techniques for self-control are learned. The child must subordinate his individual needs and goals to the group. At home, the child must strike a balance between the values and activities of his parents and those of his peer group. The peer group puts the child in a situation in which he has to reevaluate internalized values. With a partial transfer of parental roles to teachers and members of the peer group, the latency child is more critical of his parents and retracts the omnipotence he delegated to them in earlier years.

As a child passes through the latency years, his fears change from concrete, symbolic representations like ghosts, dangerous animals, and monsters, to more generalized and less symbolic substitutes for his fears of parents. His anxieties now focus more on his everyday performance, although he still tries to create a balance between his old magical world and the new world of reality. For this reason, he may temporarily regress to an earlier stage where he can utilize old behavior in the service of controlling emotional conflicts. In doing so, he intensifies reaction formations such as guilt, disgust, and shame against those infantile impulses stirred up by regressive shifts. Reaction formations now are more integrated into his developing character. In his sexual development, he must look outside the home for new models for identification. The girl looks for idealized, romantic, prestigious identificatory figures, although the early latency girl may still play out the role of mother and daughter. On the other hand, boys look for men who have status in society, people who are strong and assertive.

The peer group clustering is largely determined on the basis of sex differences, which results in a cleavage between the sexes. And, in fact, the popularity of the child in the peer group has a lot to do with the clarity of the child's sex-type activities and attitudes. Girls tend to be more obsessive, boys more compulsive, in staying within the acceptable modes of behavior of the peer group. We find that latency children pick models for identification on the basis of not only cultural factors but also the child's own personality traits and skills. In other words, he tries to imitate a prestigious figure toward whom he feels he has kinship. For instance, a boy who is well coordinated, outgoing, and strong may choose an athletic star for his model. But these gender criteria break down in late latency and early adolescence when both girls and boys consider the male as much more competent in problem solving and adapting to the world. Unfortunately, this dichotomous distinction continues through adulthood, leaving the female with a negative self-concept our society does little to dispel.

The games of the culture are vital to the latency child. For instance, games with rules (Piaget's third category of play) come into prominence during the latency years. Hobbies, which are halfway between play and work, are now selected; some lead to ego mastery and a sense of productive competence. In latency years, there is a special culture with its own rules, rhymes, riddles—games grownups are not permitted to enter. Latency rites include peculiar little superstitions, excessive counting, tongue twisters, repetitive jokes that make fun of adults, and odd collections of objects which serve as talismans. Hobbies appear early and frequently are precursors of later work. Brief coded messages are part of the clubs, packs, and gangs of latency children, all of whom pride themselves on their group solidarity and individuality. Latency play is in general more realistic and frequently based on rules that now are not immutable. But there is an upholding of one unchanging rule: the exclusion from the group of those children who do not fit into the social identity of the latency group. For instance, girls organize their clubs for the purpose of keeping out all boys and other girls, especially girls who like boys. On the other hand, boys are greatly involved in games, projects, and trips; their group concentrates on trading and gathering prize objects. In the group there is a great deal of bartering, which is another way of comparing strength and assets of members.

Toward the end of latency, children enter pubescence, which is generally regarded as a two-year interval preceding the onset of full puberty. Psychologically, pubescence is closer to the middle school years than it is to adolescence. Its onset is characterized by a spurt in physical growth, which includes physical changes in both primary and secondary sexuality. For some children, pubescence can be very short-lived, hardly observable by even the child and his parents. But usually rapid spurts in the growth of the arms, legs, and neck occur, with changes in height, increase in weight, and increased sexual impulses, along with growth of the genitalia. The triggers for pubescent growth are neuroendocrinological. After several years, at the time of actual puberty, these biological changes reach a peak characterized in the female by menarche and in the male by spermatogenesis. This is the time of development called preadolescence, a misnomer, as it is also used to designate the middle school years; in this respect it is not specific or meaningful enough to be a useful term. Pubescence, although it is close to late latency, should be regarded as part of early adolescence because of instinctual drive increases. At that time, sexuality blossoms and physical growth is rapid. Aggressive and sexual drives intensify, body concepts change, narcissistic body investment is augmented, and the pubescent child completes his cognitive shift from the concrete to the abstract. In some ways, there is a kind of irony to this change, in that developmentally he is capable of greater rationality; but at the same time, he is overwhelmed with physical discomfort from his growth and emotional uneasiness about his body. Of course, he is bombarded with sexual feelings. At this time, the pubescent boy and girl are vulnerable to regressive shifts to phallic and preoedipal fixation points. For instance, attitudes of tidiness and cleanliness slip back to dirtiness; neatness is reversed to disorder and chaos, sociability to outright boorishness; relatively stable mood swings to euphoria and depression. The adaptive calm with the parents is shattered by aggression and alienation from them. In general, there is a resurgence of dependency conflict with surface ambivalence, more marked in boys. Boys are at this time more mature and prone to regression. Girls tend to maintain a sophisticated facade, making boys feel even more inferior. At the same time, boys dread any trace of femininity in themselves and organize ego defenses around passive-active and masculine-feminine conflicts.

Thus, there occurs in latency a complicated reorganization of the defensive structures of the ego, enabling a balance between defense and drive, appropriate to the culture of the child and family, a balance that facilitates calm behavior and educability. The child now uses fantasy defensively to play out conflicts and discharge drives in thought rather than in action, thereby maintaining the balance of ego and id during latency.

REFERENCES

Bornstein, B. (1959). On latency, *Psychoanalytic Study of the Child.* New York: International Universities Press 8:279–85.

Erikson, E. H. (1959). Identity and the life cycle. *Psychol. Issues* 1:50–100.

Freud, S. (1905). *Three essays on the theory of sexuality. Standard Edition.* Vol. 7. London: Hogarth Press.

Freud, S. (1905). *On the Sexual Theories of Children. Standard Edition.* Vol. 7. London: Hogarth Press.

Galenson, E., and Roiphe, H. (1976). *J. Amer. Psychoanal. Assn.* Some suggested versions concerning early female development. 24: 19–58.

Hughes, T. (1949) *Tom Brown's School Days.* London: J. M. Dent.

Kern S. (1973). Freud and the discovery of child sexuality. *History Childhood Quarterly* 1:118–141.

Kinsey, A. C., Pomeroy, W. B., and Martin, C. E. (1948). *Sexual Behavior in the Human Male.* Philadelphia: Saunders.

Kinsey, A. C., Pomeroy, W. B., Martin, C. E., and Gebhard, P. H. (1953). *Sexual Behavior in the Human Female.* Philadelphia: Saunders.

Mahler, M. S. (1972). *Int. J. Psychoanal.* On the first three subphases of the separation-individuation process. 53:333–38.

Parens, H., Pollock, L., Stern, J., and Kramer, S. (1976). *J. Amer. Psychoanal. Assn.* On the girl's entry into the Oedipus complex. 24:79–108.

Piaget, J., and Inhelder, R. (1969). *The Psychology of the Child.* New York: Basic Books.

Plath, S. (1981). *Ariel.* New York: Harper and Row, p. 51.

Rutter, M. (1970). Normal psychosexual development. Paper presented at the British Psychological Society Meeting, Nov. 6.

Sarnoff, C. (1976). *Latency.* New York: Aronson, pp. 382–86.

Sexton, A. (1974). *The Death Notebooks.* Boston: Houghton Mifflin, p. 14.

Sullivan, H. S. (1953). *Collected Works of Harry Stack Sullivan.* Vol. 1. New York: Norton.

12

ASSESSMENT OF THE ADOLESCENT

Aaron H. Esman

Traditionally, the diagnostic assessment of emotionally disturbed adolescents has been regarded as an exceptionally difficult procedure. Anna Freud (1969), for instance, wrote of adolescence as a "developmental disturbance" and said "I . . . place the [normal] adolescent reactions . . . at an intermediary point on a line between mental health and illness." In her classic (1958) paper on adolescence she stated "The adolescent manifestations come close to symptom formation of the neurotic, psychotic or dyssocial order, and merge almost imperceptibly into borderline states, initial, frustrated or full-fledged forms of almost all the mental illnesses. Consequently the differential diagnosis between adolescent upsets and true pathology becomes a difficult task" (p. 113). Miss Freud codified in this paper the prevailing psychiatric view that "adolescent turmoil" is not merely prevalent but normative and, indeed, desirable. As a consequence, mental health professionals, as Offer and his associates (1980) have recently reported, tend to characterize the normal adolescent as more disturbed than the normal adolescent sees himself, or as more disturbed than psychiatrically ill or delinquent adolescents see themselves.

It is only in relatively recent years that this dictum has been subjected to serious reconsideration, largely on the basis of large-scale studies of normal populations. In the 1960s a number of investigations were undertaken to determine the course of adolescent development in Western populations and to assess adolescent psychopathology in the light of such considerations. Among the first such studies was that of Grinker, Grinker, and Timberlake (1962), who investigated a group of adolescents they called "homoclites," meaning those who follow the common rule. They were impressed by this group's effective adaptive capacities and by their evident lack of turmoil or psychopathology. Subsequently Douvan and Adelson (1966) reported an extensive interview and questionnaire study of average American junior high school and high school students. They found that these normative adolescents did not show evidence of ego failure and disruptions, evidenced little rebelliousness except over trivial matters, and showed no indications of a "generation gap" with parents.

Perhaps the most extensive and influential of these normative studies was that conducted by Daniel Offer and his associates (Offer and Offer 1975) with a population of male high school students in a Chicago suburb. They found that there were in essence three patterns of development, to which they referred respectively as "continuous," "surgent," and "tumultuous." The continuous developers, who represented 23 percent of their sample, showed a pattern of smooth, unruffled progression throughout adolescence and into young manhood. Their backgrounds were characterized by healthy and intact families, by parental support of their growing independence, and by a life-long pattern of stable supportive peer relations. They were generally satisfied with themselves and with their place in life and were in essence models of mental health. None of the members of this group had shown any clinical psychiatric illness. The second or surgent group, which comprised 35 percent of the total sample, was characterized by a generally sound pattern of adaptation, but with somewhat more emotional conflict with periods of some progression and regression, with a certain amount of turmoil in the early adolescent period and with some self-questioning, sexual anxiety, and mild emotional constriction. By and large, however, their development was characterized by adequate adaptation and general developmental success, though as might be expected, there was somewhat more conflict with parents than in the "continuous" group. Some 36 percent of the clinical syndromes manifested in the total population came from this surgent segment.

The third pattern was that of "tumultuous growth." These adolescents made up 21 percent of the total study population and appear closest to the classical pattern of adolescent turmoil. Many of them showed overt behavior problems, intergenerational conflict, wide mood swings, and so on. Not surprisingly, about half of the clinical cases came from this group.

A fourth group comprising about 21 percent of the total study population showed a mixed pattern, with features of two or more of these subgroups that made it difficult to classify them. Overall, however, at least two-thirds of the total group developed in a manner inconsistent with the classical picture of "adolescent turmoil."

Another perspective on this issue is provided by the clinical studies of James Masterson (1967, 1968). In brief, Masterson found that of the adolescents studied who showed clinically significant behaviors, the great majority continued to manifest clinical syndromes after a five-year follow-up period. For the most part their behavior patterns became consolidated into well-defined clinical diagnoses, and few if any of them showed substantial remission in their clinical disorders. As a result Masterson drew the conclusion that adolescent pathology was a very different thing from normal adolescent development and that the burden of proof lay on any clinician who chose to assess tumultuous or disorganized development in adolescence as "normal adolescent turmoil." Strober, Green, and Carlson (1981) have recently reported similar findings regarding the reliability of DSM-III diagnoses of adolescent patients.

A number of other studies bearing in the same direction could be cited, among them that of Michael Rutter and his associates (1976), who, from their study of a large population of rural adolescents in England, came to conclusions quite similar to those of Offer and his associates in suburban Chicago: that is, that rebelliousness was generally limited in early adolescence to trivial matters such as length of hair, staying out late, and so forth, and that by and large the path of development was relatively smooth and unmarked by the tempestuousness described in the classical view.

The current view, then, of adolescent development is that there appear to be a number of pathways through which the young person progresses from childhood to adulthood. The classical view of turbulent, tempestuous, romantically tinged turmoil is but one of these possible pathways, and in all probability, statistically the least likely. It is, however, the one most consistent with a psychopathological outcome and the one most likely to come to clinical attention. It is perhaps for this reason that, as Offer, Ostrov, and Howard (1981) have shown, mental health professionals tend to see normal adolescents as far more troubled than do the adolescents themselves.

This is not intended to minimize the stressful character of adolescence. The young person traversing this phase is confronted by a number of crucial developmental "tasks" requiring major adaptations in many aspects of life. He must experience and adapt to the biological changes of puberty, with its attendant impact on the body image and on drive organization. He must learn to deal with new patterns of social relationships, tinged as they are increasingly with sexual feelings and fantasies and the definition of sexual role patterns. The adolescent must also undergo significant changes in his relations with parents and other family members, as he tests out his capacity for autonomous living while learning to come to terms with residual dependent wishes and feelings of attachment to parents who are no longer seen as omnipotent, idealized figures (Esman 1982). Decisions must be made about future life plans, particularly in areas of education and vocation, involving identification with actual or fantasized models. There must be accommodations to new cognitive capacities, exemplified by what Piaget (1969) called "formal operational thought." All of this is subsumed under what Blos (1969) spoke of as "consolidation of character," which represents ideal end points in the process of becoming an adult. It is not an easy time, and a fair number of adolescents do succumb to the stresses of the phase or to the predisposition they bring with them from their earlier years and experience significant psychopathology. In this chapter I shall try to describe a mode of clinical assessment of such disorders that would permit the clearest possible definition of diagnosis, prognosis, and treatment planning.

PHASE-SPECIFIC CONSIDERATIONS

The adolescent is in an equivocal developmental situation. No longer dependent on his parents, he is not yet fully autonomous. In the context of a clinical situation he is most frequently a somewhat reluctant participant. Even where verbally fluent and capable of some self-reflection, he has not yet established a sense of temporal continuity and his grasp of his past is often as hazy as his conception of his future. He is still enmeshed in a network of social institutions in which his adaptive capacities are subject to scrutiny and his behavior to criticism.

In short, from the standpoint of clinical assessment as from others, the adolescent occupies a rather vague space between childhood and adulthood. Like an adult he can (if he will) communicate intelligibly and usefully about his mental state, but as with a child, his reports generally require supplementation from schools, parents, courts, hospitals, and other significant adults. Given some of his phase-specific sensitivities, however, such ancillary information should be obtained with a maximum of tact, discretion, and respect for the adolescent's concern for autonomy and confidentiality.

Accordingly, the assessment of adolescent psychopathology will commonly involve the following elements:

1) Clinical interview/s with the adolescent;
2) In many cases, a family interview, at least with the adolescent and his parents;
3) Interview/s with parents, individually and/or collectively;
4) Information from school/s, previous therapists, and other professionals;
5) Psychological testing;
6) Medical/pediatric examinations.

I shall discuss each of these in turn.

The Clinical Interview(s)

Not merely the assessment but further course of treatment (if any) may hinge on the conduct of the initial clinical contact with an adolescent. In consequence, this encounter should be arranged with the greatest care. Wherever possible, arrangements for the initial interview should be made with the adolescent himself, rather than through the parents. Even the unwilling, angry, defiant adolescent will often respond to the examiner's recognition that he has his own schedule of activities that deserves respect and accommodation. Even in hospitals, the examiner should show regard for the adolescent's need for privacy and his desire for self-determination, and arrange the initial interview so that the patient retains the highest possible level of self-respect. The adolescent should be assured that within the limits of feasibility and sound clinical judgment, whatever he says will be treated as a confidential communication.

The technique of the initial interview is largely a function of the examiner's personal style. As a recent report by Hopkinson, Cox, and Rutter (1981) points out, there is no single "right" way to conduct an interview. Aichhorn (1917) provided a classic example of virtuosity in engaging delinquent adolescents in a direct but empathic fashion. The younger adolescent is likely to be guarded and mistrustful; some effort in putting him at ease with relatively neutral conversation is often helpful, whereas older adolescents can generally be approached more directly about the presenting occasion for the interview.

However conducted, the interview should be designed to yield information in the following areas:

1) Appearance and behavior (including level of psychosexual maturation);
2) Thought content;
3) Formal aspects of speech and thought;
4) Affect (observer's judgment) and mood (patient's report);
5) Impulse control and frustration tolerance;
6) Major preoccupations, interests, and coping capacities;
7) Object relations (range and quality);
8) Capacity for self-observation
9) Characteristic defense mechanisms;
10) Level of superego development;
11) Level of cognitive function.

Needless to say, a single interview, particularly one with a balky, guarded, or manipulative adolescent, is unlikely to yield a full picture in all these areas. Further, acute toxic states resulting from drug or alcohol use, or acute organic confusions resulting from head trauma, may complicate the assessment process, so that only observation over a span of time may permit an accurate evaluation. A series of meetings may therefore be necessary to provide the data that, together with those derived from other sources, will combine to generate a usable clinical impression.

Family Interview

A major element in the psychology of adolescence is the resolution of those mutual issues of autonomy and attachment, dependence and independence, and sexual conflict that pervade the parent-child relationship. It is rare indeed for an adolescent to come to clinical attention without some significant aspect of his troubled or troubling behavior being played out in the family nexus. It is essential to assess not only the adolescent's attitudes, feelings, and behavior with respect to his parents and siblings, but equally the attitudes, feelings, and behavior of family members toward the adolescent on whom, for whatever reasons, they have focused their concern (see Anthony 1969; Counts 1967).

Traditionally, such information has been and continues to be obtained through interviews with parents, singly and/or together, and where indicated, with other family members. The growth in recent decades of interest in and understanding of family interaction processes has added a significant observational tool to the psychiatrist's armamentarium. The family interview permits an *in vivo* perspective of the ways in which the family members deal with each other in a moderately stressful situation, and it can highlight processes that might otherwise elude notice. Power relationships, patterns of communication (and noncommunication), internal alliances, projective tendencies, scapegoating—all can emerge in such an interview and richly illuminate the genetic and current dynamic aspects of the adolescent's problems (Williams 1973; Offer and Vanderstoep 1974). It is often difficult to arrange, or for many psychiatrists to conduct, an interview with all family members; this may be the case particularly where parents are divorced and antagonistic, and where there are very young children. A session with some combination of adolescent and parents is, however, a highly desirable aspect of the evaluation procedure. Where possible, a home visit in which family interactions can be observed *in situ* may be of great value.

Interviews with Parents

To obtain crucial information regarding aspects of current behavior and developmental history as well as data on the personal histories of parents and other family members, it is advisable to see parents early in the assessment process. Further, the establishment of a working relationship with the adolescent patient necessitates at least minimal support and cooperation from parents; this is likely to be fostered by permitting them some initial contact with the therapist so they do not feel totally isolated and disregarded.

The timing and tactical management of such interviews is, however, a delicate matter that requires flexibility, tact, and judgment on the part of the examiner. Wherever possible, it is desirable to obtain the adolescent's consent to such interviews, with his understanding that they are designed to help the examiner understand the problem and that the confidentiality of the patient's communications will be respected. It is often useful to offer the patient the option of being present at the session himself. It is extremely rare for an adolescent to refuse such permission when requested in this fashion, and many will decline the invitation to join in the meeting.

In certain cases, however, this program will not be feasible. For instance, where the adolescent is resistant to, refuses, or is physically unavailable for examination, or when parents are uncertain as to whether evaluation is required and seek preliminary consultation, it may be necessary to see the parents first. In such cases the examiner should, when and if he ultimately sees the adolescent, be frank and explicit about his contacts with parents, and the latter must be told that their communications will not be bound by the rule of confidentiality but may be shared with the patient.

Under any circumstances, certain kinds of information should be sought. The initial contact should wherever possible be held with both parents, so that one can observe areas of agreement and disagreement, possible conflicts between parents, and possible counteridentification. Even when parents are separated or divorced such a joint meeting is desirable unless the relationship is so acrimonious that they cannot communicate at all without fighting. The parents' respective perceptions of the adolescent and his problems, their account of his conduct at home and elsewhere, and their description of family relationships will generally occupy the hour.

Subsequent meetings should be held with each parent alone. This will allow for opportunities to obtain detailed developmental history, to permit each parent to speak more freely about their marital relationship than in the joint session, and to learn about the personal and family histories of each parent. Given present concepts of genetic influence, history of the presence of affective, schizophrenic, or alcoholic illness in family members may be particularly pertinent.

Milieu Informants

Much of the adolescent's life is played out in the context of community institutions. In particular, many of his pathological behaviors as well as his strengths and capacities will be revealed in his school performance and behavior. Should he be involved in delinquent antisocial activities, the judicial system may be the source of pertinent information, while some patients will have been treated by other therapists in childhood or earlier adolescence. In all cases, it is desirable to obtain information from such ancillary sources, any of which may provide a perspective on the patient's mental functioning that cannot be gained from the clinical situation alone. For patients in residential settings, the observations of nurses, activities therapists, school personnel, and dining room staff may be richly informative. In all instances one is interested in data bearing on ego strengths and weaknesses, favored modes of defense and adaptation, and patterns of object relations as seen in real-life situations.

Psychological Assessment

Psychological testing can make a major contribution to the assessment of the adolescent particularly in the following situations:

1) Discrimination of acute phase-related psychotic reactions from long-standing disorders;
2) Demonstration and specific delineation of learning disabilities that, often covert and long-standing, may be major contributors to psychopathological reactions in adolescence;
3) Clarification of the role of subtle organic factors not demonstrable by usual psychiatric or neurological methods.

Of course, they may also be helpful, as they are with patients of all ages, in clarifying diagnosis, assessing intelligence, and suggesting significant psychodynamic issues.

Medical/Biological Assessment

There is perhaps no period in the life cycle in which psychological and physiological processes are more intimately linked than adolescence. In particular, the hormonal changes that normally induce puberty may vary extensively in their timing, sequence, and onset and in their accompanying external manifestations (Tanner 1971). This may in turn generate a range of emotional reactions from fear and shame to pride and satisfaction. Certain endocrine disorders may present themselves primarily with emotional and behavioral symptoms (e.g., thyrotoxicosis). Further, in many severe psychiatric disorders toxic factors are often implicated or at least suspected, and must be ruled out. For all these reasons, a careful physical examination with appropriate chemical studies and a careful neurological examination are mandatory components of psychiatric evaluations of adolescents. Clinics and pediatricians specializing in adolescent medicine are appropriate resources.

EVALUATIVE CONSIDERATIONS

Since the adolescent is in a period of developmental flux, diagnostic assessment is not always easy, even when all available data are in place. Some of the issues that require careful evaluation include:

1) *Degree of Interference with Normal Adaptive Functions.* It is not unusual for concerned parents to bring for consultation an adolescent who is experimenting heavily with drugs or who appears unusually moody or defiant. Any of these complaints may herald the onset of serious psychiatric illness, but they may also be consistent with normal adolescent developmental processes. The significance can be evaluated only in the context of an overall assessment with particular emphasis on the degree to which they interfere with normal adaptive function. The adolescent whose drug experimentation is not associated with a decline in school attendance and performance; the adolescent whose moodiness is not associated with social withdrawal, day/night sleep reversal, or academic failure; the adolescent whose defiance is limited to struggles with parents around curfews and room cleaning rather than antisocial behavior—all can be considered, in the absence of data to the contrary, to be working within the usual range of adolescent conflicts, and parental concern can often be alleviated by tactful explanation and reassurance.

2) *Patterns of Defense Organization.* In adolescents as in adults a crucial consideration in assessment is the configuration of predominant defense mechanisms. The preferential use of more "primitive" defenses such as denial, projection, and withdrawal is likely to portend more serious pathology and to interfere more substantially with effective adaptation than does that of such "higher level" defenses as reaction-formation, suppression, isolation of affect, or intellectualization. Although it is the traditional wisdom that defense patterns in adolescence are shifting and unstable, more recent work (Esman 1980) suggests that the seeds of later psychopathology are clearly laid down by midadolescence, at least, and that some defensive styles and character patterns are stable parts of continuous growth patterns from childhood to adulthood (Offer 1980).

3) *Acuteness and Chronicity.* While it is true that many cases of emotional distur-

bance have their acute onset in adolescence, careful assessment will frequently reveal subtle but definite premorbid indications of impairment. Such data are particularly important in evaluating acute psychotic reactions in adolescence, which may in some cases be the initial episode in a chronic disorder but may in others be isolated, phase-related breakdowns without long-term sequelae. As Anthony and Scott (1960), Feinstein and Wolpert (1973) and others have pointed out, acute manic episodes in adolescents are commonly preceded by histories of emotional instability, moodiness, and irritability of long standing, sometimes evident in early childhood (Esman, Hertzig, and Aarons 1983). Similarly, acute schizophreniform episodes can often be distinguished from initial schizophrenic breaks by careful inquiry into patterns of object relations, earlier indications of unrealistic thinking, histories of sadistic behavior in childhood, family history of mental illness, and the like.

Thus, although estimations of possible chronicity may be difficult, and may at times have to await follow-up observations of clinical course, meticulous history taking may sometimes facilitate such judgments.

4) *Learning Disorders.* One of the principal areas of difficulty for many troubled adolescents is their academic performance. Schools are a major referral source, and breakdown of function is often shown most clearly in this area, manifested by declining achievement, truancy or school avoidance, disruptive behavior, and the like. It is mandatory, in any situation where school problems exist, to obtain a thorough educational evaluation, including not only achievement tests but also assessment of perceptual-motor integration and graphomotor function. Through this means one can often detect previously undiagnosed—and untreated—learning disabilities that play a major determining role in the adolescent's deteriorating school adjustment and behavioral difficulties (Silver 1979; Rothstein 1982). This is particularly important in cases where there is a history of head injury (Shaffer et al. 1980). Much time and therapeutic energy have been wasted with such patients where school problems have been attributed to rebelliousness, depression, or other affective factors, and where the etiological role of underlying learning disorder has been ignored or underestimated. A convenient rule of thumb is that any school-age child or adolescent of middle- or upper-class background who never reads for pleasure or who actively avoids leisure reading should be suspected of having a primary reading disability. College students, too, are not immune to such difficulties (Cohen 1983).

5) *Transience vs. Fixity.* It has long been a shibboleth in the approach to emotional and behavioral disorder in adolescence that "he'll grow out of it." This piece of folk wisdom is echoed in official psychiatric circles by the frequent use of the diagnosis "Adjustment Reaction of Adolescence," or "Transient Situational Reaction." Although it is true that some adolescents' maladaptations are transitory and related to acute situational determinants, it would be a serious error to assume such an outcome in all or even most cases that come to clinical attention. It is now well known, for instance, that many children and adolescents with attention deficit disorders ("minimal brain dysfunction") and learning disabilities continue to show evidence of impairment well into adult life (Hartocollis 1968; Weiss et al. 1985). Follow-

up studies of adolescent anorectics have shown that their eating disorders and/or dietary peculiarities continue well past the "cure" of their acute illness (Hsu, Crisp, and Harding 1979; Bruch 1973). Like the question of acuteness vs. chronicity, therefore, the prediction of transience vs. fixity of disorder requires thorough and rigorous history taking and assessment of the full range of personality structure and function; one must recognize, however, that in many cases judgment must be suspended. It is well to bear in mind Masterson's (1968) dictum that the burden of proof lies with the clinician who makes the judgment that the disturbed adolescent will "grow out of it."

6) *Social-Cultural Considerations.* Adolescents are on the front lines of social change, both as initiators and as barometers of shifts in values and mores (Esman 1975). A generation ago, for instance, the use of marijuana was confined to marginal groups in American society—particularly Blacks, Mexican-Americans, and jazz musicians and their acolytes. At that time, a white middle-class adolescent who habitually smoked marijuana would have been behaviorally deviant, and the practice would have aroused appropriate clinical concern. In the present social climate, of course, no clinical meaning can be attached to the fact of marijuana use by any adolescent; significance can be assessed only in the context of overall behavior.

Further, adolescents, where only partially acculturated, often carry on the beliefs and cultural norms of their families and the subcultures from which they derive. A 15-year-old girl from a recently arrived Cuban refugee family ascribed her suicidal gesture to the voice of her guardian angel, which, she said, regularly appeared to instruct her about her conduct. Since the belief in such phenomena is indigenous and virtually universal in her subculture, it would be injudicious to assign to it the same significance one would attach to a similar belief in an upper-class Anglo-Saxon patient.

Such considerations imply that the clinician engaged in the assessment of adolescents must have a reasonable familiarity with the influence of culture on behavior and must in addition be sensitively attuned to the peculiarities of the adolescent's peer culture. At the same time he must avoid falling into the trap of uncritical cultural relativism; certain phenomena are pathognomonic in any cultural context.

7) *Assessment of Suicidal Risk.* One of the major concerns in the evaluation of adolescents is the possibility of suicide. Data on the severity of this problem are abundant (Jacobs 1971; Petzel and Cline 1978); it is clear that adolescent suicide is a major public health problem, closely correlated with both prevalence of depressive reactions and the phase-specific action orientation and impulsivity of adolescents. Suicidal thoughts, wishes, threats, and gestures are frequent presenting problems, and the clinician may be called upon to make critical judgments in emergency situations, requiring decisions about hospitalization, medication, or other major interventions.

Such judgments are fraught with difficulty. Clinical experience indicates that many seriously suicidal adolescents may well thwart all efforts at control and treatment; on the other hand, some impulsive, histrionic patients may inadvertently succeed in an effort not consciously intended. A profile of the suicidal adolescent may be a useful guide to assessment of risk. It should be recalled that although three times as many female adolescents as male adolescents attempt suicide, three times as many males as females succeed.

The prototypical suicidal adolescent is male, over 14 years of age, and white. He is likely to have made a prior attempt, and there is likely to be a history of suicidal behavior in his family, which is probably a disorganized and chaotic one. There is also a strong possibility of his having a history of significant physical illness, either recent or past. Although college student status per se is not a significant variable, attendance at a prestigious institution appears to be one. Above all, a history of long-standing emotional problems, recent object losses, increasing isolation and withdrawal, and evidence of suicidal thought and preoccupations should alert the clinician to the presence of significant danger and the need for appropriate protective action.

8) *Sexual Identity.* A major concern of many adolescents, particularly males, is that of homosexuality. Particularly in subcultures which place strong emphasis on conventional models of virility, boys who experience any homoerotic feelings or fantasies, or who deviate in significant ways from the conventional norms of athleticism or sexual adventurism may be stigmatized, or at least be plagued with self-doubt. Even more may this be the case where early pubertal development may have been accompanied by incidents of mutual masturbation or other kinds of homoerotic play.

Categorical predictions of adult sexual role patterns are difficult during the developmental flux of adolescence. It is fairly well established, however, that the likelihood of ultimate homosexual identity is increased in the presence of the following factors:

1) Cross-dressing and preference for opposite-sex playmates in early childhood and "latency" (Zuger 1984);
2) Frequent, as opposed to occasional and isolated homosexual play, especially if it has occurred before or after early adolescence;
3) Sexual excitement manifested in dreams and masturbation fantasies, associated predominantly or exclusively with figures of the same sex (Saghir and Robins 1973).

It need hardly be said that, given the sensitivity of the subject, answers to such questions may be obtained only after extended inquiry and in the context of a well-established alliance with a tactful but persistent examiner.

It must be acknowledged that at times, circumstances dictate a more condensed, less systematic assessment procedure than that outlined above. An example is that of John, a 16-year-old sophomore at a prominent boarding school, whose father called in a virtual panic requesting immediate consultation because John had come home for spring vacation in a state of intense agitation and bewilderment. He went first to his mother's home, where he confessed that he had taken LSD the night before and felt he was having a "bad trip." After clearance by his pediatrician, a local psychiatrist to whom she had taken him recommended immediate placement in a residential drug program. I was asked for a second opinion.

John was the only son of divorced parents; the father had remarried and John spent most of his time with father and stepmother. His previous history was one of unbroken successful achievement; he had done well in elementary school and his first year at boarding school had been equally successful. He was a competent athlete with many friends, maintained a steady B average, and was well-liked by his teachers and the school administrators. He acknowledged that, along with many fellow students, he had been smoking marijuana on weekends all year, but this had not notably interfered with his academic or athletic performance. The LSD experiment was his first, and he firmly maintained that it would be his last. Although they were aware of the nature of his problem, the school was clear and explicit in its wish for him to return.

All parents were clearly concerned and devoted, and John's relations with them were warm and seemingly without major conflict. On examination two weeks after the event, John showed no sign of cognitive or affective disorder. He maintained a continuing interest in marijuana, which he had found "relaxing," but abjured interest in any other drugs. He was given to intellectualization and to somewhat pretentious and pseudomature use of language, which seemed in part designed to impress the examiner with his seriousness and the firmness of his sense of control.

It seemed clear that whatever issues might underlie John's devotion to marijuana, he was not addicted and did not have a serious drug problem. His drug use always occurred in a social context and in part at least represented conformity to peer modes. His overall level of adaptation was excellent. I therefore recommended that he return to his school and that he obtain supportive counseling there. I further reassured his distressed and overwrought parents and urged them to suggest to the school that it concern itself more effectively with the pattern of campus substance abuse, which it had hitherto sought to minimize.

TREATMENT IMPLICATIONS

The assessment of psychophathology in adolescence is not an academic exercise. For those who are troubled, and particularly for those whose troubles interfere significantly with their functioning in life, treatment may be not only appropriate, but vital. It is important to keep in mind, however, that the unique developmental issues of the adolescent period and its subphase (Blos 1962) dictate specific therapeutic approaches (Esman 1984).

The young adolescent (12 to 14) is often difficult to engage in individual psychotherapy. He is likely to be at the peak of his rebelliousness and internal turmoil and therefore guarded and suspicious with adults and inclined to externalize his problems. Family-centered approaches that minimize the designation of the early adolescent as "the patient" may prove particularly helpful at this stage, either as adjunct to or instead of individual therapy.

The midadolescent (15–18) is more likely to be capable of introspection and to be under less internal pressure, and may be better able to relate to and even welcome the assistance of a psychotherapist. Even here, however, the therapist should be prepared for the likelihood that the phase-specific pressure toward action may lead the patient to interrupt therapy as soon as his presenting symptoms are relieved. In such cases, work on what may seem to be underlying issues of a characterological nature may have to be deferred until later adolescence or young adulthood. Here too, occasional family meetings can be helpful in dealing with specific conflicts or otherwise unresolvable parent-child issues.

The older adolescent (18–21), whose personality is likely to have attained some level of consolidation and who is more capable of introspection, is usually able to work in therapy like an adult. Since he is, or developmentally should be, psychologically less dependent on parents than his younger siblings, treatment can more clearly be individually focused, with less need for concurrent family interventions. Classical analytic work is more likely to be possible in this period, though some "parameters" may be necessary with respect to continuing developmental issues (decisions about college, career plans, and so on).

In general, it should be emphasized that therapy, geared to the needs and developmental characteristics of adolescent patients, is possible and advisable, with recognition of the fact that certain issues will have to be left to await the impact of further development and, if necessary, later intervention. Of course, for the more severely disturbed adolescent, residential, hospital, and pharmacological therapies may be required (Esman 1983).

FURTHER STUDY

Although much has been learned in recent years about the assessment of adolescents, many areas remain obscure and will require further study. We certainly need more accurate and reliable ways to determine in specific cases the potential gravity of acute breakdowns. The relationship of particular forms of psychopathology to specific subphase developments (Esman 1980), to specific family constellations, and to specific hormonal and other neurochemical changes—and their potential diagnostic value—is only beginning to be explored. Further, we are far from having devised "objective" instruments that will allow us to make more confident assessments and predictions than the currently available clinical methods can do. And, finally, a variety of treatment implications for specific configurations remains unsettled—for instance, when is the adolescent best treated at home, in a residential center, in hospital, or in individual group and/or family therapy? At present, such decisions are based in large measure on the training, experience, and theoretical predilections of the evaluator; it is in any case not clear to what degree such decisions are to be reliably made on the basis of initial assessment. All these questions and others point out the need for continuing research into the complex and fascinating enterprise of diagnostic assessment of adolescents.

REFERENCES

Aichhorn, A. (1917). *Wayward Youth*. New York: Viking Press, 1948.

Anthony, E. J. (1969). The reactions of adults to adolescents and their behavior. In G. Caplan and S. Lebovici (Eds.). *Adolescence, Psychosocial Perspectives*. New York: Basic Books.

————, and Scott, P. (1960). Manic-depressive psychosis in childhood. *J. Child Psychol. and Psychiat.* 1:53–72.

Blos, P. (1962). *On Adolescence*. New York: Free Press.

————. (1969). Character formation in adolescence. *Psychoanal. Study Child* 23:245–63.

Bruch, H. (1973). *Eating Disorders*. New York: Basic Books.

Cohen, J. (1983). Learning disabilities and the college student: Identification and diagnosis. *Adol. Psych.* 2:177–78.

Counts, R. (1967). Family crises and the impulsive adolescent. *Arch. Gen. Psych.* 17:64–71.

Douvan, E., and Adelson, J. (1966). *The Adolescent Experience*. New York: Wiley.

Esman, A. (1975). Changing values: Their implications for adolescent development and psychoanalytic ideas. *Adol. Psych.* 5:18–34.

————. (1980). Midadolescence—Foundations for later psychopathology. In S. Greenspan and G. Pollock (Eds.). *The Course of Life*, Vol. 2. Bethesda, Md.: National Institute of Mental Health.

————. (1982). Fathers and adolescent sons. In S. Cath, A. Gurwitt, and J. Ross (Eds.). *Father and Child*. Boston: Little Brown.

————. (1983). *The Psychiatric Treatment of Adolescents*. New York: International Universities Press.

————. (1984). A Developmental Approach to the Psychotherapy of Adolescents. *Adol. Psychiatry* 12:119–33.

Esman, A., Hertzig, M., and Aarons, S. (1983). Juvenile manic depressive illness: A developmental perspective. *J. Am. Acad. Child Psych.* 22: 302–4.

Feinstein, S., and Wolpert, E. (1973). Juvenile manic-depressive illness. *J. Am. Acad. Child Psych.* 12:123–36.

Freud, A. (1958). Adolescence. *Psychoanalytic Study of the Child* 13:255–78.

————. (1969). Adolescence as a developmental disturbance. In *The Writings of Anna Freud* 7:39–47. New York: International Universities Press, 1971.

Grinker, R. R. Sr., Grinker, R. R. Jr., and Timberlake, J. (1962). Mentally healthy young males (homoclites). *Arch. Gen. Psych.* 6:405–53.

Hartocollis, P. (1968). The syndrome of minimal brain dysfunction in young adult patients. *Bull. Menninger Clinic* 32:102–14.

Hopkinson, K., Cox, A., and Rutter, M. (1981). Psychiatric Interviewing Techniques: III—Naturalistic Study: Eliciting Feelings. *Brit. J. Psychiat.* 138:406–15.

Hsu, L., Crisp, A., and Harding, B. (1979). Outcome of anorexia nervosa. *Lancet* 8107:61–65.

Jacobs, J. (1971). *Adolescent Suicide.* New York: Wiley–Interscience.

Masterson, J. (1967). The symptomatic adolescent five years later: He didn't grow out of it. *Am. J. Psychiat.* 23:1338–45.

———. (1968). The psychiatric significance of adolescent turmoil. *Am. J. Psychiat.* 124:1549–54.

Offer, D. (1980). Adolescent development: A normative perspective. In S. Greenspan and G. Pollock (Eds.). *The Course of Life,* Vol 2. NIMH, pp. 357–72.

———, and Vanderstoep, E. (1974). Indications and contradictions for family therapy. *Adol. Psych.* 3:249–62.

———, and Offer, J. (1975). Three developmental routes through normal male adolescence. *Adol. Psych.* 4:121–41.

———, Ostrov, E., and Howard, K. (1981). The mental health professional's concept of the normal adolescent. *Arch. Gen. Psychiat.* 38:149–52.

Piaget, J. (1969). The intellectual development of the adolescent. In G. Caplan and S. Lebovici (Eds.). *Adolescence: Psychosocial Perspectives.* New York: Basic Books.

Petzel, S., and Cline, D. (1978). Adolescent suicide: Epidemiological and biological aspects. *Adol. Psych.* 6:239–66.

Rothstein, A. (1982). An integrative perspective on the diagnosis of learning disabilities. *J. Am. Acad. Child Psych.* 21:420–26.

Rutter, M., et al. (1976). Adolescent turmoil: Fact or fiction? *J. Child Psychol. and Psychiat.* 17:35–56.

Saghir, M., and Robins, E. (1973). *Male and Female Homosexuality.* Baltimore: Williams and Wilkins.

Shaffer, D., et al. (1980). Head injury and later reading disability. *J. Am. Acad. Child Psych.* 19:592–610.

Silver, L. (1979). The minimal brain dysfunction syndrome. In J. Noshpitz (Ed.). *Basic Handbook of Child Psychiatry,* Vol. 2. New York: Basic Books.

Strober, M., Green, J., and Carlson, G. (1981). Reliability of psychiatric diagnosis in hospitalized adolescents. *Arch. Gen. Psych.* 38:141–45.

Tanner, J. M. (1971). Sequence, tempo, and individual variation in the growth and development of boys and girls aged 12 to 16. *Daedalus* 100:907–30.

Weiss, G., et al. (1985). Psychiatric status of hyperactives as adults. *J. Am. Acad. Child Psych.* 24:211–20.

Williams, F. (1973). Family therapy: Its role in adolescent psychiatry. *Adol. Psych.* 2:324–39.

Zuger, B. (1984). Early effeminate behavior in boys. *J. Neu. Ment. Dis.* 172:90–7.

IV

Developmental Disturbances of Speech, Language, and Learning

13

SPEECH PATHOLOGY IN CHILDREN

Edward D. Mysak

The purpose of this chapter is to present a clinical guide to the assessment of pathologies of speech in children. Information in this area has grown enormously in the last years and there are now whole books devoted to the various topics covered in this chapter. A single chapter devoted to child speech pathology, therefore, can only skim the surface of the area. Those readers seeking additional knowledge are invited to refer to a number of general texts in the field of communicative disorders (e.g., Travis 1971; Mysak 1976; Lass et al. 1982; Bloodstein 1984; and Shames and Wiig 1985).

This chapter is concerned with the development and disorders of speech of children from about 1 year through puberty. The chapter is divided into two parts. The first is devoted to speech simplexes characterized by relatively specific disorders of articulation, phonation, and rhythm. The second is devoted to speech complexes characterized by multiple symptoms and associated with cleft palate and various neurodevelopmental and psychodevelopmental conditions.

SPEECH SIMPLEXES

Childhood speech disorders that show a relatively specific symptom and appear confined to the speech system may be described as simplexes. For example, some children may appear equal to their peers in all respects except that they begin to speak later than expected or do not articulate some of the speech sounds well, or their voices or speech rhythms are atypical. In any regular school, upward of 5 percent of the population may fall into this category of children with speech disorders. Each discussion of a speech simplex includes developmental information, descriptions of forms of the disorder, and diagnostic and therapy considerations.

SPEECH ONSET

After the first year of life, speech sounds develop together with the comprehension and formulation of speech symbols. Various relationships exist, therefore, between the developmental patterns and the disorder patterns of speech sounds and their manner of production. There are exceptions, however, to such expected relationships.

Powers (1971, p. 843) identified at least two forms of problems with the onset of speech: infantile perseveration and delayed speech. She commented that when the child's problem is basically with speech sounds, it may be referred to as infantile perseveration. If, however, in addition to speech sound lapses, the onset of speech is late and various oral language deficiencies are present, the condition may be referred to as delayed speech. On the other hand, it has been reported that there are children with certain types of intellectual deficits in which speech sounds may be normally produced even though there is a severe limitation of verbal capacity.

Developmental Patterns. Darley and Winitz (1961) examined the results of fifteen studies of the age of appearance of the first word in twenty-six groups of children. They stated: "From the results of these studies it appears that the average child begins to say his first word by approximately one year. Delay of appearance of first word beyond 18 months may indicate a serious physical, mental, or hearing involvement."

Statements by various authorities in speech pathology on the emergence of the first spoken word follow: "Girls begin to speak about the fourteenth month after birth and boys about the fifteenth month" (West and Ansberry 1968, pp. 53–54); and "Most children begin to understand and say words in their second year, and they begin by saying only one word at a time" (Bloom and Lahey 1978, p. 129). There is apparently a range of months during which authorities expect first words to appear in normal children. In general, however, it may be said that the first word is expected by about 1 year of age.

In discussing the onset of speaking in phrases and sentences, Van Riper (1963, p. 108) stated that "any child who is not using at least a few understandable two-word phrases or sentences by the age of thirty months should be referred to a physician or speech therapist immediately." Worster-Drought (1968) stated that "most normal children can produce short sentences by the age of two years." However, he reported that "there are some exceptions when otherwise normal children are later in acquiring normal speech, even up to the end of their third year. Sometimes such a late development of speech is a family characteristic." In general, then, it is expected that the average child should be using at least simple, two-word utterances by about 30 to 36 months of age.

Disorder Patterns. A possible background for immaturity is specific, developmental language retardation, where speech sounds and spoken language develop more slowly than expected, but where all other aspects of development may be roughly within normal limits, except possibly for a family predisposition toward slow language learning.

Bloodstein (1958, pp. 23–24), describing specific language immaturity, found that among 108 children between 2 and 6 years of age he examined because of stuttering, one-third were described by their parents as "late talkers," as persisting in the use of "baby talk," or as "difficult to understand" prior to the onset of stuttering. Except for these speech symptoms, the children were relatively free of other clinical manifestations.

Diagnosis. Many questions must be considered when the speech pathologist is confronted with a problem of apparent delay in speech onset. First, is the problem physiological or pathological? If it is outside of normal limits, is it actually a case of specific, developmental language immaturity, or is it secondary to mental retardation, serious hearing loss, brain dysfunction, emotional disturbance, or some combination of these factors?

Formulating appropriate habilitation plans is also complex. For example, will the problem resolve itself as a function of time alone? If intervention is considered appropriate, is parental counseling on how to facilitate speech development sufficient? Or should there be professional intervention in the form of enrollment in a nursery school or kindergarten and/or actual speech therapy?

ARTICULATION

Powers (1971, p. 839) summarized her examination of major survey reports with the comment, ". . . it is safe to say that functional articulation defectives represent between 75 to 80 percent of all speech defectives in the school population."

The following comments by Milisen (1971, p. 624) are also informative:

> In the first grade, from 15 to 20 percent of the children are likely to be described as having defective articulation. There is a marked decrease . . . in the percentages through the first three or four grades, after which the decline is likely to become small or nonexistent. . . . Apparently, articulation is likely to improve until the age of 9 or 10; but after that age, for the most part, misarticulated sounds remain defective unless therapy is provided.

Developmental Patterns. Speech sounds emerge during at least two stages: the prespeech stage and the speech stage. The prespeech stage includes a reflexive vocalization period (approximately the first 4 to 6 weeks), a babbling period (up to about 6 months), a lalling period (up to about 9 months), and an echolalia period (up to about 12 months). During these first 12 months or so, the child theoretically utters forms of all the sounds she will need to utter during the speech stage. About three periods appear discernible in the speech stage, which extends from the period of the acquisition of about twenty words by about 18 months to the period of adult-like symbolic intercommunication by 7 or 8 years. Speech sound development is taking place throughout this 7- or 8-year period; however, only the developmental trends observed during the speech period are presented here.

The earliest age levels at which 75 percent of children tested by Templin (1957) correctly articulated certain consonant sounds are as follows: 3.0 years: M, N, NG, P, F, H, W; 3.5 years: Y; 4.0 years: B, D, K, G, R; 4.5 years: S, SH, CH; 6.0 years: T, L, V, TH; 7.0 years: TH (voiced), Z, ZH, J. Another study, by Prather, Hedrick, and Kern (1975), of the ages at which 75 percent of children correctly produced consonant sounds, indicated that sounds may be acquired earlier than reported by Templin.

As with other developmental schedules, individual differences exist from child to child. The articulatory schedule presented, however, should at least provide specialists with a general idea of when certain speech sounds are expected to develop and, perhaps more importantly, should remind them that sounds do develop as a function of time and that many appear in developmental forms before they reach full maturity.

Disorder Patterns. Since the nomenclature in speech pathology is still not well established, descriptive rather than causal terms will be used as often as possible to identify various articulatory problems. The discussion of disorder patterns is divided into two parts: the first is on articulatory immaturity patterns, or those reflecting late, slow, or incomplete development; and the second is on articulatory dysmaturity patterns, or those reflecting disturbed development.

Articulatory immaturity cases are those in which speech sound patterns typical of a younger child persist well past normal time limits and where they may remain incomplete unless there is therapeutic intervention. Powers (1971, p. 843) described articulatory immaturity as ". . . the pattern of speech sound production which research has shown to be typical of normal speech development in the first several years of life is reflected at later age levels. . . ."

Articulatory dysmaturity cases are those in which speech sound patterns reflect interference with normal maturational processes by particular pathological factors. Such factors include hearing loss (Van Riper and Emerick 1984, p. 173); developmental articulatory dyspraxia; possible disturbances in proprioceptive and tactile feedback; problems in auditory discrimination and span for speech sounds (Powers 1971, pp. 858–62); structural anomalies of the mouth, lip, tongue, and dental occlusion (Bloomer 1971, Ch. 28); isolated dysarthria (Morley 1965, pp. 178–84); reflexogenic problems (Mysak 1980, pp. 121–22); and relatively specific neurological involvement and combinations of involvement of lips, tongue, soft palate, and laryngeal and pharyngeal muscles due to congenital suprabulbar paresis, meningitis, poliomyelitis, and the Moebius syndrome (Worster-Drought 1968).

Diagnosis. The diagnostic responsibility of the speech pathologist in these cases is first to determine whether the articulatory patterns presented by the client may in fact be within normal limits. It is not infrequent for mothers or friends of the family to hear developmental varieties of S, R, L, for example, and to perceive them as defective rather than as developmental forms.

If, however, the diagnostician believes that there is a problem of some kind, then consideration should be given to whether the symptoms are of the immaturity or of the dysmaturity variety. One needs also to determine whether it is a relatively speech-specific problem or one symptom of a complex. On the basis of a thorough and complete analysis of a particular case of articulatory immaturity or dsymaturity, for example, the speech pathologist may recommend either prior orthodontic work followed by a speech therapy program in the case of misarticulation associated with a malocclusion or a speech sound stimulation program in the case of slow speech sound development.

VOICE

Voice is the carrier tone of spoken communication. It also serves as a signal system during the prespeech stage since parents often report that they can distinguish various meanings in their infants' wails and cries. Disorders of voicing are not too common among children; however, it has been estimated that about 1 to 2 percent of schoolchildren do present clinical voice problems (Wilson 1979, p. 11).

Developmental Patterns. Data on the vocal evolution and involution of the male and female voice through the lifespan have been reported by Mysak and Wilder (1981, pp. 25–29). This discussion is limited to the developmental stages for the speaking fundamental frequency of boys and girls through the postpubertal period. The developmental trends for males and females for speaking fundamental frequency is one of a progressive lowering of pitch level from 7 years until after puberty. As would be expected, the amount of lowering is much greater for males. Most of this difference can be attributed to the much greater growth and development of the larynx among boys during the pubertal period.

Metraux (1950), who studied various aspects of the speech development of 207 children at 18, 24, 30, 36, 42, 48, and 54 months, also described certain voice changes during this period. Some prominent features of voice change were as follows: 18 months: not well controlled and tends to become high-pitched and strained; 24 months: better pitch control, pitch lower, still some straining, and squeaking is common; 30 months: voice continues to show wide pitch variability, under stress voice may change quickly from a low-pitched tone to a high, thin, nasalized squeak; 36 months: usually well controlled and in general shows an even, normal loudness, begins to use whispered voice to gain attention; 42 months: normal speaking tone characterized by high, full-volumed yell, whispered voice still used but readily changes to a yell if responses to requests are slow; 48 months: voice somewhat subdued, many children (especially boys) persist in use of loud voice, inflections tend to be marked; and 54 months: voice becomes well modulated, girls' voices may become imitative of their mothers.

Developmental trends discernible in Metraux's observations are the tendency for the child to experiment with pitch, loudness, and quality dimensions of voice and the progression toward increased control and monitoring of voice, no doubt in keeping with environmental models and rewards.

Disorder Patterns. In the ensuing discussion, vocal immaturity refers to conditions that may retard the development and function of the laryngeal structures, and vocal dysmaturity refers to various conditions that may directly interfere with the development and function of the laryngeal structures.

Vocal immaturity may be caused by a number of reasons. One reason for a postpubertal adolescent to continue to speak with the voice of a child would be the dysfunctioning of the sex glands to the point of inhibiting laryngeal growth and development. There are cases of prepubertal or pubertal hoarse-husky voices that appear related to the advent of maturity rather than to some immaturity disorder. Van Riper and Irwin (1958, pp. 169–70) indicated that school speech clinicians frequently have children aged 10 to 12 years referred to them because of complaints of hoarse or husky voices. However, these vocal differences often disappear after puberty. It is acknowledged that various investigators view huskiness and hoarseness as characteristic of the prepubertal or pubertal period and as heralds of approaching voice change.

Vocal dysmaturity may be caused by a number of conditions that directly disturb vocal behavior through the pubertal period. Schwartz (1961) reported on the infantile voice involvement of congential laryngeal stridor. Possible causes include immaturity of the larynx, abnormally shaped larynx, and excessive rehearsal of the laryngeal closing reflex during aquatic fetal life. Complete or partial loss of the larynx in childhood due to cancer or trauma (rare), allergies, asthmatic conditions, and physical weakness have also been cited as contributors to childhood voice problems. Specific laryngeal pathologies have been identified that may affect voicing; among them are vocal nodules. Most authorities agree that vocal nodules are the result of abuse of the voice. Since children frequently shout and yell excessively, it is not uncommon to find "screamer's nodes" and hoarseness in childhood (Wilson 1979, p. 36). Greene (1957, p. 69) indicated that such children often suffer from chronic hoarseness and that it is common between the ages of 5 and 10 years.

Contact ulcers, also commonly the result of misuse and abuse of the cords, occur only rarely in children. Neurogenic involvement of the larynx is also a rare occurence in children (Worster-Drought 1968), except in cases of cerebral palsy. Hoarseness due to inflammation of the cords because of colds is common in children. Laryngeal webs, often congenital but also possibly due to diptheria, are a relatively uncommon condition.

Hypernasality, a rather common voice disorder, may be found in children for various reasons. One obvious reason is a congenital cleft palate. Various differences in the anatomy and physiology of the velopharyngeal closure mechanism may also account for a certain number of cases of childhood hypernasality. Hypernasality is also often found as a sequela to bulbar poliomyelitis or diphtheria (Worster-Drought 1968).

Diagnosis. The first action taken by a speech pathologist upon receiving a referral of childhood voice disorder is to make sure a laryngological examination has been performed. Following medical clearance, a judgment must be made as to whether or not the presenting phonatory pattern is a reflection of a developmental phase. If not, it must be determined whether there are possible ongoing socioemotional backgrounds for the problem. Consultation with psychiatry-psychology is important here. Regardless of the background of the vocal misuse, it must also be determined whether the misuse may eventually result in an abuse of laryngeal tissue, possibly resulting in nodes, polyps, or ulcers.

Decisions also have to be made as to whether the vocal symptoms are amenable to medical, otolaryngological, or psychiatric-psychological procedures alone or in various combinations; or whether voice symptom therapy needs to be provided because the misuse has led to tissue change once and, regardless of the medical, surgical, or psychological attention, will very likely again result in tissue change because of the habituation of an injurious phonatory pattern. The clinician must also decide whether voice symptom therapy should be provided simultaneously with psychotherapy and/or parental counseling because the child's phonatory patterns are of the nature that may eventually cause pathological tissue change.

FLUENCY

Stuttering is familiar to most adults and rather easily "diagnosed" by laymen. The incidence of the disorder among children is approximately 1 percent, and the sex ratio is about 4:1 in favor of boys. Because of its audible and visible symptomatology and its social implications, and because of the progressive increase in self-awareness of and sensitivity toward the symptoms by the child who stutters, it is perhaps one of the most painful childhood speech disorders.

Developmental Patterns. Speech fluency, like other aspects of speech production, develops as a function of time, and adultlike fluency patterns may not be observed until the latter part of the first decade of life. Johnson (1957, pp. 901–902), in summarizing the results of various studies of children's fluency, stated, "In general, these investigators have found that repetitions of sounds or syllables, whole words, and phrases or combinations of two or more words are relatively common in the speech of children from two through five years of age. . . . The range is from less than ten to approximately one hundred instances of repetition per one thousand running words, and the mean is approximately forty-five instances per one thousand words." Johnson also pointed out that these repetitions are tension-free, that the children do not appear to be conscious of them, and that the speech gradually becomes more fluent as a function of time (i.e., they may be considered to be normal, developmental disfluencies). Worster-Drought (1968) referred to these disfluencies as physiological stammering and as purely transient phenomena.

In Metraux's (1950) study of children's speech between 18 and 54 months, the following observations were made with reference to what may be termed develop-

EDWARD D. MYSAK

mental disfluency: (1) 18 months: repetition of syllables or words more frequently than not; (2) 24 months: use of "uh" and "uh, uh" before many responses and compulsive repetition of word or phrase; (3) 30 months: compulsive repetition of phrase even more marked and an increase in such repetition now caused by inter- rather than intracommunication factors (developmental stuttering evidenced for the first time at this age, i.e., repetition of syllable or first word often progressing to a tonic block that can be easily broken); (4) 36 months: return to easy repetition with- out compulsive character, use of "uh" or "um" as starter for speech, infrequent tonic block on initial syllables; (5) 42 months: frequent repetitions, developmental stuttering is again prominent, speech blocking may be accompanied by grimacing, cocking of the head, and so on; (6) 48 months: reduction in repetitions (however, repetitions and blocking episodes may continue in those children who previously manifested "developmental stuttering"); and (7) 54 months: use of "um" or "uh" at beginning of phrase, infrequent appearance of repetitions, except for those children who showed earlier tendency toward speech blocking.

Wingate (1962) summarized a review of the literature of the speech characteris- tics of young children by stating that children show considerable individual varia- tion in the type, amount, and frequency of fluency irregularities, but that certain kinds of irregularities, that is, predominantly syllable repetitions and prolongations, are found more frequently in children later identified as stutterers.

Finally, in a study of thirty-six nonstuttering males aged 2, 4, and 6 years, Wex- ler and Mysak (1982) found that the most frequently occurring disfluency types at each age level were revision, incomplete phrase, and interjections, and that the least occurring type was part-word repetitions for 2- and 4-year-olds and disrhythmic phonation for 6-year-olds. Also, for total frequency of disfluency, the mean fre- quency was 14.6 per one hundred words for 2-year-olds and 9.1 for both 4- and 6- year-olds.

Developmental patterns that emerge from this discussion of childhood fluency, at least up to 5 years or so, include:

1. Disfluencies of various kinds appear physiological in children's speech;
2. There is a progressive reduction in these nonfluencies as a function of time;
3. Amount and frequency of disfluency appear related to internal factors first (e.g., searching for a certain word or phrase) and then to external factors (e.g., attempting to gain or fearing to lose a listener's attention).

Disorder Patterns. An important development in stuttering theory has been the slow shift from the age-old physiogenic-versus-psychogenic battle over the cause of stuttering to the increased recognition that various forms of the disorder known as stuttering may exist. In summing up their discussion of the origins of stuttering, Van Riper and Emerick (1984, p. 271) stated that ". . . stuttering has many origins, many sources and that the original causes are not nearly so important as the main- taining causes, once stuttering has started." In short, there is growing acceptance that the overt symptoms identified as stuttering behavior may, like the symptom of fever, have numerous sources or combinations of sources.

This author believes it clinically useful to divide stuttering into symptomatic and idiopathic forms.

Symptomatic forms include stuttering associated with childhood neuroses, with special CNS and ANS disorders, mental retardation, and with language dysfunction.

Idiopathic forms, or common childhood stuttering, describes stuttering that develops without any apparent cause. The onset of common childhood stuttering is usually between 2 and 4 years; however, occasionally onset is associated with entrance into school. At the time of onset, stuttering almost always takes the form of developmental repetitions that are produced relatively without self-awareness or tension. It occurs most often in the presence of adults who have begun to listen to "how" rather than "what" is being said and who in some way indicate disapproval of the disfluencies. It occurs in children who are relatively free of any significant neurological or psychological symptomatology (although many have family histories of stuttering), and it occurs in children whose parents are essentially normal except perhaps for their concern about their child's speaking ability. Finally, the diagnosis of stuttering in these cases is almost always made first by a layman.

In common childhood stuttering symptoms may be observed to form and transform. If significant others respond to the child's disfluency in a punitive fashion, for example, certain symptom formation may occur. The child may eventually react in "forceful" ways to his disfluencies by attempting to reduce their number and/or frequency at a time when he is neurophysiologically unable to. This may result in heightened speech muscle tone, and consequently his easy repetitions may become clonic in nature. Similarly, his attempts at reducing syllable prolongation time may cause his prolongations to become tonic in nature. Even further symptom formation may take place in time. For example, the abnormal increase in speech muscle tone may irradiate to muscles of the face, head, neck, and so on; also, the child may begin to use "arm swings," "leg swings," "thoracic sways," and so on, as "blockbusters" and distraction devices. In addition to the acquisition of these extraneous movements, the child may develop an array of covert symptoms such as sound and word fears, fears of certain speaking situations, use of verbal "starters" and circumlocutions and synonyms for "hard words," and also the conscious avoidance of speaking situations.

Stuttering symptomatology may also undergo various transformations. One model for changes in stuttering symptomatology as a function of time was presented by Bloodstein (1960). Bloodstein described four stages of stuttering.

1. The preschool stage characterized by episodic repetitions at the beginnings of sentences and on minor parts of speech. Also the child shows little evidence of concern.
2. The early elementary school stage characterized by chronic blocks on major parts of speech. Also, the child now considers himself a stutterer but still shows little or no concern.
3. The junior high and high school stage characterized by stuttering chiefly in response to specific situations. Also, the appearance of sound and word

fears and the use of word substitutions and circumlocutions occurs, but essentially there is no avoidance of speaking situations and little or no evidence of embarrassment.

4. The high school and older stage characterized by a strong anticipation of stuttering, by feared sounds, words, and situations, by the frequent use of word substitutions and circumlocutions, and by embarrassment and avoidance of speaking situations.

Bloodstein stated that the stages are variable and are typical rather than universal, and that the changes are continuous and gradual.

Diagnosis. In suspected cases of childhood stuttering, the speech pathologist must first determine whether the problem is in the "ear of the parent" or is actually in the "mouth of the child"—is it a case of developmental disfluency, or is there an actual increase in the amount and frequency of speech repetitions and prolongations—that is, is it a case of early stuttering? In the case of suspected early stuttering, further studies should be made, for example, by pediatrics, neurology, and psychiatry-psychology, in order to determine whether the disfluency is associated with environmental speech pressures or associated with some form of neurological and/or psychological distress.

If the diagnosis points to some form of symptomatic stuttering, for example severe emotional stress, speech therapy may wait until causal psychotherapy is provided to counteract the underlying disorder. Or speech therapy may be recommended simultaneously with some other therapy in the hopes of preventing or retarding the development of reactive speech symptoms.

On the other hand, if the diagnosis is idiopathic or common childhood stuttering, therapy may take the form of parental speech counseling alone or counseling done simultaneously with fluency facilitation work for the child. If the child is older and reactive symptoms are manifested, various symptom approaches to therapy are available to the clinician (see Wall and Myers 1984, Ch. 7).

SPEECH COMPLEXES

Childhood speech disorders that appear in the form of multiple symptoms or that are associated with greater conditions may be described as complexes. The discussion of speech complexes is presented here under the following headings: cleft palate, neurodevelopmental syndromes (including mental retardation, cerebral palsy, and minimal brain dysfunction), and psychodevelopmental problems.

Cleft Palate

Much has been written in the areas of classification, incidence, embryology, etiology, anatomy and physiology, and evaluation and management (including surgical, orthodontic, prosthetic, otological, dental, psychological, and speech and hearing) of congenital cleft lip and palate. The discussion here will focus on what is considered the most important sequela of cleft palate, that is, the common disturbance of the child's speech communications. For a good overview chapter on cleft palate with special reference to speech, the reader is referred to a chapter by McWilliams (1985).

Background. Congenital clefts of the palate and lip have occurred in man for a long time. Symptoms of such clefts have been found among the remains of some early inhabitants of Egypt, and a report of a cleft lip was reported in the first century. Today the incidence of congenital clefts of the palate and/or lip has been estimated to be one in 750 or eight hundred live births. The immediate cause of such clefts is a failure in embryogenesis; specifically a failure in the complete development, by about the first eight to ten weeks, of one or more of the five embryonic processes of the face.

Clefts of the lip and palate can range from bifid uvula, or a lip pit, to a combination of complete cleft of the soft and hard palates and complete bilateral clefts of the lip. Etiology of such conditions may be divided into genetic and congenital (environmental) categories. Family histories have been reported in 27 percent of isolated cleft lip cases, in 19 percent of isolated cleft palate cases, and in 41 percent of combination cleft lip and palate cases. Possible environmental causes that have been reported include maternal radiation, thyroid deficiency, basal metabolism irregularity, dietary deficiencies, infection, and stress. Parental age, and number and recency of racial fusions in the maternal ancestry have also been cited as possible causal factors. It is not unusual for children with cleft lip and palate to exhibit multianomalies (about 20 to 25 percent), since the heart, limbs, and skeleton are also developing during the fifth to the tenth weeks of embryonal life.

Speech and Hearing. About 40 percent of children with cleft palate may exhibit hearing problems. Upper respiratory system infection and eustachian tube anomalies are the causes usually cited for these problems. Factors that may contribute to the speech syndrome include taut upper lip, missing or supernumerary teeth, various malocclusions, alveolar ridge and dental arch anomalies, oronasal fistulae, palatal vault anomalies, short and poorly functioning soft palates, and flattened nasal alae. Intellectual and socioemotional deficits may also serve as compounding factors.

In any one case, the child with cleft palate may manifest language immaturity, phonatory-resonatory irregularities due to oronasal and velopharyngeal structural anomalies, and articulatory problems associated with chronic hearing problems and with lip, alveolar ridge, dental-occlusal, and palatal vault anomalies.

Diagnosis. Evaluation and management of children with cleft lip and palate are best done through cleft palate teams. Such teams are usually composed of a pediatrician, plastic surgeon, otolaryngologist, orthodontist, prosthodontist, dentist, social worker, psychologist, audiologist, and speech pathologist.

If a child with a cleft lip and/or palate appears at a team conference within a few weeks of his birth, the role of the speech pathologist is basically one of providing speech counseling for the parents. In this regard, the writer (Mysak 1961) described techniques that might encourage the development of more normal oropneumody-namics for voice and speech sound production during the first months of life. This counseling, plus periodic demonstrations of techniques and follow-up, represents secondary preventive work designed to ensure maximum development of prespeech activities during the first 12 months of life.

The speech pathologist should also urge that palatal closure take place as early as possible. Early closure allows the infant to create intraoral breath pressure and oralized speech airstreams during at least part of the prespeech period of vocal activity, which is important to later speech development. If for one reason or another palatal surgery is planned at a year or beyond, the speech pathologist should consider requesting an interim oral prosthesis. Early and ongoing monitoring of the child's auditory behavior is also done, since these children are vulnerable to conductive hearing losses. The speech pathologist also evaluates and reports to the team on the possible speech repercussions of anomalous dentition and occlusion. Further, the clinician must be alert to all the factors that may retard the development of spoken language. This includes reduced or inappropriate speech stimulation due to frequent hospitalization and/or negative parental attitudes.

NEURODEVELOPMENTAL SYNDROMES

This discussion of neurodevelopmental speech syndromes includes descriptions of speech and hearing disorders associated with those childhood conditions referred to as mental retardation, cerebral palsy, and minimal brain dysfunction.

Mental Retardation. Retardates are those who are involved more generally with respect to motor, perceptual-conceptual, socioemotional, and speech and language developments. Wood (1964, p. 36) defined mental retardation as "a reduced ability to learn adequately from any experience within his environment, whereas children with aphasia, hearing loss, or emotional disturbance are able to learn from certain types of experience, depending upon their individual problems." Etiologies for the various brain dysfunctions in mental retardation include chromosomal abnormalities, central nervous system impairment, familial tendencies, or various combinations of these factors. With respect to relationships between speech and mental retardation, Matthews (1971, p. 802) stated, "In our own clinical experience, mental retardation has been one of the most frequently encountered factors associated with language and speech retardation."

In defining the nontrainable child, many authorities include the criterion that the child is nonverbal or capable of learning only a few monosyllabic words. Brown (1967, p. 335) stated, "In general, the degree of speech retardation parallels the degree of mental deficiency." In Darley and Winitz's (1961) review of research on the time of appearance of the first word among the mentally retarded, they report a range of approximately 30 to 60 months. They concluded, "Intelligence is apparently an important factor in the age of appearance of the first word." Myklebust (1954,

Ch. 9), in his discussion of mental deficiency and speech acquisition, indicated that those children classified as nontrainable usually do not acquire speech, while those classified as trainable may begin to use words at approximately 3 years of age and those classified as educable may begin to use words at approximately 18 to 24 months of age.

Matthews (1971, Ch. 31) offered the following conclusions based on a review of the literature of the speech and hearing of the mentally retarded:

1. On the average, the mentally retarded child acquires language considerably later than the normal child.
2. When speech does emerge, the incidence of disorders is considerably higher than in the general population.
3. There is no evidence that the disorders differ in kind from those disorders of nonretarded children.
4. There appears to be a relationship between intellectual level and degree of speech involvement.
5. The incidence of hearing loss is considerably higher than in a nonretarded population.

Of 280 children referred with delayed development of speech, Morley (1965, Ch. 7) indicated that seventy-one cases were associated with general mental retardation. The intelligence quotient was ascertained in thirty-two of seventy-one cases; the average IQ was 60, with a range of 37 to 87. The mean age for the first use of words was 3 years, and the mean age for the first use of phrases was 4 years. Morley also reported the following findings on the speech of eighty-two hospital patients with severe mental retardation: (1) the outstanding feature was the absence or poverty of speech rather than defective articulation; (2) the onset of speech was severely delayed, and when it developed it was extremely limited; and (3) speech comprehension was better than expression.

When confronted with a child with speech involvement possibly associated with mental retardation, the clinician must estimate whether the deficit is merely one part of the child's retardation in overall abilities or whether parts of the speech disorder may be attributed to hearing loss, emotional disturbance, specific types of CNS impairment, glandular dysfunction, institutionalization, and so on. For the speech pathologist to arrive at a good analysis of the child's speech and language profile, examination data from other specialists—the pediatrician, psychiatrist, psychologist, and audiologist—are required.

If the child's speech problem appears to be associated with mental retardation, the speech pathologist needs to consider how speech habilitation procedures might fit into the total management plan. Is the retardation so severe and the learning potential so limited that speech therapy is not indicated except, perhaps, in the form of some suggestions to the parents if the child is still at home? Or is the degree of retardation sufficient to require special school placement and, until this takes place, should interim speech therapy and home suggestions be provided? If a child has been placed but there is no speech service available at the school and the child shows potential for speech progress, supplementary speech therapy should be provided, and speech-stimulation suggestions should be offered to teachers and parents. There are also times when the speech pathologist determines that speech progress is in keeping with overall development and hence special speech therapy may not be indicated. There are cases in which the child may manifest interesting amounts of unactualized potential in speech and language functioning and hence becomes a candidate for special speech therapy.

With reference to speech therapy for the retarded, Brown (1967, p. 335) commented, "Of course it is possible to improve the speech of a mentally retarded child by intensive training, and it is also possible to improve his intelligence scores somewhat." Matthews (1971, Ch. 31) also concluded that speech therapy with mentally retarded children can be beneficial. Rigrodsky and Steer (1961) reported on their study with mentally retarded children designed to compare an experimental articulation therapy technique based upon Mowrer's autistic language-development theory with a traditional stimulus method. At the conclusion of speech training, the upper intellectual group (IQ scores ranging from 45 to 79) achieved better scores than the lower intellectual group (IQ scores ranging from 12 to 44) on certain articulation tests. No significant differences were found between the two groups receiving the speech therapy when compared with each other or with the control groups. Observation revealed, however, that "the children in the experimental program appeared to become more spontaneously verbal and more favorably inclined to the therapy sessions than were the children receiving the traditional therapy programs."

Cerebral Palsy. Cerebral palsy refers to a wide range of chronic childhood brain syndromes with observable sensorimotor deficits. Such children may manifest major intellectual, hearing, and emotional problems. For inclusive discussions of the multifaceted problems found in cerebral palsy—for example, neuromuscular, orthopedic, seizure disorder, visual-perceptual, social, emotional, intellectual, educational, and vocational problems, as well as problems in speech, hearing, and language—the reader is referred to a text by Cruickshank (1976). For texts more specifically concerned with the speech and hearing concomitants, the reader is referred to texts by McDonald and Chance (1964), Mecham et al. (1966), and Mysak (1980).

The first clinical description of cerebral palsy was offered by Dr. Little, an English physician, in 1843. Incidence figures today range from one to six in every one thousand births. Etiological factors include heredity and various environmental problems, of which the major ones are prematurity, anoxia, malformations, birth trauma, kernicterus, and multiple pregnancies. Types of cerebral palsy include spasticity, athetosis, rigidity, ataxia, tremor, atonia, and mixed.

The incidence of speech problems among the cerebral palsied is high. Numerous reports give figures which range from 70 to 86 percent. A high proportion of the cases are mixed and the speech of the cerebral palsied may range from a complete absence of communication to little if any differences from the normal.

Excluding the frequent complications of major problems of mental retardation and emotional disorder, cerebral palsy speech syndromes may take the form of various combinations and degrees of the following involvements: infantile breathing patterns plus paralytic breathing symptoms; symptoms of auditory immaturity and otopathology; speech sound immaturity and various forms of dysarthria; symptoms of infantile laryngeal functioning and of laryngeal paralysis; symptoms of speech rhythm immaturity as well as of pathology of speech rhythm mechanisms; and symptoms of oral language immaturity as well as of pathology. In short, cerebral palsy speech syndromes take many forms and have multiple backgrounds, and the speech pathologist must examine for every possible type and combination of speech pathology.

With respect to the speech diagnosis, the clinician must determine whether major hearing, intellectual, and emotional problems are present, and whether the presenting problem is a relatively specific dysarthria or some complex of auditory, articulatory, phonatory, rhythm, and linguistic symptoms. Further, it must be determined to what degree each symptom reflects immaturity secondary to the brain lesion and how much is due to primary paralysis directly associated with the brain involvement.

Because of the complexity of many of the speech syndromes presented by the cerebral palsied child, wide-spectrum treatment approaches to speech habilitation are usually recommended in the hopes of ensuring that each child will actualize his maximum potential for speech communication.

This means that the speech clinician should start work as soon as possible after the child is identified. Treatment should include: preventive speech therapy procedures for the prespeech period designed to minimize possible secondary problems; causal speech therapy procedures for the speech age designed to ameliorate those factors that appear to be directly responsible for certain speech symptoms; speech symptom procedures designed to ensure that the child uses all the speech sounds and symbols he is capable of at any one time in his therapy program; and speech compensatory techniques designed to help the child develop compensatory sounds when certain sounds are impossible for him to make or, when necessary, to help him use augmentative or alternative communication devices (Vanderheiden and Grilley 1976) to supplement or to replace his efforts at speech communication

Minimal Brain Dysfunction. Minimal brain dysfunction in childhood describes children who may be classified in different ways by different specialists. CNS-impaired, cerebral dysfunction, minimal brain damage, minimal chronic brain syndrome, brain-injured, perceptually handicapped, cerebrally handicapped, and learning-disabled are some of the terms used. These are the children who may not manifest observable neuromotor problems and in whom the diagnosis of childhood neurological disorder may be based entirely on behavioral manifestations. These are also the children who may show varying degrees and combinations of sensory, perceptual, integrative, motor, and behavioral symptoms—and, importantly from the standpoint of this section of the chapter, symptoms of language pathology (see Ch. 14).

It is among the children who usually fit the category of minimal brain dysfunction that developmental aphasia may be found. Such children may show the following kinds of speech and hearing symptoms in various combinations and to various degrees: (1) auditory: possible acuity loss as well as problems with span, discrimination, figure ground, and sequencing; (2) articulatory: subtle or frank neurological deficits of the tongue and velum and slow and disturbed development of speech sounds; and (3) linguistic: retardation or lack of speech formulation; problems in speech comprehension; unusual differences between speech comprehension and formulation abilities; compensatory use of speechreading and gesture to assist speech comprehension; use of agrammatisms; omission of functional or small words in speech; problems in organizing sentences and sequences of sentences; lack of or inconsistent meaning associated with verbalization; atypical verbal associations during reading or speaking; word-finding problems, use of circumlocutionary speech; echolalia; and verbal perseveration.

Worster-Drought (1968) identified two types of aphasia in children: receptive aphasia and executive aphasia. In auditory receptive aphasia, the otherwise intelligent child finds it difficult to comprehend spoken language and consequently also suffers secondary expressive problems. In executive or expressive aphasia, the child may comprehend well but is very slow or unable to express himself in spoken language; however, he usually compensates for his verbal problem with gesture and mime.

Worster-Drought believed that receptive aphasia in childhood is best termed congenital or developmental auditory aphasia. The diagnostic profile of such a child shows limited or absent speech comprehension, limited and frequently unintelligible speech expression, average nonverbal IQ, and a normal or near normal audiogram. Most of these children spontaneously acquire some sounds and words and may gradually acquire a language of their own, that is, an idioglossia understood only by those close to them (he believed congenital auditory imperception is the basis of true idioglossia); in addition, such speech is invariably telegrammatic and characterized by omissions of syllables and word endings. Also, because of their comprehension limitations, these children may echo questions directed at them and request the frequent repetition of new words (reflection of their defective auditory word memory). Some of these children attempt to speechread but do not do so consistently unless taught. Worster-Drought recognized three grades of congenital auditory imperception: (1) pure word deafness only; (2) word or language deafness with additional inability to distinguish between cruder sounds; and (3) the previous deficits plus some actual peripheral hearing loss, including those children who are impervious not only to spoken language but to any ordinary sound. The most likely cause of the problem is "a biological variation of the nature of an aplasia or agenesis affecting both sides of the brain in the temporal lobe cortex and including the auditory word area" (p. 435).

In developmental executive aphasia, speech comprehension may be adequate but speech formulation is considerably delayed and, upon its appearance, is characterized by single words usually associated with gesture; the further development of speech is marked by dysarticulation. Both kinds of aphasia may be found in acquired cases associated with head injury, brain abscess or tumor, encephalitis, and epilepsy.

The following points are made by Myklebust (1954, Ch. 7) in his discussion of childhood aphasia: Aphasia is a relatively specific disorder of symbolic functioning and reflects itself in various degrees of inability to comprehend speech (predominantly receptive aphasia), to speak (predominantly expressive aphasia), or to use language for thought (central aphasia), irrespective of whether it is congenital or acquired. Children who exhibit predominantly expressive aphasia comprehend speech well but rarely engage in vocal activities such as jargon or imitative speech. Those who have less disability may exhibit intermittent ability to use words, phrases, or sentences. Children who exhibit predominantly receptive aphasia can hear speech but cannot comprehend it. They may begin to ignore speech as well as other sounds or intermittently and unexpectedly to comprehend a word. They also experience secondary speaking problems. Those who have mixed aphasia are difficult to differentiate from those with predominantly receptive problems. In short, receptive and expressive aphasias are impairments of interverbalization, while central aphasia is an impairment of intraverbalization.

Finally, Eisenson (1968) offered some impressions of childhood aphasia based on his years of experience with nonverbal children. He indicated that relatively few children he had seen qualified as truly aphasic, and he stated, "With rare exception, developmentally aphasic children are essentially those who have auditory perceptual involvements." He stated further that unless "there is clear evidence to suspect an underlying dysarthria or oral apraxia, expressive manifestations in the child may be considered just another aspect of auditory aphasia."

The speech pathologist is often asked to diagnose relatively specific language disorders in children suspected of suffering from minimal brain dysfunction. The first task with such referrals is to determine whether the child's language development is in fact outside of normal limits. Then the clinician must determine whether the language symptoms can be explained on the basis of serious hearing loss, mental retardation, emotional disturbance, or combinations of these. Data from pediatrics, neurology, psychiatry, psychology, and otolaryngology may be required. The clinician needs these data to test the hypothesis that the language disturbance is on the basis of a relatively specific involvement of central neural mechanisms subserving language function. The length of time that a child suffers from a relatively primary language disturbance is also critical to diagnosis and habilitation, since a primary language disturbance can be expected to produce repercussions in social, emotional, and intellectual developments.

Habilitation of children with minimal brain dysfunction and relatively specific language disorder is complex. Language therapy in the form of home activities as well as professional therapy should be offered as soon as possible. Depending on the progress made in developing speech communication, special schooling and other therapies may eventually be required.

PSYCHODEVELOPMENTAL PROBLEMS

Psychodevelopmental problems can be divided into two parts: the first concerns those childhood socioemotional problems that may disturb the voicing, articulation, and rhythm aspects of spoken symbols; the second has to do with those childhood socioemotional problems that may disturb the comprehension and formulation of spoken symbols. The causes of such problems may range from meager stimulation or inappropriate reward for speech to childhood neuroses and psychoses.

Van Riper (1963, pp. 2–11) discussed the roles of speech in thinking, intercommunication, emotional expression, social control, and the identification of self. His discussion is supportive of the important and reciprocal relationships that exist among intellectual, socioemotional, and speech developments. Hence, primary socioemotional problems that may affect speech development may give rise to a vicious spiral of childhood problems as, conversely, may primary speech problems that may affect socioemotional development. Early identification and analysis for possible primary and secondary factors in a childhood behavioral disorder that includes speech symptoms are therefore important.

Speech Production Symptoms. Environmental conditions that may affect the development of the voice, articulation, or rhythm dimensions of speech may or may not seriously affect the child's emotional and social developments. Each case, however, requires careful study if the vicious spiraling previously referred to is to be avoided.

Articulatory symptoms may stem from factors such as foreign accent and non-standard speech-sound models, reduction in the amount of speech stimulation, and hospitalization during the speech-sound learning period. Regression in articulatory development is sometimes seen when certain children desire or need the amount and kind of attention a younger sibling may be receiving. These regression patterns may be surprisingly similar to those of the younger sibling. West and Ansberry (1968, p. 50) stated that speech develops earliest and best in a child whose environment provides rich speech experiences (with both children and adults), a real need and pleasure to be derived from speaking, and daily rewards for steady improvement in speech.

Phonatory symptoms can originate for various socioemotional reasons and at different periods in a child's life. For example, early negative conditioning of an infant's vocalization has been seen as one possible contributor to disturbance in vocal development. Brodnitz (1959, p. 49) stated, "Many of the deviations from normal vocal behavior that we find in the adult can be traced to the mutational change during puberty."

Perkins (1957, pp. 848–49) hypothesized about early negative conditioning of an infant's vocalization. If an infant is deprived of experiencing early contented vocalization because of being in a state of continual discomfort (stemming, for example, from colic, parental rejection, or "crying it out"), his patterns of tense vocalization may tend to be reinforced. There are not data on just how such early reinforcement of tense vocal patterns may affect later vocal maturation. Along these lines, Murphy (1964, p. 31), in discussing the genesis of abnormal voice in children, stated, "Throughout the vocal learning process, the voice acquired by the child depends upon how he imitates or identifies with important adults in his environment." He believed normal vocal development depends upon approval and success in earlier phases of communication, that is, satisfactions derived from vocal play and imitation.

Brodnitz (1959, pp. 50–51) described three types of postmutational voice disorders in males that he ascribed to psychological influences. The mutational falsetto is a relatively rare condition, in which a male with normal vocal cords speaks in a high, squeaky voice and often with a pitch that is higher than a child's voice. Incomplete mutation describes a voice that began to descend during mutation, but that leveled off before reaching the full depth of the adult male pitch. These conditions were interpreted by Brodnitz as resulting from a rejection at puberty of the maturity and responsibility of adulthood or from a refusal to accept vocal masculinity because of a rejection of the father. The mutational basso is the third type of postmutational voice disorder. It is characterized by the use of an abnormally deep voice, which, according to Brodnitz, represents an attempt to express vocally a maturity that is premature or not genuine.

Mutational voice disturbances in females have been observed less frequently. The mutational falsetto in a female is rather rare, but an upwardly displaced pitch level is more common (Brodnitz 1959, p. 52). Abnormally deep female voices are sometimes encountered and may be reflective of endocrine factors or, possibly, a male identification.

Murphy (1964, p. 31) reported his survey of the literature on personality and voice descriptions—a type concept which he believed is not very useful. The following possible relationships were found: weak voice and weak, submissive, shy personalities; loud voice and vital, aggressive, dominant personalities; thin, high voice and stingy, indecisive personalities; monotonous voice and a lack of imagination; breathy voice and fearful, passionate personalities. Other personality-voice relationships reported include harsh voices and aggressive, antagonistic, competitive, and hypertense individuals (Van Riper and Irwin 1958, p. 233); and harsh quality with high pitch and chronic feelings of anxiety and insecurity (Curtis 1967, p. 208).

Hysterical aphonia is rare in children (Wilson 1979, p. 45). Such sudden loss of voice may be precipitated by extreme fright or disappointment. Berry and Eisenson (1956, p. 232) reported that the condition occurs more frequently in girls and may appear as early as puberty (or sometimes even earlier). They believed that deeply seated emotional problems are the "true etiological agents" of hysterical aphonia. Rather simple explanations for voice differences may also exist, such as poor speech models (Curtis 1967, p. 208) and faulty vocal learning (Murphy 1964, pp. 33–34).

Fluency symptoms may also arise as a result of psychodevelopmental problems. Substantial controversy over the cause and treatment of stuttering has existed for a long time. In its simplest form, the controversy has existed among investigators who could be identified as "organicists," "environmentalists," and "interactionists." Throughout the long history of stuttering research, conclusive data have not been found to support any one position. An interesting development has been the move by many clinicians to a multicausal approach to the problem, a move that is so often necessary and productive when clinicians deal with human disorders and diseases.

That psychogenic forms of stuttering exist would be difficult to deny. The "to speak or not to speak" conflict, and hence the frequent compromise of incomplete speaking or stuttering, may arise because (1) the speaker fears that he may automatically process thoughts that are socially unacceptable into words (Travis 1971, Ch. 39), and (2) the child's attempts at speaking are accompanied by feelings of guilt or hostility (Sheehan 1975, Ch. 2). Other theories include Glauber's theory (1958, p. 78) that stuttering is a symptom of a pregenital conversion neurosis, and Eisenson's theory (1975, Ch. 6) that some stuttering may reflect a psychological perseverative manifestation. Worster-Drought (1968) reported that "purely hysterical stammer is uncommon in children." When it appears, it is more frequent in girls and usually appears at about the time of puberty or later.

Speech Content Symptoms. Speech content symptoms result from conditions that affect socioemotional development to the point where they interfere with language development. With respect to childhood emotional problems, for example, a neurosis may affect the way in which language is produced, while a psychosis may affect whether or not language is acquired. As indicated below, however, not all cases of environmentally induced language pathology are based on serious emotional disturbance.

Various environmentally based reasons for language retardation in childhood have been advanced over the years. Some of the categories of reasons given are insufficient stimulation because of absence of one or both parents (social isolation) or because of "quiet parents" ("silent environment"); reduced motivation because parents or siblings anticipate the child's needs and desires; inappropriate rewards for "baby talk"; inadequate rewards for the child's actual progress in language development; and inappropriate stimulation due to exposure to excessive verbal discipline and "angry talk," to poor language models, or to models using more than one language poorly. Other background factors cited are shock, accident, parental rejection, birth of a younger sibling, negativism, and hospitalization.

In his review of the literature on speech, thought, and communication disorders in childhood psychoses, Shervanian (1967) presented the following general information: (1) Speech and language disturbances are key symptoms of childhood psychoses. (2) Childhood psychoses are not a single disease entity; the major subtypes include the nuclear schizophrenic child, early infantile autism, the symbiotic psychotic child, the very young, severely disturbed child with unusual sensitivities, and schizophrenic adjustment to neurological dysfunction.

In terms of auditory impairment, Shervanian reported a range from hypersensitivity to a simulation of anacusis. With respect to speech, he stated:

1. There is no single entity that could be "called typical of the communication process of psychotic children"; however, there is much "to suggest the possibility of a number of syndromes of psychotic speech, thought, and communication" with variations influenced by numerous variables.
2. There may be severe language retardation from the very beginning, or normally developing speech may cease or regress.
3. "There may be a cessation of speech for communicative purposes." Other peculiarities reported include silence, except for animal sounds; long periods of silence interspersed with the utterance of complete sentences and the display of numerous voice, articulation, and rhythm defects by the speaking child; the possession of a large and complex vocabulary, which the child does not combine into usable sentences; and, finally, the production of echolalia, delayed echolalia, neologisms, logorrhea, and verbal perseveration.

For other discussions of speech and language evaluation and language symptom therapy for psychotic children, the reader is referred to articles by Rubin, Bar, and Dwyer (1967) and Ruttenberg and Wolf (1967).

One of the first concerns of the speech pathologist when a psychodevelopmental basis for presenting speech symptoms in a child is suspected is the matter of level of involvement. Is it due to insufficient or inappropriate speech stimulation? Or is it one symptom of a complex associated with some form of serious childhood emotional disorder? If in fact the disorder is of emotional origin, the speech pathologist must consider the possible role of speech therapy in the total habilitation program. Sometimes the use of language symptom therapy will be considered before, during, or after psychotherapy. When such symptom therapy is offered, the close collaboration of the psychotherapist is required.

SUMMARY

Child speech pathology is a large and complex clinical area. Diagnostic expertise requires training to the doctoral level in addition to years of clinical experience. It is no longer possible for any one speech pathologist to be equally competent in diagnosis in all aspects of this complex area. The speech pathologist must be able to function well in the team diagnostic approach.

As with other developmental areas, the speech clinician deals with developing organisms and hence with symptoms that vary in form and importance as a function of time. Also, because of the importance of speech to perceptual, conceptual, and socioemotional developments, the primacy of speech problems is not always easy to establish; conversely, when primary speech disorders are present for certain lengths of time, relatively specific speech disorders rapidly develop into childhood complexes. Further, it is more often the case that serious speech problems in childhood have multiple origins. Finally, the child speech pathologist must be prepared to formulate and enter into combination therapy approaches and to develop individualized, preventive, etiologically based, symptom focused, and compensatory speech therapy programs.

REFERENCES

Berry, M. F., and Eisenson, J. (1956). *Speech Disorders: Principles and Practices of Therapy.* New York: Appleton-Century-Crofts.

Black, M. E. (1964). *Speech Correction in the Schools.* Englewood Cliffs: Prentice-Hall.

Bloom, L., and Lahey, M. (1978). *Language Development and Disorders.* New York: Wiley.

Bloodstein, O. (1958). Stuttering as an anticipatory struggle reaction. In J. Eisenson (Ed.). *Stuttering: A Symposium.* New York: Harper.

———. (1960). The development of stuttering. II. Developmental phases. *J. Speech Hearing Disorders* 25:366–76.

———. (1984). *Speech Pathology: An Introduction.* Boston: Houghton Mifflin.

Bloomer, H. H. (1971). Speech defects associated with dental malocclusions and related abnormalities. In L. E. Travis (Ed.). *Handbook of Speech Pathology and Audiology.* Englewood Cliffs: Prentice-Hall.

Brodnitz, F. S. (1959). *Vocal Rehabilitation.* Rochester, Minn.: Whiting Press.

Brown, S. F. (1967). Retarded speech development. In W. Johnson and D. Moeller (Eds.). *Speech Handicapped School Children.* New York: Harper and Row.

Cruickshank, W. M. (Ed.). (1976). *Cerebral Palsy.* Syracuse: Syracuse University Press.

Curtis, J. F. (1967). Disorders of voice. In W. Johnson and D. Moeller (Eds.). *Speech Handicapped School Children.* New York: Harper and Row.

Darley, F. L., and Winitz, H. (1961). Age of first word: Review of research. *J. Speech and Hearing Disorders* 26:272–90.

Eisenson, J. (1968). Developmental aphasia: A speculative view with therapeutic implications. *J. Speech Hearing Disorders* 33:3–13.

———. (1975). Stuttering as perseverative behavior. In J. Eisenson (Ed.). *Stuttering: A Second Symposium.* New York: Harper and Row.

Glauber, P. I. (1958). The psychoanalysis of stuttering. In J. Eisenson (Ed.). *Stuttering: A Symposium.* New York: Harper.

Greene, M. C. L. (1957). *The Voice and its Disorders.* London: Pitman Medical.

Johnson, W. (1957). Perceptual and evaluational factors in stuttering. In L. E. Travis (Ed.). *Handbook of Speech Pathology.* New York: Appleton-Century-Crofts.

Lass, N. J., et al. (1982). *Speech, Language, Hearing,* Vol. 2. Philadelphia: Saunders.

McDonald, E. T., and Chance, B. (1964). *Cerebral Palsy.* Englewood Cliffs: Prentice-Hall.

McWilliams, J. (1985). Cleft Palate. In G. H. Shames and E. H. Wiig (Eds.). *Human Communication Disorders.* Columbus: Merrill.

Matthews, J. (1971). Communication disorders in the mentally retarded. In L. E. Travis (Ed.). *Handbook of Speech Pathology and Audiology.* Englewood Cliffs: Prentice-Hall.

Mecham, M. J., et al. (1966). *Communication Training in Childhood Brain Damage.* Springfield, Ill.: Thomas.

Metraux, R. W. (1950). Speech profiles of the preschool child 18 to 54 months. *J. Speech Hearing Disorders* 15:37–53.

Milisen, R. (1971). The incidence of speech disorders. In L. E. Travis (Ed.). *Handbook of Speech Pathology and Audiology.* Englewood Cliffs: Prentice-Hall.

Morley, M. E. (1965). *The Development and Disorders of Speech in Childhood.* Baltimore: Williams and Wilkins.

Murphy, A. T. (1964). *Functional Voice Disorders.* Englewood Cliffs: Prentice-Hall.

Myklebust, H. (1954). *Auditory Disorders in Children: A Manual for Differential Diagnosis.* New York: Grune and Stratton.

Mysak, E. D. (1961). Pneumodynamics as a factor in cleft palate speech. *Plastic and Reconstruct. Surgery* 28:588–91.

———. (1976). *Pathologies of Speech Systems.* Baltimore: Williams and Wilkins.

———. (1980). *Neurospeech Therapy for the Cerebral Palsied.* New York: Teachers College Press.

Mysak, E. D., and Wilder, C. N. (1981). Phonatory and resonatory problems of organic origin. In R. W. Rieber (Ed.). *Communication Disorders.* New York: Plenum Press.

Perkins, W. H. (1957). The challenge of functional disorders of voice. In L. E. Travis (Ed.). *Handbook of Speech Pathology.* New York: Appleton-Century-Crofts.

Powers, M. H. (1971). Functional disorders of articulation—symptomatology and etiology. In L. E. Travis (Ed.). *Handbook of Speech Pathology and Audiology.* Englewood Cliffs: Prentice-Hall.

Prather, E. M., Hedrick, D. L., and Kern, C. A. (1975). Articulation development in children aged two to four years. *J. Speech Hearing Disorders* 40:179–91.

Rigrodsky, S., and Steer, M. D. (1961). Mowrer's theory applied to speech habilitation of the mentally retarded. *J. Speech Hearing Disorders* 26:237–43.

Rubin, H., Bar, A., and Dwyer, J. H. (1967). An experimental speech and language program for psychotic children. *J. Speech Hearing Disorders* 32:242–48.

Ruttenberg, B. A., and Wolf, E. G. (1967). Evaluating the communication of the autistic child. *J. Speech Hearing Disorders* 32:314–24.

Schwartz, A. B. (1961). Congenital laryngeal stridor—speculations regarding its origin. *Pediatrics* (1985). 27:477–79.

Shames, G. H., and Wiig, E. H. (1985). *Human Communication Disorders.* Columbus: Merrill.

Sheehan, J. (1975). Conflict theory and avoidance-reduction therapy. In J. Eisenson (Ed.). *Stuttering: A Second Symposium.* New York: Harper.

Shervanian, C. C. (1967). Speech, thought, and communication disorders in childhood psychoses: Theoretical implications. *J. Speech Hearing Disorders* 32:303–14.

Templin, M. C. (1957). Certain language skills in children. *Institute of Child Welfare Monograph Series.* No. 26. Minneapolis: University of Minnesota Press.

Travis, L. E. (1971). *Handbook of Speech Pathology and Audiology.* Englewood Cliffs: Prentice-Hall.

Vanderheiden, G., and Grilley, K. (Eds.). (1976). *Nonvocal Communication Techniques and Aids for the Severely Physically Handicapped*. Baltimore: University Park Press.

Van Riper, C. (1963). *Speech Correction*. Englewood Cliffs: Prentice-Hall.

Van Riper, C., and Emerick, L. (1984). *Speech Correction: An Introduction to Speech Pathology and Audiology*. Englewood Cliffs: Prentice-Hall.

Van Riper, C. and Irwin, J. V. (1958). *Voice and Articulation*. Englewood Cliffs: Prentice-Hall.

Wall, M. J., and Myers, F. L. (1984). *Clinical Management of Childhood Stuttering*. Baltimore: University Park Press.

West, R., and Ansberry, M. (1968). *The Rehabilitation of Speech*. New York: Harper and Row.

Wexler, K. B., and Mysak, E. D. (1982). Disfluency of two-, four- and six-year-old males. *J. Fluency Disorders* 7:37–46.

Wilson, D. K. (1979). *Voice Problems of Children*. Baltimore: Williams and Wilkins.

Wingate, M. E. (1962). Evaluation and stuttering. Part I. Speech characteristics of young children. *J. Speech Hearing Disorders* 27:106–15.

Wood, N. E. (1964). *Delayed Speech and Language Development*. Englewood Cliffs: Prentice-Hall.

Worster-Drought, C. (1968). Speech disorders in children. *Devel. Med. Child Neurol.* 10:427–40.

14

LANGUAGE IN THE PRESCHOOL CHILD: DEVELOPMENT AND ASSESSMENT

Shoshana Mafdali Goldman

In the first three years of normal development, a child's cognitive, social, and affective accomplishments are reflected in spoken language. He is freed from the limits of the here and now. He thinks internally and uses symbols to represent and communicate thoughts, feelings, and events (past, present and future). He knows he is an autonomous, separate person with a particular gender identity, an "I."

Language ability is one of many forms of intelligence that vary widely among normally developing children, some of whom will excel in language and others, in other kinds of intelligence. When language development is impaired or abnormally delayed, however, overall development is at risk. Disorders of language often reflect disruptions in the cognitive, social, or affective aspects of development and can themselves disturb those aspects. It is rare to find an isolated language impairment.

Language is so essential a human characteristic that hardly any psychological assessment is possible without it. The very universality of language development has, until recent years, led us to ignore the processes by which language is acquired. It has therefore been difficult to differentiate the behaviors of the child at risk for language disorders from the wide range of normal variation among preschoolers. In recent years, however, we have learned enough about the varied courses of language development to enable us increasingly to recognize the vulnerable child. We can even prescribe therapies to foster specific language skills.

Language development is the emergence of an innate human capacity to use verbal symbols to communicate, shaped by interaction of the child's biological and psychological makeup with an environment; speech is the physical production of vocal sounds for language expression. Normal language development requires integrity of the central and peripheral nervous systems as well as adequate exposure to an appropriate socioemotional context. A language disorder is any deviant or unusually delayed acquisition or development of an aspect of language. Any delay, if unduly long, distorts normal language development. There are wide ranges of rates and styles of normal language development, and language competence may be relatively less developed than other forms of intelligence in normal children.

Language assessments use three models: medical, linguistic, or psychoneurological. The medical model, emphasizing etiology and nosology (e.g., diagnoses of mental retardation, hearing impairment, developmental aphasia, or environmental deprivation) is dealt with elsewhere and has only gross treatment implications for the language therapist. To present the distinctive and nontechnical aspects of language assessment, this chapter examines the development of language linguistically in its major dimensions (phonology, semantics, syntax, and pragmatics) and psychoneurologically in the cognitive processes by which it is learned (attention, perception, memory, symbolization, conceptualization, and socialization). Disorders of different aspects of language and some elements of the assessment process will be discussed as well.

A good assessment is directed not only at diagnosis but also at specific treatment recommendations. It will use each model, examining the development of each aspect of language in relation to psychological processes, with understanding of pathogenesis, to arrive at an intervention. Since the expertise of most language and learning evaluators is not primarily in psychosocial assessment, we will deal only briefly with that dimension.

Language assessment is at best a combination of careful history taking (including teacher reports), observation in a naturalistic setting to record a language sample, and both clinical and standardized testing. If behavior precludes testing, a visit to home and school is especially advisable. Techniques of assessment range from descriptive observation to standardized tests, but the latter alone do not accurately or reliably describe a preschooler's language abilities. Thorough understanding of language development and its relationships with cognitive, affective, and social development is required effectively to observe, record, analyze, and interpret the spontaneous language and discourse of a preschooler. In addition to listing the most useful standardized tests, this chapter will summarize significant elements of the processes of history taking, clinical observation, and informal testing.

The cognitive aspects of language are *how* language is learned, that is, the cognitive processes presumed to be responsible for the comprehension and production of the linguistic code. Cognitive aspects of language are the elements of psychoneurological or information processing models. One such model, adapted from Johnson and Myklebust (1967), states that disorders of any learning, including language learning, may occur in one or a combination of five cognitive areas: learning systems, types of experience, hierarchy of experience, sensory modality, or type of processing.

Learning systems include input, output, and integration. Experiences can be verbal or nonverbal. Experience takes the forms of sensation; attention and perception (how one *selects* and *organizes* sensation, *compares* the data with other input stored in memory, use feedback, and *assigns meanings* to new inputs and *stores* it in a category); memory (including mechanisms for experiences, concepts, words, sounds, visual and auditory events and skills); and symbolization and conceptualization. Sensory modalities are auditory, visual, kinesthetic, and tactile. Information processing is intrasensory or intersensory.

The four major linguistic dimensions of language are: phonology, semantics, syntax, and pragmatics. *Phonology* concerns the rules governing the sound system of language and their production for the expression of meaning. *Semantics* concerns the content or meaning of words and messages. It includes signifier-signified relationships and mental representations of knowledge, vocabulary, verbal and nonverbal concepts and systems of categorization, and verbal comprehension (overlapping with syntax). *Syntax* concerns the rules governing the form or structure of language, including word order for conveying meaning, grammar, and morphology. Morphemes are the smallest units of meaning and include sentences and structures such as -ing, -ed, plural and possessive /s/. *Pragmatics* concerns the use of language, primarily the communicative and noncommunicative functions of language (or why we use language) and rules that govern the changing linguistic and nonlinguistic contexts that determine language use (or discourse rules for knowing who should say what to whom, where, and how).

Each domain of language has its own system of rules. Phonological rules, for example, govern the combination and production of sounds into syllables. The sounds t, f, u, d, a, l cannot be put together to form a syllable in English, though they can in Arabic. Syllables form morphemes such as un, -ing, -tion, boy, 's, cabinet. Morphemes combined form words and sentences, and sentences combined form discourse, as in comments, requests, demands, exclamations, conversation, jokes, lectures, and so on. The task of the child is to learn the rules of these inseparable domains for comprehension and production within his biological, psychological, or environmental competencies and constraints.

Language development is affected by social and emotional factors, such as amount and type of language stimulation and communication, position in family, sociocultural and familial expectations and attitudes, and bilingualism. Language competencies and handicaps affect a family's interaction with a child. Intrapersonal factors (e.g., personal drives, desires, motivations, need to communicate, or intrapsychic conflict) as well as interpersonal relationships (e.g., development of an autonomous sense of self, quality and style of interpersonal communication, degree and type of language stimulation, attitudes and values of family and community toward language, linguistic competencies, and language disorders) as well as environmental factors all affect language development.

All the above factors continually change, not in a simple additive fashion, but by a gradual process involving qualitative changes in behavior and thought. The impact of the interaction of the child and his environment differs at different points in development. For example, the loss of a loved one or the birth of a sibling may affect aspects of language and language processing differently at age 2 months and age 2 years. There may also be "critical periods" of development for certain aspects of language, which are an issue in current research.

COGNITIVE ASPECTS OF LANGUAGE DEVELOPMENT

Communication begins with an infant's first cry, but such vocalizations only reflect states in a changing inner and outer environment (Bloom and Lahey 1978). They are not intended to represent thought or feelings. To use language that intentionally represents such change, an infant must accomplish cognitive as well as social and emotional tasks in the first years of life, in addition to linguistic tasks.

However, before these cognitive tasks can be accomplished, normal hearing acuity must be intact. Thus, the first and foremost factor to rule out in children who present with speech and language delays or language learning difficulties is a hearing loss. Careful history taking and clinical observation should alert clinicians to hearing problems. (However, it is wise to obtain an audiometric evaluation as a general rule). Children with hearing losses usually present with normal affect, curiosity, and nonverbal intellectual abilities, including play. Often, they appear to be attentive and concentrating unusually well because they are not distracted by extraneous auditory stimuli. Hard-of-hearing and deaf children want to communicate and naturally find ways to make their needs known and to understand others. They may develop an elaborate gestural system or display vivid facial expressions and body language. A history of normal cooing and babbling until age 6 months followed by a quantitative and qualitative change in vocalization may be a clue to a hearing disorder. Do not expect the high-pitched voice associated with deaf persons. This voice quality appears only after a child is taught to voluntarily control his voice. Finally, a history of chronic otitus media, especially bilaterally, should alert a clinician to possible intermittent hearing losses. Current research indicates that bilateral otitus media has long-term adverse affects on children not only audiologically but linguistically, educationally and psychologically as well (Silva et al. 1986).

Auditory Attention: Development. Attention is prerequisite and reciprocally related to all learning. By 5 or 6 weeks of life, infants begin active scanning in response to stimuli and can sustain attention to the human voice (Moerk 1977). Selective attention to the environment directs further cognitive development, and what a child learns as a result of his attention further influences to what he will direct his attention (Neisser 1967). In addition to selective scanning, aspects of attention necessary for normal language learning include set-to-attend, feedback, and inhibition of extraneous information (Beery 1969). Factors that influence attention as well as other cognitive processes include drive, motivation, exposure, and culture (Eisenson 1972).

Auditory Attention: Disorders. The relationship of attentional disorders to language disorders has not been well researched. Many writers discuss the theoretical impact of problems in attention upon learning and language (Beery 1969; Hallahan et al. 1978; Johnson and Myklebust 1967; Stark 1981). These authors suggest that, without selective attention to critical linguistic elements, information is lost affecting the learning of linguistic variables such as phonemic discrimination, morphological endings, semantics, extralinguistic factors in the communicative context, and para-linguistic factors such as discrimination of changes in intonation or unstressed inflection.

What remains unresolved is the direction of the relationship. Do problems in language learning affect the ability to attend to language or vice versa? Or perhaps both are possible. (For a full discussion of attentional disorders in children, see Kinsbourne and Caplan 1979.)

Auditory Attention: Assessment. In assessing attentional deficits in language-impaired children, one wants to specify the nature of the attention problem, whether it is modality-specific, and what is its relation to language and cognition. Clinicians should ask parents under what conditions the child does attend. Can he attend to stimuli but not shift to new stimuli, or does he have trouble maintaining his focus on stimuli and what kind of stimuli? Does attention to verbal stimuli improve if the linguistic level or semantic level is reduced, suggesting a linguistic and semantic basis to problems in attention rather than vice versa? Information from the history is crucial for learning about attentional problems, since in a one-to-one structured situation, the problems are often not as evident. Parents often report the following about their child: he repeatedly asks "what?" or "huh"; he seeks out quiet uncluttered places to work; he is "off the wall" in noisy, crowded places; he cannot sit still and is in constant motion; paradoxically he sometimes has the capacity to shut out completely what is going on around him and to focus intensely on a particular task. Associated problems of low frustration tolerance, distractibility, impulsivity, and social immaturity are often reported.

An informal clinical assessment can include observing differences in responses to structured standardized tests versus unstructured play situations. Often children with attentional problems cannot play in a purposeful and organized and planful way, or they tend to repeat actions and themes. On standardized tests, such as Goldman-Fristoe-Woodcock Auditory Skills Test Battery (1974) subtest "auditory selective attention subtest," difficulties in scanning stimuli are observed.

Some children with attentional problems *seem* to perform at a higher level on unstructured tasks than on structured tasks of the same type, but close observation reveals the child's true difficulties. One 4-year-old child with a language delay and severe attentional problems, for example, was described by his parents and teachers as a whiz at block building. Gil clearly enjoyed block construction and spent a good deal of his time in the block corner (avoiding verbal activities), but close observation indicated that he was repeating the same structures over and over. Indeed on testing he showed moderate difficulties reproducing designs on a block design test where he had to pay close attention to a given model rather than simply to produce whatever came to mind.

Auditory Perception: Development. By age two months, an infant can discriminate his mother's voice from a stranger's. Between three and seven months, he shows differential responses to intonation conveying different information. By seven months, many infants respond to specific words of familiar persons in specific contexts (Luria 1981). Studies of infant speech perception strongly suggest inborn "linguistic feature detectors or auditory templates that prepare the child to discriminate speech sounds" (Eimas and Corbit 1973). Between one and four months, infants accomplish the intersensory integration between vision and hearing (Piaget 1954).

The relationship of infant perceptual development to later perception and language is not fully understood. For example, although infants can discriminate different speech sounds such as /b/ and /p/, these are one of the last discriminations made by 2-year-olds. That is, despite precursory capabilities, children need to learn or relearn differences between speech sounds when they become more aware of language (Bloom and Lahey 1978).

Auditory Perception: Disorders. Underlying auditory perceptual processing disorders has been the richest area of research in language disorders. However, the full range of auditory perceptual disorders involving discrimination, rate, and sequencing cannot be fully discussed here.

A specific neurologically based syndrome involving the inability to process speech sounds but the intact ability to process language visually through sign language is known as "verbal auditory agnosia" and results in almost complete incomprehension of spoken language, complete or partial mutism, and secondary behavioral abnormalities. Communication intent is preserved as seen in eye contact and response to paralinguistic cues such as gesture, intonation, and facial expression. However, awareness of sound and vocalization of sound may be impaired, affecting interpersonal communication (Johnson and Myklebust 1967; Rapin and Allen 1983).

Language disorders have long been considered to be broadly related to auditory discrimination difficulties (Johnson and Myklebust 1967; Beery 1969; Wiig and Semel 1984; Carrow-Woolfolk and Lynch 1982). In a series of systematic studies of children labeled aphasic, many have been found to have problems perceiving the order of acoustic stimuli (linguistic and nonlinguistic) and discriminating acoustic (though not visual) stimuli unless the interval between stimuli is very long (Lowe and Campbell 1965; Tallal 1976; Tallal et al. 1985). However, as with attention, no cause-effect relationship between process and product (e.g., language comprehension or production and academic achievement) has been conclusively established with either aphasic children or other populations of children with language disorders. Opponents of the view that perceptual processing disorders underlie language disorders argue that language in a more general and abstract sense is disordered and is reflected in processing difficulties, that is, that they are the effect rather than the cause of the language disorder (Rees 1973).

Auditory Perception: Assessment. Whether or not tests of perception (or other psychoneurological processes as attention and memory) are used in language assessment is clearly a function of one's philosophical viewpoint. Those who maintain that linguistic knowledge shapes auditory perception feel that auditory perceptual tests are redundant and only point to the obvious fact that these children have language learning difficulties, that is, that low scores on tests of processes indicate that language in a more general sense is weak (Bloom and Lahey 1978). However, not all language disordered children have perceptual problems, at least as revealed by commercially available standardized tests. In some cases, however, knowledge of children's perceptual abilities can help plan an intervention program. For example, 4-year-old Eduardo could not hear the difference between vowel sounds. Thus the words "set" and "sat" and "book" and "back" were not differentiated. Whether or not this was the cause or the effect of his language disorder is unknown. But clearly his comprehension was affected, as was his ability to learn morphological rules. Once when told, "Give it to me back," Eduardo stared in confusion at the examiner, then handed her the "book" next to him. Clearly, Eduardo was using neither linguistic (syntactic) nor nonlinguistic contextual (what had previously taken place) cues to comprehend the statement. The focus on language therapy in this particular case was precisely on learning such strategies in addition to "auditory training."

Unless auditory perceptual problems are severe, parents' reports often overlook problems in these areas. If a perceptual problem is suspected, especially if there are speech articulation difficulties, one can ask a specific question such as, "Does your child mistake words he hears, like 'cab' for 'cap'?"

Rate of verbal processing can be explored clinically by speaking slowly or rapidly and noting any changes in response (keeping content simple and constant). (This, however, does not get into more subtle disorders of rate or perception found experimentally by Tallal and her colleagues.)

Tests used to measure auditory discrimination and sequencing in preschool children are (1) Goldman-Fristoe-Woodcock Test of Auditory Discrimination, and (2) Goldman-Fristoe-Woodcock Auditory Skills Test Battery. There is no commercially available test of rate of perception.

Auditory Memory: Development. As with perception and attention, memory is integrally related to language learning. Aspects of memory associated with language learning include short- and long-term storage, auditory sequential memory span, paired associative memory, rapid precise retrieval, retroactive and preactive inhibition, incidental learning, and "active working memory." Short-term storage holds information in mind long enough for recognition, accurate perception, judgment, corrective feedback, and comparison with past information. Auditory images are stored in long-term semantic memory (if they are words) as categories of perception (which are the building blocks of meaning relationships and conceptualization). Expressive language and communication require exact recall or retrieval of stored information. Memory functions participate in the processing, learning, and serial order production of language at all levels: phonemes, words, sentences, and discourse. According to Miller and Chomsky (1963), processing sentence structures depends primarily on short-term memory, while deriving meaning (deep structure) of a sentence depends more on long-term memory.

Infants have recognition memory but not the capacity to recall things to mind

(Piaget 1962). They recognize objects and events as familiar when these things evoke or activate previously experienced auditory, visual, kinesthetic, or motor sensations. They have no recall, since recall requires evoking absent objects and events, that is, mental representation. Anisfeld (1984) pointed out that in consequence of this, early infantile experiences, especially intense emotional ones, are hard to change, since they are retained as sensorimotor impressions that "unlike categorically coded memories are not directly subject to conscious inspection and analysis" (p. 25). By age 2, however, with advances in mental representation the child is able to use images and symbols internally and can reconstruct thought from memory.

Developmentally, serial recall changes with age both in amount remembered and in strategies used. Wiig and Semel (1984) have summarized the literature as follows. Before age 2, children do not semantically organize input for serial recall, since no categories are set up. Between ages 3 and 5, semantic categories (e.g., fruit, vehicles, toys) are used to organize recall. Below age 5 or 6 children do not have any recognition of strategies to facilitate recall, for example, rehearsing labels or chunking information into perceptual or conceptual units. By first grade, however, children can be taught to label and rehearse information they are asked to remember. It is not until approximately age 11 (around the transition from concrete to formal operational thought, according to Piagetian theory) that children spontaneously and consciously employ strategies in the sense of having knowledge and awareness of memory processes—a metememory.

Auditory Memory: Disorders. Language disorders (in particular, childhood aphasia or specific language disorders) have long been and continue to be associated with disorders in auditory memory, in addition to auditory perception. However, memory problems are often inseparable from attentional difficulties and fall into an attention-retention continuum (Myklebust 1954; Johnson and Myklebust 1967). Empirical studies (with school-age language-impaired children) have identified problems in short-term auditory sequential memory, including rote and sentence recall (Masland and Case 1968; Aten and Davis 1968; Lowe and Campbell 1965).

Critics of the position that a memory disorder is causing the language disorder argue that memory reflects the child's increasing knowledge of language and that delays or disorders of language explain the memory problems. They point out that memory for sentences is highly dependent on knowledge of semantic and syntactic aspects of the sentence (McNeil 1966; Bloom and Lahey 1978; Olson 1973). Moreover, the relationship of rote recall, including digit span, to language learning has been questioned. For example, language-impaired children identified as schizophrenic or autistic have been found to have intact or above-average memory span for unrelated, nonsyntactically connected words (e.g., dog, shoe, go, blue). However, they do worse than normal or retarded children on recalling syntactically related sentences (Hermlin and Frith 1971), suggesting that they do not use meaning and grammatical structure as a strategy to facilitate recall (Bloom and Lahey 1978).

Three memory problems, related to real-life situations and associated with language-disordered children, are difficulties in (a) word retrieval, (b) following directions, and (c) retelling stories. Problems in retrieving labels (word-finding difficulties or "dysnomia") have long been associated with language disorders in both adult and childhood aphasia (Johnson and Myklebust 1967), more recently in connection with dyslexia or specific reading difficulties, and as one symptom predictive of early decoding problems (Denckla and Rudel 1976; Jansky and DeHirsch 1972).

Difficulties following oral directions and problems around story-retelling are a common complaint of nursery school teachers and are often the first clue to a possible language problem. Both involve more complex processing of verbal information than short-term memory tasks. Story-retelling is important as it utilizes performance variables that occur in natural communication: semantic and syntactical decoding without situational cues, auditory verbal memory both short- and long-term, identifying saliency, and sequencing of verbal information (John et al. 1970), and grammar and syntax.

Auditory Memory: Assessment. Memory functions are highly interrelated with attention, motivation, level of anxiety, and context. In history taking, the examiner should look for unusual discrepancies among different memory functions. One would note, for example, excellent memory for past events (episodic memory), especially emotionally intense ones, but difficulty recalling names of persons or places, or difficulty learning, even after frequent exposure, rote sequences such as telephone numbers, addresses, and the ABCs. It is clinically significant whether the child has labels for specific items within semantic categories, (e.g., button, snap, zipper, or just button for all categories), whether he hesitates when naming objects on demand, or whether he asks to repeat questions. One way to rule out sensory-hearing problems when the child repeatedly asks "what" is not to repeat, but to remain silently attentive to the child. Often, given this extra time, the child will then answer, suggesting either an attentional-motivational problem or the need for a longer time to process or retrieve information. However, if a child repeatedly asks "what?", his hearing should be tested. In regard to memory for a new word, one can note how easily a child learns a new word and recalls it five minutes later.

Standardized testing is available for children over age three. Tests of short-term auditory memory for preschoolers include (1) Binet Sentence Memory; (2) Detroit Tests of Learning Aptitude, Auditory Attention Span for Unrelated Words; (3) Goldman-Fristoe-Woodcock Auditory Skills Battery: Auditory Memory subtest; (4) Kaufman ABC Auditory Memory subtest; and (5) French Pictorial Test of Intelligence: Immediate Recall.

Tests measuring the ability to follow directions are found in the Detroit Tests of Learning Aptitude: Oral Directions and the Stanford Binet Intelligence Scale. A story-retelling test is included in the Slingerland Pre-reading Screening Test (Kindergarten).

Preschool tests of word retrieval are found in: (1) Jansky Predictive Reading Index: Naming subtest (Kindergarten); (2) Gardner One-Word Expression Language Test; and (3) Clinical Evaluation of Language Functions: CELF: Word Confrontation (Kindergarten and up).

Symbolic Representation: Development. One of the main cognitive accomplishments following the first two years of a child's life is the ability to think in symbols. The semantic function, or the ability to know word meanings, is linked with the development of object-concept (permanence and constancy), self-other awareness and differentiation, and symbolic representation (Piaget 1962; Werner and Kaplan 1963). With the ability to symbolize, the 18- to 24-month-old child has acquired the vehicle for language learning. Symbolic representation is manifested in nonverbal cognition as well as in language, as seen in pretend play. Play thus serves as a window through which we can learn of the child's knowledge of the world and level of thought. Clinically, it can be used as a tool for measuring nonverbal symbolic thought.

Piaget (1962) provided a detailed analysis of pretend play that has been confirmed by recent empirical studies (Fenson and Ramsey 1980; Fein and Apfel 1979; Watson and Fischer 1977; Goldman 1984). These studies offer a developmental sequence of pretend play from infancy to age four, which, with his other developmental schemata, have become standard guidelines for students of child development.

What follows is an outline of Piagetian stages of symbolic play.

OUTLINE OF PIAGETIAN STAGES OF SYMBOLIC PLAY

Play Without Representation. Sensorimotor Stages 2 through 3 (from approximately 1 to 8 months of age).

Cognitive and affective development during the first 8 months of life lay the groundwork for object knowledge (including the person object) and self-other differentiation, the two critical achievements that form the bases for representation and subsequently for symbolic play. During this period, objects, events, and activities are becoming differentiated and coordinated. Play with objects is not yet decontextualized or represented. It is characterized by repetitive, joyful actions on objects, such as sharing, rolling, or throwing. Piaget calls this sensorimotor practice play. At first, practice play is related to the child's own body, e.g., repeatedly sucking for the mere pleasure of it. But soon the child begins to play with objects outside his own body, e.g., repeatedly banging and dropping things. Finally, two or more objects are related one to another, e.g., placing objects inside a container.

Presymbolic Representation in Play. Sensorimotor Stages 4 through 5 (approximately 8 to 18 months of age).

During this period, repetitive practice play behaviors with objects are sustained for longer periods of time. In addition, behaviors are beginning to be decontextualized and therefore extracted from their routine contexts or imitated and played in game-like and ritualistic ways. For example, a child may go through all the ritualistic behaviors associated with going to sleep when she sees her blanket, even though she is not ready to go to sleep. Sometime after 12 months of age, the child shows an understanding of common object use and relations that is manifested in play through brief "gestures of recognition." Examples of such presymbolic play behaviors include briefly placing an empty spoon to his mouth, a comb to his hair, or hat on his head (with no real intention to eat, groom, or go outside), or lifting the telephone receiver and placing it into ritual position, then setting it aside. According to Piaget (1962) and Werner and Kaplan (1963), such behavior constitutes a form of primitive representation and is the first step in symbolic representation and symbolic play.

Autosymbolic, the Beginning of Symbolic Representation in Play. Sensorimotor Stage 6 (approximately 18 to 24 months).

This is a period of transition into true symbolic play. During this period the child achieves the capacity to represent internally objects, actions, and events. This is reflected in the capacity to imitate objects or events no longer present to the senses ("deferred imitation"), to use language, and to represent events in action, i.e., pretend play. Pretense, however, is limited to self-related activities. That is, the child's own activities are represented outside their usual adaptive contexts, such as playfully simulating drinking from a toy cup or feigning to sleep.

True Symbolic Play. Preoperational Stage (after age 2).

Two kinds of symbolic play emerge during the early preoperational stage. The first involves the extension or projection of symbolic schemas outside the child and onto new objects. For example, the child pretends to feed his mother or to put a doll to sleep. The second kind of symbolic play involves imitating other models, presumably as part of the process of identification. For example, a child pretends to mop the floor like Mommy or telephone in a deep voice like Daddy. This is a primitive form of role-playing.

At first these symbolic games are in the form of single events, but soon symbolic schemas are combined—the child holds the phone to his ear, then dials, or feeds mother, then feeds her doll. More advanced forms include *planning and forethought* in symbolic activities and use of absent and substitute objects. For example, a child looks for a frying pan, finds it, then sets it on a toy stove, or a child announces designators such as calling a stick "spoon." Even more advanced play involves *planned combinations* of elements into a coherent sequence: the child pretends to put food into a frying pan, looks around for a spatula, finds it, stirs the food, says "eggs," then feeds mother. Verbal announcements *prior to* the activity imply planned symbolic action.

Around age 3, symbolism becomes firmly established and actions and events decontextualized. Play then rapidly advances in elaboration of realistic scenes, inclusion of language, and realistic details. Play can now function as a means of reliving emotionally difficult situations, overcoming fears, compensating for disappointments, and the like. Prior to the cognitive advancement in symbolic representation, play could not be used as a vehicle for emotional development.

Between the ages four and five play becomes more organized and orderly, imitative of reality in a more exacting way, and characterized by sophisticated and elaborate role-play.

Symbolic Representation: Disorders. The complete inability to think symbolically either verbally or nonverbally would result in severe mental retardation or a global aphasia (Myklebust 1954). Disruptions in symbolic thinking have also been associated with childhood aphasia (Morehead and Morehead 1974) and with autism. To the extent that the development of language and play is a function of a common underlying symbolic functioning, advances in both areas should be parallel. Beyond age three or four, however, language appears to be necessary for advances in pretend play, and problems in language may affect pretend play. This writer's clinical impression of language-impaired children is that children with primarily expressive difficulties (i.e., dyspraxia) but intact comprehension have less difficulty in the domain of play than children with receptive language difficulties. Children with problems in attending, planning, and organizing may evidence difficulty in pretend play after age 3 or 4. Finally, children with impaired ability to differentiate self from others are impaired in all representational abilities.

Symbolic Representation: Assessment. It is important to obtain a description of a child's use of objects and pretense at home, since anxiety often inhibits children from playing freely in an office setting. For children younger than 18 months or very delayed, ask parents if child shows "delayed imitation" of their actions, for example, sponging a table or putting on parents' clothing; can gesture or pantomime his needs; understands that things out of sight can reappear; understands and uses the pointing gesture (seen normally around 13 months of age); or uses a "transitional object" that is a function of presymbolic use of representation.

Clinically, one should give children the opportunity to manipulate realistic toy objects as well as to respond to suggestions to use less realistic objects such as blocks as substitutes for things; one should also note the level of symbolic play as discussed above. A significant discrepancy between level of pretense and level of word meanings (verbal symbolic representation) suggests a possible language delay that is not due to a disorder in symbolization, but may be related more to specific linguistic factors.

Conceptualization: Development. Forming concepts entails the use of all the cognitive mechanisms discussed above. The prelinguistic child has to attend selectively to features of his environment, discriminate invariant perceptual features, store them in memory in some form of representation or prototype, recognize other instances of the same, and generalize such information into categories or "concepts." He must also discriminate among different properties in members of the same concept in order to form subcategories of old concepts.

Several "concepts" (i.e., not abstract categories) are basic to normal language development; these include the concepts of the object, self, body, space, time, attributes (the physical properties of objects), and relationships (see Chapter 6 in this volume). Rational concepts arise as a result of the integration of concepts of self, space, and time (Piaget 1970). These involve the relations of the child to other persons, objects, and events, and the relations of these to each other. This knowledge forms the basis of the pragmatic aspects of language (Bruner 1983; Bates, Camaloni, and Volterra 1975) and cause-and-effect relations (Church 1961).

By the end of the sensorimotor period somewhere around age 2, the child has reached a point in prelinguistic conceptual development that is necessary for the emergence of language, especially for word meanings (Bloom 1970, 1973; Brown 1973; Bruner 1975; Slobin 1967; Piaget 1952) and for the development of higher levels of conceptualization.

Disorders. A specific disorder in conceptual development affects all aspects of language development. When general concept development is deficient, retardation results and all aspects of language learning are deficient.

Assessment. Assessment of conceptual skills is necessary to rule out a general intellectual retardation and to learn about areas of cognitive strengths and weaknesses. For example, some children are very well oriented in time but not in space and consequently have trouble learning spatial concepts and verbal labels of such concepts. Others are well oriented in space but not in time. Not all such children are necessarily language-impaired or learning-disabled but are within the limits of normal variation.

Clinically significant discrepancies do exist, however, and care must be taken in the selection of tools for assessing bright children with specific language deficits. A language-impaired child may have abilities in other areas, for example, mechanical or musical abilities, creativity, intuitive social perceptions, and rhythmic skills. For example, a 3-year-old boy who was extremely hyperkinetic and responded inconsistently to verbal discourse had just begun to acquire a few words (including names of opera singers). The parents reported that he was able to sit through an entire opera with apparent enjoyment, although he was unable to sit quietly during the music period at school. In subsequent language therapy, taped music became a crucial link to language acquisition, as the child first listened to, identified, and imitated the different instruments on the tape. Language learning also took place in the context of spatial-kinesthetic, highly creative and fanciful activities, since as time went on, the therapist discovered how unusually imaginative the child was. Yet he was diagnosed borderline retarded by standard IQ tests.

Standardized tests of conceptualization in infancy include: (1) Uzgiris and Hunt's Assessment of Infancy: Ordinal Scales of Psychological Development (based on Piagetian theory); (2) Bayley Scale of Infant Development; (3) Cattel Infant Intelligence Scale; (4) Denver Developmental Screening Test; and (5) Piaget Sensorimotor Scale. Standardized tests for the preschool child include:

A. Purely Nonverbal Tests
   (1) Goodenough Draw-A-Person Test;
   (2) Hiskey-Nebraska Test of Learning Aptitude;
   (3) Illinois Tests of Psycholinguistic Abilities (ITPA) Visual reception, visual association, and manual expression subtests;

      (4) Leiter International Performance Scale;
      (5) Pictorial Test of Intelligence.
    B. Nonverbal and Verbal Tests of Intelligence and Aptitude
      (1) Brigance Preschool Inventory;
      (2) Columbia Mental Maturity Scale;
      (3) Denver Developmental Screening Test;
      (4) Detroit Tests of Learning Aptitude;
      (5) McCarthy Scales of Children's Abilities;
      (6) Merrill-Palmer Scale of Mental Tests;
      (7) Stanford Binet Scale of Intelligence (highly verbally weighted);
      (8) Wechsler Preschool and Primary Scale of Intelligence.
    C. Tests of Basic Concepts
      (1) Basic Concept Inventory;
      (2) Boehm Test of Basic Concepts;
      (3) Piagetian Tasks for the Preoperational Stage.

LINGUISTIC ASPECTS OF DEVELOPMENT

Word Meanings: Development. Most writers agree that the development of word meaning is a slow process involving and reflecting qualitative changes in the child's thinking (Anisfeld 1984; Bloom 1973; Brown 1968; Luria 1981; Piaget 1962; Vygotsky 1962; Werner and Kaplan 1963). While the foundations for language learning begin at birth, it is not until the object concept is attained and representational cognition emerges that sound production and speech can take on a referential function. Words by definition are representational entities and not manipulable actions. Thus, it is not until Sensorimotor Stages 4 to 5 (roughly between 12 to 18 months), when sensorimotor representation emerges, that infants' vocal productions begin to be used for representation (Anisfeld 1984). Between the ages of 10 to 36 months, word meanings undergo changes that reflect the child's level of cognition and self-other differentiation.

The first words of children are presymbolic. They appear between 10 and 15 months and are very meager—between three and ten in number. Presymbolic words are tied, usually in a ritualistic way, to the child's actions and the particular context. Often hearing particular words effects an immediate response. For example, one toddler repeatedly put his hands to his head and made the gesture of brushing his hair each time he heard the word "brush" (Goldman 1984). The social rituals taught to infants, such as making or saying "bye-bye," are presymbolic. By their very nature such words are not generalizable. They are more like conditioned responses. These early words often may drop out of use as newer ones emerge at a higher level of meaning. Interestingly, parents of children with delayed or deviant language development frequently report that their children had a few words that they stopped using around age 18 to 24 months, but that, unlike normal children, they acquired no others. It is possible that such children have an impairment in the development of symbolization and conceptualization that precludes the normal development of words into a network of meanings.

Between 15 to 24 months, the child acquires around 50 words that are more advanced in their meanings. At this next level of symbolization the child can generalize words to new and different situations. However, these overextensions are based not on adult categories but on subjective associations and experience. For example, the word for water may refer to a pond of water and the ducks in it, or the word "kick" for any leg extension, a fluttering moth, throwing an object, and the like.

Somewhere between 18 to 24 months, the child's thinking becomes truly symbolic and words become social symbols. At this level words are generalized more systematically and based on conventional categories that are consistent with adult meanings. However, they continue to be either too narrow or too generalized. For example, "water" may refer to all liquids, "dog" to all four-legged animals, and "daddy" to all adult males. These truly symbolic words, however, result in the attainment of the "lexical principle" (Anisfeld 1984) reflected in a spurt of vocabulary growth: the number of words increases rapidly and is often accompanied by an active interest in word acquisition. The vocabulary spurt indicates that the child has realized that things are referred to by conventional words. By age 2 vocabularies range from 200 to 400 words (McCarthy 1954; Slobin 1967). Not long after this vocabulary spurt children begin to combine words, first as presyntactic successive single-word utterances and then into syntactically related two- and three-word utterances. At this point, the role of language becomes critical in the development of reasoning, socialization, and affect.

By age 3, the lexical principle is firmly established, as reflected in the average vocabulary of 900–1000 words. By age 4 a child's vocabulary has increased to approximately 1,500 words, and by age 6 to about 2,500 words.

Psycholinguists such as Bloom (Bloom and Lahey 1978), Brown (1973), and Slobin (1967) have identified universal patterns of semantic intentions, or what a child refers to at the single-word utterance stage. Carrow-Woolfolk and Lynch (1982) have compiled a list from an exhaustive review of the literature. Between 12 and 18 months, when most children speak first in single-word utterances, their meanings are the following:

1. Demonstrative Naming—e.g., this, that, mommy, juice, cup.
2. Nonexistence and Disappearance: no more, gone, all gone.
3. Recurrence: more.
4. Negation: Rejection and Denial: no, not, don't, dirty.
5. Location: here, there, up, sit-lap.
6. Notice: hi, see, look, here.

Between 18 and 22 months other meanings emerge.

7. Cessation: stop.
8. Possession by Association: my, mine, daddy car, baby nose.

  9. Question: what's that?
 10. Action: push, off, run, go, up.
 11. Attribution: hot, dirty.

Seventy-six percent of the meanings of children's first words are in the first three categories (Brown 1973). However, individual differences in styles have been found in children's first vocabularies (Nelson 1973)—those concerned with self and others express words relating to greetings or getting people to do things for them, those concerned more with naming objects and people (a more cognitive style) have many specific labels for things; and there are children with both styles.

Somewhere between 18 and 30 months, children speak in two-word utterances. At the two-word stage, meanings are expressed by the relationship between two words. For example, instead of saying "all gone," child says "all gone juice."

The following semantic relations make up most of the meanings at the two-word stage:

  1. Nomination or Existence: a, the, it, this, that see + noun, e.g., "a ball," "see baby";
  2. Recurrence: more, 'noth + noun, e.g., "more juice";
  3. Nonexistence: no, no-more, all-gone = noun or verb, e.g., "all-gone juice," "no up";
  4. Agent + action: e.g., "daddy fix," "Mommy go";
  5. Action + object: "pull train";
  6. Agent + Object: "mommy book";
  7. Action + Location: "sit chair";
  8. Entity + Location: "baby chair" (meaning baby is at the chair);
  9. Possessor + Possession: "mommy chair" (mommy's chair);
 10. Attribute + Entity or vice versa: "big ball" or "ball red";
 11. Demonstrative + Entity: "there ball."

Since these eleven relational categories have been found to exist in most languages, one can assess the early meanings of very young children in a naturalistic setting.

Between ages 3 and 5, basic categories of space, time, causality, and those that specify relationships between persons emerge, reflecting the child's expanding mental capacity to understand his world. The 2-year-old's repetitive exploration of containers containing objects "in" or "on" expands to a wider range of spatial concepts. Spatial relational adjectives appear in a well-established order: big/little, tall/short and long/short, high/low, thick/thin and wide/narrow, with the positive pole often appearing first. Meanings proceed slowly and usually from the general to the specific. Thus, for a period of time in the semantic development of the normal child, "tall," "long," and "thick" may mean the same thing as "big" (Clark 1973).

Prepositions describing location in space emerge between the ages of 3 and 4. Things are spoken about as being "on top of," "over," "near," "behind," "in back of," and "outside." During this period the child's internal cognitive map of his immediate spatial environment is developing and reflected in his vocabulary.

An even greater expansion in vocabulary is noted for time concepts. The 2-year-old lives in the here and now. By age 3, he begins to understand past, present, and future and to use words referring to time, for example, "this day," "yesterday," "tonight," "in two days," "when I'm older." Between 3 and 4 years of age, time concepts begin to be generalized and categorized, as seen in expressions such as "everyday," "on Sundays," "sometimes," "in winter time," and so on. The sequential nature of time is reflected in statements such as "Before I go to sleep I say my prayers. Then mommy gives me a kiss." Preschool children typically cannot tell time, but they begin to show an interest in the clock and to use (usually inaccurately) clock words such as "at 7 o'clock" or "in ten minutes."

Advances in the understanding of cause-effect relationships are reflected in understanding verbs such as "give," "take," "pay," "spend," "buy" or "sell." Again preschool children master these concepts in order from least to most complex, and early preschoolers make errors substituting more complex for less; e.g., understanding "buy" or "sell" as "give" and "take" (de Villiers and de Villiers 1978).

The most complex of relational words are the diectic expressions, where meaning changes as the contexts shift. Diectic expressions of space include here/there, this/that, in front of/behind. These locate objects in relation to the speaker. Diectic expressions of time locate events in time in relation to the moment of utterance. They include "now," "yesterday," "today," and "tomorrow." The pronouns I/you, me/you, and my/your involve a switch from the speaker's point of view to the hearer's (pronominal confusions autistic children characteristically persist in making).

What a child means by his linguistic references changes gradually over time. A 2-year-old's knowledge about "dog" is very different from a 4-year-old's or a 6-year-old's, but all are gradual approximations to the adult semantic system of categorization. One of the later steps in the development of word meanings (and other domains of language) is a conscious knowledge of language. By age 3 and particularly at age 4, children show an interest in playing with word meanings, using words imaginatively and even creating their own words and rhymes (e.g., "icky picky licky sticky").

Another important aspect of semantic development is a growing conscious awareness that words have meaning and stand for things. This is part of the development of cognition or metalinguistics and is reflected in the child's increasing ability to define words. Word meanings represent a hierarchical rule-governed system of relationships that are actively and gradually learned and internalized from the time the child listens to language spoken. Over- and undergeneralizations are a normal part of this evolving process and reflect the child's struggle to realize the adult's categorical system. The child's underlying conceptual system can influence how he stores, retrieves, and defines words. In assessing the child's knowledge of words, it is necessary to understand the developmental stages the child's concepts undergo and the various other dimensions that influence concept development and word meanings.

Word Meanings: Semantic Disorder. A semantic disorder is a disruption in the association between words and/or grammatical structures and their meanings in the absence of a conceptual problem (Carrow-Woolfolk and Lynch 1982). In other words, the content that language encodes is understood when presented nonverbally. However, to the extent that language facilitates conceptual development, conceptual lags will appear as the deviant child gets older. Moreover, severe disorders in semantic development will of necessity interfere with interpersonal communication and other uses of language.

Semantic disorders have been differentiated from the inability to process the phonological aspects of language, that is, "verbal auditory agnosia." However, in severe cases of semantic disorders it is difficult to differentiate the two. Both result in the inability to comprehend spoken language. Verbal agnosia, however, is much more severe and all-encompassing, resulting in mutism or a few words poorly articulated (Rapin and Allen 1983).

Semantic disorders do not usually result in mutism and may in fact involve fluent expressive language and good articulation. Semantic disorders have traditionally been referred to as "receptive language disorders" or "receptive aphasia" (Carrow-Woolfolk and Lynch 1982). Some children have difficulty understanding the referential meaning of *specific* word categories, such as action references (verbs), attribute references (adjectives), notion modifiers (adverbs), spatial and temporal references (prepositions), and references to persons, quantities, time, and space (pronouns).

Some children with receptive language disorders have underlying problems in the concepts words refer to. For example, children with difficulties in spatial discrimination may be delayed in the comprehension, use and differentiation of labels such as "in," "on," "under," "by," "at," "here" and "there." The latter two may also reflect difficulties in perceiving the rules for speaker-listener shifts in spatial perspective, illustrating the interplay between semantic and pragmatic development. Similarly, semantics and syntax interact in such difficult tasks as learning reflexive pronouns (for example, the words "myself," "yourself," or "themselves," in sentences such as "The little baby got herself all dirty," or "The ducks found themselves all alone in the pond").

In some young children one can discern problems in multiple-meaning words. These problems can reflect problems in conceptualization and tendency toward concrete thinking, limited imagery and use of symbolization, perseveration, and problems shifting from one grammatic-syntactic category to another (Wiig and Semel 1984), or difficulties in using linguistic and nonlinguistic context cues for interpreting word meaning. Normal 4- and 5-year-old children, for example, understand that a person "running" and water "running" have very different meanings. In fact, children's appreciation of multiple meanings is seen in their own verbal creations that sound poetic to an adult listener. Children who have no trouble with multiple word meanings will easily grasp new and unfamiliar uses of old words, such as an engine "running," when it is explained to them. Children with difficulties in the area often have trouble learning idiomatic phrases, such as "at 5 o'clock."

Another semantic difficulty is in understanding and using basic linguistic concepts that express logical relationships (Wiig and Semel 1984) such as:

1. Coordination: and;
2. Class exclusion: not, all;
3. Class inclusion: all, many, some, any, few;
4. Class inclusion-exclusion: either . . . or;
5. Spatial-sequential: first, last, middle;
6. Temporal-sequential: first, last, before, after, when, not . . . till;
7. Cause-effect conditions: when . . . then, if . . then;
8. Instrumental: with, without;
9. Revision: no . . . instead.

Similarly, learning linguistic relationships that express logical operations may be troublesome (Wiig and Semel 1984). These include:

1. Comparative relationships: bigger than;
2. Familial (possessive relationships: Grandpa is daddy's father);
3. Spatial relationships—especially unusual ones that may require visual imagery: The elephant sat on the mouse.
4. Temporal sequential relationships: We will eat before we go to the movies.

Verbal analogies also present problems for certain children with semantic difficulties. For example, you drive a car and you fly a————.

One of the most recognized semantic disorders is a difficulty with quick retrieval or selection of a specific word on demand. Word-finding difficulties are not generally noted in preschool children, since such young children are normally hesitant and dysfluent in their speech, expressing themselves in ways characteristic of the older dysnomics: prolonged pauses, place holders such as "uh, uhm," starters such as "and then, and then . . .," indefinites such as "this and that," and imprecise words such as "Mommy made a cake" instead of "baked." However, by age 5 to 5½ these normal hesitancies diminish considerably. Furthermore, frequent errors such as substituting words within the same category ("guitar" for "drum") are not typical of the normal child and may be indicative of difficulties in categorizations.

Word-finding problems in older, dyslexic children were found associated with problems in sentence recall and verbal repetition (Wiig and Semel 1984). In my clinical experience I have noted that many 4- and 5-year-olds who have difficulty learning nursery rhymes, prayers, and rote familiar sequences, such as the alphabet, by age 6 or 7 present with word-finding difficulties.

The dysnomic difficulties described above may result in gaps in spontaneous vocabulary and a lack of flexibility and elaboration in language. Interestingly, it may not be reflected in poor scores on standardized tests of definition, since imprecise word retrieval can be compensated for by circumlocution.

Semantic comprehension disorders will affect other areas of learning (Johnson and Myklebust 1967). Some children become "word callers" (i.e., can decode written words without comprehension). Some preschool children are "hyperlexic" (decoding beyond their ability to speak and presumably without comprehension of what they are reading). Written language will reflect comprehension deficits; it may be concrete, poorly developed and elaborated, and limited in vocabulary. Arithmetic skills may be normal for calculation but poor in numerical reasoning.

Word Meanings. Assessment Standardized Tests of Word Meaning. These include:

(1) Assessment of Children's Language Comprehension (ACLC);
(2) Boehm Test of Basic Concepts;
(3) Clinical Evaluation of Language Functions: Word Classes, Linguistic Relationships, Relationships and Ambiguities subtests;
(4) Expressive One-Word Picture Vocabulary Test;
(5) Detroit Tests of Learning Aptitude. Verbal Absurdities, Verbal Opposites, Orientation subtests;
(6) Full-Range Picture Vocabulary Test;
(7) Illinois Test of Psycholinguistic Abilities: Auditory Reception, Auditory Association, Verbal Expression subtests;
(8) Peabody Picture Vocabulary Test—Revised;
(9) Test of Auditory Comprehension of Language;
(10) Test of Language Development: Picture and Oral Vocabulary subtests;
(11) Token Test for Children;
(12) Wechsler Preschool and Primary Scale of Intelligence: Vocabulary subtest.

Tests for Word Retrieval.

(1) Boston Naming Test;
(2) Jansky Predictive Index:Naming subtest;
(3) Expressive One-Word Picture Vocabulary Test;
(4) Clinical Evaluation of Language Functions: Producing Names on Confrontation.

Syntax and Morphology: Development. Almost from the very first attempts at stringing two words together, a child's language production exhibits some kind of pattern or rule that directs his efforts. At first, these rules are not based on conventions. But the child's active use of strategies for combining words to express meanings-in-relationship pays off in at least two important ways as he approaches adultlike grammar. First, meanings—needs, thoughts, feelings, desires, demands—are more precisely expressed, which in turn results in further fine tuning these meanings for the child. Second, familiar adults do not need to guess as much from context what the child is trying to say and the child can make himself understood when speaking to unfamiliar adults, since meanings are carried more by the linguistic elements and less by context. For example, only a parent or caretaker living with a child would know what he meant if at 16 months a child pointed to his room, saying "blanky"— his usual way of saying he wants his nap in the bed, not in his crib. At 18 months, if he says "blanky bed," a stranger may have a better idea what he meant, but shades of meaning are unclear. Does he want to go to bed now? Is he merely commenting on the fact that he takes his blanket to bed? At 22 months he may say "Go bed, blanky" and at 2½, "I wanna go to bed now with my blanky."

Between ages 1½ and 4 or 5, most of the grammatical (and phonological) rules of language are mastered. During this short period of 2½ to 3½ years, speech utterances expand at a very rapid rate from two-word utterances to long, fully formed, complex sentences.

Most psycholinguists use the morpheme, the smallest unit of meaning, rather than words, as the measure of sentence length. For example, "dog" is one morpheme, "dogs" is two morphemes, and "my dogs" is three morphemes. A child's Mean Length of Utterance (MLU) is the average number of morphemes in a sample of one hundred utterances. Early syntactic development is measured on the basis of MLU (Bloom and Lahey 1978; Brown 1973). Between MLU 1.0–2.0 the child's word combinations involve the basic semantic relations discussed in the previous section. No grammatical rules are employed at this stage and no morphological endings used. The child typically chains content words (noun + noun or noun + verb) together in "telegraphic" fashion. That is, the words carrying the information are used (nouns, verbs, adjectives) but not the "functors" (prepositions, articles, conjunctions, and auxiliary verbs).

Despite the absence of conventional syntax, two-word utterances have a set of rules of their own, a regularity in word order (Bloom 1970; Braine 1963; Brown 1973; Anisfeld 1984). For example, typical two-word utterances are "big ball," "big car," "big___", "more ball," "more car," "more juice," "more___," rather than "car more," or "ball big." The "principle of word order" is attained shortly after the "lexical principle" when children realize that all things have a name (Anisfeld 1984).

Beginning from approximately when MLU is between 2.0 and 2.5 until MLU is longer than 4.0 (between ages 2 and 4 or 5), children start learning various subsystems of grammar: (1) morphological inflections; (2) negation; (3) question forms; and (4) complex syntax. The grammatical morphemes appear in the following order (Brown 1973):

(1) present progressive -ing;
(2) prepositions "in" or "on";
(3) plural /s/ on regular nouns;
(4) irregular past tense, e.g., "come" and "went";
(5) possessive /s/ on nouns, e.g., "Mommy's coat";
(6) uncontractable copula forms of "to be": am, is, are, was, were;
(7) articles a and the;
(8) regular past tense, e.g., "baby jumped";
(9) third-person regular, e.g., "baby climbs";
(10) third-person irregular forms, "does" and "has";
(11) uncontractable auxiliary, e.g., "will" and "can";
(12) contractable copula forms of "to be," e.g., "it's mine";
(13) contractable auxiliary, e.g., "I'll climb."

As can be seen, these grammatical morphemes represent ideas about location, time, possession, number, and mood or attitude of speaker. Thus, development of these linguistic features is interrelated with cognitive and pragmatic aspects of development.

As discussed above, several categories of negation have been identified in the language of children at the one- and two-word stage (Bloom 1970; Bloom and Lahey 1978). They are disappearance, nonoccurrence, cessation, rejection, prohibition, and rejection. These same contents are expressed in older preschool children by the use of more complex syntactic structures.

Question forms develop between ages 2 and 4 as children learn the transformational rules for affirmative statements (e.g., "Mommy is baking") and the transformed question form (e.g., "Why is Mommy baking?") appears in children's question forms such as "Why Mommy is baking?" or "What Daddy will play?" These transition forms include the "wh"-word but do not transpose the subject and auxiliary verb. The question forms learned are in the following approximate sequence: "where," "what," "whose," "who," "why," "how," and "when" (Ervin-Tripp 1970). Children usually learn to respond to these questions before they ask them. Both the comprehension and use of question forms are integrally related to advances in cognition and the social pragmatic functions of language.

Once MLU exceeds 3.0 children's noun and verb phrases expand and sentences combine more than one thought by the use of connectives and complex grammatical rules. Expansions such as "Daddy come home" instead of "Daddy come" or the chained phrases "Daddy home," "Come home" appear; modifiers such as "The big furry cat" instead of "The cat" also appear.

Between ages 2 and 3 connectives encoding more than one idea in a single sentence appear in the following order: "and," "then," "because," "what," "when," "but," "that," "if," and "so." For example, two kinds of connective clauses appear, coordinate and superordinate (see Bloom and Lahey 1978, for full discussion). Examples of early preschool children's complex forms are the following:

(1) "That's mine and that's mine too";
(2) "I'm gonna eat this then I'm gonna play outside";
(3) "Don't sit on that chair cause it's broken";
(4) "I gonna build a circus but I don't got not elephants";
(5) "When Daddy comes home he gonna give me a kiss";
(6) "Look what I got!";
(7) "Now I know how to do it";
(8) "Daddy sits on the chair where the window is";
(9) "Tell Mommy I want a cookie."

The preschool child's growing attention to and understanding of complex grammatical relationships exceeds his ability to produce these structures. This is obvious in his ability to sit and listen to stories with complex structures. By age 4, children can listen to stories read aloud up to twenty to thirty minutes or longer. They typically elaborate on the text, ask relevant questions, or answer questions about the story. A typical 4-year-old's story such as Hoban's *Bread and Jam for Francis* (1964) includes complex structures such as embedded clauses and transposed negative statements (" 'Aren't you worried that maybe I will get sick and all my teeth will fall out from eating so much bread and jam?' asked Francis"). The demands for attention, verbal memory, word meaning, verbal comprehension, and integration of ideas is great, yet most 4- and 5-year-olds do it effortlessly.

Syntax and Morphology: Disorders. Some young children present with a disorder of the structural aspects of language but with relatively intact conceptual abilities and knowledge about the pragmatics of language. Problems may have to do with particular morphological inflections such as tense markers or with processing structurally complex sentences such as possessive clauses ("It's my daddy's car"); transformational structures (question forms); and complex syntax ("This is what you can do," "You can't have ice cream till Daddy comes home"). Such difficulties with the structural aspects of language will eventually interfere with the development of concepts and with discourse and other pragmatic aspects of language. Moreover, parent-child relations may be interfered with if a child's difficulties are in processing or comprehending complex syntax and parents are unaware of this limitation.

Rapin and Allen (1983) observed that, in all but one of the syndromes of language disorders in children where syntax was severely affected, there was also a phonological disorder (as is also true in adult aphasia) with or without oromotor dysfunctions. This is interesting in light of Chomsky's recent nativist position on the acquisition of language. Chomsky states that innate factors account more for syntax and phonology than for the development of meaning. Rapin and Allen's (1983) groupings of language disorders in children that include a primary disorder in syntax are: (1) a phonologic-syntactic syndrome, and (2) a syntactic-pragmatic syndrome. The phonologic-syntactic syndrome is the most prevalent of language disorders in children and is characterized by a difficulty mastering the rules of phonology and grammar. Speech is characterized by substitutions and inversions in articulation. The syntactic deficiency is characterized by a very limited use of function words and inflections of nouns and verbs and very simple syntactic constructions. They pointed out that these children exhibit syntactic constructions that differ from those of normally developing younger children. For example, they may say "The baby is cry" whereas a normal child in the early stages of syntactic development would say "baby cry," "baby crying" or "a baby crying." The phonological programming problems are often compounded by a dysarthria or a dyspraxia.

Children with a syntactic-pragmatic syndrome are more rare. They exhibit impaired syntax, pragmatic use of language, and variable phonology and prosody. Picture naming, isolated semantic notions, and use of single words to express ideas are intact. These children respond to simple commands but not to why questions. Rapin and Allen speculated that this syndrome may be a stage in the recovery of children from a more severe form of language disorder.

The language comprehension of children with syntactic disorders is a function of the severity of the syntactic impairment. There are, however, children with a more pure form of expressive language disorder, where comprehension is relatively intact but expression unintelligible and expressive syntax and morphology poor.

Disorders of syntax are often associated with memory deficits. As noted above, the skilled use of language depends upon both short- and long-term memory. Language processing and comprehension appears more closely related to recognition memory, while language formulation and production requires recall and retrieval (Wiig and Semel 1984). Other processing problems found to be associated with disorders of syntax and morphology are problems of attention (Johnson and Myklebust 1967; Ross 1976), discrimination, for example, distinguishing between "in" and "on" or "He is sleeping" and "He is sleepy" (Wren 1980); symbolization (Bloom 1970; Brown 1973; Johnson and Myklebust 1967; Werner and Kaplan 1963); and conceptualization (Johnson and Myklebust 1967).

Syntax and Morphology: Assessment. Parents' descriptions of children with disorders in syntactic development reveal difficulties with or an inability to answer questions and to respond to questions that require complex formulation, such as "What did you do in school today?" On the other hand, questions such as "Did you paint a picture in school today? Did you use the green paint?" which require only yes-no answers are responded to. Parents often report an excellent vocabulary and intact nonverbal thinking. It is important to find out the extent to which children comprehend language. I often ask parents to reduce the syntactic complexity of their speech and to note whether this leads to improved comprehension, or to eliminate accompanying gestures and note if this decreases comprehension. Comprehension must be verified clinically. This is one area on which parents' reports of children frequently err.

Spontaneous language samples from naturalistic settings are critical for assessment of syntax, especially of children between the ages of 2 and 4. Tests do not cover all critical areas. For example, a child's Mean Length of Utterance can be determined only from a language sample. Issues related to sociocultural factors, bilingualism, and biculturalism must be considered in any language assessment but in particular with regard to syntax and phonology. (See Ervin-Tripp 1978; Carrow-Woolfolk and Lynch 1982; Wiig and Semel 1984).

Standardized Tests of Grammar and Syntax. These include:

(1) Assessment of Children's Language Comprehension (ACLC);
(2) Beery-Talbot Tests of Language: Comprehension of Grammar;
(3) Clinical Evaluation of Language Functions (CELF): Grammatic Understanding;
(4) Developmental Sentence Scoring and Developmental Sentence Types;
(5) Illinois Tests of Psycholinguistic Abilities (ITPA): Grammatic Closure;
(6) Northwestern Syntax Screening Test (NSST);
(7) Test of Auditory Comprehension of Language (TACL);
(8) Token Test for Children;
(9) Test of Language Development: (TOLD) Grammatic Understanding.

Tests of Sentence Imitation.

(1) Binet Sentence Repetition;
(2) Carrow Elicited Language Inventory (CELF);

(3) Detroit Tests of Learning Aptitude: Auditory Attention Span for Unrelated Syllables.

Pragmatics: Development. Neither phonological, nor semantic, nor syntactic accuracy is sufficient for effective communication to occur. Pragmatic accuracy as well is necessary. Pragmatics of language or language use includes the ability to attend to, integrate, and use various verbal, nonverbal, and contextual aspects of communication.

One facet of pragmatics is the communicative function of language. These functions begin prelinguistically; as a function of the social/communicative aspects of language, pragmatics can be viewed as part of the process of self-other differentiation. Bruner (1983) pointed out that the organismic matrix for language learning starts at birth with the mother-child interaction, the universal source of all language functions. Recent infant research has demonstrated the natural sensitivity of infants to social and affective aspects of their environment, almost as though they were at the same time "sociocentric" as well as egocentric beings. This is coupled with the intuitive sense of parents, who naturally act in tune with their infant's capabilities and resources.

One of the earliest social-communicative infant behaviors to emerge is the regulatory function of the infant's cry. As soon as the infant makes the connection between his cries and the adults as agents of comfort, his cries constitute an attempt to regulate behavior.

Another early infant communicative behavior is gaze and pleasurable vocalization. By age 2 or 3 months, pleasurable communicative acts are evident in mutual and alternating gaze and vocalization behaviors between child and mother. These acts promote and regulate shared attention and joint action (Bateson 1975; Bruner 1983; Jaffe et al. 1973; Lewis and Freedle 1973; Stern et al. 1975). For example, Stern found that 3- to 4-month-old infants' vocalizations rarely occurred in isolation (within a social situation) but as part of the communicative act.

The shared attention, joint transactions, and play routines between mother and child are the source of language functions, and, according to Bruner (1983), the source of meaning and predication as well. Bruner enumerated some of the communicative functions that develop in the early months of life, including: references-recipient, demander-complier, seeker-finder, task initiator and accomplice, and actor and prohibiter.

It is not until Piaget's Sensorimotor Stages 4 and 5 (somewhere between 9 and 12 months) that children learn or discover the "idea" of communication. That is, that gesture, eye contact, and vocalizations can be used intentionally for purposeful communication. For example, infants wave their arms to be picked up, gesture to give up objects in their hand, tug at an adult to gain attention, wave goodbye, and point to or direct their visual gaze to what they want. Pointing to designate wants is already a presymbolic gesture typical to Sensorimotor Stage 6 (between 12–18 months). It appears just prior to the onset of first words of reference (Werner and

Kaplan 1963; Bates 1976) and seems to be correlated with the size of a child's early vocabulary (Bloom and Lahey 1978).

Halliday (1975) classified five early communicative functions between ages 9 and 18 months of age on the basis of communicative intent. They are:

(1) The "interactional," whereby gestures and sound making are used in"me" and "you" interactions with others;
(2) The "personal," whereby personal feelings, interests, likes and dislikes reflect the child's self-awareness;
(3) The "instrumental" or "I want" or "here I come," whereby the child expresses and satisfies his needs to get objects or services from other;
(4) The "regulatory" or "Do what I say," whereby the child manipulates or controls the behavior of others by 13 to 14 months;
(5) The "cognitive-heuristic" or "Tell me what/where/how/why/when," whereby the child uses vocalizations to learn about his environment. It can be communicative or noncommunicative.

There are several systems for categorizing the communicative functions of language of young children (Rees 1978). Carrow-Woolfolk and Lynch (1982) integrated these into six major categories as follows:

(1) *Greetings and Social Routines.* e.g., "hi," "bye-bye," "thank you," and "sorry." These appear very early in a child's vocabulary because they are easy in the sense of varying least in form and context (Bloom and Lahey 1978). Social phrases appear to be related to direct teaching by parents (Blank-Grief and Berk-Gleason 1980) and/or parental style of communication (Nelson 1980).
(2) *Regulating.* This was discussed above in the prelinguistic stage. At age 3 the largest single subcategory of this function is requesting and demanding action from another person (Dore 1977). This function includes using language to control, persuade, request, nag, correct, convince, threaten, demand, and so on. It also appears as a noncommunicative form of self-direction as will be discussed below.
(3) *Exchanging Information.* For example, labeling objects and events, answering adult questions, asking questions, describing, explaining, comparing, associating with other experiences, asserting. Initially, the toddler only comments on the here and now and on the obvious, such as "me climbing," "my hat," and does not supply any new information. With development these remarks decrease. By 18 to 24 months, the child starts to ask "what" and "where" questions and can also give such information when asked. By 3 to 3½ the child can supply details and elaborate on observations of the past, present, and future (see section below on conversational and discourse skills).
(4) *Expressing Feelings.* Initially all feelings are expressed nonverbally through vocalization, intonation, facial expression, and body movement. Between ages 2 to 5 children express in words their emotions, likes and dislikes, feelings of empathy, protests, criticism, threats, and the like. However, la-

beling feelings is not an early development. It is the events that aroused feelings that children talk about and not how they feel about them (Bloom and Lahey 1978). From age 2½ through the preschool years, one notes adults and caretakers labeling feelings for the child as he experiences them. For example, "You look so excited" or "I know you're mad," and so on. It has been noted that adults comment with exaggerated emotion as a natural way to teach a child how to differentiate and verbalize appropriate feelings (Clark 1973). By ages 3 to 5, children can speak about feeling "hurt," "angry," or "mad," "sad, "lonely," and so forth.

Another communicative function of language is discourse. Discourse is the most complex of "speech acts," but some of the rules of discourse begin with the first mother-child interactions, for example, turn taking and reciprocity. Discourse develops as a function of increased cognitive as well as social capacities. It depends on increased attention span and verbal comprehension and decreased distractibility. It also depends on the ability to decenter and understand others. Three aspects of discourse that emerge in the preschool years are presupposition, turn taking, and diexis.

Presupposition. Presupposition has to do with the ability to know the resources of listeners in varying social situations and to establish a shared knowledge and reality. That is, a speaker adapts both the linguistic structure and the content of his speech based on what he presupposes his listener already knows and what he judges the listener needs to know in order for him to be understood (Bates 1976; Halliday 1975).

A rudimentary ability to know a listener's point of view is evident in children as young as 2 years old. Two-year-olds, for example, ask more questions to adults than to other children (Bloom and Lahey 1978). In general, however, 2-year-old children's discourse is primarily centered on their own intent and not with the intent of a listener. By age 3 and 4 much more adaptation to listener needs is evident. One study, for example, found 4-year-olds talked differently to 2-year-olds and to other 4-year-olds (Shatz and Gellman 1973). They used more concrete verbs and less complex grammar. Such factors as linguistic and cognitive sophistication, size of the child, and capacities for attention seemed to be used by the 4-year-olds to monitor what they said. Other studies show that even when speaking to adults, 3- and 4-year-olds modify their speech, for example, with blind versus sighted persons or with persons who shared the experience they are talking about versus those who did not.

Of significance to clinicians is the observation that children, especially between ages 2 and 4, speak more frequently and use longer sentences when they speak spontaneously and originate the topic and discourse. Furthermore, language varies with the context, activity, participant, and extent to which the child can control the situation (Bates 1971, cited in Bloom and Lahey 1978).

Turn Taking. Speaking in discourse is a give-and-take behavior that depends on listener feedback, an awareness of such feedback, and mutual monitoring of attention and comprehension. It is heavily influenced by parental input and monitoring in relation to a child's resources (Bloom, Rocissano, and Hood 1976). Prelinguistic conversational turn taking begins with mother-infant interactions. By age 3 children learn to frame verbal conversations using techniques for monitoring and feedback. One of the first techniques used by 2-year-olds is the vocative (calling someone's name) to gain or regain a listener's attention before continuing to speak. Even earlier, children exclaim "look" or tug at a person to draw a listener's attention. Three-to 5-year-olds use repetition and questions contingent on the prior utterance (e.g., *Where* does he live?) to regulate turn taking (Garvey 1977).

By age 3 children answer "what," "where," and "who" questions that help adults maintain conversations with children. By this age, children understand that a topic is something shared in discourse and that each time it is their turn they can give new information (Bloom, Rocissano, and Hood 1976).

Maintenance of meaning over successive exchanges increases with development. Very young children's short attention span, distractibility and limited comprehension, and self-centeredness result in their tendency to make irrelevant remarks. At age 3 about half of a child's utterances are still not semantically contingent on the prior utterance, although they may be linguistically contingent, for example: Adult: "I ride my car to work." Child: "ride a bike" instead of "I ride my bike to the park," or "Take me for a ride in your car." (Bloom, Rocissano, and Hood 1976). Between ages 4 and 5, topics are sustained over several successive exchanges. Yet, when conversation is out of context or when conversation is initiated by a general question, such as "how was school today," parents often add more specific questions to direct conversation, for example, "Did you paint a picture?", "Was Monica in school?" These questions also serve to teach children how to answer general questions (Carrow-Woolfolk and Lynch 1982).

Diexis. "Diexis is a linguistic device that anchors an utterance to the communicative setting . . ." (Carrow-Woolfolk and Lynch 1982, p. 192). Three forms of diexis are person/object, place, and time, all of which shift during conversation. That is, the role of speaker and listener and their perspective of location and time change. In infancy, these changing shifts are learned in the exchanges between mother and child (Bruner 1975). For example, in a game where objects are exchanged back and forth, the agent of action switches back and forth. In peek-a-boo games there is also a change of role. Diexis of person refers to the alternation in use of personal pronouns "I," "me," "you," "it," "yours," "mine," learned sometime between ages 2 and 3.

Diexis of place refers to the alternation of certain nouns, pronouns, and verbs as a function of the spatial orientation of speaker vis-à-vis listener. These include words like this/that, here/there, come/go, and bring/take. These words are often learned and used (often with gesture to resolve ambiguity) before children understand their shifting meaning (Nelson 1973). Some children start out using the pairs as if they meant the same thing (Clark 1973). Between ages 3 and 4, children begin to understand the contrasts, but it is not until around age 8 that there is complete mastery.

Diexis of time refers to the relativity of time as evident in concepts such as today, yesterday, and tomorrow, and the spatial adjectives that describe time: near/ far, long/short, as in "My birthday is far from now" or "It took a long time." There is very little data on the development of temporal expressions, but there is agreement that children learn words referring to space earlier than words referring to time (Clark 1973).

In addition to interpersonal-communicative functions of language, language is used for intrapersonal purposes as follows. At the intrapersonal level language gives us both "a distance from and a new intimacy with our own selves" (Peller 1966).

Pretend Play. This use of language is related to the development of symbol formation (Bruner 1975; Piaget 1962). Between ages 2 and 5 pretend play increases in frequency and becomes more social, involving role playing (Garvey 1977; Piaget 1962). Make-believe play and its accompanying language serve to explore feelings, increase excitement, reenact events for mastery and undoing disappointment, lessen fear, prepare for stressful events, rehearse social skills, catharsis, and more. Often words themselves are used as play symbols. This usually involves idiosyncratic meanings attached to anxiety-arousing events related to aggression and sexual activities and other taboo topics.

Cognitive or Learning. At the single-word utterance stage, children label objects and events with no other purpose than naming. This naming behavior is one of the first functions of children's early vocabulary (Anisfeld 1984; Halliday 1975; Bloom and Lahey 1978; de Villiers and de Villiers 1978). The "learning function" (Halliday 1975) of language continues into the two-word stage, for example, comments such as "two cars" or "red car." There is evidence that the naming function facilitates perception, frees a child for further exploration of and interaction with his environment, and reduces his "cognitive" load (Carrow-Woolfolk and Lynch 1982). Words used in such a way also direct perceptions and feelings (Anisfeld 1984; Goldman 1984).

Self-Direction. Related but somewhat different is the use of words to mediate verbally one's own actions, that is, to direct, regulate, monitor, and otherwise tell oneself what and how to perform actions (Luria 1961; Vygotsky 1962). Between 1½ and 3 years, adult language functions to direct a child's attention and action. A typical 2-year-old might say, "Don't break the cup" *after* the cup has fallen and broken, indicating that the child has not yet internalized the controls although he has learned the appropriate language for such situations. Between ages 3 and 6, a child's self-directed speech becomes increasingly more internalized, in the form of "inner speech" (Vygotsky 1962), allowing for more reflective actions and greater inhibition. From a psychoanalytic point of view, language serves not only to organize external experience, but also to facilitate conscious mastery of drives and to distance from one's self.

Magic. The magical power of words becomes notable around age 3 and often as early as age 2, when children begin to recognize taboo words (Bates 1976). Preschool children perceive words as an integral part of a thing, an act, or a wish (Vygotsky 1962). Consequently they may avoid using certain words because their expression amounts to expressing the forbidden wish or impulse (Freud 1905).

Metalinguistic. This is the last of the language functions to appear in the preschool years. It has to do with the use of language to think about and talk about language, that is, understanding language as a decontextualized object. One of the first manifestations of this function is rhyming and giving word synonyms and antonyms, which appears at about kindergarten age.

Verbal communication is a function not only of speaker-listener relationship but also of the social context. The process of socialization involves learning the rules for the use of language in different contexts. This includes appropriateness of topic and rules of etiquette for various social situations. Moreover, meaning varies with context independent of semantics or syntax. For example, the statement "Be careful with the spaghetti" can function as a command when spoken to a 2-year-old but as a social phrase when said to a guest.

By age 3, children can speak of past and future since they are less context-bound. The true sign of freedom from context is the ability to lie. Lying requires a decontextualization from the real event and the selective presentation of information that is suited to convince the listener (Piaget 1962; de Villiers and de Villiers 1978).

Pragmatics: Disorders. Interest in normal pragmatic development is new; consequently relatively little is known about pragmatic language disorders in children, particularly in the preschool years. However, clinical reports indicate that impaired children have communication deficits with either normal phonology, syntax, and semantics or with pragmatic problems in combination with, but more severe than, their other language deficits (Speckman 1983). Among children with specific language disorders or childhood aphasia there is evidence of difficulties in the various functions of language, in role-taking abilities (presuppositions), turn taking, and conversation diexis and metalinguistics. Children with problems in interpersonal communication including nonverbal communication, such as those diagnosed as autistic, schizophrenic and psychotic, evidence severe pragmatic language disorders. Analyzing their verbal communication on the basis of pragmatic variables can yield effective strategies for therapeutic intervention.

Rapin and Allen's (1983) nosology of preschool language disorders found two syndromes in which pragmatic disorders appear prominent. These are the semantic-pragmatic without autism and the syntactic-pragmatic, both of which were discussed above. The specific difficulties with communication and language use are not elaborated upon by these authors nor is any explanation offered as to why these language disorders cluster this way. One reason why syntactic and pragmatic deficits often may coexist is that the pragmatic function of language is derived, as we saw, from early instrumental and regulatory functions that also play a large role in the development of syntax, as opposed to the "learning" or cognitive function associated more with vocabulary development (Halliday 1973, 1975). Thus, one would want to explore the very early mother-child interaction, particularly the instrumental and regulatory use of "significant others" in infancy. The semantic and pragmatic syndrome may be functions of a failure to categorize and abstract in some children. In nonverbally bright children, however, the deficit may be specific to rules of language.

Speckman (1983) discussed the disorders in discourse and pragmatics that may arise from processing deficits. As noted above, attention is necessary for all learning. Children with attentional disorders, especially those who are distractible, perseverative, and disinhibited, may have difficulty learning the rules of turn taking, diexis, topic maintenance, and the like. They may fail to attend to subtle changes in intonation, stress, kinesics (body language), and so on, that are part of the communicative process. Perceptual disorders may also interfere with these paralinguistic cues as well as with pitch, tempo, and pauses. Short-term memory deficits may impede the ability to store simultaneously linguistic, paralinguistic, and extralinguistic information necessary for pragmatic rule generalization and for monitoring conversation. Problems with symbolization can affect pragmatics and discourse in various ways. The most obvious is with comprehension of discourse. However, nonverbal symbolization problems have been identified in a subgroup of learning-disabled children with "social perception" disorders (Bryan 1977; Johnson and Myklebust 1967; Minskoff 1980). These children's failure to understand the symbolic value of such behaviors as intonation, facial expression, body postures, social and spatial distance, and gestures results in inappropriate social behavior and poor interpersonal relations. For example, they may fail to respect another person's space or to recognize negative feelings in a person's voice (intonation and/or volume). Understanding symbols within a context, that is, inferring meaning from mode of presentation and/or use, is often difficult for children with nonverbal symbolization problems. This is especially true when the verbal content and nonverbal message do not agree. (Most people rely on the nonverbal message when this occurs.)

Pragmatics: Assessment. No formal or well-standardized procedures for assessing communication competencies exist. For a thorough assessment, a complete history and observation of the child in different settings and together with different people is suggested. Of course, natural settings such as the home or classroom, with parents, siblings, and/or peers is best. As yet there is no complete taxonomy of pragmatic skills. The one outlined here offers a consensus among several writers. The important point is to use some frame of reference to guide clinical observations.

The presenting problem of a language-impaired preschooler can appear to be emotional disturbance, neurological impairment, or social maladaptation.

Differential diagnosis of language impairment is possible at increasingly early ages and is critical for effective treatment. If language therapy or parent counseling is not instituted early enough, secondary learning and emotional problems usually occur. Good language assessments of preschoolers are as yet infrequent because they demand extensive familiarity with developmental issues, and much of the key research is recent. Such assessments, however, are being done. They are most useful when accompanied by detailed and specific prescriptions for language therapy, which is increasingly being adapted to succeed with preschoolers.

A full assessment of a preschooler cannot rely heavily on standardized tests. Clinical skill, experience, and understanding of overall early development are critical. Evaluators and therapists should work very closely with parents of preschoolers to teach them to extend therapy into the child's home life. Caretakers and teachers can help greatly.

The traditional pediatric attitude of "wait and see" towards language delays and disorders has begun to yield in the face of common secondary learning and emotional problems, to more prompt referrals for diagnosis to rule out language learning problems. Most children with language delays before age four are indeed not impaired, but we now have greater skill in identifying children at high risk. Poor language comprehension, socialization problems, a family history of speech, language, or learning disorders and probably attention deficit disorders or chronic *otitis media* are strong indications for diagnostic referral in the presence of language delay.

Delayed language development may be benign. Parents need to be reminded that, just as not all normal children are athletic or musical, so some bright children are not especially verbal and need to have other strengths fostered. Normal development can be facilitated by informed parents who do not add their own frustrations, pressures, or anxieties to the difficulties that create delays in learning and socialization. Parent education and guidance in appropriate school placement are possible outcomes of findings of normal variations in development.

Early findings of specific disorders or abnormal delays are making possible earlier remediation and the prevention of serious sequelae. Parents and teachers can learn to communicate more effectively with language-impaired preschoolers at their cognitive and linguistic levels, to meet their distinctive needs, to have realistic expectations of them, to reduce their frustrations and failures and intelligently to foster normal learning. Individual language therapy, supplementary services in schools, special classes, and even special schools are available for the specific needs of different language-impaired children.

Some psychiatrically impaired preschoolers routinely require language and learning therapy apart from psychotherapy, notably the autistic and schizophrenic, who are significantly impaired in pragmatics and often in other areas. A psychiatrist should seek language evaluation of any disturbed child who, after age 2½ and without gross retardation, is not presenting normal language comprehension or production. Pediatricians and neurologists should refer patients with language delays combined with oromotor dysfunctions, that is, dyspraxia and dysarthria.

REFERENCES

Anisfeld, M. (1984). *Language Development from Birth to Three.* Hillsdale, N.J.: Lawrence Erlbaum.

Aten, J., and Davis, J. (1968). Disturbances in the perception of auditory sequence in children with minimal brain dysfunction. *J. Speech Hearing Res.* 11:236–45.

Bates, E. (1976). *Language and Context: The Acquisition of Pragmatics.* New York: Academic Press.

———, Camaloni, L., and Volterra, V. (1975). The acquisition of performatives prior to speech. *Merrill-Palmer Q.* 21 (31):205–66.

Bateson, M. C. (1975). Mother-infant exchanges: The epigenesis of conversational interaction. In D. Aronson and R. Rieber (Eds.). *Developmental Psycholinguistics and Communication Disorders. Annals of the New York Academy of Sciences* 263:101–13.

Beery, M. F. (1969). *Language Disorders of Children.* New York: Appleton-Century-Crofts.

Blank, M. (1978). *The Language of Learning: The Preschool Years.* New York: Grune and Stratton.

Blank-Grief, E., and Berk-Gleason, J. (1980). Hi, thanks, and goodbye: More routine information. *Language and Soc.* 9:159–66.

Bloom, L. (1970). *Language Development: Form and Function in Emerging Grammar.* Cambridge: MIT Press.

———. (1973). *One Word at a Time: The Use of Single-word Utterances Before Syntax.* Mouton: The Hague.

———, and Lahey, M. (1978). *Language Development and Language Disorders.* New York: Wiley.

———, Lightbown, P., and Hood, L. (1975) Structure and variation in child language. *Monographs of the Society for Research in Child Development,* No. 40 (Serial No. 160).

———, Miller, P., and Hood, L. (1975). Variation and reduction as aspects of competence in language development. In A. Pick (Ed.). *Minnesota Symposia on Child Psychology,* Vol. 9. Minneapolis: University of Minnesota Press.

———, Rocissano, L., and Hood, L. (1976). Adult-child discourse: Developmental interaction between information processing and linguistic knowledge. *Cognitive Psychology* 8:521–52.

Braine, M. D. (1963). On learning the grammatical order of words. *Psychol. Rev.* 70:323–48.

Brown, R. (1968). The development of Wh questions in child speech. *J. Verbal Learning Verbal Behav.* 7:279–90.

———. (1973). *A First Language.* Cambridge: Harvard University Press.

———, Cazden, C., and Bellugi, U. (1973). The child's grammar from one to three. In C. A. Ferguson and D. I. Slobin (Eds.). *Studies of Child Language Development.* New York: Holt, Rinehart and Winston.

Bruner, J. S. (1975). The ontogenesis of speech acts. *J. Child Language* 2:1–19.

———. (1983). *Child's Talk: Learning to Use Language.* New York: Norton.

———, Olver, R., and Greenfield, P. M. (1966). *Studies in Cognitive Growth.* New York: Wiley.

Bryan, T. (1977). Learning-disabled children's comprehension of nonverbal communication. *J. Learning Disabilities* 16:501–6.

Carrow-Woolfolk, E., and Lynch, J. I. (1982) *An Integrative Approach to Language Disorders in Children.* New York: Grune and Stratton.

Chomsky, N. (1957). *Syntactic Structures.* The Hague: Mouton.

———. (1965). *Aspects of the Theory of Syntax.* Cambridge: MIT Press.

Church, J. (1961). *Language and the Discovery of Reality.* New York: Random House.

Clark, E. V. (1973). Nonlinguistic strategies in the acquisition of word meanings. *Cognition* 2:161–82.

———. (1976). What's in a word? On the child's acquisition of semantics in his first language. In T. E. Moore (Ed.). *Cognitive Development and the Acquisition of Language.* New York: Academic Press.

Clark, H. H. (1973). Space, time, semantics and the child. In T. E. Moore (Ed.). *Cognitive Development and the Acquisition of Language.* New York: Academic Press.

Denckla, M. B., and Rudel, R. G. (1976). Rapid "automatized" naming (R.A.N.): Dyslexia differentiated from other learning disabilities. *Neuropsychologia* 14:471–79.

deVilliers, J. G., and deVilliers, P. A. (1978). *Language Acquisition.* Cambridge: Harvard University Press.

Dore, J. (1977). Holphrases, speech acts, and language universals. *J. Child Language* 2:21–40.

Eimas, P., and Corbit, J. (1973). Selective adaptation of linguistic feature detectors. *Cognitive Psychol.* 4:99–109.

Eisenson, J. (1972). *Aphasia in Children.* New York: Harper and Row.

Erickson, E. (1963). *Childhood and Society.* 2d ed. New York: Norton.

Ervin-Tripp, S. (1970). Discourse-agreement: How children answer questions. In J. R. Hayes (Ed.). *Cognition and the Development of Language.* New York: Wiley.

———. (1978). Is second language learning like the first? In E. Hatch-Marcussen (Ed.). *Second Language Acquisition.* Rowley, Mass.: Newbury House.

Fagen, J. F. (1977). An attention model of infant recognition. *Child Devel.* 48:345–59.

Fein, G. G. (1979). Play and the acquisition of symbols. In L. Katz (Ed.). *Current Topics in Early Childhood Education.* Norwood, N.J.: Ablex.

Fein, G. G., and Apfel, N. (1979). Some preliminary observations on knowing and pretending. In N. Smith and M. B. Franklin (Eds.). *Symbolic Functioning in Childhood.* Hillsdale, N.J.: Lawrence Erlbaum.

Fenson, L., and Ramsey, D. (1980). Decentration and integration of play in the second year of life. *Child Devel.* 51:171–78.

Freud, S. (1905). Jokes and their relation to the unconscious. *Standard Edition,* Vol. 8. London: Hogarth Press.

Garvey, C. (1977). *Play.* Cambridge: Harvard University Press.

Goldman, S. M. (1984). Symbolic development in play, language and self-awareness. Unpublished doctoral dissertation. Yeshiva University, New York.

Hallahan, D. P., et al. (1978). Selective attention and locus of control in learning disabled and normal children. *J. Learning Disabilities* 11:231–36.

Halliday, M. A. K. (1973). *Explorations in the Functions of Language.* New York: Elsevier-North.

———. (1975). *Learning how to Mean-Explorations in the Development of Language.* London: Edward Arnold.

Head, H. (1963). *Aphasia and Kindred Disorders of Speech* (2 vols.). Cambridge: Cambridge University Press (1926). Reprinted by Hafner Publishing, New York.

Hermlin, B., and Frith, U. (1971). Psychological studies in childhood autism: Can autistic children make sense of what they see and hear? *J. Spec. Edu.* 5:105–16.

Hermlin, B., and O'Connor, N. (1965). Remembering words by psychotic and normal children. *Brit. J. Orthopsychiatry* 35:927–36.

Hoban, R. (1964). *Bread and Jam for Francis.* New York: Harper and Row.

Jaffe, J., Stern, D., and Perry, J. (1973). Conversational coupling of gaze behavior in prelinguistic human development. *J. Psycholing. Res.* 2:321–29.

Jansky, J., and DeHirsch, K. (1972). *Preventing Reading Failures: Prediction, Diagnosis, Intervention.* New York: Harper and Row.

John, V., Horner, V. M., and Berney, T. D. (1970). Story retelling: A study of sequential speech in young children. In H. Levin and H. P. Williams (Eds.). *Basic Studies on Reading.* New York: Basic Books.

Johnson, D. J., and Myklebust, H. (1967). *Learning Disabilities: Educational Principles and Practices.* New York: Grune and Stratton.

Kinsbourne, M., and Caplan, P. J. (1979). *Children's Learning and Attentional Problems.* Cambridge: Little Brown.

Lewis, M., and Freedle, R. (1973). Mother-infant dyad: The cradle of meaning. In P. Pliner (Ed.). *Communication and Affect.* New York: Academic Press.

Lowe, A. D., and Campbell, R. A. (1965). Temporal discrimination in aphasoid and normal children. *J. Speech Hearing Res.* 8:313–14.

Luria, A. R. (1961). *The Role of Speech in the Regulation of Normal and Abnormal Behavior.* New York: Pergamon Press.

———. (1981). *Language and Cognition.* New York: Wiley.

———, and Yudovich, F. I. (1971). *Speech and the Development of Mental Processes in the Child.* Baltimore: Penguin Books.

McCarthy, D. (1954). Language development in children. In L. Carmichael (Ed.). *Manual of Child Psychology.* 2d ed. New York: Wiley.

McNeil, D. (1966). Developmental psycholinguistics. In F. Smith and G. A. Miller (Eds.). *The Genesis of Language.* Cambridge: MIT Press.

Mahler, M., Pine, F., and Bergman A. (1975). *The Psychological Birth of the Human Infant.* New York: Basic Books.

Masland, M., and Case, L. (1968). Limitations of auditory memory as a factor in delayed language development. *Brit. J. Disorders Commun.* 3:139–42.

Miller, G. A., and Chomsky, N. (1963). Finitary models of language users. In R. D. Luce, R. R. Bush, and E. Galanter (Eds.). *Handbook of Mathematical Psychology,* Vol. 2. New York: Wiley.

Minskoff, E. H. (1980). Teaching approach for developing nonverbal communication skills in students with social perception deficits. Part 1: The basic approach and body language clues. *J. Learning Disabilities* 13:118–24.

Moerk, E. L. (1977). *Pragmatic and Semantic Aspects of Early Language Development.* Baltimore: University Park Press.

Morehead, D. M., and Morehead, A. (1974). From signal to sign: A Piagetian view of thought and language during the first two years. In R. L. Schiefelbusch and L. L. Lloyd (Eds.). *Language Perspectives: Acquisition, Retardation and Intervention.* Baltimore: University Park Press.

Myklebust, H. R. (1954). *Auditory Disorders in Children: A Manual for Differential Diagnosis.* New York: Grune and Stratton.

Neisser, U. (1967). *Cognitive Psychology.* New York: Appleton-Century-Crofts.

Nelson, K. (1973). Structure and strategy in learning to talk. *Monographs of the Society for Research in Child Development* 38 (1–2, Serial No. 149).

―――. (1978). Early speech in its communicative context. In F. D. Minifie and L. L. Lloyd (Eds.). *Communicative and Cognitive Abilities: Early Behavioral Assessement.* Baltimore: University Park Press.

―――. (1980). *Planning Individualized Speech and Language Intervention Programs.* Tuscon, AZ: Communication Skill Builders.

―――, and Nelson, K. (1978). Cognitive pendulums and their linguistic realization. In K. Nelson (Ed.). *Children's Language,* Vol. 1. New York: Gardner Press.

Nicolich, L. M. (1977). Beyond sensorimotor intelligence: Assessment of symbolic maturity through analysis of pretend play. *Merrill-Palmer Q.* 23(2):89–101.

Olson, G. M. (1973). Memory development and language acquisition. In T. E. Moore (Ed.). *Cognitive Development and the Acquisition of Language.* New York: Academic Press.

Peller, L. E. (1965). Language and development. In P. B. Naubaur (Ed.). *Concepts of Development in Early Childhood Education.* Springfield, Mass.: Thomas Press, p. 492.

Piaget, J. (1952). *The Origins of Intelligence in Children.* New York: International Universities Press.

―――. (1954). *The Construction of Reality in the Child.* New York: Basic Books.

―――. (1962). *Play, Dreams and Imitation in Childhood.* New York: Norton.

―――. (1970). Piaget's theory. In L. Carmichaels (Ed.). *Manual of Child Psychology.* New York: Wiley.

Rapin, I., and Allen, D. A. (1983). Developmental language disorders: Nosologic considerations. In U. Kirk (Ed.). *Neuropsychology of Language, Reading and Spelling.* New York: Academic Press.

Rees, N. S. (1973). Auditory processing factors in language disorders: A view from Procrustes' bed. *J. Speech and Hearing Disorders* 38:3.

―――. (1978). Pragmatics of language: Application to normal and disordered language development. In R. L. Schiefelbusch (Ed.). *Basis of Language Intervention.* Baltimore: University Park Press.

Ross, A. (1976). *Psychological Aspects of Learning Disabilities and Reading Disorders.* New York: McGraw-Hill.

Shatz, M., and Gellman, R. (1973). The development of communication skills: Modifications in the speech of young children as a function of listener. *Monogr. Society Res. Child Development* 38 (Serial No. 152).

Silva, P. A., Chalmers, D., and Stewart, I. (1986). Some audiological, psychological, educational, and behavioral characteristics of children with bilateral otitis media with effusion. *J. Learning Disabilities* 19 (3).

Slobin, D. I. (1967). *A Field Manual for Cross-cultural Study of the Acquisition of Communicative Competence.* Berkeley: University of California Press.

―――. (1973). Cognitive prerequisites for the development of grammar. In C. Ferguson and D. Slobin (Eds.). *Studies of Child Language Development.* New York: Holt, Rinehart and Winston.

Speckman, N. J. (1983). Discourse and pragmatics. In C. T. Wren (Ed.). *Language Learning Disabilities.* Rockville, Md.: Aspen Systems Corp.

Stark, J. (1981). Reading: What needs to be assessed? *Topics in Language Disorders* 1:87–94.

Stern, D., et al. (1975). Vocalizing in unison and in alternation: Two modes of communication within the mother-infant dyad. In D. Aronson and R. Rieber (Eds.). *Developmental Psycholinguistics and Communicative Disorders. Annals of the New York Academy of Sciences* 263:89–100.

Tallal, P. (1976). Rapid auditory processing in normal and disordered language development. *J. Speech Hearing Res.* 19:561–71.

———, and Piercy, M. (1973). Developmental dysphasia: Impaired rate of nonverbal processing as a function of sensory modality. *Neuropsychologia* 11: 389–98.

———, and Piercy, M. (1974). Developmental aphasia: Rate of auditory processing and selective impairment of consonant perception. *Neuropsychologia* 12:83–93.

———, and Piercy, M. (1975). Developmental aphasia: The perception of brief vowels and extended stop consonants. *Neuropsychologia* 13:69–74.

———, Stark, R. E., and Mellits, D. E. (1985). The relationships between auditory temporal analysis and receptive language development: Evidence from studies of developmental language disorder. *Neuropsychologia* 23(4):527–34.

Vygotsky, L. S. (1962). *Thought and Language.* Cambridge: MIT Press.

Wadsworth, B. J. (1984). *Piaget's Theory of Cognitive and Affective Development.* 3d ed. New York: Longman.

Watson, M. W., and Fisher, K. W. (1977). A developmental sequence of agent use in late infancy. *Child Devel.* 48:828–36.

Werner, H., and Kaplan, B. (1963). *Symbol Formation.* New York: Wiley.

Wiig, E. H., and Semel, E. (1984). *Language Assessment and Intervention for the Learning Disabled.* Columbus, Ohio: Merrill.

Wolf, M. (1984). Naming, reading, and the dyslexias: A longitudinal overview. *Annals of Dyslexia* 34:87–115.

Wren, C. (1980). The relationship of auditory and cognitive process to syntactic patterns in learning disabled and normal children. Unpublished doctoral dissertation, Northwestern University.

15

ASSESSMENT OF LEARNING DISABILITIES

Jeannette Jefferson Jansky

Learning disabilities is a term that refers to a diverse group of disorders. These include ineffective listening habits, an uneven course of language development, and difficulties with reasoning and with achieving proficiency in spoken and written language and in mathematics. Such disorders are viewed as being inborn manifestations of central nervous system dysfunction. Although learning disabilities may occur with other handicapping conditions, such as sensory impairment, mental retardation, emotional difficulty, sociocultural deprivation, and poor teaching, they are not caused by those conditions. (Hammill et al. 1981).

This definition acknowledges the varied forms such disabilities assume. In reflecting upon findings reported at a conference sponsored by The National Institute of Mental Health, Benton and Pearl (1978) referred to the evidence that specific dyslexia, a form of learning disability, is not a unitary disability but a group of disabilities, each with distinctive symptomatology. It should also be noted that previous definitions, and specifically the one set forth in Public Law 94-142, required a diagnosis based on discrepancy between expected and actual performances. The more recent definition omitted this requirement because of flaws in techniques used to quantify severe discrepancy.

In their review of the 1981 definition, McLoughlin and Netic (1983) recommended standard score comparisions and regression analysis as useful techniques for diagnosis. Geschwind (1982) made a point of emphasizing the talents some learning-disabled individuals show, and McLoughlin and Netic lamented the fact that the term learning disabilities has become almost synonymous with underachievement, and they suggested that efforts be made to program for special talents. In addition, the authors mentioned that elementary school students have tended to receive most attention, and they proposed that provisions be made for remediating the learning problems of adolescents and adults. Finally, they reminded the reader, as did Eisenberg (1978), that the complicating effects of environmental factors are underemphasized by the definition.

EPIDEMIOLOGY

Estimates of the prevalence of learning disability vary considerably, in part because of lack of agreement as to definition. In the case of developmental reading disability, 77.2 percent of 136 professionals who responded to a questionnaire placed the incidence below 5 percent (Tucker, Stevens, and Ysseldyke 1983). Badian (1984), who examined 550 8- to 12-year-old children in a community near Boston, found the incidence to be 4 percent (22/550). Baker and Cantwell (1985) placed the incidence of developmental arithmetic disorder at 6 percent.

Boys with reading disabilities have been found to outnumber girls at a ratio of 2:1 in large population samples and 4:1 in clinic groups (Rutter and Yule 1973). The male-to-female ratio in the Badian study was 2.5:1. Baker and Cantwell stated that the male-to-female ratio in developmental arithmetic disorder is unclear, probably because such disorders occur so frequently in children who also present developmental language disorders.

Birth order is differentiated between disabled and adequate readers in the Badian study, with 31.3 percent fifth or later-born and only 6.3 percent first-born (as compared with 11 percent later, and 27.5 percent first-born in the group of adequate readers).

Chronological age at time of school entry was not a contributor to reading status in the Badian investigation. (See also Jansky and de Hirsch 1972.) However, month of birth did significantly differentiate poor readers from adequate ones. The prevalence of reading disability for boys born in July was 20.8 percent, or 3.7 times the average rate. While the reason for the relationship is unclear, Badian cited evidence that a wide range of environmental factors influence the developing nervous system, with the male fetus more vulnerable than the female.

The incidence of reading disability among the less advantaged and in inner-city groups was reported by Rutter and Yule to be significantly higher than for controls. In the Jansky and de Hirsch study the economically disadvantaged second graders scored lower than controls on the reading comprehension test.

ETIOLOGY

Neurological Basis. Most (though by no means all) investigators subscribe to the neurological basis theory of learning disabilities. This position derives partly from reports of brain-injured *adults* who showed various forms of alexia and acalculia. Such investigations have underscored the importance of the left hemisphere for various linguistic and cognitive functions. In studying cases of developmental learning disabilities, researchers have based inferences about the relationship between brain function and performance on children's scores on neuropsychological tests.

With the advent of more sophisticated tools for measurement, observations about the relationship between structure and function have become more specific. Geschwind and Levitsky (1968), for example, documented the anatomical asymmetry of the brain, showing that the left planum temporale is significantly larger than the right one in about two-thirds of the population. Galaburda (1983) recalled that in the very earliest descriptions of the syndrome, it was suspected that brains of dyslexics develop differently from those who read adequately. With Kemper (Galaburda and Kemper 1979) he reported findings from the post-mortem architectonic analysis of the brain of a 20-year-old left-handed male dyslexic. They described various disturbances in the development and structure of the left cortex. In similar analysis of the brain of a second subject, a 14-year-old dyslexic, Galaburda (1983) found more primitive levels of architectonic development in the left brain than in analogous areas of the right hemisphere.

Hier et al. (1978) undertook CT scan studies of twenty-four dyslexics between the ages of 14 and 74 years. He found a reversal of the usual posterior hemispheric asymmetry in a significant number of dyslexic subjects. Denckla, LeMay, and Chapman (1985) pointed out that the attempts made to provide normative CT data on pediatric populations have not been entirely satisfactory. In their CT study of thirty-two children 7 to 14 years of age referred for various school difficulties, they reported that the two radiologists who read CT scans "blind" found that most of these learning-disabled children had *normal* protocols, even though the subjects had been selected for neurological lateralization characteristics typical for right and left hemisyndromes. Twenty percent of the scans were read as "slightly abnormal" by both radiologists. These basically negative results of Denckla et al. are in the same direction as those of Thompson, Ross, and Horwitz (1980), who found only one subject with an abnormal CT scan in a sample of forty-four children diagnosed as having minimal brain injury. Denckla, LeMay, and Chapman left open the possibility that with technological advance in CT, it may be feasible to identify more specific findings in developmentally impaired children.

Lubar et al. (1985) discussed the use of EEG to evaluate neurological aspects of learning disabilities. He noted that early studies found that subjects were more likely than normals to show slow activity below 8 Hz; and that subsequently, using more sophisticated methods for quantification, parietal-occipital slowing was identified in children who were at risk for minimal brain injury. In the Luber et al. study of sixty-nine children with learning disabilities and thirty-four controls, power spectral Fast Fourier analysis of the scalp EEG was obtained from three left-hemisphere and three right-hemisphere locations. The investigators found that the theta and theta-low-alpha bands tended to distinguish normal from learning-disabled children, but that other EEG frequencies did not.

The evidence for neurological difference, thus, is steadily accumulating, though it is still not possible to relate specific brain sites to specific subtypes of developmental dyslexia.

Family History. The very earliest reports noted that language disabilities frequently occur in several individuals in the same family. Hallgren (1950) was one of the first to conduct an extensive study of this association. He investigated the families of 112 reading-disabled children and concluded that the condition was due to a gene at a single locus that produced a dominant effect. In 1982 Smith et al. presented evidence based on genetic linkage analysis that showed an association between one form of dyslexia and a structural variation of chromosome 15. With additional findings from a later study, Smith provided important evidence of the genetic origin of dyslexia and support for the idea of heterogeneity based on the suggestion that there is at least one dominant form. Volger, De Fries, and Decker (1984) used Bayesian inverse probability analysis to evaluate the self-reported reading status of the families of 174 reading-disabled children and of 182 controls. It was found that the risk for reading disability is increased substantially (by a factor of from about 4 to over 13) if either parent showed delays in learning to read. In their excellent discussion of the state of the art of heritability research, Childs and Finucci (1983) posited an interaction between gene effects and experience. Convinced that a multiplicity of genetic and environmental variables account for these disabilities, they suggested that these effects operate in different ways in different people. They look forward to the time when information as to familial quality and mode of inheritance will lead to classifications that are useful for prevention and remediation.

Baker and Cantwell (1985) discussed the dearth of definitive studies of the genetic predisposition to developmental arithmetic disorder. Such evidence as exists consists of family history case reports and monozygotic twin studies showing greater-than-chance correlations with arithmetic level. They, too, consider the confounding effects of environmental factors.

LEARNING DISABILITY SUBTYPES

An Etiology-Oriented Subtype. Hynd and Hynd (1984) derived their hypothesized subtypes of reading disabilities from the results of studies of adult subjects. Their conceptualization is offered as an example of a neurological viewpoint. The Hynds' description of the normal reading process suggests that discrete zones of cortical activity work together to provide a functional system for a given cognitive process. Hynd and Hynd looked at differences between dyslexics and normals in the distribution of electrical activity as they engaged in reading and listening tasks. The dyslexics showed less efficient patterns of electrical activity than normals. The greatest differences were found in Broca's area, the left temporal region (an area roughly equivalent to Wernicke's area), and in the angular gyrus.

Hynd and Hynds' model of reading assumes that visual material is registered in the occipital lobes, where associations are made between visual stimuli and known letters or words. Information is then coordinated with input from other sensory modalities in the region of the angular gyrus. Coupled with linguistic-semantic comprehension from the region of the planum temporale and the temporal lobe, the information is shared with Broca's area via the arcuate fasciculus. Simultaneous and sequential processing are involved at different stages and probably at different levels of development. The authors emphasized that although processing in their model of normal reading appears to be sequential, it involves series of feedback loops.

The Hynds' proposed three disability subtypes: surface dyslexia, phonological dyslexia, and deep dyslexia. *Surface dyslexics* appear to access print through phonological, or nonvisual modes. While they read nonwords well, they have trouble reading meaningful ones. They process short words better than long ones, and they rely on phonological rules. They cannot access the purely visual-spatial aspects of words, or words as wholes. When phonological rules are not applicable, reading breaks down. Semantic access is problematic and comprehension is deficient. In *phonological dyslexia* the reader manages familiar words well, but has trouble with function words and nonwords, or those that must be read through a phonetic system. Grapheme-phoneme conversion is impaired. The individual can process letter strings and can understand what he reads, but he cannot read well orally. In *deep dyslexia* the reader can read familiar words (especially nouns) well, but makes many semantic paralexic errors. He might, for example, read the printed word "mitten" as "glove." Most such individuals have word-finding deficits. They misread nonwords, verbs, and abstract nouns, and rely upon imageability, concreteness, and word frequency. They can read words in context better than they read single words. Deep dyslexics have grapheme-phoneme conversion difficulty. Comprehension during silent reading is better than it is during oral reading. The pathway is presumed to follow through the right occipital region where the imageability of words is important; it proceeds from there through Wernicke's area, where words are processed as wholes and meaning is attached.

Hynd and Hynd concluded that if the distribution of neuroanatomical anomalies is truly random, then the potential number of subtypes is indeed many. The three they suggested do not incorporate all disabled readers. Dorman (1985) took issue with the Hynds' approach to subtyping on the grounds that findings based on adult patients may not be at all applicable to children.

Performance-Oriented Subtypes. As suggested earlier, not all investigators subscribe to a neurologically oriented approach to subtyping. Many prefer to base typologies on performance.

Lovett (1984) exemplified the researcher who works from a model of normal reading based on cognitive theory, where reading is conceived as one of the most interactive and complex examples of human information processing, involving simultaneous processing of many different levels of textual information. Processing units are parallel and completely bidirectional in their interaction. Lovell viewed the LaBerge and Samuels (1974) constructs, accuracy and automaticity, as cornerstones of normal reading. She noted that fluency is established only when all levels of visual to semantic decoding occur accurately and automatically. Attention is thereby freed for an uninterrupted appreciation of textual meaning.

Lovett used Rumelhart's model (1977) as a framework for sorting children according to differences in reading behavior. Rumelhart proposed six knowledge sources: letters and spelling patterns, speech sounds, letter-sound correspondences, vocabulary, syntax, and meaning. In order to read, the individual combines perceptual information from the text, with information from his six knowledge sources. As these are synthesized (processing information simultaneously, as described above), the reader accepts the most probable interpretation as the appropriate reading of the text.

Lovett's two subtypes of disabled readers are categorized according to the accuracy/automaticity (rate) criteria. In her study *accuracy/disabled* readers were found to be inferior in their understanding of oral language structure: syntax and morphology. (They were comparable to their rate-disabled peers in word knowledge and word retrieval functions.) They also had trouble associating unfamiliar pseudo-words and novel symbols, and were at a disadvantage when required to learn associations or exceptions to the rule.

The *rate-disabled* readers were found to have a basic deficit in speed of word recognition, and a more global deficit in speed of accessing and providing names for single- or multiple-element visual arrays. This speed disadvantage was specific to the rapid labeling of visual symbols or pictures, and was not evident on auditory responsive naming or associative naming measures. It was thus not attributable to a general word retrieval or lexical access problem. Decoding accuracy was worse on connected text; functional overload occurred when specific processes involved the sequential translation of continuous visual input.

The disability of the rate-disabled subtype appears to be restricted to visible language, while the handicaps of the accuracy disabled subtype include a language disability that is multifaceted and coupled with specific speech sound analysis problems and a sound symbol learning disability.

Lovett used Stanovich's interactive-compensatory model (1980) to describe the way both normal and disabled readers go about reading. Briefly, this holds that any component knowledge source may potentially be selected to compensate for deficient processing in another source. This model does not predict that compensatory alternatives will necessarily be successful; it simply recognizes the range of options available to the reader.

Task-based subtypes proposed by several other investigators will be summarized briefly. In 1973 Boder categorized children as dyseidetic or dysphonetic by observing qualitative differences in their reading and spelling performances. She found that 9 percent of the children showed an inability to perceive whole-word configurations and referred to them as dyseidetic, while 63 percent appeared handicapped by a failure to acquire phonetic word analysis and word synthesis skills, and were called dysphonetic. The rest belonged to a mixed or combined category.

Petrauskas and Rourke (1979) worked with a pool of tests tapping six categories of functioning: tactile-perceptual; sequencing; motoric; visual-spatial; auditory-verbal; and abstract-conceptual. Data based on the performance of 160 normal and disabled readers were subjected to correlation analysis and Q factor-analysis procedures. Three reliable subtypes of reading-disabled children were identified: *Subtype 1*, included the greatest number of reading-disabled subjects. These children exhibited difficulties on tests that were primarily verbal in nature. Their abilities in the tactile-perceptual, motoric, visual-spatial, and abstract-conceptual areas were within normal limits, and their WISC verbal-performance IQ discrepancy favored performance IQ. *Subtype 2* exhibited a small WISC verbal-performance IQ discrepancy. Children in this category showed the so-called ACID pattern (poor WISC Arithmetic, Coding, Information, and Digit Span subtest performances). They also performed poorly on the WRAT reading, spelling, and arithmetic subtests. Their most striking deficits were on tests for finger agnosia with the right and left hands, and on immediate memory for visual sequences. Children in Subtype 2 were viewed as having a more general sequencing difficulty. This group included half of the reading-disabled children. *Subtype 3* was the smallest reliable subtype. Subjects tended to have greater difficulty with the right than with the left hand on both the Tactual Performance Test and on the Finger Recognition Test. They were also conceptually inflexible, especially when linguistic coding was involved. Their verbal IQs were lower than their performance IQs.

Spreen and Haaf (1986) submitted test scores of two groups of learning-disabled children to cluster analysis. Although the tests used differed from those selected by other investigators, three subgroups comparable to those previously identified emerged: visuo-perceptual, linguistic, and articulo-graphic.

Baker and Cantwell (1985) reported agreement among investigators as to the multiplicity of skills that may be dysfunctional in developmental arithmetic disorder. Included were problems with recognition of numerical symbols or signs; with aligning columns of numbers, with maintaining place, with ordering series of numbers, and with the clustering of objects into groups. Children with developmental arithmetic disabilities were also reported to make such seemingly "careless" errors as omitting digits, decimals, or symbols; forgetting to add numbers to be carried; and failing to note the sign. They were also said to have trouble learning the multiplication tables and holding in mind sequences of steps for problem solving.

Baker and Cantwell observed that language and verbal difficulties are such frequent concomitants of arithmetic disorders that dyscalculia might almost be considered a language disability. Indeed, Spreen's findings led him to suggest that only a few learning-disabled subjects can be said to have "specific" reading disabilities, and even fewer to have "specific" arithmetic impairment, since the majority of subjects presented difficulty in both areas. Ackerman, Anhalt, and Dykman (1986) presented evidence to support their hypothesis that reading-disabled children are likely to become numerically imcompetent adults, given their inability to automatize basic number combinations. Baker and Cantwell cited such verbal deficits as inadequate decoding, limited vocabulary, and inability to master the terminology of arithmetic.

Rourke and Strang (1983) discussed earlier studies in which their unit identified a "specific" arithmetic disorder cluster. Children belonging to this cluster demonstrated well-developed auditory-perceptual abilities, but functioned inadequately on complex psychomotor and tactile-perceptual tasks.

Although investigators seem to be turning up similar categories, and although the subtypes appear to have some clinical validity, clinicians have been reluctant to "force" an individual disabled reader into one or another category because the number and diversity of his symptoms cross several subgroup lines. There is something haunting about Lovett's observation that the more exhaustive the effort to account for differences among subjects, the more different they are revealed to be, and the more puzzling is the problem of this heterogeneity. The goal of prescriptive teaching based on diagnostic categorizations remains elusive.

CONCOMITANTS OF LEARNING DISABILITY

Immaturity. Bender (1958) and de Hirsch (1957,1975) characterized many of the learning-disabled children they studied as neurophysiologically immature. Both viewed the child's failure to master academic skills at the expected times as evidence of a comprehensive, organismic immaturity that was manifested not only in academic failure, but also in delay all along the developmental line. Bender described lags in neurological patterning in children with severe reading disabilities. Such children were found to show awkwardness in motor control; variability in motor tone; dys-rhythmic, immature electroencephalographic patterns; disorganized and impulsive behavior; primitiveness of perceptual-motor patterning and capacity to develop *gestalten*; and immature, impulse-driven, and dependent personalities and feelings of anxiety and inadequacy that lead to various symptom formations.

De Hirsch (1975) characterized children who are unready for formal schooling as retaining the global responses of the younger child. Unready children have short attention spans, show ambiguous laterality, imprecise auditory perception, and in-attentiveness. Parents report delays in language acquisition, and later on, clinicians observe subtle deficits in comprehension and expression. De Hirsch pointed out that lags in ego development accompany lags in physiological development. Such children have trouble postponing gratification and may also exhibit a short frustration span. They may express aggression behaviorally rather than by way of language. Wish-fulfilling and magical solutions seem to be preferred approaches to problem solving. De Hirsch made the important observation that when unready children are older, some develop compensatory compulsive-obsessive-like mechanisms. It is less likely that these defenses are developed against forbidden impulses than against fear of disintegration. The defenses themselves often constitute barriers to learning.

Behavioral Difficulties. Teacher ratings of behavioral disorders are excellent predictors of learning disabilities. These ratings have tended to characterize learning-disabled children as less adept socially, less directed to task, less organized, and less responsible than non-learning-disabled children. Several behavioral subgroups were described by McKinney (1984) and by McKinney and Feagans (1983). The first subgroup included children who were dependent and unable to settle down to work. On the other hand, they had average verbal skills, only minor lags in achievement, and were quite good socially. The second group presented behavioral deficits across the board, they showed marked unevenness in cognitive profile, and scored far below expectation on achievement measures. The third group was poorly oriented to task, extroverted, and hostile. They were of average intelligence and functioned only slightly below expectation in achievement. The fourth group presented no behavioral difficulties, were of average intelligence, and were deficient only in academic achievement. The severity of the social incompetence and of the behavioral problems of the learning-disabled boys studied by McConaughty and Ritter (1985) placed these children within the clinical range for patients assigned to mental health clinics.

Many learning-disabled children are inattentive. It is unclear whether their inattentiveness represents a turning away from tasks that are too difficult, or is a manifestation of a global attention deficit disorder, or of some form of conduct disorder. Garfinkel (1986) has discussed the diagnostic difficulty of distinguishing between attention problems that belong to a separate syndrome and those that represent a subcategory of conduct or behavior disorder.

Depression. Depression in learning-disabled children has received increasing attention in recent years. The impact of deep feelings of failure experienced day after day, year after year, cannot be minimized, nor can depression in adolescent and adult dyslexics be taken lightly. Most clinicians know of at least one attempted suicide or suicide in their network of clinical contacts with dyslexic individuals.

In discussing the major depressive disorder syndrome (MDD), Livingston (1985) raised several questions about its connection with learning disability. He asked if depression causes or worsens learning disabilities. He wondered, further, whether learning disabilities are risk factors in the development of major depressive disorder. Finally, he asked if some identifiable brain dysfunction might put children at risk for both major depressive disorder and certain kinds of learning difficulties. In regard to the first question, he hypothesized a possible relationship between the time of onset of MDD and the onset or worsening of learning difficulties. A corollary would be the finding that successful treatment of MDD is accompanied by improvement in school performance. As to the second question, the author hypothesized that MDD may be more frequent in children with previously diagnosed learning problems than in controls or in children with other psychiatric conditions. Livingston discussed the third question regarding a particular brain dysfunction that underlies both risk for MDD and learning disability. He reported the suggestion that in adults MDD is associated with right-hemisphere impairment (including dyscalculia, motor development delays, poor handwriting, faulty sequencing, performance IQ lower than verbal IQ, and minor abnormalities of hand and foot posture and in performances on dichotic listening tasks). He hypothesized that children with arithmetic and visuomotor difficulties (associated with right-brain dysfunction) may develop MDD more frequently than children with other learning disabilities.

ASSESSMENT

The assessment is usually undertaken by a psychologist, special educator, or sometimes by a physician. The evaluator will have been trained to administer and interpret tests and to understand the basics of measurement theory. In some settings evaluations are undertaken by several specialists, while in others they are completed by a single individual, in a school, clinic, or private office.

The process should include a history-taking interview that will elicit information as to family history; vicissitudes of pregnancy, delivery, and development (especially of language); childhood illnesses, especially otitis media resulting in periodic reduction of auditory efficiency during the years that language develops; information as to special talents and interests; the child's relationship with siblings, parents and others; his autonomy; and the ways he handles frustration, failure, and anger. The evaluator will have the opportunity to judge the extent of the parent's active involvement in the child's day-to-day activities, and the way the parent views the child and his learning problems. The initial interview also includes a careful exploration of concerns that led up to the request for evaluation, and a review of school records and reports of relevant previous evaluations.

The testing itself will consider the child's performance on tasks or variables that are pertinent for learning. These include a test of intelligence; measures of activity level; right-left orientation; fine motor competence; graphics, spatial sequencing, and lay-out efficiency; attention; indices of language-processing competence (including assessments of the way the child takes in sounds, syllables, words, sentences and language in context; ability to follow spoken directions; comprehension of spoken language, language expression (including melody, rhythm, rate, articulation, word elicitation, maturity of sentence structure, formulation ability, and oral story summary); performance on oral and silent reading achievement tests (vocabulary and comprehension); a spelling test, a written composition, and a measure of arithmetic (computation and word problems). Such cognitive functions as memory, sequencing, organization, integration, and analysis are brought into play in the course of testing.

Various projective tests may be administered to assess the way the child sees himself in general and in relation to the disability, and to learn more about the way the child manages his academic problems. If one is to estimate outcome, it is absolutely essential to get an impression of the degree to which the child is likely to be an active participant in the remedial process.

During the follow-up visit the clinician discusses results with the parents, makes recommendations as to remedial approaches, possible shifts in class or school placements, and makes referral to appropriate specialists. The evaluator must take time to answer as many parental questions as possible and to allay parental anxiety; sometimes a second or third follow-up session may be appropriate. Information as to outcome should also be given to the child, in a way that will be constructive, useful, and informative.

The evaluation will have accomplished its purpose to the extent that it informs parents and child about the way the child learns; and to the extent that it lays the groundwork for effective intervention.

TREATMENT

The treatment of learning disabilities is primarily pedagogic. There is little solid evidence that therapies that rely primarily on medication, vitamins, diet control, eye muscle training, or motor patterning retraining are effective.

There is disagreement as to preferred methods of remediating reading disabilities. One of the best-known approaches to teaching children with reading disabilities was developed by Orton and his followers. This strategy first directs attention to associating the sound or sounds with their written correlates; to the systematic mastery of small units of language, phonemes and syllables, followed by the blending of those clusters into words and sentences. The use of techniques that engage the several senses simultaneously is recommended. The rationale for this procedure is that children's failure to learn to cope with letters and syllables is basic to their failure to learn to read. It is concluded, therefore, that by teaching phoneme-grapheme correspondence, they will teach them to learn to read. A different point of view emphasizes the importance of sentence and paragraph contexts, that is to say of meaningful units, for learning to read. Proponents of this view hold that control of letter and word perception is mediated by higher cognitive processes. There seems to be a real question as to the desirability of adhering rigidly to a single strategy. Some children may not be ready when they enter school to use an analytic decoding approach, especially if English is their second language. Such children have a poor ear for the sounds and vocabulary of their new language and a teaching strategy based on introduction to reading by way of sounds may be inadvisable. There are other children who tend to become obsessively preoccupied with details rather than with wholes. Such children find themselves caught in a maze of small units that are barriers to pulling out meaning. A feasible alternative to the sound/symbol approach is a sentence learning approach, which speaks to the child's appreciation of larger language units and introduces sight words in a sentence context. There is no doubt at all, however, about the necessity, sooner or later, to achieve a thorough mastery of melding spoken with written equivalents of single phonemes and letters, syllables, words, sentences, and larger language units. And there is no doubt about the desirability of achieving automaticity so as to attain fluency. This involves considerable practice at every step along the way. The child should work on writing and spelling at least as much as on reading. Because there is no correlation between spelling and intelligence, it is unlikely that the poor speller will ever become really proficient.

In her review of the literature Gittelman (1983) found no evidence to suggest that any one treatment method is best either for groups of children or for individual children with specific types of deficits. This is not to discount the value of intervention. Most remedial specialists use a variety of approaches, and it is relatively easy to demonstrate progress by way of teacher reports, standardized test scores, and observation of changes in the child's reading habits.

It is extremely important for the reading specialist to work closely with teachers, other professionals, and with the parents. Parental support is essential to the success of intervention. Children should be referred for psychiatric evaluation and assistance, when indicated early on, *before* they get themselves into trouble that further compromises their chances of succeeding.

It is difficult to overstate the value of early identification and intervention. The earlier the child can achieve mastery, the sooner he will be pleased with himself and with school. This is not to mention the practical benefits of learning to use reading and writing as tools for communication.

CASE VIGNETTE

Charley was the youngest of three brothers. His father had been slow to learn to read and his mother's speech was rushed and disorganized. Both of Charley's older brothers were dyslexic, as was an older half-brother. Charley was the product of an uneventful pregnancy and delivery. Developmental course was unremarkable, Charley was quite reticent, although he learned to speak ahead of schedule and used complicated constructions. He sometimes had trouble following directions because he was slow to develop right/left awareness, but general comprehension was excellent. The WPPSI administered when he was 5, showed a Full Scale IQ within the Superior range, with a twenty-point discrepancy between verbal and performance IQs in favor of the verbal score. Readiness testing at age 5 revealed that Charley was at risk for reading failure. His scores on various paper and pencil tests were low. Specifically, his pencil management was poor, and his copies of designs and letters and words were awkward and inaccurate and poorly spaced on the page. During his early years in school he reversed and transposed letters when reading and writing. He was slow to learn to associate spoken with written language units, had trouble discriminating between similar sounding words, and struggled to isolate or segment individual sounds of spoken words. His spoken language was somewhat slurred and indistinct. Although he clearly had trouble managing sounds, more conceptual aspects of language were unaffected. His vocabulary and sentence sense were excellent, his sense of humor quite sophisticated, and his general fund of information extensive. He had ongoing difficulty with numbers and arithmetic. He was inclined to daydream and his first- and second-grade teachers complained that he rarely paid attention during class discussions.

Readiness training was instituted when Charley was 5 and remedial intervention (in the case of both reading and arithmetic) continued until he was 14, when he went away to boarding school. He repeated second grade and also attended remedial camp for eight weeks during two summers. Sound/ symbol correspondences were stressed during remedial sessions. A great deal of time was spent on writing and spelling, and later on learning to type. When he was 12, he worked on vocabulary development and techniques for taking various kinds of tests. Arithmetic tutoring was undertaken by a second specialist, who drilled the mastery of number combinations, and later worked to develop a system for working through several-step problems. Charley was ambitious and his progress in reading and in writing was considerably better than it was in spelling and arithmetic. His SSAT Verbal and Reading Comprehension scores fell in the 60 to 70 percentile range, while the Quantitative score stayed within the 20th percentile band.

Charley became much better focused during remedial sessions and in the classroom as he grew older. The strategy used was to draw his attention to states in which he was and was not daydreaming. It was relatively easy for him to learn to postpone these reveries. He formed an excellent relationship with teachers, clinicians, and peers, but remained slightly passive and stubborn. After being mugged several times as a ten- and 11-year-old, Charley decided to learn to wrestle. This developed into a strong interest leading to participation on the school wrestling team. Charley was admitted to a relatively demanding boarding school where he has had to struggle (without remedial support) to sustain passing grades. At last contact he was expected to pass all of his ninth-grade courses.

Charley would probably be diagnosed by Hynd and Hynd as having a phonological dyslexia, by Lovett as showing symptoms characteristic for both rate- and accuracy-disabled readers, and by Boder as being dysphonetic. That he seems to be managing is attributable in large part to the fact that his family was able to provide intensive remediation for ten years. They were also supportive of him without being overly anxious, thanks to their experience with his older brothers. Further, they took turns in working on his behalf; in other words, they shared the responsibility for his care. Although his mother was irritated by his passivity and cynicism, she was sensitive to his need for companionship and his fondness for certain sports and for animals.

This case illustrates the fact that satisfactory progress in cases of a moderately severe learning disability depends on economic advantage, sustained parental support, and a willingness of the child to form a therapeutic relationship that will permit him to go the distance. In other words, progress depends on considerably more than the application of appropriate remedial methods. While the economically advantaged family can sometimes arrange for a felicitous learning environment, this is clearly not possible for others who are less fortunate. In these cases, responsibility falls to the school or the clinic, institutions that are themselves hard pressed. The result is that no one ever discovers the progress the child might have made because the resources for appropriate intervention simply are not available. The losses to the individual and the community are incalculable.

SUMMARY

This chapter has presented a definition of learning disabilities that leaves the way open for modification. The search for stable subtypes is the focus of much current research. The identification of subcategories should lead to more effective intervention approaches. The case description illustrates the complexity of the disorders and suggests that satisfactory resolution requires a very substantial modification of the learning environment. It is hoped that with increasing awareness schools may be able to incorporate refinements that will be beneficial not only to the learning disabled but all students.

REFERENCES

Ackerman, P., Anhalt, J., and Dykman, R. (1986). Arithmetic automatization failure in children with attention and reading disorders: Associations and sequela. *J. Learning Disabilities* 19:222–32.

Badian, N. (1984). Reading disability in an epidemiological context. Incidence and environmental correlates. *J. Learning Disabilities* 17:129–36.

Baker, L., and Cantwell, D. (1985). Developmental arithmetic disorder. In H. Kaplan and B. Sadock (Eds.). *Comprehensive Textbook of Psychiatry/4.* Baltimore/London: Williams and Wilkins.

Bender, L. (1958). Problems in conceptualization and communication in children with developmental alexia. In P. Hoch and J. Zubin (Eds.). *Psychopathology of Communication.* New York: Grune and Stratton.

Benton, A., and Pearl, D. (1978). *Dyslexia: An Appraisal of Current Knowledge.* New York: Oxford University Press.

Boder, E. (1973). Developmental dyslexia: A diagnostic approach based on three atypical reading-spelling patterns. *Devel. Med. Child Neurol.* 15:663–87.

Childs, B., and Finucci, J. (1983). Genetics, epidemiology, and specific reading disability. In M. Rutter (Ed.) *Developmental Neuropsychiatry.* New York: Guilford Press.

Denckla, M., Le May, M., and Chapman, C. (1985). Few CT scan abnormalities found even in neurologically impaired learning-disabled children. *J. Learning Disabilities* 18:132–35.

Dorman, C. (1985). Defining and diagnosing dyslexia: Are we putting the cart before the horse? *Reading Res. Q.* 20:505–08.

Eisenberg, L. (1978). Definitions of dyslexia: Their consequences for research and policy. In A. Benton and D. Pearl (Eds.). *Dyslexia: An Appraisal of Current Knowledge.* New York: Oxford University Press.

Galaburda, A. (1983). Developmental dyslexia: Current anatomical research. *Annals of Dyslexia* 33:41–53.

———, and Kemper, T. (1979). Cytoarchitectonic abnormalities in developmental dyslexia: A case study. *Annals of Neurology* 6:94–100.

Garfinkel, B. (1986). Recent developments in attention deficit disorder. *Psychiatric Annals* 16:11–15.

Geschwind, N. (1982). Why Orton was right. *Annals of Dyslexia* 32:13–30.

———, and Levitsky, W. (1968). Human brain: Left-right asymmetries in temporal speech region. *Science* 161:186–89.

Gittelman, R. (1983). Treatment of reading disorders. In M. Rutter (Ed.). *Developmental Neuropsychiatry.* New York: Guilford Press.

Hallgren, B. (1950). Specific dyslexia: A clinical and genetic study. *Acta Psychiatr. Neurol. Scan.* 1–287.

Hammill, D. D., et al. (1981). A new definition of learning disabilities. *Learning Disability Q.* 4:336–42.

Hier, D., et al. (1978). Developmental dyslexia, evidence for a subgroup with reversal of cerebral asymmetry. *Arch. Neurol.* 35:90–92.

de Hirsch, K. (1957). Tests designed to discover potential reading difficulties. *Am. J. Orthopsychiatry* 27:566–675.

———. (1975). Language deficits in children with developmental lags. In R. Eissler, et al. (Eds.). *Psychoanal. Study Child* 30:95–126.

Hynd, G., and Hynd, C. (1984). Dyslexia: Neuroanatomical/neurolinguistic perspectives. *Reading Research Q.* 19:482–98.

Jansky, J., and de Hirsch, K. (1972). *Preventing Reading Failure.* New York: Harper and Row.

LaBerge, D., and Samuels, S. (1974). Toward a theory of automatic information processing in reading. *Cognitive Psychol.* 6:293–323.

Livingston, R. (1985). Depressive illness and learning difficulties: Research needs and practical implication. *J. Learning Disabilities* 18:518–20.

Lovett, M. (1984). The search for subtypes of specific reading disability: Reflections from a cognitive perspective. *Annals of Dyslexia* 34:155–78.

Lubar, J., et al. (1985). Spectral analysis of EEG differences between children with and without learning disabilities. *J. Learning Disabilities* 18:403–8.

McConaughty, S., and Ritter, D. (1985). Social competence and behavioral problems of learning-disabled boys aged 6–11. *J. Learning Disabilities* 18:547–53.

McKinney, J., and Feagans, L. (1983). Adaptive classroom behavior of learning-disabled students. *J. Learning Disabilities* 16:360–67.

McKinney, K. (1984). The search for subtypes of specific learning disability. *J. Learning Disabilities* 17:43–50.

McLoughlin, J., and Netic, A. (1983). Defining learning disabilities: A new and cooperative direction. *J. Learning Disabilities* 16:21–23.

Petrauskas, R., and Rourke, B. (1979). Identification of subtypes of retarded readers: A neuropsychologically multivariate approach. *J. Clin. Neuropsychol.* 1:17–37.

Rourke, B., and Strang, J. (1983). Subtypes of reading and arithmetical disabilities: A neuropsychological analysis. In M. Rutter (Ed.). *Developmental Neuropsychiatry.* New York: Guilford Press.

Rumelhart, D. (1977). Toward an interactive model of reading. In S. Dornic (Ed.). *Attention and Performance* 6. Hillsdale, N.J.: Lawrence Erlbaum.

Rutter, M., and Yule, W. (1973). Specific reading retardation. In L. Mann and D. Sabatino (Eds.). *The First Review of Special Education.* Philadelphia: J.S.E. Press with Buttonwood Farms.

Smith, S., et al. (1982). *Science* 219:1345–47.

Spreen, O., and Haaf, R. (1986). Empirically derived learning disability subtypes: A replication attempt and longitudinal patterns over fifteen years. *J. Learning Disabilities* 19:170–80.

Stanovich, K. (1980). Toward an interactive-compensatory model of individual differences in the development of reading fluency. *Reading Res. Q.* 16:32–71.

Thompson, J., Ross, R., and Horwitz, S. (1980). The role of computed axial tomography in the study of the child with minimal brain dysfunction. *J. Learning Disabilities* 13:48–51.

Tucker, J., Stevens, L., and Ysseldyke, J. (1983). Learning disabilities: The experts speak out. *J. Learning Disabilities* 16:6–14.

Volger, G., DeFries, J., and Decker, S. (1984). Family history as an indicator of risk for reading disability. *J. Learning Disabilities* 17:616–21.

V

Assessment of Children and Adolescents with Special Educational Needs

16

READINESS FOR EARLY CHILDHOOD SCHOOLING

Diana Townsend-Butterworth

Recent research has indicated that early childhood schooling can help to promote a child's readiness to learn (Knox and Glover 1978) and that children from low-income homes benefit from an enriched daycare environment (Golden et al. 1978; Heber et al. 1972; Ramey and Smith 1976). However, despite the indications seen in some of the Head Start studies that age 3 may be late to effect lasting changes in the cognitive and social patterns of some children, or the arguments that home may be a better place than school for early childhood education (Moore and Moore 1972), little published research exists on readiness for early childhood school itself, before kindergarten.

Most of the research on readiness has concentrated on readiness for kindergarten or for first grade. Some studies have used self-concept measures (Flynn 1975), Piagetian measures (Becher and Wolfgang 1977; Kaufman 1971), general intelligence measures (Feshbach, Adelman, and Fuller 1974; Huberty and Swann 1974; Knox and Glover 1978; Kulberg and Gershman 1973; and Telegdy 1976), and teacher ratings (Flook and Velicer 1977; Glazzard 1977), but much of the research has concentrated on readiness for reading rather than on readiness in the more global sense for all the social, emotional, and cognitive challenges of an early childhood school.

This chapter will address some of these issues as well as questions of societal norms and parental need and it will provide guidelines for both parents and educators. I also hope to ease not only the anxiety of those urban parents who fear that unless their 2-year-old attends the right toddler group she will suffer academic and social deficits for the rest of her life, but also the worries and guilt feelings of those parents who return to work out of either choice or necessity while their children are still very young. My conclusions are drawn from a review of the relevant literature, from a series of interviews with directors of early childhood schools, pediatricians, child psychiatrists, psychologists, and parents, as well as from my own experience as the former head of a junior school and from my clinical practice as an educational consultant. The interviews were limited to New York City and the children referred to are from predominately middle- and upper-level socioeconomic backgrounds.

A QUESTION OF DEFINITION

Early childhood education is a generic term used by educators to describe a variety of programs designed to meet the social, emotional, physical, and cognitive needs of young children. They are not primarily caretaking programs.

Over the years programs for young children have been known by a confusing array of names: preschool; nursery school; kindergarten; preK; infant school; preprimary; first program; toddler program; Head Start; Extended Day; Daycare; Childcare; and Infantcare. Each of the names has a different meaning to different people in different parts of the country. In New York City the Health Department uses daycare as an umbrella word. Outside of New York City, the state prefers the term "prekindergarten education" for all programs for children under the age of approximately four years nine months, when they are eligible for kindergarten. The term "nursery school" is used in many parts of the country to refer to private schools for 3-, 4-, and 5-year-olds with half day programs. Many educators, however, find the term old-fashioned and feel it implies caregiving.

In the late sixties, the National Association for Nursery Education officially changed its name to the National Association for the Education of Young Children, and subsequently the National Association of Nursery School Directors became the National Association of Early Childhood Directors. In 1985 the New York Independent Schools Directory changed the title of a category listing Nursery Schools to Early Childhood Schools. The name changes are significant because they are indicative of an attempt to bridge two gaps: the first between daycare and nursery school; and the second between elementary school and preschool. The term daycare still carries connotations of tenement child minders and custodial day nurseries. Although the term nursery school originated in the slums of London, by the 1960s it conjured up images of children from storybook America, hardly relevent to an urban, industrial, multiethnic America where up to 60 percent of mothers with children under the age of 6 are working and one child out of every six under the age of 18 is being raised by a single parent. These parents need quality care for their children before and after, as well as during, traditional school hours. Many nursery schools are now offering full day and extended day programs. Parents who use daycare are demanding quality care that will "foster the development of the child physically, intellectually, and socioemotionally" (Caldwell and Hilliard 1983, p. 5). Distinctions between nursery school and daycare are blurring as both are reformulated into "a comprehensive service to children and families that supplements the care children receive from their families" (Caldwell and Hilliard 1983, p. 4).

The second gap to be addressed by the new definitions is that between school and preschool. Some educators find in the use of the term preschool the implication that this is not real school and that something called real school will follow—an implication that seems to belie the importance of the early years, to undermine the significance of early childhood schools, and to block communication between early childhood educators and elementary school teachers. The Kramer School Project, operated jointly by the Center for Early Development and Education at the University of Arkansas and the Little Rock Public Schools, was an attempt to bridge this gap. Children from the age of 6 months attended programs in a public elementary school. Since everyone was technically in school, the term preschool was irrelevant. Coordination between school, home, and community was emphasized as the school sought to forge new links between "early childhood education and elementary education, education and daycare, education and research, the home and the school" (Braun and Edwards 1972, p. 385).

Despite efforts of the National Association for the Education of Young Children and other educators to define the field of early childhood education and to eliminate confusing terminology, a consensus of definition has yet to be reached, and the terms preschool and nursery school are still being used in some parts of the country by educators and parents.

NURSERY SCHOOL MOVEMENT

From the beginning, the nursery school movement was closely affiliated with the science of child development, drawing freely on the new research. In 1929 Dr. Arnold Gesell, a physician at Yale, founded the Yale Guidance Nursery as a laboratory school for the Yale Psychological Clinic. Gesell's theories on the maturational nature of child development had a strong influence on nursery school educators. Many nursery schools were associated with either universities or research institutes. Nursery schools also flourished in churches, homes, community centers, shopping centers, and commercial buildings.

In 1924 there were twenty-eight nursery schools in eleven different states. By 1933 there were seventeen hundred. In the mid 1930s, "concerned educators in New York City successfully petitioned to have certain standards and regulations established by law for operating nursery schools. Since then, legal requirements have existed for operating a preschool program for more than five children" (Boegehold et al. 1977, p. 109). The rapid increase in nursery schools was a result both of the new interest in child development among middle- and upper-class parents, and also of the decision by the Work Projects Administration to use early childhood education to create jobs for unemployed teachers during the Depression. Later, during World War II, The Lanham Act provided federal funds for childcare for mothers who were working in wartime factories. While many of the new centers were more concerned with practical issues of health and safety than with child development, there were some excellent programs carefully designed to meet the needs of parents and children. Among the latter were The Kaiser Child Service Centers, built by

Edgar Kaiser with the help of Eleanor Roosevelt, for the children of workers in the Kaiser shipyards. Each center served one thousand one hundred and twenty-five children from the age of 18 months to 6 years, twenty-four hours a day, three hundred and sixty-four days a year. The centers were located at the entrances to the shipyards so parents could drop children off on the way to work and stop by to check on them during their breaks. The program was run by two child development specialists, Lois Meek Stolz and James Hymes, Jr. All the teachers had degrees in child development and salaries were equal to those of other Kaiser employees with college degrees. In 1945, when women were no longer needed in the factories, the centers closed.

The postwar period saw an attempt to return to a romanticized prewar life style. Women were told by child psychologists, as well as by ministers and politicians, that their place was in the home, not the work force. It was the mother's responsibility to see to her child's early education.

THE REDISCOVERY OF EARLY CHILDHOOD EDUCATION

The 1960s brought a rediscovery of early childhood education with a new emphasis on intellectual development and cognition as a result of the work of Jerome Bruner, Benjamin Bloom, Robert White, and Jean Piaget. Piaget criticized the noncognitive bias in early childhood education: "a few years ago the main trend . . . owing to the widespread influence of psychoanalysis was to avoid frustrating the developing child. This led to an excess of unsupervised liberty which ended in generalized play without much educational benefit. A reaction has taken place in the direction of a channeling and strengthening of cognitive activities." (Piaget 1973, p. 6).

The federal government also rediscovered early childhood education. Head Start, legislated in 1964 as part of the Economic Opportunity Act, was the first large-scale attempt to challenge the effects of poverty with a program of compensatory education for three- to five-year-olds whose family income fell below the poverty level. Head Start was followed by many other programs including: Home Start; Follow Through; The Ypsilanti Early Education Program; HOPE (Home-Oriented Preschool Education Project in Appalachia, West Virginia); BEEP (Brookline Early Education Program); The Kramer School Project in Little Rock, Arkansas; and the New Parents as Teachers Project in Missouri. There was little uniformity among programs either in philosophy or method. Some focused on general cognitive development, others on teaching specific verbal, linguistic, or sensory motor skills. All sought to overcome the multiple educational disadvantages born of poverty. All depended on the belief that by influencing a child's environment one could influence the child and her future intellectual development.

The results of early intervention programs have been studied extensively by educational researchers and "it has been consistently shown that children who attend preschool show an immediate gain in I.Q. . . . The pattern of findings suggests that the children show gains in areas and on kinds of performance that the preschool program stressed" (Shapiro and Biber 1972, p. 134). "It has also been reported that children who have gone to preschool have better attendance records in kindergarten and first grade." (Shapiro and Biber 1972, p.136).

EARLY CHILDHOOD EDUCATION TODAY

As educators and parents became increasingly aware of the research in cognitive development and the apparent positive results of compensatory education programs, they began to wonder if all children might not benefit from the experience of early childhood school and, if so, would they benefit more from an approach that provided "the child with more structured materials and activities which can help accelerate the growth of logical operations and the development of basic concepts in various areas of knowledge, such as numbers, space, time, etc." (Braun and Edwards 1972, p. 136). Educators and public officials debate proposals on public school programs for 4-year-olds. Some see the possibility of bringing the advantages of early childhood education to all children, rich and poor alike; others fear that 4-year-olds may be asked to struggle with tasks before they have the neurological maturity for success.

READINESS FOR EARLY CHILDHOOD SCHOOL

The time a child began school was traditionally determined by a combination of local law and family circumstance. There were no readiness tests or interviews in an early German kindergarten, founded by Friedrich Wilhelm Froebel in the 1840s. Maria Montessori would admit all children living in the tenement to the Children's House provided they didn't arrive "unwashed or in soiled clothing" (Braun and Edwards 1972, p. 116). Margaret McMillan, who with her sister founded a school in London, stipulated that no child was "excluded, no matter how difficult the situation" (Braun and Edwards 1972, p. 129). The concept of an individual child's readiness for a particular program or early childhood schooling is a relatively recent one. It derives in part from Gesell's theories developed in the twenties and thirties about the "innate maturational blueprints" (Braun and Edwards 1972, p. 207) present in all children and the fixed stages through which each child must pass. Any attempt to train a child to sit, to talk, to read, or to alter significantly her behavior in any way before she was ready was seen as useless and perhaps even harmful. Intelligence was regarded by many as a life-long constant based on heredity, and as "developing along genetically predetermined patterns" (Braun and Edwards 1972, p. 208) largely independent of environmental influences. The latter assumptions were challenged by the work of Harold Skeels with retarded children in the late thirties at the Iowa

Child Welfare Research Station. Thirty years later Benjamin Bloom at the University of Chicago found IQs to be significantly influenced by the following factors: verbal stimulation; affection and reward for verbal reasoning; active interaction with problems; exploration of environment; and learning new skills (Braun and Edwards 1972, p. 232). Some educators were beginning to see environmental stimulation as a major factor in the rate and extent of a child's development (Guthrie 1952; Skinner 1953; Bereiter and Englemann 1966). Other educators saw development as a balanced combination of genetic inheritance and environmental effects all modified by a child's own actions (Piaget 1970; Bruner 1960; Kohlberg 1969). While agreeing that biological maturation could not be accelerated, they believed that overall development could be enhanced by providing cognitive challenges. Bruner found that "any subject can be taught effectively in some intellectually honest form to any child at any stage of development" (Goodwin and Driscoll 1980, p. 3).

Early childhood directors maintain there is no such thing as readiness in general, only readiness for a particular program. According to Bettye Caldwell, former president of NAEYC, "children at birth and any age thereafter are ready for formal education—education that is appropriate for their stage of growth and development" (Caldwell 1983b). Directors of some early childhood schools feel that it is even a contradiction to speak of a child's readiness for their program. They believe that a good early childhood educational program should be flexible enough to meet the needs of individual children at whatever their developmental stage, and that it is important to fit the program to the child rather than the child to the program. Directors of other early childhood schools believe that, despite the flexibility of their teachers and the child-centered nature of their programs, there are nevertheless certain minimal social and verbal skills a child should possess to be comfortable in an early childhood school and to benefit from the social, emotional and cognitive challenges.

EARLY CHILDHOOD SCHOOL AT THE AGE OF 4

The 1980 census showed that 49 percent of all 4-year-olds were in some form of early childhood program. Seventy percent of these children were from families with incomes over $25,000. Some states have advocated the funding of state programs for all 4-year-olds. Currently in New York State, federally financed preK programs (Head Start) funded under the Economic Opportunity Act of 1965 are available for children from low-income families. However there are too few programs to accommodate all eligible children. New York State has additional programs under the auspices of the Elementary and Secondary Education Act for children with educational disadvantages (generally interpreted to mean children whose siblings have exhibited learning difficulties). New York State also has experimental preK programs that serve approximately ninety-three hundred children in seventy-four districts. Ninety percent of the children selected for the experimental programs must be economically disadvantaged.

Interest in publicly funded preK programs is not limited to New York State. In 1984, South Carolina allocated $2.4 million for child development programs in public schools for 4-year-olds with "predicted significant reading deficiencies" (*Education Week*, Oct. 16, 1985). In Texas, school districts are required to offer a program for 4-year-olds if they have a specified number of children who are either economically disadvantaged or not fluent in English. State officials in Illinois, Massachusetts, Missouri, Michigan, and Washington have allocated funds to identify at-risk 4-year-olds and to provide programs for them. In Vermont, former Governor Snelling proposed that "pilot projects in local districts be set up to screen all 3- to 5-year-olds for developmental problems and to provide early intervention" (Blank 1985).

Access to publicly supported early childhood schools so far has been largely determined by special needs and limited to specific segments of the population that have included: children from families with incomes below the poverty level; children raised in non-English-speaking families; children whose older siblings have learning problems; and children who have themselves been identified through screening programs as being in need of early intervention. The fact that most publicly funded preK programs begin at 4 rather than 3 is a result of economic reality rather than of educational theory.

EARLY CHILDHOOD SCHOOL AT THE AGE OF 3

Early childhood programs in independent schools typically begin at 3. A poll of ten directors of early childhood schools in New York City indicated that in their opinion three is an ideal time for most children to begin. The following factors were seen by the directors as predictive of a child's readiness for a successful adjustment to an early childhood school at the age of three: (1) a sense of confidence and security; (2) a level of independence that enables a child to begin doing things for him or herself; (3) a desire to explore and to have experiences outside the home; (4) the ability to separate from the parent or primary caregiver; (5) sufficient verbal skills to communicate with other children and adults; (6) a beginning ability to relate to other children, to share, to take turns, to be part of a group; (7) the ability to stay focused for a short period of time, to sustain an activity briefly in a goal-directed manner; (8) physical development within a normal range; and (9) the ability to deal with the physical demands of the environment, for example, going up and down stairs, using the toilet, and so on.

Alexandra Zimmer, Director of The Madison Presbyterian Day School, summed up her feelings and those of many of the other directors by saying, "a child is ready for school when she has a basic sense of trust, a sense that no matter what happens she will be taken care of and be safe—so she is able to separate from her mother and to enter a relationship with other people in another environment with new materials. If a child has trust, anything else can be taught."

PARENTAL READINESS

In my study, most of the directors found questions of parental readiness more pertinent to a child's successful adjustment to early childhood school than the child's own level of readiness. For example, Lydia Spinelli has found that "it is usually not the child but the parent who isn't ready to separate" (personal communication). Peggy Marble, Director of Christ Church Day School, feels that while "most children are ready to separate by 3, because they are able to retain a picture of their mother in their heads that they can hold on to when she isn't there and to understand that she will come back, many mothers aren't ready to let go" (personal communication). According to Jaki Williams, Director of Nursery and Kindergarten at The Town School, "sometimes a mom wants to feel needed in the classroom after she's no longer really needed by the child, and it is important that she not communicate her doubts either verbally or through body language" (personal communication). Alexandra Zimmer stressed the importance of the relationship between parent and child, "ideally a relationship in which the parents neither had unrealistic expectations for their child, nor insisted on doing everything for him, one in which the child has learned trust from his parents because they have made the child's life comfortable, happy and secure. They have come back when they said they would, they have kept their word to the child, they have let him feel that it is all right to be wrong sometimes and to take chances" (personal communication). Marlene Barron, Director of the West Side Montessori School, spoke of the importance of a sense of compatibility between parents and school and of the parents' trust in the school: "If adults don't trust the program, the child won't trust it and be able to make friends and take advantage of all that's going on" (personal communication).

For the child who doesn't go to school at 3, the differences may be slight. According to Mitten Wainwright, the child from a middle-class background who "stays home will be no less knowledgeable in the long run, but she will probably have less experience getting along with groups of children, less experience with waiting and taking turns and being part of a group and, as a result, she may be less developed socially" (personal communication).

EARLY CHILDHOOD SCHOOL AT THE AGE OF 2

"No child needs to be in school at 2," said Marlene Barron, "though a few, the ones who are hungry for new experiences, may benefit from being there" (personal communication). The other directors agreed. They also concurred with Lydia Spinelli that "a toddler program mustn't be a watered down version of a 3-year-old program. It is particularly important for teachers to adapt to a toddler rather than expect her to adapt to them. The atmosphere in a toddler program should be as home-like as possible, nurturing and secure, as well as challenging and stimulating" (personal communication). Peggy Marble and Alexandra Zimmer both emphasized that children shouldn't be expected to share or to participate in group activities before they are ready (personal communication).

Sometimes it is the parents who are in need of toddler programs. "It takes a super strong parent to keep up with one of these often adorable creatures twenty-four hours a day . . . It is important to recognize your own personal tolerances, your limits of energy" (Ames and Chase 1973, p. 164). Parents need time away from their 2-year-olds. They need time for themselves to replenish their energy and to continue their own growth, they need time for careers and time to spend with other children, and they need this time without worries about how their children are being cared for. Some parents also need the support and the sense of being part of a community of other parents with young children.

For most children participation in a toddler program, aside from helping to create an early love for school and an appetite for learning, will probably make little difference in their long-range physical, social, emotional, and cognitive development; but there are a few children for whom participation could make a difference.

Case #1

Andrew D. began school at 2. He is now 5 and just beginning to be able to relate to children in group situations. He likes children but still isn't always sure how to play with them. He is an only child and lives with his mother. Andrew's mother reports that he was a normal, happy, bright, but somewhat reserved baby. His mother, a psychologist, gave up her practice to be with him. The two were very close and spent much time alone together. His father traveled frequently on business. Just before Andrew's second birthday, his mother returned to her practice full-time. Concerned about the lack of playmates in the neighborhood and unable to find a suitable person to provide the stimulation she felt was important, his mother decided to enroll him in a toddler program five mornings a week. Although Andrew had had no trouble relating with the other children he occasionally saw on a one-to-one basis at home, he was overwhelmed at finding himself in a group of strange children in unfamiliar surroundings away from his mother and home. He became irritable and hard to please at home, and at school he was fretful and disorganized. He clung to the teacher and demanded her undivided attention. He couldn't share with the other children and didn't know how to play with them. Fortunately the school and his teacher were understanding and flexible. The teacher gave him individualized projects and arranged special play areas for him near her so he wouldn't be bothered by the other children. His mother changed her schedule so she could spend more time with Andrew after school. Slowly Andrew began to adjust to being in school and to demand less individual attention, but he continued to have trouble relating to the children and being part of the group.

For Andrew, separation from home and mother was both too soon and too abrupt. He would have benefitted from more exposure to other children in the familiar surroundings of home or in a mothers' playgroup before attending a toddler program.

The following children would be most likely to benefit from being part of a toddler program: (1) children from difficult home situations; (2) children from two career families who might otherwise spend the day at home alone with a housekeeper; (3) children without ready access to other children and to outdoor play space; (4) children from homes where English is not the primary language; (5) children from economically or socially disadvantaged backgrounds; and (6) children with special educational needs.

Yet many of the directors interviewed felt that the few children who would definitely be better off spending another year at home or in an informal playgroup were: (1) those still bonded to their mothers in such a symbiotic way that they never leave the mother's lap in a new situation despite the presence of reassuring adults and enticing materials; and (2) those children so scattered that they continually run from one activity to another rarely touching base with their mothers.

Marlene Barron stressed that "parents should know why they are sending a child to school, what their expectations are, if these expectations are realistic, and whether they are in harmony with the goals and expectations of the school. They should question not only whether the child is ready for the school, but whether the school is ready for the child. They should know whether the school has a fixed program that the child is expected to fit into or if the program will be adapted to the needs of their child."

Case #2

Thomas P. started school at 3½. All the other children had been in toddler programs and were used to being in group situations, but Thomas was unfamiliar with this situation. He didn't know how to be part of a group and he didn't know how to play with other children. Thomas was a first child and when he was 2 his mother didn't realize that other mothers were sending their children to toddler groups. She had a new baby and neither the time nor the energy to plan playdates for Thomas or to be part of a mothers' playgroup. According to his mother, Thomas had been an unusually happy, easy baby. He walked and talked at the normal time. He was large and well coordinated. When he was almost 2, his sister was born and Thomas's personality changed. He began lashing out at people, hitting, and kicking. His mother, baffled by his behavior and overwhelmed by the combination of a difficult toddler and a new baby, elected to return to work. She hired an old-fashioned nanny with a rigid approach to discipline to look after the children. Thomas never misbehaved with the nanny, but became increasingly "impossible" with his parents in the evening after she had gone home. He behaved so badly on the few playdates he had that his mother gave up trying to arrange them. When he finally started school, he didn't know how to be part of a group. He hit the other children and threw things at them to attract their attention. He became the most disruptive boy in the class and the teacher told his mother she didn't know how to handle him. The director suggested his mother pick him up half an hour early every day. His parents had chosen the school because it was convenient and some of their friends had children there. They hadn't discussed values or philosophy of child rearing. They had barely met the director. After talking to their pediatrician and an educational consultant, they decided to change schools. This time they knew what they wanted: a school whose values and philosophy they shared; a director they felt comfortable talking to and whose advice they respected. They also wanted a school with small groups, a low student-teacher ratio, and a belief in establishing clear limits. They found the school they were looking for. One of the teachers was assigned especially to Thomas, home and school communicated daily about his progress, and they coordinated on matters of discipline. Gradually things began to improve. Thomas is now in kindergarten and, while still very active and given to occasional bursts of temper, he has made friends and is part of the group. His parents' belief and trust in his new school is reflected both in Thomas's progress and in his awareness that home and school are pulling together in his behalf.

Invalid reasons for sending a child to a toddler program include parental ambition and the hope that a program for 2-year-olds "will put the child on the route to success" (personal communication). Early childhood programs, all the directors agreed, can be fun for children and they can give extended support to families, but they won't make children smarter or more successful.

EARLY CHILDHOOD SCHOOL BEFORE THE AGE OF 2

School before the age of 2 reflects the needs of parents rather than children. Given the reality of these needs and the existence of semiformalized programs for very young children, it is pertinent to examine when a child may be separated from her parents without ill effect. Representative Patricia Schroeder recently introduced a bill that would require "employers to provide at least four months of leave for a father or mother who chooses to stay home with a newborn infant" (*New York Times*, December 29, 1985). Studies by T. Berry Brazelton indicate that the end of 3 months is the earliest age at which children should be separated from their parents. By 3 months Brazelton finds the central nervous system is sufficiently mature to enable babies to reach out to their parents with "cementing as well as demanding behavior. The opportunity for positive attachment between parent and child is dramatically enhanced" (Brazelton 1984, p. 11). Brazelton also discovered that while separation of infants and parents before the end of 3 months can result in an emotional detachment on the part of the parent, this problem can be largely prevented if "each member of the care taking team, consciously works to cement parents to their children" (Brazelton 1984, p. 11). Sirgay Sanger has found in his work with infants and parents that "the role of the primary, nurturing figure in the baby's eyes isn't allotted on the basis of time but of responsiveness. And if his exchanges with his mother are the place where he finds his needs uniquely understood, encouraged and supported, the amount of physical time those exchanges occupy in his day will matter less" (Sanger 1985, p. 229).

Jerome Kagan, while recognizing the importance of the first six months of life as a time for parents to bond with their baby, feels that separation during the second six months may be more critical from the child's point of view because of his newly developing anxieties. However, only about 10 percent of all children, those who are biologically vulnerable, born to be timid, are affected by a mother's absence, according to Kagan. "Children don't need love like they need vitamins, and the way a child perceives a parent's absence may be more important than the absence itself. If a child feels the parent's absence to be a result of selfishness or rejection, it will have a negative effect on the child, but if the child thinks the parent is going off to help the sick or to do some important meaningful work, she will think what wonderful parents even if she rarely sees them" (Kagan lecture, Oct. 1, 1985).

Case #3

Karen G.'s job gave no maternity leave. After using up all her accumulated sick leave, she reluctantly returned to work when Caroline was 8 weeks old. She arranged a family daycare setting for Caroline with a woman who had a 6-month-old infant. She was careful to ensure that she and the other woman shared the same values and philosophy of child rearing and that there was continuity of routine. When Caroline was 4 months old, she moved her to a child-oriented daycare center where she would have more interaction with other children. According to Karen, the other children became like brothers and sisters for Caroline, an only child. The center was attentive to physical, social, emotional, and cognitive needs, and communication between home and center was excellent. Satisfied with the care Caroline was receiving during the day and pleased with her progress, Karen was able to relax and enjoy her time with Caroline in the evening. Now 4, Caroline is a healthy, bright child. According to her mother and teacher, she is also unusually loving, outgoing, and socially aware.

THE ROLE OF SOCIETAL NORMS

The question of when to begin school depends for some parents more on social issues and community norms than on educational needs or maturational stages. Dr. Edward A. Davies, Director of the Department of Pediatrics at Lenox Hill Hospital in New York City, finds "readiness is not an issue anymore. The age a child enters school is influenced primarily by factors outside the family. Some parents no longer ask me if their child is ready for a toddler program, they just send him because all his friends are going. There may be no one around to play with or the parents are both working and they can't find a suitable person to provide the stimulation they feel is important" (personal communication).

According to Gretchen Lengyel, co-director of The Madison Playgroup and past president of The Parents League of New York, "if most children in town Y start school at age 4, that is the time for children who live in that town to start. If, on the other hand, in town X toddler groups are the norm, most children in town X will start at 2. Out of every one hundred children, a few really should go to school and a few really shouldn't go, but for the great majority—90 percent of them, it doesn't make any long-range difference whether they go or not. A few children at 2 or 3 are physically immature or hesitant—these children need the quieter forms of tender loving care found at home. There are a few children who are so directed and motivated that challenges in play and social exchanges make them scream for joy—these children need to be in school. For most children the decision of when to start school has little to do with independence, get up and go, or maturity; it is a parental decision, and for most children there is no problem because most children are ready to go to school in the same way they are ready to go to the zoo" (personal communication).

THE ROLE OF SOCIAL NECESSITY

The *New York Independent Schools Directory 1985–86* lists forty schools with programs for children under 3 and eleven with programs for children under 2. In 1976 the same publication had only two listings for children under 3 and none for children under 2.

Demographic changes during the last decade have made early childhood school an increasingly important factor in the lives of many American children. In 1980 for the first time more American women worked outside the home than remained at home, and 45 percent of all American women held full-time jobs (*World Almanac 1981*). This is not to imply that women have not worked outside the home before, and in fact, Maria Montessori cited as one of the advantages of her Children's House the new freedom it gave mothers "to go away to work with easy minds" (Braun and Edwards 1972, p. 118). However, the percentage of women holding full-time positions of responsibility in the work force has increased dramatically in recent years. The Bureau of Labor Statistics indicates that 53.5 percent of the mothers with children under 6 and 49.5 percent of those with infants under 3 are in the labor force (*New York Times*, December 29, 1985). By 1990 an estimated 80 percent of all children under 6 will have working mothers (*Education Week*, Oct. 16, 1985). Alison Clarke-Stewart reported that "one-half of the mothers of preschool age children are using some form of childcare" (*New York Times*, May 29, 1985).

During the same decade average family size declined and the number of one-parent families rose by 107 percent *(World Almanac 1985)*. The shift from a rural to a suburban or urban lifestyle also continued. Many families experienced a rise in real estate prices in relation to family income.

The picture drawn from these statistics is of a child born in the 1980s, isolated in a smaller apartment in an urban setting, with less play space, fewer siblings with whom to play, and with less opportunity to begin the lessons of early childhood under the care and tutelage of a parent. Children from lower-level socioeconomic backgrounds may be left to fend for themselves. Senator Alan Cranston found that at least twenty thousand children under the age of 6 were looking after themselves while their parents worked (Dittman 1981, p. 143). Children from middle- and upper-level socioeconomic backgrounds may be left in the care of non-English-speaking caregivers with little knowledge of child development. For children such as these, early childhood school is not a choice but a necessity, and individual readiness for school becomes largely irrelevant. The issue instead is one of selecting a school parents can afford with an able, caring faculty trained in early childhood education and a child-centered approach that will be able to meet the child's physical, social, emotional and cognitive needs. Alternatives for those parents who decide not to send their toddler to an early childhood school include: parent-led playgroups; parent-child classes at the local Y; parent-child classes at gymnasiums and museums.

Many early childhood schools do have space for a few children with certain special needs. The description and assessment of other available programs for children with special needs is outside the realm of this chapter. Public Law 94-142, The Education for All Handicapped Children Act, gives each state the responsibility for identifying, screening, evaluating and providing appropriate educational services for all children with learning problems (Meisels 1985, p. vii). Specific information concerning local programs may be obtained from the Board of Education.

METHODS OF ASSESSING READINESS FOR EARLY CHILDHOOD SCHOOL

Many early childhood programs admit children on the basis of either chronological age or date of application—a first-come first-serve approach. Others select children based on a determination of physical, social, economic, or educational need. Some early childhood directors, particularly those in large urban areas where a choice is available, attempt to assess both a child's and her parents' readiness for and compatibility with their particular program. Several methods are in theory available for making this assessment: tests (measures of intelligence, screening instruments, readiness tests); and observational inventories (formal and informal).

Tests

In practice tests are seldom used to determine the readiness of normal children with no suspected deficits for early childhood programs prior to kindergarten, with the exception of a few programs specifically designed for gifted children, which require an IQ test for admission.

Many educators agree with Margaret M. Devine, educational consultant at The Madison Presbyterian Day School and former president of the World Organization for Early Childhood Education, that children of this age are "essentially not testable" (personal communication). Problems found with formalized testing of very young children include: limited test-taking skills; difficulty in understanding directions; eagerness to please adults; and a general failure to take tests seriously (Goodwin and Driscoll 1980, p. 111). Tests are generally used only when problems or deficits are suspected, "to identify children who may need further evaluation and educational intervention" (Meisels 1985, p. 1). According to Janet Brown McCracken, publications director for NAEYC, "testing isn't necessary for a good early childhood program unless there are strong indications of major problems" (personal communication).

Observational Measures

Formal, highly structured observational methods are used mainly in research, but the informal observation of children in small semistructured group settings is the most frequently employed method of assessing a child's readiness for a particular program. This form of admissions screening usually includes parent interviews and questionnaires as well as informal observation of the child. Children are generally observed in small groups of five or six for periods ranging from thirty to forty-five minutes. The children are given the opportunity to interact both with each other and with two or three early childhood teachers, as well as with a variety of materials designed for young children. Materials may include simple puzzles, play dough, Legos, blocks, paper and crayons, dolls, cups and plates, and other play equipment from the housekeeping corner. The teachers watch the children and note their: response to each other; response to the materials; physical behavior and expressions; use of language—whether their language is sufficiently developed to communicate their needs; approaches to problem solving; large and small motor control; tolerance for frustration; ability to focus on a task; sense of confidence and security; and interest in exploring and interacting with the environment.

Except in those few instances where the child has an obvious behavior problem or developmental deficit, the parent interview and questionnaire are more important than the observation of the child, particularly at the toddler level. During the parent interview, schools assess: family dynamics—in what ways do parents interact with each other and with the child; the parents' real knowledge about their child and the reality of their expectations; the ways in which parents deal with separation issues;

parents' reaction to their child's misbehaving; their ability to set limits; the degree of love and trust between parent and child and whether the child can look to the parents for encouragement and guidance; the compatibility of the goals of parents and school and the parents' trust and support of the school.

CONCLUSION

Most children are ready for early childhood school at 3, although some are earlier. At the age of 3, they are ready for the social, emotional, and intellectual challenges of being part of a group. They are able to interact positively with children and adults and with a variety of interesting materials in a new environment. They will grow in a school where the teachers are trained in early childhood education and where the activities are individualized enough to meet their needs in a stimulating but noncompetitive environment. Put simply, most children are ready for early childhood school because their parents have loved them and helped to make their lives comfortable, happy, and secure. As a result, they have the confidence and trust to reach out to new experiences.

For a variety of social and economic reasons that have little to do with competence or development, some children will go to early childhood school unprepared. Some of them will find the love and trust and confidence at school that others have found at home. If the school is sufficiently flexible, and the teachers and parents are caring and patient, they too will adjust in time.

When a child should begin an early childhood school is a question that cannot be answered by either parents or educators alone. The answer will not come from standardized tests or questionnaires or formal studies. It will come from a sharing of knowledge about the nature of early childhood programs and about the needs and nature of the individual child. If the child goes to school, will the experience be fun for her? Will there be a shared sense of values between home and school—a feeling that both are working together for the benefit of the child? If the child stays home, will there be children to play with and space to explore? Will there be interesting and interested adults around to serve as resources and to insure that the environment is stimulating as well as secure?

Early childhood school is oriented toward process, not toward the end result. The process should be childhood. Children can be taught many skills: they can learn to count and to say the alphabet; they can be taught to identify shapes and colors; and how to read and write their names; but their childhood must not be hurried in the process. George Z. Tokieda, Co-Chairman of the Science Department at The Brearley School in New York City, wrote "let us have the courage to let our children discover on their own and in their own time. . . . to allow them to be bored, to fail and ultimately to succeed" (Tokieda 1983). As parents and educators, we need to remember that children have many years to write their names and to study calculus, but very few to see dragons in the clouds.

REFERENCES

Ames, L. B., and Chase, J. A. (1973). *Don't Push Your Preschooler.* New York: Harper and Row.

Becher, R. M., and Wolfgang, C. (1977). An exploration of the relationship between symbolic representation in dramatic play and art and the cognitive and reading readiness levels of kindergarten children. *Psychology in the Schools.* Vol. 14: pp. 377–81.

Bereiter, C., and Engelmann, S. (1966). *Teaching Disadvantaged Children in the Preschool.* Englewood Cliffs, N.J.: Prentice-Hall.

Blank, H. (1985). Early childhood and the public schools. *Young Children.* May, Vol. 40, No. 4: pp. 52–55.

Boegehold, B. D., et al. (1977). *Education Before Five.* New York: Bank Street College of Education.

Boehn, A. E., and White, M. A. (1982). *The Parents' Handbook on School Testing.* New York: Teachers College Press.

Bowlby, J. (1969). *Attachment and Loss, Volume 2: Attachment.* New York: Basic Books.

Boyer, E. G., Simon, A., and Karafin, G. R. (1973). *Measures of Maturation.* Vols. 1–3. Philadelphia: Research for Better Schools, Inc.

Braun, S. J., and Edwards, E. P. (1972). *History and Theory of Early Childhood Education.* Belmont, Calif.: Wadsworth Publishing Company.

Brazelton, T. B. (1984). Cementing family relationships. In *Infants We Care For.* Rev. Ed. Laura Dittmann (Ed.). Washington, D.C.: The National Association for the Education of Young Children (NAEYC).

Bridgman, A. (1985). Early-childhood education: States already on the move. *Education Week.* October 16, Vol. 5, No. 7.

Bruner, J. F. (1960). *The Process of Education.* Cambridge: Harvard University Press.

Caldwell, B. M. (1967). On reformulating the concept of early childhood education—some whys needing wherefores. *Young Children.* Vol. 22, No. 6: pp. 348–56.

———. (1983a). How can we educate the American public about the child care profession. *Young Children.* Vol. 38, No. 3: pp. 11–17.

———. (1983b). Should four-year-olds go to school? *Young Children.* Vol. 38, No. 4: pp. 48–50.

———, and Hilliard, A. G. (1983). *What Is Quality Child Care.* Washington, D.C.: NAEYC.

Cohen, D. H., Stern, V., and Balahan, N. (1982). *Observing and Recording the Behavior of Young Children.* 3d ed. New York: Teachers College Press.

Dittmann, L. L. (1981). Where have all the mothers gone, and what difference does it make? In *Infants: Their Social Environments.* B. Weissbourd and J. Musick. (Eds.). Washington, D.C.: NAEYC.

Elkind, D. (1981). Child development and early childhood education: Where do we stand today? *Young Children.* Vol. 36, No. 5: pp. 2–9.

Evans, E. D. (1975). *Contemporary Influences In Early Childhood Education.* 2d ed. New York: Holt, Rinehart and Winston.

Feshbach, S., Adelman, H., and Fuller, W. W. (1974). Early identification of children with high risk of reading failure. *J. of Learning Dis.* Vol. 7: pp. 639–44.

Flook, W. M., and Velicer, W. F. (1977). School readiness and teachers' ratings: A validation study. *Psychology in the Schools.* Vol. 14: pp. 140–46.

Flynn, T. M. (1975). Behavioral components of school readiness. *J. of Experimental Ed.* Vol. 44: pp. 40–45.

Glazzard, P. (1977). The effectiveness of three kindergarten predictors for first grade achievement. *J. Learning Dis.* Vol. 10: pp. 95–99.

Golden, M., et al. (1978). *The New York City Infant Day Care Study.* New York: Medical and Health Research Association of New York City.

Goodwin, W., and Driscoll, L. A. (1980). *Handbook for Measurement and Evaluation in Early Childhood Education.* San Francisco: Jossey-Bass.

Gordon, N. J. (1982). Readiness. In H. E. Mitzel (Ed.). *Encyclopedia of Educational Research.* 5th ed. Vol. 3. New York: Free Press.

Guthrie, E. R. (1952). *The Psychology of Learning.* New York: Harper and Brothers.

Heber, R., et al. (1972). *Early Intervention as a Technique to Prevent Mental Retardation.* Madison: Rehabilitation Research and Training Center in Mental Retardation, University of Wisconsin. ED 080162.

Huberty, C. J., and Swan, W. W. (1974). Preschool classroom experiences and first grade achievement. *J. of Educ. Res.* Vol. 67: pp. 311–16.

Hymes, J. L., Jr. (1969). *Early Childhood Education.* Washington, D.C.: NAEYC.

Ilg, F. L., et al. (1978). *School Readiness Behavior Tests Used at the Gesell Institute.* New York: Harper and Row.

Kagan, J. (1984). *The Nature of the Child.* New York: Basic Books.

Kamii, C. (1985). Leading primary education toward excellence. *Young Children.* Vol. 40, No. 6: pp. 3–9.

Katz, L. G. (1970). Early childhood education as a discipline. *Young Children.* Vol. 26, No. 2: pp. 82–89.

Kaufman, A. F. (1971). A psychometric analysis of tests built from their tasks. *Child Development.* Vol. 42: pp. 1341–60.

Knox, B. J., and Glover, J. A. (1978). A note on preschool experience effects on achievement, readiness, and creativity. *Journal of Genetic Psychology.* Vol. 132: pp. 151–52.

Kohlberg, L. (1969). *Handbook of Socialization Theory and Research.* D. Goslin (Ed.). Chicago: Rand McNally.

Kulberg, J. M., and Gershman, E. S. (1973). School readiness: Studies of assessment procedures and comparison of three types of programming for immature five year olds. *Psychology in the Schools.* Vol. 10: pp. 410–20.

Leach, P. (1978). *Your Baby and Child.* New York: Knopf.

Levine, M. D., et al. (1980). The pediatric examination of educational readiness: Validation of an extended observation procedure. *Pediatrics.* Vol. 66, No. 3: pp. 341–48.

Lief, N. R., and Fahs, M. E. (1983). *The Second Year of Life.* New York: Dodd, Mead.

Marble, P. (1982). Looking at toddler programs. *Parents League Rev.* New York, Vol. 16: pp. 84–87.

Meisels, S. J. (1985). *Developmental Screening in Early Childhood: A Guide.* Washington, D.C.: NAEYC.

Moore, R., and Moore, D. (1972). *The Pre-School Movement: Panacea or Portent.* Berrien Springs, Mich.: Hewilt Research Center. ED 081477.

New York Health Code. Excerpt from Article 45. The City of New York, amended June 30, 1973.

New York Independent Schools Directory. (1985–86). New York: ISAAGNY in cooperation with the Parents League of New York.

New York State Education Department: a) Bureau of Child Development and Parent Education Position Paper, 1967; b) Evaluation of the N.Y. State Experimental Prekindergarten Program—Final Report; c) Guidelines for N.Y. State Prekindergarten Program 1985–86; d) Moffatt, Barbara. Associate in the Bureau of Child Development and Parent Education, personal communication, December 1985.

New York Times. 29 May 1985, 25 September 1985, 29 December 1985.

O'Connell, J. C. (1983). Research in review. *Young Children.* Vol. 38, No. 2: pp. 62–70.

Piaget, J. (1970). In *Carmichael's Manual of Child Psychology,* Vol. 1. P. Mussen (Ed.). New York: Wiley.

———. (1973). *To Understand Is to Invent.* New York: Viking Press.

Ramey, C. T., and Smith, B. J. (1976). Assessing the intellectual consequences of early intervention with high-risk infants. *Am. J. Mental Deficiency.* Vol. 81: pp. 318–24.

Sanger, S. (1985). *You and Your Baby's First Year.* New York: William Morrow.

Shapiro, E., and Biber, B. (1972). The education of young children: A developmental-interaction approach. *Teachers College Record.* Vol. 74, No. 1: pp. 55–79.

Skinner, B. F. (1953). *Science and Human Behavior.* New York: Macmillan.

Spock, B., and Rothenberg, M. B. (1985). *Dr. Spock's Baby and Child Care.* New York: Pocket Books.

Telegdy, G. A. (1976). The validity of IQ scores derived from readiness screening tests. *Psychology in the Schools.* Vol. 13: pp. 394–96.

Tokieda, G. Z. (1983). What's the hurry? Patience. *Parents League Review.* Vol. 17: pp. 36–40.

Weber, E. (1984). *Ideas Influencing Early Childhood Education.* New York: Teachers College Press.

Whitbread, N. (1972). *The Evolution of the Nursery-Infant School.* London/Boston: Routledge Kegan Paul.

White, B. (1975). *The First Three Years of Life.* Englewood Cliffs, N.J.: Prentice-Hall.

The World Almanac Book of Facts. (1981). New York: Newspaper Enterprise Association.

———. (1985). New York: Newspaper Enterprise Association.

Zigler, E. F., and Gordon, E. W. (1982). *Day Care: Scientific and Social Policy Issues.* Boston: Auburn House.

Zinsser, C. (1984). The best day care there ever was. *Working Mother.* Vol. 7, No. 10: pp. 76–80.

17

ASSESSMENT FOR PRIVATE BOARDING SCHOOL PLACEMENT

Alison Pedicord Schleifer

Over the past ten years, independent schools—in particular boarding schools serving children from late childhood through secondary school age—have experienced a rush of applicants and are enjoying renewed popularity. As public school systems face budget crises, teacher job actions, mandates for curricular change, changes in student populations, and possibly increased levels of violence within the schools, to name a few causes, families representing a wider range of socioeconomic backgrounds are turning toward private education for their children. This is certainly happening in urban regions; indeed, even in many suburban communities that have traditionally boasted nationally recognized school systems, this trend is evident. Moreover, the public has become increasingly aware of the tremendous diversity available among the various types, populations, educational offerings, and purposes of independent schools, both day and boarding. As families turn to the private schools, the lack of an appropriate day school option in their locale, or the advice of educators or of social service, psychological, or medical professionals working with the families may lead them for the first time to consider the boarding school as an alternative. While the well-known college preparatory boarding schools continue to serve their traditional populations of students from upper-class and educated professional middle-class families, they are increasingly serving students from all classes, from both urban and suburban situations, and from families who lack a familial tradition of independent education or who are making financial sacrifices in order to send the child to a boarding school. Frequently, as families find that they must make distinctions between schools or explore a range of unfamiliar institutions, many seek the counsel of an independent educational consultant.

This chapter focuses on the assessment of children by independent educational consultants and in particular on the assessment of those children and adolescents

The author gratefully acknowledges a wealth of practical knowledge gained from many personal conversations about the assessment process with Ruth E. Bishop, a pioneer educational consultant.

who might be candidates for private boarding school placement. While most consultants follow similar procedures, it is important to underline the word *independent*. Consultants differ as to background, training, clientele, and methodology of assessment and operation, but all are committed to making the best recommendations and referrals for each child. Each educational consultation is unique, and what may be appropriate for one child would be the wrong prescription for another. Particular assessment techniques for the learning-disabled, the retarded, the emotionally disturbed child, or for children with specialized needs are discussed at length in other sections of this book. Similarly, the variety of residential schools is so great that it would go beyond the scope of this chapter to attempt an in-depth study. Nonetheless, there is value in defining generally the nature and function of the educational consultant, describing a typical clientele, discussing some of the commonly presented situations that might be resolved by a boarding school placement, and examining some of the benefits and risks of a boarding school. The chapter will also focus briefly on an overview of the diversity of boarding schools, with some attention to specialized boarding schools that serve the learning-disabled or the socially and emotionally maladjusted child. Finally, the chapter will focus on some of the questions considered in the assessment process as the educational consultant matches child and school and makes educational recommendations.

THE INDEPENDENT EDUCATIONAL CONSULTANT

The renewed interest in private sector education in recent years has led to a growth in the number of independent educational consultants. While some consultants focus on counseling or career advising, most assist families and students seeking information about particular private schools, other academic programs, or colleges. The majority of independent educational consultants are not obligated to any institution by affiliation or receipt of commissions or finders' fees; work privately with each family or student; are informed about schools and programs from firsthand visits, from constant professional exchange, and from their own awareness of curricular and academic philosophies; are knowledgeable about assessment techniques, psychological and educational testing, and counseling techniques; and are primarily as an advocate for the child concerned with each child's educational needs. While not new, the profession has not been highly organized or systematically developed until recent years.

The consultant must be knowledgeable about a variety of fields: education, counseling, child and adolescent development, learning disabilities, and curriculum to name a few, but is not strictly bound to any particular field. Thus, there is no body of professional literature on methodology that specifically addresses educational consulting or the conduct of a practice. Consultants, working from their own interests, depend on professional literature from many fields. Most consultants come from the field of counseling or from many years of work with students in schools or other institutions, especially the boarding schools themselves.

Broadly, the independent educational consultant will review and evaluate previous academic and social records and earlier testing; interview the child and parents or guardians; recommend further assessment if it seems warranted or recommend other professionals who might assist the family with other aspects of the problem; make definite educational recommendations; perhaps facilitate contact with educational institutions; and work with the family throughout the decision-making process. In addition, many consultants maintain contact with the family and school to conduct follow-up studies of adjustment and academic progress.

CLIENTELE

A large number of cases recommended to the educational consultant involve requests for a residential or boarding school for a child. Families are usually referred by other professionals, such as the admissions officer at a school, or by friends and associates who have previously worked with an educational consultant. While some consultants adjust their fees to the client's ability to pay and the enactment of Public Law 94-142 has ensured that some families will have education fees paid by the public school district, the clients are by and large self-selected in terms of their ability to pay part or all of the standard consultation fee and future school fees. The clientele is further self-selected in terms of the type of situation being presented. Most families or professionals working with the family are aware of day school placements within a reasonable drive of the home, and, often, they have already considered these options. Obvious need for long-term custodial or physical care, needs for sheltered living arrangements, or total therapeutic environments for severe psychiatric disturbances are frequently met by recommendations from other professionals at an early age. Only rarely does a family with these requirements seek out the services of an educational consultant.

COMMONLY PRESENTED SITUATIONS

By far the largest group within most clienteles is the family that perceives some sort of difficulty or need for change with the child's current educational setting for academic, social, or emotional reasons, and that seeks assistance in selecting a boarding school. The parents may have noticed one or more of the following common signs of a need for an educational reevaluation without realizing fully what they may mean:

1. The child's academic performance changes suddenly, or there is a distinct difference in the child's personality or behavior for no apparent reason.

2. The child appears to be "marking time" in the school setting with signs of boredom or depression.
3. The child begins to show signs of giving up at school; there is anxiety, depression, or withdrawal, especially in cases in which school has always been difficult for the child.
4. The child has particular learning needs, either for advanced work or remedial work, that are not being met by the current school.
5. The child actively seeks a new school environment and is unhappy in the present school.
6. The child has a need for structure and supervision or, conversely, for greater freedom and exposure that cannot be met by the present school or family circumstances.
7. The child is deprived of a normal peer group or the provision for normal social interaction because of changes in family circumstances.
8. The child's behavior or the behavior of other family members makes problematic the possibility of the child remaining in the family unit, school, or community on a constant basis.
9. The child is developing unique talents that cannot be adequately developed in the home, present school, or community.
10. The family is advised by school personnel that the child's particular educational needs might be better served in another academic setting.

While not every case cited above will finally be resolved by a boarding school placement, there are many occasions in which the wisely chosen boarding school may mean the difference between the student's success or failure.

For children who have always attended boarding schools, the family may seek a consultation for advice about particular schools that have changed since the previous child or seek suggestions of other schools when a particular child clearly cannot meet the academic standards of the parental alma mater, or for schools that serve special talents or interests. Often, both the parents and child are committed to the idea of boarding school. Consultants frequently advise good students of average or above average ability who seem to have been lost in the shuffle of the large public high school or who need advanced work in only one or two subjects. For these students the smaller size and more personalized atmosphere of the boarding school can be especially beneficial. Similarly, a gifted student caught in a mediocre academic setting needs increased academic challenge, stimulation, and adventure and thus should consider the most competitive boarding schools, in which he or she will find a number of other gifted students. As the number of single parents increases, consultants are frequently asked about boarding schools that can provide positive role models for the noncustodial parent, especially in the case, for example, of a mother seeking to provide a more constant positive role model for her early adolescent son who sees his father for only a brief time each year. Parents or guardians who travel constantly or who live abroad in unsettled political areas will often seek the security of a consistent and loving school for a child, particularly if the child is in the elementary grades or perhaps completing secondary school and anticipating attending college in the United States. In recent years, with the advent of the alternative school and popular trends toward self-discovery, the consultant is also sometimes asked to advise and make recommendations for students who have missed time at school, taken time off to develop an alternative lifestyle, or who may not have completed high school, but who now wish further academic or terminal career-oriented guidance.

More commonly, the situation as perceived by the family is the lack of success the child is experiencing in his or her current school setting. Perhaps the child appears unmotivated or unwilling to put forth the effort, or perhaps the child is seeking success with peers in social situations that the family finds unacceptable. Some children are of only very modest intellectual ability and are having academic difficulty because in the early years of school they were able to mask their modest ability and gain praise because of pleasing personalities. They may have reached a plateau and now need a less rigorous academic setting; their parents may be unable or unwilling to accept the limited ability. The consultant may see children who are sources of tension, or who are acting out in either the home or school; children whose parents are unable or unwilling to impose consistent behavior limits and to develop structure; or children who are caught in destructive, manipulative behavior patterns because their parents lack confidence for parenting, are too narcissistic themselves, have simply abdicated the parental roles, or may be masking their own social and emotional needs. Children whose parents are separated or divorced and who find themselves caught painfully between two powerful but opposing parental forces, and children whose parents are together but who are subjected to family pressures such as financial or employment stress, physical and mental illness, alcoholism, or severe problems with siblings, often become candidates for the boarding school.

Finally, every consultant sees some children who, despite seeming harmony in the home, consciously or unconsciously feel the need to challenge authority with drugs, sex, hostile antisocial and/or delinquent acts, and openly to test parents, school, and community authorities: the child who is arrested for vandalism or theft; the young girl who is approaching term in an unwanted pregnancy and who needs another environment because of rebellion against the family; the child who has been dismissed from a school because of possession or drugs or alcohol in the school setting. These students, often characterized as "at risk" students for any school, present special problems in terms of placement, for the consultant must always consider the risk that such students pose to others and to themselves and must determine whether their primary need is for a therapeutic setting. Unfortunately, some families seek boarding school as a possible solution simply to remove the child from the home or community when a child may really need therapy or counseling. All too often then, if a regular school placement is achieved, the behavior is repeated. Frequently it is the task of the educational consultant to redirect such families toward individual or family therapy with no change in school, other educational placement options such as the therapeutic residential school, or, at least, to make the family aware of the limitations of most regular boarding schools, which do not work well with children who are at risk because they lack the therapeutic community.

BOARDING SCHOOLS: BENEFITS AND RISKS

Professionals in the social service and psychological communities as well as other educators and parents are sometimes hesitant about boarding schools. They may view them as somehow "undemocratic," only for the very wealthy, or for those with superior intellectual ability. While these perceptions may be valid for some, it is useful to explore what characterizes most boarding schools to demythologize the rather arbitrary labeling.

Traditionally, boarding schools have offered benefits not as easily found in the day school setting. Classes are generally smaller; study hours, either supervised or on an honor system, are regularized each day; teachers and support faculty who live on campus are available for enrichment and accelerated work or for remedial work and extra help at almost any time of the day or evening; and the small classes and provision for more personalized and continuous faculty attention generally lead to an atmosphere more conducive to learning. The schools are freed from bureaucratic regulation, contract-mandated class sizes, district-wide scheduling practices, and the like, which can bind curricular offerings at a public school. This freedom often allows for greater academic and curricular flexibility. The gifted student is assured that a small, single advanced placement class will meet or that a new course might be created for several students interested in pursuing a subject. In some schools students can do projects involving the use of a laboratory or computer, exchange ideas with faculty members over dinner or during free time, or engage in independent study. Similarly the student who needs help can be assured of remedial work, and does not have to rely on parents or siblings or have to wait until the next day to talk with a teacher about difficult assignments, but generally is able to get help almost immediately. The dedication of faculty to students on a twenty-four hour a day basis leads most often to a closer relationship. The overriding advantages of the boarding school are the academic specialization for a narrower group of students, the curricular flexibility, the structured setting that can lead to increased efficiency of work, and the dedication of the entire community to the development and maintenance of good study habits and motivated enthusiastic acquisition of knowledge.

The boarding school also offers a ready-made community of peers and adults for the student. Students are encouraged to participate in the total life of the school community. Academics, activities, community support, and sports in the boarding school offer wide exposure to a variety of personalities and ideas. Students have to learn to live with and adapt to people of differing natures and backgrounds. They have to begin to handle freedom and responsibility in a nonfamily but still structured milieu, and they have to begin to make decisions for themselves. The possibilities abound, therefore, for a student to strengthen talents and to develop new ones because of facilities or faculty skills that did not exist in the previous family or school setting.

For many students and their families the boarding school can be a positive experience. When the problem seems to be centered in the family setting and has not become too severe, removing a child to a boarding school can often provide a needed respite from tension; it allows for increased development of maturity in the child and a change of previous family behavior patterns that adversely affected the child's past schooling.

> Andrea, for example, first came for a consultation at age 12. Testing revealed superior intellectual ability and great curiosity coupled with a reluctance to attempt anything new for fear of failure. She had been placed in the top track in the middle school but achieved only average grades of B's and C's. A second child, born many years after her sibling, to somewhat older, professional-level parents, she felt intimidated by the parental drive for success and yet fearful of breaking strong family ties and the happiness of the home. Clearly, Andrea needed some room for self-development and confidence building. Given her and the family's fears about boarding school for grade eight, she was placed first in the summer school program of a leading elementary boarding school. Quickly she began to blossom and excel academically as she made friends with faculty and students and became involved in sports and arts activities. At the end of the summer session she asked to be allowed to return for the regular year program. The faculty, who had watched her develop new interests without fear, encouraged her. Andrea remained happily there through grade nine, when, at the top of her graduating class, she chose to continue at a secondary boarding school. The relationship with her parents blossomed as she began, with distance, to recognize that their "pressure" was not directed at her in a negative way and as she began to develop artistic interests that she had been fearful of expressing at home.

Most boarding school faculty are more than willing to give extra support and guidance to a student who is experiencing adjustment difficulties, and some but not all schools are even able to provide for outside professional psychological support services for a brief period of time. For the minor emotional or social adjustment problem such as extreme shyness, fear of failure, negative peer influence, and the like, the experience of leaving home, of having to adjust to living with a diverse group of people and new peer pressures to change behavior, and of breaking old routines and patterns of behavior, can often enable a student to develop a better self-image, to be able to confide in another sympathetic person, and to work through a period of negative behavior to achieve a fresh start. But the regular academic boarding school cannot, unless it is a total therapeutic setting, work well with or provide ongoing professional therapy for a serious emotional or social adjustment problem.

The right boarding school can often provide advanced study for the bright or gifted student without having to accelerate the student's class level in order to accommodate intellectual ability, thus providing more normal peer group relationships. The boarding school can address the need for remediation of specific academic weaknesses and can give specialized language retraining or math work to assist the learning-disabled student. A motivational problem stemming from a lack of challenge or a previous series of failures may be reversed over time at a boarding school as the student experiences success after placement at a more appropriate curricular level. Such a problem may also be resolved when a student is placed with a more motivated group of peers and begins to respond to positive peer pressure. At the very least, the faculty can often demonstrate more clearly to parents and counselors what a student's future needs may be.

> Three batteries of tests in the elementary school years had shown the family that Warren, age 13, had some learning difficulties in the reading and language areas coupled with apraxia of eye movements. The third of four closely spaced children, he also manifested poor impulse control with a tendency toward hyperactivity and presented a history of intense sibling rivalry with an older sister. Intelligence was in the high average range overall and school achievement through the elementary years, with resource room support, was at or slightly above grade level. But with the onset of puberty and the change to a very large middle school where resource room help was not continued because of achievement at grade level, he floundered, began to engage in impulsive behavior, and seemed never to be able to complete work on time, despite a short school day and plenty of time after school for homework. The family placed Warren in a regular boarding school known for its structured program, but did not seek special help since the previous school had discontinued remedial work. Within several weeks it became obvious to faculty working with Warren that he needed the special assistance of the school's learning disabilities program, and Warren was entered in the program. This program gave him at least five periods per week of intensive remedial work, without causing him to lose any other course work or activities at school. Almost immediately the family noted significant changes in Warren's behavior and attitude. The highly structured day of classes, sports, and evening supervised study, coupled with intensive remediation and the generalized strong emphasis at the school on study skills, in reading and discussion for class, helped Warren to develop organizational skills that allowed him to focus on tasks without distractions. He even found that, although he had never been known for athletic ability in his previous schools, he was able to gain a place on the third-level soccer team. Four years of intensive remediation, coupled with a traditional college preparatory program of studies in a very structured environment, allowed Warren to suc-

ceed very well and gain admission to a good small liberal arts college, where he plays soccer and is majoring in biology and environmental science.

There are risks involved in sending a student to boarding school. In general, families should be aware that they give up certain immediate parental controls for the time that the student is away and that they will miss certain events of maturation unless the school is located very close to home. Children mature when out of the home settings for long periods of time, and this fact can be a threat to many families. For some students an unsatisfactory boarding school placement can cause the child to act out. There is also the increased risk of the child's feeling abandoned or rejected, especially if the change of school was imposed by the parents or guardians. In cases in which therapy is ongoing, a move to a boarding school can disrupt the therapeutic relationship, and care should be taken not to change therapists or to discontinue therapy without a thorough consultation with the professional. Some children find that they are unable to adapt to the closeness of the community in a residential setting because their problematic area is peer relationships and social relations. For these children the boarding school may only increase anxiety. If the placement is not right, the child may experience academic failure or inability to cope with increased academic demands, with a resultant decline in self-esteem. Finally, for the student who is at risk because of the need to test authority, the boarding school often becomes yet another place to challenge rules or to test authority, with the most frequent result being suspension or dismissal. Such a child, for example, who is sent to a military academy by frustrated parents on the theory that the academy will somehow instill respect for authority through a multitude of rules, regulations, and punishments, may continue to test and experience another failure, with the result that the initial behavior is often exacerbated.

Thus, for the child who needs a specific academic challenge or period of remediation, for one who needs to be exposed to a broader community or who needs a more supportive setting, and for the child without serious emotional problems who can indeed live independently away from home, the regular academic boarding school can present a positive alternative. In most cases the benefits outnumber the risks, but in every case the pros and cons must be weighed as parents contemplate sending their child away to school and as they select an appropriate school.

BOARDING SCHOOLS: DIVERSITY OF SCHOOLS

Just as the variety of children's educational needs is great, directories abound with listings of diverse independent boarding schools that offer campus living and a variety of curricular approaches, activities, and athletics for almost any age from kindergarten through high school and beyond. (Directories such as *The Handbook of Private Schools*, published by Porter Sargent [Boston], Peterson's *Guide to Independent Secondary Schools* [Princeton, N.J.], and *The Bunting and Lyon Blue Book—Private Inde-*

pendent Schools [Wallingford, Conn.] are published annually and detail information about most of the nation's private boarding and day schools: history of the school, numbers of faculty, numbers of students, requirements, placement after graduation, admissions standards and the like. Lovejoy's *Prep and Private School Guide* [New York, Simon and Schuster, 1980] is another such guide, now in its fifth edition. Guides to select groups of schools are published by the Secondary School Admissions Test Board, *Independent Secondary Schools, A Handbook* and by the National Association of Independent Schools Committee on Boarding Schools, *Boarding Schools* [Boston, published annually]. The annual publication *Educational Register*, published by Vincent-Curtis [Boston], contains display information about selected schools and articles of general interest to families and the general public about various aspects of independent education, school and camp life.)

Schools range from the very traditional, mid-sized or large, highly competitive long-established college preparatory schools with ivy-covered buildings and famous graduates to the small, family-oriented nontraditional school of twenty students and twelve faculty located in a backwood hamlet. The most competitive schools seek highly qualified mature students who can enjoy intense academic, athletic, and social competition. For the average to above average ability student of good character there is a large group of solid middle-rank college preparatory schools that offer somewhat less competitive academic programs and a wide range of sports and activities designed to develop other talents. But academic ranking is only one measure that distinguishes schools from one another.

For those students and families who prefer a different sort of school or more specialized program there are schools that emphasize particular educational philosophies, or programs such as competitive skiing or professional level work in music and the arts in addition to college prep academics. There are schools for specialized student bodies such as dyslexic students, learning-disabled, and children from single-parent families or from a specific religious background. Some schools are single-sex; others are military in orientation. Some schools have a community-based participatory form of governance, and some allow the students little voice or choice. Some schools are based around a working farm and both students and faculty share farm chores, while others occupy urban settings. There are schools that encourage foreign travel for a term or semester or off-campus community-based hands-on learning, and others that encourage independent academic study. There are schools that require all students to do community service and participate in the maintenance of the campus and schools that still provide maid service for the student rooms; schools that require uniforms or have strict dress codes and others that allow students great latitude in dress and behavior codes.

Given the wide variety of schools, one has the impression that there may well be a school for every sort of student personality or need. In fact, this is very nearly the case. It is the task of the educational consultant to match family and student needs with the appropriate group of schools and to assist families to make decisions among schools that are: rural or urban, large or tutorial, structured or unstructured, coed or single-sex, graded or ungraded, conservative or progressive, college preparatory or career-oriented, strict or permissive, religious or nonsectarian.

BOARDING SCHOOLS: SCHOOLS FOR SPECIAL NEEDS

There are two population groups that need a more specialized academic environment, the learning-disabled student and the emotionally handicapped student. There is value in focusing briefly on some characteristics of the schools that cater to these populations.

Although there is an increasing number of regular boarding schools that offer programs for a limited number of mildly learning-disabled students, for the student whose disability is more severe, consultants and families must turn to the special school. Distinct from those institutions that work with the blind, deaf, seriously neurologically impaired or severely physically handicapped, there are some schools that work specifically with students who exhibit dyslexia, disgraphia, or visual and auditory perceptual difficulties and who, despite adequate intellectual ability, cannot perform at a level commensurate with their intellectual ability in a regular classroom. Most of the academically oriented schools for the learning disabled work with students of average or above average intelligence who are free from primary emotional problems. Since it is well recognized that early intervention is prime for this sort of student, many of these schools take younger students, usually from grades four or five onward. Some terminate after the middle school years, while a few continue through the secondary years. In most cases, the goal of the specialized learning disabilities school is to provide intensive remediation and retraining, usually for a period of one to three years, with the ultimate goal of returning the student to a regular academic program with a minimum of academic assistance.

When assessing the student with a history of learning difficulties, the consultant has to determine from testing what form the disability takes, what measures have been used to date to facilitate the child's compensation in the school setting, and what the probability is for successful remediation given the child's age. Finally the consultant must assess the student's and family's attitude toward the disability. Factors such as geographic location, size of school, coed or single-sex, competitive level of curriculum, extracurricular offerings, and the like, which form the basis for selection of the regular boarding school, become secondary as one moves into the consideration of the specialized school. The consultant must choose the particular schools that offer remedial work specifically tailored to a student's special needs. One learning disabilities school, for example, works solely with the very bright dyslexic student, while another works best with students whose disabilities lie in the visual-perceptual area. The schools, moreover, achieve their greatest success with those students who are able to recognize their disability without denial, who accept the need for specialized retraining, who are willing to adapt to change through retraining, and who have not lost because of previous school frustration the self-confidence needed for motivation. Often the educational consultant finds it necessary to assist the family to accept the need for more specialized intervention if the child is to succeed in school without feeling different and isolated.

Janet, for example, appeared from school performance to have only boarderline intellectual ability and had struggled throughout her elementary school years to remain just slightly below grade level. Subtest scores on the verbal tests of the WISC were mixed, but those on the performance tests were well below the average and with retesting over a period of years were unchanged. As a youngster she was quite uncoordinated and had difficulty with sports, but was highly motivated, got along well with peers and faculty, and showed fine singing talent with excellent ability to retain both words and music. As she entered the junior high years and faced the increased reading demands, she found that hours of drill and intense work on homework with her parents quizzing her at every stage, which had enabled her to keep up in elementary school, could not be maintained. She fell farther behind, had to give up any activities out of school, and began to be physically ill with the effort to keep up. Guidance personnel began to advise the family to consider moving her to less demanding vocational courses, yet she experienced difficulty in these courses as well.

Further investigation revealed massive visual-perceptual disabilities, including the physical lack of ability to maintain bifocal focus for more than five to ten minutes when reading. When tested orally, she showed at least average ability. Janet was placed in a specialized learning disabilities school that incorporated intense remedial work on visual-perceptual skills. The recognition that she had at least average ability, the intensive remediation, an individually planned academic curriculum that allowed for more learning through auditory processes, and a supportive faculty and staff encouraged her to regain her motivation to succeed. Quickly she regained her self-confidence, became involved in the school life, had time to develop her musical talent, and began to achieve in her academic work.

Over the past years, enormous progress has been made in schools in addressing the needs of the learning-disabled student through "resource room" and other specialized teaching, but many students still need the continuum of the boarding school experience to address their needs. Cost is a factor, since costs rise whenever there is a substantial amount of tutorial work. The tuition costs, for example, at a school for learning disabilities may be as much as three to five thousand dollars more than the cost of other boarding schools. In some cases the school district will assume the tuition costs, while in others, parents must decide whether they can assume the financial burden. It is not unusual to find a parent deciding to use resources set aside for college to finance several years of intensive remediation at the middle school level so that the learning-disabled child has the opportunity to compensate enough to attend college in the future. For families and consultants alike, resources exist to provide information about schools and programs as well as information about the process of working with the child's current school to develop an appropriate education plan under the guidelines of Public Law 94-142. (The Orton Dyslexia Society, 724 York Road, Baltimore, Maryland; The Association for Children with Learning Disabilities, 4156 Library Road, Pittsburgh, Pennsylvania, which has state chapters throughout the nation; and the National Association of Private Schools for Exceptional Children, which publishes a directory describing the services of its member schools are excellent sources of information for the public. Porter Sargent's *Directory for Exceptional Children* [Boston, 1984] and Academic Therapy Publication's *Directory of Educational Facilities for the Learning Disabled* [Novalo, Calif., published annually], are only two of the directories which give listings of specialized schools.)

In any student population there is a small but significant number of students who fail to make a satisfactory adjustment to school, home or community life, who show signs of primary emotional disturbance whether organic or substance abuse induced, and who are no longer able to function in the average home or school environment because of antisocial behavior, loss of control, or extreme withdrawal from others. Such students need the residential therapeutic school, which provides education within a therapeutic living environment. Differentiated from the hospital or psychiatric facility, which provides a closed, inpatient setting to work with a child in crisis, most of the therapeutic schools remain more open settings. Usually a student will enter such a school upon release from an inpatient facility or directly if the emotional disturbance is not so severe as to require hospitalization. Most therapeutic schools include an educational component that is flexible or ungraded and therefore can be designed to fit individual academic needs, daily or weekly individual or group psychotherapy, and a highly structured living situation that includes some degree of behavior modification under the close supervision of professional staff. At the majority of therapeutic schools the program continues on a year-round basis, with the average stay being about two years. Such schools differ in their admissions policies as to the degree of emotional disturbance they can work with effectively, and some schools operate a variety of programs or levels within the program in which they differentiate students according to the severity of disturbance. Admissions criteria also differ from school to school according to the age and sex of the child and according to whether the child is referred by a public agency or is a private admission, since some schools do not accept public funds. Normally, the goal of the residential therapeutic school is to enable the student to return as soon as possible to a less restrictive boarding or day school setting. While they differ from each other in treatment philosophy and methodology, some favoring intensive individual psychotherapy, others a behavior modification program coupled with group therapy sessions, almost all are very expensive for the average family, as much as three or four times the cost of a year at a regular boarding school. Education costs are often borne by the home school district, and in some cases costs are deductible for tax purposes or are covered by private insurance.

Alex, age 11 with average ability but a history of learning disabilities, was assessed for boarding school placement. He had attended a variety of schools while the family moved around a great deal when he was young, and the family had placed him in a quiet coed boarding school with a specialized learning disabilities program the previous year. He had recently been dismissed from the school for a series of aggressive confrontations with faculty and other students. The family requested immediate placement in a boarding setting that would give him remediation. It was impossible for him to live with the parents, who traveled world-wide on business, at times at considerable physical risk. During the interview, Alex showed intense hostility toward both the parents and consultant, refused to discuss his past school, and became alternately abusive or silent. Assessment revealed a significant learning disability, addressed with excellent remediation, but with little or no growth in academic skills for the previous three years.

Alex was described by former faculty as fearful for the parents' safety in troubled political areas yet hostile toward them, with feelings of having been abandoned. They described him as ready to burst with feelings of hostility that made every encounter in the school setting potentially explosive. Since it was obvious that Alex needed more attention than a regular school could offer and the possibility of seeing a therapist on an outpatient basis did not exist, a decision was made to recommend the residential therapeutic school as a first priority; the selection of recommended schools included those that could continue remediation of learning problems once he had begun to work through the emotional blocks to learning.

For the family, student, and consultant, the decision to turn to the residential therapeutic school is not one to be made without thorough investigation of alternatives. Such a decision usually involves the family, the consultant, other educators, and any medical personnel working with the student. It is frequently chosen as a half-way measure between a period of hospitalization and the return to the home school or other regular boarding school. Familiarity with the specific programs and philosophies of each therapeutic school is essential in order to maintain continuity of the therapeutic methodology. It is also imperative that the family understand and be supportive of such a move to a therapeutic school. (In addition to the directories previously mentioned in this section, a good source of information about a limited number of residential therapeutic schools is the directory of member schools of the American Association of Children's Residential Centers, Ben Franklin Station, Post Office Box 14188, Washington, D.C., 20044.)

ASSESSMENT

How does the educational consultant assess the child's needs and how does the consultant narrow the choices of particular schools to manageable recommendations for a student? The immediate goals of the educational consultant are to clarify the situation as it is presented by the family or referring agent, to establish a trusting and honest relationship between the consultant and the family, and to make recommendations concerning educational goals and strategy based on the consultant's best assessment of the child's needs.

The educational consultant is not necessarily a psychiatrist, psychologist, physician, social worker, or teacher, and thus is free to take an overview of the child's needs, taking into consideration the evaluations and recommendations from the other disciplines. Prior assessments and recommendations of other professionals who have worked with the child must be considered, but the consultant is in a unique position to balance those recommendations against each other and to fit them into the overall educational needs of the child. Similarly, while a client-consultant relationship must include a good working rapport and may, over time, become a very close friendship, the educational consultant does not enter into a therapeutic relationship with the child and family. It is a difficult but necessary balance that must be struck if the consultant is to be a true advocate for the child. The educational consultant is guided by professional ethical standards of confidentiality and respect for the client's welfare and reputation with regard to the institutions. Similarly, while safeguarding confidentiality, with due regard for family permission, the educational consultant must maintain professional integrity and share information with institutions and other professionals who have a right to know certain privileged and confidential information about the client.

It is difficult, therefore, to discuss assessment by the educational consultant in anything but general terms. Each consultant has preferred methods to establish a rapport and ongoing relationship with clients and to assess children's academic needs, but most good educational consultants have a large repertoire of assessment tools and cannot say which they will use at a given time for a client. The consultant must treat each case as unique; as will be discussed later, proper school placement requires a great measure of subjective judgment and matchmaking.

Intake interviews or questionnaires yield information about the child's past physical and emotional developmental history, family interactions, family, social, and economic history, and major positive and negative events in the child's life. The intake process is almost always followed by a review of previous academic records. These yield information about intellectual ability as measured by standard testing and teacher reports, school performance in prior grades, possibly academic skill levels as measured by standardized achievement testing, and school-related behavior. This step will usually include a review of any other individual psychoeducational, neurological, and physiological testing that has already been done for the child. The consultant may, in addition, recommend further assessment or evaluative testing in order to have as complete a picture as possible of the child's intellectual ability, emotional health, and physical state (including but not limited to vision performance, hearing, chemical balance in the body, and growth and development).

Almost all consultants require one or more in-depth interviews with the child and family, in which the consultant is able to get to know the child, assess on a first-hand basis any information not previously evaluated, and develop the beginnings of a trusting working relationship between consultant and family. Some consultants prefer to interview the child first and then review other assessments, while some hold separate parent and child interviews, use games, role-playing or paper and pencil tests, or simply ask questions of both child and parents. Many consultants have developed a series of questions that elicit information, while others prefer a free-form interview. Many ask the child to read a passage aloud and require a writing sample in the student's handwriting. Other consultants have particular informal techniques for the assessment of visual or auditory discrimination, neurological impairment, emotional stability and reaction to authority, and academic motivation and skill level. Almost all consultants would agree, however, that the most successful assessment is one in which the consultant is ready and able to adapt tools and assessment techniques to the client and to the special mood and atmosphere of the interview period. With one family or child, a few questions will elicit a flood of family and school related information germaine to the assessment, while with another child, it might be necessary to play a game or to use a confrontational approach to parents who are reluctant to allow the child to discuss family interpersonal relationships or the like. It is not uncommon, after an initial interview, for the child or one or both of the parents to decide to share further information about family dynamics that was hinted at in the interview but may have seemed insignificant or perhaps as too threatening to talk about. Not infrequently, when parents and children are interviewed together for a time, each will gain a new perspective on the other's attitudes and performance. For example, parents are often surprised by the insightfulness of an adolescent whom they regard as little more than a child, when the adolescent talks about peer relationships, goals the child has developed, or what interests the student wants to pursue. This review and interview process is perhaps the most significant part of the assessment of the child's needs, for it is during this process that the consultant brings together both objective data, possibly for the first time considering it as a whole and without the prejudice of any particular discipline, and subjective evaluations to answer some of the following questions and to get a clear picture of the situation, which may or may not correspond to that stated by the family or referral agent.

The consultant will try to define and differentiate those needs that can be addressed by school, family, or community resources. The consultant will also try to determine whether a stated problem is isolated or repeated and where it is evidenced. For example, can current curricular offerings or community resources provide adequate intellectual stimulation for the gifted student? Should acceleration be recommended or would that place the child at a social disadvantage among older peers and push the child toward higher education at too rapid a pace? Is there an academic placement that can meet both intellectual and social needs, and can the family afford such a placement? For another, is the child's seeming lack of motivation really due to a defense mechanism the child has established to cover an undiagnosed learning disability or gap in basic skills? Are there specific learning patterns that need direction and remediation? What are the reasonable expectations for success for this child, based on measures of overall intellectual ability, strengths and weaknesses in skill levels, previous academic background, and family and child goals for the academic program? How does the child handle the learning problem? Do the parents understand the child's needs and can they accept a remedial setting without prejudice to the child? In another situation assessment questions might focus on the child's relationship to peers and faculty in school and to peers and adults in community activities and how they might change. What school and community influences have been brought to bear on this child? Is there use or abuse of alcohol or drugs by the child or parent, what are the possible motivations for such use, and what is the extent of use? Have difficulties with a sibling or parent created such tension within the family that the child is preoccupied at school and unable to achieve, or conversely, is school the one outlet for success and acceptance that the child is unable to find in the family setting? In such cases the consultant may have to determine whether the perceived problem lies with the child or whether one or both parents may indeed be the source of a problem and may be projecting that problem onto the child. Educational consultants will also take into account the likelihood of bettering the situation or correcting a true problem. Would a solution be best achieved through a change in school or attendance in a program such as a camp or enrichment summer school program for a limited time away from home, or is it best for the child to remain at the present school? Is further evaluation, individual or family counseling, or therapy called for? Would the preferred course of action be to remove the child from the family or to leave that child in the family setting and recommend that other children be sent to boarding school? While not exhaustive, these examples give a good idea of the sorts of questions that must be considered in the assessment process. In general, the consultant will consider questions such as the child's ability and curricular needs to meet this ability; what schools or programs exist that are likely to meet these needs; the child's and family's attitude toward boarding school; what schools or programs exist that match the family values, attitudes, aspirations, and financial situation; what possible negative and positive influences a move to a boarding school would have on all members of the family; the overall benefits and risks involved in sending the child to a different school, especially the boarding school; and what reasonable expectations can be met as a result of this recommendation from the consultant.

When recommending a change to a boarding school, the consultant must match the child's educational and social needs with schools that serve those needs. Just as subjective judgments entered the definition of the situation and the decision to recommend boarding school, the consultant necessarily must use more subjective criteria in the matching of school and child. Often, for example, two consultants will have very different impressions of a school and the sort of student who fares best there. These subjective criteria are based on long-term familiarity with particular boarding schools through frequent visits to the schools, confidence in the faculty and administration, experiences with previous clients who have attended a particular school, and what some educational consultants call a "sixth sense" about whether school and child are a good match. Objective criteria include knowledge of faculty academic preparation and level of expertise as well as teaching ability and dedication, financial stability of the school and financial aid possibilities, curriculum, physical facilities, and what sports and activities are available. The subjective criteria include such intangibles as impressions of the quality of life at the school, of student faculty rapport, of the social, intellectual, and attitudinal make-up of the student body, and even impressions of the school's physical plant and how that will enhance or detract from the child's well-being. Even such seemingly unimportant questions as the quality of the food served, numbers of students in dorms, distance from home, ease of transportation to and from the school, and the number and scheduling of open weekends are questions the consultant must address in selecting schools to recommend to a family. Similarly, the consultant must consider how the child will adapt to boarding school. Is the child able to make friends easily, accept new situations, and adapt to dormitory living and shared facilities without feeling that personal privacy has been violated? Will the child be able to share in community life and find security in the boarding school?

During or after the interview the consultant will make specific recommendations and will work with the family to develop an educational strategy for the child, involving possible school placement and future educational goals. Such recommendations may also include specific suggestions for short-term, non-school-related resolutions to the present situation. Frequently the consultant serves throughout the process as an interpreter of other professionals' assessment information and recommendations. The consultant can, for example, distill information from educational testing and make scores, percentages, stanines, grade equivalent norms and the like comprehensible to the family. Often the consultant must confront a family directly and assist them as gently as possible to face a serious problem that had not been noticed in the original situation or to face a different situation entirely. The consultant may well be able to reassure a family that what they perceive as a problem is in fact not an unusual situation and not without solution. In this way, without assuming the role of therapist the consultant may become a source of support to families seeking to understand the ramifications of their child's school needs, or a facilitator of communication between the family, other professionals, and institutions. A good consultant is able to convey to other professionals and especially to possible boarding schools far more about a student's or family's needs than academic data or test scores reveal. Often the consultant can make valuable suggestions as to approaches a school might try with the student or what type of specialized program would best suit the student. Not infrequently the consultant may remain available to both family and school for further assessment and recommendation throughout the initial time at a new school. The relationship between consultant and client may well become one of lasting rapport, and it is not unusual for the consultant to be asked to advise on future college selection or to assist a second child in the family.

If the family chooses to follow up on the recommendations made by the educational consultant and if those recommendations involve a change of school, the family and child then go through a process of information gathering about the school options, visiting the recommended schools for interviews and for first-hand impressions of the schools, and selecting and making application to the schools that seem most appropriate. Although some consultants work only on a consultation basis, most continue to be available as families go through this process. They answer questions, refine recommendations, and facilitate contact between family and school. Often, as both child and family interact with the consultant and admissions officers and visit schools, the process of exploring school options helps parents learn more about their child and helps the child to be more aware of his or her role and needs in the academic world.

Barbara, age 13 and in grade 8 in an excellent suburban school district, was according to most measures a successful and happy student. She came from a well-educated, well-traveled, successful and happy, close-knit family, was a talented violinist and vocalist, participated in school and community sports and activities, had several close friends, and was respected by faculty as an achiever in the upper tracks of the competitive middle school. Her case serves as a good illustration of some of the questions considered in the assessment process. Despite her seeming success, Barbara was unhappy and felt different from her peers. In addition the guidance counselor had indicated to the family that she felt Barbara might simply be an over-achiever, for throughout her school years there was a record of substantially lowered scores on all standard testing and even occasionally on classroom tests. Since the consultant had placed her older brother in boarding school several years before, the family sought a consultation to determine whether a school change would be appropriate, given her growing unhappiness with her current situation. The school provided excellent college preparation, and they had not considered a private school for her, since she did not express a desire to attend boarding school.

Barbara was a tall, mature, and very attractive 13-year-old who quickly showed her verbal ability and her ease of conversation with adults in the interview. She talked openly and at length about her love of music, her pleasure at being a valued member of the club tennis team, her participation in her church youth group, which her close friends also attended, and her enjoyment of English and Spanish classes at school. She enjoyed getting to know teachers but indicated that this was not generally approved of by peers at her school and she did not want to be labeled as a teacher's pet. Over the past year she had also noticed that as her interest and knowledge of music deepened, many of her friends could not share that with her. Although she could not fully explain her dissatisfaction with school, she did talk at length about her frustration and anxiety in a large group testing situation and her fears that this would hamper future school success. The consultant recommended a full psychoeducational evaluation to determine more closely her intellectual potential and to assess basic skill levels and emotional state. Testing revealed a stable, emotionally healthy, high achieving girl who took pride in her work, especially when she could share it with others, and broad-based above average intellectual ability with no apparent learning difficulties. There was no evidence that she was working beyond intellectual capacity.

From the interview and testing it was apparent that Barbara needed a much smaller and more personalized school setting in which she could get to know faculty, participate in smaller classes in which contributions were expected, and in which she could be tested in a variety of ways. She had, for example, always excelled at essay examinations, which she thought of as a conversation with the instructor. The consultant recommended that she consider the small boarding school setting. Since success seemed relatively assured in most college preparatory boarding schools of middle competitive rank, recommendation decisions focused on geographic location, coed or all-girl, urban or country setting, extracurricular offerings, characteristics of the student population, and finally on the more subjective quality of school atmosphere. The consultant recommended a group of small, yet competitive, all-girl schools within a three-hour drive from her home. Barbara was very comfortable with girls of her age, but found that the boys still seemed much younger and seemed intimidated by her height and verbal maturity. The all-girl school would free her from social pressures at a time when they are most awkward for a more mature girl. She would also have more time and find greater resources to pursue her musical talents, since these particular schools all had very strong music courses, talented faculty musicians who taught voice and instrumental music, and excellent practice facilities. The consultant singled out two schools that, while maintaining high academic expectations, offered supportive and personalized environments that encouraged the girls to develop their artistic talents. Socially, Barbara would find in these schools an international student body as widely traveled and as exposed as she was. Once enrolled, Barbara found immediate friends who shared her love of music and she became a member of a small chamber group. She was able to relax and to thrive in the seminar format of the smaller classes, and found that as her test anxiety decreased even the standard college testing began to show her ability. A new interest in drama developed and she was frequently tapped for female roles, especially those involving singing in the neighboring boys' school dramatic productions. Barbara graduated with a superior grade average, an acknowledged student leader, an accomplished musician, and a much less anxious young woman who was then ready for a competitive coed college.

SUMMARY

As more families, either by personal choice or upon the recommendation of medical and psychological professionals or educators, investigate the private boarding school for their children, they are increasingly seeking the services of the independent educational consultant. The independent educational consultant, who brings together knowledge of educational options and alternatives with sensitive understanding of children in all aspects of their lives, functions as a resource to the family and as an advocate for the child. The consultant is not confined to any individual educational or psychological discipline and is not under obligation to any educational institution. Each clientele is particular to the consultant, but there are several obvious types of cases that occur frequently. Most consultants regularly see the student who is not receiving enough attention or challenge in the school setting, the student who has very specialized educational needs that are not well met in the current school, the student who is falling behind and not performing up to potential, or the student who has not made a good adjustment to school, home, or community because of emotional difficulties. Often for such children, the educational consultant will recommend the smaller size, more personalized attention, structured academic and social life that characterize the boarding school as a possible way of solving the school related problem.

The variety of private boarding schools is great in this country. Most follow a traditional academic curriculum based on college preparatory subjects. For the majority of students without serious learning or emotional difficulties that impede learning, there is enough diversity among the nation's boarding schools in terms of geographic location, size, competitive level, philosophy, and offerings and activities, to enable the educational consultant to make very specific recommendations of schools that closely match the needs, personality, and aspirations of the student. For the educationally handicapped student with learning or emotional difficulties, the educational consultant is able to recommend the more specialized school that works with the learning-disabled student or the residential therapeutic school for the student who requires a therapeutic living setting coupled with an academic setting.

The key to a good match or good recommendations for placement is the assessment process the educational consultant undertakes. A review of previous school records and consultation with other professionals who have worked with the child are coupled with the observations made in one or more interviews with the child and family to define and gain an overview of the student's educational, social, and emotional needs. At each level of the assessment there are both objective and subjective questions to be asked and decisions to be made before the consultant is able to make recommendations concerning educational options for the student. While some children become definite candidates for boarding schools, there are others for whom it is not a wise choice either because of the child or the limitations of the available boarding schools to work effectively with the child.

18

ASSESSING THE GIFTED CHILD AND ADOLESCENT

Sanford J. Cohn

INTRODUCTION

The gifted have evoked from society acclaim and inspiration as well as resentment and fear. Persons of great ability have been expected to contribute to civilization's tasks of survival and cultural advancement. At other times, those particular attributes that speak to individual differences in capabilities have frequently been obscured (Stanley 1976a). Lewis Madison Terman, acknowledged as the father of the gifted child movement in this country, observed that "it is the prevailing *Zeitgeist* that will decide, by the rewards it gives or withholds, what talents will come to flower" (Terman 1954, p. 227).

American education in the mid-1980s is said to be in crisis (*A Nation at Risk* 1983). Expectations for academic performance of school children have fallen lower than can ever be remembered, and attention is riveted on ways to enhance them (Resnick and Resnick 1985). The ablest students have been especially affected by these circumstances in the most adverse of ways (Lerner 1982). As a result, education of the gifted has received renewed interest. Gone is the well-worn axiom that gifted children simply "can make it on their own." In its place is the recognition that such seemingly benign neglect can inhibit the pace and level of our ablest children's ultimate development, destroy their inclinations toward educational pursuit in particular, and undermine their motivation to achieve.

Types and Degrees of Giftedness

The terms "gifted" and "talented" describe degrees to which an individual is endowed with certain abilities or skills. As such, they can refer to virtually any and all conceivable modes of human endeavor. It has thus been a significant problem to define the particular group of interest which special education services. An operational definition is required that will maximize educational help.

The sections of this chapter devoted to identification, assessment, and educational interventions focus on providing such a definition for academically talented youth. Inasmuch as the single characteristic "gifted" individuals have in common is the ability to learn quickly and well, the programs that result from such attempts involve the very core of the educational process.

In contrast to the many myths about gifted children, these youths are healthy and robust, physically and emotionally. Matching academic demand with assessed intellectual needs serves well in combating boredom and the acting out behavior often associated with it. When faced with scholastic challenges and provided with appropriate direction about conquering them, highly able youths exhibit eagerness and determination.

For some, years of inappropriate educational experiences have resulted in poor attitudes about school and symptoms of underachievement. For others perfectionistic compulsion to complete assignments in intricate detail has made school bearable. Dealing with such youths simply and directly yields positive results (Cohn and Finlay 1982). Most often, the task of the counselor or therapist is to mobilize some of the tremendous learning capacity such children have on behalf of their social development. They respond well to guidance about how they might behave in certain circumstances and how they might better their educational development.

Rarely is intellectual ability the cause of an emotional problem. Most often, with this population as with others, psychopathic behavior results from a troubled family setting. A child with superb reasoning ability has an excellent tool with which to work toward healthy social and emotional development.

IDENTIFICATION AND ASSESSMENT

The Optimal Match Strategy

The general principles that provide the foundation for identifying highly able children or youths, as well as for developing and implementing appropriate Individualized Educational Plans (IEP) for them, center on the appraisal of the youngster's educational characteristics (both cognitive and affective) and on the manipulation of significant educational variables (Stanley 1980) within the context of available resources. In its simplest terms, the process has as its ultimate goal the formulation of a match between a youngster's assessed academic needs and a variety of educational alternatives appropriate in pace, degree of rigor, and demand. For this reason the method has been named "The Optimal Match Strategy" (Robinson and Robinson 1982). This name was coined by the late Professor Halbert B. Robinson, former director of Child Development Research Group at the University of Washington. We have borrowed this term and intend it to be used to mean the process of assessing students' needs and matching educational experiences to meet them.

Implementing the Optimal Match Strategy requires attention to the following set of broad goals:

1. to provide a profile of a child's abilities in specific areas as accurately and precisely as possible;
2. to diagnose the status of the youngster's developed skills in curricula related to areas of outstanding ability;
3. to survey the youth's attitudes toward school in general, specific subjects, career aspirations, values, and interests;
4. to inform the youngster (whenever suitable) and his family about this profile of abilities and developed skills, and to assist them in exploring educational alternatives appropriate to the child's assessed educational needs and to help to determine which of those alternatives are feasible for them to pursue;
5. to provide documentation concerning the child's abilities, skills, and the family's desired educational options to the family and to specified agencies in which these alternatives are to be implemented;
6. to provide opportunities for follow-up assessment and counsel;
7. to refer families in need of special services (such as psychological counseling) to appropriate sources of information and counsel.

Assessment Problems to Overcome

The assessment of a highly able child's abilities in specific talent areas related to academic performance and the determination of what the student already knows in subjects related to areas of outstanding talent present several assessment problems that the professional must overcome. In particular these problems include:

1. the need for information that is relevant to immediate educational planning;
2. the limitations of age-appropriate tests in providing reliable estimates of a highly able youngster's true ability; and,
3. the phenomenon known as "the ceiling effect."

Educationally Relevant Information

In our society intellectual giftedness has become virtually synonymous with high IQ scores. A recent national survey indicates that tests of general intelligence are used for such purposes more frequently than any other selection tool (Alvino, McDonnel, and Richert 1981). Dependence on such tools can be traced back to Terman's *Genetic Studies of Genius*, a large-scale, longitudinal study of children who scored exceptionally well on his then newly devised Stanford-Binet Intelligence Scale (Terman 1925). While the knowledge garnered from the Terman studies over the past sixty-five years has served to help gifted individuals escape the many negative stereotypes that had become associated with them, and that still persist among many educators and psychologists (George 1977; Solano 1977; Pyryt 1977; Fox 1977; Cohn 1977a), one unavoidable result has also been the nearly automatic connection between giftedness and high scores on intelligence tests.

Measures of global intellectual ability like IQ fail to provide enough specifically relevant information to help plan appropriate educational experiences for highly able youths. In particular, the absence of a measure of mathematical reasoning ability leaves a blind spot. Recent studies conducted by the Study of Mathematically Precocious Youth (SMPY) at The Johns Hopkins University (Stanley, Keating, and Fox 1974; Keating 1976; Stanley, George, and Solano 1977; George, Cohn, and Stanley 1979; Benbow and Stanley 1983) and by the Project for the Study of Academic Precocity (PSAP) at Arizona State University (Cohn and Cohn 1986) have demonstrated the merit of determining a youngster's ability to reason both verbally *and* mathematically, rather than relying upon a single index of general intellectual ability (vis-à-vis the IQ) for educational planning.

Measures of verbal reasoning ability assess how well a youngster understands what he reads and the extent of his developed vocabulary. Verbal ability of this kind helps youngsters achieve well in writing, English, reading and literature, history and geography, anthropology, linguistics, psychology, philosophy, foreign languages, and the like. Measures of mathematical reasoning assess a youngster's ability to solve problems involving arithmetic reasoning, algebra, and geometry. Ability in this area helps youngsters achieve well in subjects such as arithmetic, algebra, geometry, trigonometry, calculus, statistics, probability theory, engineering, computer science, mathematical economics, mathematical psychology, mathematical sociology, and the physical sciences.

For effective educational intervention the minimum information about a child's profile of specific abilities must include measures of both mathematical and verbal reasoning ability, since all courses at the elementary, secondary, and postsecondary levels relate to some degree to one and/or the other ability dimensions. Other types of reasoning ability, such as abstract reasoning, spatial reasoning, and mechanical comprehension, are also valuable, especially for educational counseling at the secondary level (Cohn 1977b, 1980). For example, a youth who has outstanding mathematical reasoning ability, combined with excellent mechanical comprehension, might well be advised to take a difficult high school physics course (perhaps even Advanced Placement Physics) as soon as he has completed the prerequisite mathematics (in this case second-year algebra), regardless of his age at the time.

Focusing on a youth's *reasoning* abilities, as measured by aptitude tests, is critical (Stanley 1977; Fox 1981). In so doing, the assessment avoids dependence on the kinds and number of courses that a child has completed to determine levels of ability in specific talent areas. In many instances it is the most able students who become bored with the schooling process and fail to achieve at expected levels (Stanley 1978). By centering the identification process on reasoning abilities in mathematical and verbal areas in particular, one can spot such youths and help them (Stanley 1977). Similarly, the use of reasoning tests appears to identify minority children and handicapped youngsters who have outstanding abilities better than other procedures that have been attempted (Fox 1981).

Poor Reliability at the Extremes

Tests are designed so that there are a few items that nearly everyone in a specified age group is expected to answer correctly or expected to miss. For the ablest youngsters in an age group, a particular test created for that group will yield scores that show diminished reliability compared with those earned by more typical youths. Because so few answers help to discriminate individual differences at the upper levels of ability, random error can account for far more variation among the highly able group than among the more typical group.

This problem of poor reliability at the upper "tail" is exacerbated by the relatively recent development of minimal competency curricula and instruments to measure performance at minimal levels. In some of the worst cases, only five test items are available to discriminate among the top twenty-five percentile ranks of the normative group. The paucity of difficult test items maximizes the effects of random error on the able student's scores. Missing even one item on such a test might result in a highly able youth's failing to qualify for special educational services that are, in fact, appropriate for the child's learning needs.

The Ceiling Effect

The ceiling effect refers to the fact that the ablest students, almost by definition, answer all or most of the test items correctly on an instrument developed for youths their own age. They are quite literally bouncing against the ceiling of the test. In this circumstance, the test yields at best a low estimate of the youngster's actual ability or developed skills (Keating 1975).

On some tests that are currently being published, the ceiling effect is so pronounced that a perfect score yields a percentile rank of less than 90. This means that the test was designed so that more than 10 percent of the youngsters who take the test will be able to answer all of the items correctly. Inexperienced and often undereducated school personnel might incorrectly interpret the student's failure to reach a criterion of 96th percentile or better as justification for refusing to identify the child as gifted, even though reaching such a criterion is impossible! The use of such inappropriate instruments as determinants of eligibility for special educational services is an illustration of the worst possible consequences of the ceiling effect.

The ideal test to use in a procedure for assessing gifted children and adolescents is one that has plenty of difficult items so that individual differences at the uppermost levels of capability within specific talent areas can be assessed accurately and precisely. Few test publishers are willing to take the financial risk of developing very difficult tests that are destined to be used with only a small (3 to 5 percent) of any one age group. A beyond-level testing procedure can be followed, however, that compensates for the absence of tests with adequate ceiling (Stanley 1954; Keating 1975). This process is described in detail in the next section.

Overcoming Assessment Problems

A two-step identification strategy can be used when assessing gifted children and adolescents to compensate for the problems of poor reliability and ceiling effect. Articulated by Stanley (1954) and employed in his Study of Mathematically Precocious Youth (SMPY) since 1972 (Stanley 1976b, 1977; George and Solano 1976; Solano 1979; George 1979), this two-step process has its roots in the earlier work of Leta Hollingworth (1929, 1942).

The first step sets eligibility criteria for the subsequent step in such a way that the reliability problem faced when assessing highly able youngsters is minimized. The second step compensates for the ceiling effect.

Identifying Academically Gifted Children

Step One: Eligibility. The first step involves selecting a group of students who, based upon past performance, are likely to be eligible for advanced educational alternatives. It is important to avoid leaving out any possible candidate (i.e., to minimize false negatives). To accomplish this, students might be chosen according to past performance on age-appropriate tests of virtually any kind (e.g., specific academic aptitude tests, achievement tests, or even tests of general intelligence). Recommendations describing a youngster's specific accomplishments might also be solicited from teachers and parents. Total battery scores, section scores (e.g., "total math score" or "total verbal score"), even scores on subtests of aptitude or achievement test batteries that are associated with reasoning in their respective areas (e.g., math applications, math concepts, math problem solving, vocabulary development, reading comprehension, language usage) can also be used. While some age-appropriate tests are better than others, usually because they are more difficult, three factors permit the establishment of the broadest possible talent pool: (1) not specifying a particular instrument or set of instruments upon which eligibility is based; (2) using either of the two most recent administrations of a standardized measure; and (3) including recommendations (c.f. Solano 1979). Age-appropriate tests are typically used to assess able youngsters in school; this procedure minimizes the problem of their poor reliability.

Step Two: The Beyond-Level Test. The second step in the identification process is presented to youths who have qualified via Step One and who are given the choice to take a difficult test of mathematical and verbal reasoning ability designed for older students. This is called a "beyond-level" testing procedure because these tests, designed for more advanced students, are given to younger children. This use of a test adds ceiling to the assessment process by providing many items that are more difficult than those typically found on age-appropriate instruments.

The first question that one must ask when considering administering a beyond-level test is "just how far beyond level should the test be?" More than a decade of research from SMPY and over five years of similar studies undertaken by PSAP provide us with a rule of thumb of sorts: multiply the child's chronological age by 1.33 and find the level of a particular instrument you wish to use nearest to, but still below, the new figure. Table 18.1 is a sample chart based on this rule of thumb.

Instruments that have been found particularly useful in mapping a child's profile of specific abilities are typically difficult tests that have not been based upon minimal competency criteria and that yield separate scores for verbal and mathematical reasoning (in addition to whatever else is being measured).

Instruments found to be particularly helpful in mapping a child's profile of developed skills, similar to the aptitude tests described above, are typically difficult tests that have not been based on minimal competency subject matter and that have relatively wide grade-level ranges (preferably three grade levels per level of the test). They also have well-documented item-topic classification tables that provide an appropriate degree of specificity for diagnosing those aspects of particular subjects that the highly able student already knows well and for determining where and at what level instruction should begin. These instruments also include a system of standard or converted scores that allow raw scores from any one of the forms and levels of the test to be interpreted relative to the series as a whole.

TABLE 18.1   Determining Levels for the Out-of-Level Test

Student's Typical Grade-Placement and Age		Level of Out-of-Level Test	
Grade	Age (years-months)	Grade-level	Age (years-months)
Kindergarten	5-2	1st-Spring	6-8
1st Grade	6-2	3rd-Fall	8-0
2nd Grade	7-2	4th Fall	9-4
3rd Grade	8-2	5th-Spring	10-8
4th Grade	9-2	7th-Fall	12-0
5th Grade	10-2	8th-Fall	13-4
6th Grade	11-2	9th-Spring	14-8
7th Grade	12-2	11th-Fall	16-0
8th Grade	13-2	12th-Fall	17-4
9th Grade	14-2	13th-Spring	18-8*
10th Grade	15-2	15th-Fall	20-0*
11th Grade	16-2	16th-Fall	21-4*
12th Grade	17-2	17th-Fall	22-8*

*Students in grades nine through twelve can use the Scholastic Aptitude Test (SAT) as a second-step screening instrument because it has plenty of "ceiling." That is, there are many difficult items and very few individuals can get all or most of them correct. The Graduate Record Examination might be administered to those students who do extremely well on the SAT. Note: 13th grade is the freshman year of college; 14th grade, the sophomore year; etc.

The Need for Practice

As mathematical and verbal reasoning tests are not usually administered to school children as a matter of course, youngsters who are to be given such tests as part of an identification procedure require some practice with them. The primary value of such practice is the reduction of test anxiety, familiarization with the types of items involved, and, of course, a maximization of the student's performance on the test. Most instruments include a set of practice items that can be reviewed well before the testing begins. It is advisable to administer a practice test under standard conditions that are as realistic as possible.

Special Needs Populations

Particularly with non-English-speaking children or with youngsters who come from situations that might inhibit verbal functioning (either because education is not highly valued by the family or because of other social or economic circumstances that create more pressing survival priorities), special identification procedures need to be followed to determine a child's areas of strength.

It is not unusual for such youngsters to score well on difficult tests of mathematical reasoning ability. If verbal tests are available in the youth's native language, they should be administered in exactly the same way they would be to English-speaking children. The *Comprehensive Tests of Basic Skills* (CTBS), published by McGraw-Hill, and the *Wechsler Adult Intelligence Scale* (WAIS), published by the Psychological Corporation, include Spanish editions. If such tests are not available, a nonverbal reasoning test, such as Raven's (1938) *Standard Progressive Matrices* or *Advanced Progressive Matrices*, published by H. K. Lewis and Company, London and distributed by the Psychological Corporation in the United States, or the *Differential Aptitude Test* (DAT) Abstract Reasoning Subtest, published by the Psychological Corporation, can be used.

Once the child's profile of mathematical, verbal (English or native language), and abstract reasoning abilities has been established, the next step in developing an Individualized Educational Plan (IEP) designed for English as the primary language would involve administering an English language achievement test at an appropriate level to chart language ability as precisely as possible. Instruction should begin at the level determined by this diagnostic test. In such instances, the youngster's abstract reasoning level might serve to aid the instructor in setting appropriate expectations for pacing the student through curriculum in language arts (mechanics of language and expression), composition, and conceiveably literature. Once English has been mastered, verbal reasoning ability should be reassessed and further advice concerning related course work in history, philosophy, and humanities should be based on this newly acquired information. If the youth is talented mathematically, he should be allowed to take appropriately challenging mathematics courses (and possibly even quantitative science courses), as they are often easy to understand because of the universality of their symbols, even if the youngster does not know English well.

A Word About Using Checklists

Criticism of tests based on alleged bias against minority youngsters has aroused interest by some in the use of checklists to identify gifted students (e.g., Renzulli and Hartman 1971). It is unfortunate that such devices were neither developed empirically nor validated properly, as they have become enormously popular. Checklists lack a standardized frame of reference. In addition, they frequently distill ratings over several presumed different categories of behavior into a single score. In so doing, they fail to provide sufficiently detailed information for realistic educational planning. The use of checklists is not recommended, unless they focus on specific behaviors in such a way as to avoid value judgments by those individuals completing them and unless they are accompanied by detailed information about their validity and reliability.

Assessing Creativity

"It has been argued . . . that creativity cannot be demonstrated before there is mastery of a discipline, and the ability to master a discipline is better measured by tests of aptitude and achievement than by tests of creativity" (Fox 1981, p. 1108).

Much of the controversy over the concept of creativity involves the question of the extent to which it is a personality trait, a specific cognitive ability, or a type of problem-solving strategy that might be learned (Michael 1977). If it is the latter, there is less need to search for those who know the process than to teach the process to everyone.

Recent and longstanding critiques of methods for assessing creativity and the effectiveness of creativity training programs suggest that evaluation of children in this area be postponed until more evidence supports their use (Mansfield, Busse, and Krepelka 1978; Cohn 1981).

CONSIDERATIONS IN EDUCATIONAL INTERVENTION

Important Educational Variables

Stanley (1980) and Cohn (1981) stressed the importance of addressing the core aspects of the educational process if effective educational intervention is to be achieved for highly able youths. The following five factors are identified as important educational variables: onset, content, style, pacing, and context.

Onset. Onset refers to the point in a student's educational development at which a desired educational alternative should be introduced. Typically, questions regarding the student's maturity and his profile of developed academic skills are crucial when making these decisions. Concerns about a youth's readiness for advanced-level course work in specific subject areas, early entrance to school or college, or a well-planned strategy of grade skips would fall under this category.

Content. Content, within the context of The Optimal Match Strategy, refers to the actual scope and sequence of educational objectives that characterize the curricula in subjects related to a youth's area(s) of outstanding capability. Degrees of difficulty of the course work, levels of advancement, texts and other materials, assessment tools, suggested avenues for exploration and application, and concern about articulation across educational levels within institutions (e.g., elementary and secondary) and across institutions (e.g., secondary and postsecondary), and the awarding of credit for accomplishments—all are issues that fall under the heading of content.

Style. Style refers to the manner in which instruction is provided to the student. Formal lectures, casual inquiry or discovery methods, and individualized diagnostic and prescriptive instruction represent several examples of style that can be implemented to achieve an appropriate match for individual students.

Pacing. Pacing refers to the speed with which a student passes through curriculum in subject matter relevant to areas of outstanding ability and well-developed skill. Pacing has been demonstrated as a crucial variable in the successful educational facilitation of highly able students, particularly in mathematics (Stanley, Keating, and Fox 1974; Keating 1976; Stanley, George, and Solano 1977; George, Cohn, and Stanley 1979; Cohn 1980; Stanley 1980; Benbow and Stanley 1982, 1983; Cohn and Cohn, in preparation), but also in the humanities (Cohn and Cohn, in preparation). The key to appropriate pacing is student supervision by the teacher, based upon continued monitoring of the student's acquisition of important skills as he advances through the scope and sequence of the curriculum. The pace must be individualized, but determined and maintained by the instructor, rather than by the student.

Context. Context refers to the setting in which instruction is to occur, as well as the level of administrative organization (e.g., classroom, school, district, region) from which students are to be drawn. Context can embrace a single classroom setting, in which the concern might be to individualize the students' progress in the mainstream. Context might also mean that students are invited to a special classroom from different classrooms within a particular school or from different schools within a school district. When educational alternatives are offered at a college or university or by a regional educational service center or a state department of education, students might be invited from across several school systems, counties, regions, states, and even from different countries. In some circumstances, moreover, educational options might be provided by paraeducational institutions such as museums, academies of arts and sciences, or professional schools. In such cases, the regions from which participants can be drawn are determined by the agency providing the special services. The family might also become part of the implementation plan, particularly for support in the form of encouragement and transportation, as well as financial and moral support.

Thinking about issues of context allows one the freedom to entertain possibilities for educational alternatives that extend considerably beyond the limits of the public or private school systems. School is viewed as only on of many places at which learning can occur. Important flexibility is thus added to the task of finding meaningful options to meet the individual needs of highly able children and youths.

The Optimal Match Strategy emphasizes that there is no one special way to meet the educational needs of all youths who are identified as academically gifted. Instead, a smorgasbord of educational alternatives is suggested, so that students and their families can choose those particular options they feel are most appropriate to their needs and within their own constraints (e.g., finances, commitments of family members to other activities, accessibility of transportation). The Optimal Match Strategy, moreover, contends that educational facilitation of gifted children and youths needs to involve all components of the fundamental educational structure (i.e., required subjects, elective subjects, and associated support services) in a comprehensive, integrated, and well-planned fashion.

A Smorgasbord of Educational Alternatives for Highly Able Youths

Two Caveats. Prior to listing and discussing the variety of educational options that a highly able youngster and his family and school officials might wish to consider, several caveats need to be mentioned. These warnings involve two possible solutions most frequently suggested by parents and counselors: private schools and self-paced study.

Private Schools. Although many private schools are noted for their high-level academic curricula, they may not be able to allow enough flexibility for very able individuals. It clearly depends upon the specific school. One possible advantage of some private institutions might be increased individual attention within the classroom setting, if the teacher/student ratio is close to one-to-ten. Another *possible* advantage might be increased ease in arranging a curriculum specifically keyed to the students' assessed abilities and developed skills. *Flexibility is the key.* If the school is willing to place a youth in specific subject-matter classes, regardless of age, it may be a good educational investment. All options should be investigated, however. The money that would be spent in sending a child to a private school might in fact be better invested in piecing together a patchwork of several different kinds of options in several different settings.

Self-Paced Study. The belief that self-paced instruction is especially desirable for the ablest students has seldom been borne out in fact. Appropriate pacing by a teacher, usually involving some modest degree of competition with other students at or near the same ability level, seems preferable. Students who have participated in various fast-paced mathematics classes have found that their actual competition is with national norms on standardized achievement tests, but they are motivated by knowing that they are completing as much material as a classmate whom they perceive to be at their ability level. Successful individually paced instruction usually has involved a mentor or teacher who set the pace on the basis of careful diagnosis with difficult standardized tests administered beyond-level. In the most typical case, the student meets at least weekly with his mentor so that he can ask questions that come up between meetings. The instructor goes over homework outside of class, carefully annotating feedback on important points or misunderstood items. Instructional time is spent on going over new material and in dialogue.

It is not very often that secondary-age (and in many cases even college-age) students have the self-discipline to pace themselves through an entire course without regular encouragement and feedback from an outside source. For this reason even highly able youths usually fail to complete correspondence courses, although in some extremely rural settings such options might be the only context for appropriate educational facilitation of highly able youngsters.

The Smorgasbord. The options included in the following *smorgasbord* of educational alternatives for highly able students range from mild deviations from typical educational procedures to rather radical ones, such as leap-frogging as many as four or five grades or entering college full-time as much as three to five years earlier than usual. The central issue is the determination of a match between the appropriate educational alternatives and a youth's assessed educational needs.

Some options can be integrated into the regular classroom by a motivated and well-educated teacher. Such alternatives might be identified as "enrichment" strategies. Other options involve having a youngster move ahead of his more typical age-mates to attend a specific subject at a higher grade-level, or even to skip one or more grades entirely. These options might be identified as "accelerative" strategies.

Enrichment Strategies

More Complex Problem-Solving in the Regular Classroom. Students who qualify for the second step of the identification procedure but who earn chance scores or below on the actual beyond-level test are likely to benefit from course work still designed for their age level that also includes more complex ideas and problems. Such modification of the school curriculum effects a class that is much more challenging than a minimal competency-based classroom would provide.

Exploration. Two kinds of exploratory enrichment strategies are recommended. The first involves introducing youths to a variety of subjects they might be interested in pursuing at an advanced level later in their educational careers. For example, many seventh graders who are extremely talented mathematically and verbally might benefit from an introductory college-level psychology or anthropology course. The problem for these students is that they know neither what psychology or anthropology is nor what psychologists or anthropologists do. An appropriate enrichment experience might focus on a "guided tour" through such advanced-level possibilities to facilitate wise future selections.

For students in junior high school and beyond, and in some cases for younger students, career exploration is an extremely important enrichment strategy. Learning about a wide variety of careers and the attendant educational prerequisites and associated lifestyles seems to stimulate the student's involvement in the educational process by providing the possibility of long-range goals.

Role Modeling. Particularly for students in groups that are underrepresented in certain talent areas (e.g., mathematically gifted girls and verbally gifted minority students), role models can be tremendously important. Seeing a successful female mathematician or scientist who also has a family might help a young mathematically gifted girl overcome the persistent advice from virtually all corners of her life to avoid developing her outstanding abilities (Fox 1977; Fox, Brody, and Tobin 1980).

Study Skills Training. Students who have never been asked to complete substantial amounts of meaningful homework often find themselves underskilled when suddenly faced with the demand for good study skills and homework habits. For direct instruction in these academic survival skills to succeed, there must be homework assigned that is both challenging and possible to accomplish. Study skills have been identified by The College Board's Education Equality Project (College Board 1981) as extremely important in preparing youths to do well in college or university course work.

Four areas of training have been found to be particularly helpful for students who are embarking upon more strenuous academic pursuits: reading with a purpose of extracting information; taking notes; managing homework time effectively; and maximizing test performance (Cohn and Cohn, in preparation).

Communication Skills Training. "Immaturity" is most often cited as a reason for refusing to allow a child to move ahead of his age mates. In some instances immaturity means that the youngster is not as gregarious as his contemporaries. Ironically, some highly able youths, particularly those whose talent lies in mathematical reasoning ability, are characteristically stable introverts. That is, they tend to form close bonds with a few individuals and appear shy or withdrawn at parties or in large group activities.

Considerable evidence to date suggests that allowing such youngsters the prerogative to move ahead helps them not only academically but also socially (George, Cohn, and Stanley 1979; Benbow and Stanley 1983). It appears that positive experiences communicating ideas of shared importance with other individuals of any age help highly able youths to develop a sense of social mobility. They come to realize they don't always have to be the same person, using the same manner to respond to all social situations.

For those youths who are concerned about their social development and who wish some direct instruction in rather basic social skills, a communication skills workshop has demonstrated some value (Cohn and Finlay 1982; Cohn and Cohn, in preparation). The workshop focuses upon learned behaviors that tend to stimulate social effectiveness. Emphasis is placed on developing interpersonal skills, understanding small groups (including the family as a small group), and developing large-group skills.

Counseling for Educational Planning. For many highly able youths, passage through the educational system is a mysterious journey through a labyrinth of unknowns. They are well served by a systematic presentation of the structure of the elementary, secondary, and postsecondary curricula that shows key prerequisites for additional advanced educational opportunities. Once students realize that proceeding along the precalculus mathematics sequence through second-year algebra, for example, might allow them to take Advanced Placement Physics (Level B) regardless of how old they are, they have access to a powerful intrinsic motivating force—their own interests (Cohn 1980).

It is never too early for a youngster and his family to assume increased responsibility for educational planning (Benbow 1978). Gathering information about oneself, learning how to interpret such information, and learning about educational alternatives that such information might lead one to consider are all valuable activities for the highly able student.

Community Opportunities. Schools are not the only places for students to find challenging educational experiences. Many outstanding academic offerings are provided by local universities and colleges, museums, libraries, and local interest groups after school, during the summer, and on weekends (Hyman 1981).

Accelerative Strategies

People develop specific abilities at different rates. The typical school curriculum is designed to meet the needs of a youngster with average abilities. If a student's ability level in a specific talent area is highly developed, starting a course sequence related to that talent area might be a stimulating alternative. Mathematically talented youths might wish to complete the computation sequence as rapidly as possible and enter the precalculus mathematics sequence as soon as they have garnered the requisite skills. Similarly, verbally talented youngsters might want to start foreign language sequences or social studies earlier than usual.

Individuals differ in their rates of learning new material well. The usual school curriculum is paced so that a person of average ability can comprehend, remember, and use the skills being taught. If a student's ability is highly developed and he is very motivated and interested in a related subject area, he may want to investigate the possibility of compacting a sequence of relevant courses. It is not unusual, for example, for such a youth to complete a typical year or more of mathematics or foreign language study within a special five-week rigorous summer program (Cohn and Cohn, in preparation).

Sometimes schools are not able to provide special options. Under such circumstances a mentor might be able to work with one or several students to cover the material as expeditiously as possible. Negotiations with the school should be pursued so that the students can be excused from their regular class period to work on the more advanced homework. It is important to work with school officials to arrange credit for the material covered by testing the students with standardized achievement test for proficiency in the specific subject and by having the mentor communicate often with the appropriate school personnel.

Choosing an appropriate mentor is crucial. One should look for an individual with great depth and breadth in the subject as well as interest and skill in working with highly able youths. Often such individuals can be found at nearby colleges and universities. Many advanced undergraduate and graduate students have the necessary training and interest, as do retired teachers, professors, engineers, and the like.

The problem of finding appropriately challenging subject matter can be solved by having the student take a course at a nearby college or university while he remains in secondary school for other course work. Since 1976 many institutions of higher learning have established a special student status for able and ambitious youths who are younger than the typical college entrant. Starting a course sequence early or compacting a course sequence may be an even more feasible option at a college or university. An SAT score that equals or exceeds that of the average college-bound high school senior suggests that an underage student could likely succeed at an introductory college-level course in a related subject. In the past, able seventh- through tenth-grade students have successfully taken courses in astronomy, chemistry, German, precalculus, calculus, computer science, expository writing, and psychology. Highly able and eager students should also be encouraged to seek out challenging, high-level courses in all areas of study. They may wish to consider, for example, such courses as Latin, Greek, philosophy, psychology, history of the Far East, drama, fine arts, voice, and many others.

The College Board Advanced Placement courses, which prepare a student for AP tests in specific subjects, are usually the highest level courses offered in high school. In an AP course students have the opportunity to study college-level material while still in high school, and if they take the respective AP examination and do well on it, they can earn advanced standing college credits for this work.

AP examinations are currently offered in more than twenty different subjects, including computer science, music theory, and studio art. Examinations in each of these areas are offered each May. High schools differ in the number and quality of AP courses that they offer. In cases where a high school does not offer an AP course that is of interest to a particular student or fails to complete all the topics suggested by the AP course syllabus, the youth can earn AP credits on his own.

In many states students who demonstrate the prerequisite skills are allowed to enter kindergarten or first grade early. Early entrance requires documented evidence of the child's advanced abilities and developed skills. Performance on standardized tests and systematic information about the child's behaviors from the parents appear equally important (Roedell, Jackson, and Robinson 1980).

Skipping one or more grades is perhaps the most controversial alternative among the variety of options open to highly able and eager youths at present. A grade skip is *not* appropriate for all gifted youngsters and there are many important factors to consider. The four most important are the student's level of ability in both mathematical and verbal reasoning, the level of skill development in curricula related to each area, the youngster's eagerness to move ahead more rapidly than usual, and the parents' support. Often it is necessary to educate both parents and the child as to why this option might be an appropriate one to consider.

A student who has mathematical and verbal reasoning abilities and skills two to five grade levels above his grade placement would be a good candidate to skip a grade if he is eager to move into more challenging material in all areas. The student with either mathematical or verbal ability and skills significantly above grade level might be better advised to seek advanced course work in the area of strength while remaining in the typical grade level.

Grade skips need to be planned strategically to avoid possible pitfalls. There are ways to take advantage of natural breaks in the schooling process when a grade skip is being considered. One such break involves moving to a new school or school district; another, moving into a new phase of schooling (such as from elementary to middle school or junior high, from junior high to high school, or from high school to college). In each of these cases a youngster enters a new situation in which he will need to go through the process of making new friends regardless of the fact that a grade has been skipped. Often this type of strategic grade skipping lessens the potential for negative social impact by not drawing attention to the atypical advancement.

Educators and others have been overly cautious in using this technique to meet the needs of academically talented youths. Arguments that are used against grade skipping often pertain to the social and emotional maladjustment that is imagined to accompany it. Studies have shown that skipping a grade (or entering kindergarten, first grade, or college early) is *not* socially or emotionally harmful. The youngsters who were advanced were at least as well adjusted as those at the typical age-grade placement (Daurio 1979). It appears that the support of the family plays an extremely important role in fostering a youngster's social and emotional adjustment whether or not he skips a grade.

Some colleges and universities permit highly able and well-prepared underage students to enter as full-time college students (Stanley, in press; Cohn and Cohn, in preparation). In some circumstances, the student's high school automatically awards a high school diploma upon the successful completion of the first year of college. Several institutions across the country offer undergraduate students the opportunity to earn masters degrees or other advanced degrees while they are earning their baccalaureate degree. In most cases the time period required to complete both degrees is less than it would be if each degree program were pursued sequentially.

CASE STUDIES

In 1979 the author and his wife, Catherine M. G. Cohn, initiated the Project for the Study of Academic Precocity (PSAP) at Arizona State University (now known as the Center for Academic Precocity, or CAP). Part of the project included Individual Assessment Services, which provide educational counseling to families to help them design educational plans for their highly able children. The authors' five years of experience have provided hundreds of case studies of these exceptional youths demonstrating the limits of possibility. We present two case studies to represent different ages and options selected by very able youngsters and their families. The circumstances described are real; the names have been changed to protect the subjects' privacy.

Case #1

Edie first contacted PSAP in the fall of her tenth-grade year. She was 14 years old and was doing very well in school, but felt that she was not developing the kinds of skills that she would need to attend and do well at a major university. At the recommendation of the PSAP staff, she took the Scholastic Aptitude Test (SAT) the following spring. At age 15 years, 8 months, Edie earned 730 on the mathematics section of the SAT, 640 on the verbal section, and 60+ on the Test of Standard Written English (TSWE). Having taken the precalculus mathematics sequence through second-year algebra upon completion of the tenth grade in her regular school, she decided that during the subsequent summer she would take college algebra and trigonometry and introductory calculus at Arizona State University. She earned the highest grades in both classes.

When it came time to plan her eleventh-grade program, she expressed the desire to continue mathematics at the college level and take her regular high school courses in other subjects. The scheduling problem this option presented could not be overcome, so she decided to consider full-time early entrance to college. While Arizona State University was not her ultimate college goal, it would provide a richer educational environment than her high school could, even though it was recognized as one of the best in the state. The proximity of the university to her home and her family's unwillingness to see her leave home at barely 16 years of age all made Arizona State University an ideal choice for Edie's first college experience.

Edie entered Arizona State University full-time majoring in mathematics in what would have been her junior year of high school. Requesting overload schedules (more than eighteen credits per semester) in difficult subjects (science courses for science and mathematics majors), Edie completed five semesters of course work in four semesters. During that time she sang in the college chorus and was hired by a local symphony choral group and by several local dinner theaters as their professional piano accompanist. During the academic year she also worked as a staff member of PSAP. Serving as an instructor and residential aide during the summer classes offered by PSAP for highly able youngsters filled out part of her summers.

At age 17, Edie transferred to a prestigious private university with substantial financial support as an entering junior. All of the credits she had earned at Arizona State University were accepted by her new university. Her outstanding academic and personal career continued to flourish there. Three years later, Edie graduated from this major university with a B.S. degree in mathematical sciences and a masters degree in operations research.

Case #2

His parents brought Jimmy to PSAP when he was 6 years old. At age 5 he had scored 170 on the Stanford-Binet Intelligence Test, and his first-grade teacher was worried that he already knew most of what she was teaching her other students. She felt that he should not be allowed to skip a grade, however, because his penmanship was quite poor. Jimmy's mother was uncertain as to what was best for him and sought advice.

Jimmy was administered a series of ability and achievement tests designed for older students. His performance of 38 out of 60 on the Raven's Standard Progressive Matrices (the score earned by the average 12-year-old) corroborated his outstanding performance on the Stanford-Binet. His scores on the School and College Ability Test (SCAT) showed him performing mathematically like an end-of-year fourth grader and verbally like a mid-year fifth grader (on tests designed for fourth and fifth graders). The Sequential Tests of Educational Progress (STEP), Series II, were then administered in four areas: reading comprehension, writing skills, math computation, and math concepts. In each area of skill Jimmy functioned consistently like end-of-year fourth graders on achievement tests designed for fourth and fifth graders. A detailed description of Jimmy's developed skills, based on the topical organization of the achievement tests, was provided to his parents and school teachers. Based on this information, he was placed in a combination second–third-grade classroom, and his parents found a tutor for him to help improve his handwriting.

By the end of the school year Jimmy received the highest marks possible in penmanship and had been scheduled to enter fourth grade the following fall. He continued to play soccer in an outside-of-school league and got along well with his classmates and with friends more his own age in soccer practice. His academic performance was outstanding and even included first-place prizes for poetry contests in the entire school system. He asked to attend special mathematics classes that would allow him to move through arithmetic at a pace and depth more to his ability. Arrangements were made to allow him to take a special fast-paced math class with other mathematically talented youngsters at PSAP in place of his regular math class. Since this math class met only once a week, he worked on his homework from that class in the library or at the back of the room instead of going to his regular arithmetic class.

As a result of the assessment and subsequent intervention, Jimmy's mother reported that Jimmy appeared happier, performed well in school, and had many more friends than he used to have.

SUMMARY

This chapter has emphasized practical approaches to finding academically talented young people, assessing their areas of strength and relative weakness, and helping them develop educationally and personally. The strategies that are described take into account both quantitative measures of intellect and intrinsic levels of motivation and interest (Stanley 1977; Cohn 1979). They represent the most sophisticated psychometric techniques available and offer a means of distinguishing individuals at all levels of giftedness and of ensuring that participants who draw upon program resources are committed to developing their abilities. A sequence of tests becomes a set of small multiple hurdles; at each step young people have the option of deciding whether or not to proceed.

Information about an individual's profile of specific abilities gathered by the assessment procedures is then applied to the problem of designing an appropriate educational plan. Key educational variables, such as onset, content, style, pacing, and context, are manipulated to create an Optimal Match. Examples of moderate to radical educational options range from providing individualized instruction within the mainstream classroom to skipping one or more school grades or entering school or college earlier than usual.

REFERENCES

A Nation at Risk (1983). Government report by the Congressional Commission on the Study of Excellence in Education. Washington, D.C.: United States Government Printing Office.

Alvino, J., McDonnel, R. C., and Richert, S. (1981). National survey of identification practices in gifted and talented education. *Exceptional Children* 48:124–32.

Benbow, C. P. (1978). Prepare now for APP examinations. *Intellectually Talented Youth Bulletin (ITYB)* 4(5):1.

———, and Stanley, J. C. (1980). Sex differences in mathematical reasoning ability: Fact or artifact? *Science* 210:4475.

———, and Stanley, J. C. (1982). Consequences in high school and college of sex differences in mathematical reasoning ability. *American Educational Research Journal* 19:598–622.

———, and Stanley, J. C. (Eds.). (1983). *Academic Precocity*. Baltimore: Johns Hopkins University Press.

Cohn, C. M. G. (1974). *Effectiveness of Creativity Training: A Research Synthesis*. Unpublished doctoral dissertation, Arizona State University.

Cohn, S. J. (1977a). Changing teachers' attitudes and behaviors toward the gifted student. *Talents and Gifts* 19(4):23–26.

———. (1977b). Cognitive characteristics of the top-scoring participants in SMPY's 1976 talent search. *Intellectually Talented Youth Bulletin* 3(10):3–6.

———. (1979). Searching for scientifically talented youth? Look for the able, curious, and committed. *Science and Children* 17(2):18–19.

———. (1980). *Two Components of the Study of Mathematically Precocious Youth's (SMPY) Intervention Studies of Educational Acceleration*. Unpublished doctoral dissertation, The Johns Hopkins University.

———. (1981). What is giftedness? A multidimensional approach. In A. H. Kramer (Ed.). *Gifted Children: Challenging Their Potential (New Perspectives and Alternatives)*. New York: Trillium Press, pp. 33–45.

———, and Cohn, C. M. G. (1986). Taking the SAT early and often: A study of growth in mathematical and verbal reasoning among academic Talent Search participants. Unpublished report prepared for the College Board, New York, N.Y.

———, and Cohn, C. M. G. (in preparation). The Optimal Match Strategy for Educating Gifted Children: Results from a Five-year Research Program Conducted by the Project for the Study of Academic Precocity (PSAP) at Arizona State University.

———, and Finlay, P. M. (1982). Preventive and interventive strategies for counseling intellectually gifted students. Paper presented at the Sixth Annual Conference on Severe Behavior Disorders sponsored by Teacher Educators of Children with Severe Behavior Disorders, Tempe, Arizona, November.

College Board. (1981). *Project Equality.* Princeton: The College Board.

Cox, C. M. (1926). The early mental traits of three hundred geniuses. *Genetic Studies of Genius,* Vol. 2. Stanford: Stanford University Press.

Daurio, S. P. (1979). Educational enrichment versus acceleration: A review of the literature. In W. C. George, S. J. Cohn, and J. C. Stanley (Eds.). *Educating the Gifted: Acceleration and Enrichment.* Baltimore: Johns Hopkins University Press.

Eysenck, H. J. (1979). *The Structure and Measurement of Intelligence.* New York: Springer.

Fox, L. H. (1977). Changing behaviors and attitudes of gifted girls. *Talents and Gifts* 19(4):13–15, 21–22.

———. (1981). Identification of the academically gifted. *American Psychologist* 36:1103–11.

———, Brody, L. E., and Tobin, D. H. (Eds.). (1980). *Women and the Mathematical Mystique.* Baltimore: Johns Hopkins University Press.

George, W. C. (1977). Discussions of barriers to education of the gifted: Attitudes and behaviors. *Talents and Gifts* 19(4):2–4.

———. (1979). The talent-search concept: An identification strategy for the intellectually gifted. *Journal of Special Education* 13:221–37.

———, Cohn, S. J., and Stanley, J. C. (Eds.). (1979). *Educating the Gifted: Acceleration and Enrichment.* Baltimore: Johns Hopkins University Press.

———, and Solano, C. H. (1976). Identifying mathematical talent on a statewide basis. In D. P. Keating (Ed.). *Intellectual Talent: Research and Development.* Baltimore: Johns Hopkins University Press, pp. 55–89.

Hollingworth, L. S. (1929). *Gifted Children: Their Nature and Nurture.* New York: Macmillan.

———. (1942). *Children Above 180 IQ. Stanford-Binet: Origin and Development.* New York: World Book.

Hyman, M. (1981). Science museums and gifted students. *Museum News* 59(7):32–38.

Keating, D. P. (1975). Testing those in the top percentiles. *Exceptional Children* 41:435–36.

———. (Ed.). (1976). *Intellectual Talent: Research and Development.* Baltimore: Johns Hopkins University Press.

Lehman, H. C. (1953). *Age and Achievement.* Princeton: Princeton University Press.

Lerner, B. (1982). American education: How are we doing? *Public Interest* 69:59–82.

Mansfield, R. S., Busse, T. V., and Krepelka, E. J. (1978). The effectiveness of creativity training. *Review of Educational Research* 48:517–36.

Michael, W. B. (1977). Cognitive and affective components of creativity in mathematics and the physical sciences. In J. C. Stanley, W. C. George, and C. H. Solano (Eds.). *The Gifted and Creative: A Fifty-Year Perspective.* Baltimore: Johns Hopkins University Press, pp. 141–72.

Pyryt, M. C. (1977). Value congruity between gifted students and their parents. *Talents and Gifts* 19(4):9–12.

Raven, J. C. (1938). *Standard Progressive Matrices.* London: H. K. Lewis.

Renzulli, J. S., and Hartman, R. K. (1971). Scale for rating behavior characteristics of superior students. *Exceptional Children* 38:243–48.

Resnick, D. P., and Resnick, L. B. (1985). Standards, curriculum, and performance: A historical and comparative perspective. *Educational Researcher* 14(4):5–20.

Robinson, N. M., and Robinson, H. B. (1982). The Optimal Match: Devising the best compromise for the highly gifted student. In D. Feldman (Ed.). *New Directions for Child Development: Developmental Approaches to Giftedness and Creativity.* San Francisco: Jossey-Bass, pp. 79–94.

Roedell, W. C., Jackson, N. E., and Robinson, H. B. (1980). *Gifted Young Children.* New York: Teachers College Press.

Sears, P. S. (1977). Sources of life satisfactions of the Terman gifted men. *American Psychologist* 32:119–28.

———. (1979). The Terman genetic studies of genius, 1922–1972. In A. H. Passow (Ed.). *The Gifted and the Talented: Their Education and Development,* Seventy-Eighth Yearbook of the National Society for the Study of Education (NSSE), Part I. Chicago: University of Chicago Press, pp. 75–96.

———, and Barbee, A. H. (1977). Career and life satisfactions among Terman's gifted women. In J. C. Stanley, W. C. George, and C. H. Solano (Eds.). *The Gifted and Creative: A Fifty-Year Perspective.* Baltimore: Johns Hopkins University Press, pp. 28–65.

———. (1977). Teacher and pupil stereotypes of gifted boys and girls. *Talents and Gifts* 19(4):4–8.

Solano, C. H. (1977). Teacher and pupil stereotypes of gifted boys and girls. *Talents and Gifts* 19(4):4–8.

———. (1979). The first D: Discovery of talent, or needles in a haystack: Identifying the mathematically gifted child. In N. R. Colangelo and R. T. Zaffrann (Eds.). *New Voices in Counseling the Gifted.* Dubuque, Iowa: Kendall/Hunt, pp. 89–106.

———. (1976a). Concern for intellectually talented youths: How it originated and fluctuated. *Journal of Clinical Child Psychology* 5(3):38–42.

———. (1976b). Tests are better finders of great math talent than teachers are. *American Psychologist* 31:313–14.

———. (1977). The predictive value of the SAT for brilliant seventh and eighth graders. *The College Board Review* 106:2–7.

———. (1978). Educational nonacceleration: An international tragedy. *Gifted/Talented/Creative* 1(3):2–5, 53–57, 60–64.

———. (1980). Manipulate important educational variables. *Educational Psychologist* 15:164–71.

————. (In press). Young entrants to college: How did they fare? *College and University*.

Stanley, J. C., George, W. C., and Solano, C. (Eds.). (1977). *The Gifted and the Creative: A Fifty-Year Perspective*. Baltimore: Johns Hopkins University Press.

————. (1978). *Educational Programs and Intellectual Prodigies*. Baltimore: The Study of Mathematically Precocious Youth, Johns Hopkins University.

Stanley, J. C., Keating, D. P., and Fox, L. H. (Eds.). (1974). *Mathematical Talent: Discovery, Description, and Development*. Baltimore: Johns Hopkins University Press.

Terman, L. M. (1916). *The Measurement of Intelligence*. Boston: Houghton Mifflin.

————. (1925). Mental and physical traits of a thousand gifted children. *Genetic Studies of Genius*, Vol. 1. Stanford: Stanford University Press.

————. (1954). The discovery and encouragement of exceptional talent. *American Psychologist* 9:221–30.

VI

Assessment at the Pediatric Neurology-Psychiatry Interface

19

PEDIATRIC NEUROLOGICAL EVALUATION

Walter J. Molofsky and Arnold P. Gold

Boundaries between the disciplines of pediatric neurology and psychiatry are sufficiently indistinct so that often the child specialist in either field evaluates children with similar complaints. Headaches, learning disabilities, hemiparesis or even a behavioral problem may be organic or psychogenic in etiology and, not uncommonly, may have features of both. For example, the child psychiatrist may be asked to evaluate a stress-induced headache where the initial triggering factor was a vascular headache. Similarly, a behavioral problem may present that is secondary to a specific learning disability in a neurologically impaired child. As the child neurologist should be comfortable with various psychiatric techniques, the child psychiatrist, in like manner, should be knowledgeable about the changes in the developing nervous system and should be competent to perform a complete neurologic examination in all ages.

The "hands-off" approach that precludes psychiatrists from physically examining the adult may be a disservice or even catastrophic to the child patient. Regardless of psychodynamics, the child with disabling headaches, for example, has the right to a funduscopic examination. The relationship among psychiatrist, child, and parent will only be enhanced by the thoroughness of an evaluation that includes a neurologic examination. Furthermore, the knowledge that the psychiatrist is a "thorough" physician rather than only a "talking doctor" or a "shrink" may serve to help quiet parental anxiety regarding the etiology of a problem.

The developing nervous system results in an orderly acquisition of developmental milestones that primarily involve locomotion, prehension, language, and social behavior. Recognition and understanding of these changes are essential to the concept of "normality." For example, an extensor plantar response may be normal in a 2- or 3-month-old infant but would be abnormal in a 2 to 3-year-old child. The "soft neurologic signs" observed in older children are often the results of delays or even arrests in this normal progression. Physicians should be aware, however, that there is significant variability in development, not uncommonly genetic in origin, which may result in a nonpathological maturational lag.

The goal of the neurologic examination is to determine whether there is abnormality in function, and then, if that condition is determined, to localize the lesion to one or more areas of the nervous system. This localization is of primary importance in arriving at a correct etiological diagnosis. Neurological disorders have a predilection for specific areas of the nervous system that allow specific delineation.

A differential diagnosis should be possible after obtaining the history and completing the physical examination. Localization of the problem to one area of the nervous system determines the development of a differential diagnosis. Thus, a child with a gait abnormality could have a lesion of the cortex, basal ganglia, spinal cord, peripheral nerve, or muscle. Prior to defining the type of lesion, the physician must determine the site of pathology.

Psychological stress factors and the possibility of a somatizing disorder should be considered as possible etiologic factors in cases of apparently undiagnosable physical illness. In general, however, organic disorders are considered before psychogenic conditions. Psychiatrists often evaluate children with similar problems as a neurologist, and alertness to certain features in the history and the physical examination may strongly suggest an organic etiology. The association of focal neurological findings in temporal relationship to the presenting complaints would strongly suggest organicity. Common problems that may present to both psychiatrists and neurologists include developmental delay, headache, motor disturbances, mood abnormalities, and sleep disorders.

Neurological diagnosis is dependent on the evaluation of the patient's history, the performance of a neurological examination, and the utilization of appropriate diagnostic procedures. Most textbooks, even pediatric textbooks, describe primarily examination techniques for the adult. However, the pediatric neurological evaluation significantly differs from that of the adult in two ways: (1) the developing nervous system results in a continual change in neurological status so that what is normal at one age would be abnormal at a later age; (2) many factors unrelated to the neurological status of the child may seriously affect the results of the examination, such as age, verbal ability, fatigue, hunger, intercurrent illness, and cooperation. This chapter will emphasize methods that are useful in the neurological evaluation of the infant and child and will provide an approach to evaluation of some common complaints.

PEDIATRIC NEUROLOGICAL EXAMINATION

History

A detailed history is the single most important aspect of the neurological evaluation, and diagnosis can often be made by history alone. It should include a chronology of development, past medical history, and family history. When possible, the current problem's history should be obtained from the child as well as the parent. It is surprising how often even children three to four years of age can give uninhibited accounts of their problems. This information should then be supplemented by the parent's detailed history.

Table 19.1 lists the major areas of inquiry covered in the neurological history. While it is important to discuss these matters with the family, it is often more informative to gather this data via a questionnaire filled out prior to the office visit (Table 19.2).

All symptoms and abnormalities should be characterized in terms of their age of onset, severity, and evolution. The neurological review of systems should cover both previous and current levels of function. Table 19.3 lists early developmental milestones that should be reviewed. This detailed historical examination requests information on abilities that may not be demonstrated during the examination.

A detailed family history, and at times examination of the parents, may provide valuable information as to many neuropsychiatric disorders, such as tuberous sclerosis, neurofibromatous, Sturge-Weber-Dimitri and dystonia.

Physical Examination

The goal of the examination is to evaluate the child's level of function according to his chronological age and determine whether there is evidence of neurological dysfunction. Table 19.4 includes an outline of the neurological examination. This includes systematic evaluation of the following areas: mental status, cranial nerves,

TABLE 19.1 Neurological History—Outline

1) Chief complaint
2) Prenatal course
3) Neonatal course
4) Pattern of growth and development:
      Motor
      Speech
      Fine Motor
      Adaptive
5) Past medical history:
      Medicines
      Allergies
      Immunizations
      Hospitalizations
      Surgery
6) Behavioral history
7) School history
8) Family history
9) Review of systems; general
10) Review of systems; neurologic (historical examination)
11) Chronology of present illness

TABLE 19.2   Answer the Following to the Best of Your Ability with Regard to Your Child

1. *PREGNANCY:*
   _____ a) Duration of pregnancy
   _____ b) Complications of pregnancy
   _____ c) Medications during pregnancy
   _____ d) Type of labor: Spontaneous   Induced
   _____ e) Duration of labor
   _____ f) Type of delivery and/or complications
   _____ g) Birth weight
   _____ h) Apgar score
   _____ i) Complications or problems in the newborn period
         Suck
         Vomiting
         Infection
         Jaundice: Level of Bilirubin, if known
         RH factor; transfusion
         Incubator care; no. of days in nursery
         Convulsions
         Cry
         Respiratory distress
         Mucous accumulation
         Other

2. *DEVELOPMENTAL MILESTONES:* (answer when pertinent)
   (Write in age at which your child accomplished the following)
   MOTOR:
   _____ a) Dominant handedness (state whether right, left, or both)
   _____ b) Head control   _____ g) Walked unassisted
   _____ c) Turned over   _____ h) Tricycle
   _____ d) Sat alone   _____ i) Bicycle
   _____ e) Crawled   _____ j) Special shoes or braces
   _____ f) Stood alone unassisted   _____ k) Any physical or occupational therapy
   SPEECH:
         a) Difficulty with: drooling, chewing, swallowing
         Write in age at which time your child accomplished the following:
   _____ b) Spoke first words (other than ma-ma and da-da)
   _____ c) Spoke first phrase
   _____ d) Spoke in complete sentences
   _____ e) Is speech adequate for age? Articulation; Content:
   _____ f) Speech therapy, if any

3. *COMPREHENSION OR UNDERSTANDING:*
   a) Do you consider your child to understand directions and situations as well as other children his age? If no, why?

4. *TOILET TRAINING:*
   _____ a) At what age was the child toilet trained for day; for night
   _____ b) Problems

5. *COORDINATION:*
   Rate your child on the following skills:

	GOOD	AVERAGE	POOR
Walking			
Running			
Handwriting			
Catching			
Throwing			
Shoelace tying			

Buttoning
Athletic abilities
At what age did your child accomplish the following:
_____ a) Buttons own clothes
_____ b) Ties his own shoelaces

6. *SCHOOL:*
Rate your child with regard to school experiences, learning adjustment in school:

	GOOD	AVERAGE	POOR
a) Nursery school			
b) Kindergarten			
c) Current grade			

What is your child's current school grade placement? _____
Describe any school problems.
Note kinds of special therapy or remedial work the patient is currently receiving.

7. *PAST MEDICAL HISTORY:*
If your child's history includes any of the following illnesses, please write in the age when the illness occurred and any other information regarding the illness:
_____ a) Epilepsy or convulsions
_____ b) Accidents, falls, trauma (type and age)
_____ c) Hernia
_____ d) Visual or eye problems
_____ e) Childhood diseases (type and age)
_____ f) Allergies (type and age)
_____ g) Serious medical illnesses and operations (type and age)

8. *BEHAVIOR:*
Please check any of the following that apply to your child's behavior:

Hyperactive	Low frustration threshold
Poor attention span	Temper outbursts
Impulsiveness	Aggressiveness
Distractibility	Does not play well with peers
Cries easily	Sibling rivalry
Underactive	Multiple fears
Behavioral problems: Home/School	Other

HABITS:

Movements	Thumbsucking
Nailbiting	Headbanging
Masturbation	Other
Psychotherapy	

9. *FAMILY HISTORY—MOTHER:*
_____ a) Age
_____ b) Age at pregnancy with patient
_____ c) Spontaneous abortions or miscarriages
_____ d) Occupation
_____ e) Highest grade completed in school
_____ f) School problems:
      1. Learning
      2) Speech
      3) Behavior
_____ g) Medical problems, neurologic disease
_____ h) Note if any family members (not including siblings of the patient) are reported to have any of the following areas of difficulty:
      1) Learning problems
      2) Speech problems
      3) Serious illness

TABLE 19.2 *(continued)*

9. *FAMILY HISTORY—FATHER*
   _____ a) Age
   _____ b) Occupation
   _____ c) Highest grade completed in school
   _____ d) School problems:
       1) Learning
       2) Speech
       3) Behavior
   _____ e) Medical problems, neurologic disease
   _____ f) Note if any family members (not including siblings of the patient) are reported to have any
       of the following areas of difficulty:
       1) Learning problems
       2) Speech problems
       3) Serious illness
10. *SIBLINGS:* (other children)
        NAME   *AGE*   *MEDICAL, SOCIAL, OR ACADEMIC PROBLEMS*
    1.
    2.
    3.
    4.
    5.

sensory functions, coordinative skills, motor system, deep tendon reflexes, and elicitation of abnormal reflexes or signs. Evaluating the child's psychomotor development is an important aspect of pediatric neurological evaluation. Performing a systematic examination such as the Denver Development Screen helps establish the child's level of development. Familiarization with the milestones makes possible a thorough developmental evaluation in a short time period.

Flexibility and patience are the keys to performing a thorough and complete evaluation. It is preferable to allow the child to direct the order of the examination. Careful observation of the child at play or while interacting with the mother provides important details of the child's abilities and level of function. This can supply information more valuable than isolated examination of individual aspects of the nervous system.

Cranial Nerves Examination

Assessment of cranial nerve function can be ascertained by careful inspection of the infant or child while in the mother's arms. This obviates the need to touch or examine the child, which avoids inducement of crying or fear reactions.

The first cranial nerve, or olfactory nerve, is very difficult to test clinically. The usefulness of this information is generally limited so it is often omitted. Parents can be questioned about the child's ability to discriminate odors at home. Various substances, such as coffee, peppermint, toothpaste, banana, and other familiar sub-

TABLE 19.3   Developmental Milestones

ORAL AND OCULAR REFLEXES

	Age of Appearance	Age of Disappearance
Rooting	Birth	1 year
Lip and sucking	Birth	1 year
Swallowing	Birth	Persists
Lateral gaze	Birth	Persists
Upward gaze	3 months	Persists

DEVELOPMENT OF HAND SKILLS

Birth	Fists
3 months	Opens hands
4 months	Midline play
6 months	Reaches
7 months	Transfers
12 months	Pincer grasp
5 years	Rigid tripod pencil grip
8 years	Dynamic tripod pencil grip

DEVELOPMENT OF WALKING

Birth–1 month	Lifts head prone
3 months	Head control supine
5 months	Turns over
8 months	Sits without support
10 months	Crawls and stands
15 months	Walks alone
3½ years	Tricycle
6 years	Bicycle

DEVELOPMENT OF BEHAVIOR

1–2 months	Smiles
4 months	Expresses displeasure
6 months	Recognizes parents
8 months	Responds to "no"
10 months	"Patty-cake" and "Bye-Bye"
12 months	Understands names of objects
15 months	Imitates and requests by pointing
18 months	Follows simple commands
2 Years	Organized play and body parts

DEVELOPMENT OF LANGUAGE

Birth	Cries
4 months	Sounds of pleasure
5 months	Primitive sounds "ah"
8 months	Syllables "baba, dada, mama"
12 months	2–3 words
2–3 years	Sentences

TABLE 19.4   Physical Examination

NAME:_____   DATE:_____

| HEAD CIRCUMFERENCE | HEIGHT | WEIGHT | VITAL SIGNS |

BRUITS
SKIN
HEENT
NECK
HEART
CHEST
ABDOMEN
PULSES
EXTREMITIES

NEUROLOGICAL
  I. *DEVELOPMENTAL EVALUATION*
      DEVELOPMENTAL MILESTONES
      R/L HANDED
      SPEECH: COMPREHENSION
      READING LEVEL
      CALCULATIONS
      GENERAL INFORMATION
      GRAPHOMOTOR SKILLS
      MEMORY: AUDITORY/VISUAL
      PERCEPTION: AUDITORY/VISUAL
      FUND OF KNOWLEDGE

  II. *MOTOR*
      GAIT PATTERNS
      BULK, TONE, STRENGTH, ABNORMAL POSTURES, ABNORMAL MOVEMENTS

  III. *REFLEXES*

DEEP TENDON REFLEXES	ABDOMINAL
BABINSKI	ANAL
CREMASTERIC	NEONATAL REFLEX

  IV. *SENSORY*
      LIGHT TOUCH, PAIN, POSITION, VIBRATIONS, GRAPHESTHESIA, STEREOGNOSTIC

  V. *COORDINATION*
      FINGER-TO-NOSE, HEEL-TO-SHIN, RAPID ALTERNATING MOVEMENTS, ATAXIA NYSTAGMUS

  VI. *CRANIAL NERVES*

SMELL	NYSTAGMUS
VISTUAL ACUITY	CORNEAL
VISUAL FIELDS	FACIAL
FUNDUS	HEARING
PUPILS	PALATE
EXTRAOCULAR MOVEMENTS	GAG
LIDS	STERNOCLEIDOMASTOID
	TONGUE

  VII. *OTHER*

stances can be offered for identification. Children who have impairment of olfaction frequently complain of gustatory impairment.

The second cranial nerve, the optic nerve, is examined for visual acuity, visual fields, and thorough funduscopy. The latter examination is best performed toward the end of the examination, as an ophthalmoscope is often frightening to the child. In an older cooperative child who recognizes letters, shapes, or numbers, visual acuity is checked with the use of the Snellen cards. To assess vision in infants or young children, small objects are placed around the room or on a testing table to ascertain whether the infant's gaze is distracted by them. When small objects, such as a raisin, are used, an assessment of the child's visual acuity can be obtained.

Visual fields that are tested by confrontation in the older child can at times be tested in an infant. A useful technique places a finger puppet on each hand of the physician. The child is coaxed to focus on a puppet placed in front of his face. Gradually the second puppet is brought into the various quadrants of the visual field with slight movements to check when the child can detect the presence of the second puppet. This technique can often disclose any significant abnormality of the visual fields.

Funduscopic examination is the most difficult part of the cranial nerve examination. It is best accomplished with the child in the mother's arms, sitting on her lap, or held over her shoulder. The examiner should slowly approach the child with the ophthalmoscope in position in an attempt to visualize the fundus. If the instrument is kept fixed on the retina, the child's normal eye movements allow visualization of all quadrants. The examiner should persevere even with an uncooperative child, if necessary instilling a short-acting mydriatic agent in order to obtain an adequate funduscopic examination.

Third, fourth, and sixth cranial nerves, which mediate the extraocular movements, are often assessed by inspection. Puppets can be presented in various quadrants of the child's visual field to ascertain whether there are full eye movements. If the child is uncooperative, place him in such a position so that to look at his mother he would have to turn his head and his eyes in a prescribed direction. By creatively varying the child's position and placement, one can obtain an evaluation of the full range of extraocular movements.

The young infant can be held in vertical suspension and rotated clockwise or counterclockwise for several turns. This also serves to assess the extraocular muscle function and the intactness of the oculo-vestibular system. The detection of the opticokinetic response using a striped piece of cloth is also useful in assessing whether impaired visual function is present. Ptosis and nystagmus are observed by using finger puppets or other small objects that maintain the child's gaze direction. Lid function and eye movements can also be observed with the object. The corneal reflex is tested in both the infant and child by playfully blowing into the eye and observing for eyelid closure.

Seventh cranial nerve function, the facial nerve, is evaluated by observing the child for intactness and symmetry of facial movements and facial features during the examination. If the child isn't cooperative, toward the end of the examination a successful attempt to make the child cry will clearly demonstrate any facial asymmetry or abnormality.

Hearing can be tested by observing responses to noise or commands made by the mother or the examiner.

Sternocleidomastoid and trapezius function is assessed either through observation or by coaxing the child to turn his head to either side or shrug his shoulders against resistance. The tongue should be examined both at rest and in movement. A lollipop can be useful in obtaining the child's cooperation. It is often one of the only ways to obtain mouth opening and to evaluate movements of the face and tongue. Lingual movements are obtained by placing a lollipop in the different quadrants of the mouth and having the child attempt to lick it. With the mouth open and the tongue at rest, fasiculations or abnormal tongue movements can be observed.

Motor Examination

Evaluation of a child's muscle strength and function is an essential part of the neurological examination. Expected motor function as well as muscle bulk, tone, and strength need assessment, with particular attention paid to asymmetry. Table 19.3 describes the major milestones in gross motor development. The formal motor examination involves evaluation of the child's gait and hand and leg function, in addition to the examination of individual muscle groups.

Systematic observation is the key to the motor examination in infants and children. Begin the motor examination at the time of initial contact with the child, while still with the mother. Unsuspected observation of the child's gait, the manner in which clothing is removed, objects are handled, the room is explored, and so on, provides valuable information regarding the child's function and strength. Given sufficient patience and time, a rather detailed motor examination can be obtained in a child of almost any age. Objects should be carefully scattered around the room and others should be handed to the child so both locomotion and prehension can be observed. During this portion of the examination both asymmetry and appropriateness of gait should be evaluated. When the older child is cooperative, ask him to walk on toes and heels, hop, and perform tandem walking.

Abnormalities in muscle bulk and the presence of any abnormal posturing or movements should be noted. Observation and examination of arm and hand function is best accomplished by systematically handing the child objects to either hand. Prehension in the young infant can be induced by placing an article of light clothing over the infant's face. Proximal motor function is assessed as the child attempts to reach for an object placed above him. Appropriateness of grasp and at times hand dominance can then be assessed. Muscle strength can be evaluated surreptitiously by providing traction on an object handed to the child and assessing the degree of resistance provided. In this fashion, upper extremity strength and coordination can be determined. Lower extremity strength can be evaluated by observing attempts to sit, stand up, and walk, while assessment of proximal leg and abdominal muscle function is made through observation of rising from a prone or supine position. As mentioned earlier, if the child is uncooperative a detailed "historical" examination of the child's abilities may have to suffice. In addition, the physician must recognize the normal variability of acquisition of motor milestones so that mild variations in neurological development are not necessarily interpreted as abnormalities.

It is more comfortable for the small child or adolescent to have this examination performed in a T-shirt and gym shorts rather than his underwear; thus parents should be requested to bring such clothing to the office.

Deep Tendon Reflexes

Table 19.5 lists the reflexes that can be obtained in a fashion similar to that in adults. The reflex examination should be accomplished in a playful manner. It is recommended to hand the child a second reflex hammer or to demonstrate the reflexes on the child's mother in order to alleviate the fear of being struck.

The plantar response should also be evaluated. The requirements of this response are that the stimulus be somewhat painful. Use of the examiner's thumb rather than a key or reflex hammer and/or observing the movements of the toes when the child's shoe or sock is removed reduces apprehension in young patients.

The reflex examination of infants and young children includes observation of the development or disappearance of various reflex patterns. Notably, there are reflex patterns, such as the sucking and grasp reflex, that are present in the neonate and subside as the child gets older. In addition there are reflexes that are not present in a newborn but that develop as the child's nervous system matures. An example of this would be the parachute response, which is commonly seen in a 7–8-month-old child on suspension from the prone position. Table 19.5 lists developmental reflexes and their time of onset and disappearance.

TABLE 19.5 Reflex Examination

Reflex	*Segmental Level*
Tendon reflexes	
Jaw jerk	Pons: Cranial nerve V
Biceps reflex	Cervical 5–6
Brachrioradialis	Cervical 5–6
Triceps reflex	Cervical 6–7–8
Knee reflex	Lumbar 3–4
Ankle reflex	Sacral 1–2
Superficial reflexes	
Corneal	Pons: Cranial nerve V
Pharyngeal reflex	Medulla: Cranial nerve IX–X
Abdominal reflex	Thoracic 8–12
Cremasteric reflex	Lumbar 1–2

Coordination

Assessment of hand coordination in the older child is obtained by using the finger-to-nose examination and requesting the child to perform rapid alternating movements. In the small infant or child this is not feasible, so utilize play and observation. A child can be offered a small toy, allowing observation of his reach. Ability to grasp objects and to place them reflexively in his mouth is observed. Coordination of the legs is evaluated while observing the child's gait. It is important to understand that the ability to perform these tasks is a function of development. There is a great deal of variability in the degree of clumsiness normal children display, which needs to be considered when determining whether the child has significant coordinative difficulty.

Sensory Examination

Sensory examination involves evaluation of the various modalities of sensation in an attempt to determine if there is any asymmetry or evidence of abnormality in the sensory pathways. The modalities tested include light touch, pain, position, pressure, graphesthesia, two-point discrimination, and sterognosis. This is the most difficult portion of the physical examination to obtain and frequently is limited to light touch and pin sensation evaluation. Position sense can occasionally be evaluated in children as young as 3 or 4 years. Older children are examined similarly to adults. Light touch is assessed by touching the child with a Q-tip and noting whether or not head or eyes are diverted to the side of the stimulus. For the neonate or infant pain sensation is determined by lightly pricking the child in various locations and observing any subtle facial grimacing or wrinkling of the eyes and face, suggesting a response to pain.

The following section discusses some of the present complaints commonly seen by both neurologists and psychiatrists and suggests when organic etiology needs to be considered.

Developmental Delay

Developmental delay, defined as delay or deficiency in the acquisition of psychomotor milestones, may be due to static or progressive processes. Developmental history review is essential, especially to differentiate the child who has always been delayed in acquisition of milestones, suggesting a nonspecific, static encephalopathy, from the child who has had a period of normal development and failed to progress or has even regressed, suggesting a progressive metabolic or structural encephalopathy.

The major areas of development include: (1) the development of oral and ocular reflexes; (2) hand function; (3) walking; (4) behavior; and (5) language development. Physical examination should confirm the developmental status of the child.

Psychomotor development is subject to many variables including genetics, race, and sex. For example, girls are more precocious in the acquisition of expressive language, whereas boys develop motor skills earlier than girls and blacks walk earlier than whites. A family history relative to the acquisition of developmental milestones may provide invaluable etiological data relative to specific delays. Maternal factors include age, medical disorders (including diabetes, thyroid dysfunction, or venereal diseases), and prior history of stillbirth or neonatal death. Prenatal complications include hemorrhage when extensive in the first trimester or occurring during the second or third trimester, maternal infections, and medication or alcohol ingestion or smoking, all of which could contribute to neonatal morbidity and future neurological dysfunction.

Of major concern is the perinatal history. Conditions predisposing to perinatal asphyxia can result in irreversible neurological dysfunction. The premature, above all the small premature weighing less than 1500 grams, is at great risk of asphyxia and intracranial hemorrhage. The neonatal period may be complicated by asphyxia, hyperbilirubinemia, hypoglycemia, and sepsis with meningitis, all of which can delay neurological development. The older child subjected to craniocerebral trauma, meningitis, or systemic hypotension with shock may manifest delays in development. The most difficult diagnostic problem is encountered when there is evidence of chronic developmental delay and no specific etiology can be delineated. Above all, when progressive disease, either manifested by a loss of previously acquired milestones or a failure to progress, is suspected, metabolic or degenerative disorders should be considered including aminoacidopathies, leukodystrophies, and lysosomal enzyme diseases.

In these disorders there may be abnormalities on physical examination that may provide clues to diagnosis. Eye abnormalities such as cataracts, cherry red spots, corneal clouding, dislocated lenses, and glaucoma may provide clues for various metabolic disorders. Abnormalities in hair may be diagnostically suggestive, such as fine hair, kinky hair in Menke's disease, or premature gray hair as seen in ataxia-telangiectasia. Hearing abnormalities such as conductive deafness may be seen in mucopolysaccharidosis. Children with certain lysosomal storage diseases such as GM_2 gangliosidosis (Tay-Sach's disease) often show hyperacusis. Splenomegaly is seen in many of the lysosomal storage diseases. Many of the metabolic diseases such as amino acid disorders may be associated with a persistent metabolic acidosis. The presence of developmental delay in association with seizures is indicative of a structural or metabolic encephalopathy. Skin abnormalities are also an important clue. Telangectasia (dilatation of small blood vessels) suggests ataxia-telangectasi, while hypo- or hyperpigmented lesions may be seen in neurofibromatosis or tuberous sclerosis, diseases associated with developmental delays. In addition, the presence of recurrent or intermittent vomiting may be indicative of a metabolic disorder. Should any of these factors be present, further neurological workup and metabolic studies would be indicated.

In sharp contrast, isolated multiple or global delays, usually improving slowly with increasing chronological age, signify an underlying nervous system disorder of a static type. Delay in the acquisition in many or all milestones indicates diffuse involvement of the brain, with the child at risk for mental retardation or cerebral palsy. Delay in any of the three areas of development—motor, speech, and adaptive behavior—is usually indicative of specific disorders. Impaired motor function results from cerebral palsy, disorders of the spinal cord, peripheral nerve, or muscle. Speech often fails to develop normally in children with brain disorders or with hearing loss. Poor adaptive behavior usually implies a diffuse disturbance of the brain but can also occur with psychosocial deprivation.

Headaches

Chronic recurrent headaches are a common problem for which children are referred to psychiatrists. Once again detailed history is the most important aspect of the evaluation. The location, severity, time of day, duration, frequency, and character of the pain needs to be recorded. Associated complaints or symptoms need to be identified as well. Headaches can be classified according to their pathophysiological origin. Certain head pains may be due to inflammation of various structures of the head or neck. This type of recurrent headache is usually associated with evidence of a pericranial inflammatory process. Localized or generalized swelling or fever may be present. Traction headaches are due to stretching of pain-sensitive structures of the head, which includes arteries and/or veins. These headaches are commonly due to mass lesions in the head, such as abcesses, vascular mass lesions, or neoplasms. There are often present upon arising from a lying position and progress in severity over the day. They may be exacerbated by coughing or with a Valsalva maneuver, and are often associated with nausea, vomiting, and focal neurological deficits. Focal deficits in a child presenting with recurrent headaches there suggest the presence of an identifiable intracranial lesion.

Migraine headaches are common in children. It has been estimated that 4 to 5 percent of children under 15 may experience migraine headaches, often in the presence of a positive family history. These are recurrent throbbing headaches, characteristically separated by a symptom-free period. Commonly associated with abdominal pain, nausea, vomiting, and occasionally transient focal neurological abnormalities such as weakness or paresthesia, these severe head pains are generally relieved by sleep. Common migraines typically have no focal abnormalities on neurological examination, while complex migraine may be associated with deficits such as hemiplegia or ophthalmoplegia.

Headaches may be due to seizures. This relationship is obvious in the presence of a clinical seizure. However, headache may occur as the sole manifestation of a seizure. If suspected the diagnosis requires confirmation with an electroencephalogram (EEG). The distinction between migraine and convulsive headaches is often difficult. Recording an EEG during the headaches is the best diagnostic confirmation. Therapeutic response with anticonvulsants or antimigraine drugs may be helpful if the EEG cannot be performed during the headache.

Head trauma is often followed by headaches and when persistent is manifestation of a posttraumatic concussion syndrome. These children may experience recurrent headaches and dizziness, and may encounter difficulty with concentration or attention. These protracted headaches are often unresponsive to analgesics and may be complicated with psychogenic factors.

Stress is the most common cause of recurrent chronic, nonspecific headaches in children. These are generally diffuse, bilateral, have no specific pattern, and have a steady rather than throbbing type of pain. Diagnosis of stress headache is made on the basis of a normal neurological examination, the nonprogressive nature of the symptoms, and a predisposing psychosocial setting.

Motor Disturbances

Disturbances in motor function may be manifested as muscle weakness, ataxia, or abnormal involuntary movements. They may be evident from early infancy as a delay in development of motor milestones or may appear at a later age as a loss or disturbance of voluntary motor activity. Muscle weakness resulting from an upper motor neuron lesion involving the motor cortex or its outflow can cause total or partial spastic paralysis of the extremities of the opposite side. Such lesions may be either congenital static deficits or acquired disturbances due to tumors, vascular insults, or degenerative disease. With static lesions, the weakness does not increase and it may actually be improved by compensatory mechanisms over time. In acquired lesions, the sudden appearance of a hemiparesis suggests vascular disease, while a slowly developing weakness implies a tumor or degenerative disorder. Additional clinical features indicative of upper motor neuron disease are exaggerated deep tendon reflexes and the pathological extensor plantar sign (Babinski reflex) on the involved side. Lower motor neuron disturbances are characterized by a flaccid muscle weakness. Myopathies such as muscular dystrophy maximally involve the large girdle muscles. Neuropathies as polyneuritis also cause diffuse weakness, but the distal musculature of the hands and feet is more involved than is proximal girdle musculature. Anterior horn cell disease results in weakness that may be symmetric or asymmetric, involving isolated muscle groups. Lower motor neuron disease is further characterized by atrophy, a normal plantar response, and hypoactive or absent deep tendon reflexes.

Ataxia results from involvement of the cerebellum and its pathways. Unsteadiness of voluntary movements may be due to a congenital defect of the cerebellum (ataxic form of cerebral palsy). This condition is characterized by poor balance during sitting and standing and the development of unsteady gait and hand function. Acquired forms of ataxia may be either acute or insidious in onset. Acute ataxia occurs with intoxications, exanthems (particularly varicella), and nonspecific infections (acute cerebellar ataxia); or it may be episodic in nature, as in vertiginous epilepsy or vestibular neuronitis. Slowly developing ataxia may be observed with increased intracranial pressure, cerebellar and brainstem tumors, heredogenerative disorders (as in ataxia-telangiectasia and Friedreich's ataxia), and some inborn errors of metabolism (such as Hartnup disease).

Abnormal involuntary movements may be triggered by stress or other psychogenic factors as in tics, or they may be the result of extrapyramidal dysfunction, as manifested by chorea, athetosis, dystonia, tremor, and ballismus. Tics or habit spasms, the most common abnormal movement disorder, are characterized by isolated repetitive movements such as winking, grimacing, or more complex tic phenomena and may have associated vocalizations, such as coughing, barking, and clearing the throat. When the vocal component (which may be manifested as obscene language) accompanies motor tics and this combination persists for a year or more, it is often referred to as Gilles de la Tourette or Tourette Syndrome.

Chorea is characterized by sudden, irregular jerky movements that may involve any group of skeletal muscles, including the face. Chorea may occur in rheumatic fever (Sydenham's chorea), encephalitis hypoparathyroidism, and occasionally lupus erythematosus. The movements of athetosis are slow and writhing, mainly affect the muscles of the extremities, and may be accompanied by choreiform movements (choreathetosis). Athetosis is a manifestation of kernicterus and congenital defects of the brain.

Dystonia is characterized by involuntary sustained spasms of the muscles of the neck, trunk, and extremities that result in abnormal posture. Dystonic movements may be manifestations of dystonia musculorum deformans (a hereditary movement disorder), encephalitis, and birth defects. They also may be associated with rigidity in hepatolenticular degeneration (Wilson's disease). Acute dystonia is most commonly seen in children as an idiosyncratic reaction to phenothiazines.

Tremor of basal ganglial origin occurs at rest, while the cerebellar form of tremor becomes evident on volitional movement. Tremor is seen in its most benign form as familial or essential tremor and in its severe form in the "wing-beating" tremor of Wilson's disease.

Mood Abnormalities

Abnormalities in affect or moods may present as part of a neurological disorder. Metabolic disorders, degenerative disorders, and intracranial lesions such as brain tumors may present with abnormalities in behavior or mood. In fact, this may be one of the earliest signs of intracranial pathology. In most children with mood disorders due to focal neurological lesions, abnormalities are present on neurological examination. It would be important to explore a patient's psychosocial background in any event, to see whether this may play either a primary or secondary role. The diagnosis of dementia in children can include metabolic or degenerative disorders as Wilson's disease or adrenoleukodystrophy, intracranial neoplasm, or chronic infections of abcesses.

Speech and Language Abnormalities

Speech and language abnormalities may present as a chronic speech and language delay, or as deterioration of speech and language function in a previously normally functioning child. The latter problem would mandate careful consideration of neurological disorders. The presence of a focal neurological deficit would warrant further neurodiagnostic studies. Initial evaluation must assess hearing with a formal audiogram and/or a brainstem auditory evoked potential.

Sleep Disturbances

Sleep disorders are problems commonly referred to psychiatrists. These can include enuresis, hypersomnia, insomnia, narcolepsy with sleep paralysis or cataplexy, hypnogogic hallucinations, night terrors, nightmares, excessive sleep, or sleep apnea. Neurological disorders are rarely the cause of these problems in children. There is, however, a slightly higher incidence of these disorders in children with psychomotor retardation but this is usually a nonspecific finding.

SUMMARY

It behooves the child psychiatrist to be sensitive to the possibility that neurological problems will be present in a significant proportion of children referred for psychiatric evaluation and treatment. Thorough history taking should therefore address pertinent neurodevelopmental issues and focus clearly on symptomatic complaints that may be of primary neurogenic etiology. Where indicated, performance of a neurological examination by the child psychiatrist may be desirable and may enhance, rather than detract from, a sound psychotherapeutic relationship.

REFERENCES

Menkes, J. H. (1985). *Textbook of Child Neurology.* Philadelphia: Lea and Febiger.
Rowland, L. (1984). *Merritt's Textbook of Neurology.* 7th ed. Philadelphia: Lea and Febiger.
Rudolph, A. M., and Hoffman, M. D. (1982). *Pediatrics.* New York: Appleton Century Crofts, Chapter 29.
Swanson, K. F., and Wright, F. S. (1982). *Practice of Pediatric Neurology.* St. Louis: Mosby.
Volpe, J. J. (1981). *Neurology of the Newborn.* Philadelphia: Saunders.

20

PEDIATRIC NEUROPHYSIOLOGICAL ASSESSMENT

Marcia Bergtraum

ELECTROENCEPHALOGRAM IN CHILD PSYCHIATRIC ASSESSMENT

An electroencephalogram (EEG) is a record of the amplified electrical activity generated by nerve cells of the brain. Electrodes are placed on the scalp and the subsequent reading reflects collective activity of many nerve cells in a small area under each electrode. This area is on the cortex of the brain. The written record obtained reflects the rising and falling of electrical potentials called brain waves. When the potentials in many nerves are changing synchronously, various rhythms are generated, reflecting different states of cortical activity. The resulting identified rhythms may be altered by local changes or by changes in nerve cells in varying localities in the brain. It is the change in existing rhythms and amplitudes that makes the EEG a useful tool in the diagnosis of nervous system disease.

It is presently well established that there is a higher incidence of electroencephalographic abnormality among psychiatric patients than in the general population. This has been confirmed by many authors (Ritvo et al. 1970). This appears to be true for nearly all psychiatric diagnoses and has an even higher incidence when organic brain disease is associated with the psychiatric impairment.

Although there is clearly a higher incidence of EEG abnormalities in the psychiatric population, EEG patterns alone are rarely if ever diagnostic of a specific psychiatric disease entity. A double blind control study by Ritvo et al. (1970) found no specific correlation between psychiatric diagnosis and EEG findings. The EEG can only be used as a tool to assist the psychiatrist in diagnosis and treatment. It is with this in mind that this chapter will focus on the EEG findings in a broad range of psychiatric diagnostic categories.

Recording the Pediatric EEG

Pediatric electroencephalography is a difficult specialty. It requires extreme patience as well as speed on the part of the technician. Children are often uncooperative and electrode placement must be done skillfully and quickly. In the psychiatric population, it is often imperative that electroencephalograms be performed in both the awake state as well as the sleep state. A tracing in the awake state may pose problems in children, especially those with significant behavioral problems. It can be a tedious procedure to obtain an artifact-free record. Allowing a parent or a friendly face to remain in the room with the youngster may often be beneficial. Often some form of sedative must be used. It is preferable to start with a mild hypnotic, such as chloral hydrate. If this is not successful, one may often use vistaril or paraldehyde. It is imperative that all neurophysiological testing be done in a laboratory with skilled and qualified personnel. Artifacts can often be mistaken for abnormal cortical activity.

Ontogeny of the EEG in Normal Children

EEG interpretation in children is complicated by the fact that one must appreciate the normal developmental aspects of cortical activity in order to diagnose pathology. The rapid maturational changes that the human brain undergoes, particularly during the first year of life, are reflected in the changing patterns recorded in the electroencephalogram.

Electrical activity has been recorded from the brain of fetuses as early as 24 weeks after conception. The EEG of the full-term newborn is the beginning of the course of changing electrical activity that slowly matures into an adult pattern. The initial EEG is slower than that seen at a later age, with the dominant activity being in the delta and theta range, particularly in the posterior head regions. As the child matures, the posterior rhythm becomes a more clearly defined alpha rhythm like that seen in the adult. By age 3, the child has an eight Hz (cycles per second) alpha rhythm, which is similar to the slower range of normal in the adult. As the child matures, the alpha frequency may increase slowly, achieving its adult value by early adolescence. The central rhythm has a similar developmental course, with slower rhythm seen during early childhood and disappearing in adolescence.

These evolving parameters are important to understand, particularly when using the EEG as a tool to distinguish organic brain disease from other psychiatric syndromes.

Organic Disease vs. Psychiatric Illness

Many organic illnesses may manifest themselves in psychiatric symptomatology. The need to distinguish between these two entities is one of the major indications for the electroencephalogram. For instance, many encephalopathies may present with suggestions of psychiatric illnesses. These may include infections, toxic or metabolic encephalopathies, as well as the vasculitic syndromes. Although the EEGs in these diseases are often not diagnostic, they may be helpful in differentiating these diseases from closely related functional and psychiatric illness. For example, a metabolic encephalopathy may be suggested by the presence of triphasic waves on the electroencephalogram. Infections and toxic metabolic states may often show a generalized slowing of the EEG. Specific types of encephalitis, such as herpes encephalitis and subacute sclerosing panencephalitis will show periodic activity in the electroencephalogram. Conditions such as a lupus encephalitis, which is often manifested by psychiatric symptomatology, will frequently show slowing of the background of the EEG. In the case of brain tumors, which may manifest themselves with abnormal behaviors, a focal slowing may often be seen in the electroencephalogram suggestive of a space-occupying lesion. In the case of drug-induced psychosis or behavioral changes, one may often see the effects of the drug on the electroencephalogram. A discussion of drug changes on the EEG is left for a later part of this chapter. However, it is worth noting that many drugs known to cause psychotic symptomatology may cause increased fast activity on the EEG tracing.

The EEG may also be useful in the detecting of possible organic contributants to such symptomatology as depression. If there is a generalized slowing of the background an organic cause for the depression should be sought. This may include all of the above-mentioned entities.

The EEG is also an extremely useful tool in separating psychomotor seizures and absence status from psychiatric causes for changes in behavior and attention.

Controversial Electrographic Patterns

In addition to the previously described parameters seen in the normal developmental encephalogram, there are a number of EEG patterns peculiar to early adolescence and young adulthood that have received much attention in the neurological and psychiatric literature. There has been much controversy over the clinical significance of these particular patterns, which include:

14 and 6 Positive Spikes (Figure 20.1). This entity was first described by Gibbs and Gibbs in 1951. It is characterized by a rhythmic discharge of arch-shaped wave forms with a predominant positive component. This burst occurs at a rate of 14 Hz or 6 Hz and is usually one second in duration. It is most commonly seen in the posterior temporal regions. The faster 14 Hz frequency is the predominant wave form, although the 6 Hz may occur independently or in association with the faster rhythm. This discharge occurs predominantly during drowsiness and light sleep.

Gibbs and Gibbs originally described this phenomenon as representing a pathological discharge from the thalamic or hypothalamic area. This was the prevailing view until the 1960s, when papers appeared casting doubt upon the clinical significance of this pattern (Henry 1963). In the late 1960s and early '70s there was a rekindling of interest in the positive spike phenomenon. At that time, many elec-

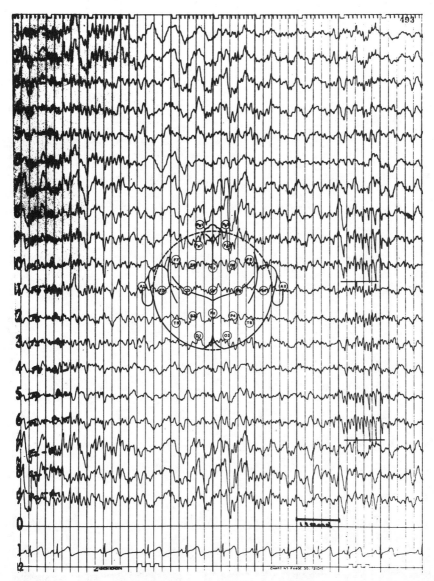

Figure 20.1. The underlined discharge is a 14 Hz positive spike occurring in the posterior parietal leads. This is a classic 14 and 6 discharge. This recording was performed in a 14 year old girl referred for headaches with no psychiatric disease.

troencephalographers studied normal populations of adolescents to determine its prevalence. Studies by Eeg-Olofson (1971) and Peterson and Eeg-Olofson (1981) all revealed an incidence of between 15 percent and 20 percent in the normal population. Lombroso's (1966) study of adolescent boys at the Phillips Andover Academy revealed that 58 percent of these students exhibited at least one example of the 14 and 6 phenomenon during drowsiness. However, studies by Hughes and Cayaffa

(1978) found a correlation between individuals with behavioral disorders and positive spikes in their EEGs.

Subsequently, Yamada et al. (1976) had described a high incidence of 14 and 6 per second spike in children with Reye's syndrome. This finding appears to be peculiar to this syndrome as it has not been found in other encephalopathies.

The literature on this subject is quite controversial. Suffice it to say that most

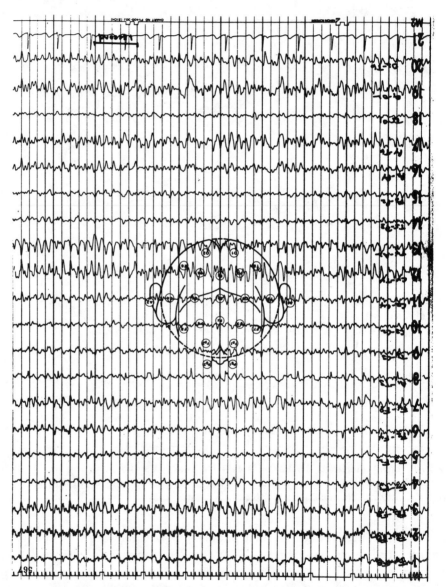

Figure 20.2. This 11 year old child was referred for intermittent explosive disorder. A 6-cycle-per-second discharge can be seen over the right hemisphere, characteristic of phantom spike and wave.

electroencephalographers do not feel 14 and 6 positive spike is anything more than a normal occurrence in adolescence during drowsiness and light sleep. A review of the cases suggesting a relationship between psychiatric disturbance and this phenomenon certainly indicates no specificity and no correlation to a specific diagnostic group.

6-Per-Second Spike and Wave Discharge (Figure 20.2). The 6-per-second spike and wave discharge or "phantom spike and wave" was first completely described by Marshall in 1955. The discharge is characterized by rapid, low voltage spikes at a rate of 6 hz. occurring maximally in the frontal region in children and the posterior regions in the adult. The discharge rarely lasts longer than one second and is activated by sleep.

Tharp (1966) found an incidence of 1.5 percent in healthy U.S. Army volunteers. This could be increased to 29 percent if subjects were given i.v. infusions of diphenhydramine. In other studies the incidence of seizures was higher (36 percent) in those patients exhibiting 6-per-second spike and wave.

Psychiatric symptoms have been found in approximately one-half of these patients (Hughes and Wilson 1983, p. 343). This, however, is much more common in adults than in children and is reported mainly in the form of behavioral disorders.

Behavioral Disorders and Disorders of Attention

The EEG does not play a major role in the management of patients with either behavioral disorders or attention deficit disorders. The most important application of the EEG here is to rule out seizures as a cause of lack of attention or behavioral indiscretion. Absence seizures and partial complex seizures can often be mistaken for daydreaming, inattention, or bizarre behavior. The yield of abnormal EEGs indicative of seizures in children with these disorders is low. However, for the rare patient in whom such a characteristic abnormality is uncovered, the results can be extremely rewarding. Treatment of the underlying disease may make all the difference in this child's functioning.

There is no EEG pattern that is diagnostic of the attention deficit disorder, hyperactivity, or behavioral abnormality. It is difficult to review the literature on this subject because of widely varying definitions of the syndrome as well as of the standards for inclusion of patients in the various studies. However, it is clear that children with behavioral disorders associated with other neurological deficits have a much higher incidence of abnormal EEGs than either their counterparts without neurological handicaps or the general population. For example, in a study by Klinkerfuss et al. (1965) EEG abnormalities were found in 53 percent of hyperkinetic children who also had other neurological deficits and in 30 percent where hyperkinesis was the only apparent problem. The EEG abnormalities in the second group consisted of nonspecific slowing and disorganization of the record, which may represent a maturational lag similar to that seen in a clinical examination. Similar findings may be seen in children with attention deficit disorder without hyperactivity.

An interesting study by Shetty (1971) compared children with hyperactivity to normal controls. This study found a higher frequency and better sustained alpha rhythm in the control subjects. The study went on to evaluate the effects of dextroamphetamine and methylphenidate on the EEG in these patients. Those children who developed increased alpha activity during i.v. infusion of these psychostimulants appeared to have a better clinical response to the drug than did those patients who experienced no change in the EEG characteristics. Magnesium pemoline was not shown to have any effect on the EEG.

In studies of delinquent children free of neurological impairment, there was no appreciable difference in EEGs when compared to age-matched controls (Wiener et al. 1966). Attempts to correlate the EEG abnormalities with other clinical data in one hundred delinquent girls proved fruitless, with an 80 percent error rate (Loomis et al. 1967).

The significance of paroxysmal abnormalities in the EEG recordings of children with behavioral disorders is also of interest. This had led some physicians to prescribe anticonvulsant therapy treatment in these disorders. Results of the use of anticonvulsants in this population has been poor. Egli and Graf (1971) reported the results of treatment of seventy-six disturbed children with spike and wave patterns without evidence of epilepsy. Fifty-seven children treated with anticonvulsants did not show an improvement in their behavior with drug therapy. Some more encouraging results have been reported recently with the use of Tegretol in this population. However, this calls for more careful study in the future.

In summary, the EEG is a helpful tool in the evaluation of children with behavioral and attentional disturbances when used to rule out seizure disorders or to document evidence of accompanying neurological impairment.

Mental Retardation and Autism

The EEG can be extremely useful in the child with mental retardation. The EEG frequency does not correlate with intelligence quotient. However, the EEG can often be helpful in the differential diagnosis of mental retardation. A deterioration of the EEG over time would be more suggestive of a degenerative disease than a static encephalopathy. Certain EEG patterns such as triphasic waves may suggest a metabolic cause for the child's difficulties. The presence of a continuous spike and wave pattern would suggest a nonconvulsant status as a cause for the child's apparent retardation (Figure 20.3). Kelloway (1952) and Gibbs and Gibbs (1962) subsequently described an unusual sleep pattern—extreme spindles—in children with cerebral palsy, mental retardation, and seizures.

Abnormal EEGs have been reported with a relatively high incidence in children with autism (Small et al. 1977). Slowing of the background, desynchronized activity, hypermature records, and paroxysmal activities have been described. None of these findings is diagnostic or really helpful in the treatment of children with this entity.

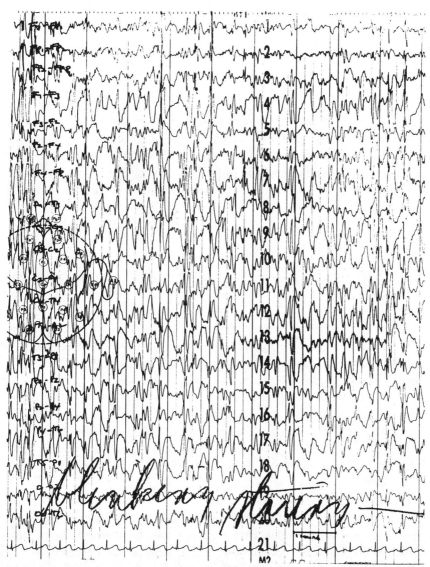

Figure 20.3. This 8 year old youngster was referred for learning disabilities, poor academic performance and daydreaming. A diagnosis of absence seizures was made, characterized by this 3-per-second spike and wave seen on the EEG. The child was staring and unresponsive during this 10-second episode.

Psychotic Disorders of Childhood

This is an extremely difficult group to assess by electrophysiological parameters. They are extremely difficult to test and require heavy sedation; often, wake recordings are virtually unobtainable. As in most areas of psychiatry, EEG abnormalities in this group are again related to coexistent neurological disease (White et al. 1964),

(Ritvo et al. 1970). Computer analysis of the electroencephalogram in these children revealed fast beta waves and slow alpha waves, but again, this is not specific and of little help in the diagnosis and treatment of these children (Itil et al. 1976).

Affective Disorders

Mania and severe depressions have been described with an onset in childhood. Some sleep studies have shown abnormalities in sleep patterns in youngsters suffering from affective disorders. Mildly disordered EEGs have been found in children suffering from mania. These disorders include a shortening of the rapid eye movements, sleep latency, and frequent awakenings during sleep recording (Weinberg and Brumback 1976).

Sleep Disorders

A full discussion of sleep recording and sleep stages is beyond the scope of this chapter. However, one should be aware that EEG studies have been performed in major sleep related disorders. The older child and adult sleep pattern is characterized by sleep cycles initiated by quiet sleep and followed by REM sleep. Quiet sleep is described in four stages, one representing drowsiness, two representing light sleep, three and four representing slow wave or deep sleep.

Somnambulism (sleepwalking), as well as somniloquy (sleep talking) occur in stage three and four sleep. The majority of patients studied with this disorder do not show any abnormality in the EEG tracing. However Pedley and Guillemaunt (1977) reported four out of six patients with this disorder with abnormal paroxysmal discharges. The patients with the paroxysmal discharges responded to treatment with anticonvulsants, primarily Dilantin and Tegretol. It is therefore important to differentiate somnambulism from a seizure equivalent.

Nightmares have been shown to occur in Rapid Eye Movement sleep. They are considered to be dreams of unpleasant nature. The individual must awaken during the period of dreaming, at which time he has a fleeting memory of the content of the nightmare. This is unassociated with any abnormal EEG pattern. By contrast, pavor nocturnus (night terror) is a disturbance seen in Stage Four of non-REM sleep. It is characterized by sudden arousal accompanied by screaming and clinical signs of fear and anxiety. These children are usually inconsolable until a full arousal and awakening takes place. This is not associated with any unusual electrical activity.

Enuresis occurs during Stage Four of quiet sleep and is considered to be a disorder of arousal. An arousal pattern of a high amplitude rhythmic delta activity can be seen as the enuretic episode takes place. No evidence of paroxysmal activity has been noted in the EEG of children with simple enuresis. However, one must differentiate enuresis of childhood from lack of bladder control as the result of a seizure during sleep. An EEG would thus be helpful in this endeavor.

Narcolepsy, which is characterized by excessive daytime sleepiness, hynagogic hallucinations, and sleep paralysis, can often be diagnosed by electroencephalographic parameters. For diagnosis of narcolepsy, a multiple sleep latency test must be performed. This test is based on the knowledge that most normal individuals who are in the adolescent or adult age group initiate sleep with slow wave patterns. Patients with narcolepsy, when recorded in the EEG laboratory during the day, have multiple episodes of sleep onsets in REM sleep patterns rather than slow wave sleep, as the normal individual would demonstrate.

Psychotropic Drugs and Their Effect on Electroencephalogram

It is of no great surprise that medication used to alter mental state and to treat psychiatric disease will often have an effect on recording of brain waves. One must differentiate the changes in electrical activity due to therapeutic levels of drugs from those produced by toxic drug intake. In the evaluation of the effects of these drugs on the EEG, one must also be aware that this may occur as the result of a number of different entities. The drug may alter the EEG because of its effect on the state of arousal of the individual. The medication may also have a direct effect on the electroencephalogram unrelated to changes in the state of arousal or consciousness. This section will include a brief description of the EEG changes noted with the use of psychotropic medication.

Neuroleptics. In general, the neuroleptics, primarily the phenothiazines induce only slight changes in the electroencephalogram even at toxic doses. These medications have been shown to cause some mild slowing of the alpha, theta, and delta frequencies. At times after the immediate initiation of these medications, a mild increase in beta may be seen. This seems to disappear with time. An increase in beta activity is also seen in drowsiness; this may be indicative of a mild sedative action, which may be seen when the drug is first initiated.

Antidepressants. The most commonly used group of antidepressants in children, the tricyclics, have only a mild effect on the normal electroencephalogram. Studies with the use of imipramine in particular have shown an increase in the delta, theta, and beta activity and a decrease in alpha activity. From a clinical standpoint this is not problematic. (Lehman and Hopes 1978). Neuralgesics as well as tricyclic antidepressants can lower the seizure threshold in vulnerable individuals.

Minor Tranquilizers. Drugs such as the benzodiazepams, as well as barbiturates, show a relatively classic drug effect. At low to moderate doses, there is a marked increase in beta activity with an increase in the distribution of beta activity. When doses approach toxic levels there is irregularity in the EEG and an increase in theta activity. As the levels increase, one may see almost continuous delta activity. If the levels are high enough to cause coma, the EEG can even show episodes of electrocerebral silence.

Lithium. Lithium is known to have a significant effect on the electroencephalogram. EEG studies have been done before, during and after treatment with lithium. These studies have indicated that no electroencephalographic changes were seen at serum lithium levels less than .76 mEg/l. For the most part, EEG changes are seen once serum lithium levels approach 1.2 mEg/l. Changes that were found with lithium appeared to become more severe with increasing serum levels (Hughes and Wilson 1983, p. 86). Lithium even at moderate levels can cause a slowing of the background frequency by 1 Hz. This is important to recognize when evaluating the EEG in these patients. Lithium has been found by some investigators to cause focal slowing and disorganization of the electroencephalogram at moderate to high dosages.

Street Drugs. Since phencyclidine use has become an increasing problem in the adolescent age group, this drug has been reported to cause significant changes in the EEG. Changes have been reported consisting of a burst of high amplitude rhythmic and arrhythmic delta similar to that seen in various forms of encephalitis (Fariello and Black 1978). The changes seem to be related to the amount of PCP ingested.

Marijuana has also been shown to cause some changes in the EEG. Of interest in the studies on marijuana is the fact that the EEG abnormalities seem to be related to the clinical experience of the subject tested. In addition, the EEG changes reflect the severity of the experience that the user is having at the time of the electroencephalogram. For instance, there appeared to be more extensive slowing of the alpha and increase in theta activity during periods of hallucinations and distortion of body images as compared to more quiescent periods (Koukkou and Lehmann 1976).

The narcotics have been shown to cause many different changes on the electroencephalogram, including decrease in alpha activity as well as an increase in amplitude and synchronization.

Naloxone has no effect on the electroencephalogram. However, when given after intake of narcotics it will reverse the EEG effects of the narcotics (Hughes and Wilson 1983, p. 90).

Epilepsy

The diagnosis of epilepsy is primarily a clinical one. It should be emphasized that a normal EEG does not rule out the diagnosis of epilepsy. Consequently, if there are clinical features suggestive of a seizure disorder, repeat EEG recordings, possibly with enhancement techniques such as sleep deprivation, should be considered. The psychiatrist is often faced with a patient who is referred for abnormal behavior, daydreaming, or inattentiveness. This group of patients may benefit from a neurological workup to rule out epilepsy if there are any clinical features suggestive of a paroxysmal alteration of consciousness. An electroencephalogram is invaluable in this workup. For instance, a child with absence seizure disorder characterized by generalized 3 to 4 per second spike and wave discharges can often be mistaken for a youngster who is inattentive or daydreaming (Figure 20.3). A child in psychomotor status can often be seen in the Emergency Room and mistaken for a child with a psychiatric fugue state or drug ingestion. An electroencephalogram in this

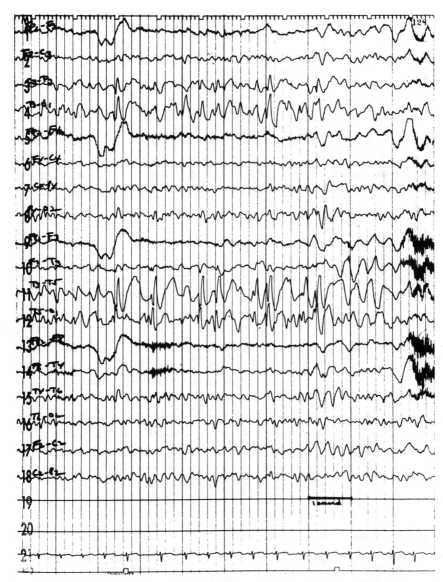

Figure 20.4. This 7 year old child was referred for episodes of bizarre behavior, including a vacant look, stereotypic movements (picking at clothing), continuously repeating the alphabet, and episodic confusion. An EEG revealed a temporal lobe seizure focus.

case may show a continuous 3 to 4 Hz rhythmic activity or spike and wave (Figure 20.4), accounting for this youngster's unexplained behavior. Patients with partial complex seizures can often manifest this in abnormal behaviors. Stereotypical behaviors, rage outburst, and atypical psychosis may all be different manifestations of a temporal lobe disorder. In such a case, an electroencephalogram done with the child sleep-deprived with nasopharyngeal leads may reveal a temporal lobe focus.

These youngsters may respond to treatment with anticonvulsants, particularly car-bamazepine.

EVOKED RESPONSES IN CHILD PSYCHIATRY

The Evoked responses are event-related electrical potentials that are recorded in a fashion similar to that used in the electroencephalogram. These responses are changes in the brain's electrical activity that are recorded in response to a sensory stimulus. These electrical potentials are not ordinarily visible in electroencephalo-graphic tracings because they are of much lower amplitude than the ongoing electrical activity of the resting brain. They can be extracted from the electroencephalo-gram by computerized techniques such as amplification and averaging. By averaging multiple responses to the same stimuli the individual recorded electrical changes summate and become large enough to be appreciated. By time-locking the response to a particular stimulus, one avoids recording random potentials and can record the evoked response.

There are several kinds of evoked potentials that are recordable from the human brain. The short latency evoked potential, such as that seen in the early time period following the stimulus, reflects electrical activity along sensory pathways and the physical properties related to that stimulus. The long latency potentials, which are recorded at a later time after the stimulus, reflect processing of information in higher cortical centers. The slow potentials known as Contingent Negative Variations (CNV) are potentially elicited under certain psychological conditions. The short latency evoked potentials have been well described and easily recorded and do not depend on the state of consciousness of the individuals. The long latency potentials, as well as the Contingent Negative Variations, are dependent upon the patient's level of arousal and concentration. It is for this reason that the longer latency potentials are much more difficult to interpret and to use in a clinical situation.

Brainstem Auditory Evoked Response

The Brainstem Auditory Evoked Response is recorded over the vertex and over the mastoids bilaterally. These responses are recorded in response to click stimuli which are delivered by earphones to the patient. When recording for approximately ten milliseconds after the click stimulus, five well-formed waves are easy to appreciate in the evaluation. The first negative wave produced is the action potential generated by the eighth nerve. The second wave produced is thought to arise either from the proximal eighth nerve or the cochlear nucleus. The third wave involved is thought to be produced in the lower brainstem in the area of the superior olive. The fourth wave is thought to be produced in the lateral lemniscus as the potential is seen traveling up the brainstem. The fifth wave is produced in the area of the mid-brain, particularly at the inferior colliculus. By recording a patient's response to sound at different decibel levels one can approximate the individual's hearing. In addition, by measuring the latency between the stimulus and the actual recording of the wave, one can approximate brainstem conduction. In the neurological setting, the Brainstem Auditory Evoked Response can be used to test for the integrity of the brainstem and the eighth nerve. It can be used in the evaluation of acoustic neuromas, brainstem tumors, and demyelinating syndromes. The responses can also be abnormally delayed in other degenerative neurological diseases.

In psychiatric patients, the Brainstem Auditory Evoked Response is a useful tool to determine the level of hearing in a patient who may be complaining of a hearing loss on a psychogenic basis. The short latency Brainstem Auditory Evoked Response has not been shown to be abnormal in any known psychiatric disorders.

Visual Evoked Response

The Visual Evoked Response is performed by recording brain waves in the occipital region of the brain. It is performed in response to the presentation of a checkerboard or flashing light stimulus to the eye. What is recorded is a single positive wave that occurs at approximately 100 milliseconds after the stimulus. The exact generator of this wave is unknown. The Visual Evoked Response can be used to determine visual acuity in patients who are uncooperative for normal visual testing. This can be performed by the use of successively smaller checkerboard patterns.

In neurological settings, the Visual Evoked Response is used in the diagnosis of optic neuritis, dymyelinating diseases involving the optic system, retinal disease, and in some of the hereditary degenerative diseases. Changes in both the amplitude and latency of the waves can be seen. In the psychiatric setting, the Visual Evoked Response can be helpful in the diagnosis of psychogenic blindness. There is no abnormality seen in the Visual Evoked potential in psychogenic blindness. However, one should be aware that in order to get a proper response the patient must be looking at the stimulus. Therefore, when testing potentially uncooperative patients, the technician must be sure that the patient is focusing in the direction of the stimulus.

Somatosensory Evoked Potential

The Somatosensory Evoked Potential is produced by electrical stimulation of the peripheral nerve. The median nerve in the wrist as well as the peroneal or posterior tibial nerve in the leg are the most commonly evaluated. Measurement of potential in response to stimuli can be measured over the entire spinal cord area as well as the cortex. However, one should be aware that stimulating a peripheral nerve is actually recording the nerve fibers conducting position and vibration sensation rather than pain and temperature. The potential volley up the spinal cord primarily tests the posterior column. The positive potential seen in approximately twenty milliseconds after stimulation, as well as the negative potential thirty milliseconds after stimulation, are thought to originate from generators in the sensory area of the cortex.

The Somatosensory Evoked Potential is a useful tool in the diagnosis of neurological disease. The Somatosensory Evoked Potential can be seen to be abnormal in diseases of the spinal cord, such as traumatic transsection or degenerative diseases (spinocerebellar degeneration). These entities may show a spinal cord potential and then either a delayed or absent cortical potential, suggestive of disease within the spinal cord. In addition, one of the degenerative diseases such as leucodystrophies, as well as damage to the cortex in children, may show abnormalities of reduced amplitude or absence of the cortical evoked potential. In diseases involving myoclonus, there is often an enhancement of the cortical wave recorded response to somatosensory stimulation.

In the psychiatric population, the Somatosensory Evoked Potential is of limited usefulness. There are, however, reports of an increase of the amplitude of Somatosensory Evoked Potentials in schizophrenic patients (Shagass 1976).

Long Latency Potentials

It is generally appreciated that after eighty to one hundred milliseconds, the Evoked Potentials are somewhat reduced in adult psychotic patients. This is true for all sensory modalities. Similar results have been found in children. However, the results of these studies are not all consistent (Fenwick 1985). It has also been found in children that neuroleptic medication can cause an increase in both the latencies and amplitude of responses. It is for this reason that the studies are difficult to interpret.

P-300 wave is a response that occurs in association with sensory stimuli of all modalities. The amplitude of this response is dependent on the patient's appreciation of the stimulus. It has been extensively studied in the adult but only on a limited basis in the child. It can be elicited in a number of ways. The most common way of eliciting this response is by use of the Auditory Evoked Response. The patient is instructed to count all of the low-pitched sounds. For instance, a high-pitched sound is delivered at a regular rate and interrupted periodically at no regular rate by a low-pitched sound. The patient is instructed to respond to or count the less frequently presented sounds. The difficulty with this Evoked Response is that the cooperation and the attention of the patient are necessary for this test. Therefore, anything that interferes with an individual's attention will tend to reduce the response. Studies of adult psychotic patients have demonstrated a marked reduction or absence of this response. Again, however, this may be related to attention. Studies in adult affective disorder patients have shown attenuation of P-300 amplitude to a lesser degree than that in schizophrenics but more than seen in the average adult. Again, whether this is related to ability to concentrate is unclear. Studies using the long latency evoked potential such as the P-300 have not been extensively done in children. However, this is a new method that is presently being studied in the younger population. Other long latency evoked potentials have been studied in children with attention deficit disorders and learning disabilities. Some of these studies have found no difference between these children and normals (Hall et al. 1976). Other studies, primarily using Auditory Evoked Response, have shown longer latencies and lower amplitudes in some of the younger patients with attention deficits. Children at older ages did not appear to show these signs (Satterfield and Braley 1977).

In children with hyperactivity and attention deficit disorder, there have been varying reports as to the use of the evoked potential in predicting the response to medication. Hall et al. found no significant difference in Visually Evoked Responses between the two responders and nonresponders, but there have been other reports to the contrary (Rutter and Hersov 1985). Suffice it to say that the literature on attention deficit disorder and evoked potentials is inconclusive and demands further study.

Computerized Topographical Brain Mapping

Computerized Topographical Brain Mapping is a relatively new electrodiagnostic technique that may greatly improve the information available for the recording of cortical potentials. Although the EEG is an important diagnostic tool, it has been poor in detecting diseases manifesting more subtle changes in brain activity. Part of the limitation in the conventional EEG has been due to the difficulty of visual analysis of the wave forms.

One of the goals of brain mapping is to overcome the limitations of the conventional EEG tracing. The EEG and Evoked Potentials are obtained from multiple scalp electrodes. The data is then processed by computer, which interprets the activity between electrode sites and produces an array of colors on the video screen. This procedure allows the reader to visualize easily even low amplitude activity seen at the scalp. The computer also allows for complicated mathematical processing producing spectral analysis, spatial analysis, and temporal analysis as well as statistical analysis.

Psychiatry is frequently criticized for its lack of hard scientific data for some of its diagnoses and treatment. Topographic brain mapping has the potential to offer a new mode of scientific inquiry that may be valuable to the psychiatrist. This test, like the EEG, is noninvasive and is performed in a similar manner to the classic EEG. The initial evaluation utilizes segments of the standard EEG in various states (eyes closed, eyes open, concentrating, staring, reading, etc.). The computer then generates a power spectral analysis of the different frequencies, creating a map of energy present at varying frequencies.

In the evoked potential, the brain mapping allows us to anatomically locate the electrical activity over the entire cortex at a given moment in time in response to varying stimuli. With this tool, one can localize and quantify the response of particular areas of the brain to particular stimuli. The technique of brain mapping has been applied to many of the major areas of psychiatric illness. In the pediatric age group there have been only limited studies published. The major portion of studies in children has been in the learning-disabled population.

Computerized Topographic Brain Mapping offers a new method to view data obtained from electrical activity of the brain. One can only speculate as to what the future may hold for the understanding of psychopathology in terms of cortical activity. The application of brain mapping to psychiatric disease is a new and exciting endeavor.

CONCLUSION

Neurophysiological testing, when one understands its application and limitations, can be of substantial assistance to the child psychiatrist. The electroencephalogram is of most value in helping to identify that psychiatric population in which there is an associated organic disorder. The EEG, coupled with Evoked Potential, may be useful in the diagnosis of conversion disorders, factitious disorder, or malingering. There is no psychiatric disorder in which neurophysiological testing alone can be exclusively diagnostic.

Newer modalities of testing, such as computerized EEG, brain electrical mapping, and positive emission tomography, offer new ways to study the higher functioning of the brain. They promise to add significantly to our understanding and appreciation of the conscious and unconscious mind, both in health and disease.

With multiple modalities now available for clinical evaluation of patients, one needs remember that neurophysiological techniques are only one of the many types of tools in the armamentarium of the physician.

REFERENCES

Eeg-Olofson, O. (1971). The development of the electroencephalogram in normal children from age 1 through 15: 14 and 6 Hz. positive spike phenomenon. *Neuropediatric* 2:405–27.

Egli, M., and Graf, I. (1971). The use of anticonvulsant treatment of behaviorally disturbed children with bioelective epilepsy. *Acta Paedopsychiat.* 41:541–69.

Fariello, R. G., and Black, J. A. (1978). Pseudoperiodic bilateral EEG paroxysm in a case of phenycledine intoxication. *J. Clinical Psychiatry* 39:579–81.

Fenwick, P. (1985). The EEG in child psychiatry. In M. Rutter and L. Hersov (Eds.). *Child and Adolescent Psychiatry—Modern Approaches.* London: Blackwell, p. 297.

Gibbs, E. L., and Gibbs, F. A. (1951). Electroencephalographic evidence of thalamic and hypothalamic epilepsy. *Neurology* 1:136–44.

———. (1962). Extive spindles: Correlation of electroencephalographic sleep patterns with mental retardation. *Science* 138:1106–7.

Hall, R. A., et al. (1976). Evoked Potential Stimulus intensity and drug treatment in hyperkinesis. *Psychophysiology* 13:405–18.

Henry, C. E. (1963). Positive spike discharges in the EEG and behavior abnormality. In G. H. Glaser (Ed.). *EEG and Behavior*. New York: Basic Books, pp. 315–44.

Hughes, J. R. (1960). The 14 and 7 per second positive spikes—A reappraisal following a frequency count. *Neurophysiol.* 42:776–84.

———, and Cayaffa, J. J. (1978). Positive Spikes revisited—In the adult. *Clin. Electroencephalography* 2:52–59.

———, and Wilson, W. P. (1983). *EEG and Evoked Potentials in Psychiatry*. Woburn, Mass.: Butterworth.

Itil, T. M., Sineon, J., and Coffin, C. (1976). Qualitative and quantitative EEG in psychotic children. *Diseases of the Nervous System* 37:247.

Kelloway, P. (1952). The development of sleep spindles and arousal patterns in infants and their characteristics in normal and certain abnormal states. *Neurophysiol.* 4:639 (Abstract).

Klinkerfuss, G. H., et al. (1965). Electroencephalographic abnormalities of children with hyperactive behavior. *Neurology* 15:833–91.

Koukkou, M., and Lehmann, D. (1976). Human EEG before and during cannabis hallucinations. *Biol. Psychiatry* 11:663–77.

Lehman, E. I., and Hopes, H. (1978). The effects of imipromine and lofepromine on EEG and their dependence on relative alpha frequency. *Neuropsych. Pharm.* 11:128–33.

Lombroso, C. T., et al. (1966). Ctenoids in healthy youths: Controlled study of 14- and 6-per-second positive spiking. *Neurology* 16:1152–58.

Loomis, S. D., Bohnert, P. J., and Huncke, S. S. (1967). Prediction of EEG abnormalities in adolescent delinquents. *Arch. Gen. Psychiatry* 17:494–97.

Marshall, C. (1955). Some clinical correlates of the wave and spike phantom. *Clin. Neurophysiol.* 7:633–36.

Pedley, T. A., and Guillemaunt, C. (1977). Episodic nocturnal wandering responsive to anticonvulsant drug therapy. *Am. Neurol.* 2:30–35.

Petersen, I., and Eeg-Olofson, O. (1981). Longitudinal study of the EEG in normal children and adolescents. *Clin. Neurophysiol.* 52:561 (Abstract).

Ritvo, E. R., et al. (1970). Correlation of psychiatric diagnosis and EEG findings: A double blind study. *Amer. J. Psychiatry* 126:988–96.

Rutter, M., and Hersov, L. (Eds.). (1985). *Child and Adolescent Psychiatry—Modern Approaches*. London: Blackwell, p. 298.

Satterfield, J. H., and Braley, B. W. (1977). Evoked potentials and brain maturation in hyperactive and normal children. *Electroenceph. Clin. Neurophysiol.* 43:43–51.

Shagass, C. (1976). An electrophysiological view of schizophrenia. *Biol. Psychiatry* 11:3–30.

Shetty, J. (1971). Alpha rhythms in the hyperkinetic child. *Nature* 324:476.

Small, J. G., et al. (1977). Electroencephalographic and clinical studies of early infantile autism. *Clin. Electroencephalog.* 8:27–35.

Tharp, B. R. (1966). The 6-per-second spike and wave complex. *Arch. Neurol.* 15:533–37.

Weinberg, W. A., and Brumback, R. A. (1976). Mania in childhood: Case studies and literature review. *Amer. J. Dis. Child* 130:380–85.

White, P. T., Demyer, W., and Demyer, M. (1964). EEG abnormalities in early childhood schizophrenia—A double blind study of psychiatrically disturbed children
during promomine sedation. *Amer. J. Psychiatry* 120:950–58.
Wiener, J. M., Delano, J. G., and Klass, D. W. (1966). An EEG study of delinquent
and nondelinquent adolescents. *Arch. Gen. Psychiatry* 15:144–50.
Yamada, T., Gordon, M., and Spillers, E. (1976). Further observation of positive
bursts in a comatose patient with Reye's Syndrome. *Proc. Am. EEG Soc.* 17.

21

THE NEUROLOGICALLY IMPAIRED CHILD AND ADOLESCENT

Helen Hanesian, Patricio Paez, and Daniel T. Williams

There has been a recent upsurge in interest in exploring the clinical terrain at the neuropsychiatry interface. In fact, entire volumes have been devoted to the subject (Trimble 1981; Pincus and Tucker 1985; Trimble 1985a; Hales and Yudofsky 1987). As we understand more about the neurophysiological underpinnings of both normal and psychopathological human behavior, there is a yearning to move beyond phenomenological description and categorization of emotional and behavioral disturbances to an elucidation of underlying mechanisms. This, in turn, presents the possibility of fashioning treatment strategies that derive not only from prior empirical trials of clinical intervention with certain types of disturbed behavior, but eventually from a grasp of the underlying pathophysiology.

For example, when a child presents with a recent onset of episodic confusion, bizarre behavior, and hallucinatory experiences, the sophisticated clinician can now do much more than take a routine history and mental status examination, and offer speculations about possible psychological causes of the patient's psychotic symptoms and a prescription for neuroleptic medication. Being alert to the fact that many disparate biological influences can lead to similar symptomatic manifestations leads the clinician first to pointed inquiries regarding possible toxic ingestions, seizure manifestations, or indications of possible trauma, infection or metabolic insults to the central nervous system. Appropriate physical and laboratory evaluations can quickly put the clinician in a more informed position to narrow differential diagnostic possibilities and commence appropriate treatment. In order to proceed along this course, however, the clinician must be imbued with a psychobiological perspective so that pertinent differential diagnostic possibilities are called to mind.

There is substantial evidence that children with documented organic brain disorders are more susceptible to environmental stresses, family disharmony, and toxicity from psychotropic medications (Rutter 1981; Shaffer 1985; Rubinstein and Shaffer 1985). While there is a wide array of studies that support this contention from the epidemiological standpoint, the clinical focus of the current chapter leads to the selection of only three representative clinical entities, which will be discussed in some detail. It is hoped that the reader can extend the perspective developed to the myriad of other entities to be encountered at the pediatric neuropsychiatry interface.

EPILEPSY

Epilepsy is a condition characterized by sudden, recurrent, and transient disturbances of mental functions or body movements that result from excessive discharging of groups of brain cells (Goldensohn et al. 1984). As such, epilepsy does not refer to a specific disease but rather to a group of symptoms that have many different causes in different individuals. In some individuals the underlying causes are static and in some they are progressive. All of the underlying causes of epilepsy have in common the quality of causing cerebral neurons to become excessively excited. The statistically more common causes of this neuronal hyperexcitability generally involve either structural abnormality of the brain or biochemical aberrations of a metabolic, infectious, or other physical etiology. Nevertheless, a review of the literature on the psychogenic precipitants of neurogenic seizures (Williams 1982) clarifies that numerous studies in both experimental animals and in patients have substantiated the capacity of emotional stress to precipitate neurogenic seizures in predisposed subjects where an organic vulnerability exists. Hence there is an important role for the psychiatrist not only in helping patients and their families to cope with the troubling psychiatric consequences of epilepsy, but also in intervening in some cases with regard to influencing pathogenesis.

The signs and symptoms of epilepsy are manifold. Among the most common manifestations are episodes of partial or complete loss of consciousness, localized or generalized muscular spasms or jerks, or apparently purposeful behavior performed while awareness is depressed. The multifaceted modes of clinical manifestation, and the fact that electroencephalographic recordings are not always diagnostic, leads to the relatively frequently encountered problem of pseudoseizures as another major diagnostic and therapeutic challenge at the neuropsychiatric interface.

Epidemiology

Estimates based on epidemiologic studies indicate that up to 1 percent of the population in the United States have epilepsy and that new cases appear at an annual rate of 40 per 100,000 (Hauser et al. 1983). Furthermore, the rate is highest in children younger than 5, with another peak of incidence at the age of puberty. Thus, it is clear that children and adolescents merit special consideration with regard to developmental issues that interact with the psychiatric complications of epilepsy.

There is evidence that socioeconomic factors play an important role in the development of epilepsy. For example, the incidence was found to be higher in black children (1.96 percent) than in white children (0.95 percent) living in New Haven, Connecticut (Hauser et al. 1983). Yet the cause of this difference is uncertain; the relative importance of perinatal factors, trauma, nutrition, other environmental influences, or genetics is unknown.

In this context, the role of inheritance in epilepsy is controversial. It is often difficult to distinguish social and economic factors from primary genetic predisposition, since poor nutrition and inadequate perinatal care, for example, frequently run in families. However, several studies indicate that, in patients with generalized epilepsy, close relatives have a two-to-four-fold increase in incidence of convulsive disorders, strongly suggesting a genetic component of vulnerability.

Classification of Epileptic Seizures

A recently revised International Classification of Seizures, which has served to improve professional communication based on a more contemporary understanding of seizure pathophysiology, is summarized as follows (Proposal for Revised Clinical and Electroencephalographic Classification of Epileptic Seizures 1981):

I. *Partial Seizures* (seizures beginning locally)
  A. Simple partial seizures (consciousness not impaired)
    1. With motor symptoms
    2. With somatosensory or special sensory symptoms
    3. With autonomic symptoms
    4. With psychic symptoms
  B. Complex partial seizures (with impairment of consciousness)
    1. Beginning as simple partial seizures and progressing to impairment of consciousness
    2. With impairment of consciousness at onset
  C. Partial seizures secondarily generalized
II. *Generalized Seizures* (bilaterally symmetric and without local onset)
  A. Absence seizures
  B. Myoclonic seizures
  C. Clonic seizures
  D. Tonic seizures
  E. Tonic-clonic seizures
  F. Atonic seizures
III. *Unclassified Epileptic Seizures* (due to incomplete data)

Space limitations preclude more detailed consideration of these clinical subtypes here, but it clearly behooves the psychiatrist working with a seizure patient to be cognizant of the specific seizure manifestations and associated clinical and prognostic features, as well as medication requirements connoted by the patient's specific seizure type.

Psychological and Psychiatric Assessment

Cognitive Functioning. A review of several studies in this area (Stores 1981) indicates that although many children with epilepsy function normally at school, proportionately more of them have learning problems than do nonepileptic children. In the Isle of Wight Study, for example, which concentrated on nine- to eleven-year-old children, over twice as many of those with epilepsy showed serious specific reading retardation than did nonepileptic children.

Developmental considerations appear pertinent here. O'Leary et al. (1981) administered a neuropsychological test battery to forty-eight children aged nine to twelve with tonic-clonic seizures. The children with seizures of early onset (before age five) were significantly impaired relative to the children with later onset on eight of the fourteen measures in the battery. The deficits were seen on tasks whose requirements included attention and concentration, memory, complex problem solving, and motor coordination.

Seizure type, duration, and degree of seizure control also seem pertinent. Farwell et al. (1985) did detailed neuropsychological testing of one hundred eighteen epileptic children ages six to fifteen and a control group of one hundred children without seizures. The Wechsler full-scale IQ of seizure patients was significantly lower than that of controls and was related to seizure type. Children with minor motor or atypical absence seizures had the lowest average FSIQ. All seizure types except classic absence alone were associated with below-control intelligence. Intelligence was also correlated with degree of seizure control. A highly significant inverse correlation between years with seizures and intelligence was found. Finally, children with seizures had been placed in special education or had repeated a grade in school almost twice as frequently as controls, and their academic achievement was behind grade placement more often than in controls.

Data from a large longitudinal study (the Collaborative Perinatal Project of the National Institute of Neurological and Communicative Disorders and Stroke) confirm the observation that as a group children with seizure disorders have lower scores on intelligence tests than other children (Ellenberg et al. 1986). However, the large sample size, use of controls, and longitudinal follow-up allowed clarification that the excess of retardation among children with seizures was accounted for by children who had neurologic abnormalities before the first seizure. Thus, among ninety-eight children with seizures, the mean score on IQ tests at seven years was not significantly different from the mean score of their siblings. Hence, it is clearly important not to assume that the presence of a seizure disorder implies intellectual impairment.

Anticonvulsant drugs, especially in combination, have been shown in recent years to interfere in significant ways with cognitive function, including attention, concentration, memory, motor and mental speed, and mental processing (Reynolds 1985). These sometimes subtle effects are easily overlooked, but may accrue to the point of substantial impairment, particularly for children in learning situations.

Recent studies have shown that most epileptic patients can be controlled on single-drug therapy and that there is very little difference in antiepileptic efficacy among the major antiepileptic drugs within designated seizure categories (Reynolds 1985). Consequently, the relative influence of each drug on cognitive function may prove to be a most important factor in the choice of an anticonvulsant drug. In this regard, it should be noted that several studies have shown significant associations between long-term use of phenytoin and phenobarbital, and cognitive deterioration in children (Corbet et al. 1985). By contrast, carbamazepine has been noted to be markedly less prone to contribute to cognitive impairments in both short- and long-term use in both normal volunteers and seizure patients.

From the above, it can readily be discerned that primary attention should be given to periodic formal monitoring of the cognitive functioning of seizure patients, with particular view to picking up signs of progressive cognitive impairment that might otherwise be overlooked. It is certainly within the purview of a psychiatrist treating such a patient to ascertain that such monitoring has occurred, to ascertain that therapeutic serum anticonvulsant levels have been documented, and to discuss with the treating neurologist the possible need for a change in anticonvulsant regimen when indicated by the patient's level of cognitive functioning.

Behavior and Personality. The literature on personality changes in epilepsy has been prolific, longstanding, and controversial (Trimble 1985b). According to some estimates, for example, 30 to 40 percent of patients with temporal lobe epilepsy (complex partial seizures) experience persistent psychiatric symptoms that, more frequently than uncontrolled seizures, become the most incapacitating aspect of the illness (Baer et al. 1984). Multiple clinical reports in adult temporal lobe seizure patients have delineated characteristic features, including deepened emotions, changes in sexual function, aggressivity, development of intense religious or philosophic interests, circumstantiality, and interpersonal viscosity. One fascinating neuropsychiatric correlate in this regard was the finding in adults of a different constellation of personality features in right versus left temporal lobe seizure patients (Baer and Fedio 1977).

A recent study of this issue in children with unilateral temporal lobe seizure foci failed to disclose characteristic differences in cognitive or personality features between right and left temporal lobe seizure patients (Camfield et al. 1984). Yet when the two groups of unilateral seizure patients were combined, ten out of twenty-seven patients (five with left, five with right focus) were seen to have personality maladjustment on formal assessment. Furthermore, the group as a whole showed significantly lower neuropsychological test functioning than normally adjusted children.

Developmental considerations may help understand the evolution of certain psychopathological correlates of the seizure state over time. Thus, Flor-Henry (1983) has studied severe psychopathological syndromes (psychosis) seen in adult seizure patients. He found that schizophreniform psychosis in these patients was related to pathology in the dominant hemisphere, whereas depressive psychosis (and neurosis) related to pathology of the nondominant hemisphere. In relation to this, Lindsay et al. (1979) did a long-term outcome study of one hundred children with temporal lobe seizures. In childhood, mental deficiency, the hyperkinetic syndrome, and cataclysmic rage outbursts were prominent. Indeed, only fifteen of the one hundred probands were wholly free from psychological problems in childhood. Yet follow-up indicated that the occurrence of overt psychiatric disorder in adult life was relatively low: Of those survivors who were not gravely mentally retarded, 70 percent were regarded as psychiatrically healthy. Overt schizophreniform psychoses developed in 10 percent of the survivors. Males with continuing epilepsy and left-sided foci were at special risk: 30 percent of such patients became psychotic. In consonance with the above noted findings of Flor-Henry and others, no patient coded as having a right-sided focus in childhood became psychotic by the time of follow-up thirteen years later. Lindsay et al. emphasized the surprising and hopeful change from the overwhelming presence of psychopathology in the childhood sample to the predominance of relative psychological intactness by adulthood. They noted that the majority of their patients received psychiatric intervention in their early years and emphasized the importance of providing such service in the appropriate management of epileptic children.

Further indications of the probable role of central nervous system (CNS) dysfunction in the psychiatric vulnerabilities of patients with epilepsy are reflected in a recent study by Hoare (1984a). Two groups of epileptic children, one newly diagnosed and one with chronic epilepsy, were contrasted with two comparable groups of diabetic children and with a nonpatient sample in order to evaluate the development of psychiatric disorder. The results confirm previous findings that children with chronic epilepsy are significantly more disturbed than both children with chronic physical illness not involving the CNS and those in the general population. Children with newly diagnosed epilepsy were also significantly more disturbed than both those with newly diagnosed diabetes and those in the general population. In both groups of epileptic children, those with focal EEG abnormalities and/or complex partial seizures were particularly vulnerable to psychiatric disturbance. The development of inappropriate dependency was also greater in the two epileptic groups of children than in the comparison groups (Hoare 1984b).

From the above it is clear that youngsters with epilepsy are at increased risk with regard to the development of psychiatric disturbance. Certainly not every youngster with epilepsy requires psychiatric attention, but a substantial proportion do and stand to benefit therefrom. A psychiatrically sophisticated neurologist who routinely follows these youngsters and can make appropriate early referral for psychiatric assessment when needed is probably the best conduit for such intervention. Once this has been done, assessment follows a routine age-appropriate format for the patient and family, with special focus on those areas of vulnerability which have been noted above. As noted below, these considerations may have application at times to the issue of seizure control.

Psychogenically Precipitated Neurogenic Seizures and Pseudoseizures

Substantial evidence points to the enhanced cognitive and emotional vulnerability of youngsters with epilepsy; it is not surprising that one manifestation of this vulnerability would be a worsening of their presenting seizure symptoms under circumstances of emotional stress. It is important for the clinician to be thoughtful and sensitive in exploring this domain, because of the many complexities that abound in the areas of differential diagnosis and treatment.

Williams (1982) reviewed several studies pointing to the role of environmental stress and emotional experiences as precipitants of true neurogenic seizures. These included reports of the emotional activation of the EEG in patients with convulsive disorder, particularly those with sensory (simple partial) and complex partial seizures when exposed to stress interviews. Furthermore, the direct emotional activation of seizures has been documented in several animal species when seizure-prone animals were exposed to various forms of environmental stress.

In contrast to the above, the term pseudoseizures has been used to designate seizure-like phenomena of purely psychological origin that are produced by patients with varying degrees of conscious or unconscious intentionality for a vast array of psychological motivations. While these are reviewed in detail elsewhere (Williams and Mostofsky 1982), brief notation is made here of the general categories of diagnostic classification to be considered in the process of assessment. These include somatoform disorders, factitious disorders, and malingering. (See Chapter 35 in this text.)

It may sometimes be extremely difficult for the clinician (neurologist, psychiatrist or other), even after a thorough review of the history, physical exam, and laboratory findings, to be certain about the distinction between neurogenic seizures, whether psychogenically precipitated or not, and pseudoseizures. This is so not only because of the protean manifestations of epileptic phenomena, but also because of the frequently artful capacity of many patients to mimic neurogenic seizures on a conscious or unconscious basis.

Simultaneous videotape and EEG recording has been a significant aid in the differential diagnosis of epilepsy and pseudoseizures (Feldman et al. 1982). The procedure focuses one camera on the patient who is wired with electrodes connected to an electroencephalograph, while a second camera is focused on the EEG write-out. The picture of the patient and the simultaneous EEG tracing appear on a split-screen videomonitor. This combined recording is stored on the videotape for future analysis and interpretation. Studies using this technique have disclosed that even in patients with clearly documented pseudoseizures there may be a coexisting neurogenic seizure disorder in from 10 percent (Lesser et al. 1983) to 37 percent (Krumholz and Niedermayer 1983) of patients.

It should be emphasized that errors in diagnosis are common in both directions in differentiating between neurogenic and psychogenic seizures. Often, ongoing assessment of the patient and family over time and close collaboration between the neurologist and mental health professional are needed to clarify the issue and to formulate an effective treatment plan.

CASE VIGNETTE

Paul was seen in psychiatric consultation at age nineteen because of persistent uncontrolled seizures after sixteen years of continuous anticonvulsant treatment with many different medications. The referring neurologist, aware of numerous markedly abnormal EEGs dating back to early childhood, was puzzled by a progressive improvement in the EEG over time, but a persistence of uncontrolled seizures, despite his maintaining the patient on therapeutic levels of three simultaneous anticonvulsants. Further, he noted the patient's report that many of the seizures were precipitated under circumstances of emotional stress.

The medical history included an episode of postvaccination encephalitis in infancy, with hospitalization and subsequent recovery. When he was three, in the setting of a conflict with his age-peer cousin, whom he injured, his grandmother shrieked, which coincided with the precipitation of a seizure in Paul. Many other seizures followed, and Paul was maintained on various anticonvulsants over time, with variable degrees—never quite complete—of seizure control. Paul experienced learning problems in school, which led to reprimands and pressure from his parents. He also was embarrassed by the experience of having uncontrolled seizures, including occasional incontinence, in view of his peers at school. He became socially withdrawn and evermore emotionally dependent on his family, particularly his articulate and domineering father, a self-made successful business entrepreneur. On finishing high school, Paul began working in his father's business. He also took some college courses but found his concentration and memory impaired, presumably by the substantial doses of the three anticonvulsants he was taking, superimposed on his previously reported learning difficulties.

On psychiatric evaluation, Paul appeared to be of average intelligence and manifested no thought disorder nor any other psychotic features. His mood was mildly depressed, and he expressed many concerns regarding his capacities for normal social, vocational, and educational functioning. The misguided nature of his father's overly intrusive and directive interventions was exemplified in his arranging for Paul to play the lead role in a pornographic film to enhance his confidence in his sexual competence.

During the course of ongoing exploratory psychotherapy, a pattern emerged in Paul's description of his seizures suggesting that they often appeared at times when he was anxious about the prospect of asserting himself in a social, school, or family setting. Particularly with his father, the seizures seemed precipitated by actual or impending criticisms or confrontations and seemed to engender a backing off by his father in the face of the seizure.

These observations led to the scheduling of a video-EEG monitoring session. Since both Paul and his father believed the events reported at age three to have been important emotional precipitants of the seizure problem, these were used as part of a diagnostic trial to try to precipitate a seizure during video-EEG monitoring, using hypnotic age-regression. (See Chapter 54 on hypnosis.) Indeed, when the patient was asked to visualize and experience in trance the events of that first seizure, a "seizure" was precipitated which turned out to have no EEG seizure correlates. This was the first documentation of the presence of pseudoseizures in Paul, and it constituted a dramatic turning point in his treatment. Because Paul was eager to diminish his anticonvulsant regimen, an agreement was worked out among the patient, the neurologist, and the psychiatrist for a gradual tapering of anticonvulsants, provided that Paul could establish a relatively seizure-free state with the help of ongoing psychotherapeutic support. Using this behavior modification framework of positive reinforcement for symptom relinquishment, together with individual and conjoint family sessions as well as hypnosis, Paul was progressively tapered off all three anticonvulsant medications over a six-month period. He continued in supportive psychotherapy for another seven months and has remained seizure-free off all anticonvulsants over two years in follow-up.

Epilepsy, Aggression, and Violence

There is controversy in the literature regarding the association between epilepsy on the one hand and aggression and violence on the other. One well-controlled study of eighty-three children with epilepsy found an association between the presence of anterior temporal lobe epileptiform spike activity and increased aggression scores on the Achenbach Child Behavior Checklist (Whitman et al. 1982). The authors note, however, that such biological variables predictive of behavioral disorder accounted for only small amounts of the variance in their comparison of children with temporal lobe and generalized epilepsies. In this regard, they recommend that more consideration be given to delineating the "situation-centered" variables predictive of behavioral disorder in children with epilepsy.

Using a different research strategy, clinical studies of violent incarcerated adolescents by Lewis et al. (1982) have suggested that epilepsy, especially psychomotor (complex partial, temporal lobe) epilepsy, is more prevalent in young offenders than in the general population. Furthermore, psychomotor epilepsy in this population was particularly associated with violence. In a clinical study of ninety-seven incarcerated boys, eleven had psychomotor seizures and an additional eight were thought most probably to have psychomotor seizures. Of the eleven boys with definite seizure disorders, all had been seriously assaultive; five had committed acts of violence during seizures as well as at other times. The authors reviewed some of the diagnostic difficulties inherent in establishing the diagnosis of psychomotor seizures in an individual where such a clinical diagnosis may interact with the perception of legal responsibility for a violent act. Despite some of the imprecision inherent in diagnosing psychomotor seizures, however, added circumstantial support for the diagnosis was lent by the very frequent history of severe central nervous system trauma such as perinatal difficulty, CNS infection, head injury, or a history of frank grand mal seizures. Of note also was the frequent association of a number of psychotic symptoms, as well as the frequent association of reports of severe physical abuse in the histories of these youngsters. The latter association in particular certainly addresses the probable role of situational variables in fostering violence in youngsters biologically at risk by virtue of a greater predisposition to impulsivity and aggression. Most importantly, the authors emphasized that a clinician called on to evaluate a violent delinquent may render a valuable service in identifying potentially treatable neuropsychopathology so that appropriate intervention can occur.

Treatment

In view of the generally acknowledged enhanced psychological vulnerability of epileptic patients, particularly to the effects of anxiety and depression (Betts 1981), it is clearly advisable to provide appropriate intervention when such symptoms are in evidence. In this regard, the elevated risk of suicide in epileptic patients is noteworthy (Barraclough 1981). Psychotherapeutic interventions in such patients should be geared to the nature of the presenting symptomatology, while taking note of the relevance of the patient's epileptic condition. Consideration of psychopharmacological agents requires attention to a potential impact on seizure threshold, as noted below.

A somewhat unique psychotherapeutic challenge in this population is that of treating psychogenically precipitated neurogenic seizures and pseudoseizures. There are many reports of successful psychotherapeutic or psychobiological treatment interventions for purposes of seizure control (Mostofsky and Balaschak 1977; Williams et al. 1978 and 1979; Williams and Mostofsky 1982). It should be emphasized that appropriate differential diagnostic assessment is a prerequisite to appropriate treatment planning in this area. The various treatment approaches utilized can be summarized under the following broad headings: conditioning techniques, psychodynamic approaches, relaxation and hypnosis, and biofeedback. As outlined in the case vignette above, often several such approaches may be usefully integrated in the service of maximizing therapeutic impact to facilitate symptom relinquishment and foster improved adaptation by the patient.

Special psychopharmacological considerations are also noteworthy in this area. Already noted is the need for the clinician to be aware of potentially cognitive-impairing effects of various anticonvulsants, particularly phenytoin and phenobarbital. Additionally, the frequently observed capacity of phenobarbital to generate hyperactivity, irritability, and aggressivity in children should be borne in mind. Consequently, it is clearly important to advocate the lowest reasonable dose of the least toxic anticonvulsant consonant with good seizure control. Carbamazepine has been reported in a number of studies to manifest mood stabilizing as well as anticonvulsant properties (Post et al. 1986). It may thus be advisable in a patient who is experiencing disturbance of mood or behavior, while being treated with another anticonvulsant, to consider switching to carbamazepine if anticonvulsant efficacy is comparable.

In many epileptic patients, however, even when the anticonvulsant regimen is optimized, there may still be indications for the additional use of psychotropic medication. Benzodiazepines have a valid place when minor tranquilization is needed. The value of intravenous diazepam in status epilepticus is well known, so there is clearly no danger of its lowering the seizure threshold, but the capacity to enhance sedation by interaction with coexisting anticonvulsants should be noted.

Major tranquilizers do have a place in the treatment of interictal psychoses in patients with epilepsy (Trimble 1985c). It should be noted, however, that several neuroleptics, particularly chlorpromazine, have a significant capacity to lower the seizure threshold and induce seizures. Of the neuroleptics currently available, molindone appears to be the safest in this regard.

Most antidepressants also have the capacity to lower the seizure threshold and induce seizures. A recent study, however, notes a marked variability among various antidepressants in this respect (Luchins et al. 1984). This study used an in vitro technique involving drug influence on spike activity in perfused guinea pig hippocampal slices. Imipramine, amitryptiline, nortryptiline, maprotiline, and desipramine tended to increase spike activity in a descending order of effect. Doxepine increased spike activity at lower concentrations, but reduced it at higher concentrations, whereas protriptyline and trimipramine reduced spike activity with increasing concentrations.

There is clinical evidence of the potential benefit of adding propranolol to the medication regimen of epileptic patients with uncontrolled aggressive outbursts that have not been controlled by optimal anticonvulsant medication adjustment (Williams et al. 1982). Although this has not yet been subjected to controlled study, open clinical experience to date suggests that a significant proportion of such patients demonstrate improved behavioral control of aggressive behavior and irritability. As long as titration is gradual with appropriate monitoring of EKG, pulse, and blood pressure and with cognizance of the relevant contraindications to using B-adrenergic blocking medication, side effects are minimal and well-tolerated.

An important consideration in treating any child or adolescent with epilepsy and an associated psychiatric problem is the need to take into account family dynamics pertinent to the genesis of the problem as well as family resources that can be mobilized in the service of effective treatment. This is particularly relevant in light of the frequently encountered problem of heightened dependency needs in such patients, noted previously. Finally, we cannot overemphasize the importance of maintaining open lines of communication between the neurologist and mental health practitioner to assure appropriate psychobiological treatment integration.

CEREBRAL PALSY

Definition and Brief History

The complex problem of cerebral palsy leads to confusion regarding the term, for it is comprised of medical, psychological, and social concerns. A survey of the literature reveals a wide range of definitions from a restricted focus on physical components to a more useful definition, which views physical symptoms as "one component of a broader brain damage syndrome comprised of neuromotor dysfunction, psychological dysfunction, convulsions, and behavior disorder of organic origin" (Minear 1956). Cerebral palsy refers to a nonprogressive central nervous system deficit with the lesion in either single or multiple locations of the brain. It is a static motor deficit with associated handicaps (Scherzer and Tscharnuter 1982).

More than one hundred years ago, W. J. Little (1862) studied approximately two hundred cases of the disorder and related "spastic rigidity" to "abnormal parturition and asphyxia at birth." He described a number of concomitant traits observed such as: impaired intellect, problems of speech, convulsions, irritability, and impulsive nervous condition. The term "Little's disease" was applied to cerebral palsy until the latter term became popular in the United States early in the 1940s. Little's thinking, however, was influenced by earlier physicians; the disorder was observed in ancient times and was referred to in the Bible (Acts 3:1,2).

In 1947, a team of specialists comprised of an orthopedist, a pediatrician, a physiatrist, an internist, a neurophysiologist, and a neurologist founded the American Academy of Cerebral Palsy, which has been an important influence in bringing the understanding of the disorder to its present level and has further influenced those in related disciplines to give attention to the problem.

Etiology and Prevalence

The underlying static encephalopathy of cerebral palsy has many possible causes and should be considered in differential diagnosis. Denhoff (1976) reported an etiologic classification based on time of onset and cause of the cerebral malformation or injury. These factors are:

1. *Prenatal*—hereditary, chromosomal and congenital (acquired in utero) abnormality, maternal illnesses or disorders affecting the fetus;
2. *Perinatal*—asphyxia, trauma, consequences of "small for date" babies, isoimmunization, hemolytic disorders and obstetrical complications;
3. *Postnatal/early infancy*—trauma, infections, toxins, nutritional, and metabolic factors.

Cerebral palsy may have its origin in any one of the periods listed above, or in combination. Mixed factors are frequent.

Data on the prevalence of cerebral palsy are varied and it is presently even more difficult to get an estimate, because since 1970 cerebral palsy is often included under the term developmental disabilities. Paneth and Kiely (1984), in an international review of population studies since 1950, reported an estimate of 2.0 per one thousand school age children. Only 10 percent of these cases are estimated to be of postnatal origin.

Cruickshank (1976) cited a 1951 survey in the state of New Jersey that reported that factors related to birth injury and developmental problems of a postnatal nature comprised more than 50 percent of the 1,105 cases. Other studies of that period also found that perinatal insults were a predominant cause of cerebral palsy (Crothers and Paine 1959). More recent investigations, however, give less importance to the factor of birth injury. In a study of 142 cerebral-palsied children born in the northwest United States after 1970, Holm (1982) reported that causes were prenatal for 50 percent, perinatal for 33 percent, and postnatal for 10 percent, while 7 percent were mixed. Etiological factors of a retrospective study for 1,503 patients seen in the St. Louis, Missouri, area revealed prematurity to be the most prominent factor, and 39 percent of the causes were prenatal in origin (O'Reilly and Walentynowicz 1981). These findings are in keeping with a recent study, based on 681 cases in Sweden, which concluded, "The factors associated with the greatest risk of developing cerebral palsy are to be born too soon and too small" (Hagberg and Hagberg 1984). Holm (1982) attributed the apparent discrepancy in relative proportion of etiologies "to differences in interpretation of medical findings prompted by recent advances in knowledge of fetal development and implications of obstetric and neonatal events." Research in prenatal development, clinical genetics, and health education were emphasized toward prevention.

Classification of Cerebral Palsy

Classification of cerebral palsy is difficult, for there is neither a single cause nor a characteristic course. More important, the description of the motor disability may not give any insight into associated handicaps such as cognitive functioning and emotional disturbance. Review of the literature reveals a multitude of systems devised by individuals (Crothers and Paine 1959; Ingram 1984) and groups such as the Little Club and the American Academy of Cerebral Palsy (Minear 1956). The most prevalent system of classification has been that of Phelps, whose work was incorporated in the system devised by the American Academy of Cerebral Palsy (Minear 1956).

The basic classification of clinical types adopted by the American Academy of Cerebral Palsy include the following:

1. *Spasticity*—characterized by stiffness of musculature and slow movement. There is a tendency toward greater involvement and contractures affecting antigravity muscles.
2. *Athetosis* —characterized by an abnormal amount and type of involuntary motion. It is further differentiated into several subgroups.

3. *Rigidity* —characterized by decreased motion. The muscles are partially contracted all of the time. The antagonists to the antigravity muscles are involved.
4. *Ataxia*   —characterized by incoordination due to disturbance in the sense of balance.
5. *Tremor*   —characterized by involuntary motions of a rhythmical manner due to agonist and antagonist contractions.
6. *Atonia*   —characterized by lack of tone and failure of muscles to respond to stimulation.

These types are followed by the topographical involvement of: monoplegia, paraplegia, hemiplegia, triplegia, quadriplegia, diplegia, and double hemiplegia.

As indicated earlier, along with the neuromuscular deficit there are often other disabilities present. Although investigators differ as to the prevalence of related disabilities, Scherzer and Tscharnuter (1982) noted that associated handicaps appear frequently. "These include abnormalities of vision (25 percent), hearing and speech (greater than 50 percent), seizure disorders (one-third), mental retardation (50 to 75 percent depending on motor severity), learning disabilities among the vast majority, and frequent social, emotional, and interfamily problems. In every sense, therefore, the term conveys the concept of a multiply handicapping condition."

Psychological and Psychiatric Assessment

The multiple handicaps of children with cerebral palsy require comprehensive assessment of a transdisciplinary nature. Various disciplines of medicine including physical, occupational and speech therapies, as well as psychology and education are integral elements of an effective program. While the motor deficit is often the most obvious disability, it may not be the predominant handicap; the high frequency of associated dysfunctions has been established. Shapiro et al. (1983) in citing Tablan, reported 88 percent of cerebral-palsied youngsters have three or more disabilities. The more frequently associated dysfunctions are: cognitive deficits, communication disorders, visual dysfunction, seizures, emotional and behavioral disorders, sensory impairments, and orthopedic deformities. It is therefore clear that for a thorough understanding of cerebral palsy, it is necessary not only to identify the individual disabilities but also the interaction of these disabilities as they affect one person. It is this complicating factor that makes assessment a difficult and challenging task.

Cognitive Functioning. The most common associated deficit of cerebral palsy is that of cognitive dysfunction. Mental retardation occurs in approximately 50 to 75 percent, while more subtle problems exist manifested in learning disabilities (Scherzer and Tscharnuter 1982). Results from the Isle of Wight studies (Rutter et al. 1976) indicated that children with cerebral palsy tended to be retarded readers even when their intelligence was average.

In an attempt to attend to this problem, the 1975 Education for All Handicapped

Children Act, Public Law 94-142, mandated that every child with a handicapping condition receive a thorough evaluation to determine his educational needs. Under this law all school age children are guaranteed an appropriate education with placement decisions based on nonbiased assessment. Although school systems have attempted to implement these regulations, the extent to which assessment is possible or unbiased for the multiply handicapped child has been questioned.

The standard psychological test battery used by the majority of urban public schools usually includes a measure for:

1) cognitive functioning, such as the Wechsler Intelligence Scale for Children-Revised;
2) visual-motor organization, such as the Bender-Gestalt Reproductions;
3) scholastic achievement, such as the Wide Range Achievement Test or Peabody Individual Achievement Test;
4) personality characteristics, such as the Draw-A-Person Test.

This standard evaluation, which is usually scheduled and completed in one block of time, may not be appropriate for many youngsters with cerebral palsy.

It is well established that intellectual ability is a measurement construct that attempts to quantify such abilities as reasoning, problem solving, verbal comprehension, and functional grasp of concepts and to express the composite score in terms of intelligence or IQ. With increasing age, however, and with handicapped populations, in particular, intelligence becomes differentiated. This multidimensional aspect of intellectual abilities varies such that a profile of functional strengths and weaknesses needs to be delineated (Ausubel et al. 1978). These cognitive abilities are difficult to assess in the cerebral-palsied child who may, for example, have a quadriplegic motor handicap and is nonvocal due to neuromuscular involvement. Because of the multiple deficits, this youngster is at a serious disadvantage in a standard psychological evaluation, which would probably place his functioning within the profound range of mental retardation. His severe deficits may further give him a label of "untestable." It is understandable, therefore, that in the early 1900s, Elizabeth Lord, a pioneer in the psychological evaluation of cerebral-palsied children, strongly disparaged a solely quantitative psychometric approach to these youngsters.

In order to meet this challenge two primary principles of psychological evaluation for the multiply handicapped are necessary:

1. adaption and understanding of standard measurement;
2. systematic observation of the child in the test situation and in the classroom environment.

Standardized Measurement. The purpose of psychological evaluation of the child with cerebral palsy is to assess the current level of intellectual functioning and social/emotional development. The information is communicated to all involved in working with the youngster and it is incorporated into the Individual Education Plan

(IEP) mandated by Public Law 94-142. Psychological measurement has been standardized and validated with specific directions for administration. The psychologist must be knowledgeable about the design and research of the tests in order to use clinical expertise for appropriate test selection and modification for use with a handicapped child. If standard measures are misused, test results will be unreliable and invalid.

The following case presentation provides an example of test selection and adaptation for a severely involved youngster.

CASE VIGNETTE

Jimmy was 8 years, 4 months of age, with a diagnosis of cerebral palsy, spastic type quadriplegia, ataxic, athetoid. He was severely involved from the neck down and had no speech. He communicated through facial expressions and relied on adaptive headgear (a pointer attached around the forehead) for making responses to questions. The tests used for diagnosis were: the Columbia Mental Maturity Scale; the Peabody Picture Vocabulary Test; and the Illinois Test of Psycholinguistic Abilities-Auditory Reception, Visual Reception.

The test results were as follows: Overall motor and language deficits seriously limited Jimmy's ability to perform on standardized tests. Current level of intellectual functioning on the Columbia Mental Maturity Scale was at the low average level (Age Deviation Score = 90). For the Columbia test, which measured general reasoning ability, he indicated with his headpointer the picture, "Which one does not belong?" On the Peabody Picture Vocabulary Test, a measure of receptive word knowledge, he obtained a Mental Age score of 5 years, 5 months (IQ 75). Here, he pointed to the appropriate picture in response to directions such as "Show me running." On selected subtests of the Illinois Test of Psycholinguistic Abilities, he obtained a mental age of 4 years, 10 months for auditory reception. He was asked questions such as, "Do boys play?" "Do chairs play?" He indicated a "yes" or "no" answer by pointing to the word on his lap board. On the visual reception subtest, which measures concepts through matching, he received a mental age of 4 years, 7 months. At the time of evaluation, Jimmy could clearly indicate a response of "yes" or "no" and was being trained in the Bliss Symbols communication method, a nonoral second language system.

A few of the more commonly used standardized instruments for cognitive assessment with cerebral-palsied youngsters are:

1. Columbia-Mental Maturity Scale;
2. Hishey-Nebraska Test of Learning Aptitudes;
3. Leiter International Performance Scale;
4. Peabody Picture Vocabulary Test;
5. Raven Progressive Matrices;
6. Illinois Test of Psycholinguistic Abilities.

Systematic Classroom Observation. It has been shown that techniques of naturalistic observation are useful to describe what occurs in the classroom and have practical implications for teaching (Hanesian 1973). An observational study of response patterns of brain-injured children showed that a child's competence, cognitive, and response styles influenced teaching style (Diller et al. 1977). Children of varying medical diagnoses behaved differently in an evaluation situation and classroom setting. For example, the cerebral-palsied child when in the classroom tended to be less active, less work-oriented, and an observer rather than a participant in contrast to the other groups. Teachers in turn responded less to this apparent passivity.

Systematic classroom observation can be targeted on an individual youngster as a useful supplement to formal evaluation, especially because the reliability and validity of test results for handicapped children has been questioned. In the assessment of Jimmy (case vignette above), a systematic classroom observation was conducted as part of the evaluation. Five, ten-minute samples of behavior were taken over a period of five days. The child's style of response and the teacher's number and type of interventions were recorded. The findings indicated that although Jimmy was restricted in motor movement and was nonvocal, he was responsive to his environment and to interpersonal relationships. Through facial expressions he communicated in an alert and personable manner. The majority of his behaviors were classified as "work" as opposed to "nonwork" because they were active listening and purposeful looking behaviors. The alertness and animation in facial expression reflected intellectual functioning results of the Columbia Mental Maturity Scale. It was recommended that along with training in the Bliss Symbols, reading should be taught through basic sight words and learning of letters, beginning with consonants relevant to words in his sight vocabulary.

Social/Emotional Development. Children with cerebral palsy are at high risk for development of emotional and behavioral disturbance. A review of the literature, however, reveals that most systematic psychological investigations are more concerned with the study of cognitive, perceptual, and visuomotor handicaps than with emotional characteristics. The paucity of data with regard to emotional disturbance is probably due to the complex nature of cerebral palsy seen as a heterogeneous group of disorders with associated handicaps. Among those researchers who have attempted to study the variable of emotional disturbance, some have surveyed the frequency of behavioral problems related to cerebral palsy, others have examined various factors that might lead to the development of emotional disorders, while few investigators have directed their attention to specific types of psychiatric problems. In general, most of these investigators have not used systematic, controlled methodology, and thus yield inconclusive results.

Based on a study from several years of clinical experience, Freeman (1970) concluded that while individuals with brain damage may show a higher incidence of perceptual disorders and problems with emotional control, there is no typical psychiatric category that can be considered characteristic of adolescents with cerebral palsy. Emotional disturbance in the adolescent with cerebral palsy is seen frequently, manifesting the full range of disorders found in the nonhandicapped population. In a more systematic, extensive study of brain-injured children (including cerebral-palsied) on the Isle of Wight, Rutter et al. (1970) reported psychiatric disorder to be five times higher than in the general population and three times higher than in children who had physical disorders not involving the brain. Similarly, Nielsen (1966), in a study that compared cerebral-palsied children of normal intelligence with a control group matched for age, sex, IQ, and socioeconomic status having no evidence of brain damage, found that three times as many cerebral-palsied youngsters displayed signs of moderate or severe personality disorders. Although the kinds of disturbances varied greatly, the cerebral-palsied children showed some common features such as difficulties in interpersonal relations, expectation of hostility and rejection from others, and low tolerance for frustration. When they felt frustrated they revealed tendencies to defiance and aggression. Rutter et al. (1970) also examined the association of organic brain dysfunction with specific types of psychiatric problems. The varieties of the psychiatric problems were similar to those found in any group of youngsters with psychiatric disorder and no known organic brain dysfunction. The majority of these cases showed neurotic or antisocial behaviors. When the variable of psychiatric disorder was controlled, there were few features of behavior, emotions, or relationships that were characteristic of youngsters with organic brain dysfunction. There was a tendency, however, for children with organic brain dysfunction without psychiatric disorder to show poorer concentration than youngsters in the general population, and there was a weak but significant relationship between hypoactivity and organic brain dysfunction. Using the same measures, Anderson et al. (1982) reported a preponderance of neurotic type as compared to antisocial type disorders. In a three-year longitudinal study of physically handicapped fifteen-year-olds (approximately 75 percent with cerebral palsy), the main psychological problems shown were depression, fearfulness, lack of self-confidence, and worry with anxiety related to school and aspects of the handicap. Emotional problems were also manifested in general irritability with some cerebral-palsied adolescents giving vent to tantrums or rages.

The possible causes leading to development of emotional disorders in cerebral-palsied children range from physical and cognitive limitations to environmental and societal circumstances. As was noted earlier, most of these variables have not been subjected to systematic investigation; the result is controversy among researchers.

In the course of growing up, the child, due to restricted movement and disturbances in perception and ability to react, might fail to engage in normal interactions with objects in the environment, with resultant delays in cognitive development (Shere and Kastenbaum 1966). Social interactions might also be less frequent and meaningful than those of other children due to factors such as parental overprotection and sporadic school attendance (Barker et al. 1953). This might result in a history of diminished and distorted interpersonal feedback (Richardson 1964) such that the child's social development is impoverished, superficial, and immature. A pattern of passivity may have been unwittingly imposed on the child from his earliest years.

For the adolescent with cerebral palsy, emotional problems are usually greater and more serious. Normal developmental concerns of peer-group acceptance, relationships with the opposite sex, and striving for independence are compounded by the multiple disabilities. This is further complicated by conflicts deriving from parental inclination toward overprotection, on the one hand, and their concern for the disabled youngster's potential for independence in adult life on the other. In a study that examined mothers' expectations and the children's performance on social, vocational, and intellectual measures, it was found that mothers underestimated the youngsters' levels of functioning. The adolescents' own predictions were even lower (Nussbaum 1966). In a teenage sample of British students, not only the parents but also the school and medical services failed to encourage independence. Sixty percent of the cerebral-palsied adolescents did not know the name of their condition and had little accurate information about it (Anderson et al. 1982). Similarly, Minde (1978), in a follow-up study of thirty-four adolescents with cerebral palsy, also found that poor communication, emotional withdrawal, and distancing existed among parents, siblings, and the cerebral-palsied youngsters regarding the nature of the disability. The development of these children, ages ten to fourteen, was highlighted by an increased awareness that their handicap was permanent and their consequent search for personal and occupational identity, which in general did not extend beyond a hope to finish school. They showed low self-esteem and the beginning of general passivity. Later, in adult life, it was found (Klapper and Birch 1966) that 25 percent of cerebral-palsied individuals are socially isolated and fewer than 10 percent marry.

The effect of visible physical disability on a child's emotional response and development of self-esteem has been subject to consideration. Some researchers see the visible disability of cerebral palsy as a major variable in determining the social reactions and attitudes a child encounters, thereby affecting self-concept (Cruickshank et al. 1976; Freeman 1970). Cruickshank et al. (1976) reported that children with a cardiac condition, a nonvisible disability, function similarly to physically normal children in several social situations. In contrast, cerebral-palsied children with visible handicaps were observed to have different personality characteristics when compared to physically normal peers.

Results from the Isle of Wight studies (Rutter et al. 1976) also indicated that children with cerebral palsy showed more psychiatric disorder than did children with asthma and chronic lung or heart disease. It was postulated, however, that visibility of disability may not be the relevant variable, since psychiatric disorder was similar for children with visible orthopedic disability and those with nonvisible physical conditions. On the other hand, children with cerebral palsy showed more psychiatric problems than those children with physical disability that did not involve the brain. The variable of organic brain dysfunction rather than visible physical disability was seen as the major factor which might result in deficient social perceptions. In an investigation with a specific focus on development of self-concept, Teplin et al. (1981) compared fifteen cerebral-palsied children ages four to eight with a control group matched for age, sex, ethnicity, IQ, and socioeconomic status. The children with cerebral palsy began to see themselves as different by age four, while the potentially negative effect on self-esteem crystallized during the primary grades at school.

The social and emotional development of the child is a complex process closely related to cognitive abilities. When these factors are complicated by the diverse neurophysiological problems of cerebral palsy, the potential for healthy personality development is jeopardized. Because cognitive and personality characteristics are closely interwoven, the assessment of emotional characteristics of the cerebral-palsied is similar to those procedures used for evaluating cognitive functioning, including measures for perceptual-conceptual abilities, projective materials, interview techniques, rating scales, and observational methods.

Treatment

The concept of cerebral palsy as a multiply handicapping condition in need of a transdisciplinary approach has led to legislation for provision of services. These laws, which grant rights to handicapped persons and their families, not only mandate services but also, as importantly, reflect public acceptance of responsibility for the disabled. Although there is need for improvement, there has never been a time of more availability of services.

Early intervention programs, beginning with children as young as two months of age, are increasingly available. In these comprehensive care programs, direct parental participation is not only stressed but is a mandatory condition of the program (Varella and Lazarus 1984). While effectiveness of these programs is subject to investigation, most agree that early involvement of parents enhances their ability to cope with a handicapped child.

For those 3 to 21 years old, the Education for all Handicapped Children Act requires that every child with a handicapping condition receive an appropriate education. Under these regulations the child is entitled to related services in addition to special education. These include various specialized services, some of which are: early identification and assessment of disabilities; physical, occupational and speech therapies; and psychological services as well as parent counseling and training. Within this orientation, psychotherapeutic intervention is an integral part of treatment.

It has been reported that family stress related to a handicapped youngster can be expected during periods of transition such as time of diagnosis, entrance to school, change in school placement, puberty, graduation, and transition to adult life (Anderson et al. 1982). The problems were found to be even greater for those mothers from lower socioeconomic background (Breslau 1983). In order to meet these needs many schools and medical facilities offer a variety of services, which include individual and peer-group therapy, family counseling, and group work for siblings and parents. A helpful technique is behavior modification used to reduce inappropriate behavior and teach adaptive behavior through principles of positive and negative reinforcement (Schofield and Wong 1975). Home and school follow-through are initiated with family and educational staff involvement. Hypnotic imagery has also been used as a tool in working with children with cerebral palsy (Lazar 1977). In addition, respite care, which allows parents time away from their handicapped child, has been a positive resource (Ptacek 1982). Because transition to adult life is even more difficult for the disabled, the cerebral-palsied youngster needs specific social skills training and comprehensive sex education, for general functioning as well as disability-related problems. The provision of appropriate psychopharmacological intervention when psychiatrically indicated is another important consideration.

It is important to note that the social milieu in which the child lives is the critical factor for healthy emotional development. While the physical and psychological components of disability often can be modified only slightly, the attitudes of parents, siblings, peers, and society have potential for greater change and should, therefore, be the focus for therapeutic intervention.

LEAD ENCEPHALOPATHY

Historical Development and Present Status

Among all the heavy metals that have been used in medicine (arsenic, antimony, cadmium, silver, gold, copper, mercury, and zinc), lead is the only one historically with no known therapeutic application (Goodman and Gilman 1985). Recently it has been recognized that even smaller amounts of lead than thought previously are toxic.

The typical diagnosis of lead intoxication in the past was associated with adult males and a known, relatively severe exposure to lead. The cluster of symptoms and signs (nausea, vomiting, abdominal cramps with constipation, headaches, personality changes and various degrees of confusion, dementia, and peripheral neuropathy), with an occupational history of exposure to lead and blood lead levels (PbB) above forty micrograms per deciliter of whole blood (μg/100 dl.), would nowadays present an unequivocal diagnostic picture.

It is only with the advent of the industrial revolution and the widespread use of man-made sources of inorganic and organic lead components, that the documented incidence and prevalence of lead intoxication became a public health problem. The average urban environment in most industrialized cities contains small but measurable amounts of lead in the air, water, and food. It has also been shown that city air has higher lead concentration than rural air. A similar correlation occurs between PbB of people who live in the city as opposed to those who live in rural settings. Yet lead toxicity is a problem not confined exclusively to inner-city children nor limited to one specific geographical area. All American children are exposed to lead in the air, in dust, and in the normal diet (U.S. Dept. of Health 1985). This exposure to environmental lead, however, cannot explain by itself the high prevalence of PbB considered to be pathogenic. Additional sources of exposure, particularly oral ingestion by children, are most often involved; an example is pica, the eating of nonedibles, specifically flakes and chips of old lead paint-coated surfaces. Pica of lead-based paint and lead-containing dust from old dilapidated homes is still the major direct source of high-dose exposure to environmental lead. To complicate the issue even further, lead comes in different forms, shapes, and colors: lead toys; lead paint, plaster; lead pipes and plumbing; lead-lined and lead-glazed pottery used to store food and drinking water; lead jewelry and cosmetics; lead dust from sanding; lead flames from the burning of lead-painted wood, old battery casings, and colored newspapers; sniffing of leaded gasoline and inhalation of fumes from car exhausts; moonshine whisky distilled through lead-containing car radiators; foundries and lead-smelting plants, among others (Nelson 1983).

Prevalence

A recent nationwide survey indicated that 3.9 percent of all American children under the age of five years had levels of 30 μg/dl or more of lead in their blood (U.S. Dept. of Health 1985). These data, applied to the entire population of American children, indicate that an estimated 675,000 children six months to five years of age have concentrations of lead in their blood that, according to the current norms for assessing pathogenicity, need medical treatment in order to minimize the likelihood for neurological damage.

Children's exposure to environmental lead tends to be most prevalent during the summer months in socioeconomically disadvantaged groups and within the age range of nine months to six years. This age distribution is probably associated with this group's developmental tendency to mouth nonfood items.

Etiology and Family Factors

Lead can gain access to the bloodstream through oral ingestion (Goodman and Gilman 1985), inhalation of fumes or dust and, less commonly, through intact skin (organic components only). Pica accounts for most of the documented cases of domestic lead intoxications. The inhalation route, the quickest, is most prevalent among adolescents who become toxic with a rapidly rising PbB following an attempt to get a drug-induced "high."

Once in the bloodstream, nearly all the circulating inorganic lead is associated with the erythrocyte. Then it is distributed in the soft tissues, mostly the kidneys and the liver. In acute intoxications with high concentrations of circulating lead, a Fanconi syndrome (hyperaminoaciduria, glucosuria, hyperphosphaturia) may result from proximal renal tubular damage. Later, lead is redistributed and stored in bones, teeth, hair, and nails.

As an indirectly acting neurotoxin, lead's pathogenicity appears to be related to a blockage of GABA-ergic pathway as well as to direct effect on the synthesis of heme (Silbergeld 1983). There is a partial inhibition of the enzyme 6–aminolevulinic acid (ALA) synthase and dehydrase. It also affects the metabolism of erythrocyte pyrimidine. These considerations are important because the two most useful screening tests for toxicity are lead blood levels (PbB) and erythrocyte protoporphyrin (EP). PbB measures recent absorption and circulating lead. EP-tests measure the level of EP in blood and, at a level of 35 μg/dl or more, indicate impaired heme synthesis. This elevated EP may be due to the toxic effects of lead or to iron deficiency. Therefore, the correlation between both tests in one child gives a more accurate representation of the potential risk of lead toxicity.

Studies in growing animals have shown that the impact of lead ingestion can be magnified by facilitating its absorption (Nelson 1983). There are certain dietary conditions that accelerate the naturally slow rate of lead absorption from the gastrointestinal tract, which occurs mostly in the small intestine. These conditions, in turn, are also associated with the nutritional practices of the lower socioeconomic groups: diets that are high in fat and low in protein, iron, calcium, magnesium, and copper. It is not a coincidence that in black families with an annual income of less than $6,000 living in the cores of large cities, the prevalence of levels of 30 μg/dl or more among their children was found to be 18.6 percent. The lower-income white families also showed a prevalence of elevated levels among their children that was as high as eight times that of families with higher incomes (U.S. Dept. of Health 1985).

Classification

The current official definitions for the measurements of different categories of lead exposure, insult, and toxicity are presented by the January 1985 Center for Disease Control's (CDC's) statement, "Preventing Lead Poisoning in Young Children" (U.S. Dept. of Health 1985): (1) *elevated PbB:* 25 μg/dl or greater; and (2) *lead toxicity:* elevated PbB with an EP of 35 μg/dl or greater. These are the recently accepted guidelines for treatment and follow-up of identified cases. On occasion, and especially in cases of recent exposure, the PbB can be higher than 100 μg/dl in the absence of clearly detectable clinical signs.

Clinical Features

The most severe clinical presentation of lead toxicity in children is that of an acute encephalopathy. Excitement, confusion, ataxia, tonic-clonic seizures, and coma may be present with levels as low as PbB 60–80 μg/dl. This is a medical emergency that requires immediate inpatient treatment directed to lower PbB quickly. Maintained high levels or chronicity will signal serious neurological damage, which may include mental retardation and a clinical picture approximating that of a pervasive developmental disorder. In less severe situations early signs and symptoms of lead toxicity are nonspecific: irritability, anorexia, behavioral changes, fatigue, and vague abdominal complaints. Unless the clinician includes plumbism in the differential diagnosis and explores it with a good history taking and laboratory data, it may be easily missed. Often the earliest recognition of the syndrome comes indirectly from the teacher who refers the child to medical care because of symptoms of attention deficit disorder, usually with hyperactivity.

CASE VIGNETTE

V.G., the only child in a single-parent family supported by public assistance, was seven years old and repeating first grade when first seen by a child psychiatrist because of "behavioral problems." He had been recently rehospitalized, with the diagnosis of "recurrent plumbism" with PbB of 68 μg/dl and EP of 267 μg/dl (both markedly elevated). The clinical presentation associated with his elevated levels of PbB included episodes of headaches, vomiting, constipation with vague abdominal discomfort, and a state of mind that fluctuated between lethargy and irritability.

The neurological evaluation performed on that last readmission was without signs of focal deficits but suggestive of a static encephalopathy secondary to lead intoxication. X rays, including an AP view of the knees, showed metaphyseal lines of slightly greater thickness than normal, which may have represented Pb lines. V. was chelated with BAL 4 mg/kg I.M. $\times$ 1 dose followed four hours later by Ca-Na-2 EDTA 50 mg/kg/d I.V. $\times$ 5 days. His response to that treatment was good with a decrease of PbB to 44 μg/dl on his first follow-up after his short hospitalization. He continued with his outpatient care at the PICA clinic, where his PbB levels were monitored while social services continued with the family's education about sources of lead that could account for the persistence of his condition. Psychometrics performed on him gave him a mental age of 4 years, 10 months compared to his chronological age of 7½ years; the IQ test classified him as mildly mentally retarded (63, Stanford-Binet).

It was not until the age of 11½ years that V. was seen at the Pediatric Neuropsychiatry Clinic at the Medical Center; he was referred by his pediatrician because of "oversensitivity, enuresis and nightmares." V. himself denied any troubles, worries, difficulties, or problems. He said he had suffered from "lead in the blood" but that was an old, "resolved problem." His baseline Conners Teachers Questionnaire was strongly suggestive of an Attention Deficit Disorder with Hyperactivity (ADDH). The teachers' comments were unanimous in labeling him as inattentive, short-tempered, and unable to sit still. His mother complained that his behavior at home was "in constant motion."

The use of stimulant medications was discussed with the patient and his mother, but both expressed vague concerns about them and requested to continue psychiatric treatment without medicines. With some coaxing, a therapeutic trial with methylphenidate was initiated. V. did show clinical improvement as measured by the changes in the Conners Teachers Questionnaire when compared to his baseline. A decrease in non–goal-oriented activity and fidgety behavior was also noticed by his mother and the treating physician.

However, V. stopped the medicine because he "didn't like it." The treatment plan was therefore revised to try to strengthen the therapeutic alliance with V. and his mother and to establish a contract for a longer, more reliable period of pharmacotherapy for his ADDH. After a year of biweekly family psychotherapy sessions, where the issues of resentment, control, deprivation and vulnerability were discussed, he agreed to "give the medicine another chance." Ritalin was reinstated with an immediate improvement in attention span and hyperactivity.

For the last three years, his PbB has been well below 20 μg/dl, which is compatible with what is presently accepted on the biological threshold for lead toxicity (U.S. Dept. of Health 1985).

Another category of clinical presentation, and the subject of intense scrutiny by researchers, is the asymptomatic, silent carrier. There seems to be an exposure and effect relationship that has emerged in epidemiological studies between body lead concentrations that have been previously considered to be safe and measurable cognitive and behavioral changes (U.S. Dept. of Health 1985).

In one illustrative study in this area (Needleman 1983), children without a documented history of lead intoxication who would not be considered to be at high risk were screened for the amounts of lead that had been stored in the dentine of their shed deciduous teeth. The dentine lead levels were significantly higher in those children who had been previously identified by their teachers as not performing well enough for the expectations of their chronological age. The overall academic performance showed an impaired organizational quality; their habitual behavior in class was described as distractable, with frequent off-task activities. Neuropsychological test results with these children were consistent with the behavioral observations that they were functioning at a lower level than age-matched controls. The clinical presentation in this group closely resembles the DSM-III (Diagnostic and Statistical Manual 1980) diagnostic criteria for ADD without hyperactivity.

The actual range of the neuropsychiatric effects of lead in children has been shown to be significantly wider than what was commonly accepted a few decades ago. The old conviction that children who demonstrated prompt recovery from the acute symptoms of lead intoxication were subsequently unmarked is not holding up well. In an even more worrisome context, groups of clinically healthy children who were assessed to be at risk but were free of symptoms or signs were neurologically worked up for detections of exposure effect; the documented slowing down of motor nerve conduction velocity was seen as evidence of a subclinical neuropathy (Seppäläinen 1982; Feldman 1982). Hence a public health problem of significant proportions is apparently involved.

Treatment

Deleading children with heavy metal antagonists is the quickest way to eliminate both the circulating and the stored lead (Goodman and Gilman 1985; Nelson

1983). The three most commonly used chelating agents are: (1) Ca-Na-2 EDTA (Disodium Calcium Edtate); (2) BAL (British anti-Leucite or Dimencaprol); and (3) D-PCA (D-Penicillamine). Their therapeutic use is based on the competitive affinity they present for heavy metals, with which they form a more stable metal-chelator complex. However, these agents are not devoid of toxic, unwanted side-effects, as they also tend to bind to the alkaline-earth metals (Fe^{++}, Ca^{++}, Cu^{++}, Mg^{++}), although to a lesser degree. The loss of these physiologically active metals, widely distributed in the normal biochemistry of the human body, carries the implication of clinical pictures arising from the depletion of these essential metals. Because lead chelation is a short-term treatment designed to mobilize it quickly and excrete it by diuresis, the problem of secondary losses is, for the most part, preventable and treatable.

D-Penicillamine, the only commercially available chelator that is effective orally, is not licensed by the Food and Drug Administration for lead intoxication. It has been estimated that approximately 20 percent of the patients (Piomelli et al. 1984) who have been treated with it present toxic side-effects that resemble those of penicillin sensitivity.

Lately, the promise of a new agent that is safer and significantly easier to use than the current ones has received much attention. DMSA (2, 3-Dimer-captosuccinic acid), a compound classified as an orphan drug by the USFDA, has been extensively studied in this country after encouraging reports from the People's Republic of China, the Soviet Union, and Japan (Graziano et al. 1985). DMSA is orally active, remarkably free of unwanted side-effects, relatively specific for heavy metals and rapidly eliminated (Graziano 1985). The present clinical studies suggest that it may replace the BAL-Ca-Na-2 EDTA therapy as the treatment of choice not only with lead intoxication but with inorganic mercury, methylmercury, and arsenic poisoning as well.

Socioeducational Management

The current state of knowledge about this totally preventable disorder, with a chemical etiology and a documented neuropsychiatric pathogenicity, supports the long-standing claim that the use of lead in either of its known forms should be eliminated (U.S. Dept. of Health 1985; Piomelli et al. 1984). It appears to be common sense that the real health hazard it creates more than outweighs its industrial applications, for which less toxic alternatives are available. Ideally, primary prevention by educating parents on the dangers of plumbism and how to avoid lead exposure in their young children can help to reduce the incidence of this problem. Until this goal is achieved, a greater public awareness of the magnitude of the problem and a more aggressive stand for the expansion of the use of interim measures that will curb its use will provide a firmer control over this biosocial problem.

One of the most significant positive measures in this regard has been the sharp reduction in the use of leaded gasoline. It is estimated that this measure alone is probably responsible for the nationwide findings of reduced PbB levels in children (Annest et al. 1983).

Lead-base paint has been eliminated from the market. However, this measure does not correct and child-proof all the surfaces that were painted prior to its removal. In fact, smooth surfaces are not considered an immediate health hazard, but it is only a function of time and wear for them to begin to loosen, peel, scale, chip, or crack.

Cans with a lead-soldered side and glazed pottery used for storing or cooking food are potential sources of contamination through leachable lead. Their present use is lower than a decade ago, but they are still found in the domestic market. The occupational exposure of industrial workers and secondarily of their families is currently supervised by the Occupational Safety and Health Administration (OSHA) (U.S. Dept. of Health 1985) but unfortunately, this protective rule applies only to industries covered by OSHA regulations.

In short, the complexities that the management of this problem presents are enormous, going far beyond the treating physician's domain. One particular facet, however, should be a basic feature of the child psychiatrist's differential diagnostic perspective: patients who appear to fit the diagnostic configuration for ADD, learning disabilities, and/or mental retardation may in reality be nonidentified subclinical cases of lead intoxication. A greater awareness of the actual magnitude of the problem will help the clinician both to meet the needs of individual patients and their families and to support appropriate public health measures that address this issue.

CONCLUSION

The neurologically impaired child presents complex diagnostic and treatment challenges when problems in psychosocial functioning require assessment. The evaluating clinician clearly needs to be well versed with the unique clinical features of the youngster's primary neurological condition and how these may be expected to interact with the vicissitudes of individual, family, academic, and social development. In many instances, independent assessments by a neurologist, psychologist, psychiatrist, and sometimes others must be effectively integrated for an adequate assessment and appropriate treatment plan to be formulated. The three syndromes discussed here illustrate the need for an informed, multivariate perspective in approaching problems at the pediatric neuropsychiatry interface.

REFERENCES

American Psychiatric Association. (1980). *Diagnostic and Statistical Manual of Mental Disease.* 3d Ed. Washington, D.C.: American Psychiatric Press.

Anderson, E. M., Clarke, L., and Spain, B. (1982). *Disability in Adolescence.* London: Methuen.

Annest, J., et al. (1983). Chronological trend in blood lead levels between 1976 and 1980. *N. Eng. J. Med.* 308:1373–77.

Ausubel, D. P., Novak, J. D., and Hanesian, H. (1978). *Educational Psychology: A Cognitive View.* 2d Ed. New York: Holt, Rinehart and Winston.

Baer, D., and Fedio, P. (1977). Quantitative analysis of interictal behavior in temporal lobe epilepsy. *Arch. Neurol.* 34:454–67.

Baer, D., Freeman, R., and Greenberg, M. (1984). Behavior alterations in patients with temporal lobe epilepsy. In D. Blumer (Ed.). *Psychiatric Aspects of Epilepsy.* Washington, D.C.: American Psychiatric Press, pp. 197–227.

Barker, R. G., et al. (1953). Adjustment to physical handicap and illness: A survey of the social psychology of physique and disability. Rev. Ed. New York: Social Science Research Council.

Barraclough, B. (1981). Suicide and epilepsy. In E. Reynolds and M. Trimble (Eds.). *Epilepsy and Psychiatry.* Edinburgh: Churchill Livingstone, pp. 72–76.

Betts, T. (1981). Depression, anxiety and epilepsy. In E. Reynolds and M. Trimble (Eds.). *Epilepsy and Psychiatry.* Edinburgh: Churchill Livingstone, pp. 60–71.

Breslau, N. (1983). Family care: Effects on siblings and mothers. In J. P. Hill (Ed.). *Minnesota Symposia on Child Psychology* 2:74–109.

Camfield, P., et al. (1984). Comparison of cognitive ability, personality profile, and school success in epileptic children with pure right versus left temporal lobe EEG foci. *Am. Neurol.* 15:122–26.

Corbet, J., Trimble, M., and Nicol, T. (1985). Behavioral and cognitive impairment in children with epilepsy: The long-term effects of anticonvulsant therapy. *J. Am. Acad. Child Psychiat.* 24:17–23.

Crothers, B., and Paine, R. S. (1959). *The Natural History of Cerebral Palsy.* Cambridge: Harvard University Press.

Cruickshank, W. M. (1976). The problem and its scope. In W. M. Cruickshank (Ed.). *Cerebral Palsy: A Developmental Disability.* 3d Ed. Syracuse: Syracuse University Press.

Cruickshank, W. M., Hallahan, D. D., with Bice, H. V. (1976). Personality and behavioral characteristics. In W. M. Cruickshank (Ed.). *Cerebral Palsy: A Developmental Disability.* 3d Ed. Syracuse: Syracuse University Press.

Denhoff, E. (1976). Medical aspects. In W. M. Cruickshank (Ed.). *Cerebral Palsy: A Developmental Disability.* 3d Ed. Syracuse: Syracuse University Press.

Diller, L., et al. (1977). Response patterns in brain-damaged children and teaching style. *JSAS Catalog of Selected Documents in Psychology,* 7 August.

Ellenberg, J., Hirtz, D., and Nelson, K. (1986). Do seizures in children cause intellectual deterioration? *N. Eng. J. of Med.* 314:1085–88.

Farwell, J., Dodrill, C., and Batzel, L. (1985). Neuropsychological abilities of children with epilepsy. *Epilepsia* 26:395–400.

Feldman, R. (1982). Neurological picture of lead poisoning. *Acta Neurol. Scandinav.* Suppl. 92, 66:185–99.

Feldman, R., Paul, N., and Cummins-Ducharme, J. (1982). In T. Riley and A. Roy (Eds.). *Pseudoseizures.* Baltimore: Williams and Wilkins, pp. 122–31.

Flor-Henry, P. (1983). *Cerebral Basis of Psychopathology.* Boston: John Wright.

Freeman, R. D. (1970). Psychiatric problems in adolescents with cerebral palsy. *Devel. Med. Child Neurol.* 12:64–70.

Goldensohn, E., Glaser, G., and Goldberg, M. (1984). Epilepsy. In L. Rowland (Ed.). *Meritt's Textbook of Neurology*. Philadelphia: Lea and Febiger, pp. 629–49.

Goodman, L., and Gilman, A. (1985). *The Pharmacological Basis of Therapeutics*. 7th Ed. New York: Macmillan.

Graziano, J. (1985). Personal communication.

Graziano, J., et al. (1985). 2-3 Dimercaptosuccinic acid as an antidote for lead intoxication. *Clinical Pharm. and Therapeutics* 37(3):431–38.

Hagberg, B., and Hagberg, G. (1984). Prenatal and perinatal risk factors in a survey of 681 Swedish cases. In F. Stanley and E. Alberman (Eds.). *The Epidemiology of the Cerebral Palsies: Clinics in Developmental Medicine*. Philadelphia: Lippincott.

Hales, R., and Yudofsky, S. (1987). *Textbook of Neuropsychiatry*. Washington, D.C.: American Psychiatric Press.

Hanesian, H. (1973). Response patterns in brain-injured children and teaching style. *Proceedings of the 81st American Psychological Association Annual Convention* 8:677–78.

Hauser, W., Annegers, J., and Anderson, V. (1983). Epidemiology and genetics of epilepsy. *Res. Publ. Assoc. Res. Nerv. Ment. Dis.* 61:267–94.

Hoare, P. (1984a). The development of psychiatric disorder among schoolchildren with epilepsy. *Devel. Med. Child Neurol.* 26:3–13.

Hoare, P. (1984b). Does illness foster dependency? A study of epileptic and diabetic children. *Devel. Med. Child Neurol.* 26:20–24.

Holm, V. A. (1982). The causes of cerebral palsy: A contemporary perspective. *J. Am. Med. Assoc.* 247(10):1473–77.

Ingram, T. T. S. (1984). A historical review of the definition and classification of the cerebral palsies. In F. Stanley and E. Alberman (Eds.). *The Epidemiology of the Cerebral Palsies*. Philadelphia: Lippincott.

Klapper, Z., and Birch, H. (1966). The relation of childhood characteristics to outcome in young adults with cerebral palsy. *Devel. Med. Child Neurol.* 8:645–56.

Krumholz, A., and Niedermeyer, E. (1983). Psychogenic seizures: A clinical study with follow-up data. *Neurology* 33:498–502.

Lazar, B. S. (1977). Hypnotic imagery as a tool in working with a cerebral-palsied child. *Int. J. Clin. Exper. Hypnosis* 25(2):78–87.

Lesser, R., Leuders, H., and Dinner, D. (1983). Evidence for epilepsy is rare in patients with psychogenic seizures. *Neurology* 33:502–4.

Lewis, D., et al. (1982). Psychomotor epilepsy and violence in a group of incarcerated adolescent boys. *Am. J. Psychiatry* 139:882–87.

Lindsay, J., Ounsted, C., and Richards, P. (1979). Long-term outcome in children with temporal lobe seizures. 3: Psychiatric aspects in childhood and adult life. *Devel. Med. Child Neurol.* 21:630–36.

Little, W. J. (1862). On the influence of abnormal parturition, difficult labours, premature birth, and asphyxia neonatorum, on the mental and physical condition of the child, especially in relation to deformities. *Trans Obstetrical Society* (London) 3:293–344.

Luchins, D., Oliver, P., and Wyatt, R. (1984). Seizures with antidepressants: An in vitro technique to assess relative risk. *Epilepsia* 25:25–32.

Minde, K. K. (1978). Coping styles of 34 adolescents with cerebral palsy. *Am. J. Psychiatry* 135(11):1344–49.

Minear, W. (1956). A classification of cerebral palsy. *Pediatrics* 18:841.

Mostofsky, D., and Balaschak, B. (1977). Psychological control of seizures. *Psychol. Bull.* 84:723–50.

Needdleman, H. (1983). Lead at low dose and the behavior of children. *Acta Psychiat. Scand.* 67, Suppl. 303:26–37.

Nelson, W. (1983). *Textbook of Pediatrics.* 12th Ed. Philadelphia: Saunders.

Nielsen, H. H. (1966). *A Psychological Study of Cerebral-Palsied Children.* Copenhagen: Munksgaard.

Nussbaum, J. (1966). Self-concept of adolescents with cerebral palsy: The relationship between self-concept, mothers' concept and reality orientation. *Cerebral Palsy J.* 27:5–7.

O'Leary, D., Seidenberg, M., and Boll, T. (1981). Effects of age of onset of tonic-clonic seizures on neuropsychological performance in children. *Epilepsia* 22:197–204.

O'Reilly, D., and Walentynowicz, J. E. (1981). Etiological factors in cerebral palsy: A historical review. *Devel. Med. Child Neurol.* 23:633–42.

Paneth, N., and Kiely, J. (1984). The frequency of cerebral palsy: A review of population studies in industrialized nations since 1950. In F. Stanley and E. Alberman (Eds.). *The Epidemiology of the Cerebral Palsies.* Philadelphia: Lippincott.

Pincus, J., and Tucker, G. (1985). *Behavioral Neurology.* 3d Ed. New York: Oxford University Press.

Piomelli, S., et al. (1984). Management of childhood lead poisoning. *J. Pediatrics* 105(4):523–32.

Post, R., et al. (1986). Antidepressant effect of carbamazepine. *Am. J. Psychiatry* 143:29–34.

Proposal for Revised Clinical and Electroencephalographic Classification of Epileptic Seizures (1981). *Epilepsia* 22:489–501.

Ptacek, L. J. (1982). Respite care for families of children with severe handicaps: An evaluation study of parent satisfaction. *J. Community Psychology* 10(3):222–27.

Reynolds, E. (1985). Antiepileptic drugs and psychopathology. In M. Trimble (Ed.). *The Psychopharmacology of Epilepsy.* New York: Wiley, pp. 49–64.

Richardson, S. A. (1964). The social environment and individual functioning. In H. G. Birch (Ed.). *Brain Damage in Children: The Biological and Social Aspects.* New York: Williams and Wilkins, pp. 100–183.

Rubinstein, B., and Shaffer, D. (1985). Organicity in child psychiatry: Signs, symptoms and syndromes. *Psychiatric Clin. N. Am.* 8:755–77.

Rutter, M. (1981). Psychological sequelae of brain damage in children. *Am. J. Psychiatry.* 138:1533–41.

Rutter, M., Graham, P., and Yule, W. (1970). *A Neuropsychiatric Study in Childhood.* Clinics in Developmental Medicine Nos. 35, 36. London: Heinemann.

Rutter, M., et al. (1976). Research Report: Isle of Wight Studies, 1964–1974. *Psychological Med.* 6:313–32.

Scherzer, A. L., and Tscharnuter, I. (1982). *Early Diagnosis and Therapy in Cerebral Palsy: A Primer on Infant Developmental Problems.* New York: Marcel Dekker.

Schofield, L. J., and Wong, S. (1975). Operant approaches to group therapy in a school for handicapped children. *Devel. Med. Child Neurol.* 17(4):425–33.

Seppäläinen, A. M. (1982). Lead poisoning: Neurophysiological aspects. *Acta Neurol. Scandinav.* Suppl. 92, 66:177–84.

Shaffer, D. (1985). Brain damage. In M. Rutter and L. Hersov (Eds.). *Child and Ado-lescent Psychiatry—Modern Approaches*. Oxford: Blackwell Scientific Pubs., pp. 129–51.

Shapiro, B. D., et al. (1983). Associated dysfunctions. In G. H. Thompson, I. L. Rubin, and R. M. Bilenker (Eds.). *Comprehensive Management of Cerebral Palsy*. New York: Grune and Stratton.

Shere, E., and Kastenbaum, R. (1966). Mother-child interaction in cerebral palsy. Environmental and psychological obstacles to cognitive development. *Genetic Psychology Monographs*. 73:255–335.

Silbergeld, E. (1983). Indirectly acting neurotoxins. *Acta Psychiat. Scand.* Supp. 303(67):16–25.

Stores, G. (1981). Problems of learning and behavior in children with epilepsy. In E. Reynolds and M. Trimble (Eds.). *Epilepsy and Psychiatry*. Edinburgh: Churchill Livingstone, pp. 33–48.

Teplin, S. W., Howard, J. A., and O'Connor, M. J. (1981). Self-concept of young children with cerebral palsy. *Devel. Med. Child Neurol.* 23:730–38.

Trimble, M. (1981). *Neuropsychiatry*. Chinchester, England: Wiley.

Trimble, M. (1985a). *Interface Between Neurology and Psychiatry*. Basel, Switzerland: Karger.

Trimble, M. (1985b). Psychosomatic aspects of epilepsy. *Adv. Psychosom. Med.* 13:133–50.

Trimble, M. (1985c). The psychoses of epilepsy and their treatment. In M. Trimble (Ed.). *The Psychopharmacology of Epilepsy*. Chinchester, England: Wiley, pp. 83–94.

U.S. Department of Health and Human Services. Preventing Lead Poisoning in Young Children, 1985. Second Revision of the Statement by the Centers for Disease Control.

Varella, J. T., and Lazarus, P. J. (1984). Survey of services provided by United Ce-rebral Palsy agencies and the effects of PL 94-142 on preschool handicapped children. *Psychological Reports* 54:183–88.

Whitman, S., et al. (1982). Psychopathology and siezure type in children with epi-lepsy. *Psychological Med.* 12:843–53.

Williams, D. (1982). The treatment of seizures: Special psychotherapeutic and psy-chobiological techniques. In H. Sands (Ed.). *Epilepsy: A Handbook for the Mental Health Professional*. New York: Brunner/Mazel, pp. 58–74.

Williams, D., and Mostofsky, D. (1982). Psychogenic seizures in childhood and ad-olescence. In T. Riley and A. Roy (Eds.). *Pseudoseizures*. Baltimore: Williams and Wilkins, pp. 169–84.

Williams, D., Spiegel, H., and Mostofsky, D. (1978). Neurogenic and hysterical sei-zures in children and adolescents. *Am. J. Psychiatry*. 135:82–86.

Williams, D., et al. (1979). The impact of psychiatric intervention on patients with uncontrolled seizures. *J. Nerv. Ment. Dis.* 167:626–31.

Williams, D., et al. (1982). The effect of propranolol on uncontrolled rage outbursts in children and adolescents with organic brain dysfunction. *J. Am. Acad. Child Psychiatry*. 21:129–35.

22

THE RETARDED CHILD AND ADOLESCENT

Ludwik S. Szymanski

INTRODUCTION

The objective of psychiatric assessment of a retarded child is to assess the possible presence of mental disorder coexisting with the retardation. However, the diagnostician must understand well the cognitive functioning of the child and the consequences of the diagnosis of retardation. Therefore, the principles underlying this diagnosis as well as current philosophy of the services for retarded persons will be briefly reviewed.

The DSM-III description of the essential features of mental retardation (which is based on the definition of mental retardation established by the American Association on Mental Deficiency; Grossman 1973), states:

"1) significantly subaverage general intellectual functioning, 2) resulting in, or associated with, deficits or impairment in adaptive behavior, 3) with onset before the age of eighteen. The diagnosis is made regardless of whether or not there is a coexisting mental or physical disorder."

The significantly subaverage intellectual functioning is defined as IQ of 70 or below, obtained on standardized individual intelligence tests. It was previously defined as more than two standard deviations below the mean for the particular test. The impairments in adaptive behavior are defined as significant limitations in individuals functioning, considering age level and cultural background. This is usually assessed clinically, although standardized scales exist.

Mental retardation is thus not a specific disease that one may or may not have. It is a behavioral syndrome reflecting cognitive and adaptive functioning below an arbitrarily defined level. It does not have a single cause, mechanism or prognosis. A specific underlying disorder can be diagnosed in a majority of severe cases and in a minority of mild ones. Retarded persons do not form a homogeneous group in terms of personality patterns, behaviors, abilities, or prognosis. These depend on the associated biological, psychological, and environmental factors (particularly educational and other services that the retarded person receives). Thus the maladaptive behavioral patterns of retarded persons are not simply a result of their retardation or "organicity."

The principles underlying the current philosophy of care for retarded children have a direct effect on the changing roles of psychiatry in this field. The normalization principle requires the use of culturally normative means to produce behaviors as culturally normative as possible (Wolfensberger 1972). The developmental approach stresses the inherent ability of every child, including the retarded one, to learn and to progress developmentally, which leads to improvement in function and quality of life. The civil rights movement led to benefits for developmentally disabled children as well. Class action suits and legislation (such as the Massachusetts Chapter 766 law of 1972 and the federal Education for All Handicapped Children Act of 1975) gave special-needs children the right to obtain, at public expense, the necessary educational and related services in the least restrictive setting. Retarded children are no longer routinely admitted to public residential institutions and in some states there are even laws expressly forbidding such practice (although some families might still place a young child in a private institution). Instead, it is expected that with available services these children will live with their families or if necessary, in foster or adoptive homes, and that in most cases they will be mainstreamed in the schools in the community.

These changes in society's attitudes have led to two major changes in the roles expected of psychiatrists in the mental retardation field. Their major responsibilities have become clinical: diagnosis, treatment, and prevention of mental disorders in retarded persons (rather than diagnosis of mental retardation itself). The need for these clinical psychiatric services is being increasingly recognized, since a number of studies have shown that behavioral disorders are the major cause of failure of community placement of retarded persons. Second, psychiatrists are increasingly seen as members of an interdisciplinary team, rather than as solo consultants or administrators.

DIAGNOSIS AND EPIDEMIOLOGY OF MENTAL RETARDATION

Traditionally, psychiatrists have diagnosed mental retardation solely on the basis of low scores on IQ tests. However, there are many individuals who test within the retarded range (mainly moderate and mild), but whose social adaptation, self-support, and other skills are similar to others' in their socioeconomic class and who do not receive services for retarded persons. Thus, diagnosing them as retarded would be inappropriate.

Mentally retarded persons often have other associated functional handicaps (such as motor, communication, and sensory deficits, as well as seizures). In a nationwide large-scale survey in 1971 of retarded persons living in both community and institutions, only 12 percent were found to be free of problems besides retardation (Conroy and Derr 1971). These handicaps are particularly frequent in the severely and profoundly retarded.

The biases inherent in the diagnosis of mental retardation solely by means of standard psychological testing have been clearly shown in the studies of Mercer (1973). Mexican-American children, when diagnosed by means of standard intelligence tests alone, had a 14.9 percent rate of mental retardation. This dropped to 6 percent when adaptive behavior testing was added to the diagnostic battery and to 1.53 percent when culturally adjusted norms were used in place of standard norms (standardized largely on the middle-class, English-speaking population).

The figures on the prevalence of mental retardation differ, depending on the manner in which they were obtained. Statistically one can expect that 3 percent of the population will have IQ below two standard deviations below the mean. However, as pointed out by Tarjan et al. (1973), the situation is complicated by several important facts. Only a fraction of retarded children are diagnosed in infancy; these are usually the more severely retarded, with an easily diagnosed syndrome such as Down Syndrome. Because the diagnosis depends on both IQ and adaptive behavior, one can expect that the prevalence of diagnosed cases will change over time, reflecting the changes in adaptive behavior. Many children diagnosed as retarded at school age due to academic failure can lose this diagnosis in adulthood if they adapt well, engage in gainful, even if simple, work, and live relatively independently. Even in childhood their retardation might be obvious only during school hours because of the level of their academic failure, but not after school, because of the level of their social adaptation. For these reasons, terms such as "the six hours retarded" and "the disappearing retarded" (adults) have been used. Also, the mortality of retarded persons varies. It is higher than average for the severely/profoundly retarded who have an underlying severe physical disorder, but average for those without such disorder, who are mildly/moderately retarded. Last but not least, the exclusion of borderline intelligence from the mental retardation range (Grossman 1973) instantly reduced the prevalence of mental retardation. Based on a survey of a community of 100,000, Tarjan et al. (1973) estimated the prevalence of mental retardation (by current definition) to be 1 percent. This is the currently accepted figure and it has been confirmed recently in surveys of large populations. Baird and Sadovnick (1985) have recently studied the population of British Columbia utilizing the Health Surveillance Registry. They investigated all births in the 1952 to 1966 cohort (ages 15 to 29 at the time of the study). Inclusion in the registry meant that the individual came to the attention of a special service. The minimum prevalence for all levels of retardation was calculated at 7.7/1,000, which was not far from the Tarjan et al. (1973) estimates.

EPIDEMIOLOGY OF MENTAL DISORDERS IN RETARDED CHILDREN

When one evaluates occurrence of mental disorders in retarded children one has to consider several questions, important among them are: the prevalence of mental disorders in this population; their types; the distribution of these disorders in relation to the severity of the retardation. Unfortunately these questions cannot be answered accurately on the basis of the existing studies, for reasons such as the inconsistent and varied use of the diagnostic criteria for mental retardation and mental disorders and biased selection of study samples, usually based on institutional or clinic populations (Szymanski 1980). This selection might lead to overestimates of the frequency of mental disorders in this population. Yet ignorance of the presence and manifestations of those disorders might lead to underdiagnosing. This last mechanism is essentially what Reiss et al. (1982) called a "diagnostic overshadowing": a tendency of clinicians to miss the diagnosis of mental disorder if they know that the patient is retarded.

Menolascino (1965, 1966) evaluated 616 children referred because of the suspicion of retardation. Of the 31 percent who were found to be disturbed, 24.5 percent were also retarded. Philips (1966) assessed 170 children referred with suspicion of retardation and concluded that it was uncommon to see a child who was not disturbed. A similar conclusion was reached by Webster (1970), who evaluated 159 referrals to a nursery for retarded children. He felt that all had a degree of disturbance in emotional development. Chess and Hassibi (1970) and Chess (1977) evaluated and followed fifty-two mildly or borderline retarded children living with their families. They diagnosed a psychiatric disorder in 60 percent initially and in 40 percent in a follow-up study. Categories such as "behavior disorder due to neurological damage" (27.3 percent), "psychosis" (6.9 percent), "neurotic behavior disorder" (4.5 percent), and "reactive behavior disorder" (2.3 percent) were diagnosed. Philips and Williams (1975) retrospectively analyzed records of one hundred children referred to a psychiatric clinic for assessment of their retardation. In eighty-seven diagnosis of a psychiatric disorder was made. In thirty-eight diagnosis of a disorder "of psychotic proportion" was made; in twenty-six "behavior disorder"; in sixteen a personality disorder; in five a neurotic disorder; and a transient situational disorder in two. Corbett et al. (1975) studied 140 children functioning on a moderate or lower level of retardation. A behavioral disorder was diagnosed in 43 percent and the following diagnoses were made: psychosis (13 percent), hyperkinesis (12 percent), conduct disorder (9 percent), stereotypies (5 percent), neurosis (3 percent). In another study Reid (1980) reported on sixty mentally handicapped children and adolescents referred to psychiatric clinic. He used a multiaxial classification system of the World Health Organization, similar to DSM-III. On Axis I the following diagnoses were made: conduct disorder (45 percent), neurotic disorder (42 percent), hyperkinesis (15 percent), childhood psychosis (8 percent), adjustment reaction (4 percent). Janicki and Jacobson (1979) studied data on thirty thousand developmentally disabled persons identified because they were recipients of specialized services. Although that sample was not really representative, the results were interesting. While Jacobson calculated that only 13.7 percent of the children could be identified as having a psychiatric disorder, it was estimated that 47.7 percent of that sample exhibited a behavioral problem.

Several studies focused on nonselected populations. In the Isle of Wight Study,

Rutter et al. (1970) assessed the entire population of 9- to 11-year-old children. The diagnosis of retardation was based on IQ level only. Based on results of parental and teacher questionnaires, emotional disorders were found four to five times more frequently in children with IQ below 70 than in those with normal intelligence. Their frequency was related to the level of cognitive development, in that the more retarded individuals were apt to be more frequently disturbed. In fact, this relationship held true for all IQ levels, not only for the retarded range. Koller et al. (1983) assessed retrospectively by means of parental questionnaire all children born in the years 1951 to 1955 in a city in England. Of the retarded persons, 61 percent were considered to have a behavioral disorder in childhood, and in 36 percent it was judged to be of a moderate or severe degree. Comparable rates in a matching sample of nonretarded children were 24 percent and 5 percent. No specific psychiatric diagnoses were made, but broad categories of behavioral disturbance were described. Aggressive behavior was found in 33 percent, emotional disturbance in 29 percent, antisocial behavior in 27 percent, hyperactive behavior in 12 percent. Among children with IQ below 50, 58 percent were estimated to be disturbed, as opposed to 81 percent of those with IQ above 70. This finding, different from Rutter et al. (1970), may be due to the fact that children who are less handicapped are referred for specialized services primarily because of coexisting behavioral disturbance and thus could be overrepresented in this study. The only reported study of a nonselected group of retarded persons that employed DSM-III criteria for mental disorders was one of Gostason (1985); it focused, however, on the 20- to 60-year-old group. The subjects were assessed in a psychiatric interview and through the Comprehensive Psychopathological Rating Scale. Thirty-three percent of the mildly retarded, 71 percent of the more significantly retarded, and 23 percent of control cases received at least one DSM-III diagnosis.

In our clinic (Developmental Evaluation Clinic of The Children's Hospital, Boston), we have used the DSM-III classification since its introduction in 1980. All children are diagnosed by a child psychiatrist experienced in mental retardation either as a primary clinician or as a supervisor of a fellow in child psychiatry. The patients are referred to this clinic for a comprehensive, interdisciplinary evaluation and not specifically to a psychiatrist, who sees them as a member of an interdisciplinary team (Tanguay and Szymanski 1980). The diagnostic findings in that population were as follows (Table 22.1).

In this sample psychiatric disorders were diagnosed less frequently in children who were more severely retarded, contradicting most studies cited above. This seemed to be explained by the referral patterns: The more severely handicapped children were younger and were referred primarily for initial medical assessment. The mildly retarded or nonretarded children were those with severe academic problems often secondary to psychiatric disorders and learning disabilities.

The existing studies, although at times yielding different results, do agree on two essential points. The first is that mental disorders are considerably more prevalent in retarded than in nonretarded children. The second is that virtually all types of mental disorders are seen in this population.

TABLE 22.1

	Mildly/ moderately retarded N = 88	Severely/ profoundly retarded N = 33	Not retarded N = 111
Adjustment disorders	14 (16%)	3 (9%)	25 (23%)
Affect disorders*	12 (14%)	2 (6%)	2
Attention deficit disorders	11 (13%)	1	11 (10%)
Pervasive developmental disorders	11 (13%)	9 (27%)	9 (8%)
Anxiety disorders	7 (8%)		12 (11%)
Conduct disorders	5 (6%)	1	9 (8%)
Organic brain disorders	3	1	6 (5%)
No Axis I diagnosis	23 (26%)	19 (58%)	20 (18%)

*Includes dysthymic and adjustment disorders with predominantly depressive mood.
Additionally, a smaller number of children had other diagnoses which included atypical psychosis, schizophrenia, oppositional disorder, and reactive attachment disorder of infancy.

In summary, retarded persons do not form a homogeneous group in terms of personality patterns, behaviors, abilities, and prognosis, which depend on the involved biological, psychological, and environmental factors. Thus the maladaptive behavioral patterns of retarded persons are not simply a result of their retardation or "organicity" and they suffer the same spectrum of mental disorders as nonretarded persons.

THE DIAGNOSTIC PROCESS

A major difficulty in the diagnosis of children's mental disorders has been a lack of clear and universally accepted diagnostic terminology. This has been a particular obstacle in work with retarded individuals, who are often multiply handicapped and for whom a number of diagnoses might be necessary to describe adequately the clinical condition. For them the "diagnostic label" of a mental disorder will not be sufficient, even if it is useful in grouping disorders for administrative or research purposes. For clinical purposes one needs a more elaborate and expanded diagnostic formulation that describes the individual's problems, strengths, environment, and so on. For this reason the DSM-III has been useful with this population. Its multiaxial system permits coding of different types of information, which provides a more detailed and individualized description of the patient. An assessment that results in such expanded diagnosis is probably the most important phase of mental health care of retarded children, since it will lead to a preventive or treatment intervention tailored to the multiple needs of the child.

The following section is based on the clinical experience of the staff at the Developmental Evaluation Clinic at The Children's Hospital, Boston. It is an interdisciplinary facility encompassing fifteen medical psychosocial disciplines. It provides both primary assessments and treatment as well as second opinion consultations. Many psychiatric clinics where retarded children are seen will obviously not have such multiple specialty services, nor will most of their patients need them. However, the principle of integrating the total biopsychosocial knowledge of the patient into a comprehensive diagnostic formulation remains the same in any setting.

In this section the stages of the assessment process will be reviewed in detail.

The Referral Stage

Children as well as retarded persons of all ages are usually referred and brought in for the evaluation by a caregiver. A frequent reason for such referral is a behavior objectionable to others, such as aggression, disruptiveness, self-stimulation, or self-injury. It is less frequent that retarded persons who are "quietly" disturbed (so that others are not disturbed by them) are referred (such as persons who are withdrawn and depressed, Szymanski and Biederman 1984). A behavior that is not considered a problem with a nonretarded person might be a source of concern if exhibited by a retarded one—for example, a retarded adolescent's interest in sexuality. Often the child had been subjected to a variety of interventions, and if they fail a psychiatric referral is made as a last resort (Menolascino and Bernstein 1970). Sometimes the referral is the result of the caregiver's frustration, "burnout," or anger, for example, because of a reduction in staffing at the school or institution. Szymanski (1977, 1980) described manifest and latent complaints (or agendas) that underlie a referral. The former are overt and verbalized, while the latter are not, and might be the unconscious real reason for the referral. For example, the teacher may wish to have a retarded child (whom she considers it ungratifying to teach) diagnosed as disturbed and removed from the classroom.

Planning the Assessment

The history accompanying the referral is often incomplete due to the referring person's ignorance or wish to emphasize only his own concerns and agendas. Frequently it is not even mentioned that the patient has been treated by another psychiatrist, and in some cases access to past history is denied under the guise of expecting an "unbiased opinion." In institutions with poorly maintained records, and whose multiple and frequently changing caretakers may know only about the client's behavior during their shift, obtaining adequate information can be a difficult problem. Not infrequently we found that a client referred because of "aggression" and "attention getting" had a history of schizophrenia and multiple hospitalizations. After reviewing the initial information the clinician might ask for additional data and decides what tests and consultations should be included in the assessment plan.

The Comprehensive Approach

A psychiatric diagnostic evaluation of a retarded person has to be comprehensive (Menolascino and Bernstein 1970; Szymanski 1977, 1980). This does not necessarily mean that in each case a complete workup should be done, but the clinician should assess the presenting symptoms and findings in the light of comprehensive biopsychosocial and developmental knowledge of the patient. In some cases a critical review of past evaluations by other disciplines might be sufficient, while in others a full interdisciplinary assessment may be needed. Therefore the diagnostician should be the most trained professional available, preferably a child psychiatrist who has training in the biological, psychosocial, and developmental domains.

Interview with the Caregivers

For the reasons described above, a comprehensive history should be obtained from all available sources, besides the primary caregivers who bring the child to the clinician. These might include teachers, various therapists, siblings, and if the patient lives in a residential school, direct careworkers. The history should be longitudinal, correlated with other concurrent events such as environmental stresses, medical illnesses and procedures, and administration of psychotropic medications. Graphic visualization of the data may be particularly helpful. For instance, it might help to resolve a question of whether a symptom is a reaction to a life event, or whether there is a cyclicity in the clinical manifestations. The clinician should be cautious not to give leading questions that might reflect his own misconceptions. For instance, some psychiatrists not infrequently ask the parents about their reaction to the "catastrophe" of having a retarded child, while this child might be a source of gratification for the parents no less than a bright sibling. Such a mistake may doom establishing an alliance with the family.

Interview with the Patient

Interviewing techniques with retarded children have been extensively described elsewhere (Philips 1966; Menolascino and Bernstein 1970; Szymanski 1977, 1980) and therefore will only be summarized here. The patient should be seen both alone and together with the family or caregivers, in order to assess the various aspects of their relationship, such as support for the patient's quest for independence versus overt or covert overprotection. Considerable direction is often necessary with retarded persons who tend to be passive and might see a silent psychiatrist as criticizing them, or whose anxiety about the interview might be expressed in overactivity and confusion. However, spontaneous expression should be encouraged and leading questions, to which retarded persons are particularly susceptible, should be avoided (Sigelman et al. 1981). In children in general and in retarded children in particular both verbal and nonverbal interviewing techniques have to be used. Retarded patients often have associated communication deficits, and the clinician has to assess their communication patterns and "tune in" to them through first observing how the child and the parents communicate. Surprisingly, many clinicians, especially those with a psychodynamic background, do not expect that one can talk to a retarded person and hence neglect this part of the assessment (Szymanski 1980). However, most retarded patients who have verbal capacities, if approached supportively, can talk about their experiences and feelings, including reactions to being handicapped, teased, and rejected. Play techniques are a valuable interviewing tool and an expressive medium for nonverbal patients.

In some cases a home or school visit is necessary, especially with severely/profoundly retarded persons who are more dependent on routine and familiar environment and whose behavior in the clinic might reflect their reaction to the stress of the interview setting rather than the patient's baseline psychopathology.

Diagnostic Formulation

The collected clinical data are analyzed at this stage and then synthesized into a meaningful whole, according to the principles of interdisciplinary approach (Cushna et al. 1980). The symptomatic behaviors have to be assessed in light of the patient's cognitive level, social experience, learning, life experience, and circumstances. For instance, are the abnormal behaviors site–specific? Are they related to certain antecedents and/or to the reactions of the caregivers? Bizarre verbalizations might not necessarily reflect a psychotic thought disorder, but a language disorder or even what the patient was taught to believe, such as that a deceased grandmother would watch him from heaven and will tell him if he is "good." In overcrowded classrooms and institutions bizarre and aggressive behaviors might in fact be adaptive if they are the only means of attracting a caregiver's response. However, abnormal behaviors should not be dismissed as an expected part of the retardation and "organicity" (Philips 1966).

A formal DSM-III diagnosis should and can be made. Additionally, a descriptive diagnostic formulation should detail the patient's strengths, weaknesses, environmental problems and supports, and other important information.

Utilization of the DSM-III criteria in specific disorders will be discussed in the following sections.

Intervention Plan

The diagnostic assessment will obviously be useless unless it results in a realistic plan for intervention. This should be comprehensive and realistic, take into consideration all the needs of the child, and be well integrated with recommendations of other disciplines.

Informing Conference

Sadly, this phase of the assessment process is frequently neglected. However, it is essential and ethical to do so. The diagnostician must review carefully with the caregivers and the patient (whenever possible) the referral questions, the findings, and the recommendations, in a manner understandable to them. In particular, the child's and the family's strengths should be highlighted. Specific techniques useful at this stage have been described elsewhere (Szymanski 1980).

Follow-up

Even if the referral were purely for a consultation, it is the diagnostician's responsibility to follow up on the recommendations at least in making appropriate referral for recommended services.

OTHER DIAGNOSTIC TOOLS AND TECHNIQUES

Recently, structured interview schedules and rating scales have been used in assessment of mental disorders in nonretarded persons, such as DIS, K-SADS and others, but reports on their reliability are still contradictory (Anthony et al. 1985; Helzer et al. 1985; Klerman 1985). Some instruments have been used with retarded persons. Kazdin et al. (1983) have described the use of the Beck Depression Inventory, Zung Self-Rating Depression Scale, and the Psychopathology Instrument for Mentally Retarded Adults and reported that they correlated significantly with each other and with the clinical diagnosis. Senatore et al. (1985) developed a psychopathology assessment instrument for retarded adults that seemed to be of value in screening individuals for referral for a more comprehensive assessment. Aman et al. (1985) has developed an Aberrant Behavior Checklist for retarded persons, which might be useful for follow-up on effects of treatment, rather than for making a diagnosis.

ASSESSMENT OF THE MEDICAL STATUS

As a group, retarded persons often have other associated disorders. A nationwide survey had indicated that 88 percent of retarded persons had at least one additional handicapping problem and in 35 percent such a problem was severe (Conroy and Derr 1971). More recently, in a population survey in British Columbia, 75 percent of mildly and 91.6 percent of profoundly retarded persons were reported to have another disability (excluding Down syndrome and neural tube defects) (Baird and Sadovnick 1985). Additionally, physical disorders are often associated with psychiatric illness, as shown in the classic studies of Hall et al. (1978, 1980). For these reasons evaluation of a retarded child's somatic status is an important part of psychiatric assessment. The associated disorders might be: a mental retardation syndrome (e.g., Down syndrome); a mental retardation syndrome of which a behavioral disorder is a part (e.g., phenylketonuria with psychosis, Lesh Nyhan syndrome with self-injurious behavior, Rett's syndrome with autistic symptoms); an associated disorder causative of psychiatric symptoms (e.g., hypothyroidism in a depressed person with Down syndrome); another handicap that may exacerbate the basic disability and psychiatric symptoms (e.g., progressive visual handicap in a retarded child with congenital rubella); a coexisting painful condition that may cause a nonverbal child to communicate the distress through disturbed behavior (e.g., self-abuse). Additionally, retarded persons often receive multiple medications whose unrecognized side-effects might include behavioral symptoms.

For these reasons a thorough evaluation of medical status is most important. Blanket acceptance of a statement that the child has been "medically cleared" by a family physician is unacceptable. Careful review of past assessments and consultations and repeating of those deemed necessary should be done. In some cases certain diagnostic techniques did not exist when previous assessments were done (e.g., chromosomal analysis for fragile–x, sphenoidal probes in EEG examination for temporal lobe epilepsy).

SPECIFIC DIAGNOSTIC CATEGORIES

In this section the occurrence and the diagnosis of major diagnostic categories of mental disorders in retarded children and adolescents will be reviewed.

Mental Retardation

Generally, children are rarely referred to a psychiatrist solely with a question of the diagnosis of retardation. Such diagnosis requires broader, interdisciplinary assessment than is possible by any one discipline. Still, when a child who functions below age level is seen by a psychiatrist this diagnosis should be considered, and if preexisting, should be critically reviewed. However, the psychiatrist's responsibility is primarily for assessment of the presence of a coexisting, other mental disorder.

In the DSM-III mental retardation is included as a mental disorder. Its diagnostic definition is three-dimensional (criteria include cognitive level, adaptation, and age of onset) and is essentially the same as that of the American Association on Mental Deficiency (Grossman 1973). The reliability of this diagnosis is generally high (Cantwell et al. 1979; Mattison et al. 1979). The placement of this diagnosis on Axis I has been criticized. Rutter and Shaffer (1980) pointed out that mental retardation reflects abnormal level rather than type of functioning and therefore should be coded on a separate axis (Rutter et al. 1975). Empirical studies have shown that grouping two major diagnoses on one axis reduces the possibility that both, if coexisting, would be diagnosed (Russell et al. 1979; Cantwell et al. 1979). For these reasons it has been suggested that the diagnosis of mental retardation be coded on Axis II (Kendell 1980, 1983), which would thus group it with other lifelong and relatively stable handicaps (Williams 1985). This change will appear in the revised version of DSM-III.

In the current version of DSM-III there is a fifth digit in the code for mental retardation. It is designed for behavioral symptoms requiring attention or treatment, which are not a part of another disorder. Theoretically it could describe nonspecific behaviors that can be attributed to mental retardation alone. This reflects, however, the early misconceptions described by Philips (1966), that a maladaptive behavior of a retarded person is simply a function of the retardation. In fact this fifth digit designation could prevent a diagnostician from attempting to diagnose accurately the coexisting mental disorder. No behavior is unique to mental retardation, and different individuals with the same level of retardation manifest a broad spectrum of behaviors just as nonretarded ones do. If a behavior is of such severity that treatment is required a specific diagnosis should be made.

Pervasive Developmental Disorders (PDD)

The PDD is a new category introduced in the DSM-III. It includes infantile autism (IA); PDD-childhood onset (differentiated from IA mainly by arbitrary age of onset over thirty months); and "atypical PDD." The broad PDD category has been relatively useful for clinical purposes, but its subcategories do not seem to reflect clinical reality. Tanguay (1984) proposed instead to classify these disorders by developmental profile.

The relationship of the pervasive developmental disorders to psychotic disorders has been a focus of controversy for years. Infantile autism in particular has been seen as an early form of schizophrenia. However, follow-up studies (Rutter et al. 1967; DeMyer et al. 1981; Kolvin 1971) are convincing in that these are separate disorders; this seems to be the accepted view at the present (Campbell and Green 1985). The DSM-III excludes the diagnosis of a PDD if hallucinations are present. However, some of these children might in later life develop a psychotic disorder and then both diagnoses should be coded. The Revised Version of the DSM-III divides PDD into Autistic Disorder (infantile or childhood onset) and PDD, Not Otherwise Specified, which seems to be better adapted to the clinical realities.

Children who are severely disturbed and retarded are not infrequently referred to a psychiatrist to determine a diagnosis of retardation versus infantile autism. This question is of course inappropriate. Not only are these conditions not mutually exclusive, but they often coexist and most children with autism are also retarded (Tanguay 1980).

The diagnostic criteria of DSM-III and DSM-III-R for PDD are equally applicable to retarded and nonretarded children. The most prominent feature distinguishing a PDD, in particular in infantile autism (IA), from uncomplicated mental retardation, is impairment in interpersonal relatedness. Philips (1966), who spoke then of psychotic children, stated: "The children with mental deficiency, regardless of etiology, relate quickly to the examiner, play meaningfully with toys and objects, and relate to each other. The psychotic child is part of the group, but never in the group." A common mistake made by lay and professional people alike is to consider the self-stimulatory behaviors of a retarded child as evidence of IA, when other symptoms of IA are lacking. Another mistake is to miss the diagnosis of retardation in an autistic child who has some "islands of intelligence" and is therefore considered to be potentially bright. In connection with that, it should be remembered that diagnosis of retardation is based on current level of functioning and not on theoretical potential.

Psychiatrists also see these individuals in adolescence or in adulthood when the residual form of IA might be diagnosed. However, this diagnosis is often missed, especially if adequate past history is not obtained. Eaton and Menolascino (1982) did not find this diagnosis in their sample of 168 retarded persons, 6 to 76 years of age. Philips and Williams (1975), in a study of one hundred retarded children, did not diagnose IA but apparently included it in the category of "psychiatric problems of psychotic proportions." In the two studies of unselected populations (Rutter et al. 1970—the Isle of Wight Study; Koller et al. 1983) specific diagnostic categories were not described. In the third, Gostason (1985) did not diagnose a PDD in his sample of 132 retarded adults. In our sample of 237 children there were nine PDD cases (five IA and four other PDD) among 111 nonretarded and twenty PDD cases (nine IA and eleven other PDD) among 126 retarded children.

Psychotic Disorders

The diagnosis of schizophrenia in retarded persons may be difficult if one adheres to the DSM-III criteria, which reflect Schneiderian first-rank symptoms and require the presence of delusions, hallucinations, or thought disorder, which cannot be documented unless a certain degree of communicative, particularly verbal, ability is present (although Eaton and Menolascino [1982] described a patient who communicated paranoid ideation through drawings and gestures). However, for the same reason overdiagnosis of psychosis in retarded persons is frequent, since many psychiatrists tend to diagnose it on the basis of strange behaviors alone, such as self-stimulation, talking to self, or aggressive outbursts.

In the past, the distinction between retardation and schizophrenia was not that clear (Reid 1972). In 1896 Kraepelin, cited by Reid (1972), considered the manneristic movements of retarded persons as diagnostic of early schizophrenia and proposed the term *propfschizophrenie* for these cases. Others thought that retarded persons could not develop genuine schizophrenia (May 1931) or that they suffer from a special type of psychosis (Earl 1934). No evidence for that has been shown, however. The earlier view that schizophrenia in childhood might result in some degree of retardation (O'Gorman 1954; Garrard and Richmond 1967) received support in the recent study of Russell and Tanguay (1981), who have shown that psychotic process in children might negatively affect their learning and cognitive skills. Schizophrenia in retarded patients can be diagnosed on the basis of the usual criteria, but this diagnosis may be difficult or impossible in patients unable to communicate sufficiently verbally (Reid 1972; Heaton-Ward 1977). The same problems exist with diagnosis of schizophrenia in young children (Cantor 1982). In summary, in verbally retarded children and adolescents the usual diagnostic criteria of schizophrenia may be used, with the usual precautions in exploring and interpreting the delusional and other statements (Szymanski 1977, 1980). The specific diagnosis of a subcategory of the disorder may, however, be more difficult. In nonverbal patients the residual DSM-III category of Atypical Psychosis can be used if symptoms such as gross disorganization of behavior, behavioral episodes suggesting hallucinations, and deterioration exist.

In many past studies psychosis in retarded persons was described utilizing a variety of diagnostic criteria (Szymanski 1980; Russell 1985) and the patient samples were usually preselected. Menolascino (1969), using DSM-I criteria, diagnosed chronic brain syndrome with or without psychosis in the majority of his sample and a functional psychosis in 3 percent. In twenty-four of one hundred sixty-eight retarded persons aged 6 to 76, Eaton and Menolascino (1982) noted that altered affect, bizarre rituals, and interpersonal distancing were judged to be a clear mark of schizophrenia. Philips and Williams (1975) diagnosed thirty-eight of one hundred retarded children as psychotic on the basis of very disturbed and disorganized behavior, including in this category autism and chronic brain syndrome. Corbett et al. (1975) diagnosed psychosis (including infantile autism) in 13 percent of children whose IQ was below the mild retardation level. Reid (1980), using WHO criteria, diagnosed psychosis in 8 percent of sixty retarded children and adolescents. Gostason (1985) diagnosed schizophrenic and paranoid disorders in four of fifty-one retarded persons. In our sample, by strict DSM-III criteria, psychosis (atypical) was diagnosed in two of 126 retarded (although possibly some of those diagnosed as atypical PDD would turn out later to have childhood schizophrenia).

A retarded child or adult may be a lonely, isolated individual, who may talk to himself and voice unrealistic ideas and expectations, such as that a deceased relative will talk to him. On closer questioning and observation it becomes evident that no genuine hallucinations nor delusions are present, but that the patient has an "imaginary friend," not inappropriate developmentally. The second, reverse problem occurs in institutions when a patient acting bizarrely is labeled by the staff as an "attention getter," but on close assessment progressive deterioration and disorganization can be found. Not infrequently both psychotic and depressive symptoms coexist, and one can mask the other.

In summary, the available knowledge indicates that the same psychotic disorders occur both in retarded and nonretarded persons; in both groups they may result in cognitive impairment to some degree. These psychotic disorders may be diagnosed in mildly retarded and verbal persons by the usual criteria but in the more severely handicapped mainly on the basis of general and severe behavioral and social disorganization.

Affective Disorders

Our understanding of depression in retarded persons has followed the developments concerning depression in nonretarded children (although with a considerable delay). For years it was thought that depression could not occur below a certain developmental level. Gardner (1967) reviewed the earlier literature and noticed contradictory theoretical predictions: some had recognized the high vulnerability of retarded persons to depression, due to their experiences of rejection, failure, and inconsistent mothering; whereas others had believed that retarded persons could not become depressed because their low intelligence precluded development of low self-esteem. Since then, the psychiatric literature (mainly case reports) has reported on cases of depression in retarded persons (Sovner and Hurley 1983). Still, such reports have been infrequent, particularly concerning retarded children. More attention has been given to "psychotic depression" (Reid 1972). Menolascino (1970) described "unresolved grief reaction" in five of ninety-five institutionalized persons with Down syndrome (which could have been an expression of a depressive disorder). Philips and Williams (1975), who reported on one hundred retarded children, and Eaton and Menolascino (1982) did not diagnose any depressive disorders in their respective samples. Gostason (1985) diagnosed only one case of atypical depression in seventy-five mildly and none among fifty-seven moderately or severely retarded persons.

Depressed retarded persons are often unnoticed by their caregivers, since they usually do not disturb others; their depressed mood is confused with the passivity "expected" of a retarded child, and a harassed teacher might even welcome the presence of one child who is quiet. For these reasons and because of professionals' ignorance of the clinical presentation of depression in retarded persons, the presence of a depressive disorder is frequently missed (Szymanski and Biederman 1984).

Manic-depressive illness has been described in retarded persons since the latter part of the last century in spite of views that it could not occur in them. Recently Reid (1976), Heaton-Ward (1977), and Rivinus and Harmatz (1979) reported on retarded patients with the diagnosis of manic-depressive illness. Gostason (1985), using DSM-III criteria, diagnosed cyclothymic disorder in two of his cases.

In our clinic a depressive disorder was diagnosed in 14 percent of mildly/moderately and in 6 percent of severely/profoundly retarded children (it included dysthymic disorder and adjustment disorders with predominance of depressive mood).

The problem with use of DSM-III criteria here is similar to one described earlier concerning diagnosis of psychosis—namely their reliance on verbalized complaints. Although DSM-III states that the clinical presentation may be affected by the developmental level, it does not describe how the symptomatology might change. The DSM-III criteria can be used for diagnosis of affective disorders in retarded persons, but one should allow for the fact that the clinical presentation depends on the patient's communication skills, particularly verbal-conceptual. The mildly retarded person might be able to verbalize dysphoric mood, low self-image, or "feeling sick."

With the less verbal one has to rely on behavioral and vegetative symptoms, as well as on intensification of preexisting aggressive, self-stimulatory, and self-abusive behaviors. Sad appearance and family history positive for depression will support the diagnosis. Thus, the suggestions of Cytryn and McKnew (1974) that there may be different levels of expression of depression in children, ranging from behavioral to verbal, apply here as well. Recently, the use of the dexamethasone suppression test has been reported in retarded patients (Szymanski and Biederman 1984), but there is no reason to expect that it will be more specific and sensitive here than with nonretarded patients. In some cases one might have to resort to a therapeutic trial with antidepressants.

Szymanski and Biederman (1984) pointed out two important differential diagnoses of depression in retarded persons: dementia (particularly Alzheimer's) and reaction to relocation. These are less frequently encountered in retarded children, but the question of dementia might sometimes be raised with adolescents with Down syndrome, in whom Alzheimer's disease has been described as occurring more frequently than in the general population (Miniszek 1983). However, while the neuropathological findings (neocortical plaques and neurofibrillary tangles) of Alzheimer's disease have been found in up to 100 percent of adults with Down syndrome over forty years of age (Malamud 1972) they are not necessarily associated with clinical dementia (Ropper and Williams 1980; Cutler et al. 1985). Some memory impairment and other cognitive changes are found in persons with Down syndrome, but usually not before the mid-forties. Careful history and observation of the patient helps to differentiate between an actual loss of memory and skills versus the loss of motivation of a depressed patient. Neurological examination, including computerized tomography and perhaps a positron emission tomography (PET scan) may be helpful as well.

In some profoundly retarded individuals who were seen in our clinic, symptoms such as interpersonal withdrawal, hypomotility, irritability, and loss of weight were noticed, especially following a loss of a close caregiver. These cases were very similar to Reactive Attachment Disorder of Infancy. However, the DSM-III limits the use of this diagnosis to cases with onset in the first 8 months of life. (This was changed in DSM-III-R to 5 years.)

Last, but not least, undiagnosed medical disorders such as hypothyroidism (e.g., in persons with Down syndrome, who are prone to it) might include symptoms similar to depression.

Organic Disorders

The diagnoses of "organicity" have been misused and overdiagnosed in the mental retardation field. That was due to factors such as psychiatrists' obsession with dividing mental disorders into the organic and nonorganic (Woodward et al. 1970), the misconception that all disordered behaviors of retarded persons are due to "brain damage," and the inadequacies of previous classification systems. The increased prevalence of brain pathology in mentally retarded persons (particularly in those who are severely and profoundly retarded) is well known. In most of the lower grades of retardation, structural brain disorder can be documented. The Isle of Wight Study has shown that 34 percent of children with documented brain disorder had evidence of mental disorder, as opposed to 12 percent of those with physical, non-brain-related disorder (Rutter et al. 1970).

The DSM-III has been a step forward in the classification of these disorders. It acknowledges that labeling a disorder as nonorganic does not imply that it is independent of brain processes, since all psychological processes depend on brain function. It removes the misleading and overgeneralizing DSM-II subdivision of organic brain disorders into "psychotic," "nonpsychotic," reversible, and irreversible (Lipowski 1980). It requires that for establishing an "organic" diagnosis, the clinical presence of the brain syndrome be recognized and that specific organic factors judged etiologically related to the organic mental state be demonstrated (rather than implied, except in certain clear circumstances). Thus, if a person is retarded, exhibits an abnormal behavior, and even has an associated neurological disorder such as epilepsy, an automatic "organic" diagnosis is not justified, unless a temporal or other association can be documented for an etiological connection between the neurological and behavioral disorders. Such association may be implied when behavioral syndrome that is present is well known to be specifically associated with a particular brain dysfunction, such as the personality change of "frontal lobe syndrome" or temporal lobe epilepsy (Bear 1979; Bear et al. 1984) (the "Geschwind syndrome," characterized by obsessive religiosity, hypergraphia, hypo- or hypersexuality, "stickiness" of mental functioning). However, in the mental retardation literature the "organic" diagnoses have been used liberally and idiosyncratically. Typically, children with retardation, seizures, or "soft signs," under- or overactivity, impulsivity, and poor judgment were often diagnosed in this manner.

For these reasons the reported prevalence of these disorders has varied greatly. Menolascino (1970), surveying ninety-five persons with Down syndrome, diagnosed "chronic brain syndrome with behavioral reaction" in seventeen who exhibited behaviors such as hyperactivity, impulsiveness, and short attention span. An additional four who manifested periods of uncontrollability and withdrawal were given a diagnosis of "chronic brain syndrome with psychotic reaction." Chess (1977) diagnosed "behavior disorder due to neurological damage" in 27.3 percent of mildly retarded children who exhibited behaviors such as jumping and hand waving, asked repetitive questions, and had a history of seizures, anoxia at birth, and "soft signs." On the other hand, Philips and Williams (1975), who noticed neurological findings in forty-eight of one hundred retarded children, found little association between them and the clinical presentation. Eaton and Menolascino (1982) diagnosed "organic brain syndrome with behavioral reaction " in 18.4 percent and with "psychotic reaction" in 11.4 percent of their sample, on the basis of factors such as history of neurological, etiologically significant factors and symptoms such as inappropriate acting out, impulsivity, and frequent tantrums. Their psychotic patients differed from schizophrenic ones in that they did not have hallucinations and did not show "progressive involvement of multiple segments of functioning." Gostason (1985) diagnosed atypical organic brain syndrome in twenty-seven of fifty-seven moderately retarded and below, and in two of seventy-five mildly retarded, on the basis of symptoms such as perseveration, lassitude, indecision, and agitation. In contrast, Russell et al. (1979), in their field study of DSM-III, used an organic designation for two patients: one with hallucinations following encephalitis and one with thought disorder following onset of seizures. This approach was consistent with the DSM-III criteria. In our clinic, using similar DSM-III interpretation, we diagnosed an organic disorder in approximately 4 percent of retarded patients and 5 percent of non-retarded ones.

In summary, better definition of organic disorders (or better adherence to DSM-III intention) is needed, as well as better assessment of retarded patients for the presence of organic structural and physiological factors, including iatrogenic ones (such as side-effects of psychotropic medication). In order to achieve that, the diagnostic assessment should be comprehensive and biobehavioral. The precipitous diagnosis of organicity should be avoided, since it often leads to therapeutic nihilism (Lipowski 1980).

Effects of Diagnostic Labeling

Physicians are trained to consider the diagnosis of the patient's problems as an important step necessary for proper treatment. Undoubtedly this perception is accurate in most cases, even though it does not always lead to a specific treatment. Other positive effects of the formal diagnosis (diagnostic "label") include improving communication between professionals and obtaining epidemiological data important for administrative and research purposes. However, the physicians are rarely trained to recognize the psychosocially negative effects of the diagnostic label. These are particularly relevant in respect to mental disorders, which still carry a stigma in our culture. The diagnosis of mental retardation also carries such stigma and moreover might lead to "tracking" the child along certain developmental patterns expected of him. It is therefore reasonable to expect that the double stigma of these two diagnoses will be even more potentially handicapping to the patient. So far little is known of the effects of combined diagnoses of mental retardation and mental disorder on attitudes of others toward the labeled individual. However, we know about the many negative effects of each diagnostic label separately. These are based chiefly on ignorance and the use of the diagnosis to classify and stereotype people rather than disorders. Mentally retarded and mentally ill people are often feared, rejected, met with stereotypical (usually negative and lowered) expectations, and excluded from services and segregated, in contradiction to the principles of normalization and mainstreaming and against the individual's long-term interests. The recently coined, illogical, and unscientific term "dual diagnosis" lumps together a mildly depressed retarded person and a floridly psychotic, severely retarded one, but tells us nothing about their problems and needs (Szymanski and Grossman 1984). Unfortunately, this term has already been used as if it were denoting a special and specific class of persons who should be segregated and effectively denied services they could well use. One must hope clinicians will avoid such general terms and will use instead clinically sound, nonstigmatizing, and descriptive nomenclature. This may pave the way to classifying retarded/disturbed persons solely on the basis of needs and not on the basis of diagnostic labels alone.

CONCLUSION

Clinical assessment of retarded children and adolescents clearly requires a thorough documentation of their cognitive and communicative abilities and limitations. Doing so, however, should not obscure the need also to evaluate coexisting psychopathology, which is more commonly encountered in retarded youngsters than in those of average intelligence. Interview of both the patient and caregivers is a prerequisite for adequate diagnostic assessment and subsequent treatment planning.

REFERENCES

Aman, M. G., et al. (1985). The aberrant behavior checklist: A behavior rating scale for the assessment of treatment effects. *Amer. J. Mental Defic.* 89:485–91.

Anthony, J. C., et al. (1985). Comparison of the lay interview schedule and a standardized psychiatric diagnosis. *Arch. Gen. Psychiat.* 42:667–75.

Baird, P. A., and Sadovnick, A. D. (1985). Mental retardation in over half-a-million consecutive livebirths: An epidemiological study. *Amer. J. Mental Defic.* 89:323–30.

Bear, D. M. (1979). Temporal lobe epilepsy—A syndrome of sensory-limbic hyperconnection. *Cortex* 15:537–84.

————, Freeman, R., and Greenberg, M. (1984). Behavioral alterations in patients with temporal lobe epilepsy. In D. Blumer (Ed.). *Psychiatric Aspects of Epilepsy.* Washington, D.C.: American Psychiatric Press.

Campbell, M., and Green, W. H. (1985). Pervasive developmental disorders of childhood. In H. I. Kaplan and B. J. Sadock (Eds.). *Comprehensive Textbook of Psychiatry.* Baltimore: Williams and Wilkins.

Cantor, S. (1982). *The Schizophrenic Child.* Montreal: Eden Press.

Cantwell, D. P., et al. (1979). A comparison of DSM-II and DSM-III in the diagnosis of childhood psychiatric disorders: I. Agreement with expected diagnosis. *Arch. Gen. Psychiat.* 36:1208–13.

Chess, S. (1977). Evolution of behavior disorders in a group of mentally retarded children. *J. Amer. Acad. Child Psychiat.* 16:5–18.

————, and Hassibi, M. (1970). Behavior deviations in mentally retarded children. *J. Amer. Acad. Child Psychiat.* 9:282–97.

Conroy, J. W., and Derr, K. E. (1971). *Survey and Analysis of the Habilitation and*

Rehabilitation Status of the Mentally Retarded with Associated Handicapping Conditions. Washington, D.C.: DHEW.

Corbett, J. A., Harris, E., and Robinson, R. (1975). Epilepsy. In J. Wortis (Ed.). *Mental Retardation and Developmental Disabilities,* vol. 7. New York: Brunner/ Mazel.

Cushna, B., Szymanski, L. S., Tanguay, P. E. (1980). Professional roles and unmet manpower needs. In L. S. Szymanski and P. E. Tanguay (Eds.). *Emotional Disorders of Mentally Retarded Persons.* Baltimore: University Park Press.

Cutler, N. R., et al. (1985). Alzheimer's disease and Down's syndrome: New insights. *Annals Int. Med.* 103:566–78.

Cytryn, L., and McKnew, D. H. (1974). Factors influencing the changing clinical expression of the depressive process in children. *Amer. J. Psychiat.* 131:878–81.

DeMyer, M. K., Hintgen, J. N., and Jackson, R. K. (1981). Infantile autism reviewed: A decade of research. *Schizophrenia Bull.* 7:388.

DSM-III. *Diagnositc and Statistical Manual of Mental Disorders* (1980). Washington, D.C.: American Psychiatric Association.

Eaton, L. F., and Menolascino, F. J. (1982). Psychiatric disorders in the mentally retarded: Types, problems and challenges. *Amer. J. Psychiat.* 139:1297–1303.

Earl, C. J. (1934). The primitive catatonic psychosis of idiocy. *British J. Med. Psychology* 14:231–53.

Gardner, W. I. (1967). Occurrence of severe depressive reactions in the mentally retarded. *Amer. J. Psychiat.* 124:142–44.

Garrard, S. D., and Richmond, J. B. (1967). Diagnosis in mental retardation and mental retardation without biological manifestations. In C. H. Carter (Ed.). *Medical Aspects of Mental Retardation.* Springfield, Ill.: Charles C. Thomas.

Gostason, R. (1985). Psychiatric illness among the mentally retarded: A Swedish population study. *Acta Psychiat. Scand.* Supplement.

Grossman, H. J. (Ed.). (1973). *Manual on Terminology and Classification in Mental Retardation.* Washington, D.C.: American Association on Mental Deficiency.

Hall, R. C. V., et al. (1978). Physical illness presenting as psychiatric disease. *Arch. Gen. Psychiat.* 35:1315–20.

———, et al. (1980). II. Physical illness manifesting as psychiatric disease. *Arch. Gen. Psychiat.* 37:989–95.

Heaton-Ward, A. (1977). Psychosis in mental handicap. *Brit. J. Psychiat.* 130:525–33.

Helzer, J. E., et al. (1985). A comparison of clinical and diagnostic interview schedule diagnoses. *Arch. Gen. Psychiat.* 42:657–66.

Janicki, M. P., and Jacobson, J. W. (1979). *New York's Needs Assessment and Developmental Diasabilities: Preliminary Report* (Technical Monograph No. 78-10). Albany: OMRDD.

Kazdin, A. E., Matson, J. L., and Senatore, V. (1983). Assessment of depression in mentally retarded adults. *Amer. J. Psychiat.* 140:1040–43.

Kendell, R. E. (1980). DSM-III: A British perspective. *Amer. J. Psychiat.* 137:1630–31.

———, (1983). DSM-III: A major advance in psychiatric nosology. In R. L. Spitzer, J. B. W. Williams, and A. E. Skodol (Eds.). *International Perspectives on DSM-III.* Washington, D.C.: American Psychiatric Press.

Klerman, G. L. (1985). Diagnosis of psychiatric disorders in epidemiologic field studies. *Arch. Gen. Psychiat.* 42:723–24.

Koller, H., et al. (1983). Behavior disturbance since childhood among a 5-year birth cohort of all mentally retarded young adults in a city. *Amer. J. Mental Defic.* 87:386–95.

Kolvin, I. (1971). Psychoses in childhood—A comparative study. In M. Rutter (Ed.). *Infantile Autism: Concepts, Characteristics and Treatment.* Edinburgh: Churchill Livingstone.

Lipowski, Z. J. (1980). A new look at organic brain syndromes. *Amer. J. Psychiat.* 137:674–78.

Malamud, N. (1972). Neuropathology of organic brain syndromes associated with aging. In C. M. Gaitz (Ed.). *Aging and the Brain.* New York: Plenum Press.

Mattison, R., et al. (1979). A comparison of DSM-II and DSM-III in the diagnosis of childhood psychiatric disorders: II. Interrater agreement. *Arch. Gen. Psychiat.* 36:1217–22.

May, J. V. (1931). The dementia praecox-schizophrenia problem. *Amer. J. Psychiat.* 11:401–46.

Menolascino, F. J. (1965). Emotional disturbance and mental retardation. *Amer. J. Mental Defic.* 70:248–56.

———. (1966). The facade of mental retardation. *Amer. J. Psychiat.* 122:1227–35.

———. (1969). Emotional disturbances in mentally retarded children. *Amer. J. Psychiat.* 126:168–79.

———. (1970). Down's syndrome: Clinical and psychiatric findings in an institutionalized sample. In F. J. Menolascino (Ed.). *Psychiatric Approaches to Mental Retardation.* New York: Basic Books.

———, and Bernstein, N. R. (1970). Psychiatric assessment of the mentally retarded child. In N. R. Bernstein (Ed.). *Diminshed People.* Boston: Little Brown.

Mercer, J. R. (1973). *Labeling the Mentally Retarded: Clinical and Social Systems Perspectives on Mental Retardation.* Berkeley: University of California.

Miniszek, N. A. (1983). Development of Alzheimer's disease in Down syndrome individuals. *Amer. J. Mental Defic.* 87:377–85.

O'Gorman, G. (1954). Psychosis as a cause of mental defect. *J. Ment. Sci.* 100:934–43.

Philips, I. (1966). Children, mental retardation and emotional disorder. In I. Philips (Ed.). *Prevention and Treatment of Mental Retardation.* New York: Basic Books.

———, and Williams, N. (1975). Psychopathology and mental retardation: A study of 100 mentally retarded children: I. Psychopathology. *Amer. J. Psychiat.* 132:1265–71.

Reid, A. H. (1972). Psychoses in adult mental defectives: II. Schizophrenic and paranoid psychoses. *Brit. J. Psychiat.* 120:205–12.

———. (1976). Psychiatric disturbances in the mentally handicapped. *Proc. Royal Soc. Med.* 69:509–12.

———. (1980). Psychiatric disorders in mentally handicapped children: A clinical and follow-up study. *J. Mental Defic. Research* 24:287–98.

Reiss, S., Levitan, G. W., and Szyszko, J. (1982). Emotional disturbance and mental retardation: Diagnostic overshadowing. *Amer. J. Mental Defic.* 86:567–74.

Rivinus, T. M., and Harmatz, J. S. (1979). Diagnosis and lithium treatment of affective disorder in the retarded: Five case studies. *Amer. J. Psychiat.* 136:551–54.

Ropper, A. H., and Williams, R. S. (1980). Relationship between plaques, tangles and dementia in Down's syndrome. *Neurology* 30:639–44.

Russell, A. T. (1985). The mentally retarded emotionally disturbed child and adolescent. In M. Sigman (Ed.). *Children with Emotional Disorders and Developmental Disabilities.* New York: Grune and Stratton.

———, et al. (1979). A comparison of DSM-II and DSM-III in the diagnosis of childhood psychiatric disorders: III. Multiaxial features. *Arch. Gen. Psychiat.* 36:1223–26.

———, and Tanguay, P. E. (1981). Mental illness and mental retardation: Cause or coincidence? *Amer. J. Mental Defic.* 85:570–74.

Rutter, M., Graham, P., and Yule, W. (1970). *A Neuropsychiatric Study in Childhood.* London: Heinemann.

———, Greenfeld, D., and Lockyer, M. (1967). A five- to fifteen-year follow-up study of infantile psychosis. II. Social and behavioral outcome. *Brit. J. Psychiat.* 113:11–83.

———, Shaffer, D., and Shepherd, M. (1975). *A Multiaxial Classification of Child Psychiatric Disorders.* Geneva: World Health Organization.

———, and Shaffer, D. (1980). DSM-III: A step forward or back in terms of the classification of child psychiatric disorders? *J. Amer. Acad. Child Psychiat.* 19:371–94.

Senatore, V., Matson, J. L., and Kazdin, A. E. (1985). An inventory to assess psychopathology of mentally retarded adults. *Amer. J. Mental Defic.* 89:459–66.

Sigelman, C. K., et al. (1981). When in doubt say yes: Acquiescence in interviews with mildly retarded persons. *Mental Retardation* 18:53–58.

Sovner, R., and Hurley, A. (1983). Do the mentally retarded suffer from affective illness? *Arch. Gen. Psychiat.* 40:61–67.

Szymanski, L. S. (1977). Psychiatric diagnostic evaluation of mentally retarded individuals. *J. Amer. Acad. Child Psychiat.* 16:67–87.

———. (1980). Psychiatric diagnosis of retarded persons. In L. S. Szymanski and P. E. Tanguay (Eds.). *Emotional Disorders of Mentally Retarded Persons.* Baltimore: University Park Press.

———, and Biederman, J. (1984). Depression and anorexia nervosa of persons with Down syndrome. *Amer. J. Mental Defic.* 89:246–51.

———, and Grossman, H. (1984). Dual implications of dual diagnosis. *Mental Retardation* 22:155–56.

Tanguay, P. E. (1980). Early infantile autism and mental retardation: Differential diagnosis. In L. S. Szymanski and P. E. Tanguay (Eds.). *Emotional Disorders of Mentally Retarded Persons.* Baltimore: University Park Press.

———. (1984). Toward a new classification of serious psychopathology in children. *J. Amer. Acad. Child Psychiat.* 23:373–84.

———, and Szymanski, L. S. (1980). Training of mental health professionals in mental retardation. In L. S. Szymanski and P. E. Tanguay. (Eds.). *Emotional Disorders of Mentally Retarded Persons.* Baltimore: University Park Press.

Tarjan, G., et al. (1973). Natural history of mental retardation: Some aspects of epidemiology. *Amer. J. Mental Defic.* 77:369–79.

Webster, T. G. (1970). Unique aspects of emotional development in mentally retarded children. In F. J. Menolascino (Ed.). *Psychiatric Approaches to Mental Retardation*. New York: Basic Books.

Williams, J. (1985). The multiaxial system of DSM-III: Where did it come from and where should it go?: I. Its origins and critiques. *Arch. Gen. Psychiat.* 42:175–80.

———. (1985). The multiaxial system of DSM-III: Where did it come from and where should it go?: II. Empirical studies, innovations and recommendations. *Arch. Gen. Psychiat.* 42:181–86.

Wolfensberger, W. (1972). *The Principle of Normalization in Human Services*. Toronto: National Institute on Mental Retardation.

Woodward, K. F., Jaffe, N., and Brown, D. (1970). Early psychiatric intervention for young mentally retarded children. In F. J. Menolascino (Ed.). *Psychiatric Approaches to Mental Retardation*. New York: Basic Books.

23

PERVASIVE DEVELOPMENTAL DISORDERS

Wayne H. Green

INTRODUCTION

The Pervasive Developmental Disorders (PDDs) entered the psychiatric nosology as a diagnostic category in 1980 with DSM-III. The PDDs include the diagnoses of Infantile Autism, Full Syndrome Present; Infantile Autism, Residual State; Childhood Onset Pervasive Developmental Disorder, Full Syndrome Present; Childhood Onset Pervasive Developmental Disorder, Residual State; and Atypical Pervasive Developmental Disorder. These disorders are characterized by severe and concomitant "distortions in the development of multiple basic psychological functions that are involved in the development of social skills and language, such as attention, perception, reality testing, and motor movement" (DSM-III 1980, p. 86). Thus, there are varying degrees of symptom overlap among the PDDs and other psychiatric disorders of infancy and childhood. It should be noted that neither etiology nor the level of intellectual functioning is taken into account in making the diagnosis of a PDD.

After a brief discussion of the diagnosis and etiology of the PDDs, the assessment of the infant/child who is being evaluated for a PDD will be reviewed. Those biological aspects that are at the interface of psychiatry and neurology will be particularly emphasized. At least one recent study for each general area will be cited and, when available, one or more references that review the area or present more detailed information and methodology will be given.

Some of the investigations described are at the forefront of research in the biology of the PDDs. Consequently, not all may be appropriate for every child and some are available only in a very few major medical research centers. Those examinations and studies that are most appropriate for a given child must be determined after review of that child's history and from an ongoing critical assessment of that child's positive and negative findings as the evaluation proceeds. In conclusion, the relationship of the evaluation to the treatment plan and its implementation will be discussed briefly.

For a comprehensive review of the Pervasive Developmental Disorders and Infantile Autism in particular, Rutter and Schopler (1978); DeMyer, Hingtgen, and Jackson (1981); Campbell and Green (1985); and Rutter (1985b) are recommended.

DIAGNOSIS

Historically, Kanner's 1943 delineation of a new psychiatric syndrome in his classic article, "Autistic Disturbances of Affective Contact," was the first description of Infantile Autism. The psychiatric nomenclature of the childhood psychoses, of which Infantile Autism was considered one, was in considerable disarray until the advent of the ninth revision of the World Health Organization's Manual of the International Statistical Classification of Diseases, Injuries, and Causes of Death (ICD-9) (1977) and DSM-III (1980). Both nosologies distinguish for the first time between children who meet criteria for schizophrenic disorder as seen in adults, and other childhood psychoses. Prior to this time, several clinical syndromes of childhood psychosis, both descriptively distinct as well as some with overlapping symptomatology, had often been confused by subsuming them all under the taxon "childhood schizophrenia." Thus Bender's (1947) childhood schizophrenics, Kanner's (1943) autistics, Mahler's (1952) symbiotic psychotics, the "unusually sensitive" children described by Bergman and Escalona (1949), Ekstein's borderline child (Ekstein and Wright 1952), Beata Rank's (1949) children with "atypical development," and children who today would be diagnosed schizophrenic disorder by DSM-III criteria were all at one time assigned "childhood schizophrenia." Adding to the confusion is the fact that some authorities, among them Bender (1971) and Fish (1979), feel that infantile autism and schizophrenic disorder with childhood onset, in the DSM-III meaning of the terms, are the same pathological entity manifested by different symptoms according to age of onset and severity. The work of Rutter (1967) and Kolvin and his colleagues (Kolvin 1971; Kolvin et al. 1971a, 1971b, 1971c, 1971d, 1971e) was influential in establishing infantile autism and schizophrenic disorder as two distinct disease entities in the current official psychiatric nomenclature (DSM-III 1980). Green and his coworkers have replicated many of these findings (Green et al. 1984a; Green and Padron-Gayol 1986). For review see Kestenbaum (1978); Fish (1979); Fish and Ritvo (1979); Campbell and Green (1985); and Cohen and Volkman (1986).

An extremely small number of children has been reported who met diagnostic criteria for Infantile Autism before 30 months of age and who subsequently, during latency or early adolescence, developed symptoms meeting criteria for schizophrenic disorder (Fish 1979; Petty et al. 1984). These few children possibly comprise a small, etiologically distinct, subgroup with significant symptom overlap with infantile autism and a maturational inability to express those differentiating symptoms of schizophrenic disorder that require the more mature levels of development present only in older children. This should not be allowed to obfuscate the fact that Infantile Autism and Schizophrenic Disorder are almost mutually exclusive diagnoses.

Some researchers have added additional criteria for what they consider infantile autism. For example, Coleman and Gillberg (1985) felt that "abnormal response to sensory stimuli" must be present to diagnose a "complete autistic syndrome" and that, if this is absent, they would make the diagnosis of "partial autistic syndrome." Similarly, Ornitz (1985) considered disturbances of sensory modulation and motility to be an essential part of the autistic syndrome, although they are not specified among the DSM-III criteria. He noted that these symptoms are most prominent in the 2- to 4-year-old age group, may be manifested by over- or underreactivity to sensory stimuli in all modalities, and may diminish as the children grow older. Clinically, the present author has also noted similar abnormalities in many cases. Although not given as specific examples by DSM-III, many of these symptoms may be subsumed under "bizarre responses to various aspects of the environment" and should be explored while taking the history.

Infantile Autism will be considered the prototype of the pervasive developmental disorders, as it is the only PDD for which there is a substantial body of clinical and research data. Childhood Onset Pervasive Developmental Disorder and Atypical Pervasive Developmental Disorder are apparently rarer than Infantile Autism; their relationship to Infantile Autism is uncertain and their diagnostic validity has yet to be demonstrated (Campbell and Green 1985).

Autism is diagnosed three to four times more frequently in males than in females; however, there is some evidence that autistic females, in general, may be more severely affected and have an increased familial incidence of cognitive problems (Campbell and Green 1985; Lord et al. 1982; Tsai et al. 1981).

Differential diagnosis may include childhood onset of schizophrenic disorder, mental retardation with behavioral disorder, severe hearing loss or deafness, the receptive type of developmental language disorder, disintegrative psychoses (Heller's disease), Rett's syndrome (Hagberg et al. 1983; Gillberg 1986), and attachment disorders of infancy and early childhood (Green 1985). For review, see Campbell and Green (1985) and Rutter (1985a, 1985b).

ETIOLOGY

As is evident from the diagnostic criteria at the present time, etiology is not taken into consideration in making the diagnosis of Infantile Autism or any pervasive developmental disorder. Most researchers consider Infantile Autism to be etiologically heterogeneous although caused by neurophysiological dysfunction of the central nervous system of either genetic and/or organic origin (Sanua 1984). Sanua (1984) also found that birth complications were felt to be of considerable etiological importance by most psychiatrists and psychologists in the United States, but by fewer of both professionals in Europe. Interestingly, about one-third of American psychiatrists and one-quarter of American psychologists still felt parental psychopathology was an important etiological factor, while even more European psychiatrists (54 percent) and psychologists (50 percent) felt this to be the case (Sanua 1984). This may be the vestiges of the psychogenic theories of autism touted by such influential proponents as Bruno Bettelheim, which implicated the parents or "refrigerator" mothers as the cause of their child's autism. (For a critical review of some of Bettelheim's work, Schopler (1976) is recommended.) Psychogenic theories have not held up to any scientifically rigorous scrutiny, and the parents of autistic children have been found to resemble the parents of normal children in infant acceptance, warmth, nurturing, feeding, and general and tactile stimulation (DeMyer et al. 1972).

No known etiology can be determined for most cases of Infantile Autism; however, many medical conditions have been reported to be associated with it and may increase the likelihood of developing Infantile Autism (for review, see especially Coleman and Gillberg 1985). Whenever a concomitant medical condition is present, it should be diagnosed on Axis III of DSM-III. The clinical course of Infantile Autism may vary according to the etiology. For example, Chess (1979) has reported a greater than usual recovery rate in children with congenital rubella who were diagnosed autistic. DeLong, Bean, and Brown (1981) reported the development of a reversible autistic syndrome in three older children, ages 5, 7½, and 11, following acute encephalopathic illnesses.

Despite the fact that most autistic children will not be found to have an identifiable etiology for their PDD, an evaluation that approaches the "state-of-the-art" is recommended to rule out any known organic etiologies. This is for several important reasons: 1) to determine any etiology for which there is an available treatment to ameliorate the condition; 2) to aid in counseling parents who are considering having more children as to genetic (e.g., fragile X-chromosome) or other risks; 3) to help dispel any guilt of the parents that they either were partially responsible for their child's condition or that they have not done everything within their capabilities to provide the best possible treatment; 4) to further our understanding of the etiopathogenesis of the PDDs.

ASSESSMENT OF THE INFANT/CHILD WITH INFANTILE AUTISM

Data including family history, a history of all the mother's pregnancies, prenatal and birth complications, and the child's personal developmental, medical, and psychiatric histories, in particular any prior medications administered, are most frequently obtained in the initial or first few interviews and may provide some guidance in the subsequent assessment of the child. First, pertinent history taking will be discussed. This will be followed by the behavioral, psychological, physical (pediatric), and neurological assessments of the child. Following this, treatment implications and the treatment modalities available will be briefly summarized.

History Taking

Family History. There is considerable evidence for an increased incidence of delayed or deficient language and cognitive development in siblings and parents of autistic children (Bartak, Rutter, and Cox 1975; Folstein and Rutter 1978; August, Stewart, and Tsai 1981; Minton et al. 1982). Baird and August (1985) reported that siblings of severely retarded (IQ < 35) autistic probands had a significantly greater (p ≥ .01) incidence of autism, nonspecific intellectual retardation, or specific cognitive impairment than did siblings of less severely impaired autistic children (IQ ≥ 35). The authors suggested that a familial genetic component, perhaps a factor influencing general cognition, exists in the families of some low-functioning autistic children. Between 2 and 3 percent of siblings of autistic children are themselves autistic; this is about fifty times the rate in the general population (Rutter 1967; DSM-III 1980; August et al. 1981; Minton et al. 1982).

Although an increased incidence of the upper social classes was reported in the early studies of the parents of autistic children, in more recent studies the incidence of social class has been found increasingly to resemble the normative distribution; it is likely the initial increase was a referral artifact (Kanner 1943; Kolvin et al. 1971d; Schopler, Andrews, and Strupp 1979; Wing 1980; Green et al. 1984a).

Pregnancies, Prenatal and Delivery Complications. A complete and detailed history of all the mother's pregnancies, including all drug use and/or abuse whether prescribed, over-the-counter, or illicit, and complications of pregnancy, is essential. Records of the mother's prenatal care and hospitalization for delivery as well as the child's birth record should be obtained, as information may be revealed of which the mother is unaware or which has been distorted either unconsciously or purposefully. Difficulties in conceiving should not be overlooked. Significantly increased occurrence of infertility and of two or more spontaneous abortions has been reported in parents of autistic children compared to the general population (Funderburk et al. 1983). There has been a reported increase in complications of pregnancy, especially midtrimester bleeding, and perinatal risk factors in autistic children (Kolvin, Ounsted, and Roth 1971e; Torrey, Hersh, and McCabe 1975; Gillberg and Gillberg 1983; Green et al. 1984a).

The Rochester Research Obstetrical Scale (RROS) (Zax, Sameroff, and Babigian 1977) is useful in assessing difficulties during the pregnancy, delivery, and neonatal period. This is a twenty-seven–item scale comprised of three subscales: the prenatal, delivery, and infant. Each item is scored 1 or 2 depending on the severity. The prenatal scale includes items on maternal age, parity, abortions, medications taken during pregnancy, and chronic physical disorders and infections. The delivery scale rates cesarean section, induction of labor, premature rupture of membranes, nonvertex presentations, difficulties with umbilical cord or placenta, abnormalities of amniotic fluid, multiple gestation, use of forceps, analgesia and anesthesia, and duration of labor. Finally, the infant scale consists of items on birth weight, premature birth, abnormal fetal an neonatal heart rates, need for resuscitation, Apgar score, and gross physical abnormalities and physical disorders.

Children's Behavioral and Developmental Symptom History. The large majority of autistic children appear to have been abnormal at birth. However, since most symptoms typical of autistic children are failures or deviations in normal developmental processes, they become evident only with the passage of time. In particular, the development and current status of social relatedness, language, and unusual behaviors should be explored. Typically, milestones in these areas are delayed and young autistic children may not make eye contact, assume an anticipatory posture, develop a social smile, or become attached to the parents. Although there is no substitute for working directly with autistic children and their parents to become familiar with most useful avenues of pursuit, Kanner's (1943) original case reports provide amazingly rich and full descriptions of the early developmental deviations typical of autistic children; with Rutter's (1985a) review of history taking in the autistic child, it is recommended for reading.

It should be noted that a few parents of autistic children report relatively normal development until a specific time or an event to which they attribute the onset of autism. In many of these cases, however, with sufficiently detailed history taking, earlier abnormalities are uncovered. The defenses of denial and suppression may be operating in some parents, and the event may be focused upon as an identifiable and acceptable cause of their child's abnormalities, thus diminishing their guilt sufficiently to permit them to recognize consciously their child's deviations for the first time.

One possible confounding factor is that autistic children are often erratic and unpredictable in their behavior and their use of language. For example, some may use a word once and never use it again. Others will use a word appropriately at times and in other similar situations seem incapable of using it. On the other hand, some autistic children do regress. Some have shown loss of speech before the age of 30 months; Kurita (1985) noted that a large majority of these had spoken only single words prior to speech loss and had other preexisting abnormalities in development.

Child's Medical History. A thorough medical history is essential with special emphasis on any symptoms characteristic of infections that may be indicative of central nervous system pathology. Kolvin, Ounstead, and Roth (1971e) reported that massive infantile spasms preceded the onset of infantile psychosis (infantile autism) in about 10 percent of cases. Autistic children may differ from normal children when physically ill; Campbell and Green (1985) noted that clinically, some autistic children may not develop a fever, show malaise, or complain of pain either overtly or by behavior. Even more remarkably their relatedness and behavior may improve noticeably while they are ill and return to baseline following recovery.

Some autistic children show evidence of an increased threshold to pain. Gillberg, Terenius, and Lonnerholm (1985) reported that twelve (60 percent) of twenty autistic children showed evidence of decreased sensitivity to pain. They also found ten of the twelve autistics with diminished pain sensitivity had at some time shown self-destructiveness; two additional children who never showed evidence of decreased pain sensitivity also showed self-destructiveness.

It is essential to have a good history of previous drug administration before selecting an appropriate psychotropic agent if one is necessary and, because of the increased incidence of stereotypies and mannerisms in autistic children, to differentiate these movements from abnormal involuntary movements as in tardive dyskinesia.

Psychiatric and Behavioral Assessments

Psychiatric (Mental Status) Examination. As in any psychiatric condition, the psychiatric mental status examination is the most fundamental assessment and the foundation upon which further evaluation must stand. For this, a thorough knowledge of normal child development is a prerequisite. Only then can the delays and deviations in development characteristic of Infantile Autism be appropriately evaluated.

One particular caveat is offered to the reader who has not evaluated many autistic children. Autistic children may appear extraordinarily different from each other, one major reason being that they may have IQs ranging from below 20 to above average. The examiner must compare each child to the development expected for a child of similar IQ without psychiatric disorder to appreciate the autistic child's psychopathology. If a very low-functioning autistic child is compared with a much higher-functioning autistic child, the distortions and deviations of the latter child may be seriously underestimated. This is because the higher-functioning child will indeed have some communicative language and appear to relate much better than the more retarded child. The striking inadequacies of the higher-functioning autistic child will become highlighted only when compared to a normal child of the same age and intelligence.

Parks (1983) has critically reviewed five rating instruments designed specifically to assess autistic symptomatology: Rimland's Diagnostic Checklist for Behavior-Disturbed Children (Form E-2) (Rimland 1971); Behavior Rating Instrument for Autistic and Atypical Children (BRIAAC) (Ruttenberg et al. 1977); Behavior Observation Scale for Autism (BOS) (Freeman et al. 1978, 1984); Childhood Autism Rating Scale (CARS) (Schopler et al. 1980); and the Autism Screening Instrument for Educational Planning (ASIEP), a component of which is the Autism Behavior Checklist (ABC) (Krug, Arick, and Almond 1980). She notes that interrater reliability has not been evaluated for Form E-2 but is adequate for the four other scales. All five scales were felt to lack rigorous studies of content validity and/or discriminant validity. For example, the BRIAAC distinguished among autistic, retarded, and normal children, but not among disturbed children with more similar symptoms (primary childhood autism, secondary childhood autism, developmental aphasia, early childhood psychosis, and mental retardation [Cohen et al. 1978]).

Other rating scales that have been found useful in assessing autistic children include the first twenty-eight items of the Children's Psychiatric Rating Scale (CPRS), the Clinical Global Impressions (CGI), and the Nurse's Global Impressions (NGI), all of which are described in the special issue of the *Psychopharmacology Bulletin* (1973) devoted to the pharmacotherapy of children.

Psychological Assessment

Although the IQ or level of intellectual functioning is not taken into consideration in making the diagnosis of Infantile Autism, it should be noted that approximately fifty percent of autistic children have IQs of 50 or below and are moderately, severely, or profoundly mentally retarded. About 25 percent of autistic children are mildly retarded and the remaining 25 percent have IQs of 70 or more and have borderline, average, or, rarely, above-average intelligence (Kanner 1943; Campbell and Green 1985). IQs of autistic children obtained on follow-up have shown about the same degree of stability and predictive use as for other groups of children (Bartak and Rutter 1976).

The clinical manifestations and prognosis of autism appear to vary in accordance with the IQ (Bartak and Rutter 1976; Freeman et al. 1981; Freeman, Ritvo, and Schroth 1984). For example, self-injurious behaviors, stereotypies, hyperactivity, seizure disorders, and poorer outcome are more common in the more retarded autistic children, while obsessional symptoms are more frequent in the more intelligent autistic children (Campbell and Green 1985).

There are certain characteristic patterns in the psychological testing, however, that are typical of autistic children whatever their level of intellectual functioning. Usually there is a marked unevenness in their test profiles, with scores measuring language development and verbal abilities being the lowest and those assessing social relatedness and appropriateness being somewhat better. Autistic children usually perform next best on items measuring fine motor tasks, especially those requiring visuospatial abilities and dexterity in manipulating objects, while gross motor test scores are highest. This markedly uneven pattern may be helpful in differentiating autistic retarded children from children who are only retarded.

Some autistic children show so-called islets of preserved intelligence, islets of precocity, or splinter functions. These were first noted in the initial case histories reported by Kanner (1943) and may include extraordinary rote memories and fluent reading (decoding) without comprehension of what is read. Usually the area of precocity ceases to develop at an accelerated rate; thus their peers overtake and surpass them as they develop. The idiot savant with prodigious memory or calculating ability, however, may result in rare cases.

Some autistic children exhibit stimulus overselectivity, paying attention to sensory cues in primarily one modality (e.g., visual) while ignoring others (e.g., auditory) (Kolko, Anderson, and Campbell 1980).

All the psychological tests available and the mechanics of their administration will not be reviewed here. For such information, the reader is referred to the appropriate sections of this book, the specific test manuals, and the standard references on the psychological testing of children. Whatever tests are used, it should be emphasized that they must be administered by a psychologist or other person who is experienced in the testing of autistic children if reliable results are to be obtained.

Because of the uneven abilities typical of autistic children of all ages, it is usually preferable to use an intelligence test that provides subtests or scores in various areas and that distinguishes, in particular, the verbal and the performance areas, rather than one that gives a single composite IQ score. The Gesell Developmental Schedules (Gesell and Amatruda 1947), which provide developmental quotients in four areas (motor, adaptive, language, and personal-social), are especially useful in testing children up to age five and occasionally for very retarded autistic children who are over five, although normative standards do not exist for these older children. Similarly, the appropriate Wechsler intelligence test (the Wechsler Preschool and Primary Scale of Intelligence [WPPSI] for children ages 4.0 to 6½ years, or the Wechsler Intelligence Scale for Children–Revised [WISC-R] for children ages 6.0 to 16¹¹⁄₁₂ years) will usually provide more useful information than an intelligence test such as the Stanford-Binet Intelligence Scale, which provides a single score.

The above tests have a verbal component. Since communicative language is usually the weakest area of the autistic child, it may be useful to administer tests that do not require the child to use or understand speech. Thus, the Peabody Picture Vocabulary Test–Revised (PPVT-R) or the Leiter International Performance Scale (LIPS) may be employed. Shah and Holmes (1985) reviewed the use of the LIPS in autistic children and found a positive correlation between the Leiter IQ and the WISC-R performance IQ but not the WISC-R verbal IQ in the eighteen autistic children they tested.

The examiner may select other psychological tests to further access the autistic child's relative strengths and/or weaknesses. In some cases, projective and educational achievement tests may also be appropriate.

For a review of the entire area of the relationship of cognitive deficits to the pathogenesis of autism, a recent review by Rutter (1983) is recommended.

Physical Assessment

Complete Physical Examination. The physical appearance of the autistic child is usually normal. Kanner (1943) noted the children's "intelligent physiognomies." Although purely retarded children with very low IQs are frequently stigmatized and look unusual, severely and profoundly retarded autistic children often appear superficially normal or even more physically attractive than average. Some autistic children toe-walk; many seem to enjoy vestibular stimulation and may spontaneously spin themselves or delight in being swung, lifted, or spun by the examiner.

Dermatological manifestations of diseases affecting the central nervous system (e.g., sebaceous adenoma and/or hypopigmented lesions typical of tuberous sclerosis or neurofibroma of von Recklinghausen's disease) should be sought carefully.

Minor Physical Anomalies (Congenital Stigmata). Waldrop and Halverson's (1971) Minor Physical Anomalies Scale has been used to assess autistic children. Weighted scores are given for anomalies of hair, head circumference, epicanthus, hypertelorism, low-seated ears, adherent ear lobes, malformed or asymmetrical ears, palate abnormalities, furrowed tongue, clinodactyly, simian line, and toe abnormalities. These anomalies appear to result from difficulties in the first trimester of pregnancy. As ectoderm differentiates into both the neural plate, from which both nerve cells and their supporting elements develop, as well as the epidermis and hair, it is hypothesized that some of these observable anomalies may reflect an intrauterine environment that also caused abnormal concomitant central nervous system development. An increased incidence of minor physical anomalies in autistic children as compared to their siblings or normal controls has been found (Walker 1977b; Links et al. 1980). Coleman (1976) reported that low-set ears, hypertelorism and syndactyly were significantly more frequent in autistics than normal controls.

Higher anomaly scores were associated with lower IQ and more frequent hospitalizations of the autistic child, increased age of the mother, and families with less psychiatric illness, alcohol and drug abuse, and criminality compared to lower anomaly scores (Links et al. 1980; Links 1980).

Complete Neurological Evaluation. A complete evaluation would include the following: a classical neurological examination, skull films (to look for intracranial calcifications which can sometimes result as sequelae of tuberous sclerosis or congenital toxoplasmosis), and special neurological tests.

Ornitz (1983, 1985) has reviewed in detail the neurophysiology of Infantile Autism, in particular "brainstem-diencephalic" studies that may explain some autistic symptoms resulting from the autistic child's inability to modulate adequately sensory input and motor output. He noted that consistent differences in brainstem transmission time (BSTT) of brainstem auditory evoked responses (BAER) were not found between groups of autistics and controls, but that subgroups of 33 to 56 percent of autistics were found to have prolonged BSTTs in three studies.

Although most autistic children have normal hearing and normal pure tone audiometric thresholds, auditory brainstem evoked responses with increased latency and markedly increased variability have been found in about one-third of autistic children, suggesting brainstem dysfunction (Rosenblum et al. 1980; Gillberg, Rosenhall, and Johansson 1983).

Ornitz (1985) also calculated the gain and the time constant of the primary nystagmus response to acceleration in twenty-two autistic and twenty-five normal children as these reflect transmission through the vestibular nucleus and brainstem reticular formation (BSRF). The autistic children showed normal gain but prolonged time constants suggesting dysfunction of a multisynaptic neuronal network in the autistic's BSRF (Ornitz 1985).

Hearing Evaluation. Autistic children often appear to be uninterested in spoken language, may not attend to the human voice, and may seem oblivious of sudden loud noises that would cause a startle response in a normal person. Consequently, they frequently are suspected of having a significant hearing deficit or of being deaf. A careful history, however, may reveal selective response to low decibel sounds that interest the child, for example, a watch ticking or cellophane's being crumpled. Autistic children may be difficult to test on audiography; a technician experienced in working with autistic children and an accompanying person who is familiar to the autistic child will maximize the likelihood of a successful test. If necessary, auditory brainstem evoked responses can be obtained. Most autistic children have been found to have normal pure tone audiometric threshold, although a few are found to have peripheral hearing deficits (Rosenblum et al. 1980; Gillberg, Rosenhall, and Johansson 1983).

Electroencephalogram (EEG). No EEG abnormalities have been identified that are pathognomonic of autism, although most studies have found that between 10 and 83 percent of autistic children have abnormal EEGs (Campbell and Green 1985). Small (1975) reported nearly two-thirds of 147 autistic children as compared to only 5.8 percent of normal controls had abnormal EEGs. The abnormal EEG findings correlated significantly with other indicators of brain dysfunction such as lower IQ, positive neurological findings, and poorer follow-up status (Small 1975).

Between 4 and 32 percent of autistic children develop seizures in the course of their illnesses (Campbell and Green 1985). Risk of developing seizures is over five times greater in severely retarded autistic children than in those with normal nonverbal IQs (Bartak and Rutter 1976). Bartak and Rutter (1976) reported that approximately one-third of autistic children whose IQs are below 70 develop seizures during adolescence. Deykin and MacMahon (1979) found that about 23 percent of 132 autistics developed a seizure disorder before age 18; age of peak onset was unusual, between 11 and 14 years, when the incidence usually lessens in nonautistic children.

Dawson, Warrenburg, and Fuller (1982) reported that seven of ten autistics were significantly different from controls and demonstrated deficient left hemispheric specialization for linguistic functions, as indicated by a reduction of alpha activity in left hemispheric EEG activation during linguistic tasks and right hemisphere dominance for both verbal and spatial functions.

Ogawa et al. (1982) found a marked delay in the lateralization of the EEG during Stage II sleep in autistic children 2 to 8 years of age compared to normal controls.

In the only study comparing the EEGs of autistic and COPDD children, Caparulo and her associates (1981) found that six (27.3 percent) of twenty-two autistic children and twelve (70.6 percent) of seventeen children with nonautistic pervasive developmental disorder satisfying five of the seven DSM-III criteria for COPDD had abnormal EEGs. Corbett (1982) has reviewed EEG findings and epilepsy in the early childhood psychoses.

Computerized Tomography (CT), Positron Emission Tomography (PET), and Regional Cerebral Blood Flow (rCBF). These techniques look for physical abnormalities or asymmetries (CT scan and rCBF) or abnormalities in the rate of cerebral metabolism in various areas in the brain (PET scan).

Results of CT scan studies are discrepant, revealing no consistent abnormalities of brain anatomical structure in children diagnosed autistic. This may be due in part to diagnostically heterogeneous samples with differing ages and neurological statuses (including seizures, focal neurological deficits, and hydrocephalus), the presence or absence of significant mental retardation, and inadequate controls (Rosenbloom et al. 1984).

Although no consistent abnormalities have been found, two studies have found a subgroup of autistic children with mild to moderate ventricular enlargement (Campbell et al. 1982b; Rosenbloom et al. 1984).

Prior, Tress, and Hoffman (1984) published the results of computed tomographic (CT) scans in nine autistic males, ages 9 to 16 years, with borderline or normal intelligence and no evidence of organic dysfunction. These boys did, however, perform more poorly on tests that reflected left hemispheric functioning than mental age-matched or younger controls. The CT scans were judged essentially normal, and no evidence was found of physical abnormality or asymmetry that might reflect the poor performance on left hemisphere related tasks. The authors emphasized that in these cases of classic autism without significant mental retardation or any evidence of organic dysfunction, all had minimal evidence of any CT scan abnormalities.

Another recently performed study (Harcherik et al. 1985) computed axial tomographic (CAT) scans on sixteen subjects with infantile autism, twenty-two subjects with attention deficit disorder, nine with language problems, nineteen with Tourette's disorder, and a control group of twenty; most subjects were teenagers. The authors found no group differences in total ventricular volume, right-left ventricular volume ratio, asymmetry of ventricles, ventricle-brain ratios, or brain density. They concluded that unless other neurological problems are present, autistic children are not likely to have quantifiable CAT scan abnormalities. These results were similar to those of a previous study (Caparulo et al. 1981), which found only four (18 percent) of twenty-two autistic males to have abnormal CT scans. In the same study, ten (59 percent) of seventeen children with a nonautistic pervasive developmental disorder (satisfying a minimum of five of the seven DSM-III criteria for COPDD) had abnormal CT scans (Caparulo et al. 1981).

The CT scan seems most appropriate for the autistic child with an abnormal neurological examination, significant EEG abnormalities, or evidence of a marked change in clinical status.

Regional cerebral blood flow (rCBF) was determined in seven autistic subjects 18 to 33 years of age, compared with thirteen control subjects (Sherman, Nass, and Shapiro 1984). The autistic subjects showed significantly lower gray matter cerebral blood flow in both right and left hemispheres, abnormal resting landscapes, and other deviances.

Rapoport and Ismond (1982) noted that the amount of radiation exposure secondary to positron emission tomography (PET) scanning is unacceptably high for research in pediatric age groups. Using PET scanning, Rumsey et al. (1985) compared resting cerebral glucose utilization rates of ten autistic men (ages 18 to 36, with normal CT scans) who had been diagnosed autistic during childhood, with fifteen normal controls. As a group, the autistics had significant elevation of glucose utilization in widespread regions of the brain, but there was considerable overlap with the normal controls. None of the autistic subjects had brain regions with lowered glucose utilization. The absolute metabolic rates of the autistic subjects were significantly higher than the controls in all nineteen (61 percent) of thirty-one circumscribed regions of interest that were significantly different ($p<.05$). Analyses of relative metabolic rates (asymmetry ratios) showed five autistics but no controls with at least one score over four Standard Deviations from the normal mean.

Measures of Laterality (Usually Handedness). Laterality is measured, as there is evidence that an increased incidence of nonrighthandedness may be indicative of brain damage, cerebral (hemispheric) dysfunction, developmental delays, and some speech and language disorders, for example, developmental dysphasia (Colby and Parkinson 1977; Boucher 1977; Gillberg 1983). There is also evidence that increased lefthandedness and vulnerability to language disorders runs in some families (Boucher 1977). Bartak, Rutter, and Cox (1975) have reported a history of speech delay in the families of about 25 percent of autistic children. As youngsters who are mentally retarded only may also show an increased incidence of delay in establishment of laterality, control groups with similar IQs are desirable.

Colby and Parkison (1977) have published a relatively simple battery of tests consisting of weighted scores in performing fourteen items usually associated with handedness, for example, drawing, writing, and the hand used to wind thread on a spool, and throwing. As not all autistic children will perform all tasks, the percentage of the time a given hand is preferred rather than a numerical score is used in determining handedness. Annett (1970) has also developed a test of hand preference with only seven items.

Colby and Parkison (1977) reported nonright-handedness in 65 percent of twenty autistic children, compared to only 12 percent of normal children; age range of all children was from 2.2 to 6.9 years (mean 4.3 years). Boucher (1977) compared handedness in forty-six retarded autistic children with Annett's (1970) normative data and with two control groups matched for sex, age, and mental age. In one control group mental age was estimated by nonverbal ability, in the other by verbal ability. No significant differences in hand preference were found among the groups. Boucher noted, however, that the verbally matched controls over age 11 had a normal distribution of hand preference; the advanced age at which they attained this was attributed to a simple maturational delay caused by their mental retardation. In contrast, autistics over 11 years of age continued to have a decreased incidence of righthandedness, although this was not statistically significant. This suggested that factors other than mental retardation per se were responsible for this persisting abnormality in the older autistic subjects. Gillberg (1983) assessed handedness in twenty-six autistic subjects an fifty-two controls matched for age, sex, and IQ; age range was from 7 to 21 years. More autistic subjects (62 percent) were nonright-handed than controls (37 percent). Six autistics (23 percent) but only three controls (6 percent) were left-handed (p<.05). An additional interesting finding was that five of the six left-handed autistics (83 percent) showed marked delayed echolalia, while only 15 percent of all ambidextrous and right-handed children did so (p<.02) (Gillberg 1983).

Tsai (1983) examined handedness in seventy autistic children ages 2 years 10 months to 13½ years (mean 6.2 years). He found that their handedness tended to stabilize at age 5 years. Those autistic children who developed hand lateralization tended to have better cognitive, language, and visual spatial abilities than children with mixed handedness. Hence, Tsai felt the presence or absence of hand lateralization by age 5 could be a useful predictor of outcome.

Dermatoglyphics. Walker (1977a) found significant differences between seventy-eight autistic subjects ages 4 to 25 and seventy-eight normal controls. Autistic children showed in particular reduced number of whorls, increased number of arches, lowered ridge counts, and less distinctness in formation of ridge line. Only 6.4 percent of autistic subjects had normal dermatoglyphics while 55.1 percent of controls did so.

Sank and Firschein (1979) analyzed fingerprint pattern frequencies in forty-four autistic children. They differed significantly from patterns of control populations and adult schizophrenics.

Chromosome Studies. The most common chromosomal abnormality reported in Infantile Autism is an X-linked recessive disorder, the fragile-X syndrome, which is typically characterized by mental retardation, large ears, elongated face, minor malformations of the hands and feet, and postpubertal macroorchidism. Watson et al. (1984) found a frequency of 5.3 percent fragile-X chromosome in seventy-six autistic males and noted this incidence was similar to that in nonautistic severely retarded males. Gillberg and Wahlstrom (1985) reported that 20 percent of forty autistic boys had fragile-X(q27); in seven of the eight cases, it was associated with mental retardation. Other chromosomal abnormalities were also reported in these forty autistic children, including fragile sites at the 16q23 and 16q26 locations, fragile-X(p22), XYY, trisomy 21, and long Y chromosomes (Gillberg and Wahlstrom 1985).

Blomquist et al. (1985) found that thirteen (16 percent) of eighty-three autistic males but none of nineteen autistic females had fragile-Xq27 chromosomes. Autistic male siblings with fragile-X syndrome have also been reported (Brown et al. 1982; August and Lockhart 1984).

Coleman and Gillberg (1985) recommend that all male autistic children have a chromosomal culture in folic acid deficient medium. Gillberg and Wahlstrom (1985) noted that some cases of fragile X(q27) may be missed in the parents of autistic children if methotrexate is not added to the culture medium.

Growth. Because abnormalities in growth, most commonly an increased proportion of children falling below the third percentile, have been reported in autistic children (Dutton 1964; Campbell et al. 1980) it is essential to record height and weight at baseline. Use of the National Center of Health Statistics Growth Charts (Hamill et al. 1976) is recommended. These baselines are particularly important, as in practice many autistic children receive psychotropic medication that may affect their growth; thus height and weight should be carefully monitored during the course of treatment.

In two short-term, double-blind, placebo-controlled studies comprising a total of seventy-six autistic children ages 2.0 to 7.6 years, haloperidol was administered in daily dosages of 0.25 to 3.0 mg/day (0.1 to 0.217 mg/kg/day) for a maximum total of eight weeks (Green et al. 1984b). Most children gained weight over the course of treatment but there was no significant change in either mean height or weight. A subgroup of forty-two of these patients entered a long-term treatment program; after their receiving haloperidol for a total of from seven to eight months, the mean percentile for weight increased by 8.2 points (p<0.05) and the mean percentile for height decreased by 4.7 points (N.S.) (Green et al. 1984a).

Fenfluramine, a drug with both stimulating and sedating properties that is used as an anorectic in adults, has recently begun to be used in the treatment of autism because of its antiseritonergic properties. Its long-term effects on growth are not yet known, but they may be more adverse than those of the neuroleptics, and they require close monitoring. At the present state of our knowledge, all autistic children, especially those receiving any medication, should have their growth recorded regularly.

Bone Age. Bone age was determined in eighty-four autistic children ages 2.0 to 7.0 years according to the methods of Greulich and Pyle (1959) by Campbell and her associates (1980). Eighty percent were within ± 1 Standard Deviation (SD) of the mean for age, while 12 percent were between 1 and 2 SDs below the mean and 6 percent were below two SDs; only a total of 2 percent were 1 or more SDs above the mean. Dutton (1964) reported that 17 percent of twenty-five psychotic (autistic) boys ages 6 to 20 years have bone ages more than 2 SDs below the norm for their chronological ages.

Laboratory Studies. These would be routine as per usual hospital admission: serum glutamic oxaloacetic transaminase (SGOT), serum glutamic pyruvic transaminase (SGPT), alkaline phosphatase, lactic dehydrogenase (LDH), creatine phosphokinase (CPK), total bilirubin, total protein, albumin, cholesterol, urinanalysis, complete blood count, differential, hematocrit, serum test for syphilis (STS), lead level, uric acid.

Cohen, Johnson, and Caparulo (1976) found significantly elevated blood lead levels in autistic children compared to their siblings and nonautistic psychotic children. Campbell et al. (1980) reported that fifteen (19.5 percent) of seventy-seven autistic subjects had lead levels above 35 micrograms/100 ml; although none was in the toxic range, intellectual functioning correlated negatively with lead levels.

Special Tests. For a general review of biochemical studies in autism including neurotransmitters (dopamine, serotonin, and norepinephrine); enzymes (e.g., monoamine oxidase [MAO], dopamine β-hydroxylase [DBH]); and blood, spinal fluid, and urinary metabolites (e.g., homovanillic acid [HVA], the principal dopamine metabolite, and 5-hydroxyindoleacetic acid [5-HIAA], the principal serotonin metabolite), Piggott (1979), Young et al. (1982), Green et al. (1985), and Coleman and Gillberg (1985) are suggested.

1. Abnormal metabolites: Blood and urine screening for inborn errors of metabolism, e.g., phenylketonuria, abnormal purine metabolism (e.g., hyperuricosuria). For review see Coleman and Gillberg (1985, pp. 144–63).

2. Endorphin levels: Gillberg, Terenius, and Lonnerholm (1985) determined cerebrospinal fluid endorphin levels in twenty autistic children ages 2 to 13 years. Mean CSF endorphin fraction II levels were higher in eleven (55 percent) of autistics than in any of the eight normal controls. There was also a trend toward correlation between high endorphin fraction II levels and self-destructiveness and decreased pain sensitivity.

3. Antibody titer screening: titers for herpes, mumps, cytomegalovirus, and rubella, for example. Stubbs (1976) reported that five of thirteen autistic children had undetectable antibody titers following a challange with rubella vaccine despite previous vaccination, whereas all eight controls had detectable titers. The author suggested the altered immune responsivity of the autistic children might have occurred as a sequela of a prenatal viral infection. For review of this area, see Coleman and Gillberg (1985, pp. 107, 131–39).

4. Immunological studies: Stubbs et al. (1977) reported a significantly depressed T-lymphocyte transformation response to phytohemagglutinin (PHA) in twelve autistic children compared with thirteen control subjects ($p < .01$). This suggested that some autistic children have a relative T-cell deficiency and that prenatal viral infection and/or immunopathology was a possible cause.

Weizman and his coworkers (1982) found thirteen (76.5 percent) of seventeen autistic, 7- to 22-year-old subjects had cell-mediated immune responses to brain tissue (human myelin basic protein) as demonstrated by inhibition of macrophage migration whereas none of eleven nonautistic controls did so. The authors suggested an undetectable brain lesion associated with autoimmunity may be important in the pathogenesis of autism.

5. Vitamins, Co-enzymes, and Co-factors: Gentile et al. (1983) found significantly elevated levels of magnesium and potassium in autistics' hair compared to that of controls. For review of this area see Coleman and Gillberg (1985, pp. 93–103, 182–85).

Neuroendocrine Studies. Neuroendocrine studies attempt to identify central hypothalamic dysfunction and possible neurotransmitter abnormalities by measuring basal and stimulated levels of hormones secreted by the pituitary. For review, Piggott (1979), Young et al. (1982), Coleman and Gillberg (1985), and Green, Deutsch, and Campbell (in press) are recommended.

1. Hormonal studies: Thyroxine (T4), Triiodothyronine (T3), Luteinizing hormone (LH), Follicle-stimulating hormone (FSH), Growth hormone (GH), Prolactin.

Endocrine studies in autistic children are of particular interest, as they may reflect brain dysfunction including neurotransmitter and hypothalamic abnormalities.

In recent reviews it was noted that although various endocrine abnormalities supporting hypothalamic-pituitary dysfunction occur in individual autistic children, no peripheral hormonal abnormalities have been found that characterize homogeneous subgroups of autistic children (Campbell et al. 1982a; Green, Deutsch, and Campbell, in press).

2. Neurotransmitters: serotonin and dopamine.

Several studies have found that about 30 percent of autistic children have hyperserotonemia; however, there is evidence that this may be related to concomitant mental retardation rather than autism per se (Campbell et al. 1975).

Gillberg, Svennerholm, and Hamilton-Heilberg (1983) reported significantly elevated levels of homovanillic acid (HVA) in the CSF of autistic children (p<.01) compared to controls matched for sex and approximate age and a group of children with "simple" mental retardation only.

Deutsch and colleagues (1985) assessed the response of twenty-two autistic children to oral L-Dopa. At least 30 percent showed a blunted plasma growth hormone response suggesting hypothalamic dysregulation and dopaminergic abnormalities.

Coleman and Gillberg (1985, pp. 75–104) have recently reviewed studies of serotonin, catecholamines, and relevant enzymes in autistic children.

Baseline (or Other) Assessment of Abnormal Movements

Because of the high incidence of stereotypies and mannerisms in autistic children, it is of crucial importance to make a baseline assessment of abnormal movements so as to be able to distinguish them from any abnormal involuntary movements that may result as a side effect of neuroleptic medication. This is particularly important as neuroleptics may decrease or eliminate stereotypies and/or mannerisms, which may then reappear when the neuroleptic is decreased or discontinued. This recrudescence may readily be confused with tardive dyskinesia if baseline measurements have not been recorded and made available for reference. The potential for misdiagnosis of movement disorders is especially great when the physician responsible for the child's treatment changes during the time the child is receiving medication. For review of this topic, see Campbell et al. (1983a).

In the only prospective study in the literature of the effect of long-term administration of haloperidol on autistic children, thirteen of fifty-eight children (22 percent) aged 3.6 to 7.8 years developed mild to moderate drug-related abnormal movements following cumulative maintenance on haloperidol in daily doses of 0.5 to 3.0 mg (mean 1.0 mg) or 0.02 to 0.22 mg/kg (mean 0.05 mg/kg) for from 3.5 to 42.5 months (Campbell et al. 1983b; Perry et al. 1985). Four of the children developed the abnormal movements while receiving haloperidol, while nine children developed abnormal involuntary movements during a period when they were receiving placebo. The movements developed de novo in eleven children; two children had preexisting stereotypies although in different topographies. The movements remitted spontaneously in ten of the children. In the other three, they ceased following resumption of haloperidol administration. The movements stopped within as few as sixteen days and by nine months in all cases (Perry et al. 1985).

The following rating scales are useful in making baseline assessments, periodic reassessments including during routine scheduled withdrawals of medication, and in following the course of any abnormal movements which may develop. The use of these and other rating scales in children has been reviewed by Campbell, Green, and Deutsch (1985).

1. Abnormal Involuntary Movement Scale (AIMS) (Guy 1976);
2. Abbreviated (Simpson) Dyskinesia Rating Scale (Simpson et al. 1979);
3. Dosage Record and Treatment Emergent Symptoms (DOTES) (*Psychopharmacology Bulletin 1973*);
4. Treatment Emergent Symptoms Write in Scale (*Psychopharmacology Bulletin 1973*).

Videotaping may be especially useful in evaluating children's abnormal movements, both baseline and any that develop during the course of treatment, as they can be reviewed and compared as well as seen by other raters not present at the live ratings.

TREATMENT

The goals in treating autistic children may be subsumed under two general areas: amelioration of abnormal behaviors and promoting or enhancing normal development. Most authorities agree that this is best accomplished by enrolling the autistic child at as young an age as practical, about 3 years old, in a highly structured therapeutic nursery staffed with teachers specially trained to work with autistic children. Ideally, the nursery should be a full-day program meeting at least five days a week and emphasizing a psychoeducational approach with special emphasis on language acquisition and social interaction. In conjunction with this, a group focusing on counseling the parents of the autistic child and, when possible, other family members should be an integral part of the treatment plan. One of the most helpful therapeutic interventions for the family of the autistic child is to dispel any irrational parental guilt that their personalities have caused their child's autism. As noted above under etiology, parental psychopathology or parent-child psychodynamics are not considered important factors in the etiology of autism. This, however, does not mean that psychodynamics are not important in the treatment of the autistic child. Autistic children, like all human beings, obviously respond to their psychosocial environments in significant and clinically relevant ways. The therapist should strive to help the entire family understand and achieve optimal interactions with the autistic child.

Although behavioral therapy techniques have been employed with autistic children with some success, Werry (1979) has pointed out three major problems: a relatively great amount of time must be invested in the individual treatment of each child; the positive results may not generalize to other environments (e.g., the autistic child's home) or times; and the autistic child still remains conspicuous. Training parents to continue the behavioral reinforcement in the home may be helpful but is also very time consuming. Lovaas (1977) has reviewed in considerable detail the use of behavioral techniques to foster language development in autistic children and has also noted the problem with maintenance of verbal behavior once it has been acquired. Blank and Milewski (1981) have reported an interesting case study of a higher-functioning 4½-year-old autistic boy whose communicative language, both spontaneous and elicited, improved remarkably after a year of two to three times weekly operant conditioning sessions of about thirty minutes duration. Importantly, this child showed considerable generalization of his gains and used language in a variety of situations with various people. However, he became confused when confronted with novel linguistic patterns and was unable to sustain a conversation. During the course of treatment symbolic play, which had been absent, developed and stereotyped routines markedly decreased.

Other more specific treatments will be only briefly considered here, as they are particularly related to the biological findings. For a more generalized consideration of treatment issues in autism, Rutter and Schopler (1978) and Rutter (1985a) are recommended. The abnormal social behaviors of autistic individuals and various methods of enhancing social skills and ameliorating existing deficits have been recently reviewed (Schopler and Mesibov 1986). Developmental and treatment issues pertaining especially to adolescent and young adult autistics have also been recently addressed (Schopler and Mesibov 1983).

Any concurrent medical conditions, including a seizure disorder, must be adequately treated. Pharmacotherapy may decrease maladaptive behaviors and facilitate relatedness in some autistic children, thereby enhancing their abilities to benefit from concomitant therapeutic interventions. It is to be expected that as our understanding of neurotransmitter abnormalities in subgroups of autistic children progresses, psychopharmacological agents may be chosen more specifically and rationally. At present, however, no drug is entirely satisfactory.

In a double-blind, placebo-controlled study, haloperidol, a dopamine antagonist, was shown to be effective in low doses (0.5 to 3.0 mg/day) in significantly reducing behavioral symptoms such as stereotypies and hyperactivity, which may be related to hyperdopaminergic activity (Anderson et al. 1984). In addition, haloperidol significantly decreased withdrawal, abnormal object relationships, fidgetiness, negativism, and angry and labile affects, and improved ratings on global clinical improvement outside the laboratory. In the laboratory, haloperidol had no significant effect on duration of stereotypies, hyperactivity, or carpet activity; however, it enhanced discrimination learning and its retention. On average, autistic children receiving haloperidol performed as well as autistic children on placebo who had developmental quotients twenty points higher on the language part of the Gesell Developmental Schedules. This suggests that enhancement of learning was independent of reduction of stereotypies or hyperactivity and secondary to a direct positive effect on attentional or other learning processes (Anderson et al. 1984).

Haloperidol has also been shown to have a synergistic interaction with behavioral therapy in reducing behavioral symptoms and facilitating language acquisition and retention in a controlled study of forty autistic children (Campbell et al. 1978). Haloperidol is almost certainly the most thoroughly studied psychotropic drug frequently used in autistic children, including double-blind, placebo-controlled, short-term studies and long-term follow-up. Improvement, although significant, is usually modest. In addition, significant numbers of children (22 percent) have developed tardive or withdrawal dyskinesias in a prospective study in which 0.5 to 3.0 mg/day of haloperidol was administered for from 3½ to 42½ months (Perry et al. 1985). Hence, other drugs with greater therapeutic efficacy and without adverse long-term sequelae continue to be sought.

Two drugs currently under investigation are fenfluramine and naltrexone. Fenfluramine, an antiserotonergic agent with both stimulating and sedating properties, has recently been reported to show positive therapeutic effects in some autistic children. It was tried initially because of the reports of hyperserotonemia in about one-third of autistic children. Curiously, however, the most favorable clinical responses correlated with low blood serotonin levels and high verbal IQs (Ritvo et al. 1984). Naltrexone, a potent long-acting opiate antagonist, might be a potentially useful agent in a subgroup of autistic children who have elevated endorphin (opioid peptides) levels. Positive effects of naltrexone have been reported in an open study of a severely disturbed 5-year-old autistic male who had no communicative language and exhibited severe withdrawal, stereotypies, aggressiveness, and hyperactivity (Campbell et al. 1986). At the present time, however, although some initial encouraging results have been reported, both of these drugs remain investigational, and further evaluation of their clinical efficacy and safety must be undertaken with satisfactory results before either can be recommended.

For review of psychopharmacological treatment of infantile autism, Green et al. (1985); Campbell, Green, and Deutsch (1985); and Campbell et al. (in press) are recommended.

CASE VIGNETTE

Family History and Present Illness

Henry, a 4-year-old black male who was admitted to an inpatient therapeutic nursery, is the youngest of five siblings; an older sibling died at age 3 months of unknown cause. His father is a successful, college-educated professional and his mother is a housewife with much less education. There is no family history of psychiatric illness, learning disorder, or seizures. However, a school psychologist reports that one older sibling has emotional problems and another sibling was described as hyperactive, socially immature, and learning-disabled, with a poor memory and short attention span.

His mother was 35 years old at the time of Henry's birth. Pregnancy was reported to be uncomplicated. Labor was about eight hours, presentation was vertex and delivery was at forty weeks gestation with midforceps. APGAR was 8 at one minute and 9 at five minutes. Mother and child were discharged after three days. Neonatal period was unremarkable. The patient was breastfed and reportedly nursed and slept normally.

The parents became concerned when Henry failed to sit, walk, and talk at the usual time. Henry first began to take steps without support at age 16 months. Babbling began at age 2 years; when admitted, he still had no communicative speech, although at times he would unpredictably say "dada." By the time he was 2, his parents were convinced he could hear and smell, and he followed objects visually and bottlefed himself. By age 3 he had begun to use a spoon and drink from a cup. At age 4 he has still not developed a pincer grasp. At times he would urinate in the toilet; however, bowel control had not been achieved at admission and he was still frequently incontinent of urine. He has no awareness of danger.

Henry recognized and differentiated his parents and siblings, but seemed more interested in inanimate objects than in people. He became preoccupied with the toilet; he would constantly flush it and frequently tried to flush various objects down it, much to his parents consternation.

Hyperactivity and impulsivity began soon after independent locomotion. Because of their severity and his delayed developmental milestones, the parents consulted a pediatric neurologist when Henry was 3½. At that time, an "ash leaf" hypopigmented lesion was noted on his trunk and he was worked up for possible tuberous sclerosis. There was no history of seizures, and classical neurological examination showed no focal findings. EEG, skull films, and a CT scan of the head with contrast were read as within normal limits. An abdominal X ray following the CT scan showed normal excretion of dye and no renal mass or deformity. Thus tuberous sclerosis was ruled out.

Admission to an inpatient therapeutic nursery at age 4 years followed Henry's breaking loose from his mother while out walking and recklessly endangering his life, nearly being killed. He had always lived at home and had never been in a nursery program of any type. On admission he had no difficulty separating from his parents, but he tried frequently to run out of the nursery or off the ward whenever he had an opportunity. He made sounds but had no communicative speech and did not respond to his name or follow simple commands. He exhibited stereotypic behaviors such as holding things close to his eyes and rotating them, collecting objects and putting them in enclosed spaces, and some grimacing and turning his head to the side. He made only fleeting or no eye contact and directed his interest toward objects, for example, the physician's watch or photo ID badges rather than toward people.

Physical Examination

Physical examination was within normal limits except for dermatological findings, the hypopigmented lesion mentioned above, and several eczematous patches. Height and weight fell between the 50th and 75th percentiles.

Other Evaluations

Laboratory tests including CBC, electrolytes, liver function tests, iron and iron binding capacity, lead level, serum test for syphilis, thyroid function tests, glucose, creatinine and urea nitrogen were all within normal limits.

Dermatoglyphic analysis showed a total ridge count that was low for a male and a slightly increased atd angle. No unusual palmar patterns were noted. Chromosomal studies were suggested because of the decreased ridge count. Sex chromatin analysis of the buccal mucosa showed male sex chromosome pattern. Intrachromosomal banding patterns revealed a pericentric inversion of the Y chromosome, which has been reported to occur in about 1 per 1000 in the general population and has not been associated with mental or physical disorders. The rest of the karyotype conformed to the expected pattern.

Hearing evaluation revealed hearing to be essentially within normal limits bilaterally at 500 to 4000 Hz. Impedence testing revealed normal conductive mechanism mobility in the right ear and could not be completed successfully in the left ear because of lack of cooperation.

Bone age determined from bilateral wrist X rays was 5 years, with a standard deviation of 8.4 months for a chronological age of 4½ years.

Handedness: Henry used his left and right hands interchangeably but used the right hand more frequently, perhaps indicative of a beginning laterality preference.

Psychological Testing

The Gesell Developmental Schedules were administered. He achieved the following basal and ceiling scores and developmental quotients (DQs) (DQ = maturity age/chronological age X 100). Motor: 18 months, 42 months, DQ 63; Adaptive: 18 months, 48 months, DQ 57; Language: 8 months, 21 months, DQ 20; and Personal-Social: 56 weeks, 42 months, DQ 45. Thus his level of functioning ranged from very severely retarded in language and moderately retarded in personal-social areas, to mildly retarded in the adaptive and motor areas.

Hospital Course

About five days after admission, Henry pulled one of the nursery teachers to some posters illustrating the numbers one to ten. The teacher recited them and after a delay of one to two minutes, Henry echoed them. Echoing, however, remained infrequent. On two of the rare occasions when he said anything other than letters and numbers, he echoed "toy time" and "tree." He used single words spontaneously on only a very few occasions; for example, he said toy and cookie in an appropriate context but was unable to continue using them. His greatest linguistic feat was echoing "walking around with my feet" during movement session but this was never repeated. He showed a special interest in letters and seemed to enjoy his teacher's telling them to him. One day, he spontaneously took a box of plastic letters and placed them correctly in order from A to P and from Z to Q, the latter group correctly but backwards. This corresponded to the placement of letters A to P on one wall of the nursery and of Q to Z on another wall. It appears he learned one group as he walked correctly from A to P and the other as he walked in the opposite direction from Z to Q! He learned to name some letters correctly and also some numbers. It should be emphasized that his performance, even in these areas of relative interest, was quite unpredictable, could not be elicited on demand, and often was not engaged in for days at a time. He resisted entering into group activities such as music and dance with the other children. He became aggressive toward new children when they entered the nursery. Throughout his approximately five-month stay in the nursery, he showed modest gains. He understood simple commands used in context, used a few words appropriately, learned to use basic program materials including puzzles, matching colors, shapes and some lotto cards, and engaged in simple representational play with cars and dolls. Shortly before discharge Henry was placed on very low doses of haloperidol, which seemed to decrease his impulsivity, distractability, and aggressiveness. Henry was discharged home and enrolled in a special therapeutic nursery school for autistic children. His discharge diagnoses were Pervasive Developmental Disorder, Infantile Autism, Full Syndrome Present and Severe Mental Retardation.

CONCLUSION

In this chapter, Infantile Autism has been used as the prototype of the pervasive developmental disorders. It is a behavioral syndrome caused by as yet poorly understood central nervous system pathology and appears to be of heterogeneous etiology. Biological investigations at the interface of neurology and psychiatry are being published at an increasingly rapid rate. Although many abnormalities have been reported, none is pathognomonic of autism. This is not unexpected. Because of the heterogeneous nature of its causes, progress will most likely advance more rapidly only as distinct, homogeneous subgroups of autistics are identified and characterized on psychoneuroendocrine parameters. To this end, it is essential that those involved in the assessment of autistic children remain abreast of current findings, consider their applicability to the specific children they are evaluating, and, whenever feasible, attempt to perform a state-of-the-art evaluation.

REFERENCES

Anderson, L. T., et al. (1984). Haloperidol in the treatment of infantile autism: Effects on learning and behavioral symptoms. *Amer. J. Psychiat.* 141(10):1195–1202.

Annett, M. (1970). The growth of manual preference and speed. *Brit. J. Psychology* 61:544–58.

August, G. J., and Lockhart, L. H. (1984). Familial autism and the fragile-X chromosome. *J. Autism and Devel. Disorders* 14(2):197–204.

———, Stewart, M. A., and Tsai, L. (1981). The incidence of cognitive disabilities in the siblings of autistic children. *Brit. J. Psychiat.* 184:416–22.

Baird, T. D., and August, G. J. (1985). Familial heterogeneity in infantile autism. *J. Autism and Devel. Disorders* 15(3):315–21.

Bartak, L., and Rutter, M. (1976). Differences between mentally retarded and normally intelligent autistic children. *J. Autism and Childhood Schizophrenia* 6(2):109–20.

———, Rutter, M., and Cox, A. (1975). A comparative study of infantile autism and specific developmental receptive language disorder: I. The children. *Brit. J. Psychiat.* 126:127–45.

Bender, L. (1947). Childhood schizophrenia. *Amer. J. Orthopsychiat.* 17:40–56.

———. (1971). Alpha and Omega of childhood schizophrenia. *J. Autism and Childhood Schizophrenia* 1(2):115–18.

Bergman, P., and Escalona, S. K. (1949). Unusual sensitivities in very young children. *Psychoanal. Study Child* vols. 3–4. New York: International Universities Press, pp. 333–52.

Blank, M., and Milewski, J. (1981). Applying psycholinguistic concepts to the treatment of an autistic child. *Applied Psycholinguistics* 2:65–84.

Blomquist, H. K., et al. (1985). Frequency of the fragile X-syndrome in infantile autism. A Swedish multicenter study. *Clinical Genetics* 27(2):113–17.

Boucher, J. (1977). Hand preference in autistic children and their parents. *J. Autism and Childhood Schizophrenia* 7(2):177–87.

Brown, W. T., et al. (1982). Autism is associated with the fragile-X syndrome. *J. Autism and Devel. Disorders* 12(3):303–8.

Campbell, M., and Green, W. H. (1985). Pervasive developmental disorders of childhood. In H. I. Kaplan and B. J. Sadock (Eds.). *Comprehensive Textbook of Psychiatry/IV*. 4th Ed. Baltimore: Williams and Wilkins, pp. 1672–83.

———, Green, W. H., and Deutsch, S. I. (1985). *Child and Adolescent Psychopharmacology*. Beverly Hills, Calif.: Sage.

———, et al. (1975). Blood serotonin in schizophrenic children: A preliminary study. *Int'l. Pharmacopsychiatry* 10:213–21.

———, et al. (1978). A comparison of haloperidol and behavior therapy and their interaction in autistic children. *J. Amer. Acad. Child Psychiat.* 17:640–55.

———, et al. (1980). Some physical parameters of young children autistic children. *J. Amer. Acad. Child Psychiat.* 19:193–212.

———, et al. (1982a). Psychiatry and endocrinology in children: Early infantile autism and psychosocial dwarfism. In P. J. V. Beumont and G. D. Burrows (Eds.). *Handbook of Psychiatry and Endocrinology*. Amsterdam: Elsevier Biomedical Press, pp. 15–62.

———, et al. (1982b). Computerized axial tomography in young autistic children. *Amer. J. Psychiat.* 139:510–12.

———, et al. (1983a). Neuroleptic-induced dyskinesias in children. *Clinical Neuropharmacol.* 6:207–22.

————, et al. (1983b). Long-term therapeutic efficacy and drug-related abnormal movements: A prospective study of haloperidol in autistic children. *Psychophar-macol. Bull.* 19(1):80–83.

————, et al. (1986). Pharmacotherapy in infantile autism: Efficacy and safety. In C. Shagass, et al. (Eds.). *Biological Psychiatry: Proceedings of the IVth World Congress of Biological Psychiatry.* New York: Elsevier, pp. 489–91.

————, et al. (In press). Overview of drug treatment in autism. In E. Schopler and G. B. Mesibov (Eds.). *Neurobiological Issues in Autism.* New York: Plenum Press.

Caparulo, B. K., et al. (1981). Computed tomographic brain scanning in children with developmental neuropsychiatric disorders. *J. Amer. Acad. Child Psychiat.* 20(2):338–57.

Chess, S. (1979). Follow-up report on autism in congenital rubella. *Autism and Child-hood Schizophrenia* 7(1):69–81.

Cohen, D. J., et al. (1978). Agreement in diagnosis: Clinical assessment and behavior rating scales for pervasively disturbed children. *J. Amer. Acad. Child Psychiat.* 17:589–603.

————, Johnson, W. T., and Caparulo, B. K. (1976). Pica and elevated blood lead level in autistic and atypical children. *Amer. J. Diseases of Children* 130:47–48.

————, and Volkman, F. R. (Eds.). (1986). Special section on issues in the diagnosis and phenomenology of the pervasive Developmental Disorders. *J. Amer. Acad. Child Psychiat.* 25(2):158–220.

Colby, K. M., and Parkison, C. (1977). Handedness in autistic children. *J. Autism and Childhood Schizophrenia* 7(1):3–9.

Coleman, M. (Ed.). (1976). *The Autistic Syndromes.* Amsterdam: North-Holland.

————, and Gillberg, C. (1985). *The Biology of the Austistic Syndromes.* New York: Praeger.

Corbett, J. A. (1982). Epilepsy and the electroencephalogram in early childhood psy-choses. In J. K. Wing and L. Wing (Eds.). *Handbook of Psychiatry, Vol. 3: Psy-choses of Uncertain Aetiology.* Cambridge: Cambridge University Press, pp. 198–202.

Dawson, G., Warrenburg, S., and Fuller, P. (1982). Cerebral lateralization in individ-uals diagnosed as autistic in early childhood. *Brain and Language* 15:353–68.

DeLong, G. R., Bean, S. C., and Brown III, F. R. (1981). Acquired reversible autistic syndrome in acute encephalopathic illness in children. *Arch. Neurol.* 38:191–94.

DeMyer, M. K., Hingtgen, J. N., and Jackson, R. K. (1981). Infantile autism re-viewed: A decade of research. *Schizophrenia Bull.* 7:388–451.

————, et al. (1972). Parental practices and innate activity in normal, autistic, and brain-damaged infants. *J. Autism and Childhood Schizophrenia* 2(1):49–66.

Deutsch, S. I., et al. (1985). Plasma growth hormone response to oral L-dopa in infantile autism. *J. Autism and Devel. Disorders* 15(2):205–12.

Deykin, E. Y., and MacMahon, B., (1979). The incidence of seizures among children with autistic symptoms. *Amer. J. Psychiat.* 136:1310–12.

Dutton, G. (1964). The growth pattern of psychotic boys. *Brit. J. Psychiat.* 110:101–3.

Ekstein, R., and Wright, D. C. (1952). The space child. *Bull. Menninger Clinic* 16:211–24.

Fish, B. (1979). The recognition of infantile psychosis. In J. G. Howells (Ed.). *Modern*

Perspectives in the Psychiatry of Infancy. New York: Brunner/Mazel, pp. 450–74.

———, and Ritvo, E. R. (1979). Psychoses of childhood. In J. D. Noshpitz (Ed.). *Basic Handbook of Child Psychiatry*, Vol. II. New York: Basic Books, pp. 249–304.

Folstein, S., and Rutter, M. (1978). A twin study of individuals with infantile autism. In M. Rutter and E. Schopler (Eds.). *Autism: A Reappraisal of Concepts and Treatment.* New York: Plenum Press, pp. 219–41.

Freeman, B. J., Ritvo, E. R., and Schroth, P. C. (1984). Behavior assessment of the syndrome of autism: Behavior observation system. *J. Amer. Acad. Child Psychiat.* 23(5):588–94.

———, et al. (1978). The Behavior Observation Scale for Autism: Initial methodology, data analysis, and preliminary findings on 89 children. *J. Amer. Acad. Child Psychiat.* 17:576–88.

———, et al. (1981). Behavioral characteristics of high- and low-IQ autistic children. *Amer. J. Psychiat.* 138(1): 25–29.

Funderburk, S. J., et al. (1983). Parental reproductive problems and gestational hormonal exposure in autistic and schizophrenic children. *J. Autism and Devel. Disorders* 13(3):325–32.

Gentile, P. S., et al. (1983). Brief report: Trace elements in the hair of autistic and control children. *J. Autism and Devel. Disorders* 13(2):205–6.

Gesell, A., and Amatruda, C. S. (1947). *Developmental Diagnosis.* 2d Ed. New York: Harper and Row.

Gillberg, C. (1983). Autistic children's hand preferences: Results from an epidemiological study of infantile autism. *Psychiatry Res.* 10:21–30.

———. (1986). Autism and Rett's syndrome: Some notes on differential diagnosis. *Amer. J. Med. Genetics* 24: Suppl. 1, 127–31.

———, and Gillberg, I. C. (1983). Infantile autism: A total population study of reduced optimality in the pre-, peri-, and neonatal period. *J. Autism and Devel. Disabilities* 13(2):153–66.

———, Rosenhall, U., and Johansson, E. (1983). Auditory brainstem responses in childhood psychosis. *J. Autism and Devel. Disorders* 13(2):181–95.

———, Svennerholm, L., and Hamilton-Heilberg, C. (1983). Childhood psychosis and monoamine metabolites in spinal fluid. *J. Autism and Devel. Disorders* 13(4):383–96.

———, Terenius, L., and Lonnerholm, G. (1985). Endorphin activity in childhood psychosis: Spinal fluid levels in 24 cases. *Arch. Gen. Psychiat.* 42:780–83.

———, and Wahlstrom, J. (1985). Chromosomal abnormalities in infantile autism and other childhood psychoses: A population study of 66 cases. *Devel. Med. and Child Neurol.* 27:293–304.

Green, W. H. (1985). Attachment disorders of infancy and early childhood. In H. I. Kaplan and B. J. Sadock (Eds.). *Comprehensive Textbook of Psychiatry/IV.* 4th Ed. Baltimore: Williams and Wilkins, pp. 1722–31.

———, Deutsch, S. I., and Campbell, M. (In press). Psychosocial dwarfism, infantile autism, and attention deficit disorder. In C. B. Nemeroff and P. T. Loosen (Eds.). *Handbook of Clinical Psychoneuroendocrinology.* New York: Guilford Press.

———, et al. (1984a). A comparison of schizophrenic and autistic children. *J. Amer. Acad. Child Psychiat.* 23(4):399–409.

———, et al. (1984b). Effects of short- and long-term haloperidol administration on growth in young autistic children. Paper presented at the 31st Annual Meeting of the American Academy of Child Psychiatry, Toronto, Canada.

————, et al. (1985). Neuropsychopharmacology of the childhood psychoses: A critical review. In D. W. Morgan (Ed.). *Psychopharmacology: Impact on Clinical Psychiatry.* St. Louis: Ishiyaku EuroAmerica, pp. 139–73.

————, and Padron-Gayol, M. (1986). Schizophrenic disorder in childhood: Its relationship to DSM-III criteria. In C. Shagass, et al. (Eds.). *Biological Psychiatry 1985: Proceedings of the IVth World Congress of Biological Psychiatry.* New York: Elsevier, pp. 1484–86.

Greulich, W. W., and Pyle, S. I. (1959). *Radiographic Atlas of Skeletal Development of the Hand and Wrist.* 2d Ed. Stanford: Stanford University Press.

Guy, W. (1976). *ECDEU assessment manual for psychopharmacology.* Rev. Ed. Publications (ADM) 76-338. Rockville, Md.: Department of Health, Education and Welfare.

Hagberg, B., et al. (1983). A progressive syndrome of autism, dementia, ataxia, and loss of purposeful hand use in girls: Rett's syndrome: Report of 35 cases. *Annals of Neurol.* 14(4):471–79.

Hamill, P. V. V., et al. (1976). *N.C.H.S. Growth Charts.* Monthly Vital Statistics Reports, Health Examination Survey Data. National Center for Health Statistics Publication (HRA) 76-1120, Vol. 25, Suppl. 3, 1–22.

Harcherik, D. F., et al. (1985). Computed tomagraphic brain scanning in four neuropsychiatric disorders of childhood. *Amer. J. Psychiat.* 142(6):731–34.

Kanner, L. (1943). Autistic disturbances of affective contact. *Nervous Child* 2:217–50.

Kestenbaum, C. J. (1978). Childhood psychosis: Psychotherapy. In B. J. Wolman, J. Egan, and A. O. Ross (Eds.). *Handbook of Treatment of Mental Disorders in Childhood and Adolescence.* Englewood Cliffs, N.J.: Prentice-Hall, pp. 354–84.

Kolko, D. J., Anderson, L. T., and Campbell, M. (1980). Sensory preference and overselective responding in autistic children. *J. Autism and Devel. Disorders* 10(3):259–71.

Kolvin, I. (1971). Studies in the childhood psychoses: I. Diagnostic criteria and classification. *Brit. J. Psychiat.* 118:381–84.

————, Garside, R. F., and Kidd, J. S. H. (1971a). Studies in the childhood psychoses: IV. Parental personality and attitude and childhood psychoses. *Brit. J. Psychiat.* 118:403–6.

————, Humphrey, M., and McNay, A. (1971b). Studies in the childhood psychoses: VI. Cognitive factors in childhood psychoses. *Brit. J. Psychiat.* 118:415–19.

————, Ounsted, C., and Roth, M. (1971e). Studies in the childhood psychoses: V. Cerebral dysfunction and childhood psychoses. *Brit. J. Psychiat.* 118:407–14.

————, et al. (1971c). Studies in the childhood psychoses: II. The phenomenology of childhood psychoses. *Brit. J. Psychiat.* 118:385–95.

————, et al. (1971d). Studies in the childhood psychoses: III. The family and social background in childhood. *Brit. J. Psychiat.* 118:396–402.

Krug, D. A., Arick, J., and Almond, P. (1980). Behavior checklist for identifying severely handicapped individuals with high levels of autistic behavior. *J. Child Psychol. and Psychiat.* 21:221–29.

Kurita, H. (1985). Infantile autism with speech loss before the age of thirty months. *J. Amer. Acad. Child Psychiat.* 24(2):191–96.

Links, P. S. (1980). Minor physical anomalies in childhood autism. Part II. Their relationship to maternal age. *J. Autism and Devel. Disorders* 10(3):287–92.

———, et al. (1980). Minor physical anomalies in childhood autism. Part I. Their relationship to pre- and perinatal complications. *J. Autism and Devel. Disorders* 10(3):273–85.

Lord, C., Schopler, E., and Revick, D. (1982). Sex differences in autism. *J. Autism and Devel. Disorders* 12(4):317–30.

Lovaas, O. I. (1977). *The Autistic Child: Language Development Through Behavior Modification.* New York: Irvington Publishers.

Mahler, M. (1952). On child psychosis and schizophrenia: Autistic and symbiotic infantile psychosis. *Psychoanal. Study Child* 7:286–305. New York: International Universities Press.

Minton, J., et al. (1982). Cognitive assessment of siblings of autistic children. *J. Amer. Acad. Child Psychiat.* 21(3):256–61.

Ogawa, T., et al. (1982). Ontogenic development of EEG-asymmetry in early infantile autism. *Brain Development* 4:439–49.

Ornitz, E. M. (1983). The functional neuroanatomy of infantile autism. *Inter'l. J. Neuroscience* 19:85–124.

———. (1985). Neurophysiology of infantile autism. *J. Amer. Acad. Child Psychiat.* 24(3):251–62.

Parks, S. L. (1983). The assessment of autistic children: A selective review of available instruments. *J. Autism and Devel. Disorders* 13(3):255–67.

Perry, R., et al. (1985). Neuroleptic-related dyskinesias in autistic children: A prospective study. *Psychopharmacol. Bull.* 21(1):140–43.

Petty, L. K., et al. (1984). Autistic children who become schizophrenic. *Arch. Gen. Psychiat.* 41:129–35.

Piggott, L. R. (1979). Overview of selected basic research in autism. *J. Autism and Devel. Disorders* 9(2):199–218.

Prior, M. R., et al. (1984). Computed tomographic study of children with classic autism. *Arch. Neurol.* 41:482–84.

Psychopharmacology Bulletin (1973). Special Issue, Pharmacotherapy of Children, DHEW Publication No. (HSM) 73-9002. Rockville, Md.: Department of Health, Education and Welfare.

Rank, B. (1949). Adaptation of the psychoanalytic technique for the treatment of young children with atypical development. *Amer. J. Orthopsychiat.* 19:130–39.

Rapoport, J. L., and Ismond, D. R. (1982). Biological research in child psychiatry. *J. Amer. Acad. Child Psychiat.* 21(6):543–48.

Rimland, B. (1971). The differentiation of childhood psychoses: An analysis of checklists for 2,218 psychotic children. *J. Autism and Childhood Schizophrenia* 1(2):161–74.

Ritvo, E. R., et al. (1984). Study of fenfluramine in outpatients with the syndrome of autism. *J. Pediatrics* 105(5):823–28.

Rosenbloom, S., et al. (1984). High resolution CT scanning in infantile autism: A quantitative approach. *J. Amer. Acad. Child Psychiat.* 23(1):72–77.

Rosenblum, S. M., et al. (1980). Auditory brainstem evoked responses in autistic children. *J. Autism and Devel. Disorders* 10(2):215–25.

Rumsey, J. M., et al. (1985). Brain metabolism in autism: Resting cerebral glucose utilization rates as measured with positron emission tomography. *Arch. Gen. Psychiat.* 42(5):448–55.

Ruttenberg, B. A., et al. (1977). *BRIAAC: Behavior-Rating Instrument for Autistic and Other Atypical Children.* Rev. Ed. Philadelphia: Developmental Center for Autistic Children.

Rutter, M. (1967). Psychotic disorders in early childhood. In A. J. Coppen and A. Walk (Eds.). *Recent Developments in Schizophrenia: A Symposium* (*British Journal of Psychiatry*, Special Publication 1). Ashford, Kent, England: Royal Medico-Psychological Association, Headley Brothers, pp. 133–58.

———, (1983). Cognitive deficit in the pathogenesis of autism. *J. Child Psychol. Psychiat.* 24:513–31.

———, (1985a). Infantile autism. In D. Shaffer, A. A. Ehrhardt, and L. L. Greenhill (Eds.). *The Clinical Guide to Child Psychiatry.* New York: Free Press, pp. 48–78.

———, (1985b). Infantile autism and other pervasive developmental disorders. In M. Rutter and L. Hersov (Eds.). *Child and Adolescent Psychiatry: Modern Approaches.* 2d Ed. Oxford: Blackwell Scientific Pubs., pp. 545–66.

———, and Schopler, E. (Eds.). (1978). *Autism: A Reappraisal of Concepts and Treatment.* New York: Plenum Press.

Sank, D., and Firschein, B. D. S. (1979). Fingerprints and laterality preferences of early onset autism. In W. Wertelecki and C. C. Plato (Eds.). *Dermatoglyphics— Fifty Years Later.* (The National Foundation—March of Dimes. Birth Defects: Original Articles Series, Vol. 15, No. 6). New York: Alan R. Liss, pp. 679–95.

Sanua, V. D. (1984). An international survey of mental health professionals on the etiology of infantile autism. In J. D. Call, E. Galenson, and R. L. Tyson (Eds.). *Frontiers of Infant Psychiatry*, Vol. 2. New York: Basic Books, pp. 428–32.

Schopler, E. (1976). The art and science of Bruno Bettelheim. *J. Autism and Childhood Schizophrenia* 6(2):193–202.

———, Andrews, C. E., and Strupp, K. (1979). Do autistic children come from upper middle-class parents? *J. Autism and Childhood Schizophrenia* 9(2):139–52.

———, and Mesibov, G. B. (1983). *Autism in Adolescents and Adults.* New York: Plenum Press.

———, and Mesibov, G. B. (1986). *Social Behavior and Autism.* New York: Plenum Press.

———, et al. (1980). Toward objective classification of childhood autism: Childhood Autism Rating Scale (CARS). *J. Autism and Devel. Disorders* 10(1):91–103.

Shah, A., and Holmes, N. (1985). Brief report: The use of the Leiter International Performance Scale with autistic children. *J. Autism and Devel. Disorders* 15(2):195–203.

Sherman, M., Nass, R., and Shapiro, T. (1984). Brief report: Regional cerebral blood flow in autism. *J. Autism and Devel. Disorders* 14(4):439–46.

Simpson, G. M., et al. (1979). A rating scale for tardive dyskinesia. *Psychopharmacology (Berlin)* 64(2):171–79.

Small, J. G. (1975). EEG and neurophysiological studies of early infantile autism. *Biolog. Psychiat.* 10:385–97.

Stubbs, E. G. (1976). Autistic children exhibit undetectable hemagglutination-inhibition antibody titers despite previous rubella vaccination. *J. Autism and Childhood Schizophrenia* 6(3):269–74.

———, et al. (1977). Depressed lymphocyte responsiveness in autistic children. *J. Autism and Childhood Schizophrenia* 7(1):49–55.

Torrey, E. F., Hersh, S. P., and McCabe, K. D. (1975). Early childhood psychosis and bleeding during pregnancy. *J. Autism and Childhood Schizophrenia* 5:287–97.

Tsai, L. Y. (1983). The relationship of handedness to the cognitive, language, and visuo-spatial skills of autistic patients. *Brit. J. Psychiat.* 142:156–62.

———, Steward, M. A., and August, G. (1981). Implications of sex differences in the familial transmission of infantile autism. *J. Autism and Devel. Disorders* 11(2):165–73.

Waldrop, M. F., and Halverson, C. F. (1971). Minor physical anomalies and hyperactive behavior in young children. In J. Hellmuth (Ed.). *Exceptional Infants: Studies in Abnormalities,* Vol. 2. New York: Brunner-Mazel, pp. 343–80.

Walker, H. A. (1977a). A dermatoglyphic study of autistic patients. *J. Autism and Childhood Schizophrenia* 7(1):11–21.

———, (1977b). Incidence of minor physical anomalies in autism. *J. Autism and Childhood Schizophrenia* 7(2):165–76.

Watson, M. S., et al. (1984). Fragile X in a survey of 75 autistic males. *New Eng. J. Med.* 310:1462.

Weizman, A., et al. (1982). Abnormal immune response to brain tissue antigen in the syndrome of autism. *Amer. J. Psychiat.* 139(11):1462–65.

Werry, J. S. (1979). The childhood psychoses. In H. C. Quay and J. S. Werry (Eds.). *Psychopathological Disorders of Childhood.* 2d Ed. New York: Wiley, pp. 43–89.

Wing, L. (1980). Childhood autism and social class: A question of selection? *Brit. J. Psychiat.* 137:410–17.

Young, J. G., et al. (1982). Clinical neurochemistry of autism and associated disorders. *J. Autism and Devel. Disorders* 12(2):147–65.

Zax, M., Sameroff, A. J., and Babigian, H. M. (1977). Birth outcomes in the offspring of mentally disordered women. *Amer. J. Orthopsychiat.* 47:218–30.

24

TICS AND THE TOURETTE SYNDROME

Alexander R. Lucas and John E. Huxsahl

Assessment of the child and adolescent with tics is based on history and clinical examination. Tics are to be identified and differentiated from other motor phenomena. First, it is necessary to distinguish normal physiological manifestations from pathological symptoms. The aim of assessment is to determine whether tic as a symptom is indicative of stress in the child's environment or of a disease process in the child, and to determine the nature of such stress or disease. Evaluation of the child and adolescent with tics cuts across the medical specialties of child psychiatry, pediatrics, and neurology. Children with tics may present to any one of those specialists as well as to family practitioners, depending upon the parents' perceptions of what the symptom may indicate. In a child, tics are often the primary reason for requesting an evaluation. At other times tic is one of several symptoms for which a child is referred. Alternatively, it may be an incidental finding in a child seen for entirely different reasons.

GENERAL CONSIDERATIONS

Tic is an abrupt, repetitive, patterned involuntary movement involving the same muscle groups over and over again. It may be isolated and limited to a single muscle or circumscribed muscle group, or tics may be widespread, involving any and all parts of the body. It may present at almost any age but is more common during certain developmental phases of childhood than during others. It may be fleeting and transitory in occurrence or episodic, or may become chronically fixed. Since tic as a symptom may be present in a wide variety of conditions, and since its severity can range from mild to severe, evaluation of children with tics involves many of the same questions and ramifications as does the evaluation of children with other symptoms and disorders. Tic can occur as a normal developmental phenomenon, reflect a temporary tension state, be seen in a reactive disorder, and as a symptom in many psychiatric disorders such as neuroses and psychotic conditions. It is seen in children with acute or chronic brain disorders, and may be a manifestation of certain encephalopathies. Throughout the editions of his classic textbook of child psychiatry, Kanner (1972) made the statement that no happy, secure child ever develops tics. That statement can no longer be accepted as credible, although one is well advised to seek for sources of tension and unhappiness in children presenting with tics.

The current classification of tic disorders outlined by DSM-III is probably the most widely used. This classification is determined by age of onset, duration of symptoms, and the presence of vocal/phonic tics in addition to motor tics. *Transient Tic Disorder* has its onset during childhood or early adolescence and consists of recurrent, involuntary, repetitive, purposeless motor tics. The tics vary in intensity over weeks or months; they have been present for at least one month but less than one year. The tics are under, at least temporary, voluntary control. (Most tics, although not volitional, can be suppressed at least partially, or for limited time periods, through conscious effort.) *Chronic Motor Tic Disorder* is characterized by tics involving no more than three muscle groups at any one time (a distinction that seems somewhat arbitrary). The intensity of the symptoms is constant over time, and they have been present for at least one year. Vocal tics may be infrequently present. *Tourette's Disorder* has an age of onset between 2 and 15 years. In addition to motor tics the presence of vocal tics is required for the diagnosis. Coprolalia (the irresistible utterance of obscenities) is present in 30 to 60 percent of cases. Recent studies have identified the association of obsessive-compulsive behavior and attention deficit disorder in patients with Tourette's Disorder. Twenty-five to 50 percent of children with Tourette's Disorder satisfy criteria for the diagnosis of attention deficit disorder. At least 40 percent of Tourette's Disorder patients manifest obsessions and compulsions. The incidence of Obsessive-Compulsive Disorder is undoubtedly less.

EPIDEMIOLOGY/GENETICS

The incidence and prevalence of tics in the general population is quite high. Tics occur more commonly in children than in adults. Their frequency increases until age 6 in girls and 7 in boys, after which it declines. Macfarlane, Allen, and Honzik (1954) found that in a sample of 252 normal children between 21 months and 14 years of age, tics and mannerisms occurred in 10 percent of girls and 11 percent of boys at the peak age. As many as one-quarter of boys and girls had a record of tics at some age. A somewhat lower figure of 12 percent was found by Lapouse and Monk (1958) in an epidemiologic study of 482 children between the ages of 6 and 12. Many of these children, who have tics recognized to be physiological variants or tension phenomena, never come to psychiatric attention. However, in one percent of five hundred consecutive children and adolescents evaluated in a psychiatric outpatient clinic the reason for referral was tics (Shaw and Lucas 1970). Incidence of Tourette's Disorder is in the range of 1 to 12/1,000,000 and prevalence has been estimated from 5 to 800/ 1,000,000 (Lucas et al. 1982).

The familial nature of Tourette's Disorder was actually recognized by Gilles de la Tourette himself. Recent genetic studies (Pauls et al. 1981, 1984) support a strong genetic contribution to Tourette's Disorder and chronic motor tic. The incidence of both Tourette's Disorder and chronic motor tic is increased in first-degree relatives of index cases. Family study data suggests a 10.7 percent incidence of Tourette's Disorder in first-degree relatives of patients with the disorder. It appears that female probands have a higher incidence of positive family history, suggesting that females may require more genetic loading to express Tourette's Disorder. It has been speculated that Tourette's Disorder has a single dominant gene with variable penetrance mode of inheritance, although definitive genetic studies have yet to be done.

DEVELOPMENTAL PERSPECTIVE

Tic is a form of movement neurophysiologically directed by the motor system. Movements begin in the human fetus at only a few weeks of age. Flexion and extension of the limbs occur, and automatic movements such as swallowing begin. At birth automatic movements necessary for survival, such as respiratory and swallowing movements, occur regularly. The skeletal movements are not yet very complex or purposeful. From these simpler movements postural control is acquired to overcome gravity effects, and chain reactions become important in the development of complex movements and the determination of patterns of movements. Finally, infants acquire an awareness of their movement and the ability to control them.

The last step requires sensorimotor integration. Afferent stimuli from joints, tendons, muscles, and skin are interpreted by the brain and result in modification of the limb movement. In addition to kinesthetic stimuli, visual, auditory, and tactile sensory motor links develop to provide information that reveals the results of movements and enables the brain to modify the position of movements. The aim of these processes is to achieve mastery over one's movements and, thus, over the environment.

Tics are involuntary movements that occur incidental to, or interfere with, the voluntary movements. Thus, they represent an unnecessary or undesirable motor act and are presumed to be pathological. Very little is as yet known about the neurophysiological origin of tics and about their precise causes.

From the simplest movements that begin in the early weeks of embryonic life, neuromuscular development progresses in a predictable manner as a function of age. Increasingly complex fine and gross motor skills are acquired as the infant and child progresses through developmental stages. The unfolding of progressively more complex skills proceeds in predictable sequences with characteristic patterns evident at each stage. Children of one or two years of age experiment freely with their newly learned motor skills when given the opportunity. The second and third years of life constitute the period of most rapid development of motor skill. Motility is one of the most important avenues for exercising such functions as mastery, integration, reality testing, and control of impulses (Lucas 1980).

Transient tics were described by Mahler (1949) to occur at age 4. It is generally believed that between 4 and 6 years of age such tics are common, and their frequency peaks around ages 6 and 7. Presumably the child's neuromuscular system is most sensitive to their development at this point, with increased irritability perhaps related to the stage of neuronal myelinization. Beyond that age general level of muscular activity increases and the frequency of tics diminishes. Perhaps this inverse relationship has to do with channels for tension discharge.

Macfarlane, Allen, and Honzik (1954) found that a significant proportion of mothers of normal children identified boys in particular to be overactive throughout the first decade of life. The peak for overactivity came at age 4 and 5 years, with the frequency 44 percent and 46 percent for boys and 35 percent for girls at those ages. The frequency gradually declined to 11 percent at age 14 years for boys, and it dropped more rapidly for girls to none identified as hyperactive by the age of 13. At certain stages children are characteristically active. Gesell, Ilg, and Ames (1956) described the 11-year-old as extremely wiggly, bouncy, and active, virtually in constant motion.

Activity level, in addition to varying at different ages, also shows markedly different patterns in individual children. Evaluation of children with tics needs to be done against the backdrop of developmental changes and individual differences.

PROCESS OF EVALUATION

The child may come for evaluation specifically because of the tics. A child with severe psychopathology as the presenting problem may also have tics of varying severity, and in some children seen for evaluation, mild tics may be an incidental finding. But often the concern of the parents and family or referring person will be the tics themselves, with questions as to their origin and meaning. Quite often they are termed "nervous tics" or "habit spasms," implying something of their origin. The child psychiatrist may be consulted directly about the child with tics, or referral may come from the family physician or other specialist. Almost always, the request for evaluation comes from someone other than the patient because the symptom is often bothersome to others. It is rare for even an older adolescent to seek evaluation because of tics.

In taking the history from the parents, one carefully inquires about the chief complaint and reason for requesting the evaluation. One tries to determine whether the symptoms are chiefly disturbing to those around the child or whether they seem to cause anxiety for the child and significantly interfere with his school and social functioning. The history of present illness and past and developmental history is systematically obtained, as it is in the evaluation of a child with any other problems. Particular attention should be given to the prenatal and birth history as well as to the developmental history, with appropriate questioning about symptoms of movement disorder and events that could result in insult to the central nervous system.

Of particular importance is the sequential history of the development of tics, starting with the age at onset, the description of particular tic manifestations including the muscle group and body part affected, the nature of the tic, and its severity. The longitudinal course, with fluctuations in the severity, and whether or not tics have been present continuously or intermittently, is explored. Evidence as to whether the symptoms are stable, have improved, or have become progressively more severe is reviewed. The use of the Yale Tourette Syndrome Symptom List (Cohen, Leckman, and Shaywitz 1985) may facilitate the history taking process. History of hyperkinesis, impulsiveness and aggressiveness, and other symptoms commonly associated with organic brain damage or dysfunction are identified. Signs and symptoms suggesting an active brain process, including infection, space occupying lesion, and degenerative disease are elicited.

The child's school history is reviewed, with emphasis on academic skills and achievement, as is the child's history of social interaction. When the history and examination of the child suggests the need for it, speech and hearing evaluation, academic achievement testing, and/or psychologic testing should be obtained.

The family history is explored, with emphasis on interaction of family members, attitudes and personality characteristics of the parents, and evidence of significant conflict in the marriage or family. Family history for the occurrence of tics, movement disorders, and hyperkinesis should be carefully explored. In patients with severe tics, nearly half the cases will show family history positive for tics (Shapiro et al. 1978). The family psychodynamics show considerable variability (Lucas, Kauffman, and Morris 1967).

A general pediatric evaluation and/or pediatric neurological examination may be indicated. Laboratory tests are not routinely obtained. Their indication depends upon the findings of the history and the physical and neurological examination.

There are times when the tic symptom continues to be the primary focus of the evaluation, but other times when evidence of significant psychopathology or learning problems in the child, and major disturbance in the family will guide the psychiatrist to shift the focus to those areas. Whether the tic symptom means that there is underlying psychopathology, whether it is a tension manifestation in response to environmental stress, or whether it has a purely neurophysiological basis are questions often difficult to answer. Tics may be isolated phenomena or they may be part of a child's broader organic or psychopathological condition. Tics are of course also seen in essentially normal children. When the examination of the child reveals such normality and the tic has no serious organic implications, interpretation of that information and reassurance to the family and child is indicated. Some parents readily accept such explanations, but others are excessively focused on the symptom as a reflection of their own anxieties or hostilities and cannot accept having a normal child.

The direct interview of the child with tics first involves careful observations of his appearance and behavior. The type, location, and frequency of tics are noted. A general child psychiatric interview is carried out appropriate to the age of the child involving observation, play, and/or conversational interview techniques. At some point the child should be asked about his awareness of tics, using suitable terms such as "jerking," "muscle twitching," and "noises" to explore his awareness and nature of the tics. Many children and adolescents are very much ashamed and embarrassed by their tics, particularly vocal noises including coprolalia, and are reluctant to talk about them. Not infrequently they fear that their symptoms indicate they are mentally ill or "crazy." Therefore, much supportive reassurance may be required before the child will talk about the tics. It may be necessary to reassure the child specifically that other people have them, that tics do not indicate that one is crazy, and that they are something the child cannot help or completely control.

In the interview the child can be observed under numerous conditions. He is observed during the structured verbal part of the interview. The examiner notes the occurrence of tics and whether their timing seems random or related to conflict-laden and anxiety-provoking content. The child can be observed in a free-play situation, and again observations are made as to whether the circumstances alter the frequency and nature of tics. The influence of the presence of others, particularly parents, on the child's activity level and tics is noticed. Whether or not the level and type of environmental stimulation influences the child's symptoms and behavior is observed.

Environmental precipitating events that may be related temporally to the onset of tics are explored. It has generally been assumed that events producing great stress or psychic trauma can manifest themselves symptomatically in tics, although this assumption has not been proven. Thus, Freud and Burlingham (1943) described the development of tics as the condensation of motor actions and gestures into symbolic expressions when circumstances prohibit children from playing out the underlying conflicts. Similarly, Gerard (1946) described the occurrence of tic following experiences arousing fear of being injured and representing a defensive response in aggression-inhibited children. Mahler (1949) characterized some tics as neurotic symptoms representing in some cases conversion symptoms and, in other cases, compulsions in an obsessive-compulsive neurosis. In contradistinction to children with symptomatic tic, Mahler identified children whose multiple tics were part of an impulse or character neurosis. She classified these children as having tic syndrome.

To gain the most thorough understanding of a child with tic in the context of his or her family, family relationships and family psychodynamics are explored. The child's fantasies, fears, and hopes are assessed through direct and projective interview techniques. The child psychiatrist can then build hypotheses and draw tentative conclusions about the development of symptoms and the origins of the child's anxiety. One must be on guard, nonetheless, against the supposition that the coexistence of events and conditions means that one caused the other.

PSYCHOLOGICAL, ACADEMIC, AND LABORATORY TESTS

Psychometric and projective psychological tests usually are indicated as part of the evaluation of children with tics to help understand the child's capacities and thought processes. Intelligence among such children takes a normal distribution, but among children with severe tics there is more variability in inter- and intratest functioning on psychometric testing than expected. Fifty percent of patients with Tourette's Disorder as compared with 14 percent of control patients had a difference of 15 points or more between verbal and performance scale IQ scores (Shapiro et al. 1978). The tics themselves, as well as impaired visuomotor functioning, may markedly interfere with reproduction of the Bender-Gestalt figures. Projective tests are of use to elaborate on the degree and nature of psychodynamic conflicts in individual children.

Academic achievement tests, like tests of intelligence and projective psychological tests, may indicate perfectly normal functioning in children with tics, but such tests often indicate moderate to severe learning deficits. The school history will suggest whether or not such testing needs to be done. A good number of children with severe tics have significant learning deficits of the types seen in children with specific learning disabilities and in brain-damaged children, while others show impairment in their school performance secondary to anxiety, poor self-esteem, and depression, or as a consequence of medication effect when they are receiving psychotropic drugs.

There are no laboratory tests that are definitive or diagnostic for tics. For this reason the electroencephalogram is not routinely indicated in the evaluation of children with tics. However, EEG abnormalities occur more often among children with severe tics than expected in the general population. Since the abnormal findings are generally nonspecific, they are usually of no practical value for diagnostic or treatment purposes, unless seizure disorder is suspected.

THE QUESTION OF PSYCHOGENICITY

The possible psychogenic etiology of tics, once accepted as a matter of fact, has come under much question in light of the current emphasis on neurochemical mechanism (Friedhoff and Chase 1982). It is a difficult question to resolve. Gerard described a series of cases whose tics began in reaction of psychic trauma during the era when such causes were pursued intensively through psychoanalytic exploration (Gerard 1946). The timing, form, and location of the tics had psychodynamic meaning and the clinical material was convincingly presented. One case example was that of a 4-year-old boy who developed an eye tic in the form of widening of both pal-pebral fissures followed by rapid blinking of both eyelids the day after first seeing his father's amputated leg. Psychodynamically this represented both the wish to see and the desire to shut out the view by closing his eyes.

A 6-year-old boy was severely slapped by his father when caught masturbating. He developed a tic involving placing his hand over his genitals and jerking his head back and to the side as if avoiding a blow. Gerard was successful in relieving the tics through psychoanalytic treatment with interpretation of their meaning. Others have not been as impressed with the response of tics to psychotherapeutic interven-tion.

DIFFERENTIAL DIAGNOSIS

The differential diagnosis of tic involves neurological and psychiatric conditions. Tics can be confused with myoclonic jerks, which are seizure phenomena. Clinically they may resemble tics, but unlike tics they occur at night. The mistaken diagnosis of Sydenham's chorea was frequently made in children who were then inappro-priately treated. The disorders can be clinically differentiated, with chorea being manifested by quick, jerky, twitching movements that are rarely exactly duplicated as in tic. Natural gestures and movements of expression of the face are grossly ex-aggerated in chorea. Speech also becomes irregular in rhythm and articulation indis-tinct. Other manifestations of rheumatic fever, including fever, arthritis, cardiac findings, and abnormal laboratory studies are not present in children with tics (Lu-cas, Kauffman, and Morris 1967). Like tics, choreiform movements disappear during sleep. The patient with tics generally has the ability to suppress the movements partially or totally for limited periods of time. This ability is markedly diminished or absent in other neurologically based movement disorders.

In rare cases, a tic can represent a symptom of progressive neurological disease. The following case study illustrates this and highlights the need for a CT scan where there is evidence of clinical deterioration in a patient with known tics.

> Robert was 9 years of age when he presented to a children's psychiatric outpatient clinic with jerky movements, involving chiefly the right arm, vo-cal tics, and coprolalia. Body spasms resembling tonic neck reflex were ac-centuated by emotional stimuli and disappeared during deep sleep. Two weeks later, prior to his admission to the inpatient unit, he developed in-coordination and staggering gait and falling. Confused thinking was noted at times. His behavior at home had become unruly and unmanageable.
>
> Psychological testing revealed intellectual functioning at a Verbal IQ of 70, Performance IQ of 44, and Full Scale IQ of 54 on the Wechsler Intelli-gence Scale for Children. The Bender-Gestalt Test showed severe impair-ment of form. The human figure was depicted in a fragmented, discon-

nected way, demonstrating severe disturbance of body image. Testing at the age of 5 had revealed an IQ of 122.

Examination in the hospital showed generalized hyperactivity, jerky movement alternately involving all the extremities, and a tic-like cough. Neurological evaluation and electroencephalogram confirmed the presence of a severe disturbance of cerebral function. A deteriorating course followed.

Children with Pervasive Developmental Disorder may have peculiar manner-isms resembling tics, sometimes choreoathetoid-like hand movements. Bizarre vo-calizations and coprolalia may be present in these children, but the diagnosis rests on the demonstration of developmental delay in social relationships and severe anx-iety.

Generalized hyperactivity and restlessness can be confused with tics. They are differentiated by careful observations to determine whether there are the abrupt involuntary movements of circumscribed muscle groups that characterize tics. A considerable number of children with tics are also diffusely hyperactive and impul-sive. Certain drugs, such as amphetamines, which have stimulating effects, and those that enhance dopamine activity in the brain, such as levodopa, can cause tic-like muscle twitching, blepharospasm, and facial grimacing.

The actual precipitation of Tourette's Disorder by treatment with stimulant med-ications (dextroamphetamine, methylphenidate, pemoline) has been well described (Lowe et al. 1982). This association has led many clinicians to recommend avoiding stimulants in patients with any type of tic. In the patient with minor tics who fulfills diagnostic criteria for Attention Deficit Disorder, the need for stimulants may exceed the potential risk of increased tics.

Eschewing psychogenesis of tics, Shapiro and coworkers classified tics as acute simple or transient tic of childhood, chronic simple tic, subacute or persistent simple or multiple tics, and chronic multiple tic or Gilles de la Tourette's syndrome (Shapiro et al. 1978). *Acute Simple or Transient Tic of Childhood* is the frequently observed "habit spasm," synonymous with what one of the authors has called "mild tension tic" occurring in at least 12 percent of all children, as frequently in girls as in boys (La-pouse and Monk 1958). Shapiro and his colleagues stated that they spontaneously remit within two weeks to a year. *Chronic Simple Tic* is designated as one or two involuntary muscular movements that do not progressively change over time and persist throughout life. These are also common "habits" that often become accepted mannerisms. They are of unknown etiology or can be the sequel of encephalitis. Subacute or persistent simple or multiple tics of childhood or adolescence were char-acterized by Shapiro and coworkers as involving one or two muscular tic-like move-ments or verbal tics, or multiple tics that persist for longer than a year but that disappear by or during adolescence. Shapiro et al. maintained that these tics are indistinguishable from Tourette's Disorder except by their temporal course. Chronic multiple tic Tourette's Disorder, according to Shapiro and colleagues, is a chronic but fluctuating illness that begins in childhood between the ages of 2 and 15, twice as frequently in boys as in girls, and unlike subacute multiple tic is chronic and lifelong. The first symptom is a single or simple tic in approximately 50 percent of patients, most frequently involving the eyes, head, or face. All patients ultimately develop multiple tics and noises, but only slightly more than half develop coprolalia.

ETIOLOGY AND OUTCOME

Some patients with chronic tics have an encephalitic etiology, and some have a family history suggesting aberrant neurotransmitter function, but often the underlying cause remains obscure. Multiple etiological factors have been implicated as illustrated in Fig. 24.1 (Lucas 1979). Recent evidence supports a neurochemical basis for tic syndrome (Cohen et al. 1979). This evidence includes the clinical response to haloperidol (suggesting dopamine hypersensitivity) and findings of reduced level of dopamine metabolite in the cerebrospinal fluid of patients.

When tic first appears and occurs as a single, simple tic or as a few multiple tics, the outcome is impossible to predict. Most tics are self-limited within weeks or months, but some persist and become progressively more severe until chronic tic syndrome is recognized. The family history may be of some help in predicting outcome, but generally observations of the child over a long period of time will reveal the outcome with certainty. In Tourette's Disorder the severity and frequency of tics usually reach their worst level in early adolescence. Tics usually diminish in adulthood and may almost abate. In some instances they persist throughout adulthood, but their violence is usually diminished. Social and personality adjustment often continues to be poor, especially in those who had signs of encephalopathy and severe learning deficits in childhood (Lucas 1976).

CASE VIGNETTES

Although the etiology of tics cannot always reliably be established, the history, precipitating events, and clinical course often provide clues as to their origin and meaning. Examples of children whose tics can be classified with reasonable certainty are given.

Transient Tic Disorder. A competent, socially outgoing boy of 7 years, Sheldon was the youngest of four children in a highly achievement-oriented family. Shortly after he began violin lessons he developed tics of his arms, shoulder, and head resembling a shrugging movement. He had earlier been prone to making snorting sounds during upper respiratory infections, and these sounds recurred in full force. After several months his parents recognized the stress produced by enforced violin practice and discontinued lessons, much to

Sheldon's relief. The tics promptly disappeared, although snorting noises recurred when he had a stuffy nose. Now 16 years old, he is an honor student, well liked by his peers, with many interests, none of which is musical.

Chronic Tic Disorder with Psychogenic Precipitants. Paul was seen at age 14 years because of tics. He had onset of facial grimaces and movements of his nose at age 5 years. These symptoms began shortly after the death of a favorite uncle. His mother reported that he had seen many doctors over the years, who were baffled by his symptoms. She gave an elaborately dramatic account of how Paul threw himself about, breaking furniture during his attacks, and she described coprolalia, although obscenities were never heard during his examination and subsequent hospital stay.

During the initial interview tics involving many muscle groups throughout his body were noted. Their frequency and intensity increased when discussing somatic complaints and his fears of serious physical illness and death. They became particularly violent when he talked about his mother, all the more so when she was present in the room. The mother was an ambitious, domineering, and aggressive woman, while the father was passive and insecure, with obsessive traits. Paul was an only child.

Upon separating from his parents and entering the hospital, Paul showed marked diminution in the frequency and intensity of his tics, but they did not totally cease. Small doses of haloperidol diminished his tics further, but it was noted that he reported a distinct feeling of relief within seconds of swallowing the pill, confirming his high degree of suggestibility. Boarding school placement was recommended on his dismissal from the hospital to ensure the continuation of his improvement away from the stresses of conflicts at home.

Chronic Tic Disorder with Postencephalitis Onset. Alvin had an episode of fever of 105°F associated with delirium lasting for a week when he was 4 years of age. He was unable to recognize his parents and did not respond to questions. A month after his febrile illness he had a recurrence of a high fever, this time accompanied by a generalized major convulsion. Within a year after these episodes Alvin developed a cough-like throat-clearing tic while attending kindergarten. Next he developed a skipping maneuver that occasionally interrupted his gait. This was followed by eye-rolling after the fashion of an oculogyric crisis. Other tics came and went during the succeeding years. They involved flicking his hands as if shaking water from them, clicking his teeth, and a head-jerking movement. At age 12 he was seen in a child psychiatric outpatient clinic, with throat-clearing noises and guttural warbling sounds. The occurrence of the tics seemed unrelated to stress. Phenobarbital and chloradiazepoxide had been tried unsuccessfully to relieve his many tics.

Psychologic testing revealed a Verbal IQ of 111, a Performance IQ of 106, with a Full Scale IQ of 109 on the Wechsler Intelligence Scale for Children. Alvin was the third of six siblings in a relatively comfortable, albeit slightly controlled, family situation. The parents were judged to be free of psychiatric disturbance.

Haloperiodol was started with limited success. Alvin continued to be followed beyond high school graduation for supportive psychotherapy related to coping with his tics, which varied in severity, but they were never well controlled with medication.

Tourette's Disorder. At 9 years of age Yvonne was evaluated in a child psychiatric outpatient clinic. From a middle-class suburb of a large metropolitan area, she had begun to have manneristic opening and closing of her mouth at age 6 and excessive blinking of her eyes. Various facial grimaces developed, accompanied by sniffling sounds and sucking on her cheeks. These habits became progressively more frequent and noticeable and began to be a source of annoyance in the classroom. At the time of her evaluation tics had involved other parts of her body and included a peculiar sudden spreading of her thighs while flexing the knees as she stood or walked. Other tics involved licking of the lips, a jumping movement as she sat in a chair, and a jerky nodding movement of the head. The onset of vocal noises had prompted the evaluation. These first resembled throat-clearing and then became progressively louder in the form of explosive high-pitched barking noises. They became so incessant and of such volume that they were intolerable in the classroom. Inarticulate sounds gradually became recognizable four-letter obscenities.

There was no history of serious medical illness, but school difficulties were evident from the early grades. Yvonne had a severe learning disability, which affected all of her subjects. Psychometric testing revealed a Verbal IQ of 94, Performance IQ of 90, and Full Scale IQ of 91 on the WISC.

Family history indicated gross family turmoil involving asocial acting-out behavior. Yvonne had an older brother who was delinquent and carried a handgun. There was severe marital strife punctuated by frequent furious arguments. The father had temper outbursts during which he was physically agressive toward his son as well as his daughter. The mother's behavior was dramatically hysterical, and she suffered from frequent conversion symptoms. Child-rearing practices directed toward the patient were highly inconsistent, vacillating between punitiveness and overindulgence.

Yvonne was admitted to a children's psychiatric inpatient unit at age 10, when she was treated in a therapeutic milieu for seven months. Severe multiple tic manifestation continued to be present, characterized by body tics and very frequent explosive high-pitched barking tics associated with diaphragmatic spasms. The majority of barking noises were inarticulate, but others took the form of the coarsest obscenities. Treatment with haloperidol resulted in considerable improvement of tics, particularly the vocal noises.

Learning problems and family conflicts continued for years after her dismissal, but tics were moderately well controlled by medication until her early

20s, when there was an exacerbation of tics complicated by conversion symptoms.

TIC IN BIOPSYCHOSOCIAL CONTEXT

As can be seen from the above case histories, tic varies considerably in severity among children and can occur within markedly different family situations. The historical view of its cause has alternated between the organic and psychogenic. At various times, with the swing of the etiological pendulum, tic has been characterized as either a neurological disease or a psychological illness based on psychodynamic mechanisms. Such dualistic thinking in medicine, persisting in today's predominantly biomedical view, has been criticized by Engel, who proposed a biopsychosocial model as the most accurate and inclusive framework within which to view the cause and clinical progression of any illness (Engel 1977). Rather than tracing the specific origin of tics to either organic or psychodynamic causes, multiple factor interaction can best be conceptualized and studied within the biopsychosocial model. Hereditary factors, neurochemical changes, intrapsychic conflicts, family influences, and social/interpersonal factors all can be viewed as interdependent variables that lead to symptoms and influence each individual and his symptoms differently. Perhaps tics are best viewed as phenomena in and of themselves, aggravated by internal or external stresses, tensions, and anxiety. Children who have tics have a visible barometer telling observers of their stage of tension and arousal. The same is true of children who are hyperactive. Thus, these children wear their feelings on their sleeves, while other children, more quiet, restrained, and less action-prone, are much more difficult to read.

In addition to varying in severity, tics also may vary in the extent to which they are influenced by biological and psychological factors. If the strength of biological factors influencing tics is plotted along the abscissa of a graph, ranging from 0 (representing an absence of biological factors) to 10 (indicating the strongest biological influence) and the strength of psychological factors is similarly plotted along the ordinate, a diagram such as shown in Figure 24.1 can be conceptualized. Various combinations of weak and strong biological and psychological influences can then be postulated. For example, the mild tension phenomena involving facial muscle twitching have relatively weak biological and psychological components. A child with postencephalitic tic may have very strong organic basic for his tic, with little environmental and psychological influence. However, another child with postencephalitic tic may have a more problematic environment, perhaps contributing to the severity of the tic. If purely psychogenic tic exists, as in the individual who develops an eye-blinking tic after witnessing a fatal auto accident, this is represented in the upper left quadrant of the diagram. Finally, severe tic syndrome with strong biological and psychological components is represented in the upper right quadrant. Some

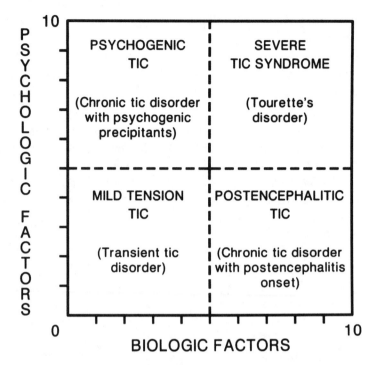

Figure 24.1. Conceptual diagram relating the strength of biological and psychological influences on the expression of tic disorders.

children with severe tic syndrome clearly have psychologically sound families and qualify for conceptual representation in the lower right quadrant. More often, though, the stress and annoyance resulting from such severe symptomatology influences peers and family in such a way and has such devastating effects on the child's own self-concept, that the family situation places additional stress upon the child, which further accentuates his symptomatology. The mutual interdependence and interaction of biological vulnerability, psychological predisposition, and social influences leading to neuromuscular hyperreactivity and culminating in tic is shown in the biopsychosocial scheme of Figure 24.2.

TREATMENT

The decision to treat a child with tics or Tourette's Disorder should primarily be based on the degree to which the disorder is interfering with the child's normal development. Many children with multiple tics and some with Tourette's Disorder are making appropriate progress in development; for them treatment is generally not indicated. Reassurance is the most appropriate approach (Cohen, Leckman, and Shaywitz 1985). For those children with incapacitating symptoms affecting development in the realm of family relationships, peer relationships, or school performance,

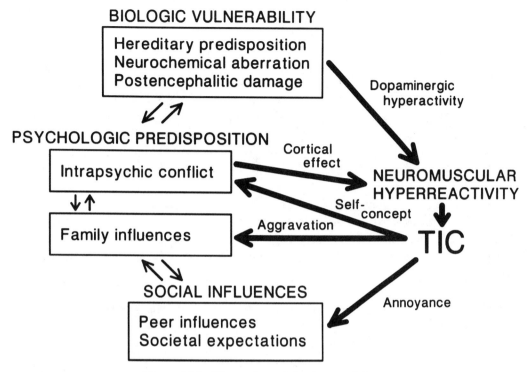

Figure 24.2. **Biopsychosocial scheme of tic.**

treatment is indicated. Treatment should initially begin with education and supportive discussion for both parent and child. Once the treatment decision has been made, it is generally worthwhile to observe the child for several weeks before initiating specific therapy. The purpose of this observation period is to establish a baseline of symptoms and to identify any associated difficulties in school, family, and peer relationships.

Pharmacological intervention is currently the only effective means of ameliorating the chronic motor and phonic symptoms of tic disorders. Presently, several classes of medication are used in the treatment of tic disorders.

Haloperidol, a butyrophone, has been the mainstay of treatment since the early 1960s. The efficacy of haloperidol is 75 to 85 percent, with vocal tic generally being most responsive, although good control of motor tics can also be expected. The usual starting dose is 0.5 mg/day and is gradually increased to 3 to 4 mg/day. Some patients may need higher doses (10 to 12 mg/day) to achieve improvement in symptoms. However, at these doses side-effects may limit the drug's usefulness. Long-term studies have shown that only 30 percent of responders will continue to take haloperidol regularly, primarily due to the side-effects. The most common side-effects include sedation, depression, excessive weight gain, intellectual dulling, and extrapyramidal reactions. Extrapyramidal reactions are effectively treated with diphenhydramine or antiparkinsonism agents. Tardive dyskinesia may develop with long-term use, but its occurrence may be decreased by utilizing the lowest possible dose and by allowing for drug holidays.

Clonidine, an imidazoline derivative, is an alpha-adrenergic agonist shown to be effective and virtually free of side-effects (Cohen et al. 1980). The efficacy of clonidine is reported to be 40 to 70 percent, but response is less rapid than to halo-peridol or pimozide. The usual starting dose is 0.05 mg/day with increase of 0.05 mg every four to seven days. The ultimate dose based on clinical response is 0.15 to 0.30 mg/day. The major side effect of clonidine is sedation, which lasts for thirty to ninety minutes after a dose is given. Recent clinical studies indicate that clonidine may be most effective for patients with the combination of tics and attention deficit disorder (Hunt et al. 1985).

Pimozide, a diphenylbutylpiperidine, is a potent neuroleptic that has been shown to be at least as effective as haloperidol in the treatment of Tourette's Disorder (Shapiro et al. 1983). The drug has only recently become available in the United States. Pi-mozide should be started at 2 mg/day and can be increased on clinical indications to 6 to 12 mg/day for children and 20 mg/day for adults. The side-effects are similar to those of haloperidol, although there seems to be less sedation noted with pimozide. Pimozide causes EKG changes in up to 25 percent of patients including T wave inversion, U waves, and QT prolongation. The development of T wave inversion or U waves calls for discontinuation of the medication.

The use of psychotherapy is most effective in dealing with the psychological issues created by the child having a chronic illness. There is no evidence to support the belief that psychotherapy alone will effectively alleviate the syndrome. But it is reasonable to use psychotherapy for isolated tics that have psychogenic meaning, such as those described by Gerard (1946) and Mahler (1949).

Academic intervention is frequently an important avenue of treatment. Those children with attention and learning problems may require special education. Communication with the school system is frequently necessary to educate teachers regarding the ways in which chronic tics or Tourette's Disorder affect learning, since many of these children will not meet school systems' criteria for learning disabilities.

The families of children with Tourette's Disorder should be given appropriate information about the Tourette's Syndrome Association (see references), a national organization with regional chapters, which has provided much information and service to patients and their families.

CONCLUSION

The assessment of children with tics involves a comprehensive evaluation including medical examination of the child, family and social history, and school evaluations. Psychological and academic testing are relevant areas of inquiry in addition to the direct clinical observations of the child. Based upon an understanding of the child's biopsychosocial adaptation, a multifaceted treatment plan is set up, designed to optimize the child's functioning in his environment.

REFERENCES

Tourette Syndrome Association, Inc., 41–02 Bell Boulevard, Bayside, NY 11361. (718) 224–2999.

Cohen, D. J., et al., (1980). Clonidine ameliorates Gilles de la Tourette Syndrome. *Arch. Gen. Psychiat.* 37:1350–57.

———, Leckman, J., and Shaywitz, B. (1985). The Tourette Syndrome and other tics. In D. Shaffer, A. A. Erhardt, and L. L. Greenhill (Eds.). *The Clinical Guide to Child Psychiatry.* New York: Free Press.

———, et al. (1979). Central biogenic amine metabolism in children with the syndrome of chronic multiple tics of Gilles de la Tourette: Norepinephrine, serotonin and dopamine. *J. Amer. Acad. Child Psychiat.* 18:320–41.

Engle, G. L. (1977). The need for a new medical model: A challenge for biomedicine. *Science* 1996:129–36.

Freud, A., and Burlingham, D. T. (1943). *War and Children.* New York: International Universities Press.

Friedhoff, A. J., and Chase, T. N. (Eds.). (1982). *Advances in Neurology.* Vol. 35, *Gilles de la Tourette Syndrome.* New York: Raven Press.

Gerard, M. W. (1946). The psychogenic tic in ego development. *Psychoanal. Study Child* 2:133–62.

Gesell, A., Ilg, F. L., and Ames, L. B. (1956). *Youth: The Years from Ten to Sixteen.* New York: Harper.

Hunt, R. D., Minderaa, R. B., and Cohen, D. J. (1985). Clonidine benefits children with attention deficit disorder and hyperactivity: Report of a double-blind placebo-crossover therapeutic trial. *J. Amer. Acad. Child Psychiat.* 24:617–29.

Kanner, L. (1972). *Child Psychiatry.* 4th Ed. Springfield, Ill.: Charles C. Thomas.

Lapouse, R., and Monk, M. (1958). An epidemiologic study of behavior characteristics in children. *Amer. J. Pub. Health* 48:1134–44.

Lowe, T., et al. (1982). Stimulant medications precipitate Tourette's Syndrome. *J. Amer. Med. Assoc.* 47:1729–31.

Lucas, A. R. (1976). Follow-up of tic syndrome. In F. S. Abuzzahab and F. O. Anderson (Eds.). *Gilles de la Tourette's Syndrome: International Registry,* Vol. 1. St. Paul: Mason, pp. 13–17.

———. (1979). Tic: Gilles de la Tourette's Syndrome. In J. D. Noshpitz (Ed.). *Basic Handbook of Child Psychiatry,* Vol. 2. New York: Basic Books, pp. 667–84.

———. (1980). Muscular control and coordination in minimal brain dysfunctions. In H. E. Rie and E. D. Rie (Eds.). *Handbook of Minimal Brain Dysfunctions.* New York: Wiley, pp. 235–52.

Lucas, A. R., Kauffman, P. E., and Morris, E. M. (1967). Gilles de la Tourette's Disease: A clinical study of fifteen cases. *J. Amer. Acad. Child Psychiat.* 6:700–22.

———, et al. (1982). Gilles de la Tourette Syndrome in Rochester, Minnesota, 1968–1979. In A. J. Friedhoff and T. N. Chase (Eds.). *Advances in Neurology,* Vol. 35. *Gilles de la Tourette Syndrome.* New York: Raven Press, pp. 267–69.

Macfarlane, J. W., Allen, L., and Honzik, M. P. (1954). *A Developmental Study of the Behavior Problems of Normal Children Between Twenty-One Months and Fourteen Years.* Berkeley: University of California Press.

Mahler, M. S. (1949). A psychoanalytic evaluation of tic in psychopathology of children: Symptomatic and tic syndrome. *Psychoanal. Study Child* 3/4:279–310.

Pauls, D. L., et al. (1981). Familial pattern and transmission of Gilles de la Tourette Syndrome and multiple tics. *Arch. Gen. Psychiat.* 38:1091–93.

———, et al. (1984). The risk of Tourette's Syndrome and chronic multiple tics among relatives of Tourette's Syndrome patients obtained by direct interview. *J. Amer. Acad. Child Psychiat.* 23:134–37.

Shapiro, A. K., Shapiro, E., and Eisenkraft, M. A. (1983). Treatment of Gilles de la Tourette Syndrome with pimozide. *Psychiatry* 140:1183–86.

———, et al. (1978). *Gilles de la Tourette Syndrome.* New York: Raven Press.

Shaw, C. R., and Lucas, A. R. (1970). *The Psychiatric Disorders of Childhood.* 2d Ed. New York: Appleton-Century-Crofts.